# Pro SQL Server 2008 Relational Database Design and Implementation

Louis Davidson

With Kevin Kline, Scott Klein, and Kurt Windisch

Apress®

**Pro SQL Server 2008 Relational Database Design and Implementation**

**Copyright © 2008 by Louis Davidson**

ISBN-13 (pbk): 978-1-4302-0866-2

ISBN-13 (electronic): 978-1-4302-0867-9

Printed and bound in the United States of America 9 8 7 6 5 4 3 2 1

Lead Editor: Jon Gennick
Technical Reviewers: Wayne Snyder, Evan Terry, Don Watters
Editorial Board: Clay Andres, Steve Anglin, Ewan Buckingham, Tony Campbell, Gary Cornell,
    Jonathan Gennick, Matthew Moodie, Joseph Ottinger, Jeffrey Pepper, Frank Pohlmann,
    Ben Renow-Clarke, Dominic Shakeshaft, Matt Wade, Tom Welsh
Project Manager: Tracy Brown Collins
Copy Editors: Heather Lang, Kim Wimpsett
Associate Production Director: Kari Brooks-Copony
Production Editor: Ellie Fountain
Compositor: Lynn L'Heureux
Proofreader: Patrick Vincent
Indexer: Broccoli Information Management
Artist: Kinetic Publishing Services, LLC
Cover Designer: Kurt Krames
Manufacturing Director: Tom Debolski

Distributed to the book trade worldwide by Springer-Verlag New York, Inc., 233 Spring Street, 6th Floor, New York, NY 10013. Phone 1-800-SPRINGER, fax 201-348-4505, e-mail orders-ny@springer-sbm.com, or visit http://www.springeronline.com.

For information on translations, please contact Apress directly at 2855 Telegraph Avenue, Suite 600, Berkeley, CA 94705. Phone 510-549-5930, fax 510-549-5939, e-mail info@apress.com, or visit http://www.apress.com.

Apress and friends of ED books may be purchased in bulk for academic, corporate, or promotional use. eBook versions and licenses are also available for most titles. For more information, reference our Special Bulk Sales–eBook Licensing web page at http://www.apress.com/info/bulksales.

The source code for this book is available to readers at http://www.apress.com.

*To my father-in-law, Verlin Wheeler. He passed away during the writing of this book, and I really never got to know him as I was told he was in his younger days. At the very least, he rivaled my love for gadgets and was an early adopter of lots of technology, like satellite dishes and even computers. I use his computer every day to manage my media collection—he probably would have liked that, though I think he would have preferred to have used the media in the library.*

# Contents at a Glance

# Contents

# Foreword

**D**atabase design is a passion that Louis and I share. This fall, I will be fortunate to share a stage with my friend, Louis Davidson. We're copresenting at DevLink in Louis's hometown of Nashville and then again at PASS in Seattle. Both times, we'll discuss, debate, and celebrate the topic of database design and how critical it is for any datacentric application.

Database design is part science and part art. There's a science to normalization, but determining the scope of the entity is an art form best learned from working with a broad repertoire of databases. There's a simple beauty to an elegant solution. Louis is more than an author or database designer; Louis is a master artisan, and in this book, you'll discover hidden within the words a call to improve your craft, to sculpt databases that stand the test of time, and to create virtual worlds of data that enable developers to play their best game.

Database design is the foundation of every datacentric application. An elegant database design makes the data obvious and easy to query and sets up the developer for success with efficient set-based queries. But, no amount of code can compensate for a poor database design or add features missing from the database. No role is more critical to any datacentric application than the role of the data modeler. User interfaces come and go, but data lasts for generations of application languages, and today's database schema errors will be cursed by programmers not yet born using languages and tools not yet invented. It's worth spending a little extra time to polish your database design under the tutelage of my good friend, Louis.

So it's with great pleasure that I welcome you to this third edition of Louis's field guide to the greatest job in the world of software.

Paul Nielsen
*SQL Server MVP*

# About the Author

**LOUIS DAVIDSON** has over 15 years of experience as a corporate database developer and architect. Currently, he is the data architect for the Christian Broadcasting Network and NorthStar Studios in Nashville, Tennessee. Nearly all of Louis's professional experience has been with Microsoft SQL Server, from the early days to the latest version currently in beta. Louis has been the principal author on four editions of a book on database design. Louis's primary areas of interest are database architecture and coding in T-SQL, and he has experience designing many databases and writing thousands of stored procedures and triggers through the years.

# About the Contributing Authors

**KEVIN KLINE** is the technical strategy manager for SQL Server solutions at Quest Software. A Microsoft SQL Server MVP since 2004, Kevin is a founding board member and past president of the international Professional Association for SQL Server (PASS). He has written or cowritten several books including *SQL in a Nutshell* (O'Reilly, 2004), *Pro SQL Server 2005 Database Design and Optimization* (Apress, 2006), and *Database Benchmarking: Practical Methods for Oracle & SQL Server* (Rampant, 2007). Kevin contributes to *SQL Server Magazine* and *Database Trends and Applications* and blogs at SQLBlog.com and SQLMag.com. Kevin is also a top-rated speaker at conferences worldwide, such as Microsoft Tech Ed, the PASS Community Summit, Microsoft IT Forum, DevTeach, and SQL Connections, and has been active in the IT industry since 1986.

**SCOTT KLEIN** is an independent consultant with a passion for all things SQL Server, .NET, and XML. He is the author of several books, including *Professional SQL Server 2005 XML* (Wrox, 2006) and *Professional LINQ* (Wrox, 2008), and he writes the biweekly feature article for the *SQL PASS Community Connector*. He has also contributed articles for several web sites, including Wrox (http://www.wrox.com) and TopXML (http://www.topxml.com). He frequently speaks to SQL Server and .NET user groups around Florida. Scott lives in Wellington, Florida, and when he is not sitting in front of a computer, he can be found hanging out with his family or aboard his Yamaha at the local motocross track. He can be reached at ScottKlein@SqlXml.com.

**KURT WINDISCH** is the applications supervisor for the internal IT department at Levi, Ray, and Shoup, Inc., a global provider of technology solutions with headquarters in Springfield, Illinois. He has more than 17 years of experience in the IT industry. He spent five years serving on the board of directors for the Professional Association for SQL Server, has written for several SQL Server magazines, and has presented at conferences internationally on the topic of database programming with SQL Server.

# About the Technical Reviewers

**WAYNE SNYDER** is recognized worldwide as a SQL Server expert and Microsoft Most Valued Professional (MVP), and he has over 25 years of experience in project management, database administration, software design, performance measurement, and capacity planning. He is a sought-after speaker, consultant, writer, and trainer. Wayne is the current president of the Professional Association for SQL Server (PASS) (www.sqlpass.org) and a managing consultant for Mariner, a business intelligence company (www.mariner-usa.com). He also plays keyboard for a regional cover band named SoundBarrier (www.soundbarrierband.com).

**EVAN TERRY** is a lead consultant working at The Clegg Company, specializing in data modeling, data quality, and information management. His past and current clients include the State of Idaho; Albertsons; American Honda Motors; and Toyota Motor Sales, USA. He is the coauthor of Apress's *Beginning Relational Data Modeling* (2005) and was a presenter at the 2006 and 2007 IAIDQ conferences and at the 2008 DAMA International Conference on the subject of data quality. He can be reached at evan_terry@cleggcompany.com.

**DON WATTERS** is a Staff Software Engineer at the Walt Disney Internet Group in Seattle, Washington. He has been working on Microsoft SQL Server products since version 6.5, and has over 10 years of experience with the product. He has extensive administrative and developer experience with very large OLTP and OLAP systems and enjoys learning and applying his knowledge to new and interesting database challenges. In his free time, Don enjoys spending time with his children, playing music and video games, and of course, studying all things related to Microsoft SQL Server. He can be reached at DonRWatters@aol.com.

# Acknowledgments

*If I have seen further, it is by standing on the shoulders of giants.*

—Sir Isaac Newton

I am not a genius, nor am I some form of pioneer in the database design world. I acknowledge that the following "people" have been extremely helpful in making this book happen. Some helped me directly, while others probably don't even know that this book exists. Either way, they have all been an important part of the process.

Far above anyone else, *Jesus Christ*, without whom I wouldn't have had the strength to complete the task of writing this book: I know I am not ever worthy of the love that You give me.

My wife *Valerie Davidson* and daughter *Amanda Davidson* for putting up with this craziness for a fourth time (and helping me with the picture for the cover). My mom for just being there to keep me entertained with information about the world around her, and my mother-in-law, too, for helping us out at times.

My best friend in the world who got me started with computers back in college when I still wanted to be a mathematician. I miss him far more than he will probably ever know; some day, I need to find him again and thank him where he might actually see it.

My mentors *Mike Farmer*, *Chip Broecker*, and *Don Plaster* for the leadership they gave me in my early years.

*Gary Cornell* for giving me a chance to write the book that I wanted to write.

*Frank Castora* and *Don Watters* for doing beta reads of the book on their own time. (Don later became a full technical editor on the book!) *Evan Terry* and *Wayne Snider* for their technical edits, even if the process when a little off center and didn't end up as we started.

My current manager *Rob Murdoch* for giving me time to go to several conferences that really helped me to produce as good of a book as I did. All of my coworkers at CBN and the now-defunct Compass, who gave me many examples for the book.

*Scott Klein*, *Kevin Kline*, and *Kurt Windisch* for taking up the slack with topics I didn't want to (OK, couldn't) tackle.

*Paul Nielsen* for offering and taking the time to write a foreword to this book.

The fantastic editing staff I've had, including *Jonathan Gennick* who (figuratively) busted my lip a few times over my poor use of the English language and without whom the writing would sometimes appear to come from an illiterate baboon. Most of these people are included on the copyright page, but I want to say a specific thanks to *Tony Davis* (who had a big hand in the book last time) for making this book great, despite my frequently rambling writing style.

*Raul Garcia*, who works on the Microsoft SQL Server Engine team, for information about using `EXECUTE AS` and certificate-based security.

*Isaac Kunen* for the discussions at Tech Ed that helped me understand spatial datatypes better.

*James Manning* for the advice on `READ COMMITTED SNAPSHOT`.

*Chuck Heinzelman* for being such a good friend and giving me the chance to write the article for SQL Server Standard around the time of this book coming out.

All the MVPs that I've worked with over the past year and a half. Never a better group of folks have I found. *Steven Dybing, Ben Miller*, and now *Ali Brooks* have been great to work with. I want to list a few others individually for things they've specifically done to help me out: *Dejan Sarka* and *Andrew Watt* reviewed the previous version of the book with incredible vigor and didn't let me slide on even small points. *Hugo Kornelis* gave me the most negative criticism of the previous version of the book; he really opened my eyes to some of the weaknesses (if only I could have gotten him to as one of the technical reviewers!). *Steve Kass* gave me the code for demonstrating what's wrong with the money datatypes, as well as cool solutions to problems in newsgroups that made me think. *Erland Somarskog* helped me understand a bit more about how error handling works, and many other topics (not to mention providing his great website, http://www.sommarskog.se/). *Adam Machanic* helped me with many topics on my blog and in newsgroups. *Aaron Bertrand* deserves thanks for his great website http://www.aspfaq.com and the shoe memories. Thanks to *Kalen Delaney* for all she has done for me and the community and to *Dr. Greg Low* for putting me on his http://www.sqldownunder.com podcast. *Kim Tripp* provided a wonderful paper on SNAPSHOT isolation levels, and *Arnie Rowland* got me the two gigs with Microsoft Learning that helped me out in parts of the book. Thanks to *Allen White* for the times at Tech Ed and the horrible interview and to *Jason Follas* for the time at Tech Ed where I listened to you talking about the spatial types. I also want to thank *Tony Bain, Hillary Cotter, Mike Epprecht, Geoff Hiten, Tom Moreau, Andrew Kelly, Tony Rogerson, Linchi Shea, Paul Nielson, Tibor Karaszi, Greg Linwood, Peter Debetta, Dr. Tom Moreau, Dan Guzman, Jacco Schalkwijk, Anith Sen, Jasper Smith, Ron Talmage, Christian Lefter*, and *Kent Tegels*, because all of you have specifically helped me out over the past years in the newsgroups, teaching me new things to make my book far better.

To the academics out there who have permeated my mind with database theory, such as *E. F. Codd, Chris Date, Fabian Pascal, Joe Celko*, my professors at the University of Tennessee at Chattanooga, and many others: I wouldn't know half as much without you. And thanks to *Mr. Date* for reviewing Chapter 1; you probably did more for the next version of this book than the current one.

And to *Jim Gray* and *Ken Henderson*, who both were amazing advocates of SQL Server and have inspired me over the years.

Even with this large number of folks I have mentioned here, I am afraid I may have missed someone. If so, thank you!

Louis Davidson

# Introduction

I often ask myself, "Why do I do this? Why am I writing another edition of this book? Is it worth it? Couldn't I help Mario save the princess faster if I just chucked the book and played Nintendo?" These questions were answered again for me by a fellow MVP at the Microsoft MVP Summit in 2008. He thanked me for writing this book and said that he'd tried to read the academic books on the subject and they were hard for him to follow.

"Oh yeah," I thought, "that was why I started out to do this thing in the first place." When I was first getting started designing databases, I learned from a few great mentors, but as I wanted to progress, I started looking for material on database design, and there wasn't much around. The best book I found was Chris Date's *An Introduction to Database Systems* (Addison Wesley, 2003), and I read as much as I could comprehend. The problem, however, was that I quickly got lost and started getting frustrated that I couldn't readily translate the theory of it all into a design process that really is quite simple once you get the ideas down. In Chris's book, and in other textbooks I had used, it became clear that a lot of theory, and even more math, went into creating the relational model.

If you want to be a theorist, Chris's book is essential reading, along with lots of other books (here is a good place to start looking for more titles: http://www.dbdebunk.com/books.html). The problem is that most of these books have far more theory than the average practitioner wants (or will take the time to read), and they don't really get into the actual implementation of a real database system. My book's goal is simply to fill that void and bridge the gap between academic textbooks and the purely implementation-oriented books that are commonly written on SQL Server—my intention is not to knock those books, not at all; I have numerous versions of those types of books on my shelf. This book is more of a technique-oriented book than a how-to book teaching you the features of SQL Server. I will cover many the most typical features of the relational engine, giving you techniques to work with. I can't, however, promise that this will be the only book you need on your shelf.

If you have previous editions of this book, you might question why you need this edition, and I know the feeling. I spent a lot of time trying to figure out why you should buy this new edition, and my reason isn't the obvious one—that now I cover 2008 features. Clearly, that is a part of it, but the biggest thing is that I continue to come up with new content to make your job easier. I've added another chapter about patterns of development (Chapter 7), and every chapter has a good amount of new material to help enhance your database designs.

Oscar Wilde, the poet and playwright, once said, "I am not young enough to know everything." It is with some chagrin that I must look back at the past and realize that I thought I knew everything just before I wrote my first book, *Professional SQL Server 2000 Database Design*. It was ignorant, unbridled, unbounded enthusiasm that gave me the guts to write the first book. In the end, I did write that first edition, and it was a decent enough book, largely due to the beating I took from my technical editing staff. And if I hadn't possessed the enthusiasm initially that drove me to finish, I likely would not be writing this fourth edition of the book. However, if you had a few weeks to burn and you went back and compared each edition of this book, chapter by chapter, section by section, to the current edition, you would notice a progression of material and a definite maturing of the writer.

There are a few reasons for this progression and maturity. One reason is the editorial staff I have had over the past two versions: first Tony Davis and now Jonathan Gennick. Both of them were *very* tough on my writing style and did wonders for the structure of the book. Another reason is simply experience, as over eight years have passed since I started the first edition. But most of the reason that the material has progressed is that it's been put to the test. While I have had my share of nice comments, I have gotten plenty of feedback on how to improve things (some of those were not-nice comments!). And I listened very intently, keeping a set of notes that start on the release date. I am always happy to get any feedback that I can use (particularly if it doesn't involve any anatomical terms for where the book might fit). I will continue to keep my e-mail address available (louis@drsql.org), and you can leave anonymous feedback on my website if you want (drsql.org). You will also find an addendum there that covers any material that I wish I had known at the time of this writing.

# Purpose of Database Design

What is the purpose of database design? Why the heck should you care? The main reason is that a properly designed database is straightforward to work with, because everything is in its logical place, much like a well-organized cupboard. When you need paprika, it's easier to go to the paprika slot in the spice rack than it is to have to look for it everywhere until you find it, but many systems are organized just this way. Even if every item has an assigned place, of what value is that item if it's too hard to find? Imagine if a phone book wasn't sorted at all. What if the dictionary was organized by placing a word where it would fit in the text? With proper organization, it will be almost instinctive where to go to get the data you need, even if you have to write a join or two. I mean, isn't that fun, after all?

You might also be surprised to find out that database design is quite a straightforward task and not as difficult as it may sound. Doing it right is going to take more time at the beginning of a project than just slapping together the data storage as you go along, but it pays off throughout the full life cycle of a project. This brings me to one of the most challenging things about doing database design right: it takes more time than not doing it (this is a battle that can occur frequently in project planning meetings). Because there's nothing visual to excite the client, database design is one of the phases of a project that often gets squeezed to make things seem to go faster. Even the least challenging or uninteresting user interface is still miles more interesting to the average customer than the most beautiful data model. Programming the user interface takes center stage, even though the data is generally why a system gets funded and finally created. It's not that your colleagues won't notice the difference between a cruddy data model and one that's a thing of beauty. They certainly will, but the amount of time required to decide the right way to store data correctly can be overlooked when programmers need to code. I wish I had an answer for that problem, because I could sell a million books with just that. This book will assist you with some techniques and processes that will help you through the process of designing databases, in a way that's clear enough for novices and helpful to even the most seasoned professional.

This process of designing and architecting the storage of data belongs to a different role from those of database setup and administration. For example, in the role of data architect, I seldom create users, perform backups, or set up replication or clustering. Little is mentioned of these tasks, which are considered administration and the role of the DBA. It isn't uncommon to wear both a developer hat and a DBA hat (in fact, when you work in a smaller organization, you may find that you wear so many hats your neck tends to hurt), but your designs will generally be far better thought out if you can divorce your mind from the more implementation-bound roles that make you wonder how hard it will be to use the data. For the most part, database design looks harder than it is.

■**Note**  To be safe, I have to make one thing clear: if you've done any programming, you'll undoubtedly disagree with some of the opinions and ideas in this book. I fully accept that this book is hardly the gospel of St. Louis of Katmai. My ideas and opinions have grown from more than 16 years of working with and learning about databases, supplemented with knowledge from many disparate people, books, college classes, and seminars. I thank many of these sources in the Acknowledgements, but there have been hundreds more whose names I've forgotten, although I've had some tidbit of knowledge imprinted on my brain from them. The design methodology presented in this book is a conglomeration of these ideas. I hope it proves a useful learning tool, and that through reading this book and other people's works, plus a healthy dose of trying out your own ideas, you'll develop a methodology that will suit you and will make you a successful database designer.

# Structure of This Book

This book is composed of the following chapters:

*Chapter 1: Introduction to Database Concepts*: This chapter provides a basic overview of essential terms and concepts.

*Chapter 2: The Language of Data Modeling:* This chapter serves as the introduction to the main tool of the data architect—the model. In this chapter, I introduce one modeling language (IDEF1X) in detail, as it's the modeling language that's used throughout this book to present database designs. I also introduce a few other common modeling languages, for those of you who need to use these types of models for preference or corporate requirements.

*Chapter 3: Conceptual Data Modeling:* In conceptual modeling, the goal is to discuss the process of taking a customer's set of requirements and to put the tables, columns, relationships, and business rules into a data model format where possible.

*Chapter 4: The Normalization Process:* The next step in the database design process is normalization. The goal of normalization is to take the set of tables, columns, relationships, and business rules and format them in such a way that every value is stored in one place and every table represents a single entity. Normalization can feel unnatural the first few times you do it, because instead of worrying about how you'll use the data, you must think of the data and how the structure will affect that data's quality. However, once you've mastered normalization, not storing data in a normalized manner will feel wrong.

*Chapter 5: Implementing the Base Table Structures:* This is the first point in the database design process in which we fire up SQL Server and start building scripts to build database objects. In this chapter, I cover building tables—including choosing the datatype for columns—as well as relationships. Part of this discussion notes how the implemented structures might differ from the model that we arrived at in the normalization process.

*Chapter 6: Protecting the Integrity of Your Data:* Beyond the way data is arranged in tables and columns, other business rules may need to be enforced. The front line of defense for enforcing data integrity conditions in SQL Server is formed by CHECK constraints and triggers, as users cannot innocently avoid having constraints and triggers do their validations. I also discuss the various other ways that data protection can be enforced using stored procedures and client code.

*Chapter 7: Patterns and Query Techniques:* Beyond the basic set of techniques for table design, there are several techniques that I use to apply a common data/query interface for my future convenience in queries and usage. This chapter will cover several of the common useful patterns as well as taking a look at some patterns that some people will use to make things easier to implement the interface that can be very bad for your query needs.

*Chapter 8: Securing Access to the Data:* Security is high in most every programmer's mind these days, or it should be. In this chapter, I cover some strategies to use to implement data security in your system, such as employing views, triggers, encryption, and even using SQL Server Profiler.

*Chapter 9: Table Structures and Indexing:* In this chapter, I show the basics of how data is structured in SQL Server, as well as some strategies for indexing data for better performance.

*Chapter 10: Coding for Concurrency:* Part of the database design and implementation process is to step beyond the structures and consider how to maximize resource utilization among many users. In this chapter, I describe several strategies for how to implement concurrency in your data access and modification code.

*Chapter 11: Considering Data Access Strategies:* In this chapter, many of the concepts and concerns of writing code that accesses SQL Server are covered. I cover *ad hoc* SQL versus stored procedures (including all the perils and challenges of both, such as plan parameterization, performance, effort, optional parameters, SQL injection, and so on), as well as discussing whether T-SQL or CLR objects are best, including samples of the different types of objects that can be coded using the CLR. The material on the CLR was provided by Kurt Windisch, as was the downloadable CLR sample code.

*Chapter 12: Database Interoperability:* Finally, in this chapter written by Kevin Kline, the challenges of building databases that have to run on not only SQL Server but also other database server platforms are discussed. *This chapter can be found on the Apress website, where it's available as a bonus download.*

*Appendix A: Codd's 12 Rules for an RDBMS:* In this appendix, I present Codd's original 12 rules for how a database should be implemented. As hardware improves, we are getting closer to finally realizing his dreams.

*Appendix B: Scalar Datatype Reference:* In this appendix, I present all of the types that can be legitimately considered scalar types, along with why to use them, their implementation information, and other details.

*Appendix C: Beyond Relational Datatype:* In this appendix, the so-called beyond relational types are discussed. Included are XML, the spatial types geography and geometry, and the hierarchyId type. The XML and spatial types sections were written by Scott Klein. *This chapter can be found on the Apress website, where it's available as a bonus download.*

Again, please don't hesitate to give me feedback on the book anytime (well, as long as you don't call me at three in the morning). I'll try to improve any sections that people find lacking and publish them to my blog (http://sqlblog.com/blogs/louis_davidson) with the tag DesignBook as well as to my website (http://drsql.org/ProSQLServerDatabaseDesign.aspx). I'll be putting more information in both places as it becomes available pertaining to new ideas, goof ups I find, or additional materials that I choose to publish because I think of them once this book is no longer a jumble of bits and bytes and is an actual instance of ink on paper.

# CHAPTER 1

# Introduction to Database Concepts

*And then she understood the devilish cunning of the enemies' plan. By mixing a little truth with it they had made their lie far stronger.*

—C. S. Lewis, *The Last Battle*

From the beginning of my career as a data architect to just yesterday (no matter what day you read this, what I'm about to say is extremely unlikely to change), I have encountered one reality that was completely difficult to beat. Doing things right is never an easy sale to a management system where the clock on the wall is the primary driver for all projects. Couple that with the fact that there are usually many times more functional programmers waiting on the database, all telling management that they can't do anything until the database is designed and at least started to be implemented. If that isn't enough, this is about the time that a little inaccuracy infects the mind-set of the project team: "Database design is not that important."

It is rarely said explicitly in those words (though it is sometimes!) but generally is mixed in with good talk about how the user interface (UI) needs to show this and this button needs to go there. The design of the system starts to feel like a photo-realistic artist painting a picture, rather than a project that needs to follow solid engineering practices, starting with answering the questions of *what* needs to be done and *then* how to do it. Even worse, since the database is the backbone of almost any software project, it compounds the problem, which will often rear its ugly near the end of the development process. If you are involved in designing the database, then it is important to understand the fundamental answer to the question, "why?"

Look at it this way, would you drive on a bridge designed by an engineer who did not understand physics? Or would you get on a plane designed by someone who didn't understand the fundamentals of flight? Sounds quite absurd, right? So, would you want to store your important data in a database designed by someone who didn't understand the fundamentals of database design?

The first four chapters of this book are devoted to the distinct phases of relational database design and how to carry out each phase effectively so you are able to arrive at a final design that can fulfill the business requirements and ensure the integrity of the data in your database. However, before starting this design process in earnest, you need to explore a few core relational database concepts. Therefore, this chapter discusses the following topic areas:

- *Database design phases*: The next section provides an overview of the four major phases of relational database design: conceptual, logical, implementation, and physical. For time and budget reasons, it is often tempting to skip the earlier database design phases and move straight to the implementation phase. This chapter will explain why skipping any or all of these phases can lead to an incomplete and/or incorrect design, as well as one that does not support high-performance querying and reporting.

- *Relational data structures*: This chapter will provide concise descriptions of some of the fundamental database objects, including the database itself, as well as tables, columns, and keys. These objects are likely familiar to most, but there are some common misunderstandings in their usage that can make the difference between a mediocre design and a high-class, professional design. In particular, misunderstanding the vital role of keys in the database can lead to severe data integrity issues and to the mistaken belief that such keys and constraints can be effectively implemented outside the database. (Here is a subtle clue: they can't.)

- *Relationships*: We will briefly survey the different types of relationships that can exist between relational tables.

- *SQL*: We will discuss the need for a single, standard, set-based language for interrogating relational databases.

- *Dependencies*: Finally, we will discuss the concept of dependencies between values and how they shape the process of designing databases later in the book.

As a side effect of this discussion, we will reach agreement on the meaning of some of the important terms and concepts that will be used throughout the book when discussing and describing relational databases. Some of these terms are misunderstood and misused by a large number (if not a majority) of people. If we are not in agreement on their meaning from the beginning, then eventually you might end up wondering what the heck we're talking about. In other words, it is important that we get on the same page when it comes to the concepts and basic theories that are fundamental to proper database design.

# Database Design Phases

Too often when I sit down to build a system that requires data storage, the knee-jerk reaction is to start thinking in terms of how to fulfill an immediate need. Little regard is given to the future data needs, and even less is given to the impact the design will have on future business needs, reporting requirements, and, most crucial of all, the integrity of the data. I admit it is easy to succumb to quick versus good when you have a manager breathing coffee breath on the back of your neck every 10 minutes asking, "Done yet?"

The problem with this mind-set is that obvious things are commonly missed, and late in the project you have to go back and tweak (and re-tweak) the design, and often tweaking means adding several major tables, splitting tables apart, or even nearly starting over (assuming there is time ). Too often, too much time is spent deciding how to build a system as quickly (and cheaply!) as possible, and too little time is spent considering the desired outcome. Clearly, the goal of any organization is to work efficiently, but it is still important to get things as right as possible the first time, partly because of the shackles of backward compatibility, which makes it harder and harder to actually make changes to your systems as more users exist. Maintenance programming is far more expensive (and an order of magnitude less fun) than initially creating the system.

A thorough database design process will undergo four distinct phases, as follows:

- *Conceptual*: This is the "sketch" of the database that you will get from initial requirements gathering and customer information. During this phase, you attempt to identify what the user wants. You try to find out as much as possible about the business process for which you are building this data model, its scope, and, most important, the business rules that will govern the use of the data. You then capture this information in a conceptual data model consisting of a set of "high-level" entities and the interactions between them.

- *Logical*: The logical phase is a refinement of the work done in the conceptual phase, transforming what is often a loosely structured conceptual design into a full-fledged relational database design that will be the foundation for the implementation design. During this stage, you fully define the required set of entities, the relationships between them, the attributes of each entity, and the domains of these attributes (i.e., the sort of data the attribute holds and the range of valid values).

- *Implementation*: In this phase, you adapt the logical model for implementation in the host relational database management system (RDBMS; in our case, SQL Server).

- *Physical*: In this phase, you create the model where the implementation data structures are mapped to physical storage. This phase is also more or less the performance tuning/optimization phase of the project because it is important that your implementation should function in the same way no matter what the physical hardware looks like. It might not function very fast, but it will function. It is during this phase of the project that indexes, disk layouts, and so on, come into play, and not before this.

The first four chapters of this book are concerned with the conceptual and logical design phases, and I make only a few references to SQL Server. Generally speaking, the logical model of any relational database will be the same, be it for SQL Server, Oracle, Informix, DB2, MySQL, or anything else based, in some measure, on the relational model.

---

■**Note** A lot of people use the name *physical* to indicate that they are working on the SQL Data Definition Language (DDL) objects, rather than the meaning I give, where it is the layer "below" the SQL language. But lumping both the DDL and the tuning layers into one "physical" layer did not sit well with some readers/reviewers, and I completely agree. The implementation layer is purely SQL and doesn't care too much about tuning. The physical layer is pure tuning, and nothing done in that layer should affect the meaning of the data.

---

# Conceptual

The conceptual design phase is essentially a process of analysis and discovery, the goal being to define the organizational and user data requirements of the system. Note that there are other parts to the overall design picture beyond the needs of the database design that will be part of the conceptual design phase (and all follow-on phases), but for this book, the design process will be discussed in a manner that may make it sound as if the database is all that matters. (As a reader of this book who is actually reading this chapter on fundamentals, you probably feel that way already.)

Two of the core activities that make up this stage are as follows:

- Discovering and documenting a set of entities and the relationships between them

- Discovering and documenting the business rules that define how the data can and will be used and also the scope of the system that you are designing

Your conceptual design should capture, at a high level, the fundamental "sets" of data that are required to support the business processes and users' needs. Entity discovery is at the heart of this process. *Entities* correspond to nouns (people, places, and things) that are fundamental to the business processes you are trying to improve by creating software. Consider a basic business statement such as the following:

**People** *place* **orders** *in order to buy* **products.**

Immediately, you can identify three conceptual entities (in bold) and begin to understand how they interact. Note too, phrases such as "in order" can be confusing, and if the writer of this spec were writing well, the phrase would have been "**People** place **orders** to buy **products**."

---

■**Note** An entity is *not* the same thing as a table. A table is an implementation-specific SQL construct. Sometimes an entity will map directly to a table in the implementation, but often it won't. Some conceptual entities will be too abstract to ever be implemented, and sometimes they will map to two or more tables. It is a major (if somewhat unavoidable because of human nature) mistake at this point of the process to begin thinking about how the final database will look.

The primary point of this note is simply that you should not rush the design process by worrying about implementation details until you start to flip bits on the SQL Server. The next section of this chapter will establish the terminology in more detail. In the end, one section had to come first, and this one won.

---

During this conceptual phase, you need to do the requisite planning and analysis so that the requirements of the business and its customers are met. The conceptual design should focus steadfastly on the broader view of the system, and it may not correspond to the final, implemented system. However, it is a vital step in the process and provides a great communication tool for participants in the design process.

The second essential element of the conceptual phase is the discovery of *business rules*. These are the rules that govern the operation of your system, certainly as they pertain to the process of creating a database and the data to be stored in the database. Often, no specific tool is used to document these rules, other than Microsoft Excel or Word. It is usually sufficient that business rules are presented as a kind of checklist of things that a system must or must not do, for example:

- Users in group X must be able to change their own information.
- Each company must have a ship-to address and optionally a bill-to address if its billing address is different.
- A product code must be 12 characters in length and be in the format XXX-XXX-XXXX.

From these statements, the boundaries of the final implemented system can be determined. These business rules may encompass many different elements of business activity. They can range from very specific data-integrity rules (e.g., the newly created order date has to be the current date) to system processing rules (e.g., report X must run daily at 12 a.m.) to a rule that defines part of the security strategy (e.g., only this category of users should be able to access these tables). Expanding on that final point, a security plan ought to be built during this phase and used to implement database security in the implementation phase. Too often, security measures are applied (or not) as an afterthought.

> **■Note** It is beyond the scope of this book to include a full discussion of business rule discovery, outside of what is needed to shape and then implement integrity checks in the data structures. However, business rule discovery is a very important process that has a fundamental impact on the database design. For a deeper understanding of business rules, I suggest getting one of the many books on the subject.

During this process, you will encounter certain rules that "have to" be enforced and others that are "conditionally" enforced. For example, consider the following two statements:

- Applicants must be 18 years of age or older.

- Applicants should be between 18 and 32 years of age, but you are allowed to accept people of any age if you have proper permission.

The first rule can easily be implemented in the database. If an applicant enters an age of 17 years or younger, the RDBMS can reject the application and send back a message to that effect.

The second rule is not quite so straightforward to implement. In this case, you would probably require some sort of workflow process to route the request to a manager for approval. T-SQL code is not interactive, and this rule would most certainly be enforced outside the database, probably in the user interface (UI).

It pays to be careful with any rule, even the first. No matter what the initial rules state, the leeway to break the rules is still a possibility. Unfortunately, this is just part of the process. The important thing to recognize is that every rule that is implemented in an absolute manner can be trusted, while breakable rules must be verified with every usage.

> **■Note** Ideally, the requirements at this point would be perfect and would contain all business rules, processes, and so forth, needed to implement a system. The conceptual model would contain in some form every element needed in the final database system. However, we do not live in a perfect world. Users generally don't know what they want until they see it. Business analysts miss things, sometimes honestly, but often because they jump to conclusions or don't fully understand the system. Hence, some of the activities described as part of building a conceptual model can spill over to the logical modeling phase.

# Logical

The logical phase is a refinement of the work done in the conceptual phase. The output from this phase will be an essentially complete blueprint for the design of the relational database. Note that during this stage you should still think in terms of entities and their attributes, rather than tables and columns. No consideration should be given at this stage to the exact details of "how" the system will be implemented. As previously stated, a good logical design could be built on any RDBMS. Core activities during this stage include the following:

- Drilling down into the conceptual model to identify the full set of entities that define the system.

- Defining the attribute set for each entity. For example, an `Order` entity may have attributes such as `Order Date`, `Order Amount`, `Customer Name`, and so on.

- Applying normalization rules (covered in Chapter 4).

- Identifying the attributes (or a group of attributes) that make up candidate keys (i.e., sets of attributes that could uniquely identify an instance of an entity). This includes primary keys, foreign keys, surrogate keys, and so on (all described in Chapter 5).

- Defining relationships and associated cardinalities.

- Identifying an appropriate domain (which will become a datatype) for each attribute and whether values are required.

While the conceptual model was meant to give the involved parties a communication tool to discuss the data requirements and to start seeing a pattern to the eventual solution, the logical phase is about applying proper design techniques. The logical modeling phase defines a blueprint for the database system, which can be handed off to someone else with little knowledge of the system to implement using a given technology (which in our case is likely going to be some version of Microsoft SQL Server).

■**Note** Before we begin to build the logical model, we need to introduce a complete data modeling language. In our case, we will be using the IDEF1X modeling methodology, described in Chapter 2.

## Implementation

During the implementation phase, you fit the logical design to the tool that is being used (in our case, an RDBMS, namely, SQL Server). This involves choosing datatypes, building tables, applying constraints, writing triggers, and so on, to implement the logical model in the most efficient manner. This is where platform-specific knowledge of SQL Server, T-SQL, and other technologies becomes essential.

Occasionally this phase will entail some reorganization of the designed objects to make them easier to implement or to circumvent some inherent limitation of the RDBMS. In general, I can state that for most designs there is seldom any reason to stray a great distance from the logical model, though the need to balance user load and hardware considerations can make for some changes to initial design decisions. Ultimately, one of the primary goals is that no data that has been specified or integrity constraints that have been identified in the conceptual and logical phases will be lost. Data can (and will) be added, often to handle the process of writing programs to use the data. The key is to not affect the designed meaning or, at least, not to take anything away from that original set of requirements.

It is at this point in the project that constructs will be applied to handle the business rules that were identified during the conceptual part of the design. These constructs will vary from the favored declarative constraints such as defaults, check constraints, and so on, to less favorable but still useful triggers and occasionally stored procedures. Finally, this phase includes designing the security for the data we will be storing. We will work through the implementation phase of the project in Chapters 5, 6, 7, and 8.

■**Note** In many modeling tools, the physical phase denotes the point where the logical model is actually generated in the database. I will refer to this as the *implementation phase* because the physical model is also commonly used to describe the process by which the data is physically laid out onto the hardware. I also do this because it should not be confusing to the reader what the implementation model is, regardless of the name they use to call this phase of the process.

## Physical

The goal of the physical phase is to optimize data access—for example, by implementing effective data distribution on the physical disk storage and by judicious use of indexes. While the purpose of the RDBMS is to largely isolate us from the physical aspects of data retrieval and storage, it is still very important to understand how SQL Server physically implements the data storage in order to optimize database access code.

During this stage, the goal is to optimize performance, but to not change the logical design in any way to achieve that aim. This is an embodiment of Codd's eleventh rule, which states the following:

> *An RDBMS has distribution independence. Distribution independence implies that users should not have to be aware of whether a database is distributed.*

---

■**Note** We will discuss Codd's rules in Appendix A.

---

It may be that it is necessary to distribute data across different files, or even different servers, but as long as the published logical names do not change, users will still access the data as columns in rows in tables in a database.

---

■**Note** Our discussion of the physical model will be reasonably limited. We will start by looking at entities and attributes during conceptual and logical modeling. In implementation modeling, we will switch gears to deal with tables, rows, and columns. The physical modeling of records and fields will be dealt with only briefly (in Chapter 8). If you want a deeper understanding of the physical implementation, check out *Inside Microsoft SQL Server 2005: The Storage Engine* by Kalen Delaney (Microsoft Press, 2006) or any future books she may have released by the time you are reading this.

---

# Relational Data Structures

This section introduces the following core relational database structures and concepts:

- Database and schema
- Tables, rows, and columns
- The Information Principle
- Keys
- Missing values (nulls)

As a person reading this book, this is probably not your first time working with a database, and as such, you are no doubt somewhat familiar with some of these concepts. However, you may find there are quite a few points presented here that you haven't thought about—for example, the fact that a table consists of unique rows or that within a single row a column must represent only a single value. These points make the difference between having a database of data that the client relies on without hesitation and having one in which the data is constantly challenged.

## Database and Schema

A *database* is simply a structured collection of facts or data. It need not be in electronic form; it could be a card catalog at a library, your checkbook, a SQL Server database, an Excel spreadsheet, or even just a simple text file. Typically, when a database is in an electronic form, it is arranged for ease and speed of search and retrieval.

In SQL Server, the database is the highest-level container that you will use to group all the objects and code that serve a common purpose. On an instance of the database server, you can have multiple databases, but best practices suggest using as few as possible for your needs. At the next level down is the *schema*. You use schemas to group objects in the database with common themes or even common owners. All objects on the database server can be addressed by knowing the database they reside in and the schema (note that you can set up linked servers and include a server name as well):

```
databaseName.schemaName.objectName
```

Schemas will play a large part of your design, not only to segregate objects of like types but also because segregation into schemas allows you to control access to the data and restrict permissions, if necessary, to only a certain subset of the implemented database.

Once the database is actually implemented, it becomes the primary container used to hold, back up, and subsequently restore data when necessary. It does not limit you to accessing data within only that one database; however, managing data in separate databases becomes a more manual process, rather than a natural, built-in RDBMS function.

---

■**Caution** The term *schema* has another common meaning that you should realize: the entire structure for the databases is referred to as the *schema*.

---

## Tables, Rows, and Columns

The object that will be involved in all your designs and code is the *table*. In your designs, a table will be used to represent *something*, either real or imaginary. A table can be used to represent people, places, things, or ideas (i.e., nouns, generally speaking), about which information needs to be stored.

The word *table* has the connotation of being an implementation-oriented term, for which Dictionary.com (`http://dictionary.reference.com`) has the following definition:

> *An orderly arrangement of data, especially one in which the data are arranged in columns and rows in an essentially rectangular form.*

A basic example of this form of table that most people are familiar with is a Microsoft Excel spreadsheet, such as that shown in Figure 1-1.

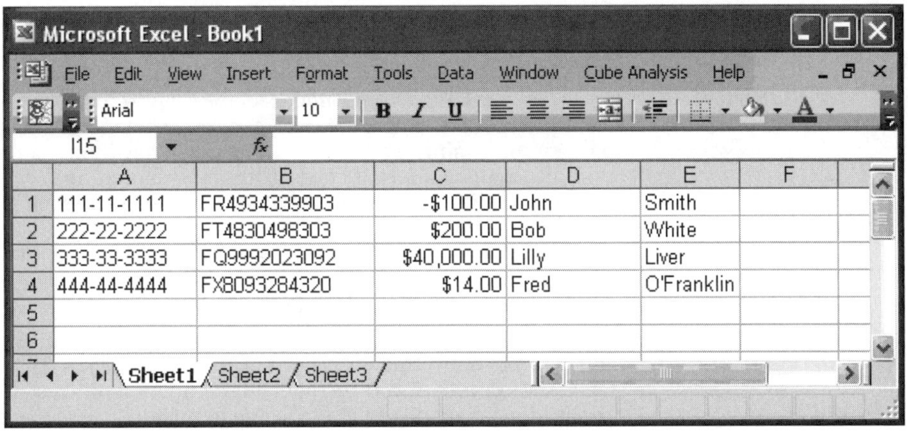

**Figure 1-1.** *Excel table*

In Figure 1-1, the rows are numbered 1–6, and the columns are lettered A–F. The spreadsheet is a table of accounts. Every column represents an attribute of an account (i.e., a single piece of information about the account); in this case, you have a Social Security number, an account number, an account balance, and the first and last names of the account holder attributes. Each row of the spreadsheet represents one specific account. So, for example, row 1 might be read as follows: "John Smith, holder of account FR4934339903, with SSN 111-11-1111, has a balance of –$100." (No offense if there is actually a John Smith with SSN 111-11-1111 who is broke—I just made this up!) This data could certainly have been sourced from a query that returns a SQL table.

However, this definition does not actually coincide with the way you *should* think of a table when working with SQL. In SQL, tables are a representation of data from which all the implementation aspects have been removed. The goal of relational theory is to free you from the limitations of the rigid structures of an implementation like an Excel spreadsheet.

In the world of relational databases, these terms have been somewhere between slightly and greatly refined, and the different meanings can get quite confusing. Let's look at the different terms and how they are presented from the following perspectives:

- Relational theory
- Logical/conceptual
- Implementation
- Physical

Table 1-1 lists all of the names that tables are given from the various viewpoints.

**Table 1-1.** *Table Term Breakdown*

| Viewpoint | Name | Definition |
|---|---|---|
| Relational theory | Relation | This term is seldom used by nonacademics, but some literature uses this term exclusively to mean what most programmers think of as a table. It consists of rows and columns, with no duplicate rows. There is absolutely no ordering implied in the structure of the relation, neither for rows nor for columns.<br>*Note: Relational databases take their name from this term; the name does not come from the fact that tables can be related. (Relationships are covered later in this chapter.)* |
| Logical/ conceptual | Entity | An entity can be loosely represented by a table with columns and rows. An entity initially is not governed as strictly as a table. For example, if you are modeling a human resources application, an employee photo would be an attribute of the `Employees` entity.<br>During the logical modeling phase, many entities will be identified, some of which will actually become tables, and some of which will become several tables. The formation of the implementation tables is based on a process known as *normalization*, which we'll cover extensively in Chapter 4. |
| Implementation | Recordset/ rowset | A *recordset/rowset* is a table that has been made physical for a use, such as sending results to a client. Most commonly, it will be in the form of a tabular data stream that the user interfaces/middle tier objects can use.<br>Recordsets do have order, in that usually (based on implementation) the columns and the rows can be accessed by position and rows by their location in the table of data. (However, it's questionable that they should be accessed in this way.) Seldom will you deal with recordsets in the context of database design.<br>A *set* in relational theory terms has no ordering, so technically a recordset is not a set per se. I didn't come up with the name, but it's common terminology. |
| Implementation | Table | The term *table* is almost the same as a relation. It is a particularly horrible name, because the structure that this list of terms is in is also referred to as a *table*. These tables, much like the Excel tables, have order. It cannot be reiterated enough that tables have *no* order (the section "The Information Principle" later in this chapter will clarify this concept further).<br>Another concern is that a table may technically have duplicate rows. It is up to you as the developer to apply constraints to make certain that duplicate rows are not allowed.<br>Tables also have another usage, in that the results of a query (including the intermediate results that occur as a query is processing multiple joins and the other clauses of a query) are also called tables, and the columns in these intermediate tables may not even have column names.<br>*Note: This one naming issue causes more problems for new SQL programmers than any other.* |
| Physical | File | In many database systems (such as Microsoft FoxPro), each operating system file represents a table (sometimes a table is actually referred to as a *database*, which is just way too confusing). Multiple files make up a database. |

During the conceptual and logical modeling phases, the process will be to identify the entities that define the system. Each entity is described by a unique set of attributes. An entity is often implemented as a table (but, remember, there is not necessarily a direct relationship between the two), with the attributes defining the columns of that table. You can think of each instance of an entity as analogous to a row in the table.

Drilling into the table structure, we next will discuss columns. Generally speaking, a column is used to contain some piece of information about a row in a table. *Atomic* or *scalar* is the common term used to describe the type of data that is stored in a column. The key is that the column represents data at its lowest level that you will need to work with in SQL. Another, clearer term—*nondecomposable*—is possibly the best way to put it, but *scalar* is quite often the term that is used by most people.

Usually this means a single value, such as a noun or a word, but it can mean something like a whole chapter in a book stored in a binary or even a complex type such as a point with longitude and latitude. The key is that the column represents a single value that resists being broken down to a lower level than what is defined. So, having a column that is defined as two independent values, say `Column.X` and `Column.Y`, is perfectly acceptable, while defining a column to deal with values like `'1,1'` would not be, because that value needs to be broken apart to be useful.

---

■**Note** The new datatypes, like XML, spatial types (`geography` and `geography`), `hierarchyId`, and even custom-defined CLR types, really start to muddy the waters of atomic, scalar, and nondecomposable column values. Each of these has some value, but in your design, the initial goal is to use a scalar type first and one of the commonly referred to as "beyond relational" types as a fallback for implementing structures that are overly difficult using scalars only.

---

Table 1-2 lists all the names that columns are given from the various viewpoints, several of which we will use in the different contexts as we progress through the design process.

**Table 1-2.** *Column Term Breakdown*

| Viewpoint | Name | Definition |
|---|---|---|
| Logical/ conceptual | Attribute | The term *attribute* is common in the programming world. It basically specifies some information about an object. In early logical modeling, this term can be applied to almost anything, and it may actually represent other entities. Just as with entities, normalization will change the shape of the attribute to a specific basic form. |
| Implementation | Column | A column is a single piece of information describing what the row represents. Values that the column is designed to deal with should be at their lowest form and will not be divided for use in the database system. The position of a column within a table must be unimportant to their usage, even though SQL does define a left-to-right order of column. All access to a column will be by name, not position. |
| Physical | Field | The term *field* has a couple of meanings. One meaning is the intersection of a row and a column, as in a spreadsheet (this might also be called a *cell*). The other meaning is more related to early database technology: a field was the physical location in a record (we'll look at this in more detail in Table 1-3). There are no set requirements that a field store only scalar values, merely that it is accessible by a programming language. |

Finally, Table 1-3 describes the different ways to refer to a row.

**Table 1-3.** *Row Term Breakdown*

| Viewpoint | Name | Definition |
|---|---|---|
| Relational theory | Tuple (pronounced "tupple," not "toople") | This is a finite set of related named value pairs. By "named," I mean that each of the values is known by a name (e.g., Name: Fred; Occupation: Gravel Worker). *Tuple* is a term seldom used except in academic circles, but you should know it, just in case you encounter it when you are surfing the Web looking for database information. In addition, this knowledge will make you more attractive to the opposite sex. (Yeah, if only . . .) Ultimately, *tuple* is a better term than *row*, since a row gives the impression of something physical, and it is essential to not think this way when working in SQL Server with data. |
| Logical/ conceptual | Instance | Basically this would be one of whatever was being represented by the entity. |
| Implementation | Row | This is essentially the same as a tuple, though the term *row* implies it is part of something (in this case, a row in a table). Each column represents one piece of data of the thing that the row has been modeled to represent. |
| Physical | Record | A record is considered to be a location in a physical file. Each record consists of fields, which all have physical locations. This term should *not* be used interchangeably with the term *row*. A row has no physical location, just data in columns. |

If this is the first time you've seen the terms listed in Tables 1-1 through 1-3, I expect that at this point you're banging your head against something solid, trying to figure out why such a great variety of terms are used to represent pretty much the same things. Many a newsgroup flame war has erupted over the difference between a field and a column, for example. I personally cringe now whenever a person uses the term *field*, but I also realize that it isn't the worst thing if a person realizes everything about how a table should be dealt with in SQL but misuses a term.

## The Information Principle

The first of Codd's rules for an RDBMS states simply that:

*All information in a relational database is represented explicitly at the logical level in exactly one way—by values in tables.*

This rule is known as the Information Principle (or Information Rule). It means that there is only one way to access data in a relational database, and that is by comparing values in columns. What makes this so important is that in your code you will rarely need to care where the data is. You simply address the data by its name, and it will be retrieved. Rearranging columns, adding new columns, and spreading data to different disk subsystems should be transparent to your SQL code. In reality, there will be physical tuning to be done, and occasionally you will be required to use physical hints to tune the performance of a query, but this should be a relatively rare occurrence (if not, then you are probably doing something wrong).

For example, the only way of knowing that employee A works for department B is by comparing the values in the relevant columns. There should be no backdoor way of finding this out (e.g., by accessing the data directly on disk).

This leads nicely to Codd's second rule, known as the Guaranteed Access Rule:

*Each and every datum (atomic value) in a relational database is guaranteed to be logically accessible by resorting to a table name, primary key value, and column name.*

The second thing that the Information Principle implies is that there is no order on tables in the database. Just because rows are retrieved from a table and seem to be in a given order, there is no contract between you and SQL Server to return rows in any given order, unless a given order is specified in a retrieval operation. Hence, it is not possible to access the row by its position in the table. There are two implications here. First, you should not need to go further than the column name to get a piece of data. So, encoding values in a column is considered wrong. Second, the physical order of the data that a table uses shall be unimportant to the use of the data. This allows you to reorder the physical structures with no worry of causing problems for the implementation, a concept that you will find extremely useful when you need to do performance tuning. Imagine if you had to access your data by the directory in which it was located. I would rather not.

The concept of order can be a big sticking point for many programmers. The confusion is made worse by the fact that data is always viewed in an arraylike format. For example, consider a table T with columns X and Y:

```
SELECT  X, Y
FROM    T
```

This returns the following (assuming of course, that the table T consists of these values, which we will assume it does!):

```
X       Y
---     ---
1       A
2       B
3       C
```

It is easy to assume that this data is in this fixed order in the file where it is stored. A more "accurate" (but admittedly not easier) way to picture data storage is as a group of values floating about somewhere in space, as shown in Figure 1-2.

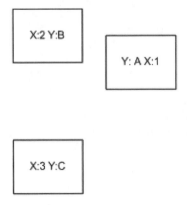

**Figure 1-2.** *Logical view of table data*

As such, how the rows are output is a cross between the function of the commands you use to retrieve them and how it is easiest for the database engine to get to the data. So, the following view of the data is equivalent to the previous table shown:

```
X     Y
---   ---
2     B
1     A
3     C
```

It is, of course, the same data—it's just ordered differently. Any database server has the right to return data in a different order if it is more convenient for it to do so. If you desire a guaranteed order, you must use an ORDER BY clause:

```
SELECT  X, Y
FROM    T
ORDER   BY X DESC
```

which now returns the data in the order specified:

```
X     Y
---   ---
3     C
2     B
1     A
```

And, for completeness, the very same data is returned by this:

```
SELECT  Y, X
FROM    T
ORDER   BY Y
```

```
Y     X
---   ---
A     1
B     2
C     3
```

Keep in mind that although the output of a SELECT statement has order, since the tables being selected from do *not* have order, a particular order cannot be assumed unless the order is forced by using an ORDER BY clause. Assuming the ordering of the result of a SELECT statement is one of the common mistakes made when dealing with SQL Server. Many programmers think that since they always receive the same results on their sandbox server (often a single processor/single disk channel arrangement) that they will be guaranteed to get back data in the same order every time. Or they try to include an ORDER BY clause in a view definition (considered a virtual table in the SQL standards) only to get back the data in a different order once the physical representation changes.

Not to beat a dead horse (or even a live one), but the lack of data ordering in a relational database is an extremely important point to understand for your future implementation.

# Domains

The *domain* of a column is the set of valid values that the column is intended to store. For example, consider a column that is intended to store an employee's date of birth. The following list covers the types of data and a few boundaries that you need to consider:

- The value must be a calendar date with no time value.
- The value must be a date prior to the current date. (Otherwise, the person will not have been born yet.)
- The value of the date value should evaluate such that the person is at least 16 or 18 years old, since you couldn't legally (and likely wouldn't want to!) hire a 10-year-old, for example.
- The value of the date value should be less than 70 years ago, since rarely will an employee (especially a new employee) be that age.
- The value must be less than 120 years ago, since we certainly won't have a new employee that old. Any value outside these bounds would clearly be in error.

Together, these points could be taken to define the domain of the DateOfBirth column. In Chapter 6, we'll cover how you might implement this domain, but in the logical phase of the design, you just need to document the domain.

A great practice (not just a best practice!) is to have *named domains* to associate common attributes. For example, in this case there could be an employeeBirthDate domain. Every time the employee birth date is needed, it will be associated with this named domain. Admittedly, it is not always possible to do this, particularly if you don't have a tool that will help you manage it.

Domains do not have to be so specific, though. For example, you might have the following named domains:

- positiveInteger: Integer values 1 and greater
- date: Any valid date value
- emailAddress: A string value that must be formatted as a valid e-mail address
- 30CharacterString: A string of characters that can be no longer than 30 characters

Keep in mind that if you actually define the domain of a string to any positive integer, the maximum is theoretically infinity. Today's hardware boundaries allow some pretty far out maximum values (e.g., 2,147,483,647 for a regular integer, and a really large number for a bigint type). It is fairly rare that a user will have to enter a value approaching 2 billion, but if you do not constrain the data within your domains, then reports and programs will need to be able handle such large data. It is a bit less rare that you might use a bigInt for a key of some sort, but frankly, in either case, the domain documentation will play a key role in the testing phase of system implementation.

---

**Note** Domains and columns need not contain only single scalar values. As long as the values are accessible only through predefined operations, you can have fixed vector values, such as a point in a plane (e.g., longitude and latitude). The ability to represent these values in SQL Server data was actually new to SQL Server 2005 and will be discussed in Chapter 5. In 2008, we now have spatial datatypes that represent a scalar (a point or a shape), but the internals can require a nonfixed number of points. The spatial datatypes are a bit of a challenge to the concept of a "fixed vector" of values, a topic we will discuss in more detail in Appendix C when the spatial datatypes are being introduced.

---

# Metadata

Metadata is data stored to describe other data. Knowing how to find information about the data stored in your system is very important. Codd's fourth rule states the following:

> *The database description is represented at the logical level in the same way as ordinary data, so that authorized users can apply the same relational language to its interrogation as they apply to regular data.*

This means you should be able to interrogate the system metadata using the same language you use to interrogate the user data (i.e., SQL).

According to relational theory, a relation consists of two parts:

- *Heading*: The set of column name/datatype name pairs that define the columns of the table
- *Body*: The rows that make up the table

In SQL Server—and most databases—it is common to consider the catalog as a collective description of the tables and other structures in the database. SQL Server exposes the heading information in a couple of ways:

- In a set of views known as the *information schema*. It is best to use this as the primary means of viewing the properties of the objects in your database as far as is possible. It consists of a standard set of views used to view the system metadata and should exist on all database servers of any brand.
- In the SQL Server–specific *catalog* (or *system*) *views*. These views give you information about the implementation of your objects and many more physical properties of your system.

# Keys

In relational theory, a relation is not allowed to have duplicate tuples. In all RDBMS products, however, there is no limitation that says that there must not be duplicate rows. However, it is strongly recommended that all tables have at least one candidate key defined to make certain that all rows are unique. SQL Server does not have to be used in a proper relational manner, and some people don't mind having duplicate rows (if you are one of these people and still think that way after reading this book, please send us an e-mail at louis@drsql.org). However, in general, not defining keys and therefore allowing duplicate rows is very poor practice, as we will discuss in the next section.

> ■**Note** Having a table without keys is useful when doing some operations, such as when you need to import data from a text file; then if uniqueness were enforced strictly in an RDBMS, you would have to do the cleansing of duplicate data in the text file. It can be much easier to import the data and do the cleansing inside the database using SQL commands.

## Purpose of Keys

Every table should have at least one *candidate key*—an attribute (or combination of attributes) that can uniquely and unambiguously identify each instance of an entity (or, in the implementation model, each row in the table). In order to enforce this, the implementation of keys in the RDBMS will prevent duplicate values.

Consider the following table, T, with columns X and Y:

```
X    Y
---  ---
1    1
2    1
```

If the design allowed the following INSERT operation:

```
INSERT T (X,Y)
VALUES (1,1)
```

then there would be two identical rows in the table. This would be problematic for a couple of reasons:

- Remember that rows in a table are unordered. Hence, without keys, there would be no way to tell which of the rows with value (1,1) in the preceding table was which. Hence, it would be impossible to distinguish between these rows, meaning that there would be no logical method of accessing a single row. This makes it tricky to use, change, or delete an individual row without resorting to "tricks" that Microsoft has allowed in SQL Server (such as the TOP operator in statements).

- If more than one row has the same values, it describes the same object, so if you try to change one of the rows, then the other row should also change, and this becomes a messy situation.

If you had defined a key on column X, then the previous INSERT would fail, as would any other insert of a value of 1 for the X column, such as VALUES (1,3). Alternatively, if you create a key based on both columns X and Y (known as a *composite key*), the (1,3) insert would be allowed, but the (1,1) insert would still be forbidden.

---

**Note** In a practical sense, no two rows can really be the same, because there are hidden attributes in the implementation details that prevent this situation from occurring (such as a row number or the exact location in the physical storage medium). However, this sort of physical thinking has no place in relational database design.

---

In summary, a key defines the uniqueness of rows over a column or set of columns. A table may have as many keys as is required to maintain the uniqueness of its rows, and a key may have as many columns as is needed to define its uniqueness. The name *candidate key* might seem odd for this item, but it is so named because the keys defined may be used either as a primary key or as an alternate key.

## Primary and Alternate Keys

A *primary key* (PK) is used as the primary identifier for an entity. It is used to uniquely identify every instance of that entity. It may be that you have more than one key that can perform this role, in which case, after the primary key is chosen, each remaining candidate key would be referred to as an *alternate key* (AK).

For example, in the United States, you wouldn't want two employees with the same Social Security number (unless you are trying to check "IRS agent" off your list of people you haven't had a visit from). Every employee probably also has a unique, company-supplied identification number. One of these could be chosen as a PK (most likely the employee number), and the other would then be an AK.

The choice of primary key is largely a matter of convenience and what is easiest to use. We'll discuss primary keys later in this chapter in the context of relationships. The important thing to remember is that when you have values that should exist only once in the database, you need to protect against duplicates.

## Choosing Keys

While keys can consist of any number of columns, it is best to try to limit the number of columns in a key as much as possible. For example, you may have a `Book` table with the columns `Publisher_Name`, `Publisher_City`, `ISBN_Number`, `Book_Name`, and `Edition`. From these attributes, the following three keys might be defined:

- `Publisher_Name`, `Book_Name`, `Edition`: A publisher will likely publish more than one book. Also, it is safe to assume that book names are not unique across all books. However, it is probably true that the same publisher will not publish two books with the same title and the same edition (at least, we assume that this is true!).

- `ISBN_Number`: The ISBN number is the unique identification number assigned to a book when it is published.

- `Publisher_City`, `ISBN_Number`: Because `ISBN_Number` is unique, it follows that `Publisher_City` and `ISBN_Number` combined is also unique.

The choice of (`Publisher_Name`, `Book_Name`) as a composite candidate key seems valid, but the (`Publisher_City`, `ISBN_Number`) key requires more thought. The implication of this key is that in every city, `ISBN_Number` can be used again, a conclusion that is obviously not appropriate. This is a common problem with composite keys, which are often not thought out properly. In this case, you might choose `ISBN_Number` as the PK and (`Publisher_Name`, `Book_Name`) as the AK.

---

■**Note**  It is important to not confuse unique indexes with keys. There may be valid performance-based reasons to implement the `Publisher_City`, `ISBN_Number` index in your SQL Server database. However, this would not be identified as a key of a table. In Chapter 6, we'll discuss implementing keys, and in Chapter 8, we'll cover implementing indexes for data access enhancement.

---

Having established what keys are, we'll next discuss the two main types of keys: natural keys (including smart keys) and surrogate keys.

## Natural Keys

Wikipedia (http://www.wikipedia.com) defines the term *natural key* as "a candidate key that has a logical relationship to the attributes within that row" (at least it did when this chapter was written). In other words, it is a "real" attribute of an entity that the user logically uses to uniquely identify each instance of an entity. From our previous examples, all of our candidate keys so far—employee number, Social Security number (SSN), ISBN, and the (`Publisher_Name`, `Book_Name`) composite key—have been examples of natural keys.

Some common examples of good natural keys are as follows:

- *For people*: Driver's license numbers (including the state of issue), company identification number, or other assigned IDs (e.g., customer numbers or employee numbers).

- *For transactional documents (e.g., invoices, bills, and computer-generated notices)*: These usually have some sort of number assigned when they are printed.

- *For products for sale*: These could be product numbers (product names are likely not unique).

- *For companies that clients deal with*: These are commonly assigned a customer/client number for tracking.

- *For buildings*: This is usually the complete address, including the postal code.

- *For mail*: These could be the addressee's name and address and the date the item was sent.

Be careful when choosing a natural key. Ideally, you are looking for something that is stable, that you can control, and that is definitely going to allow you to uniquely identify every row in your database.

One thing of interest here is that what might be considered a natural key in your database is often not actually a natural key in the place where it is defined, for example, the driver's license number of a person. In the example database, this is a number that every person has (or may need before inclusion in our database, perhaps). However, the value of the driver's license number is just a series of integers. This number did not actually occur in nature tattooed on the back of the person's neck at birth. In the database where that number was created, it was actually more of a surrogate key (which we will define in a later section).

Given that three-part names are common in the United States, it is usually relatively rare that you'll have two people working in the same company or attending the same school who have the same three names. (Of course, if you work in a company with 200,000 people, the odds will go up that you will have duplicates.) If you include prefixes and suffixes, it is a bit less likely, but "rare" or even "extremely rare" cannot be implemented in a manner that makes it a safe key. If you happen to hire two people called Sir Lester James Fredingston III, then the second of them probably isn't going to take kindly to being called Les for short just so your database system isn't compromised.

One notable profession where names must be unique is acting. No two actors who have their union cards can have the same name. Some change their names from Archibald Leach to something more pleasant like Cary Grant, but in some cases the person wants to keep his or her name, so in the actors database they add a *uniquifier* to the name to make it unique.

A uniquifier might be some meaningless value added to a column or set of columns to give you a unique key. For example, five people (up from four, last edition) are listed on the Internet Movie Database site (http://www.imdb.com) with the name Gary Grant (not Cary, but Gary). Each has a different number associated with his name to make him a unique Gary Grant. (Of course, none of these people has hit the big time, but watch out—it could be happening soon!)

---

**Tip** We tend to think of names in most systems as a kind of semiunique natural key. This isn't good enough for identifying a single row, but it's great for a human to find a value. The phone book is a good example of this. Say you need to find Ray Janakowski in the phone book. There might be more than one person with this name, but it might be a "good enough" way to look up a person's phone number. This semiuniqueness is a very interesting attribute of a table and should be documented for later use, but only in rare cases would you use the semiunique values and make a key from them using a uniquifier.

---

## Smart Keys

A commonly occurring type of natural key in computer systems is a *smart* or *intelligent key*. Some identifiers will have additional information embedded in them, often as an easy way to build a unique value for helping a human identify some real-world thing. In most cases, the smart key can be disassembled into its parts. In some cases, however, the data will probably not jump out at you. Take the following example of the fictitious product serial number XJV102329392000123:

- *X*: Type of product (LCD television)
- *JV*: Subtype of product (32-inch console)

- *1023*: Lot that the product was produced in (the 1023rd batch produced)
- *293*: Day of year
- *9*: Last digit of year
- *2*: Color
- *000123*: Order of production

The simple-to-use smart key values serve an important purpose to the end user, in that the technician who received the product can decipher the value and see that in fact this product was built in a lot that contained defective whatchamajiggers, and he needs to replace it. The essential thing for us during the logical design phase is to find all the bits of information that make up the smart keys because each of these values is likely going to need to be stored in its own column.

Smart keys, while useful in some cases, often present the database implementor with problems that will occur over time. When at all possible, instead of implementing a single column with all of these values, consider having multiple column values for each of the different pieces of information and calculating the value of the smart key. The end user gets what they need, and you in turn get what you need, a column value that never needs to be broken down into parts to work with.

A big problem with smart keys is that it is possible to run out of unique values for the constituent parts, or some part of the key (e.g., the product type or subtype) may change. It is imperative that you be very careful and plan ahead if you use smart keys to represent multiple pieces of information. When you have to change the format of smart keys, it often becomes a large validation problem to make sure that different values of the smart key are actually valid.

---

**Note** Smart keys are useful tools to communicate a lot of information to the user in a small package. However, all the bits of information that make up the smart key need to be identified, documented, and implemented in a straightforward manner. Optimum SQL code expects the data to all be stored in individual columns, and as such, it is of great importance that you needn't ever base computing decisions on decoding the value. We will talk more about the subject of choosing implementation keys in Chapter 5.

---

## Surrogate Keys

*Surrogate keys* (sometimes described as *artificial keys*) are kind of the opposite of natural keys. The word *surrogate* means "something that substitutes for," and in this case, a surrogate key substitutes for a natural key. Sometimes there may not be a natural key that you think is stable or reliable enough to use, in which case you may decide to use a surrogate key. In reality, many of our examples of natural keys were actually surrogate keys in their original database but were elevated to a natural status by usage in the "real" world.

A surrogate key can uniquely identify each instance of an entity, but it has no actual meaning with regard to that entity other than to represent existence. Surrogate keys are usually maintained by the system. Common methods for creating surrogate key values are using a monotonically increasing number (e.g., an Identity column), some form of hash function, or even a globally unique identifier (GUID), which is a very long identifier that is unique on all machines in the world.

The concept of a surrogate key can be troubling to purists. Since the surrogate key does not describe the row at all, can it really be an attribute of the row? Nevertheless, an exceptionally nice aspect of a surrogate key is that the value of the key should never change. This, coupled with the fact that surrogate keys are always a single column, makes several aspects of implementation far easier.

The only reason for the existence of the surrogate key is to identify a row. The main reason for an artificial key is to provide a key that an end user never has to view and never has to interact with. Think of it like your driver's license number, an ID number that is given to you when you begin to drive. It may have no other meaning than a number that helps a police officer look up who you are when you've been testing to see just how fast you can go in sixth gear (although in the United Kingdom it is a scrambled version of the date of birth). The surrogate key should always have some element that is just randomly chosen, and it should never be based on data that can change. If your driver's license number were a smart key and decoded to include your hair color, the driver's license number might change frequently (for some youth and we folks whose hair has turned a different color). No, this value is good only for looking you up in a database.

Usually a true surrogate key is never shared with any users. It will be a value generated on the computer system that is hidden from use, while the user directly accesses only the natural keys' values. Probably the best reason for this definition is that once a user has access to a value, it then may need to be modified. For example, if you were customer 0000013 or customer 00000666, you might request a change.

---

**■Note** In some ways, surrogate keys should probably not even be mentioned in the logical design section of this book, but it is important to know of their existence, since they will undoubtedly still crop up in some logical designs. A typical flame war on the newsgroups (and amongst the tech reviewers of this book) is concerning whether surrogate keys are a good idea. I'm a proponent of their use (as you will see), but I try to be fairly open in my approach in the book to demonstrate both ways of doing things. Generally speaking, if a value is going to be accessible to the end user, my preference is that it really needs to be modifiable and readable. You can also have two surrogate keys in a table: one that is the unchanging "address" of a value, the other that is built for user consumption (that is compact, readable, and changeable if it somehow offends your user).

---

Just as the driver's license number probably has no meaning to the police officer other than a means to quickly call up and check your records, the surrogate is used to make working with the data programmatically easier. Since the source of the value for the surrogate key does not have any correspondence to something a user might care about, once a value has been associated with a row, there is not ever a reason to change the value. This is an exceptionally nice aspect of surrogate keys. The fact that the value of the key does not change, coupled with the fact that it is always a single column, makes several aspects of implementation far easier. This will be made clearer later in the book when choosing a primary key.

Thinking back to the driver's license analogy, if the driver's license card has just a single value (the surrogate key) on it, how would Officer Uberter Sloudoun determine whether you were actually the person identified? He couldn't, so there are other attributes listed, such as name, birth date, and usually your picture, which is an excellent unique key for a human to deal with (except possibly for identical twins, of course). In this very same way, a table ought to have other keys defined as well, or it is not a proper table.

Consider the earlier example of a product identifier consisting of seven parts:

- *X*: Type of product (LCD television)
- *JV*: Subtype of product (32-inch console)
- *1023*: Lot that the product was produced in (the 1023rd batch produced)
- *293*: Day of year
- *9*: Last digit of year
- *2*: Color
- *000123*: Order of production

A natural key would consist of these seven parts. There is also a product serial number, which is the concatenation of the values such as XJV102329392000123 to identify the row. Say you also have a surrogate key on the table that has a value of 3384038483. If the only key defined on the rows is the surrogate, the following situation might occur:

```
SurrogateKey  ProductSerialNumber
------------  --------------------
10            XJV102329392000123
3384038483    XJV102329392000123
3384434222    ZJV104329382043534
```

The first two rows are not duplicates, but since the surrogate key values have no real meaning, in essence these are duplicate rows, since the user could not effectively tell them apart.

This sort of problem is common, because most people using surrogate keys do not understand that only having a surrogate key opens them up to having rows with duplicate data in the columns where the data has some logical relationship to each other. A user looking at the preceding table would have no clue which row actually represented the product he or she was after, or if both rows did.

**Note** When doing logical design, I tend to model each table with a surrogate key, since during the design process I may not yet know what the final keys will in fact turn out to be. This approach will become obvious throughout the book, especially in the case study presented throughout much of the book.

## Missing Values (NULLs)

If you look up the definition of a "loaded subject" in a computer dictionary, you will likely find the word NULL. In the database, there must exist some way to say that the value of a given column is not known or that the value is irrelevant. Often, a value outside of legitimate actual range (sometimes referred to as a *sentinel* value) is used to denote this value. For decades, programmers have used ancient dates in a date column to indicate that a certain value does not matter, they use a negative value where it does not make sense in the context of a column, or they simply use a text string of 'UNKNOWN' or 'N/A'. These approaches are fine, but special coding is required to deal with these values, for example:

```
IF (value<>'UNKNOWN') THEN ...
```

This is OK if it needs to be done only once. The problem, of course, is that this special coding is needed *every time* a new type of column is added. Instead, it is common to use a value of NULL, which in relational theory means an empty set or a set with no value. Going back to Codd's rules, the third rule states the following:

> NULL *values (distinct from empty character string or a string of blank characters or zero) are supported in the RDBMS for representing missing information in a systematic way, independent of data type.*

There are a couple of properties of NULL that you need to consider:

- Any value concatenated with NULL is NULL. NULL can represent any valid value, so if an unknown value is concatenated with a known value, the result is still an unknown value.

- All math operations with NULL will return NULL, for the very same reason that any value concatenated with NULL returns NULL.

- Logical comparisons can get tricky when NULL is introduced.

Let's expand this last point somewhat. When NULL is introduced into Boolean expressions, the truth tables get more complex. When evaluating a condition, there are three possible outcomes: TRUE, FALSE, or UNKNOWN. Only if the search condition evaluates to TRUE will a row appear in the results. If one of your conditions is NULL=1, you might be tempted to assume that the answer to this is FALSE, when in fact this actually resolves to UNKNOWN. Remember that I said that NULL values represent missing values—"missing" implies that a value *may* exist.

This is most interesting because of queries such as the following:

```
SELECT CASE WHEN 1=NULL or NOT(1=NULL) THEN 'True' ELSE 'NotTrue' END
```

Many people would expect NOT(1=NULL) to evaluate to TRUE, but in fact 1=NULL is UNKNOWN, and NOT(1=NULL) is also UNKNOWN. The opposite of unknown is not, as you might guess, known. Instead, since you aren't sure if UNKNOWN represents TRUE or FALSE, the opposite might also be TRUE or FALSE.

Table 1-4 shows the truth table for the NOT operator.

**Table 1-4.** *NOT Truth Table*

| Operand1 | NOT(Operand1) |
| --- | --- |
| TRUE | FALSE |
| UNKNOWN | UNKNOWN |
| FALSE | TRUE |

Table 1-5 shows the truth tables for the AND and OR operators.

**Table 1-5.** *AND and OR Truth Table*

| Operand1 | Operand2 | AND | OR |
| --- | --- | --- | --- |
| TRUE | TRUE | TRUE | TRUE |
| TRUE | FALSE | FALSE | TRUE |
| TRUE | UNKNOWN | UNKNOWN | TRUE |
| FALSE | FALSE | FALSE | FALSE |
| FALSE | UNKNOWN | FALSE | UNKNOWN |

I just want to point out that NULLs exist and are part of the basic foundation of relational databases; I don't intend to go too awfully far into how to program with them. The goal in your designs will be to minimize the use of NULLs, but unfortunately it is impossible to completely ignore them, particularly because they begin to appear in your SQL statements even when you do an outer join operation. This section will help you avoid the worst problems that you are bound to encounter.

# Relationship Between Entities

I have established what an entity is and how entities are structured (especially with an eye on the future tables you will create), but entities are just the beginning. To make entities more interesting, and especially to achieve some of the structural requirements to implement tables in the desired shapes, you will need to link entities together (sometimes even linking an entity to itself). You do this by recognizing and defining the relationship between the entities. Without the concept of a relationship, it would be necessary to simply put all data into a single entity, which would be a very bad idea because of the need to repeat data over and over (repeating groups of data is the primary no-no in good database design).

A term that we need to establish before getting started is one that you no doubt will already have heard as a reader of this book. It is a *foreign key*. A foreign key is used to establish a link between two tables by stating that a set of column values in one table is required to match the column values in a candidate key in another (commonly the primary key, but any declared candidate key will do).

The foreign key is one of the most important tools to maintaining the integrity of the database, but it does not deal with *all* relationship types, only the simple ones. A common mistake when discussing relationships is to think that all relationships between entities can directly correspond to a foreign key. During the logical design phase, this is often not going to be the case, and sometimes it will require additional tables to be created to implement a relationship, and sometimes you will not be able to implement a relationship using simple SQL constructs.

When defining the relationship of one entity to another, several factors are important:

- *Involved entities*: The entities that are involved in the relationship will be important to how easy the relationship is to work with. The number of related entities need not be two. Sometimes it is just one entity, such as an employee table where you need to denote that one employee works for another, or sometimes it is more than two; for example, Book Wholesalers, Books, and Book Stores are all commonly related entities.

- *Ownership*: It is common that one entity will "own" the other entity. For example, an invoice will have invoice line items. Without the invoice, there would be no line items.

- *Cardinality*: Cardinality indicates the number of instances of one entity that can be related to another. For example, a person might be allowed to have only one spouse (would you really want more?), but a person could have any number of children.

For an example of a relationship between two tables, consider the relationship between a Parent table, which stores the SSNs and names of parents, and a Child table, which does the same for the children, as shown in Figure 1-3. Bear in mind a few things. First, this is a simple example that does not take into full consideration all of the intricacies of people's names. Second, the parent and child might be located in the same table. This will be discussed more later in the book.

**Parent**

| Parent SSN | Parent Name |
|---|---|
| 111-11-1111 | Larry Bull |
| 222-22-2222 | Fred Badezine |

**Child**

| Child SSN | Child Name | Parent SSN |
|---|---|---|
| 333-33-3333 | Tay | 111-11-1111 |
| 444-44-4444 | Maya | 222-22-2222 |
| 555-55-5555 | Riely | 222-22-2222 |

**Figure 1-3.** *Sample Parent and Child tables*

In the Child table, the Parent SSN is the foreign key (denoted in these little diagrams using a double line). It is used in a Child row to associate the child with the parent. From these tables, you can see that Tay's dad is Larry Bull, and the parent of Maya is Fred Badezine.

The fact that we used parents and children as an example was not happenstance. Not only is it an example that everyone can understand, but also it introduces two common terms that are central to the implementation of relationships. The table containing the primary key is known as the *parent* table, and the table that receives the primary key and uses it as the foreign key is the *child* table. These terms will be used quite often throughout the book. The copying of the key from the parent to the child to establish the relationship is referred to as *migrating the key*.

---

**Note** For a little history, I should mention that the Integrity Independence Rule (Codd's twelfth rule) requires that for all nonoptional foreign key values in the database, there must be a matching primary key value in the related table.

---

There are several additional things to note about this. First, there is the matter of ownership. Clearly, it is not politically correct to say that a parent "owns" their child, but in reality, it does follow that without a parent, there would be no child. So, if you did have a `Parent` and `Child` table, the `Parent` would own the `Child`. (Please don't start any cults based on this book unless the focus is strictly on database design.)

Cardinality is the next question. The realities of the relationship between parent and child dictate that:

- One parent can have any number of children, even zero.

- Depending on the purpose of the database, the child can have a limited number of parents: a fixed number of 2 if the database stores biological parents and 0 or more if you are talking about guardians, living parents, and so on.

The key to this whole section is that even for such a seemingly simple scenario, things are quite complicated. And we didn't even broach the subject of whether a child could also be a parent, in which case we would change the structure such that we had an entity for person and then allow for a relationship to exist between instances of the entity.

In this section, we'll discuss the logical relationship types, and we'll cover how to implement the relationships later. These relationships can be divided at this point into two basic types:

- Binary relationships
- Nonbinary relationships

The distinction between the two types lies in the number of tables involved in the relationship. A *binary relationship* involves two entities (or one table related to itself). A *nonbinary relationship* involves more than two entities. This may seem like a small distinction, but it really is not.

When you are doing your conceptual design, you need to keep this distinction in mind and learn to recognize each of the possible relationships. When we introduce data modeling in Chapter 2, you'll learn how to represent each of these in a data model.

## Binary Relationships

The number of rows that may participate in each side of the relationship is known as the *cardinality* of the relationship. Different cardinalities of binary relationships will be introduced in this section:

- One-to-many relationships
- Many-to-many relationships

Each of these relationship types and their different subtypes has specific uses and specific associated challenges.

### One-to-Many Relationships

One-to-many relationships are the class of relationships whereby one table migrates its primary key to another table as a foreign key. As discussed earlier, this is commonly referred to as a *parent/child* relationship and concerns itself only with the relationship between exactly two tables. A child may have at most, one parent, but a parent may have many children. Note too that the name *one-to-many* is a general term used, but when implementing the relationship, a more specific specification of cardinality is done, where the *one* part of the name really can mean zero or one, and *many* can mean zero, one, a specific amount, or an unlimited amount.

It should be immediately clear what when the type of relationship starts with one, as in one-to . . . One row is related to some number of other rows. However, sometimes a child row can be related to zero parent rows. This is often referred to as an *optional relationship*. If you consider the earlier Parent/Child example, if this relationship was optional, it would mean that a child may exist without a parent. If the relationship between parent and child were optional, it would be OK to have a child named Sonny who did not have a parent, as shown in Figure 1-4.

**Parent**

| Parent SSN | Parent Name |
|---|---|
| 111-11-1111 | Larry Bull |
| 222-22-2222 | Fred Badezine |

**Child**

| Child SSN | Child Name | Parent SSN |
|---|---|---|
| 333-33-3333 | Tay | 111-11-1111 |
| 444-44-4444 | Maya | 222-22-2222 |
| 555-55-5555 | Riely | 222-22-2222 |
| 666-66-6666 | Sonny | |

**Figure 1-4.** *Sample table including a parentless child*

The missing value would be denoted by NULL, so the row for Sonny would be stored as (NULL, Larry). Optional relationships are covered in Chapter 2. For the general case, we (and most others in normal conversation) will speak in terms of one-to ____ relationships, just for ease of discussion.

For the rest of this section on binary relationships, we will discuss several different variations that have different implications later during implementation:

- *One-to-many*: The general case, where many can be between zero and infinity.

- *One-to-exactly N*: In this case, one parent row is required to be related to a given number of child rows. For example, a child can have only two biological parents. The common case is one-to-zero or one.

- *One-to-between X and Y*: Usually the case that X is 0 and Y is some boundary set up to make life easier. For example, a user may have a maximum of two usernames.

### One-to-Many (the General Case)

The one-to-many relationship is the most common and the most important relationship type. For each parent row, there may exist unlimited child rows. An example one-to-many relationship might be Customer to Orders, as illustrated in Figure 1-5.

| Customer Number | Name |
|---|---|
| 1 | Joe's Fisheteria |
| 2 | Betty's Bass Shop |
| 3 | Fred Fish |

| Customer Number | Order Number | Order Date |
|---|---|---|
| 1 | 100000002 | 20070510 |
| 1 | 100000004 | 20070511 |
| 2 | 100000008 | 20070522 |
| 2 | 100000009 | 20070701 |
| 2 | 100000022 | 20070531 |
| 3 | 100000028 | 20070613 |

**Figure 1-5.** *One-to-many example*

Quite often, a one-to-many relationship will implement a relationship between two tables that indicates that the parent "has" (or "has-a") child. For example, a parent has a child. A team has players. A class has students. This category generally indicates ownership by the parent of the child. "Has" relationships often indicate an attribute of the parent that has many values.

A special case of a one-to-many relationship is a *recursive relationship*. In a recursive relationship, the parent and the child are in the same table. This kind of relationship is used to model a tree data structure using SQL constructs. As an example, consider the classic example of a bill of materials. Take something as simple as a ceiling fan. In and of itself, a ceiling fan can be considered a part for sale by a manufacturer, and each of its components is, in turn, also a part that has a different part number. Some of these components also consist of parts. In this example, the ceiling fan could be regarded as made up recursively of each of its parts, and in turn each part consists of all of its constituent parts.

The following table is small subset of the parts that make up a ceiling fan. Each of the parts 2, 3, and 4 are all parts of a ceiling fan. You have a set of blades and a light assembly (among other things). Then part 4, the globe that protects the light, is part of the light assembly. (OK, I had better stop here, or some of you might get turned on to go to The Home Depot rather than read the rest of the book!)

```
Part Number    Description          Used In Part Number
-----------    -----------          -----------
1              Ceiling Fan
2              White Fan Blade Kit   1
3              Light Assembly        1
4              Light Globe           3
```

### One-to-Exactly N Relationship

Often, instead of allowing unlimited children, there is some limit required by the situation being modeled, or a business rule. For example, a business rule might state that a user must have two e-mail addresses. Figure 1-6 shows an example of a one-to-two relationship cardinality. (It's not particularly a likely occurrence to have names like this, but the point here is that each relationship has one parent and two children and that examples of this type are pretty rare.)

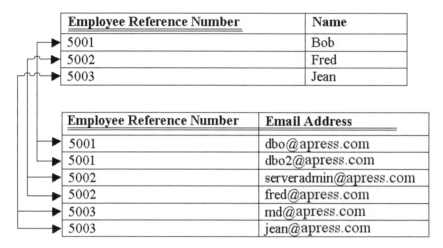

| Employee Reference Number | Name |
|---|---|
| 5001 | Bob |
| 5002 | Fred |
| 5003 | Jean |

| Employee Reference Number | Email Address |
|---|---|
| 5001 | dbo@apress.com |
| 5001 | dbo2@apress.com |
| 5002 | serveradmin@apress.com |
| 5002 | fred@apress.com |
| 5003 | md@apress.com |
| 5003 | jean@apress.com |

**Figure 1-6.** *Example of a one-to-two relationship*

The most typical version of a one-to-N relationship type that gets used on occasion is a one-to-one relationship. This states that for any given parent, there may exist exactly one instance of the child. Another example here is that a child has only two biological parents, but it gets trickier going the other direction, because a parent has no logical limitation on the number of children they can have (other than the amount of sleep they need, that is).

A one-to-one relationship may be a simple "has-a" relationship like this example (i.e., a house has a location), or it may be what is referred to as an "is-a" relationship. "Is-a" relationships indicate that one entity extends another. For example, say there exists a person entity and an employee entity. Employees are all people (in most companies); thus, they need the same attributes as people, so we will use a one-to-one relationship: employee is a person.

### Many-to-Many Relationships

The final type of binary relationship is the many-to-many relationship. Instead of there being a single parent and one or more children, there would be more than one parent with more than one child. For example, a child has (biologically, at least) more than one parent: a mother and a father. This mother and father may have more than one child, and each mother and father can have children from other relationships as well.

Another common example of a many-to-many relationship is a car dealer. Pick nearly any single model of car, and you'll see that it is sold by many different car dealers. Then take one car dealer. It in turn sells many different car models.

Note also that a large number of relationships between entities you will encounter will actually be many-to-many relationships. For example, it seems that relationships like an album's relationship to a song is simply one-to-many when you begin defining your entities, yet a song can be on many albums. And once you start to include concepts such as singers, musicians, writers, and so on, into the equation, you will see that it requires a lot of many-to-many relationships to adequately model those relationships. An important part of the design phase is to examine the cardinality of your relationships and make sure you have considered how entities relate to one another in reality, as well as in your computer system.

The many-to-many relationship is not directly implementable using a simple SQL relationship but is typically implemented by introducing another relationship table. Instead of the key from one table being migrated to the other table, the keys from both tables in the relationship are migrated to a new table that is used to implement the relationship. In Chapter 2, we'll present more examples and discuss how to implement the many-to-many relationship.

### Nonbinary Relationships

Nonbinary relationships involve more than two tables in the relationship. Nonbinary relationships can be very problematic to discover and model properly, yet they are far more common than you might expect, for example:

> A **room** is used for an **activity** in a given **time period.**

> **Publishers** sell **books** through **bookstores**.

Each of these will often begin with three entities and one associative entity/relationship that relates all tables together:

```
Room (room_number)
Activity (activity_name)
Time_Period (time_period_name)
Room_Activity_TimePeriod (room number, activity_name, time_period_name)
```

From there, it may or may not be possible to break down the relationships between these tables (commonly known as a *ternary* relationship because of the three tables) further into a series of relationships between the entities that will satisfy the requirements in an easy-to-use manner. Often, what starts out as a complex ternary relationship is actually discovered to be a couple of binary relationships that are easy to work with. This is part of the normalization process that will be covered in the "Advanced Normalization" section of Chapter 4. During the earlier, conceptual phases of design, it is enough to simply locate the existence of the different types of relationships.

# Data Access Language (SQL)

One of the more important aspects of relational theory is that there must be a high-level language through which all data access takes place. Codd's fifth rule states the following:

> A relational system may support several languages and various modes of terminal use (for example, the fill-in-blanks mode). However, there must be at least one language whose statements are expressible, by some well-defined syntax, as character strings, and whose ability to support all of the following is comprehensive: data definition, view definition, data manipulation (interactive and by program), integrity constraints, and transaction boundaries (begin, commit, and rollback).

This language has been standardized over the years in SQL. Throughout this book, we will use most of the capabilities listed in the fifth rule in some way, shape, or form:

- *Data and view definition*: Chapters 5 and 6
- *Integrity constraints*: Chapter 6

- *Transaction boundaries*: Chapter 9
- *Data manipulation*: Chapter 10

---

■**Note** SQL that is used to define objects is commonly referred to as Data Definition Language (DDL), and SQL that is used to manipulate data is known as Data Manipulation Language (DML). In this book, I assume you have used SQL before, so you know that most everything done is handled by four statements: SELECT, INSERT, UPDATE, and DELETE.

---

SQL is a *relational* language, in that you work on relations or *sets* of data at a time, rather than on one row at a time. This is an important concept. Codd's seventh rule states the following:

> *The capability of handling a base relation or a derived relation as a single operand applies not only to the retrieval of data but also to the insertion, update, and deletion of data.*

What is amazingly cool about SQL as a language is that one very simple statement almost always represents hundreds and thousands of lines of code being executed. Most of this code executes in the physical realm, accessing data on disk drives, moving that data into registers, and performing operations in the CPU (envision Tim Allen on *Home Improvement* grunting here, please).

An overarching goal of efficient SQL usage is to do as much work on data in our tables using set-based operations. SQL tables are built to effectively work on lots of data at one time. Where a normal language might be optimized for running many single statements over and over, SQL is optimized for running one statement that does many things.

Finally, the last point we'll try to make here early in the book relates to Codd's twelfth rule, called the Nonsubversion Rule. It states the following:

> *If an RDBMS has a low-level (single-record-at-a-time) language, that low-level language cannot be used to subvert or bypass the integrity rules or constraints expressed in the higher-level (multiple-records-at-a-time) relational language.*

While the fifth rule (mentioned earlier) states that a language must exist that operates within a certain set of parameters and boundaries, supporting several types of constructs and objects, it does not preclude other languages from existing. The twelfth rule does state that all languages that act on the data must follow the rules that are defined on the data.

# Understanding Dependencies

Beyond basic database terms, I want to introduce a few mathematical concepts now before they become necessary later. They center on the concept of *dependencies*. The structure of a database is based on the idea that given one value, you can find related values. For example, take a person. If you can identify the person, you can also determine other information about the person (such as hair color, eye color, height, or weight). These values for each of these attributes may change over time, but unless the data is changed in the database, the values will be the same every time you ask the question. For example, at any given instant, there can be only one answer to the question, "what is the person's weight?"

We'll discuss three different concepts related to this in the sections that follow: functional dependency, and determinant. Each of these is based on the idea that one value depends on the value of another.

## Functional Dependency

*Functional dependency* is one of those terms that sounds more complicated than it is. It is actually a very simple concept. It basically means that if you can determine the value of attribute A given a value of attribute B, then B is dependent on A. For example, say you have a function, you execute it on one value (let's call it Value1), and the output of this function is *always* the same value (Value2). Then Value2 is functionally dependent on Value1.

In a table, consider the functional dependency of nonkey columns to key columns. For example, consider the following table T with a key of column X:

```
X     Y
---   ---
1     1
2     2
3     2
```

You can think of column Y as functionally dependent on the value in X, or fn(x) = y. Clearly, Y may be the same for different values of X, but not the other way around. This is a pretty simple yet important concept that needs to be understood. As you will see quite clearly in Chapter 4, poorly understood functional dependencies are at the heart of many database problems, for example:

```
X     Y     Z
---   ---   ---
1     1     1
2     2     4
3     2     4
```

In this example, fn(x) = y, but as far as it appears in this small subset of data, f(y) = z. Consider that f(y) = z, and you want to modify the z value to 5 for the second row:

```
X     Y     Z
---   ---   ---
1     1     1
2     2     5
3     2     4
```

Now there is a problem with our stated dependency of f(y) = z because f(2) = 5 AND 4. A common example of this is the date of birth attribute and an age attribute. The date a person is born determines his or her current age, yet a person's age does not determine his or her birth date (it does indicate a range of values, but not the value itself).

## Determinant

A term that is related to functional dependency is *determinant*, which can be defined as "any attribute or set of attributes on which any other attribute or set of attributes is functionally dependent." So, in our previous example, X would be considered the determinant. Two examples of this come to mind:

- Consider a mathematical function like 2 * X. For every value of X, a particular value will be produced. For 2 you will get 4; for 4 you will get 8. Anytime you put the value of 2 in the function, you will always return a 4, so 2 functionally determines 4 for function (2 * X). In this case, 2 is the determinant.

- In a more database-oriented example, consider the serial number of a product. From the serial number, additional information can be derived, such as the model number and other specific, fixed characteristics of the product. In this case, the serial number functionally determines the specific, fixed characteristics, and as such, the serial number is the determinant in this case.

If this all seems kind of familiar, it is because any key of a table will functionally determine the other attributes of the table, and each key will be a determinant, since it functionally determines the attributes of the table. If you have two keys, such as the primary key and alternate key of the table, each will be a determinant of the other.

# Summary

In this chapter, I introduced some of the basics of database objects and some aspects of theory. It's very important that you understand most of the concepts discussed in this chapter, since from now on, we'll assume you understand them.

We went over a road map for the different phases our database design will go through. This road map will, in fact, be the process that will be used throughout the rest of the book and is how the book is organized. The road map phases are as follows:

- *Conceptual*: Identify what the user needs.

- *Logical*: Design the database only in terms of what the user needs in a manner that is conducive to straightforward implementation.

- *Implementation*: Design and implement the database in terms of the tools used (in the case of this book, SQL Server 2005).

- *Physical*: Design and lay out the data on physical storage based on usage patterns and what works best for SQL Server.

Of course, the same person will not necessarily do every one of these steps. Some of these steps require different skill sets, and not everyone can know everything, or so we're told.

We introduced relational data structures and defined what a database is. Then we covered what tables, rows, and columns are. From there, we discussed the Information Principle (which defines that data is accessible *only* in tables and that tables have no order), defined keys, and introduced NULLs and relationships. We also presented a basic introduction to the impetus for how SQL works.

Finally, we discussed some of the mathematical concept of dependencies, which basically is concerned with noticing when the existence of a certain value requires the existence of another value. This information will be used again in Chapter 4 as we reorganize our tables for optimal usage in our relational engine.

In the next few chapters, as we start to formulate a conceptual and then a logical design, we will primarily refer to entities and their attributes. After we have logically designed our tables in the logical design phase, we'll shift gears to the implementation phase and speak of tables, rows, and columns. Here is where the really exciting part comes, because the database construction starts and our database starts to become real. Then all that is left is to load our data into a well-formed, well-protected relational database system and set our users loose!

It all starts with the material presented here, though: understanding what a table is, what a row is, and so on. As a last reminder, tables have no order. None.

# CHAPTER 2

■■■

# The Language of Data Modeling

*The Simpsons is filmed before a live studio audience.*

—"Lisa's Sax," *The Simpsons*

If the database that is being modeled is done correctly, the data model is often the best form of documentation a system gets. It gives you an overview of the foundation of the system, and programmers and end users alike can read it to get an idea of how their system works and how tables are related. Best of all, using a good tool, you can practically design the basics of a system live, right with your clients as they describe what you want (hopefully, someone else would be gathering other requirements that are not data structure related).

The first step, however, is to get a grasp on the language that the graphical depiction your model will convey. In this chapter, I will introduce the basic concept of *data modeling*, in which a representation of your database will be produced that shows the objects involved in the database design and how they interrelate. It won't be as cool as watching *The Simpsons* drawn right in front of your eyes, but then again, the writers of *The Simpsons* were more than likely making a joke. Note too that this representation, much like an episode of *The Simpsons*, is more than just pictures. It is really a description of the database, with a graphical representation being just one facet of the model. The graphical part of the model is probably the most interesting to most people, especially since it does give a very quick and easy-to-work-with overview of your objects and their relationships.

In the next section, I'll provide some basic information about data modeling and introduce the modeling tool I prefer for data modeling: IDEF1X. I'll then cover how to use the IDEF1X methodology to model and document the following:

- Entities
- Attributes
- Relationships
- Descriptive information

Finally, I'll briefly introduce several other alternative modeling methodology styles, including Information Engineering and the Chen Entity Relationship Model (ERD) methodology. I'll also show an example of the diagramming capabilities built into SQL Server Management Studio.

## Introduction to Data Modeling

Data modeling is a skill at the foundation of database design. In order to start designing databases, it is very useful to be able to effectively communicate the design as well as make it easier to visualize. Most of the objects introduced in Chapter 1 have graphical representations that make it easy to get an overview of a vast amount of database structure and metadata in a very small amount of space. As mentioned earlier, a common misconception about the data model is that it is solely about the graphical display. In fact, the model itself can exist without the graphical parts; it can consist of just textual information. Almost everything in the data model can be read in a manner that makes grammatical sense. The graphical nature is simply there to fulfill the baking powder prophecy—that a picture is worth a thousand words. It is a bit of a stretch, because as you will see, the data model will have lots of words on it!

---

■**Note** There are many types of models or diagrams: process models, data flow diagrams, data models, sequence diagrams, and others. For the purpose of database design, however, I will focus only on data models.

---

Several popular modeling languages are available to use, and each is generally just as good as the others at the job of communicating a database design. When choosing my data modeling methodology, I looked for one that was easy to read and could display and store everything required to implement very complex systems. The modeling language I use is Integration Definition for Information Modeling (IDEF1X).

IDEF1X is based on Federal Information Processing Standards Publication 184, published September 21, 1993. To be fair, the other major methodology, Information Engineering, is pretty much just as good, but I like the way IDEF1X works, and it is based on a publicly available standard. IDEF1X was originally developed by the U.S. Air Force in 1985 to meet the following requirements:

- Support the development of data models
- Be a language that is both easy to learn and robust
- Be teachable
- Be well tested and proven
- Be suitable for automation

---

■**Note** At the time of this writing, the full specification for IDEF1X is available at `http://www.itl.nist.gov/fipspubs/idef1x.doc`. The exact URL of this specification is subject to change, but you can likely locate it by searching the `http://www.itl.nist.gov` site for "IDEF1X."

---

While the selection of a data modeling methodology may be a personal choice, economics, company standards, or features usually influence tool choice. IDEF1X is implemented in many of the popular design tools, such as the following, which are just a few of the products available that claim to support IDEF1X (note that the URLs listed here were correct at the time of publication, but are subject to change in the future):

- *AllFusion ERwin Data Modeler*: `http://www.ca.com/us/products/product.aspx?ID=260`
- *Toad Data Modeler*: `http://www.quest.com/toad-data-modeler/`
- *ER/Studio*: `http://www.embarcadero.com/products/erstudio`
- *Visible Analyst DB Engineer*: `http://www.visible.com/Products/Analyst/vadbengineer.htm`
- *Visio Enterprise Edition*: `http://www.microsoft.com/office/visio`

Let's next move on to practice modeling and documenting, starting with entities.

# Entities

In the IDEF1X standard, *entities* (which, as discussed previously, are loosely synonymous with tables) are modeled as rectangular boxes, as they are in most data modeling methodologies. Two types of entities can be modeled: *identifier-independent* and *identifier-dependent*, usually referred to as *independent* and *dependent*, respectively.

The difference between a dependent entity and an independent entity has to do with how the primary key of the entity is structured. The independent entity is so named because it has no primary key dependencies on any other entity or, to put it in other words, there are no foreign key columns from other entities in the primary key.

Chapter 1 introduced the term "foreign key," and the IDEF1X specification introduces an additional term: *migrated*. The term "migrated" can be misleading, as the definition of *migrate* is "to move." The primary key of one entity is not actually moving; rather, in this context the term refers to the primary key of one entity being copied as an attribute in a different entity, establishing a relationship between the two entities.

If the primary key of one entity is migrated into the primary key of another, it is considered dependent on the other entity, because one entity is dependent on the existence of the other to have meaning. If the attributes are migrated to the nonprimary key attributes, they are "independent" of any other entities. All attributes that are not migrated as foreign keys from other entities are referred to as *owned*, as they have their origins in the current entity. Other methodologies and tools may use the terms "identifying" and "nonidentifying" instead of "owned" and "independent," as well as "dependent."

For example, consider an invoice that has one or more line items. The primary key of the invoice entity might be `invoiceNumber`. So, if the invoice has two line items, a reasonable choice for the primary key would be `invoiceNumber` and then `lineNumber`. Since the primary key contains `invoiceNumber`, it would be dependent upon the invoice entity. If you had an `invoiceStatus` entity, and it was related to `invoice`, it would be independent, as an invoice's existence is not really predicated on the existence of a status (even if a value for the `invoiceStatus` to `invoice` relationship *is* required).

An independent entity is drawn with square corners, as follows:

The dependent entity is the converse of the independent entity, as it will have the primary key of one or more entities migrated into its primary key. It is called "dependent" because its identifier depends on the existence of another entity. It is drawn with rounded-off corners, as follows:

> ■**Note** The concept of dependent and independent entities lead us to a bit of a chicken and egg paradox (not to mention, a fork in the road). The dependent entity is dependent on a certain type of relationship, yet the introduction of entity creation can't wait until after the relationships are determined, since the relationships couldn't exist without entities. If this is the first time you've looked at data models, this chapter may require a reread to get the full picture, as the concept of independent and dependent objects are linked to relationships.

One of the most important aspects of designing or implementing any system is how objects, variables, and so forth are named. If you have ever had to go back and work on code that you wrote months ago, you understand what I mean. For example, `@x` might seem like an OK variable name when you first write some code, and it certainly saves a lot of keystrokes versus typing `@holdEmployeeNameForCleaningInvalidCharacters`, but the latter is much easier to understand after a period of time has passed (for me, this period of time is approximately 14.5 seconds, but your mileage may vary).

Naming database objects is no different, and actually, it is really quite more important to name database objects clearly than it is for some other programming objects, as quite often your end users will get used to these names: the names given to entities will be translated into table names that will be used by programmers and users alike. The conceptual and logical model will be considered your primary schematic of the data in the database and should be a living document that you change before changing any implemented structures.

Most discussions on how objects should be named can get heated because there are several different "camps," each with different ideas about how to name objects. The central issue is plural or singular. Both ways have merit, but one way has to be chosen. I choose to follow the IDEF1X standard, which says to use singular names. The name itself refers to an instance of what is being modeled, but some folks believe that the table name should name the set of rows. Is either way more correct? Not really—just pick one and stick with it. The most important thing is to be consistent and not let your style go all higgledy-piggledy as you go along. Even a bad set of naming standards is better than no standards at all.

In this book, I will follow these basic guidelines for naming entities:

- *Entity names should never be plural.* The primary reason for this is that the name should refer to an instance of the object being modeled rather than the collection. This allows you to easily use the name in a sentence. It is uncomfortable to say that you have an "automobiles row," for example—you have an "automobile row." If you had two of these, you would have two automobile rows.

- *The name given should directly correspond to the essence of what the entity is modeling.* For instance, if you are modeling a person, name the entity `Person`. If you are modeling an automobile, call it `Automobile`. Naming is not always this cut and dried, but it is wise to keep names simple and to the point. If you need to be more specific, that is fine, too. Just keep it succinct (unlike this explanation!).

Entity names frequently need to be made up of several words. During logical modeling, it is acceptable to include spaces, underscores, and other characters when multiple words are necessary in the name, but it is not required. For example, an entity that stores a person's addresses might be named `Person Address`, `Person_Address` or, using the style I have recently become accustomed to and the one I'll use in this book, `PersonAddress`. This type of naming is known as *Pascal case* or *mixed case*. (When you don't capitalize the first letter, but capitalize the first letter of the second word, this style is known as *camelCase*.) Just as in the plural/singular argument, there really is no "correct" way, just the guidelines that I will follow to keep everything uniform.

Regardless of any style choices you make, no abbreviations should generally be used in the logical naming of entities. Every word should be fully spelled out, as abbreviations lower the value of the names as documentation and tend to cause confusion. Abbreviations may be necessary in the implemented model because of some naming standard that is forced on you or an industry standard term. If you do decide to use abbreviations in your names of any type, make sure that you have a standard in place to ensure the names use the same abbreviation every time. One of the primary reasons to avoid abbreviations is so you don't have to worry about different people using Description, Descry, Desc, Descrip, and Descriptn all for the same attribute on different entities. We'll delve into naming things in the implementation model further in Chapter 5.

On the other side of the spectrum, you also don't want to go too far in the direction of long, descriptive sentence names for an entity. A name such as LeftHandedMittensLostByKittensOn➥ SaturdayAfternoons (obviously quite different from LeftHandedMittensLostByKittensOnSunday➥ Mornings) will be painful to use even in the logical model. In the implementation model, the name will definitely become something that programmers and users alike will hate you for (and for good reason!). A better entity and name might be simply mitten. Much of what is encoded in that name will likely turn out to be attributes of the mitten entity: mitten status, mitten hand, mitten used by, and so forth. The breakdown of what is an attribute or column actually falls more under the heading of normalization, which I'll discuss in detail in Chapter 4.

It is often the case that novice database designers elect to use a form of *Hungarian notation* and include prefixes and or suffixes in names—for example, tblEmployee or tblCustomer. Prefixes like this are generally considered a very bad practice, because names in relational databases are almost always used in an obvious context. Using Hungarian notation is a good idea when writing functional code (like in Visual Basic or C#), since objects don't always have a very strict contextual meaning that can be seen immediately upon usage, especially if you are implementing one interface with many different types of objects. With database objects, however, it is rare that there is a question as to whether a name refers to a column or a table. Plus, it is very easy to query the system catalog to determine what the object is if it is not obvious. Not to go too far into implementation right now, but you can use the sys.objects catalog view to see the type of any object. For example, this query will list all of the different object types in the catalog (your results may vary; this query was executed against the AdventureWorks2008 database we will use for some of the examples in the book):

```
SELECT  distinct type_desc
FROM    sys.objects
```

Here's the result:

```
type_desc
--------------------------------------------
CHECK_CONSTRAINT
DEFAULT_CONSTRAINT
FOREIGN_KEY_CONSTRAINT
INTERNAL_TABLE
PRIMARY_KEY_CONSTRAINT
SERVICE_QUEUE
SQL_SCALAR_FUNCTION
SQL_STORED_PROCEDURE
SQL_TABLE_VALUED_FUNCTION
SQL_TRIGGER
SYNONYM
SYSTEM_TABLE
UNIQUE_CONSTRAINT
USER_TABLE
VIEW
```

We will use sys.objects more in Chapter 5 and beyond to view properties of objects that we create.

# Attributes

All attributes in the entity must be uniquely named within it. They are represented by a list of names inside of the entity rectangle:

```
AttributeExample
┌──────────────────┐
│ Attribute1       │
│ Attribute2       │
└──────────────────┘
```

---

■**Note**  The preceding image shows a technically invalid entity, as there is no primary key defined (as required by IDEF1X). I'll cover the notation for keys in the following section.

---

At this point, you would simply enter all of the attributes that have been defined in the discovery phase. In practice, it is likely that you would have combined the process of discovering entities and attributes with the initial modeling phase. It will all depend on how well the tools you use work. Most data modeling tools cater for building models fast and storing a wealth of information to document their entities and attributes.

In the early stages of logical modeling, there can be quite a large difference between an attribute and what will be implemented as a column. As I will demonstrate in Chapter 4, the attributes will be transformed a great deal during the normalization process. For example, the attributes of an Employee entity may start out as follows:

```
Employee
┌──────────────────┐
│ EmployeeNumber   │
│ FirstName        │
│ LastName         │
│ Address          │
│ PhoneNumber      │
└──────────────────┘
```

However, during the normalization process, tables like this will often be broken down into many attributes (e.g., address might be broken into number, street name, city, state, zip code, etc.) and possibly many different entities.

---

■**Note**  Attribute naming is one place where I tend to deviate from IDEF1X standard. The standard is that names are unique within a model. This tends to produce names that include the table name followed by the attribute name, which can result in unwieldy, long names that look archaic. There are many naming standards, some with specific abbreviations, name formats, and so forth. For example, a common one has each name formed by a descriptive name and a class word, which is an abbreviation like EmployeeNbr, ShipDt, or HouseDesc. For sake of nonpartisan naming politics, I pretty much am happy to say that any decent naming standard is acceptable, as long as it is followed.

---

Just as with entity names, there is no need to include Hungarian prefixes or suffixes in the attribute names now or in implementation names. The type of the attribute can be retrieved from the system catalog if there is any question about it.

In the following sections, we will go over the following aspects of attributes on your data model.

- Primary keys
- Alternate keys
- Foreign keys
- Domains
- Attribute naming

## Primary Keys

As noted in the previous section, an IDEF1X entity must have a primary key. This is convenient for us, as in Chapter 1 an entity was defined such that each instance must be unique. The primary key may be a single attribute, or it may be a composite of multiple attributes. A value is required for every attribute in the key (logically speaking, no nulls are allowed in the primary key).

The primary key is denoted by placing attributes above a horizontal line through the entity rectangle. Note that no additional notation is required to indicate that the value is the primary key.

```
PrimaryKeyExample
┌──────────────────────┐
│ PrimaryKey           │
├──────────────────────┤
│ Attribute1           │
│ Attribute2           │
└──────────────────────┘
```

For example, consider the `Employee` entity from the previous section. The `EmployeeNumber` attribute is going to be unique, so this would be an acceptable primary key:

```
Employee
┌──────────────────────┐
│ EmployeeNumber       │
├──────────────────────┤
│ FirstName            │
│ LastName             │
│ Address              │
│ PhoneNumber          │
└──────────────────────┘
```

The choice of primary key is an interesting one. In the early logical modeling phase, I generally do not like to spend time choosing the final primary key attribute(s). The main reason for this is to avoid worrying too much about what the key is going to be. I tend to add a simple surrogate primary key to migrate to other entities to help me see when there is any ownership. In the current example, `EmployeeNumber` clearly refers to an employee, but not every entity will be so clear, not to mention there may be more advanced business rules where `EmployeeNumber` is not always unique. Having to go back and change this in the logical model can be a tiresome activity, particularly when you have a very large model.

Also, you may have multiple things that identify a given instance of an entity. As an example, consider an entity that models a product manufactured by a company. The company may identify the product by the type, style, size, and series:

```
       Product
     ┌──────────────┐
     │ Type         │
     │ Style        │
     │ Size         │
     │ Series       │
     ├──────────────┤
     │ ProductName  │
     └──────────────┘
```

The name may also be a good key, and more than likely there is also a product code. Which is the best key—or which is even truly a key—may not become apparent until later in the process. There are many ways to implement a good key, and the best way may not be instantly recognizable.

Instead of choosing a primary key during this part of the process, I add a value to the entity for identification purposes (this value is also known as a *surrogate key* and will be discussed in more depth in Chapter 3). I then model all candidate keys (or unique identifiers) as alternate keys (which I will discuss in the next section). The result is that it is very clear in the logical model what entities are in an ownership role to other entities, since the key that is migrated contains the name of the modeled entity. I would model this entity as follows:

```
       Product
     ┌──────────────┐
     │ ProductId    │
     ├──────────────┤
     │ Type         │
     │ Style        │
     │ Size         │
     │ Series       │
     │ Name         │
     └──────────────┘
```

───────────────────────────────────────────────────────────────

■**Note** Using surrogate keys is certainly not a requirement in logical modeling; it is a personal preference that I have found a useful documentation method to keep models clean, and it corresponds to my method of implementation later. Not only is using a natural key as the primary key in the logical modeling phase reasonable, but also many architects find it preferable. Either method is perfectly acceptable.

───────────────────────────────────────────────────────────────

## Alternate Keys

As defined in Chapter 1, an alternate key is a set of one or more attributes whose uniqueness needs to be guaranteed over all of the instances of the entity. Alternate keys do not have a specific location in the entity graphic like primary keys, nor are they migrated for any relationship. They are identified on the model in a very simple manner:

AlternateKeyExample

| PrimaryKey |
| --- |
| AlternateKey1 (AK1)<br>AlternateKey2Attribute1 (AK2)<br>AlternateKey2Attribute2 (AK2) |

In this example, there are two alternate key *groups*: group AK1, which has one attribute as a member, and group AK2, which has two attributes. Thinking back to the product example, the two keys would then be modeled as follows:

Product

| ProductId |
| --- |
| Type (AK1)<br>Style (AK1)<br>Size (AK1)<br>Series (AK1)<br>Name (AK2) |

One extension that Computer Associates' ERwin adds to this notation is shown here:

AlternateKeyExample

| PrimaryKey |
| --- |
| AlternateKey1 (AK1.1)<br>AlternateKey2Attribute1 (AK2.1)<br>AlternateKey2Attribute2 (AK2.2) |

A position number notation is tacked onto the name of the key (AK1 and AK2) to denote the position of the attribute in the key. In the logical model, technically the order of attributes in the key should not be considered and certainly should not be displayed. It really does not matter which attribute comes first in the key; all that really matters is that you make sure there are unique values across multiple attributes. When a key is implemented, the order of columns *will* become interesting for performance reasons, as SQL Server implements uniqueness with an index, but uniqueness will be served no matter what the order of the columns of the key is.

---

■**Note** The discussion of indexes is left to Chapter 9, and during the conceptual and logical modeling phases, it is best practice (though perhaps completely unrealistic) to completely ignore performance tuning needs until the physical modeling phase (which also includes the tuning, indexing, and disk layout phases of the project).

---

# Foreign Keys

Foreign key attributes, as I've alluded to, are also referred to as migrated attributes. They are primary keys from one entity that serve as a reference to an instance in another entity. They are again a result of relationships (which we'll look at later in the chapter). They are indicated much like alternate keys by adding the letters "FK" after the foreign key:

```
ForeignKeyExample
┌─────────────────────────┐
│ PrimaryKey              │
├─────────────────────────┤
│ ForeignKey (FK)         │
└─────────────────────────┘
```

For example, consider an entity that is modeling a music album:

```
Album
┌─────────────────────────┐
│ AlbumId                 │
├─────────────────────────┤
│ Name (AK1)              │
│ ArtistId (FK)(AK1)      │
│ PublisherId (FK)(AK1)   │
│ CatalogNumber(AK2)      │
└─────────────────────────┘
```

The `artistId` and `publisherId` represent migrated foreign keys from the artist entity and the publisher entity. We'll revisit this example in the "Relationships" section later in the chapter.

One tricky thing about this example is that the diagram doesn't show what entity the key is migrated from. This can tend to make things a little messy, depending on how you choose your primary keys. This lack of clarity about what table a foreign key migrates from is a limitation of most modeling methodologies, as it would be unnecessarily confusing if the name of the entity where the key came from was displayed, for a couple of reasons:

- There is no limit (nor should there be) on how far a key will migrate from its original owner entity (the entity where the key value was not a migrated foreign key reference).

- It is not completely unreasonable that the same attribute might migrate from two separate entities, especially early in the logical design process. This is certainly not a design goal, but it is technically possible.

One of the reasons for the primary key scheme I will employ in logical models is to add a key named <entityName>Id as the identifier for entities so that the name of the entity is easily identifiable, and it lets us easily know where the original source of the attribute is, and we can see the attribute migrated from entity to entity even without any additional documentation.

# Domains

The term "domain" is regrettably used in two very similar contexts in the database parlance. In Chapter 1, a domain referred to a set of valid values for an attribute. In IDEF1X, you can define named, reusable specifications known as domains, for example:

- `String`: A character string

- `SocialSecurityNumber`: A character value with a format of *###-##-####*

- `PositiveInteger`: An integer value with an implied domain of 0 to `max(integer value)`
- `Truth`: A five-character value with a domain of (`'FALSE'`,`'TRUE'`)

Domains in the specification not only allow us to define the valid values that can be stored in an attribute, but also provide a form of inheritance in the datatype definitions. *Subclasses* can then be defined of the domains that inherit the settings from the base domain. It is a good practice to build domains for any attributes that get used regularly, as well as domains that are base templates for infrequently used attributes. For example, you might have a character type domain where you specify a basic length, like 60. Then you may specify common domains like *name* and *description* to use in many entities. For these, you should choose a reasonable length for the values, plus you should require that the data cannot be an empty string.

Regardless of whether or not you are using an automated tool, it is useful to define common domains that you use for specific types of things (applying a common pattern to solve a common problem). For example, a person's first name might be a domain. The reason that this is so cool is that you don't have to think "Hmm, how long to make a person's name?" more than once. After you make a decision, you just use what you have used before.

---

■**Note** Defining common domains also fights against `varchar(50)` syndrome, where every column in a database stores textual data in columns of exactly same length. Putting in some early thought on the minimum and maximum lengths of data is easier than doing it when the project manager is screaming for results later in the process and the programmers are chomping at the bit to get at your database and get coding.

---

In conceptual/logical modeling, you'll commonly want to gather a few bits of information, such as the general type of the attribute: character, numeric, logical, or even binary data. It's also important to document in some form the legal values for an attribute that is classified as being of the domain type. This is generally done using some pseudocode or in a textual manner, either in your modeling tool or even in a spreadsheet.

It is extremely important to keep these domains as implementation-independent datatype descriptions. For example, you might specify a domain of `GloballyUniqueIdentifier`, a value that will be unique no matter where it is generated. In SQL Server, a unique identifier could be used (GUID value) to implement this domain. In another operating system (created by a company other than Microsoft, perhaps) where there is not exactly the same mechanism, it might be implemented differently; the point is that it is a value that is statistically guaranteed to be unique every time the value is generated. The conceptual/logical modeling phase should be done without too much thinking about what SQL Server can do, if for no other reason than to prevent yourself from starting to impose limitations on the future solution prior to understanding the actual problem.

When you start implementation modeling, you will use the same domains to assign the implementation properties. This is the real value in using domains. By creating reusable template attributes that will also be used when you start creating columns, you'll spend less effort and time building simple entities, which make up the bulk of your work. Doing so also provides a way for you to enforce companywide standards, by reusing the same domains on all corporate models (predicated, of course, on you being diligent with your data model over time!).

Later on, implementation details such as datatype, constraints, and so forth will be chosen, just to name a few of the more basic properties that may be inherited. Since it is very likely that you will have fewer domains than implemented attributes, the double benefit of speedy and consistent model assembly is achieved. However, it is not reasonable or even useful to employ the inheritance mechanisms when building tables by hand. Implementation of domains is way too much trouble to do without a tool.

As an example of a domain hierarchy, consider this set of character string domains:

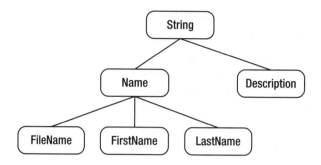

Here, String is the base domain from which you can then inherit Name and Description. FileName, FirstName, and LastName are inherited from Name. During logical modeling, this might seem like a lot of work for nothing, because most of these domains will share some basic details, such as not allowing NULLs or blank data. However, FileName may be optional, whereas LastName might be mandatory. It is important to set up domains for as many distinct attribute types as possible, in case rules or datatypes are discovered that are common to any domains that already exist.

Domains are a nice feature of IDEF1X (and other methodologies or tools that support them). They provide an easy method of building standard attribute types, reducing both the length of time required for repeating common attribute types and the number of errors that occur in doing so. Specific tools implement domains with the ability to define and inherit more properties throughout the domain chain to make creating databases easier. During logical modeling, domains can optionally be shown to the right of the attribute name in the entity:

DomainExample

| AttributeName: DomainName |
| --- |
| AttributeName2: DomainName2 |

So if I have an entity that holds domain values for describing a type of person, I might model it as follows:

Person

| PersonId: SurrogateKey |
| --- |
| Description: Description<br>FirstName: PersonFirstName<br>LastName: PersonLastName |

To model this example, I defined four domains:

- SurrogateKey: The surrogate key value. (Implementation of the surrogate should not be implied by building a domain, so later this can be implemented in any manner.) I could also choose to use a natural key.

- Description: The same type of domain as the name domain, except to hold a description (can be 60 characters maximum).

- PersonFirstName: A person's first name (30 characters maximum).

- PersonLastName: A person's last name (50 characters maximum).

The choice of the length of name is an interesting one. I searched on Google for "person first name varchar" and found lots of different possibilities: 10, 35, unlimited, 25, 20, 15—all on the first page of the search! Just as you should use a consistent naming standard, you should use standard lengths every time like data is represented, so when you hit implementation the likelihood that two columns storing like data will have different definitions is minimized.

During the implementation phase, all of the domain will get mapped to some form of datatype or, in some cases, a user-defined type. The point of a domain in the logical model is to define common types of storage patterns that can be applied in a common manner, including all of the business rules that will govern their usage.

## Naming

Attribute naming is a bit more interesting than entity naming. I stated earlier that my preference is to use singular, not plural, entity names. The same issues that apply in entity naming are technically true for attribute naming (and no one disagrees with this!). However, until the logical model is completed, the model may still have attribute names that are plural. Leaving a name plural can be a good reminder that you expect multiple values. For example, consider a Person entity with a Children attribute identified. The Person entity would identify a single person, and the Children attribute would identify sons and daughters of that person.

The naming standard I follow is very simple:

- Generally, it is not necessary to repeat the entity name in the attribute name, though it is common to do so with some primary key attributes, particularly surrogate keys, since it is specific for that table. For most attributes, the entity name is implied by the attribute's inclusion in the entity.

- The chosen attribute name should reflect precisely what is contained in the attribute and how it relates to the entity.

- As with entities, no abbreviations are to be used in attribute names, certainly not for the conceptual/logical model. Every word should be spelled out in its entirety. If for some reason an abbreviation must be used (e.g., due to the naming standard currently in use), then a method should be put into place to make sure the abbreviation is used consistently, as discussed earlier in the chapter. For example, if your organization has a ZRF "thing" that is commonly used and referred to in general conversation as a ZRF, you might use this abbreviation. In general, however, I recommend avoiding abbreviations in all naming unless the client is insistent.

- The name should contain absolutely no information other than that necessary to explain the meaning of the attribute. This means no Hungarian notation of the type of data it represents (e.g., LastNameString) or prefix notation to tell you that it is in fact an attribute.

---

**Note** Attribute names in the finalized logical and implementation models will not be plural, but we'll work this out in Chapter 4 when normalizing the model. At this point it is not a big deal at all.

---

Consistency is the key to proper naming, so if you or your organization does not have a standard naming policy, it's worthwhile to develop one. The overarching principles of my naming philosophy is to keep it simple and readable and to avoid all but universally standard corporate abbreviations. This standard will be followed from logical modeling into the implementation phase. Whatever your standard is, establishing a pattern of naming will make your models easy to follow, both for yourself and for your programmers and users. Any standard is better than no standard.

# Relationships

Up to this point, the constructs we have looked at have been pretty much the same across most data modeling methodologies. Entities are always signified by rectangles, and attributes are quite often words within the rectangles.

Relationships are where things start to get confusing, as many of the different modeling languages approach representing relationships graphically a bit differently. To make the concept of relationships clear, I need to go back to the terms "parent" and "child." Consider the following definitions from the IDEF1X specification's glossary (these are remarkably lucid definitions to have been taken straight from a government specification!):

- *Entity, Child*: The entity in a specific connection relationship whose instances can be related to zero or one instance of the other entity (parent entity)

- *Entity, Parent*: An entity in a specific connection relationship whose instances can be related to a number of instances of another entity (child entity)

- *Relationship*: An association between two entities or between instances of the same entity

In IDEF1X, every relationship is denoted by a line drawn between two entities, with a solid circle at one end of that line to indicate where the attribute is migrated to. In the following image, the primary key of the parent is migrated to the child. This is how to denote a foreign key on a model.

Relationships come in several different flavors that indicate *how* the parent table is related to the child. We will look at examples of several different types of relationships in this section:

- *Identifying*, where the primary key of one table is migrated to the primary key of another. The child will be a dependent entity.

- *Nonidentifying*, where the primary key of one table is migrated to the nonprimary key attributes of another. The child will be an independent entity as long as no identifying relationships exist.

- *Optional identifying*, when the nonidentifying relationship does not require a child value.

- *Recursive relationships*, when a table is related to itself.

- *Subtype* or *categorization*, which is a one-to-one relationship used to let one entity extend another.

- *Many-to-many*, where an instance of an entity can be related to many in another, and in turn many instances of the second entity can be related to multiples in the other.

We'll also cover the *cardinality* of the relationship (how many of the parent relate to how many of the child), *role names* (changing the name of a key in a relationship), and *verb phrases* (the name of the relationship).

Relationships are a key topic in database design, but not a completely simple one. A lot of information is related using a few dots and lines.

> **▮Tip** All of the relationships (except the last one) discussed in this section are of the one-to-many variety, which encompasses *one-to-zero, one, many,* or perhaps *exactly-n* relationships. Technically, it is more accurately *one-to-(from M to N)*, as this enables specification of the *many* in very precise (or very loose) terms as the situation dictates. However, the more standard term is "one-to-many," and I will not try to make an already confusing term more so.

## Identifying Relationships

The concept of a relationship being *identifying* is used to indicate that the essence (defined as the intrinsic or indispensable properties that serve to characterize or identify something) of the child instance is defined by the existence of a parent. Another way to look at this is that generally the child in an identifying relationship is an inseparable part of the parent. Without the existence of the parent, the child would make no sense.

The relationship is drawn as follows:

To implement this relationship in the model, the primary key attribute(s) are migrated to the primary key of the child. Because of this, the key of a parent instance is needed to be able to identify a child instance record, which is why the name *identifying relationship* is used.

In the following example, you can see that the ParentId attribute is a foreign key in the Child entity, from the Parent entity.

The child entity in the relationship is drawn as a rounded-off rectangle, which, as mentioned earlier in this chapter, means it is a dependent entity. A common example is an invoice and the line items being charged to the customer on the invoice:

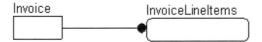

Without the existence of the invoice, the line items would have no purpose to exist. It can also be said that the line items are identified as being part of the parent.

## Nonidentifying Relationships

In contrast to identifying relationships, where  relationship indicated that the child was an essential part of the parent entity, the *nonidentifying relationship* indicates that the child represents a more informational attribute of the parent. Often, a nonidentifying relationship is used because an attribute of one table requires more than a single value.

When implementing the nonidentifying relationship, the primary key attribute is not migrated to the primary key of the child. It is denoted by a dashed line between the entities. Note too that the rectangle representing the child now has squared off corners, since it stands alone, rather than being dependent on the `Parent`:

This time, the key attribute will not migrate to the primary key; instead, it will be in the nonprimary-key attributes.

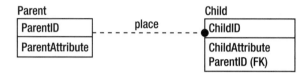

Taking again the example of an invoice, consider the vendor of the products that have been sold and documented as such in the line items. The product vendor does not define the existence of a line item, because with or without knowing the exact vendor the product originates from, the line item still makes sense.

The difference between identifying and nonidentifying relationships can be tricky but is essential to understanding the relationship between tables and their keys. If the parent entity defines the need for the existence of the child (as stated in the previous section), then use an identifying relationship. If, on the other hand, the relationship defines one of the child's attributes, then use a nonidentifying relationship.

Consider the following examples:

- *Identifying*: You have an entity that stores a contact and an entity that stores the contact's telephone number. The `Contact` defines the phone number, and without the contact, there would be no need for the `ContactPhoneNumber`.

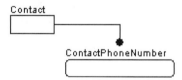

- *Nonidentifying*: Consider the entities that were defined for the identifying relationship, along with an additional entity called `ContactPhoneNumberType`. This entity is related to the `ContactPhoneNumber` entity, but in a nonidentifying way, and defines a set of possible phone number types (`Voice`, `Fax`, etc.) that a `ContactPhoneNumber` might be. The type of phone number does not identify the phone number; it simply classifies it. Even if the type wasn't known, recording the phone number could still be valid, as the number still has informational merit. However, a row associating a contact with a phone number would be useless information without the contact's existence.

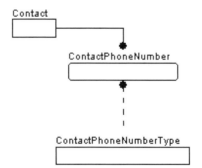

The `ContactPhoneNumberType` entity is commonly known as a *domain entity* or *domain table*, or sometimes as a *lookup table*. Rather than having a fixed domain for an attribute, an entity is designed that allows programmatic changes to the domain with no recoding of constraints or client code. As an added bonus, you can add columns to define, describe, and extend the domain values to implement business rules. It also allows the client user to build lists for users to choose values with very little programming.

---

■**Tip**  Child instances that have no corresponding parent instance are called o*rphaned rows.*

---

While every nonidentifying relationship defines the domain of an attribute of the child table, sometimes when the row is created it's not necessary that the values are selected. For example, consider a database where you model houses, like for a neighborhood. Every house would have a color, a style, and so forth. However, not every house would have an alarm company, a mortgage holder, and so on. The relationship between the alarm company and bank would be optional in this case, while the color and style relationships would be mandatory.

---

■**Note**  Here, I assume you would need an entity for both color and style. Whether or not creating a table for simple domains is a good idea will be discussed in the next couple of chapters (hint: I usually think it is a good idea).

---

The difference in the implemented table will be whether or not the child table's foreign key will allow nulls. If a value is required, then it is considered *mandatory*. If a value of the migrated key can be null, then it is considered *optional*.

The optional case is signified by an open diamond at the opposite end of the dashed line from the black circle, as shown here:

In the mandatory case, the relationship is drawn as before, without the diamond. Note that an optional relationship may have a cardinality of zero, while a mandatory relationship must have a cardinality of one or greater (cardinality refers to the number of values that can be related to another value, and the concept will be discussed further in the next section).

So why would you make a relationship optional? Consider once again the nonidentifying relationship between the invoice line item and the product vendor. The vendor in this case may be required or not required as the business rules dictate. If it is not required, you should make the relationship optional.

---

■**Note**  You might be wondering why there is not an optional identifying relationship. This is due to the fact that you may not have any optional attributes in a primary key, which is true in relational theory and for SQL Server as well.

---

For a one-to-many, optional relationship, consider the following:

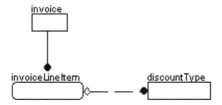

The `invoiceLineItem` entity is where items are placed onto an invoice to receive payment. The user may sometimes apply a standard discount amount to the line item. The relationship then from the `invoiceLineItem` to the `discountType` entity is an optional one, as no discount may have been applied to the line item.

For most optional relationships like this, there is another possible solution, which can be modeled as required, and in the implementation a row can be added to the `discountType` table that indicates "none." An example of such a mandatory relationship could be genre to movie in a movie rental shop's database:

The relationship is genre `<classifies>` movie, where the `genre` entity represents the one and `movie` represents the many in the one-to-many relationship. Every movie being rented must have a genre, so that it can be organized in the inventory and then placed on the appropriate rental shelf.

## Role Names

A *role name* is an alternative name you can give an attribute when it is used as a foreign key. The purpose of a role name is to clarify the usage of a migrated key, because either the parent entity is very generic and a more specific name is needed or the same entity has multiple relationships. As attribute names must be unique, assigning different names for the child foreign key references is often necessary. Consider this example:

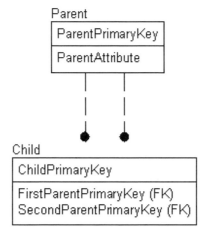

In this diagram, the Parent entity and the Child entity share two relationships, and the migrated attributes have been role named as FirstParentPrimaryKey and SecondParentPrimaryKey.

In diagrams, you can indicate the original name of the migrated attribute after the role name, separated by a period (.), as follows:

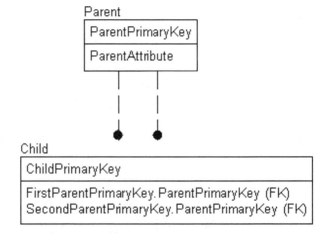

As an example, say you have a User entity, and you want to store the name or ID of the user who created a DatabaseObject entity instance as well as the user that the DatabaseObject instance was created for. It would then end up as follows:

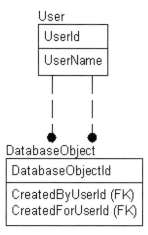

Note that there are two relationships to the DatabaseObject entity from the User entity. Due to the way the lines are drawn on a diagram, it is not clear from the diagram which foreign key goes to which relationship. Once you name the relationship with a verb phrase, it will be easier to determine, but often determining which line indicates which child attribute is simply trial and error.

## Relationship Cardinality

The cardinality of the relationship denotes the number of child instances that can be inserted for each parent of that relationship. Cardinality may seem like a fringe topic, since the logic to implement can be tricky, but the reality is that if the requirements state the cardinality, it can be important to document the cardinality requirements and to implement restrictions on cardinality in the database constraints where possible. At this point however, logical modeling is not about how to implement but about documenting what should be. We will talk implementation of data constraints in Chapter 6.

The following set of figures shows the six possible cardinalities that relationships can take on (see Figures 2-1 through 2-6). The cardinality indicators are applicable to either mandatory or optional relationships.

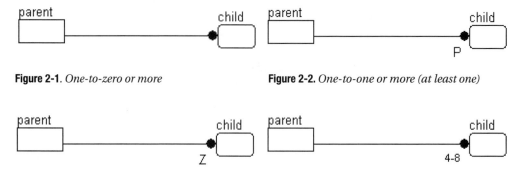

**Figure 2-1.** *One-to-zero or more*

**Figure 2-2.** *One-to-one or more (at least one)*

**Figure 2-3.** *One-to-zero or one (no more than one)*

**Figure 2-4.** *One-to-some fixed range (in this case, between 4 and 8 inclusive)*

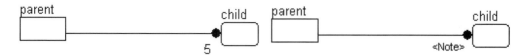

**Figure 2-5.** *One-to-exactly N (in this case, 5, meaning each parent must have five children)*

**Figure 2-6.** *Specialized note describing the cardinality*

For example, a possible use for the one to one-or-more might be to represent the relationship between a guardian and a student in a school database:

This is a good example of a zero-or-one to one-or-more relationship, and a fairly complex one at that. It says that for a guardian instance to exist, a student must exist, but a student need not have a guardian for us to wish to store the guardian's data. Note that I did not limit the number of guardians in the example, since it is not clear at this point if there is a limit.

Next, let's consider the case of a club that has members with certain positions that they should or could fill, as shown in Figures 2-7 through 2-9.

**Figure 2-7.** *One-to-many—allows unlimited positions for the member*

**Figure 2-8.** *One-to-one*

**Figure 2-9.** *One-to-zero, one, or two*

Figure 2-7 shows that a member can take as many positions as are possible. Figure 2-8 shows that a member can serve in no position or one position, but no more. Finally, Figure 2-9 shows that a member can serve in zero, one, or two positions. They all look pretty similar, but the Z or 0–2 is important in signifying the cardinality.

---

■**Note** I considered including examples of each of these cardinality types, but in most cases, they were too diffi-cult or too silly. It is a fairly rare occurrence that I have needed anything other than the basic one-many, one-zero, or one relationship types.

In the following subsections, I will introduce a few special types of one-to-many relationships as well as many-to-many relationships.

---

## Recursive Relationships

One of the more difficult—but most important—relationship types to implement is the *recursive relationship*, also known as a *self-join*, *hierarchical*, *self-referencing*, or *self-relationship*. This is modeled by drawing a nonidentifying relationship not to a different entity, but to the same entity. The migrated key of the relationship is given a role name. (I generally use a naming convention of adding "parent" to the front of the attribute name, but this is not a necessity.)

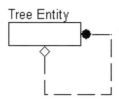

The recursive relationship is useful for creating tree structures, as in the following organizational chart:

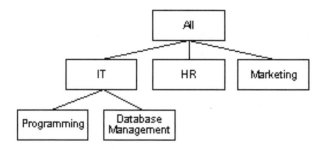

To explain this concept fully, I will show the data that would be stored to implement this hierarchy:

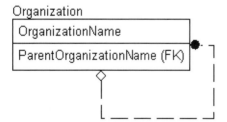

Here is the sample data for this table:

```
organizationName       parentOrganizationName
--------------------   ---------------------------
All
IT                     All
HR                     All
Marketing              All
Programming            IT
Database Management    IT
```

The organizational chart can now be traversed by starting at All and getting the children to ALL, for example: IT. Then you get the children of those values, like for IT one of the values is Programming.

As a final example, consider the case of a Person entity. If you wanted to associate a person with a single other person as the first person's spouse, you might design the following:

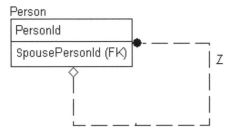

Notice that this is a one-to-zero or one relationship, since (in most places) a person may have no more than a single spouse, but need not have one. If you require one person to be related as a child to two parents, an associative entity is required to link two people together.

## Subtypes

*Subtypes* (also referred to as *categorization relationships*) are another special type of one-to-zero or -one relationship used to indicate whether one entity is a specific type of a generic entity. Note also that there are no black dots at either end of the lines; the specific entities are drawn with rounded corners, signifying that they are indeed dependent on the generic entity.

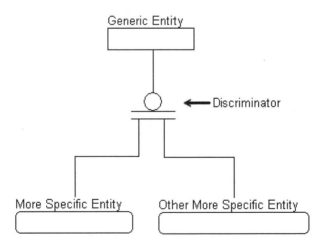

There are three distinct parts of the subtype relationship:

- *Generic entity*: This entity contains all of the attributes common to all of the subtyped entities.
- *Discriminator*: This attribute acts as a switch to determine the entity where the additional, more specific information is stored.
- *Specific entity*: This is the place where the specific information is stored, based on the discriminator.

For example, let's look at a video library. If you wanted to store information about each of the videos that you owned, regardless of format, you might build a categorization relationship like the following:

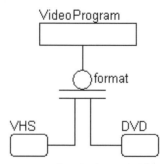

In this manner, you might represent each video's price, title, actors, length, and possibly description of the content in the Video entity, and then, based on format, which is the discriminator, you might store the information that is specific to VHS or DVD in its own separate entity (e.g., special features and menus for DVDs, long or slow play for VHS tapes, etc.).

---

■**Tip** The types of relationships in this example are what I referred to earlier as "is-a" relationships: a VHS is a video, and a DVD is also a video.

---

There are two distinct category types: *complete* and *incomplete*. The complete set of categories is modeled with a double line on the discriminator, and the incomplete set is modeled with a single line (see Figure 2-10).

**Figure 2-10.** *Complete (left) and incomplete (right) sets of categories*

The primary difference between the complete and incomplete categories is that in the complete categorization relationship, each generic instance must have one specific instance, whereas in the incomplete case this is not necessarily true. An instance of the generic entity can be associated with an instance of only one of the category entities in the cluster, and each instance of a category entity is associated with exactly one instance of the generic entity. In other words, overlapping subentities are not allowed.

For example, you might have a complete set of categories like this:

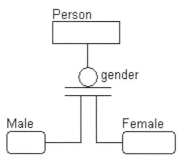

This relationship is read as follows: "A Person *must* be either Male or Female." This is certainly a complete category. This is not to say that you know the gender of every person in every instance of all entities. Rather, it simply means that if the instance has been categorized, any person must fall in one of the two buckets (male or female).

However, consider the following incomplete set of categories:

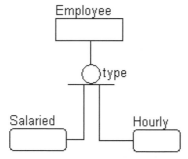

This is an incomplete subtype, because employees are either salaried or hourly, but there may be other categories, such as contract workers. You may not need to store any additional information about them, though, so there is no need to implement the specific entity. This relationship is read as follows: "An Employee can be either Salaried or Hourly or other."

## Many-to-Many Relationship

The many-to-many relationship is also known as the *nonspecific relationship*, which is actually a better name, but far less well known. It is common to have quite a few many-to-many relationships in the data model, particularly in the early conceptual model. These relationships are modeled by a line with a solid black dot at either end:

There is one real problem with modeling a many-to-many relationship: it is often necessary to have more information about the relationship than that simply many EntityX instances are connected to many EntityY instances. So the relationship is usually modeled as follows:

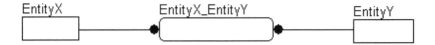

Here, the intermediate EntityX_EntityY entity is known as an *associative entity* or *resolution entity* (names like *tweener, joiner,* and other slang terms are not uncommon either). In early modeling, I will often stick with the former representation when I haven't identified any extended attributes to describe the relationship and the latter representation when I need to add additional information to the model.

---

■**Tip**  I should also note that you can't implement a many-to-many relationship in the relationship model without using a table for the resolution. This is because there is no way to migrate keys both ways. You will notice when you use a many-to-many relationship that no key is migrated from either table, so there would be no data to substantiate the relationship. In the database, you are required to implement all many-to-many relationships using a resolution entity.

---

To clarify the concept, let's look at the following example:

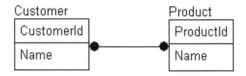

Here, I have set up a relationship where many customers are related to many products. This is a common situation, as in most cases companies don't create specific products for specific customers; rather, any customer can purchase any of the company's products. At this point in the modeling, it is reasonable to use the many-to-many representation. Note that I am generalizing the customer-to-product relationship. It is not uncommon to have a company build specific products for only one customer to purchase.

Consider, however, the case where the Customer need only be related to a Product for a certain period of time. To implement this, you can use the following representation:

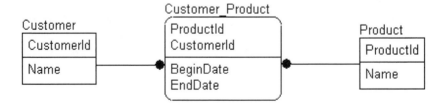

In fact, almost all of the many-to-many relationships tend to require some additional information like this to make them complete. It is not uncommon to have no many-to-many relationships modeled with the black circle on both ends of a model, so you will need to look for entities modeled like this to be able to discern them.

**■Note** For architects who use surrogate keys for all entities, many-to-many relationships can disappear from the implementation model entirely, so recognizing such relationships in the final model can take a discerning eye.

## Verb Phrases (Relationship Names)

Relationships are given names, called *verb phrases*, to make the relationship between a parent and child entity a readable sentence and to incorporate the entity names and the relationship cardinality. The name is usually expressed from parent to child, but it can be expressed in the other direction, or even in both directions. The verb phrase is located on the model somewhere close to the line that forms the relationship:

The relationship should be named such that it fits into the following general structure for reading the entire relationship:

*parent cardinality – parent entity name – relationship name – child cardinality – child entity name*

For example, the following relationship

would be read as

*One contact is phoned using zero, one, or more phoneNumber(s).*

Of course, the sentence may or may not make perfect grammatical sense, as this one brings up the question of how a contact is phoned using zero phone numbers. If presenting this phrase to a nontechnical person, it would make more sense to read it as follows:

*One contact can have either no phone number or one or more phoneNumbers.*

The modeling language does not take linguistics into consideration when building this specification, but from a technical standpoint, it does not matter that the contact is phoned using zero phone numbers, since it follows that they have no phone number.

Being able to read the relationship helps you to notice obvious problems. For instance, consider the following relationship

It looks fine at first glance, but when read like this

*One contactType classifies zero or one contacts.*

it doesn't make logical sense. It means to categorize all of the contacts it would be required to have a unique `ContactType` row for each `Contact`, which clearly is not at all reasonable. This would be properly modeled as follows:

which now reads

*One contactType classifies zero or more contacts.*

Note that the type of relationship, whether it is identifying, nonidentifying, optional, or mandatory, makes no difference when reading the relationship.

You can also include a verb phrase that reads from child to parent. For a one-to-many relationship, this would be of the following format:

*One child instance (relationship) exactly one parent instance.*

In the case of the first example, you could have added an additional verb phrase:

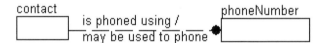

The parent-to-child relationship again is read:

*One contact is phoned using zero, one, or more phoneNumber(s).*

You can then read the relationship from child to parent. Note that when reading in this direction, you are in the context of zero or one phone number to one and only one contact.

*Zero or one phoneNumber(s) may be used to phone exactly one contact.*

Since this is going from many to one, it is assumed that the parent in the relationship will have one related value, and since you are reading in the context of the existence of the child, you can also assume that there is zero or one child record to consider in the sentence.

For the many-to-many relationship, the scheme is pretty much the same. As both entities are parents in this kind of relationship, you read the verb phrase written above the line from left to right and from right to left for the verb phrase written below it.

---

**Tip** Taking the time to define verb phrases can be troublesome, because they are not actually used in the implementation of the database, and often people consider doing work that doesn't produce code directly to be a waste of time. However, well defined verb phrases make for great documentation, giving the reader a good idea of why the relationship exists and what it means.

---

# Descriptive Information

It has been said many times by many people that "a picture is worth a thousand words" (originally said in a Royal Baking Powder commercial, not by Confucius), and it is very true. Take a picture of a beautiful mountain, and it will inspire thousands of words about the beauty of the trees, the plants, the babbling brook (my relative ability to describe a landscape being one of the reasons I write technical books). What it *won't* tell you is how to get there yourself, what the temperature is, and whether you should bring a sweater and mittens or your swim trunks.

Data models are the same way. You can get a great start on understanding the database from the model, as I have discussed in the previous sections of this chapter. We started the documentation process by giving good names to entities, attributes, and the relationships, but even with well-formed names, there will still likely be confusion as to what exactly an attribute is used for and how it might be used.

For this, we need to add our own thousand words (give or take) to the pictures in the model. When sharing the model, descriptions will let the eventual reader—and even a future version of yourself—know what you originally had in mind. Remember that not everyone who views the models will be on the same technical level: some will be nonrelational programmers, or indeed users or (nontechnical) product managers who have no modeling experience.

Descriptive information need not be in any special format. It simply needs to be detailed, up to date, and capable of answering as many questions as can be anticipated. Each bit of descriptive information should be stored in a manner that makes it easy for users to quickly connect it to the part of the model where it was used, and it should be stored either in a document or as metadata in a modeling tool.

You should start creating this descriptive text by asking questions such as the following:

- What is the object supposed to represent?
- How will the object be used?
- Who might use the object?
- What are the future plans for the object?
- What constraints are not specifically implied by the model?

The scope of the descriptions should not extend past the object or entities that are affected. For example, the entity description should refer only to the entity, and not any related entities, relationships, or even attributes unless necessary. An attribute definition should only speak to the single attribute and where its values might come from.

Maintaining good descriptive information is equivalent to putting decent comments in code. As the eventual database that you are modeling is usually the central part of any computer system, comments at this level are more important than at any others. We can also say that this is the bread and butter of having a logical model. For most people, being able to go back and review notes that were taken about each object and why things were implemented is invaluable, especially true for organizations that bring in new employees and need to bring them up to speed on complex systems.

For example, say the following two entities have been modeled:

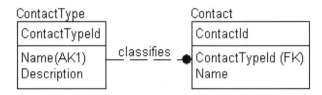

The very basic set of descriptive information in Tables 2-1 and 2-2 could be stored to describe the attributes created.

**Table 2-1.** *Entities*

| Entity | Attribute | Description |
|---|---|---|
| **Contact** | | **Persons That Can Be Contacted to Do Business With** |
| | ContactId | Surrogate key |
| | ContactTypeId | Primary key reference for a contactType, classifies the type of contact |
| | Name | The full name of a contact |
| **ContactType** | | **Domain of Different Contact Types** |
| | ContactTypeId | Surrogate key |
| | Name | The name that the contact type will be uniquely known as |
| | Description | The description of exactly how the contact should be used as |

**Table 2-2.** *Relationships*

| Parent Entity Name | Phrase | Child Entity Name | Definition |
|---|---|---|---|
| ContactType | Classifies | Contact | Contact type classification. |

# Alternative Modeling Methodologies

In this section, I will briefly describe a few of the other modeling methodologies that you will likely run into when looking for database information on the Web or perhaps in other tools you may be using to design databases. You will see a lot of similarities among them—for example, most every methodology uses a rectangle to represent a table, and a line to indicate a relationship. You will also see some big differences among them, such as how the cardinality and direction of a relationship is indicated. Where IDEF1X uses a filled circle on the child end and an optional diamond on the other, one of the most popular methodologies uses multiple lines on one end and several dashes to indicate the same things.

All of the examples in this book will be done in IDEF1X, but knowing about the other methodologies may be helpful when you are surfing around the Internet, looking for sample diagrams to help you design the database you are working on. (Architects are often particularly bad about not looking for existing designs, because frankly, solving the problem at hand is one of the best parts of the job. However, don't reinvent the wheel every time!)

I will briefly discuss the following:

- *Information Engineering (IE)*: The other main methodology, which is commonly referred to as the *crow's feet* method

- *Chen Entity Relationship Model (ERD)*: The methodology used mostly in academic texts

- *Visio*: A tool that many developers have handy that will do an admirable job of helping you to design a database

- *Management Studio database diagrams*: The database object viewer that can be used to view the database as a diagram right in Management Studio

---

**Note** This list is by no means exhaustive. For example, several variations loosely based on the Unified Modeling Language (UML) class modeling methodology are not listed. These types of diagrams are common, particularly with people who use the other components of UML, but these models really have no standards. Some further reading on UML data models can be found in Clare Churcher's book *Beginning Database Design* (Apress, 2007), on Scott Adler's AgileData site (http://www.agiledata.org/essays/umlDataModelingProfile.html), and on IBM's Rational UML documentation site (http://www.306.ibm.com/software/rational/uml/resources/documentation.html), and many others. (The typical caveat that these URLs are apt to change applies.)

---

## Information Engineering

The *Information Engineering* (IE) methodology is well known and widely used. Like IDEF1X, it does a very good job of displaying the necessary information in a clean, compact manner that is easy to follow. The biggest difference is in how this method denotes relationship cardinalities, using a crow's foot instead of a dot, and lines and dashes instead of diamonds and some letters.

Tables in this method are denoted as rectangles, basically the same as in IDEF1X. According to the IE standard, attributes are not shown on the model, but most models show them the same as in IDEF1X—as a list, although the primary key is denoted by underlining the attributes, rather than the position in the table. (I have seen other ways of denoting the primary key, as well as alternate/foreign keys, but they are all very clear.) Where things get very different using IE is when dealing with relationships.

Just like in IDEF1X, IE has a set of symbols that have to be understood to indicate the cardinality and ownership of the data in the relationships. By varying the basic symbols at the end of the line, you can arrive at all of the various possibilities for relationships. Table 2-3 shows the different symbols that can be employed to build relationship representations.

**Table 2-3.** *Information Engineering Symbols*

| Symbol | Relationship Type | Description |
|---|---|---|
| ⟶< | Many | The entity on the end with the crow's foot denotes that there can be greater than one value related to the other entity. Alternatively, for a one-to-one relationship, the crow's foot can be replaced by a single line that looks like the required symbol, which is shown in Figure 2-13. |
| + | Required | The key of the entity on the other end of the relationship is required to exist. A line on both ends indicates that a child is required for a parent row to exist, just like a "P" on the end of an IDEF1X model. |
| ─○─ | Optional | This symbol indicates that there does not have to be a related instance on this end of the relationship for one to exist on the other. It can appear at the parent or the child. |
| - - - - - | Nonrequired | A set of dashed lines on one end of the relationship line indicates that the migrated key may be null. |

Figures 2-11 through 2-14 show some examples of relationships in IE.

**Figure 2-11.** *One-to-many: Specifically, one row in Table A may be related to zero, one or more rows in Table B. A related row must exist in Table A for a row to exist in Table B.*

**Figure 2-12.** *One-to-many: Specifically, one Row in Table A may be related to one or more rows in Table B*

**Figure 2-13.** *One-to-one: Specifically, zero or one row in Table A can be related to zero or one row in Table B. A row needn't exist in Table A for a row to exist in Table B (the key value would be optional).*

**Figure 2-14.** *Many-to-many relationship*

I have never felt that this notation was as clean as IDEF1X, as much of the symbology seems a bit arcane. It conveys the information well though and is likely to be used in some of the documents that you will come across in your work as a data architect or developer. IE is also not always fully implemented in tools; however, usually the circle, dashes, and crow's feet are implemented properly.

---

■**Tip** You can find more details about the Information Engineering methodology in the book *Information Engineering, Books 1, 2, and 3* by James Martin (Prentice Hall, 1990).

---

## Chen ERD

The Chen Entity Relationship Model (ERD) methodology is quite a bit different from IDEF1X, but it's pretty easy to follow and largely self-explanatory. You will seldom see this methodology anywhere other than in academic texts, but since quite a few of these types of diagrams are on the Internet, it's good to understand the basics of the methodology. Here's a very simple Chen ERD diagram:

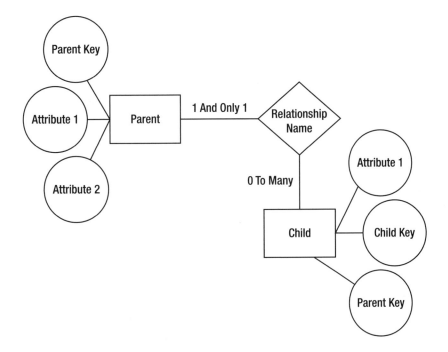

Each entity is again a rectangle; however, the attributes are not shown in the entity but are instead attached to the entity in circles. The primary key either is not denoted or, in some variations, is underlined. The relationship is denoted by a rhombus, or diamond shape.

The cardinality for a relationship is denoted in text. In the example, it is 1 and Only 1 Parent rows <relationship name> 0 to Many Child rows. The primary reason for including the Chen ERD format is for contrast. Several other modeling methodologies—for example, Object Role Modeling (ORM) and Bachman—implement attributes in this style, where they are not displayed in the rectangle.

While I understand the logic behind this approach (entities and attributes are separate things), I have found that models I have seen using the format with attributes attached to the entity like this seemed overly cluttered, even for fairly small diagrams. The methodology does, however, do an admirable job with the logical model of showing what is desired and also does not rely on overcomplicated symbology to describe relationships and cardinality.

---

■**Note**  You can find further details on the Chen ERD methodology in the paper "The Entity Relationship Model—Toward a Unified View of Data" by Peter Chen (it can be found by performing a Google search for the title of the paper).

Also, note that I am not saying that such a tool to create Chen diagrams does not exist; rather I personally have not seen the Chen ERD methodology implemented in a mainstream database design tool other than some early versions of Microsoft Visio. Quite a few of the diagrams you will find on the Internet will be in this style, however, so it is interesting to understand at least the basics of the Chen ERD methodology.

---

# Visio

Visio is a tool that many developers use for designing databases; often, they already have it in their tool belt for other types of drawings and models (such as process flow diagrams). By nature, Visio is a multipurpose drawing tool and as such does not lend itself well to being a fully featured database design tool. That said, Visio is not the world's worst tool to design a database either. It does lack a refined manner of going from conceptual to logical and finally to an implemented database, but unless you are doing serious enterprise-level designs, this limitation may not matter much to you (and, like many of us, you may not have the ducats to shell out for a more fully featured tool, and using Visio is better than just using Management Studio's diagrams).

Models created using Visio have a distinctive style that shares some features with object-oriented design tools. While the tool supports many of the features of more powerful tools, the picture of the model is pretty basic:

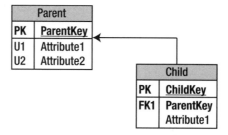

The arrow points to the parent in all cases but does not indicate ownership, cardinality, or even optionality. It does tell you what columns are primary keys in two ways (using the line and the "PK"), as well as telling you what columns are part of foreign keys with "FK" plus a number, in case there are more than one. Alternate keys are denoted with "U" plus a number. In the preceding model, the Parent entity/table has two alternate keys.

Visio implements a good amount of detail to define columns, include comments, and set cardinalities via dialogs and editors. All in all, the tool is not a terrible choice for modeling if it is the only one available.

# Management Studio Database Diagrams

The database diagramming capability built into SQL Server Management Studio is not a modeling tool, though often it can be a developer's only available tool for modeling. It is a very useful tool to provide a graphical view the structure of an implemented database (a picture really *is* worth a thousand words!), but because it works directly against the implemented tables, it is not overly useful for design but only for the final implementation. You can use this view to modify structures as well, but I would not suggest it. Use T-SQL code in the Management Studio query window to make table changes. (All table structures in this book will be done in this way, and doing so is a best practice for repeatability purposes. I will talk more on this in the latter half of the book.) You could do this design on an empty database, but it is seriously too clunky of a tool for design.

The following is an example of a one-to-many relationship in Management Studio:

The primary keys are identified by the little key in an attribute. The relationship is denoted by the line between the entities, with the one end having a key and the many end having an infinity sign.

You can display the entities in several formats by just showing the names of the entities or by showing all of the attributes with datatypes, for example:

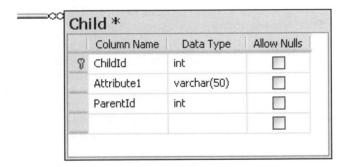

While the database diagram tool does have its place, I must stress that it isn't a full-featured data modeling tool and shouldn't be used as such if you can avoid it. I included coverage of the SQL Server modeling capabilities here because it's included in SQL Server and in some situations it's the best tool you may have access to. It does give access to all implementation-specific features of SQL Server, including the ability to annotate your tables and columns with descriptive information. Unfortunately, if you decide to implement a relationship in a trigger, it will not know that the trigger exists. (I cover triggers in Chapter 6, so if you have no idea what a trigger is right now, don't worry.)

In most cases, the SQL Server tool isn't the optimal way to see actual relationship information that is designed into the database, but it does offer a serviceable look at the database structure when needed.

> ■**Note** In the Business Intelligence tools for SQL Server 2005 and 2008, there is also another tool that resembles a data model in the Data Source view. It is used to build a view of a set of tables, views, and (not implemented) queries for building reports from. It is pretty much self-explanatory as a tool, but it uses an arrow on the parent end of the relation line to indicate where a primary key came from, much like Visio does. This tool is not pertinent to the task of building or changing a database, but I felt I should at least mention it briefly, as it does look very much like a data modeling tool.

# Best Practices

The following are some basic best practices that can be very useful to follow when doing data modeling:

- *Pick a model language and understand it*: This chapter has been a whirlwind coverage of much of the symbology of the IDEF1X modeling language. IDEF1X is not the only modeling language, and the one you use can be as divisive of a decision as any you will make in programming. Many of us have a flavor that we like, and we don't like the others (guess which one I like best). The plain fact is that they almost all have merit. The important thing is that you understand your chosen language and can use it to communicate with users/programmers at the level they need.

- *Entity names*: There are two ways you can go with these: plural or singular. I feel that names should be singular (meaning that the name of the table describes a single instance, or row, of the entity, much like an OO object name describes the instance of an object, not a group of them), but many other highly regarded data architects and authors feel that the table name refers to the set of rows and should be plural. Whichever way you decide to go, it's most important that you are consistent. Anyone reading your model shouldn't have to guess why some entity names are plural and others aren't.

- *Attribute names*: It's generally not necessary to repeat the entity name in the attribute name, except for the primary key. The entity name is implied by the attribute's inclusion in the entity. The chosen attribute name should reflect precisely what is contained in the attribute and how it relates to the entity. And as with entities, no abbreviations are to be used in the logical naming of attributes; every word should be spelled out in its entirety. If any abbreviation is to be used, due to some naming standard currently in place, for example, then a method should be put into place to make sure the abbreviation is used consistently, as discussed earlier in the chapter.

- *Relationships*: Name relationships with verb phrases, which make the relationship between a parent and child entity a readable sentence. The sentence expresses the relationship using the entity names and the relationship cardinality. The relationship sentence is a very powerful tool for communicating the purpose of the relationships with nontechnical members of the project team (e.g., customer representatives).

- *Domains*: Define domains for your attributes, implementing type inheritance wherever possible to take advantage of domains that are similar. Using domains gives you a set of standard templates to use when building databases that ensures consistency across your database and, if used extensively, all of your databases.

# Summary

The primary tool of a database designer is the data model. It's such a great tool because it can show the details not only of single tables at a time, but the relationships between several entities at a time. Of course it is not the only way to document a database; each of the following is useful, but not nearly as useful as a full-featured data model:

- Often a product that features a database as the central focus will include a document that lists all tables, datatypes, and relationships.
- Every good DBA has a script of the database saved somewhere for re-creating the database.
- SQL Server's metadata includes ways to add properties to the database to describe the objects.

A good data modeling tool (often a costly thing to purchase but definitely well worth it) will do all of these things and more for you. I won't give you any guidance there, as this is not an advertisement for any tool (not even for the basic Microsoft tools that you likely have your hands on already, and frankly they are *not* the best in class tools that you need to get). Clearly, you need to do a bit of research and find a tool that suits you. It doesn't matter if your tool uses IDEF1X or any of the other model methodologies I outlined, such as Information Engineering, Chen ERD, and Microsoft Management Studio, or even something else like UML, or a new one that pops up after this book is published.

I know several very talented data architects who don't use any kind of tools to model with, sticking with SQL scripts to create their databases, so using a modeling tool is not necessary to get the database created. However, a graphical representation of the data model is a very useful tool to share the structure of the database with developers and even end users very quickly. And the key to this task is to have common symbology to communicate on a level that all people involved can understand on some level.

In this chapter, I presented the basic process of graphically documenting the objects that were introduced in the first chapter. I focused heavily on the IDEF1X modeling methodology, taking a detailed look at the symbology that will be used through database designs. The base set of symbols outlined here will enable us to fully model logical databases (and later physical databases) in great detail

All it takes is a little bit of training, and the rest is easy. For example, take the model in Figure 2-15.

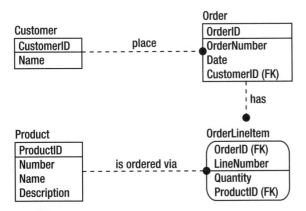

**Figure 2-15.** *Reading this basic model is not difficult at all, if you simply apply the explanations from this chapter.*

Customers place orders. Orders have line items. The line items are used to order products. With very little effort, nontechnical users can understand your data models, allowing you to communicate very easily, rather than using large spreadsheets as your primary communication method. The finer points of cardinality and ownership might not be completely clear, but usually, those technical details are not as important as the larger picture of knowing which entities relate to which.

If you have named attributes well, users won't be confused about what most attributes are, but if so, your spreadsheet of information should be able clear up confusion about the finer points of the model.

Now that we've considered the symbology required to model a database, I'll use data models throughout the book to describe the entities in the conceptual model (see Chapter 3), the logical model (see Chapter 4), and throughout the implementation presented in the rest of the book as shorthand to give you an overview of the scenario I am setting up, often in addition to scripts.

# CHAPTER 3

■■■

# Conceptual Data Modeling

DILBERT: © Scott Adams/Dist. by United Feature Syndicate, Inc.

**A**h, Mr. Adams, I wish you weren't so darn accurate sometimes. Too often computer projects have roots so tangled and goofy that they make this cartoon seem rather tame in comparison. Trade magazines might be great tools to the discerning mind, but in the hands of a high-level manager, all the buzz words affect them in the same manner that whiteboard markers affect programmers: they make them euphoric to do "something." (It's a good thing whiteboard markers are nontoxic!)

When tasked to design a database system, you have to be mindful that users often aren't technologists. So when you start to gather requirements, relying on users to know what they want, and how to implement it, is almost always complete folly. On the flip side, keep in mind that you're building a system to solve a business problem for the user (as well as the people who sign the checks), not for yourself, so you must consider what the user wants. There's an old saying that you shouldn't build users a Cadillac when all they want is a Volkswagen (though when this saying was coined, a VW wasn't quite as expensive as it is today). Even worse, though, is when you make your users a Cadillac convertible when what they needed was a dump truck. These two things are similar in that they're both vehicles with an open top, but they have very different uses.

This chapter is entitled "Conceptual Data Modeling" because the goal is to get the concepts for the final product into a document, not to start designing the final model you will implement, since we are still really early in the process. In this book, my focus is on the database designer, but you also might have to gather requirements other than just those that are data related. This can be a hard task because of the (seemingly) conflicting needs of the database designer (data integrity) and the UI designer (useful interface that is easy to use), but they aren't conflicting needs in the end. Frankly, taken as a challenge, it actually makes your job interesting. No matter what, the most important need is to give users a useful interface that manipulates their data and maintains data integrity.

# Understanding the Requirements

Without the designer having a solid understanding of the requirements, the system will essentially be based on guesses. It isn't necessary to gather every requirement about every area of a large system initially; the system can be broken down into portions, often called *subject areas*. The size of the subject area is based upon the needs of the team and development methodology used. For example, the Scrum methodology breaks down everything into (generally speaking) 30-day units for designing, coding, and testing, while something like the Waterfall methodology would expect you to design the entire system first and then start coding. If Scrum were your team's methodology, the subject area might be small, function-oriented subject areas based on a set of user needs. Or you might break things down into larger functional areas, such as an accounts-payable module in an accounting system or a user-management module for a website. The important thing is that all development methodologies will tell you one thing: design *before* you code. Sure, there is a good amount of variability when it comes to how much design you need, but you still don't start typing until you know where you are going.

For gathering requirements, there are many tools and methodologies for documenting processes, business rules, and database structures. The Unified Modeling Language (UML) is one possible choice; the Microsoft Solutions Framework (which employs UML) is another. There are also several model types in the IDEF family of methods; as covered in Chapter 2, I'll employ the Entity-Relationship (E-R) modeling method IDEF1X to model databases. I won't be covering any of the other modeling languages for the nondatabase structure parts of the project but will rather be using a manual spreadsheet method, which is by far the most common method of documenting requirements—even in medium-sized organizations where spending money on documentation tools can be harder than teaching your cat to play "fetch."

Regardless of the tools used to document the requirements, the needs for the database design process are the same. Specifications need to be acquired for the following:

- Entities and relationships
- Attributes and domains
- Business rules that can be enforced in the database
- Processes that require the use of the database

Without these specifications, you'll either have to constantly go back to the client and ask a bunch of questions (which they will sometimes answer three different ways for every two times they are asked, teaching you discernment skills) or start making guesses. Although guessing wrong a few times is a good education in how not to do things, it's certainly no way to work efficiently (unless you happen to be the Amazing Kreskin and guess right 99.9 percent of the time).

As a major part of this process, the data architect's goal will be to produce a graphical model of the database. (As stated in the previous chapter, I'll be using IDEF1X-based diagrams, but you can use whatever methodology your tool supports, even if it is just a piece of paper and a No. 2 pencil.)

---

**▪Tip** A word of caution when gathering requirements: common structures and solutions to problems will immediately come to mind, and you might want to just start coding right away. From experience, you might already have some idea of how to structure tables and how to format the tables. Soon you stop listening to the client drone on about something to which you should be paying attention and start hacking away at a solution while they are telling you important bits of information that may invalidate the design you have already fallen in love with.

During the early parts of a project, figuring out the "what" and "why" comes first; then you can work on the "how." Once you know the details of what needs to be built, the process to get it built will be reasonably natural, and you can possibly apply preexisting patterns to the solution.

---

In this chapter, I'll get the project started by going through the following steps to determine what the database system will do:

- *Documenting the process*: I'll briefly introduce the types of concerns you'll have throughout the project process in terms of documenting requirements.

- *Looking for requirements*: Here I'll talk about the places to find information and some techniques for mining this information.

- *Identifying objects*: You'll go through the documentation and build the conceptual model, as well as identify tables, relationships, and columns as they exist in the requirements.

- *Identifying business rules and processes*: You'll look for the rules that form the boundaries for our system usage, as well as common processes that need to be designed for.

- *Following up/reviewing with the client*: This section will cover the final steps in the conceptual design process, which center largely around communicating with the client to make sure you don't just start building like crazy something they really don't want, usually because they didn't understand what it is you were planning.

For those readers who are new to database design, you should initially follow the principles outlined in this chapter unaltered to ensure the best result for your project. Take care that I said "new to database design," not new to creating and manipulating tables in SQL Server. Although these two things are interrelated (I'll spend more than a third of this book looking at creating and manipulating tables in SQL Server), they are distinct and different steps of the same process.

The process taken in this book will probably seem a bit rigid, and this is a valid argument. Must the process be so strict? Of course not, and most accomplished database designers are likely to acquire "shortcuts" that make sense and that move quickly from requirements to logical model to implemented database. However, the results achieved are always far better the more methodically I take these preliminary steps prior to firing up SQL Server Management Studio and "building stuff." In my experience, the more time I spend on design, the less time I spend trying to go back and change my ideas to match the desires of the client.

---

■**Tip** Throughout the process of design and implementation, you'll no doubt find changes to the original requirements. Make sure to continue to update your documentation, because the best documentation in the world is useless if it's out of date.

---

# Documenting the Process

Before going too deeply into gathering requirements or building a conceptual model, it's important to say a bit about documentation and communications with clients. If you've ever traveled to a place where no one speaks the same language as you, you know the feeling of being isolated based solely on communication. Everything everyone says sounds weird to you, and no matter how often you ask where the bathroom is, all you get is this blank look back. It has nothing to do with intelligence; it's because you aren't speaking the same language.

Information technology professionals and our clients tend to have these sorts of conversations, because frequently we technology types don't speak the same language as our clients. Clients tend to think in the language of their industry, and we tend to think in terms of computer solutions. No place is this clearer than when it comes to SQL Server's tools. We relational programmers have trouble communicating to the tool designers what we want in SQL Server's tools. They do a good job, but it is clear they aren't completely on the same page as the users.

During this process of analysis, you should adopt one habit early on: document, document, document as much of the information that you acquire as reasonably possible. It's horrible to think about, but you might get hit by a bus tomorrow, and every bit of information in your head will be rendered useless while you recover. Less morbidly, if a project team member decides to take a month off, someone else will have to take over his or her work (or you just might have to wait to make any progress until they get back, leading to long, working weekends!). So, you should document, document, document; do it during a meeting or immediately after it. Without documentation, you will quickly risk forgetting vital details. It's imperative that you don't try to keep everything in your head, because even people with the best memories tend to forget the details of a project (especially if they're hit by that bus I talked about earlier).

The following are a few helpful tips as you begin to take notes on users' needs:

- Try to maintain a set of documents that will share system design and specification information. Important documents to consider include design-meeting notes, documents describing verbal change requests, and sign-offs on all specifications, such as functional, technical, testing, and so on.

- Beyond formal documentation, it's important to keep the members of your design team up to date and fully informed. Develop and maintain a common repository for all the information, and keep it up to date.

- Note anywhere that you add information that the users haven't given you or outwardly agreed to.

- Set the project's scope early on, and keep it in mind at all times. This will prevent the project from getting too big or diverse to be achievable within a reasonable period of time and be within the budget. (Hashing out changes that affect the budget early in the process will avoid future animosity!)

Once you document something, there's a crucial step that follows: making sure the client agrees with your version of the documentation. As you go through the entire system design process, the client will no doubt change his mind on entities, data points, business rules, user interface, colors—just about anything he can—and you have to prepare yourself for this. Whatever the client wants or needs is what you have to endeavor to accomplish. The client is in ultimate control of the project, and you have to be flexible enough to run with any proposed changes, whether minor or major (though they do need to be realistic).

Clients change their minds, and sometimes it seems to be more than a daily occurrence. Most frequently, they want more and more features. The common term for this is *scope creep*. The best way to avoid conflict is to make sure you get your client's approval at regular stages throughout the design process. This is sometimes known as the *principle of CYA*, which I think has something to do with covering all your bases, though the letters probably have a more sinister meaning.

In addition to talking to the client, it's important to acquire as many notes, printouts, screen shots, CD-ROMs loaded with spreadsheets, database backups, Word documents, e-mails, handwritten notes, and so on, that exist for any current solution to the problem. This data will be useful in the process of discovering data elements, screens, reports, and so on, that you'll need to design into your applications. Often you'll find information in the client's artifacts that's invaluable when putting together the data model.

# Requirements Gathering

One of the primary jobs of the design team is to get a handle on the scope (mission statement or mission objectives) that describes what's supposed to be accomplished. The design team will likely consult this document during the design and implementation and upon completion (and in many cases the scope changes at least a few times during the course of a project). However, if the project's objectives and aims aren't decided to some reasonable level early in the process and nothing is written down, there's a strong chance there will be conflicts between your design team and your clients as your ideas and theirs diverge. This will be of particular concern when the invoices start to roll in and you want to get your payments.

Vagueness or indecision may cause unnecessary discussions, fights, or even lawsuits later in the process. So, make sure your clients understand what you're going to do for them, and use language that will be clearly understood but that's specific enough to describe what you learn in the information-gathering process. This kind of process is beyond the scope of this book; I'll assume that it has been done by the business analysts.

Throughout the process of discovery, *artifacts* will be gathered and produced that will be used throughout the process of implementation as reference materials. Artifacts are any kind of documents that will be important to the design, for example, interview notes, e-mails, sample documents, and so on. In this section, I'll discuss the following types of artifacts or activities in some detail:

- Client interviews
- Prototypes and existing systems
- Various other types of documentation

By no means is this an exhaustive list of where to find and acquire documentation; in fact, it's far from it. The goal is simply to get your mind clicking and thinking of information to get from the client so your job will be easier.

## Client Interviews

It's often the case that the person designing the data storage (commonly referred as the *data architect*) will never meet the user, let alone be involved in formal interviews. The project manager, business analyst, and system architect might provide all the required information. Other projects might involve only a data architect or a single person wearing more hats than the entire Fourth Army on maneuvers. I've done it both ways: I've been in the early design sessions, and I've worked from documentation. The better the people you work with, the more pleasant the latter is. In this section, I'll talk quickly about the basics of client interviews, because on almost any project you'll end up doing some amount of interviewing the client.

Client interviews are commonly where the project really gets started. It's where the free, unstructured flow of information starts. However, it's also where the communication gap starts. Many clients generally think visually—in terms of forms, web pages, and simple user interfaces in particular. As the data architect, your job is to balance the customers' perceived need with their real need: a properly structured database that sits nicely behind a user interface and captures what they are really after: information to make their business lives easier and more lucrative. Changing a form around to include a new text box, label, or whatever, is a relatively simple task, giving the user the false impression that creating the entire application is an easy process. If you want proof, make the foolish mistake of demonstrating a polished-looking prototype application with non-hard-coded values that makes the client think it actually works. The clients might be impressed that you've put together something so quickly and expect you to be nearly done. Rarely will they understand that what exists under the hood—namely, the database and the middle-tier business objects—is where all the main work takes place.

**Tip** While visual elements are great places to find a clue to what data a user will want, as you go along in the process you'll want to be careful not to center your design around a particular interface. The structure of the data needs to be dictated on what the data means, not on how it will be presented. Presentation is more of an interface design task, not a database design one.

Brainstorming sessions can also yield great results for gathering a lot of information at once, as long as the group doesn't grow too large. The key here is to make sure that someone is facilitating the meeting and preventing the "alpha" person from beating up on the others and giving only his or her own opinion. Treat information from every person interviewed as important, because each person will likely have a different viewpoint. Sometimes the best information comes not from the executive, but from the person who does the work. Don't assume that the first person speaks for the rest, even if they're all working on the same project or if this individual is the manager (or even president or owner of a major corporation, though a great amount of tact is required sometimes to walk that tightrope).

In many cases, when the dominant person cannot be controlled or the mousey person cannot be prodded into getting involved, one-on-one sessions should probably be employed to allow clients to speak their mind, without untimely interruptions from stronger-willed (though sometimes not stronger-minded) colleagues. Be mindful of the fact that the loudest and boldest people might not have the best ideas and that the quiet person who sits at the back and says nothing might have the key to the entire project. Make sure to at least consider everybody's opinions.

The more that's written down and filed away, rather than just committed to memory, the more information will be available later after 20 long, sleepless weeks so the clients can verify the information by reviewing it. This means that not only can you improve relations with your clients, but you also enhance your chances of identifying the data they'll want to see again, as well as provide the design team with the information required to design the final product.

This part of the book is written with the most humility, because I've made more mistakes in this part of the design process than any other. The client interview is one of the most difficult parts of the process that I've encountered. It might not seem a suitable topic for experienced analysts, but even the best of us need to be reminded that jumping the gun, bullying the clients, telling them what they want before they tell you, and even failing to manage the user's expectations can lead to the ruin of even a well-developed system. If you have a shaky foundation, the final product will likely be shaky as well.

## Questions to Be Answered

The following are some questions that are important to the database design aspects of a system's development. Again, this isn't an exhaustive list, but it's certainly enough to get you started.

### What Data Is Needed?

If the data architect is part of the design session, some data is clearly needed for the system. Most users, at a high level, know what data they want to see out of the system. For example, if they're in accounting, they want to see dollars and cents summarized by such-and-such a group.

### How Will the Data Be Used?

Knowing what your client is planning to use the data in the system for is an important piece of information indeed. Not only will you understand the process, but you can also begin to get a good picture of the type of data that needs to be stored.

For example, imagine you're asked to create a database of contacts for a dental office. You might want to know the following:

- Will the contact names be used just to make phone calls, like a quick phone book?
- Will the client be sending e-mail or posting to the members of the contact lists? Should the names be subdivided into groups for this purpose?

- Will the client be using the names to solicit a response from the mail, such as appointment reminders?
- Is it important to have family members documented? Do they want to send cards to the person on important dates?

## What Rules Govern the Use of the Data?

Taking our previous example of contacts, you might discover the following:

- Every contact must have a valid e-mail address.
- Every contact must have a valid street address.
- The client checks every e-mail address using a mail routine, and the contact isn't a valid contact until this routine has been successfully executed.
- Contacts must be subdivided by the type of issues they have.

It's important not to infer too many rules from documentation. At least be sure and confirm them with the client before assuming them to be true. Something might seem obvious to you but could be wrong (business rules are far too often made to be broken).

Case in point: what is a "valid" e-mail address? Well, it's the e-mail address that accurately goes with the contact. Sure, but how on Earth do you validate that? The fact is, you don't. Usually this means that something like the e-mail address is valid, in that it has an ampersand character between other characters and a dot (.) between one or more alphanumeric values (such as %@%.%, plus all characters between A and Z, 0 and 9, an underscore, and so on), but the value is completely up to interpretation.

If you're too strict, your final product might be unacceptable because you've placed a rule on the data that the client doesn't want or you've missed a rule that the client truly needs. I made this mistake in a big way once, which torpedoed a system for several weeks, early in the system's life. Rules that the client had seemingly wanted to be strictly enforced needed to be occasionally overridden on a case-by-case basis, based on their client's desires. Unfortunately, our program didn't make it possible for the user to override these rules, so teeth were gnashed and sleep was lost fixing the problem (even worse, it was a fixed-bid contract where these kinds of overages meant no more money, completely eating away any possible bonus. And no, I didn't make that deal).

Some rules might have another problem: the client wants the rule, but it isn't possible or practical to implement it. For example, the client might request that all registered visitors of the client's website have to insert a valid mobile phone number, but is it certain that visitors would provide this data? And what exactly is a valid mobile number? How can you validate that—by format alone, or does it have to be validated by calling it? Or checking with the phone company? What if users provide a landline instead? Implementability is of no concern at this point in the process. Someone will have to enforce the rule, and that will be ironed out later in the process.

## Who Will Use the Data?

The answer to the question of who will use the data might indicate other people who might need to be interviewed and will likely be of importance when you come to define the security for the system.

## What Do You Want to See on Reports?

Reports are often one of the most frequently forgotten parts of the design process. Many novice developers leave implementing them until the last minute (a mistake I've made more than once over the years). However, users are probably more interested in the reports that are generated from the data than anything else you do. For the user, reports are where data becomes information and are used as the basis of vital decision making and can make or break a company.

Looking back at the contact example, what name does the client want to see on the reports?

- First name, last name
- First name, middle name, last name
- Last name, first name
- Nickname

It's important to try to nail such issues down early, no matter how small or silly they seem to you. They're important to the client, who you should always remember is paying the bill. And frankly, the most important rule for reporting is that you cannot report on data that you do not capture.

From a database design standpoint, the content of the reports is extremely important, because it might help to discover data requirements that aren't otherwise thought of. Avoid being concerned with the physical design of the reports yet, because it might lead to the temptation of coding and away from modeling.

---

**■Tip** Don't overlook existing reports. They're the most important part of any system, and you'll often discover that clients have important data in reports that they never even think about when they're expressing needs. One of my company's clients is rebuilding its database systems, and it has hundreds of reports currently in production.

---

## Where Is the Data Now?

It is nice once in a while to have the opportunity to create a totally new database with absolutely no preexisting data. This makes life so easy and your job a lot of fun. Unfortunately, this is almost never the case, except possibly when building a product to be sold to end users in a turnkey fashion (then the preexisting data is their problem or yours if you purchase their system). For almost every system I have worked on, I was creating a better version of some other system, so we had to consider converting existing data that's important to the end users. (Only one major system was a brand new system. That was a wonderful experience for many reasons; not only didn't we have to deal with data conversion, but we didn't have to deal with existing processes and code either.)

Every organization is different. Some have data in one centralized location, while others have it scattered in many (many) locations. Rarely, if ever, is the data already in one well-structured database that you can easily access. If that were the case, why would the client come to you at all? Clients typically have data in the following sundry locations:

- *Mainframe or legacy servers*: Millions of lines of active COBOL still run many corporations.
- *Spreadsheets*: Spreadsheets are wonderful tools to view, slice, and dice data but are wildly inappropriate places to maintain complex data. Most users know how to use a spreadsheet as a database but, unfortunately, are not so experienced in ensuring the integrity of their data, so this data is undoubtedly going to give you a major headache.

- *Desktop databases such as Microsoft Access*: Desktop databases are great tools and are easy to deploy and use. However, this often means that these databases are constructed and maintained by nontechnical personnel and are poorly designed, potentially causing many problems when the databases have to be enlarged or modified.

- *Filing cabinets*: Even now in the 21st century, many companies still have few or no computers used for anything other than playing solitaire and instead maintain stockpiles of paper documents. Your project might simply be to replace a filing cabinet with a computer-based system or to supply a simple database that logs the physical locations of the existing paper documents.

Data that you need to include in the SQL Server database you're designing will come from these and other weird and wonderful sources that you discover from the client. (Truth is commonly stranger than fiction.) Even worse, spreadsheets, filing cabinets, and poorly designed computerized databases don't enforce data integrity (and often desktop databases, mainframe applications, and even existing SQL Server databases don't necessarily do such a perfect job either), so always be prepared for dirty data that will have to be cleaned up before storage in your nice new database.

## Will the Data Need to Be Integrated with Other Systems?

Once you have a good idea of where the client's important data is located, you can begin to determine how the data in your new SQL Server solution will interact with the data that will stay in its original format. This might include building intricate gateway connections to mainframes, linking server connections to other SQL Servers or Oracle boxes, or even linking to spreadsheets. You can't make too many assumptions about this topic at this point in your design. Just knowing the architecture you'll need to deal with can be helpful later in the process.

---

■**Tip**  *Never* expect that the data you will be converting or integrating with is going to have *any* quality. Too many projects get their start with poor guesses about the effort required, and data cleanup has been the least well-guessed part of them all. It will be hard enough to understand what is in a database to start with, but if the data is bad, it will make your job orders of magnitude more difficult. If you have promised to do the work for $1,000 and it ends up taking 500 hours, you would have been better off with a spatula working midnights at the Waffle House.

---

## How Much Is This Data Worth?

It's also important to place value judgments on data. In some cases, data will have great value in the monetary sense. For example, in the dental office example that will be presented later in this chapter, the value lies in the record of what has been done to the patient and how much has been billed to the patient and his or her insurance company. Without this documentation, it might take hours and days to dig this data out and eventually get paid for the work done. This data has a specific monetary value, because the quicker the payment is received, the more interest is drawn, meaning more profits. If the client shifts the turnover of payments from one month to one week because of streamlining the process, this might be worth quite a bit more money.

On the other hand, just because existing data is available doesn't necessarily mean that it should be included in the new database. The client needs to be informed of all the data that's available and should be provided with a cost estimate of transferring it into the new database. The cost of transferring legacy data can be high, and the client should be offered the opportunity to make decisions that might conserve funds for more important purposes.

# Existing Systems and Prototypes

If you're writing a new version of a current database system, then access to the existing system can be both a blessing and a curse. Obviously, the more information you can gather about how any previous system and its data was previously structured, the better. All the screens, data models, object models, user documents, and so on, are important to the design process.

However, unless you're simply making revisions to an existing system, often the old database system is reasonable only as a reference point for completeness, not as an initial blueprint. On most occasions, the existing system you'll be replacing will have many problems that need to be fixed, not emulated. If the system being replaced had no problems, why is the client replacing the existing system?

Prototypes from the early design process might also exist. Prototypes can be useful tools to communicate how to solve a real-world problem using a computer or when you're trying to reengineer how a current process is managed. Their role is to be a "proof of concept"—an opportunity to flesh out with the design team and the end users the critical elements of the project on which success or failure will depend.

The real problem with prototypes is that if a database was created for the prototype, it is rarely going to be worth anything. So, by the time database design starts, you might be directed to take a prototype database that has been hastily developed and "make it work" or, worse yet, "polish it up." Indeed, you might inherit an unstructured, unorganized prototype, and your task will be to turn it into a production database in no time flat (loosely translated, that means to have it done yesterday or sooner).

Bear in mind that you should consider prototypes only as interactive pictures to get the customer to sign a contract with your company. Sometimes you might be hired to implement the prototype (or the failed try at a production system that's now being called a prototype) that another consultant was hired to create (or worse yet, an employee who still works there and has a chip on his shoulder the size of a large Asian elephant that spends all day eating bonbons and watching soap operas). It's better to start from scratch, developing the final application using structured, supported design and coding standards. As a data architect, you must work as hard as possible to use prototype code *only* as a working model—a piece of documentation that you use to enhance your own design. Prototypes help you to be sure you're not going to miss out on any critical pieces of information that the users need—such as a name field, a search operation, or even a button (which might imply a data element)—but they may not tell you anything about the eventual database design at all.

# Other Types of Documentation

Apart from interviews and existing systems, you can look to other sources to find data rules and other pieces of information relevant to the design project. Often the project manager will obtain these documents; or sometimes they will not be available to you, and you just have to take someone else's word for what is said in them. In these cases, I find it best to get into writing your understanding and make sure it is clear who said what about the meaning of documentation you cannot see. Ordinarily I try not to worry about the later "blame factor," but it is essential to worry when you are working from a translation that may later come under dispute.

## Early Project Documentation

If you work for a company that is creating software for other companies, you'll find that early in the project there are often documents that get created to solicit costs and possible solutions. For example:

- *Request for quote (RFQ)*: A document with a fairly mature specification, which an organization sends out to determine how much a solution would cost
- *Request for proposal (RFP)*: For less mature ideas for which an organization wants to see potential solutions and get an idea about its costs

Each of these documents contains valuable information that can help you design a solution because you can get an idea of what the client wanted before you got involved. Things change, of course, and not always will the final solution resemble the original request, but a copy of an RFP or an RFQ should be added to the pile of information that you'll have available later in the process. Although these documents generally consist of sketchy information about the problem and the desired solution, you can use them to confirm the original reason for wanting the database system and for getting a firmer handle on what types of data are to be stored within it.

No matter what, if you can get a copy of these documents, you'll be able to see the client's thought pattern and why the client wants a system developed.

## Contracts or Client Work Orders

Getting copies of the contract can seem like a fairly radical approach to gathering design information, depending on the type of organization you're with. Frankly, in a corporate structure, you'll likely have to fight through layers of management to make them understand why you need to see the contract at all. Contracts can be inherently difficult to read because of the language they're written in (sort of like a terse version of a programming language, with intentional vagueness tossed in to give lawyers something to dispute with one another later). However, be diligent in filtering out the legalese, and you'll uncover what amounts to a basic set of requirements for the system—often the requirements that you must fulfill exactly or not get paid.

What makes the contract so attractive is simple. It is, generally speaking, the target you'll be shooting at. No matter what the client says, or what the existing system was, if the contract specifies that you deliver some sort of watercraft and you deliver a Formula 1 race car because the lower-level clients change their minds without changing the contract, your project could still be deemed a failure (figuratively speaking, of course, since who doesn't like Formula 1 race cars?).

## Level of Service Agreement

One important section of contracts that's important to the design process is the required level of service. This might specify the number of pages per minute, the number of rows in the database, and so on. All this needs to be measured, stored, tested for, and so on. When it comes to the optimization phase, knowing the level of service can be of great value. You may also find some data that needs to be stored to validate that a service level is being met.

## Audits Plans

Don't forget about audits. When you build a system, you must consider whether the system is likely to be audited in the future and by whom. Government, ISO 9000 clients, and other clients that are monitored by standards organizations are likely to have strict audit requirements. Other clients may also have financial audit processes. Of particular concern are all the various privacy policies, child data restrictions, credit card encryption rules, and so on. All of these will not only require that you follow rules that regulatory bodies set but that you document certain parts of your operation. These audit plans might contain valuable information that can be used in the design process.

### Reports, Forms, and Spreadsheets

A large percentage of computer systems are built around the filling out of forms—government forms, company forms, all kinds of forms. You can guarantee that all this data is going to be scattered around the company, and it's imperative to find it *all*. It's virtually certain that these sources will contain data that you'll need for your project, so make sure the client gives you all such items.

It's kind of ironic that I spend only such a small amount of text on this topic, because it will take up a good amount of your time. There are so many forms—new forms, old forms, proposed forms, and so on. Dealing with forms is a simple thing, but depending on the size of the user community and the number of reports and screens in an application, it can be a long process indeed. Every distinct physical piece of output that you can find that the existing system produced will be useful.

One system I'm working on has more than 800 distinct reports (hopefully by the time this book is published I will refer to it as the "successful project"). It was a terrible mess to catalog all the reports, and it was thankfully the job of several of my colleagues. It was a tedious process but essential. The information retrieved from those reports helps to run the business.

# Identifying Objects and Processes

The process of discovery is *theoretically* complete at this point. Someone has interviewed all the relevant clients, documented the outcome, and gathered artifacts ranging from previous system documentation to sketches of what the new system might look like to prototypes to whatever is available. Assuming you were not part of the team that gathered this documentation, now the fun part starts: sifting through all the documentation and looking for database entities and attributes. In the rest of this chapter, I'll introduce the following processes:

- *Identifying entities*: Looking for all the "things" that need to be modeled in the database.

- *Identifying relationships between entities*: Relationships between entities are what make entities useful. Here the goal is to look for natural relationships between high-level entities.

- *Identifying attributes and domains*: Looking for the individual data points that describe the entities.

- *Identifying business rules*: Looking for the boundaries that are applied to the data in the system that go beyond the domains of a single attribute.

- *Identifying fundamental processes*: Looking for different processes (code and programs) that the client tends to execute that are fundamental to its business.

---

**■ Note** Calling these *processes* is a bit of a stretch really. In this section I'm going to approach these activities in a linear manner, identifying all entities first, all attributes next, and so on. This is just done for illustrative purposes to make you think about the individual parts of the process one at a time. Realistically, you'll likely look for all at the same time in a more natural approach.

---

Going through these identification processes can be the most difficult part of the overall process of building a database system, because as technical people, our deep-down desire is to "build stuff." I know I didn't start writing SQL code with a mind to write and read loads of mind-numbing documentation. But if you tear off and start designing structures and writing code, you'll likely find out that you missed something that gave you important insight into the client's structures and needs, leading you to restructure your solution. When you waste time doing that once, you will not want to repeat the process, particularly because you will have a boss and a gaggle of programmers all giving you heck because you are spending time that they had expected to be coding!

Throughout the rest of the chapter, the following example piece of documentation will be used as the basis of our examples. In a real system, this might be just a single piece of documentation that has been gathered. (It always amazes me how much useful information you can get from a few paragraphs, though to be fair I did write—and rewrite—this example more than a couple of times.)

*The client manages a couple of dental offices. One is called the Chelsea Office, the other the Downtown Office. The client needs the system to manage its patients and appointments, alerting the patients when their appointments occur, either by e-mail or by phone, and then assisting in the selection of new appointments. The client wants to be able to keep up with the records of all the patients' appointments without having to maintain lots of files. The dentists might spend time at each of the offices throughout the week.*

*For each appointment, the client needs to have everything documented that went on and then invoice the patient's insurance, if he or she has insurance (otherwise the patient pays). Invoices should be sent within one week after the appointment. Each patient should be able to be associated with other patients in a family for insurance and appointment purposes. We will need to have an address, a phone number (home, mobile, and/or office), and optionally an e-mail address associated with each family, and possibly each patient if the client desires. Currently the client uses a patient number in its computer system that corresponds to a particular folder that has the patient's records.*

*The system needs to track and manage several dentists and quite a few dental hygienists who the client needs to allocate to each appointment as well. The client also wants to keep up with its supplies, such as sample toothpastes, toothbrushes, and floss, as well as dental supplies. It has had problems in the past keeping up with when it's about to run out of supplies and wants this system to take care of this for both locations. For the dental supplies, we need to track usage by employee, especially any changes made in the database to patient records.*

Through each of the following sections, our goal will be to acquire all the pieces of information that need to be stored in our new database system. Sounds simple enough, eh? Well, although it's much easier than it might seem, it takes time and effort (two things every programmer has in abundance, right?).

# Identifying Entities

*Entities* are the most straightforward objects to identify while you're scanning through documentation. Entities generally represent people, places, objects, ideas, or things referred to grammatically as nouns. For example, our dental office includes the following:

- *People*: A patient, a doctor, a hygienist, and so on
- *Place*: Dental office, patient's home, hospital
- *Object*: A dental tool, stickers for the kids, toothpaste
- *Idea*: A document, insurance, a group (such as a security group for an application), the list of services provided, and so on

There's clearly overlap in several of the categories (for example, a building is a "place" or an "object"), and don't be surprised if some objects fit into several of the subcategories below them that I will introduce. It isn't critical to identify that an entity is a person, place, object, or idea. However, if it fits nicely within a specific group, it can help to assign some attributes, such as a name for a person or an address for the location of a building.

Things will be classified as people, places, and objects, and this will help to define some basic information needed later when defining attributes. Also, this will help ensure that all the documentation necessary is available to describe each entity.

---

■**Tip**  How an entity is implemented in a table might be different from the initial entities you specify. It's better not to worry about this at this stage in the design process—you should try hard not to get too wrapped up in the eventual database implementation. This sounds simple enough but can be the hardest thing to do. When building the initial design, you want the document to come initially from what the user wants. Then you'll fit what the user wants into a common mold later if possible. However, at this point, a change in the design is a click and a drag away, because all you're doing is specifying the foundation; the rest of the house shouldn't be built yet.

---

Let's look at each of these types of entities and see what kinds of things can be discovered from the documentation sample in each of the aforementioned entity types.

## People

Nearly every database needs to store information about people. Most databases have at least some notion of users (generally thought of as people, though not always). As far as real people are concerned, a database might need to store information about many different types of people. For instance, a school's database might have a student entity, a teacher entity, and an administrator entity.

In our example, four people entities can be found—patients, dentists, hygienists, and employees:

*. . . the system to manage its **patients** . . .*

Also

*. . . manage several **dentists, and quite a few dental** hygienists . . .*

Patients are clearly people, as are hygienists and dentists (yes, even the ones with the tiny pitchforks who dig around looking for ways to hurt you are actually people). Because they're people, specific attributes can be inferred (such as that they have names, for example).
Also:

*. . . we need to track usage by **employee** . . .*

Dentists and hygienists have already been mentioned. It's clear that they'll be employees as well. For now, document that there are four new entities: patients, hygienists, dentists, and employees. Our model starts out as shown in Figure 3-1.

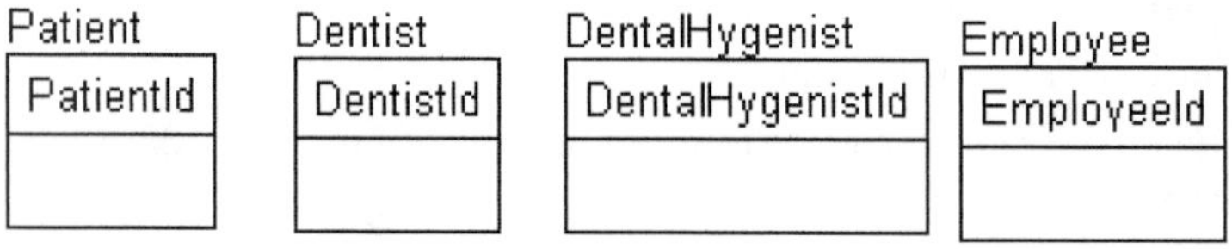

**Figure 3-1.** *Four new entities*

---

**■Tip** Note that I have started with giving each entity a surrogate key. This serves as the placeholder while I do the modeling, particularly to make it clearer when I start relating tables to one another. This is shorthand I use to show ownership of the relationship in the conceptual and logical model. Feel free to use any key you want during this process to make the model clear to yourself.

---

## Places

Users will want to store information in many different types of places. One obvious place entity is in our sample set of notes:

> ... *manages a couple of dental **offices** ...*

From the fact that these are places, later we'll be able to infer that there's address information about the office and probably phone numbers, staffing concerns, and so on. It also gives us an idea that the two offices aren't located too close to each other, so there might be business rules about having appointments at different offices, or even preventing the situation in which a dentist might be scheduled at two places at one time. "Inferring" is just slightly informed guessing, so verify all inferences with the client.

I add the Office entity to the model, as shown in Figure 3-2.

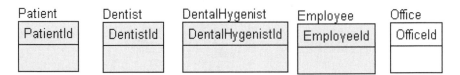

**Figure 3-2.** *Added Office as an entity*

---

**■Note** In the models, things that haven't changed from the previous step in the process are in gray, while new things aren't shaded at all.

---

## Objects

Objects refer primarily to physical items. In our example, there are a couple different objects:

> ... *with its **supplies, such as sample toothpastes, toothbrushes, and floss, as well as** dental supplies ...*

Supplies, such as sample toothpastes, toothbrushes, and floss, as well as dental supplies, are all things that the client needs to run its business. Obviously, most of the supplies will be simple, and the client won't need to store a large amount of descriptive information about them. For example, it's possible to come up with a pretty intense list of things you might know about something as simple as a tube of toothpaste:

- *Tube size*: Perhaps the length of the tube or the amount in grams
- *Brand*: Colgate, Crest, or some off-brand
- *Format*: Metal tube, pump, and so on
- *Flavor*: Mint, bubble gum (the nastiest of all flavors), cinnamon
- *Manufacturer information*: Batch number, expiration date, and so on

This could go on and on, but it's unlikely that the users will have a business need for this information, because they probably just have a box of whatever they have and give it out to their patients (to make them feel better about the metal against enamel experience they have just gone through). At this point, we need to apply "selective ignorance" to the process and ignore the different attributes of things that have no business interest. It is a good idea to drill into the client's process to make sure what they actually want.

Only one entity is necessary—Supply—but document that "Examples given were sample items, such as toothpaste or toothbrushes, plus there was mention of dental supplies. These supplies are the ones that the dentist and hygienists use to perform their job."

So I add the Supply entity to the model, as shown in Figure 3-3.

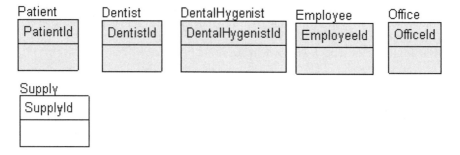

**Figure 3-3.** *Added the Supply entity*

## Ideas

No law requires that entities should be real objects or even exist physically. At this stage of discovery, you need to consider information on objects that the user wants to store that don't fit the already established "people," "places," and "objects" categories and that might or might not be physical objects.

For example, consider the following:

> *. . . and then invoice the patient's **insurance**, if he or she has insurance (otherwise the **patient pays**) . . .*

Insurance is an obvious important entity. Another entity name looks like a verb rather than a noun in the phrase "patient pays." From this we can imply that there might be some form of payment entity to deal with.

---

■**Tip** Not all entities will be adorned with a sign flashing "Yo, McGillicuddy, I am an entity!" A lot of the time, you'll have to read into what has been documented and sniff it out like a pig on a truffle.

---

The model now looks like Figure 3-4.

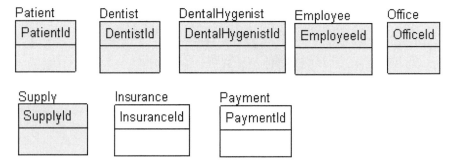

**Figure 3-4.** *Added the Insurance and Payment entities*

## Documents

For many, the term *documents* seems to refer to tangible pieces of paper containing information that the client needs to keep track of. This might seem like splitting hairs, but what if someone makes a copy of the piece of paper? Does that mean there are two documents, or are they both the same document? Usually it isn't the case, but sometimes people do need to track physical pieces of paper and, just as often, versions and revisions of a document.

On the other hand, most of the time, even though it's a piece of paper, it merely represents something intangible:

> . . . and then **invoice** the patient's insurance, if he or she has insurance (otherwise the patient pays) . . .

Invoices are pieces of paper (or e-mails) that are sent to a customer after the services have been rendered. However, no mention was made as to how invoices are delivered. They could be e-mailed or postal mailed—it isn't clear—nor would it be prudent for the database design to force it to be done either way unless this is a specific business rule. At this point, just identify the entities and move along; again, it usually isn't worth it to spend too much time guessing how the data will be used. This is something you should interview the client for.

> . . . appointments, **alerting** the patients when their appointments occur, either by e-mail or by phone . . .

This type of document almost certainly isn't delivered by paper but by an e-mail message or phone call. The e-mail is also used as part of another entity, an Alert. The alert can be either an e-mail or a phone alert.

---

**Note** If you are alert (no pun intended), you probably are thinking that Appointment, Email, and Phone are all entity possibilities, and you would be right. In my teaching process here I am looking at the types in a bubble. In the real process you would just look for nouns linearly through the text.

---

Next we add the Invoice and Alert entities to the model, as shown in Figure 3-5.

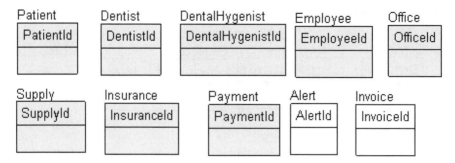

**Figure 3-5.** *Added the Alert and Invoice entities*

## Groups

Another idea-type entity is a group of things, or more technically, a grouping of entities. For example, you might have a club that has members or certain types of products that make up a grouping that seems more than just a simple attribute. In our sample we have one such entity:

> *Each patient should be able to be associated with other patients in a **family** for insurance and appointment purposes.*

Although a person's family is an attribute of the person, it's more than that. So, we add a Family entity, as shown in Figure 3-6.

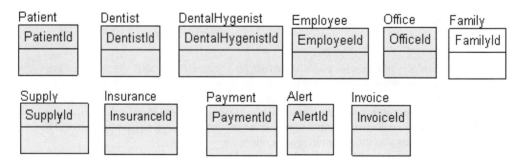

**Figure 3-6.** *Added the Family entity*

## Other Entities

The following sections outline some additional common objects that are perhaps not as obvious as the ones that have been presented. They don't always fit a simple categorization, but they're pretty straightforward.

### Audit Trails

Audit trails, generally speaking, are used to track changes to the database. You might know that the RDBMS uses a log to track changes, but this is off-limits to the average user. So, in cases where the user wants to keep up with who does what, entities need to be modeled to represent these logs.

They would be analogous to a sign-in/out sheet, a library card (remember those?) with which users check books out and back in, or just a list of things that went on in any order.

Consider the following example:

*For the dental supplies, we need to track usage by employee, and especially any changes made in the database to the patient records.*

In this case, the client clearly is keen to keep up with the kinds of materials that are being used by each of its employees. Perhaps a guess can be made that the user needs to be documented when dental supplies are taken (the difference between dental supplies and nondental supplies will certainly have to be discussed in due time). Also, it isn't necessary at this time that the needed logging be done totally on a computer, or even by using a computer at all.

A second example of an audit trail is as follows:

*For the dental supplies, we need to track usage by employee, **and especially any changes made in the database to the patient records.***

A typical entity that you need to define is the audit trail or a log of database activity, and this entity is especially important when the data is sensitive. An audit trail isn't a normal type of entity, in that it stores no user data and, as such, should generally be deferred to the implementation design stage. The only kinds of entities to be concerned with at this point are those that users wish to store in directly. As such, you shouldn't deal with these types of statements at this stage but leave them until the implementation phase.

## Events

Event entities generally represent verbs or actions:

*For each **appointment**, the client needs to have everything documented that went on . . .*

An appointment is an event, in that it's used to record information about when patients come to the office and have something done to them. For most events, appointments included, it's important to have a schedule of when the event is (or was) and where the event will occur. It's also not uncommon to want to have data that documents an event's occurrence (what was done, how many people attended, and so on). Hence, many event entities will be tightly related to some form of document entity. In our example, appointments are more than likely scheduled for the future, and when the appointment occurs, a record of what was done is made, so the dentist can get paid.

There are all sorts of events to look for beyond the obvious examples, such as meter readings, weather readings, equipment measurements, and so on. Also consider that an event isn't necessarily so grand a thing that it has to have people attend it. It's just something that happens at a given point in time—an occurrence.

## Records and Journals

The last of the entity types to examine at this stage is a record or journal of activities. Note that I mean "record" in a nondatabase sort of way. A record could be any kind of activity that a user might previously have recorded on paper. In our example, the user wants to keep a record of each visit:

*The client wants to be able to keep up with the **records of all the patients' appointments without having to maintain lots of files.***

This kind of thing is one of the main advantages of building database systems: eliminating paper files and making data more accessible. How many times must I tell the doctor what medicines I'm taking, all because her files are insane clutters used to cover her billing process, rather than being a useful document of my history? Covering one's self by doing due diligence is fine, but by leveraging the RDBMS, the information our computer systems are constantly gathering comes alive, and trends can be seen instantly in ways it would take hours to see on paper.

This is another entity type that's similar to an audit log but would potentially contain more information, such as notes about a contact, rather than just a record that a contact had taken place.

The model after the changes looks like Figure 3-7.

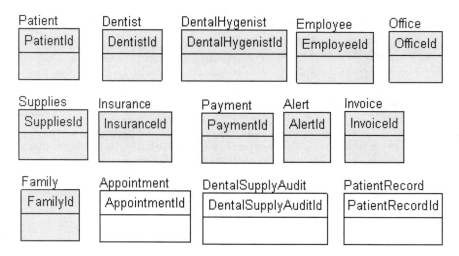

**Figure 3-7.** *Added the Appointment, DentalSupplyAudit, and PatientRecord entities*

## Entity Recap

So far we've discovered the list of preliminary entities shown in Table 3-1. It makes a pretty weak model, but this will change in the next section as we begin adding attributes.

Before progressing any further, stop, define, and document the entities as shown in Table 3-1.

**Table 3-1.** *Entity Listing*

| Entity | Type | Description |
| --- | --- | --- |
| Patient | People | The people who are the customers of the dental office. Services are performed, supplies are used, and patients are billed for them. |
| Family | Idea | A group of patients grouped together for convenience. |
| Dentist | People | People who do the most important work at the dental office. Several dentists are working for the client's practice. |
| Hygienists | People | People who do the basic work for the dentist. There are quite a few more hygienists than dentists. *(Note: Check with client to see whether there are guidelines for the number of hygienists per dentist. Might be needed for setting appointments.)* |

| Entity | Type | Description |
|---|---|---|
| Employee | People | Any person who works at the dental office. Dentists and hygienists are clearly a type of employee. |
| Office | Places | Locations where the dentists do their business. They have multiple offices to deal with and schedule patients for. |
| Supplies | Objects | Examples given were sample items, such as toothpaste or toothbrushes, plus there was mention of dental supplies. These supplies are the ones that the dentist and hygienists use to perform their job. |
| Insurance | Idea | Used by patients to pay for the dental services–rendered work. |
| Payment | Idea | Money taken from insurance or patients (or both) to pay for services. |
| Invoice | Document | A document sent to the patient or insurance company explaining how much money is required to pay for services. |
| Alert | Document | E-mail or phone call made to tell patient of an impending appointment. |
| Dental Supply Audit | Audit Trail | Used to track the usage of dental supplies. |
| Appointment | Event | The event of a patient coming in and having some dental work done. |
| Patient Record | Record | All the pertinent information about a patient, much like a patient's chart in any doctor's office. |

*Implementation modeling note: log any changes to sensitive/important data.*

The descriptions are based on the facts that have been derived from the preliminary documentation. Note that the entities that have been specified are directly represented in the customer's documentation.

## Relationships Between Entities

Next we will look for the ways that the entities relate to one another, which will then be translated to relationships between the entities on the model. The idea here is to find how each of the entities will work with one another to solve the client's needs. I'll start first with the one-to-N type of relationships and then cover the many-to-many. It's also important to consider elementary relationships that aren't directly mentioned in your requirements, but be careful not to make too many inferences at this point in the process.

### One-to-N Relationships

In each of the one-to-N (commonly one-to-one or one-to-many) relationships, the table that is the "one" table in the relationship is considered the parent, and the "N" is the child or children rows.

The one-to-N relationship is used almost exclusively in implementation, but most of the natural relationships that users tell you about turn out to be many-to-many relationships. It is important to really consider the cardinality of all relationships you model so as not to limit future design considerations by missing something that is very natural to the process.

I'll classify some of our relationships as has-a or is-a, but not all will fit in this mold. I'll present examples of each type in the next couple sections.

---

■**Tip** A good deal of the time required to do database design may be simple "thinking" time. I try to spend as much time thinking about the problem as I do documenting/modeling a problem, and often more. It can make your management uneasy (especially if you are working an hourly contract) since "thinking" looks a lot like "daydreaming," but working out all the angles in your head is definitely worth it.

---

### The "Has-A" Relationship

The main special type of relationship is the "has-a" relationship. It's so named because the parent table in the relationship has one or more of the child entities employed as attributes of the parent. In fact, the "has-a" relationship is the way you implement an attribute that often occurs more than once.

In our example paragraph, consider the following:

*. . . then invoice the **patient's insurance, if he or she has insurance** . . .*

In this case, the relationship is between the Patient entity and the Insurance entity. It's an optional relationship, because it says "if he or she has insurance." Add the following relationship to the model, as shown in Figure 3-8.

**Figure 3-8.** *Added the relationship between the Patient and Insurance entities*

Another example of a "has-a" relationship is found in the following example:

*Each **patient should be able to be associated with other patients in a** family for insurance and appointment purposes.*

In this case, we identify that a family has patients. Although this sounds odd, it makes perfect sense in the context of a medical office. Instead of maintaining ten different insurance records for each member of a family of ten, the client wants to have a single one where it makes sense. So, we add a relationship between family and patient, stating that a family instance may have multiple patient instances.

That the family is covered by insurance is also a possible relationship in Figure 3-9. It has already been specified that patients have insurance. This isn't unlikely, because even if a person's family has insurance, one of the members might have an alternative insurance plan. It also doesn't contradict our earlier notion that patients have insurance, although it does give them two different paths to identify the insurance. This isn't necessarily a problem, but when two insurance policies exist, you might have to decide which one takes precedence. Again, this is something to discuss with the client and probably not something to start making up.

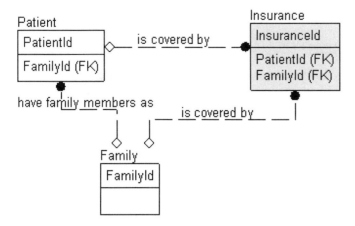

**Figure 3-9.** *Relationships added between the Patient, Insurance, and Family entities*

Here's another example of a has-a relationship, shown in Figure 3-10:

> *... **dental offices ... The client needs the system to manage its patients and** appointments ...*

In this case, make a note that each dental office will have appointments. Clearly, an appointment can be for only a single dental office, so this is a has-a relationship. One of the attributes of an event type of entity is a location. It's unclear at this point whether a patient comes to only one of the offices or whether the patient can float between offices. This will be a question for the clients when you go back to get clarification on your design.

Now add the relationship shown in Figure 3-10.

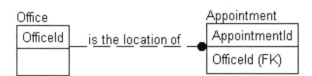

**Figure 3-10.** *Relationship added between the Office and Appointment entities*

## The "Is-A" Relationship

The idea behind an "is-a" relationship is that the child entity in the relationship "extends" the parent. For example, cars, trucks, RVs, and so on, are all types of vehicles, so a car *is a* vehicle. The cardinality of this relationship is always one-to-one, because the child entity simply contains more specific information that qualifies this extended relationship. The reason for having this sort of relationship is conceptual. There would be some information that's common to each of the child entities (stored as attributes of the parent entity) but also other information that's specific to each child entity (stored as attributes of the child entity).

In our example, the following snippets exist:

> *... manage several **dentists,** and quite a few **dental hygienists** who the client ...*

and

> *. . . track usage by* **employee**, *and especially . . .*

From these statements, you can see there are three entities, and there's a relationship between them. A dentist is an employee, as is a dental hygienist. There are possibly other employees for whom the system needs to track supply usage as well. Figure 3-11 represents this relationship.

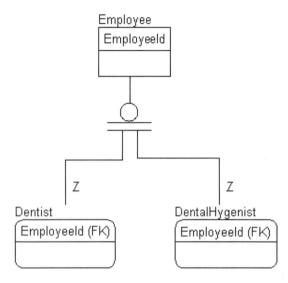

**Figure 3-11.** *Identified subtyped relationship between the Employee, Dentist, and DentalHygenist entities*

---

**■Note**  Because the subtype manifests itself as a one-to-one identifying relationship (remember from Chapter 2, the Z on the relationship line indicates a one-to-one relationship), separate keys for the Dentist and DentalHygienist entities aren't needed.

This use of keys can be confusing in the implementation since you might have relationships at any of the three table levels and since the key will be the same name. These kinds of issues are why you maintain a data model for the user to view as needed to understand the relationships between tables.

---

## Many-to-Many Relationships

Many-to-many relationships are far more prevalent than you might think. In fact, as you refine the model, a great number of relationships may end up being many-to-many relationships as the real relationship between entities is realized. However, early in the design process, only a few many-to-many relationships might be recognized. In our example, one is obvious:

> *The dentists might spend time at each of the offices throughout the week.*

In this case, multiple dentists can work at more than one dental office. A one-to-many relationship won't suffice; it's wrong to state that one dentist can work at many dental offices, because this implies that each dental office has only one dentist. The opposite, that one office can support many dentists, implies dentists work at only one office. Hence, this is a many-to-many relationship (see Figure 3-12).

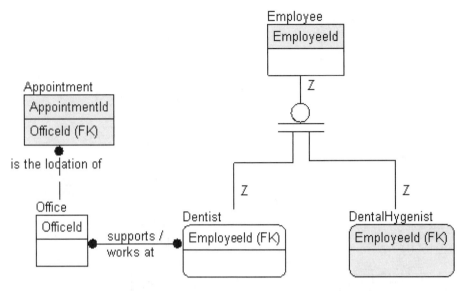

**Figure 3-12.** *Added a many-to-many relationship between Dentist and Office*

This is an additional many-to-many relationship that can be identified:

*. . . dental supplies, we need to track usage by employee . . .*

This quote says that multiple employees can use different types of supplies, and for every dental supply, multiple types of employees can use them. However, it's possible that controls might be required to manage the types of dental supplies that each employee might use, especially if some of the supplies are regulated in some way (such as narcotics).

The relationship shown in Figure 3-13 is added.

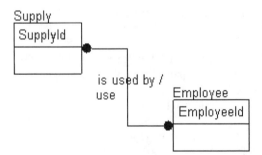

**Figure 3-13.** *Added a many-to-many relationship between the Supply and Employee entities*

I'm also going to remove the DentalSupplyAudit entity, because it's becoming clear that this entity is a report (in a real situation you'd ask the client to make sure, but in this case I'm the client, and I agree).

## Listing Relationships

Figure 3-14 shows the model so far.

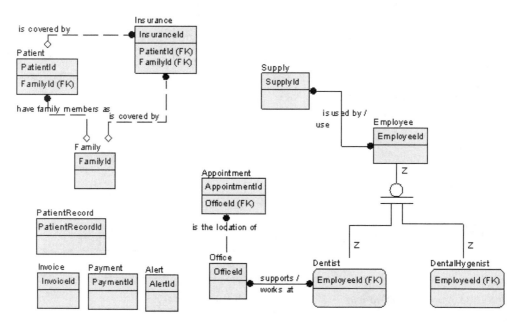

**Figure 3-14.** *The model so far*

There are other relationships in the text that I won't cover explicitly, but I've documented them in the descriptions in Table 3-2, which is followed by the model with relationships identified and the definitions of the relationships in our documentation (note that the relationship is documented at the parent only).

**Table 3-2.** *Initial Relationship Documentation*

| Entity | Type | Description |
|---|---|---|
| Patient | **People** | **The people who are the customers of the dental office. Services are performed, supplies are used, and the patient is billed for these services.** |
| | Is covered by Insurance | Identifies when the patient has personal insurance. |
| | Is reminded by Alerts | Alerts are sent to patients to remind them of their appointments. |
| | Is scheduled via Appointments | Appointments need to have one patient. |
| | Is billed with Invoices | Patients are charged for appointments via an invoice. |
| | Makes Payment | Patients make payments for invoices they receive. |
| | Has activity listed in PatientRecord | Activities that happen in the doctor's office. |

| Entity | Type | Description |
|---|---|---|
| Family | **Idea** | **A group of patients grouped together for convenience.** |
| | Has family members has Patients | A family consists of multiple patients. |
| | Is covered by Insurance | Identifies when there's coverage for the entire family. |
| Dentist | **People** | **People who do the most important work at the dental office. There are several dentists working for the client's practice.** |
| | Works at many Offices | Dentists can work at many offices. |
| | Is an Employee | Dentists have some of the attributes of all employees. |
| | Do work during Appointments | Appointments might require the services of one dentist. |
| Hygienists | **People** | **People who do the basic work for the dentist. There are quite a few more hygienists than dentists. *(Note: Check with client to see if there are guidelines for the number of hygienists per dentist. Might be needed for setting appointments.)*** |
| | Is an Employee | Hygienists have some of the attributes of all employees. |
| | Have Appointments | All Appointments need to have at least one hygienist. |
| Employee | **People** | **Any person who works at the dental office. Dentists and hygienists are clearly a type of employee.** |
| | Use Supplies | Employees use supplies for various reasons. |
| Office | **Places** | **Locations where the dentists do their business. They have multiple offices to deal with and schedule patients for.** |
| | Is the location of Appointments | Appointments are made for a single office. |
| Supplies | **Objects** | **Examples given were sample items, such as toothpaste or toothbrushes, plus there was mention of dental supplies. These supplies are the ones that the dentist and hygienists use to perform their job.** |
| | Are used by many Employees | Employees use supplies for various reasons. |
| Insurance | **Idea** | **Used by patients to pay for the dental services rendered.** |
| Payment | **Idea** | **Money taken from insurance or patients (or both) to pay for services.** |
| Invoice | **Document** | **A document sent to the patient or insurance company explaining how much money is required to pay for services.** |
| | Has Payments | Payments are usually made to cover costs of the invoice (some payments are for other reasons). |
| Alert | **Document** | **E-mail or phone call made to tell patient of an impending appointment.** |
| Appointment | **Event** | **The event of a patient coming in and having some dental work done.** |
| PatientRecord | **Record** | **All the pertinent information about a patient, much like a patient's chart in any doctor's office.** |

Figure 3-15 shows how the model has progressed.

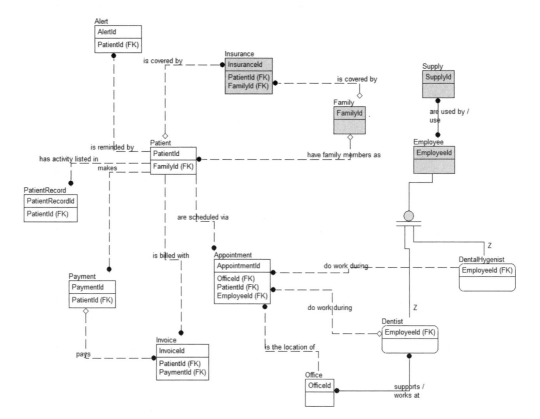

**Figure 3-15.** *The model after adding entities and relationships*

You can see at this point that the model is starting to gel and look like a data model. In the next section, we will start adding attributes to the tables, and the model will really start to take form. It is not 100 percent complete, and you could probably find a few things that you really want to add or change (for example, the fact that Insurance *pays* Invoice stands out is a definite possibility). However, note that we are trying our best in this phase of the design (certainly in this exercise) to avoid adding value/information to the model. That is part of the process that comes later as you fill in the holes in the documentation that you are given from the client.

## Identifying Attributes and Domains

Next, the goal is to look for items that identify, make up, and describe the entity you're trying to represent, or—to put this into more computing-like terms—the properties of an entity. For example, if the entity is a person, attributes might include driver's license number, Social Security number, hair color, eye color, weight, spouse, children, mailing address, and e-mail address. Each of these things serves to represent the entity in part.

Identifying which attributes to associate with an entity requires a similar approach to identifying the entities themselves. You can frequently find attributes by noting adjectives that are used to describe an entity you have previously found. Some attributes will simply be discovered because of the type of entity they are (person, place, and so on).

Domain information for an attribute is generally discovered at the same time as the attributes, so at this point you should identify domains whenever you can conveniently locate them.

The following is a list of some of the common types of attributes to look for during the process of identifying attributes and their domains:

- *Identifiers*: Any information used to identify a single instance of an entity. This is loosely analogous to a key, though identifiers won't always make proper keys.

- *Descriptive information*: Information used to describe something about the entity, such as color, amounts, and so on.

- *Locators*: Identify how to locate what the entity is modeling, such as a mailing address or, on a smaller scale, a position on a computer screen.

- *Values*: Things that quantify something about the entity, such as monetary amounts, counts, dates, and so on.

As was true during our entity search, these aren't the only places to look for attributes, but they're a good place to start. The most important thing for now is that you'll look for values that make it clearer *what* the entity is modeling. Also, it should be noted that all of these have equal merit and value, and there may be overlaps in groupings. Lots of attributes will not fit into these groupings (even if all of my example attributes all too conveniently will). These are just a set of ideas to get you started looking for attributes.

## Identifiers

Identifier attributes are the attributes that you will use to identify one instance from another. I start here because they are some of the most important attributes. Every entity needs to have at least one identifying attribute or set of attributes. Without attributes, there's no way that different objects can be identified later in the process. These identifiers are keys, as defined in Chapter 1.

For example, here are some common examples of good identifiers:

- *For people*: Social Security numbers (in the United States), full names (not always a perfect identifier), or other IDs (such as customer numbers, employee numbers, and so on).

- *For transactional documents (invoices, bills, computer-generated notices)*: These usually have some sort of externally created number assigned for tracking purposes.

- *For books*: The ISBN numbers (titles definitely aren't unique, not even always by author).

- *For products*: Product numbers for a particular manufacturer (product names aren't unique).

- *For companies that clients deal with*: These are commonly assigned a customer/client number for tracking.

- *For buildings*: The complete address including ZIP/postal code.

- *For mail*: The addressee's name and address and the date it was sent.

There are many more examples, but by now you should understand what identifiers mean. Thinking back to the relational model stuff in Chapter 1, each instance of an entity must be unique. Identifying unique natural keys in the data is the first step in implementing a design.

Take care to really discern whether what you think of as a unique item is actually unique. Look at people's names. At first glance they almost seem unique, but there are hundreds of Louis Davidsons in the United States, and that isn't *that* common of a name. Thousands, if not millions, of John Smiths are out there!

In our example, the first such example of an identifier is found in this phrase:

*The client manages a couple of dental offices. One is called the **Chelsea Office**, the other the **Downtown Office**.*

Usually when something is given a name such as this, it's a good attribute to identify the entity, in our case Name for Office. This makes it a likely candidate for a key because it's unlikely that the client has two offices that it refers to as its "Downtown Office," because that would be confusing. So, I add the following attribute to the Office entity in the model (shown in Figure 3-16). I'll create a generic domain for these types of generic names, for which I generally choose 60 characters as a reasonable length. This isn't a replacement for validation, because the client might have specific size requirements for attributes, though most of the time the client doesn't have a clear idea at design time.

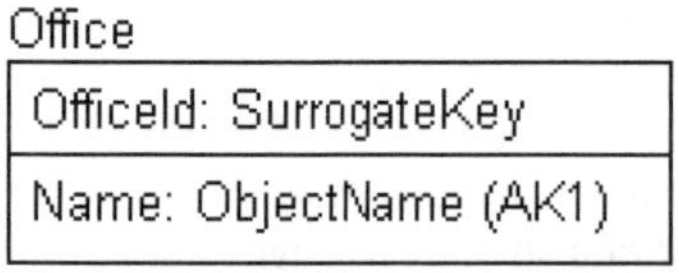

Office

| OfficeId: SurrogateKey |
| Name: ObjectName (AK1) |

**Figure 3-16.** *Added the Name attribute to the Office entity*

Another identifier is found here:

*Currently the client uses a patient number in its computer system that corresponds to a particular folder that has the patient's records.*

Hence, the system needs a patient number attribute for the Patient entity. Again, this is one of those places where querying the client for the specifications of the patient number is a good idea. For this reason, I'll create a specific domain for the patient number that can be tweaked if needed. The client is using eight-character patient numbers from the existing system, on further discussion with the client (see Figure 3-17).

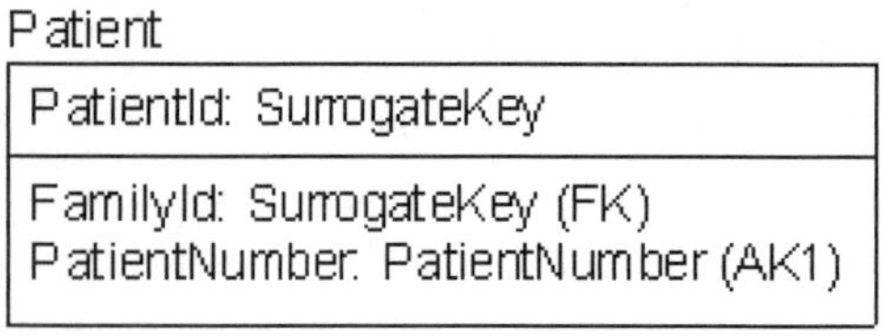

Patient

| PatientId: SurrogateKey |
| FamilyId: SurrogateKey (FK)<br>PatientNumber: PatientNumber (AK1) |

**Figure 3-17.** *Added the PatientNumber attribute to the Patient entity*

---

■**Note** I used the name PatientNumber in this entity, even though it repeated the name of the table. I did this because it's a common term to the client. It also gives clarity to the name that Number would not have. Other examples might be terms like PurchaseOrderNumber or DriversLicenseNumber, where the meaning sticks out to the client. No matter what your naming standards, it's generally best to make sure that terms that are common to the client appear as the client normally uses them.

---

For the most part, it's usually easy to discover an entity's identifier, and this is especially true for the kinds of naturally occurring entities that you find in user-based specifications. Most everything that exists naturally has some sort of way to differentiate itself, although differentiation can become harder when you start to dig deeper.

A common contra-positive to the prior statement about everything being identifiable is things that are managed in bulk. Take our dentist office—although it's easy to differentiate between toothpaste and floss, how would you differentiate between two different tubes of toothpaste? And do you really care? It's probably a safe enough bet that no one cares which tube of toothpaste is given to little Johnny, but this knowledge might be important when it comes to the narcotics that might be distributed. More discussion with the client would be necessary, but my point is that differentiation isn't always simple. During conceptual design, the goal is to do as best as you can. Some details like this can become implementation details. For narcotics, we might require a label be printed with a code and maintained for every bottle. For toothpaste you may have one row and an estimated inventory amount. In the former, the key might be the code you generate and print, and in the latter, the name "toothpaste" might be the key.

## Descriptive Information

*Descriptive information* refers to the common types of adjectives used to describe things that have been previously identified as entities and will usually point directly to an attribute. In our example, different types of supplies are identified, namely, sample and dental:

> ... *their supplies, such as **sample toothpastes, toothbrushes, and floss, as well as** dental supplies.*

Another thing you can identify is the possible domain of an attribute. In this case, the attribute is "Type Of Supply," and the domain seems to be "Sample" and "Dental." Hence I create a specific special domain: SupplyType (see Figure 3-18).

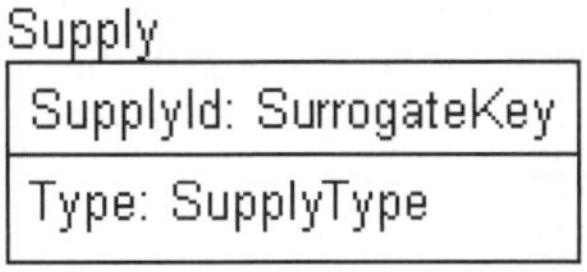

```
Supply
┌─────────────────────────────┐
│ SupplyId: SurrogateKey       │
├─────────────────────────────┤
│ Type: SupplyType             │
└─────────────────────────────┘
```

**Figure 3-18.** *Added the Type attribute to the Supply entity*

## Locators

The concept of a locator is not unlike the concept of a key, except that instead of talking about locating something within the electronic boundaries of our database, the locator finds the geographic location, physical position, or even electronic location of something.

For example, the following are examples of locators:

- *Mailing address*: Every address leads us to some physical location on Earth, such as a mailbox at a house or even a post office box in a building.

- *Geographical references*: These are things such as longitude and latitude or even textual directions on how to get to some place.

- *Phone numbers*: Although you can't always pinpoint a physical location using the phone number, you can use it to locate a person.

- *E-mail addresses*: As with phone numbers, you can use these to locate and contact a person.

- *Websites, FTP sites, or other assorted web resources*: You'll often need to identify the website of an entity or the URL of a resource that's identified by the entity; such information would be defined as attributes.

- *Coordinates of any type*: These might be a location on a shelf, pixels on a computer screen, an office number, and so on.

Anything that's a place is bound to have one or more of these attributes, because a nonmoving target can always be physically located with an address or geographic coordinates. Figure 3-19 shows an example of an implied locator, which I'm implying from the following bit of text from our sample document:

*... manages a couple dental offices ...*

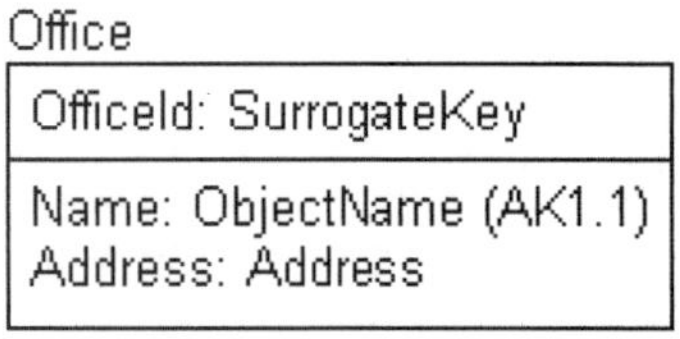

Office

| OfficeId: SurrogateKey |
|---|
| Name: ObjectName (AK1.1)<br>Address: Address |

**Figure 3-19.** *Added an Address attribute to the Office entity*

Because an office is a place, it must have an address where it's located. Hence, the dental Office entity will also have an attribute for the specific location information about the different offices. Each office can have only one address that identifies its location, so the address is a specific locator. Also important is that the domain for this address be a physical address, not a post office box.

However, places aren't the only things you can locate. People are locatable as well. In this loose definition, a person's location can be a temporary location or a contact that can be made with the locator, such as addresses, phone numbers, or even something like GPS coordinates, which might change quite rapidly. In this next example, there are three typical locators:

*... have an **address**, a phone number (home, mobile, and/or office), and optionally an **e-mail address associated with each family, and possibly patient if the client desires** ...*

Most customers, in this case the dental victims—er, patients—have phone numbers, addresses, and e-mail address attributes. The dental office uses these to locate and communicate with the patient for many different reasons, such as billing, making and canceling appointments, and so on. Note also that often families don't live together, because of college, divorce, and so on, but you might still have to associate them for insurance and billing purposes. From these factors you get these sets of attributes on families and patients; see Figure 3-20.

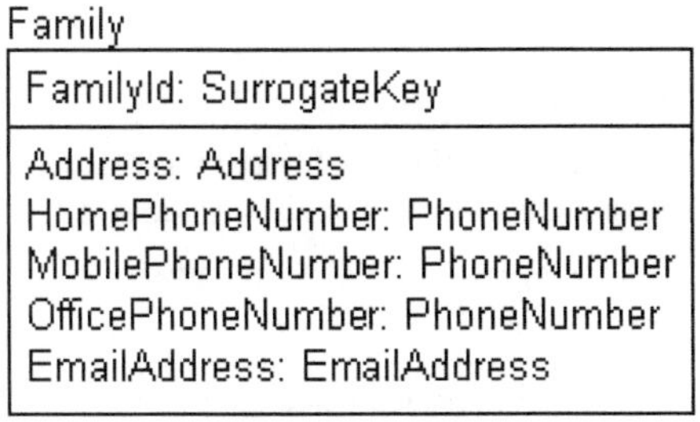

Family

| FamilyId: SurrogateKey |
| --- |
| Address: Address<br>HomePhoneNumber: PhoneNumber<br>MobilePhoneNumber: PhoneNumber<br>OfficePhoneNumber: PhoneNumber<br>EmailAddress: EmailAddress |

**Figure 3-20.** *Added location-specific attributes to the Family entity*

The same is found for the patients, as shown in Figure 3-21.

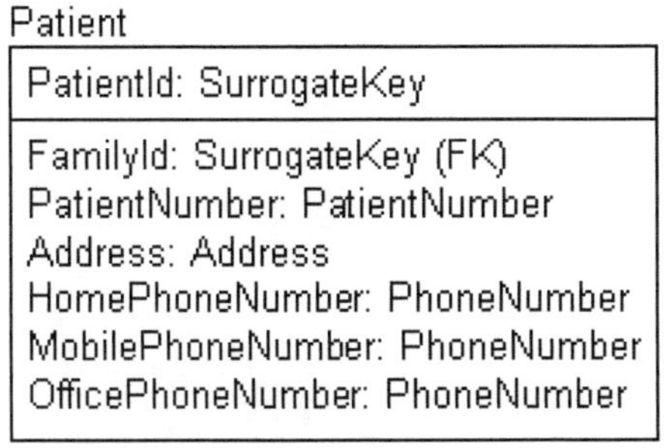

Patient

| PatientId: SurrogateKey |
| --- |
| FamilyId: SurrogateKey (FK)<br>PatientNumber: PatientNumber<br>Address: Address<br>HomePhoneNumber: PhoneNumber<br>MobilePhoneNumber: PhoneNumber<br>OfficePhoneNumber: PhoneNumber |

**Figure 3-21.** *Added location-specific attributes to the Patient entity*

This is a good place to reiterate one of the major differences between a column and an attribute. An attribute doesn't really have any specific requirement for its shape. It might be a scalar value, it might be a vector, and it might be a table in and of itself. A column in your implemented database needs to fit a certain mold of being a scalar or fixed vector and nothing else. In conceptual modeling, the goal is documentation. The normalization process shapes all our attributes into the proper shape for implementation in our relational database.

It's enough in conceptual modeling to realize that when users see the word *address* in the context of this example, they think of a generic address used to locate a physical location. In this manner, you can avoid any discussion of how the address is implemented, not to mention all the different address formats that might need to be dealt with when the address attribute is implemented later in the book.

## Values

Numbers are some of the most powerful attributes, because often math is performed with them. Get the number of dependents wrong for a person, and his or her taxes will be messed up. Or get your wife's weight wrong on a form, and she might just beat you with some sort of cooking device (sad indeed).

Values are generally numeric, such as the following examples:

- *Monetary amounts*: Financial transactions, invoice line items, and so on
- *Quantities*: Weights, number of products sold, counts of items (number of pills in a prescription bottle), number of items on an invoice line item, number of calls made on a phone, and so on
- *Other*: Wattage for light bulbs, size of a TV screen, RPM rating of a hard disk, maximum speed on tires, and so on

Numbers are used all around as attributes and are generally going to be rather important (not, of course, to minimize the value of other attributes!). They're also likely candidates to have domains chosen for them to make sure their values are reasonable. If you were writing a package to capture tax information about a person, you would almost certainly want a domain to state that the count of dependents must be greater than or equal to zero. You might also want to set a likely maximum value, such as 30. It might not be a hard and fast rule, but it would be a sanity check, because most people don't have 30 dependents (well, most sane people, before, or certainly not after!). Domains don't have to be hard and fast rules at this point (only the hard and fast rules will likely end up as database constraints, but they have to be implemented somewhere, or users can and will put in whatever they feel like at the time).

In our example paragraphs, there's one such attribute:

*The client manages a **couple of dental offices.***

The question here is what attribute this would be. In this case, it turns out it won't be a numeric value, but instead some information about the cardinality of the dental Office entity.

## Relationship Attributes

Every relationship that's identified might imply bits of data to support it. For example, consider a common relationship such as Customer pays Invoice. That's simple enough; this implies a relationship between the Customer entity and the Invoice entity. But the relationship implies that an invoice needs to be paid; hence (if you didn't know what an invoice was already), it's now known that an invoice has some form of amount attribute.

As an example in our database, in the relationship Employees use Supplies for various reasons, the "for various reasons" part may lead us to the related-information type of attribute. What this tells us is that the relationship isn't a one-to-many relationship between Person and Supplies, but it is a many-to-many relationship between them. However, it does imply that an additional entity may later be needed to document this fact, since it's desired to identify more information about the relationship.

---

■**Tip**  Don't fret too hard that you might miss something essential early in the conceptual design. Often the same entity, attribute, or relationship will crop up in multiple places.

---

## A List of Entities, Attributes, and Domains

Figure 3-22 shows the conceptual graphical model as it stands now.

Table 3-3 shows the entities, along with descriptions and column domains. The attributes of an entity are indented within the Entity/Attribute column (I've removed the relationships found in the previous document for clarity). Note I've taken the list a bit further to include all the entities I've found in the paragraphs and will add the attributes to the model after the list is complete.

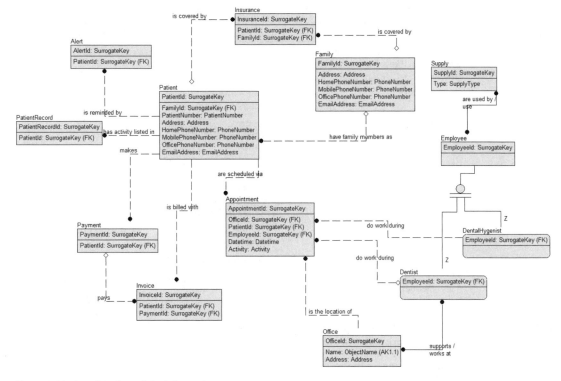

**Figure 3-22.** *Graphical model of the patient system*

Table 3-3 lists the descriptive metadata.

**Table 3-3.** *Final Model for the Dental Office Example*

| Entity/Attribute | Description | Column Description | Column Domain |
|---|---|---|---|
| Patient | **The persons who are the customers of the dental office. Services are performed, supplies are used, and they are billed for them.** | | |
| | PatientNumber | Used to identify a patient's records, in the computer | Unknown, generated by the current computer system |
| | HomePhoneNumber | Phone number to call patient at home | Any valid phone number |
| | MobilePhoneNumber | Phone number to call patient away from home | Any valid phone number |
| | OfficePhoneNumber | Phone number to call patient during work hours *(Note: Do we need to know work hours for the patient?)* | Any valid phone number |
| | Address | Postal address of the family | Any valid address |
| | EmailAddress | Electronic mail address of the family | Any valid e-mail address |

*Continued*

**Table 3-3.** *Final Model for the Dental Office Example*

| Entity/Attribute | Description | Column Description | Column Domain |
|---|---|---|---|
| Family | **Groups of persons who are associated, likely for insurance purposes.** | | |
| | HomePhoneNumber | Phone number to call patient at home | Any valid phone number |
| | MobilePhoneNumber | Phone number to call patient away from home | Any valid phone number |
| | OfficePhoneNumber | Phone number to call patient during work hours *(Note: Do we need to know work hours for the patient?)* | Any valid phone number |
| | Address | Postal address of the family | Any valid address |
| | EmailAddress | Electronic mail address of the family | Any valid e-mail address |
| | FamilyMembers | Patients that make up a family unit | Any patients *(Note: Can patient only be a member of one family?)* |
| Dentist | **Persons who do the most important work at the dental office. There are several dentists working for the client's practice.** | | |
| Hygienists | Persons who do the basic work for the dentist. There are quite a few more hygienists than dentists. *(Note: Check with client to see if there are guidelines for the number of hygienists per dentist. Might be needed for setting appointments.)* | | |
| Employee | Any person who works at the dental office. Dentists and hygienists are clearly a type of employee. | | |
| Office | Locations where the dentists do their business. They have multiple offices to deal with and schedule patients for. | | |
| | Address | Physical address where the building is located | Address that is not a PO box |
| | Name | The name used to refer to a given office | Unique |
| Supply | **Examples given were sample items, such as toothpaste or toothbrushes, plus there was mention of dental supplies. These supplies are the ones that the dentist and hygienists use to perform their job.** | | |
| | Type | Classifies supplies into different types | "Sample" or "Dental" identified |

| Entity/Attribute | Description | Column Description | Column Domain |
|---|---|---|---|
| Insurance | **Used by patients to pay for the dental services rendered work.** | | |
| Payment | **Money taken from insurance or patients (or both) to pay for services** | | |
| Invoice | **A document sent to the patient or insurance company explaining how much money is required to pay for services.** | | |
| | SentTo | To whom the invoice was sent | "Insurance" or "Patient" |
| Alert | **E-mail or phone call made to tell patient of an impending appointment.** | | |
| | Type | How the alert is to be sent | "E-mail," "Home Phone," "Mobile Phone," or "Office Phone" |
| | SendTo | The patient that the alert is sent to | Any patient |
| Appointment | **The event of a patient coming in and having some dental work done.** | | |
| | DateTime | The point in time when the appointment will start, or started | Valid date |
| | Activity | Identifies the different procedures and examinations that a patient has had during an appointment | |

*Implementation modeling note: log any changes to sensitive or important data. The relationship between employees and supplies will likely need additional information to document the purpose for the usage.*

---

**Tip** Consider carefully the use of the phrase "any valid" or any of its derivatives. The scope of these statements needs to be reduced to a reasonable form. (In other words, what does "valid" mean? The phrases "valid dates" indicates that there must be something that could be considered invalid. This in turn could mean the "November 31st" kind of invalid or that it isn't valid to schedule an appointment during the year 1000 BC. Common sense can take us a long way, but computers seriously lack common sense without human intervention.)

---

Note that I added another many-to-many relationship between Appointment and Supply to document that supplies are used during appointments. Figure 3-23 shows the final graphical model.

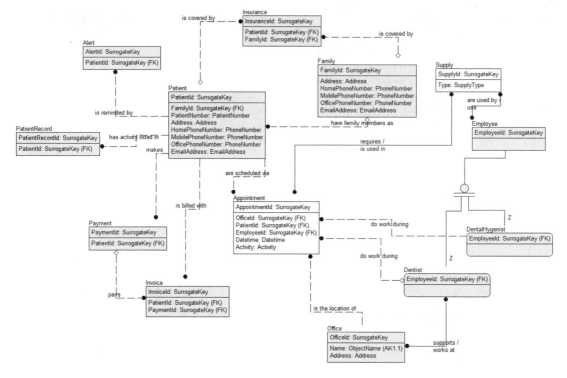

**Figure 3-23.** *Model with all entities, attributes, and relationships*

At this point, the entities and attributes have been defined. Note that nothing has been added to the design that wasn't explicitly stated in the single requirement artifact we started with. When doing this kind of activity in a "real" setting, all the steps of finding entities, relationships, and attributes would likely be handled at one time. In this chapter, I've performed the steps in a deliberate, step-by-step process only to focus on one at a time to make the parts of the process clearer. If this had been a real design session, whenever I found something to add to the model, I would have added it immediately.

It might also be interesting to note that the document is now several pages long—all from analyzing three small paragraphs of text. When you do this in a real project, the resulting document will be much larger, and there will likely be quite a bit of redundancy in much of the documentation.

# Identifying Business Rules and Processes

In this section, the process moves from defining the structural parts of the conceptual database design to the parts that cause us to define some of the constraints and usage of the data, as well as documenting attributes to support parts of the process (like intermediate data). I'll introduce the following concepts:

- Identifying business rules
- Identifying fundamental processes

# Identifying Business Rules

Business rules can be defined as statements that govern and shape business behavior. Depending upon an organization's methodology, these rules can be in the form of bulleted lists, simple text diagrams, or other formats (too often they are stored in a key employee's head). A business rule's existence doesn't imply the ability to implement it in the database at this point in the process. The goal is to get down all data-oriented rules for use later in the process.

When defining business rules, there might be some duplication of rules and attribute domains, but this isn't a real problem at this point. Get as many rules as possible documented, because missing business rules will hurt you more than missing attributes, relationships, or even tables. You'll frequently find new tables and attributes when you're implementing the system, usually out of necessity, but finding new business rules at a late stage can wreck the entire design, forcing an expensive rethink or an ill-advised "kludge" to shoehorn them in.

Recognizing business rules isn't generally a difficult process, but it is time-consuming and fairly tedious. Unlike entities, attributes, and relationships, there's no straightforward, specific grammar-oriented clue for identifying all the business rules. In essence, everything we have done so far in this chapter is, in fact, just specialized versions of business rules.

However, my general practice when I have to look for business rules is to read documents line by line, looking for sentences including language such as "once . . . occurs," ". . . have to . . . ," ". . . must . . . ," ". . . will . . . ," and so on. However, documents don't always include every business rule. You might look through a hundred or a thousand invoices and not see a single instance where a client is credited money, but this doesn't mean it never happens. In many cases, you have to mine business rules from two places:

- *Old code*: It's the exception, not the rule, that an existing system will have great documentation. Even the ones that start out with wonderful system documentation tend to have their documentation grow worse and worse as time grows shorter and client desires grow. It isn't uncommon to run into poorly written spaghetti code that needs to be analyzed.

- *Client experience*: Using human memory for documentation can be as hard as asking teenagers what they did the night before. Claims of forgetting, or simply making up stuff that they think you want to hear, is just part of human nature. I've already touched on how difficult it is to get requirements from users, but when you get into rules, this difficulty grows by at least an order of magnitude because most humans don't think in details, and a good portion of the business-rules hunt is about minute details.

Getting business rules from either of these sources is rarely on the top of the list of things to do on a Saturday night or even instead of a trip to the proctologist. If you're lucky, you'll be blessed by a business analyst who will take care of this process, but in a lot of cases the business analyst won't have the programming experience to ferret out subtle business rules from code, and a programmer will have to handle this task. That's not to mention that it's hard to get to the minute details until you understand the system, something you can do only by spending lots of time thinking, considering, and digesting what you are reading. Rare is the occasion to spend enough time to do a good job going to be afforded you.

In our "snippet of notes from the meeting" example, a few business rules need to be defined. For example, I've already discussed the need for a customer number attribute but was unable to specify a domain for the customer number. Take the following sentence:

*For each appointment, the client needs to have everything documented that went on . . .*

You can derive a business rule such as this:

*For every appointment, it is required to document every action on the patient's chart so it can be charged.*

Note that this rule brings up the likelihood that there exists yet another attribute of a patient's chart—Activity—and another attribute of the activity—ActivityPrices. This relationship between Patient, PatientRecord, Activity, and ActivityPrices gives you this feeling that it might be wrong. It will be wrong to implement it in code this way, very wrong. Normalization corrects this sort of dependency (see, I promised in the previous chapter that it would come up again). It's logical that there exists an entity for activities with attributes of name and price that relate back to the PatientRecord entity that has already been created. Either way is acceptable during conceptual modeling, as long as it makes sense to the readers of the documents. I'll go ahead and add an Activity entity with a name and a price for this requirement.

Another sentence in our example suggests a further possible business rule:

*The dentists might spend time at each of the offices throughout the week.*

Obviously a doctor cannot be in two different locations at one time. Hence, we have the following rule:

*Doctors must not be scheduled for appointments at two locations at a time.*

Another rule that's probably needed is one that pertains to the length of time between appointments for doctors:

*The length of time between appointments for dentists at different offices can be no shorter than X.*

Not every business rule will manifest itself within the database, even some that specifically deal with a process that manages data. For example, consider this rule:

*Invoices should be sent within one week after the appointment.*

This is great and everything, but what if it takes a week and a day, or even two weeks? Can the invoice no longer be sent to the patient? Should there be database code to chastise the person if someone was sick and it took a few hours longer than a week? No; although this seems much like a rule that could be implemented in the database, it isn't. This rule will be given to the people doing system documentation and UI design for use when designing the rest of the system. The other people working on the design of the overall system will often provide us with additional entities and attributes.

The specifics of some types of rules will be dealt with later in Chapters 5 and 6, as you implement tables and integrity constraints.

## Identifying Fundamental Processes

A process is a coherent sequence of steps undertaken by a program that uses the data that has been identified to do something. It might be a computer-based process, such as "process daily receipts," where some form of report is created, or possibly a deposit is created to send to the bank. It could be something manual, such as "creating new patient," which details that first the patient fills out a set of forms, then the receptionist asks many of the same questions, and finally the nurse and doctor ask the same questions again once arriving in the room. Then some of this information is keyed into the computer after the patient leaves so the dental office can send a bill.

As a reasonable manual-process example, consider the process of getting a driver's license (at least in Tennessee):

1. Fill in learner's permit forms.
2. Obtain learner's permit.
3. Practice.
4. Fill in license forms.
5. Pass eye exam.
6. Pass driving exam.
7. Have picture taken.
8. Receive license.

Processes might or might not have each step well enumerated during the conceptual or even logical phase, and many times a lot of processes are fleshed out during the implementation phase in order to accommodate the tools that are available at the time of implementation. I should mention that most processes have some amount of *process rules* associated with them (which are business rules that govern the process, much like those that govern data values). For example, you must complete each of those steps (taking tests, practicing driving, and so on) before you get your license. Note that some business rules are also lurking around in here, because some steps in a process might be done in any order (the eye exam could be before the driving exam and the process would remain acceptable), and others must be done in order (as originally noted, if you received the license without passing the exams, that would be kind of stupid).

In general, I would include the datatype rules in the database design but would probably avoid most of the process rules, because far too often a process rule either can be overridden or can change. It might be that you store just a value that states that the process was followed or the person who overrode it.

In the license process, not only do you have the explicit order that some tasks must be performed, but there are other rules, such as that you must be 15 to get a learner's permit, you must be 16 to get the license, you must pass the exam, practice must be with a licensed driver, and so on. If you were the business analyst helping to design a driver's license project, you would have to document this process at some point.

Identifying processes (and the rules that govern them) is relevant to the task of data modeling. Many procedures in database systems require manipulation of data, and processes are critical in these tasks. Each process usually translates into one or more queries or stored procedures, which might require more data than has been specified.

In our example, there are a few examples of such processes:

*The client needs the system to manage its patients and appointments . . .*

This implies that the client needs to be able to make appointments, as well as manage the patients—presumably the information about them. Making appointments is one of the most central things our system will do, and you will need to answer questions like these: What appointments are available during scheduling? When can appointments be made?

This is certainly a process that you would want to go back to the client and understand:

*. . . and then invoice the patient's insurance, if he or she has insurance (otherwise the patient pays).*

I've discussed invoices already, but the process of creating an invoice might require additional attributes to identify that an invoice has been sent electronically or printed (possibly reprinted). Document control is an important part of many processes when helping an organization that's trying to modernize a paper system. Note that sending an invoice might seem like a pretty inane event—press a button on a screen, and paper pops out of the printer.

All this requires is selecting some data from a table, so what's the big deal? However, when a document is printed, we might have to record the fact that the document was printed, who printed it, and what the use of the document is. We might also need to indicate that the documents are printed during a process that includes closing out and totaling the items on an invoice. The most important point here is that you shouldn't make any major assumptions.

Here are other processes that have been listed:

- *Track and manage dentists and hygienists*: From the sentence, "The system needs to track and manage several dentists, and quite a few dental hygienists who the client needs to allocate to each appointment as well."

- *Track supplies*: From "The client has had problems in the past keeping up with when it's about to run out of supplies, and wants this system to take care of this for both locations. For the dental supplies, we need to track usage by employee, and especially any changes made in the database to the patient records."

- *Alert patient*: From "alerting the patients when their appointments occur, either by e-mail or by phone . . ."

Each of these processes identifies a unit of work that you must deal with during the implementation phase of the database design procedure.

# Finishing the Conceptual Model

In this section, I'll briefly cover the steps involved in completing the task of establishing a working set of documentation. There's no way that we have a complete understanding of the documentation needs now, nor have we yet discovered all the entities, attributes, relationships, business rules, and processes that the final system will require. However, the better the job you do, the easier the rest of the process of designing and implementing the final system will be.

On the other hand, be careful, because there's a sweet spot when it comes to the amount of design needed. After a certain point, you could keep designing and make little—if any—progress. This is commonly known as *analysis paralysis*. Finding this sweet spot requires experience. Most of the time too little design occurs, usually because of a deadline that was set without any understanding of the realities of building a system. On the other hand, without strong management, I've found that I easily get myself into analysis paralysis (hey, the book focuses on design for a reason; to me it's the most fun part of the project).

The final steps of this discovery phase remain (the initial discovery phase anyhow, because you'll have to go back occasionally to this process to fill in gaps that were missed the first time). There are a few more things to do, if possible, before starting to write code:

1. Identify obvious additional data needs.

2. Review the progress of the project with the client.

3. Repeat the process until satisfied *and* the client is happy and signs off on what has been designed.

These steps are part of any system design, not just the data-driven parts.

## Identifying Obvious Additional Data Needs

Up until this point, I've been reasonably careful not to broaden the information that was included from the discovery phase. The purpose has been to achieve a baseline to our documentation, staying faithful to the piles of documentation that were originally gathered. Mixing in our new thoughts prior to agreeing on what was in the previous documentation can be confusing to the client, as well as to us. However, at this point in the design, you need to change direction and begin to add the attributes that come naturally. Usually there's a fairly large set of obvious attributes and, to a lesser extent, business rules that haven't been specified by any of the users or initial analysis. Make sure any assumed entities, attributes, relationships, and so on, stand out from what you have gotten from the documentation.

For the things that have been identified so far, go through and specify additional attributes that will likely be needed. For example, take the `Patient` entity, as shown in Table 3-4.

**Table 3-4.** *Completed Patient Entity*

| Entity | Description | Domain |
|---|---|---|
| **Patient** | **The people who are the customers of the dentist office. Services are performed, supplies are used, and they are billed for them.** | |
| **Attributes** | | |
| PatientNumber | Used to identify a patient's records, in the current computer system | Unknown; generated by computer and on the chart. |
| Insurance | Identifies the patient's insurance carrier. | Unknown *(Note: Check for common formats used by insurance carriers, perhaps?)* |
| **Relationships** | | |
| | Has Alerts | Alerts are sent to patients to remind them of their appointments. |
| | Has Appointments | Appointments need to have one patient. |
| | Has Invoices | Patients are charged for appointments via an invoice. |
| | Makes Payment | Patients make payments for invoices they receive. |

The following additional attributes would be desirable:

- *Name*: The contact's full name is probably the most important attribute of all.

- *Birth date*: If the person's birthday is known, a card might be sent on that date. This is probably also a necessity for insurance purposes.

You could certainly add more attributes for the `Patient` entity, but this set should make the point clearly enough. There might also be additional tables, business rules, and so on, to recommend to the client. In this phase of the design, document them and add them to your lists.

One of the main things to do is to identify when you make any large changes to the customer's model. In this example, the client might not want to keep up with the birth dates of its patients (though as noted, it's probably an insurance requirement that wasn't initially thought of).

The process of adding new stuff to the client's model based on common knowledge is essential to the process and will turn out to be a large part of the process. Rarely will the analyst think of everything.

## Review with the Client

Once you've finished putting together this first-draft document, it's time to meet with the client. Show the client where you've gotten to in your design, and have the client review every bit of this document. Make sure the client understands the solution that you're beginning to devise for it.

It's also worthwhile to devise some form of sign-off process/document, which the client signs before you move forward in the process. In some cases, your sign-off documents could well be legally binding documents and will certainly be important should the project go south later for one reason or another. Obviously, the hope is that this doesn't happen, but projects fail for many reasons, and a good number of them are not related to the project itself. It's always best if everyone is on the same page, and this is the place to do that.

## Repeat Until the Customer Agrees with Your Model

It isn't likely you'll get everything right in this phase of the project. The most important thing is to get as much correct as you can and get the customer to agree with this. Of course, it's unlikely that the client will immediately agree with everything you say, even if you're the greatest data architect in the world. It is also true that often the client will know what they want just fine but cannot express it in a way that gets through your thick skull. In either event, it usually takes several attempts to get the model to a place where everyone is in agreement, and every iteration should move you and the client closer to your goal.

There will be many times later in the project that you might have to revisit this part of the design and find something you missed or something the client forgot to share with you. As you get through more and more iterations of the design, it becomes increasingly important to make sure you have your client sign off at regular times; you can point to these documents when the client changes his or her mind later.

If you don't get agreement, often in writing or in a public forum, such as a meeting with enough witnesses, you can get hurt. This is especially true when you don't do an adequate job of handling the review and documentation process and there's no good documentation to back up your claim versus the clients. I've worked on consulting projects where the project was well designed and agreed upon but documentation of what was agreed upon wasn't made too well (a lot of handshaking at a higher level to "save" money). As time went by and many thousands of dollars were spent, the client reviewed the agreement document, and it became obvious that we didn't agree on much at all. Needless to say, that whole project worked out about as well as hydrogen-filled dirigibles.

---

■**Note** I've been kind of hard on clients in this chapter, making them out to be conniving folks who will cheat you at the drop of a hat. This is seldom the case, but it takes only one. The truth is that almost every client will appreciate you keeping him or her in the loop and getting approval for the design at reasonable intervals.

---

# Best Practices

The following list of some best practices can be useful to follow when doing conceptual modeling:

- *Be diligent*: Look through everything to make sure that what's being said makes sense. Be certain to understand as many of the business rules that bind the system as possible before moving on to the next step. Mistakes made early in the process can mushroom later in the process.

- *Document*: The point of this chapter has been just that. Document every entity, attribute, relationship, business rule, and process identified (and anything else you discover, even if it won't fit neatly into one of these buckets). The format of the documentation isn't really all that important, only that the information is there, that it's understandable by all parties involved, and that it will be useful going forward toward implementation.

- *Communicate*: Constant communication with clients is essential to keep the design on track. The danger is that if you start to get the wrong idea of what the client needs, every decision past that point might be wrong. Get as much face time with the client as possible.

---

■**Note** This mantra of "review with client, review with client, review with client" is probably starting to get a bit old at this point. This is one of the last times I'll mention it, but it's so important that I hope it has sunk in.

---

# Summary

In this chapter, I've presented the process of discovering the entities that would eventually make up the dental-office database solution. We've weeded through all the documentation that had been gathered during the information-gathering phase, doing our best not to add our own contributions to the solution until we processed all the initial documentation, so as not to add our personal ideas to the solution. This is no small task; in our initial example, we had only three paragraphs to work with, yet we ended up with several pages of documentation from it.

First I introduced some of the basics of documentation and requirements gathering. This is the most important part of the process, because it's the foundation of everything that follows. If the foundation is solid, the rest of the process has a chance. If the foundation is shoddy, the rest of the system that gets built will likely be the same. The purpose of this process is to acquire as much information about what the client wants out of its system. As a data architect, this might be something that's delivered to you, or at least most of it. Either way, the goal is to understand the user's needs.

Once you have as much documentation as possible from the users, the real work begins. Through all this documentation, the goal is to discover as many of the following as possible:

- Entities and relationships

- Attributes and domains

- Business rules that can be enforced in the database

- Processes that require the use of the database

From this, a conceptual data model will emerge that has many of the characteristics that will exist in the actual implemented database. In the upcoming chapters, the database design will certainly change from this conceptual model, but it will share many of the same characteristics.

# CHAPTER 4

■■■

# The Normalization Process

*The Atomic Age is here to stay—but are we?*

—Bennett Cerf

**N**ormalization is the process of taking the entities and attributes that have been discovered and making them suitable for the relational database system. The process does this by removing redundancies and shaping the data in the manner that the relational engine desires to work with it. Once you are done with the process, working with the data will be more natural using the set-based SQL language.

In computer science terms, *atomic* means that the value cannot (or more reasonably should not) be broken down into smaller parts. If you want to get technical, most any value can be broken down into smaller parts. For the database definition, consider *atomic* to refer to a value that needn't be broken down any further for use in the relational database. Our eventual goal will be to break down the piles of data we have identified into values that are atomic, that is, broken down to the lowest form that will need to be accessed in Transact SQL (T-SQL) code.

Normalization often gets a bad rap, and there are many misconceptions about it. I should refute a few things that normalization may seem like but clearly is not:

- *Myth*: It's primarily a method to annoy functional programmers (though this does tend to be a fun side effect, if you have the clout to get away with it).

- *Myth*: It's a way to keep database professionals in a job.

- *Myth*: It's a silver bullet to end world suffering or even global warming.

The process of normalization is based on a set of levels, each of which achieves a level of correctness or adherence to a particular set of "rules." The rules are formally known as *forms*, as in the *normal forms*. There are quite a few normal forms that have been theorized and postulated, but I'll focus on the primary six that are commonly known. I'll start with First Normal Form (1NF), which eliminates data redundancy (such as a name being stored in two separate places), and continue through to Fifth Normal Form (5NF), which deals with the decomposition of ternary relationships. (One of the normal forms I'll present isn't numbered; it's named for the people who devised it.) Each level of normalization indicates an increasing degree of adherence to the recognized standards of database design. As you increase the *degree of normalization* of your data, you'll naturally tend to create an increasing number of tables of decreasing width (fewer columns).

In this chapter, I'll start out by addressing two fundamental questions:

- *Why normalize?*: I'll take a detailed look at the numerous reasons why you should normalize your data. The bottom line is that you should normalize to increase the efficiency of, and protect the integrity of, your relational data.

- *How far should you normalize?*: This is always a contentious issue. Normalization tends to optimize your database for efficient storage and updates, rather than querying. It dramatically reduces the propensity for introducing update anomalies (different records displaying different values for the same piece of data), but it increases the complexity of your queries, because you might be forced to collect data from many different tables.

My answers to these questions will be followed by a look at each of the normal forms in turn, explaining with clear examples the requirements of each one, the programming anomalies they help you avoid, and the telltale signs that your relational data is flouting that particular normal form. It might seem out of place to show programming anomalies at this point, since the first four chapters of the book are specifically aligned to the preprogramming design, but it can help reconcile to the programming mind what having data in a given normal form can do to make the tables easier to work in SQL. I'll then wrap up with an overview of some normalization best practices.

# Why Normalize?

Before discussing the mechanics of the normalization process, I'll discuss some of the things that normalization will do for you, if done correctly. In the following sections, I'll discuss reasons that might not be obvious, even after finishing the sections on how to normalize, such as the following:

- Eliminating data that's duplicated, increasing the chance it won't match when you need it

- Avoiding unnecessary coding needed to keep duplicated data in sync

- Keeping tables thin, increasing the number of values that will fit on an 8K physical database page (which will be discussed in more detail in Chapter 9) and decreasing the number of reads that will be needed to read data from a table

- Maximizing the use of clustered indexes, allowing for more optimum data access and joins

- Lowering the number of indexes per table, because indexes are costly to maintain

Many of these are implementation issues or even pertain more to physical modeling (how data is laid out on disk). Since this is a professional book, I'm assuming you have some knowledge of such things. If not, later chapters of the book will give overviews of these issues and direct you to additional reading on the subject.

It is also true that normalization has some negative effects on performance for some operations. This fact is the basis of many arguments over how far to normalize. However, the costs are nearly always outweighed by the positives of having to make sure that data is not corrupted by operations that *seem* correct, but aren't because of poor design decisions.

## Eliminating Duplicated Data

Any piece of data that occurs more than once in the database is an error waiting to happen. No doubt you've been beaten by this once or twice in your life: your name is stored in multiple places, then one version gets modified and the other doesn't, and suddenly you have more than one name where before there was just one.

The problem with storing redundant data will be obvious to anyone who has moved to a new address. Every government authority requires citizens to change address information individually on tax forms, drivers' licenses, auto registrations, and so on, rather than making one change centrally. Getting this information updated for a simple move can be a complicated process.

## Avoiding Unnecessary Coding

Extra programming in triggers, in stored procedures, or even in the business logic tier can be required to handle poorly structured data, and this in turn can impair performance significantly. Extra coding also increases the chance of introducing new bugs by causing a labyrinth of code to be needed to maintain redundant data.

## Keeping Tables Thin

When I refer to a thinner table, the idea is that a relatively small number of columns are in the table. Thinner tables mean more data fits on a given page in the database, therefore allowing the database server to retrieve more rows for a table in a single read than would otherwise be possible. This all means that there will be more tables in the system when you're finished normalizing. However, there's a commonsense cut-off point (for example, there are only a few cases where a table has only a single column, such as the sequence table I will build in Chapter 7).

## Maximizing Clustered Indexes

Clustered indexes order a table natively in SQL Server. Clustered indexes are special indexes in which the physical storage of the data matches the order of the indexed data, which allows for better performance of queries using that index. Typically, you use them to order a table in a convenient manner to enhance performance. Each table can have only a single clustered index. The more clustered indexes in the database, the less sorting needs to be performed, and the more likely it is that queries can use the MERGE JOIN—a type of join technique that requires sorted data and can join large sets of data very quickly. Sorting is a costly operation that you should avoid if possible. Chapter 9 will cover clustered indexes, and indexes in general, in great detail.

The concept of clustered indexes applies to normalization in that you'll have more tables when you normalize. The increased numbers of clustered indexes increase the likelihood that joins between tables can use merge joins, which are the fastest types of joins.

## Lowering the Number of Indexes Per Table

The fewer indexes per table, the less maintenance is required to maintain the indexes. Although that statement probably merits entry to the obvious statement of the year contest, another less obvious factor is moving data in and out of memory. In SQL Server, data and indexes are broken up and stored on 8K pages (Chapter 9 covers this in more detail). SQL Server usually cannot keep the whole database in RAM at any one time. It keeps a "snapshot" of what's recently been looked at. To keep the illusion of having the whole database in memory, SQL Server moves the pages in and out of a high-speed fast-access storage space when they're required, but this space can contain only a limited number of pages at any one time. Therefore, SQL Server moves the pages in and out of the space on the principle that the most frequently accessed remain in. The operation of moving pages in and out of memory onto physical storage is costly in terms of performance and especially painful if clients are twiddling their thumbs waiting for operations to complete. So, to keep performance as high as possible, the goal is to minimize physical page transfers. Normalization helps keep indexing to a minimum by keeping tables thin and specific, rather than having lots of columns to deal with.

# How Far to Normalize?

As I noted in the introduction to this chapter, database normalization can be a polarizing topic for the database architect, especially when dealing with other developers. If you have no idea what normalization is, ignore this section for now, but almost every person who has any knowledge of databases has heard about the normal forms, and disagreements (aka knock-down, drag-out fights) often arise between database architects and client developers over how to store data. They're hard to resolve, mainly because there's never a single indisputably "correct" design. Furthermore, normalization appears to be a complex process, and certainly, it takes a lot of time and planning initially to build applications on top of *properly structured* tables. However, in my opinion, you simply cannot afford *not* to put some time and effort into your data design and to normalize your data correctly as far as necessary. There's no magic number or completely ideal process to follow.

---

■**Caution** I know that many of you reading this book will already have a preconceived notion of the magical level of normalization, but the answer I give is probably not the one you will expect, especially if you have read any trade literature on the subject.

---

I mention a magic number because it's commonly thought that Third Normal Form is that magic level, but truly, this is rarely the case. Even without you knowing it, most databases turn out to be in Fourth Normal Form, and even Fifth. Having basic knowledge of what these normal forms are makes it easier to look out for the pitfalls that they do cover (they're not just something that super mathematician database geeks came up with to make themselves look cool to the opposite sex).

The original sin of most every new database designer is to fall (to some level or another) for the false logic that the fewer tables the data is stored in, the less code required and the fewer user interfaces needed. So, a solution with 200 tables will take a lot longer than a database with 20 tables, right? Although this thinking seems very logical, it's completely wrong on many far more important levels. Relationships between the different data elements have to be understood and dealt with, and this is what normalization is all about.

Normalization isn't that complex a subject, and with a little effort you can achieve an efficient, durable design that you won't find yourself needing to chop and change and that won't be subject to data-integrity issues. I'm not saying that once the design has been implemented, it can't or won't need to be changed. Expansions and changes in business practices are common. However, it's easier to add new information and new entities to a well-normalized database.

So, what is the answer to the question, how far to normalize? Although Third Normal Form is an absolute must, it is essential to consider how each entity fits the rules of Fourth Normal Form and strongly consider normalizing to that level. The thing is, the problems that Fourth Normal Form are designed to solve are extremely crucial to the structure of any database design and will bite you just as hard as those of any of the lower forms. So, now that you know how this thing ends, you can just relax and read the rest of the chapter.

# The Process of Normalization

The process of normalization is really quite straightforward: take entities that are complex and extract simpler entities from them. The process continues until every table in the database represents one thing and every column describes that thing. This will become more apparent throughout the chapter, as I work through the different normal forms.

In 1970, in his now-famous paper, "A Relational Model of Data for Large Shared Data Banks," E. F. Codd presented the world with First Normal Form, based on the shape of the data, and the Second and Third Normal Forms, based on functional dependencies in the data. Codd and R. Boyce further refined these as the Boyce-Codd Normal Form (BCNF). Finally, the Fourth and Fifth Normal Forms deal with multivalued and join dependencies in the data. I'll break down normalization into three categories of steps:

- Entity and attribute shape
- Relationships between attributes
- Multivalued and join dependencies in entities

Note that the conditions mentioned for each step should be considered for every entity you design, and preferably in order, because each normal form is built upon the precept that the lower forms have been done.

# Entity and Attribute Shape: First Normal Form

First Normal Form is centered on making sure entities and attributes are shaped properly for the relational languages that manipulate them (most importantly SQL). For an entity to be in First Normal Form, it must have the following characteristics:

- All attributes must be atomic, that is, only a single value represented in a single attribute in a single instance of an entity.
- All instances of an entity must contain the same number of values.
- All instances of an entity must be different.

First Normal Form violations often manifest themselves in the implemented model with data handling being far less optimal, usually because of having to decode multiple values stored where a single one should be or because of having duplicated rows that cannot be distinguished from one another.

## All Attributes Must Be Atomic

The goal of this part of First Normal Form is that each attribute should represent only one value, not multiple values. This means there should be nothing like an array, no delimited lists, and no other types of multivalued attributes that you could dream up represented by a single attribute. For example, consider a group of data like 1, 2, 3, 6, 7. This likely represents five separate values. This group of data might not actually be multiple values as far as the design is concerned, but for darn sure it needs to be looked at.

One good way to think of atomicity is to consider whether you would ever need to deal with part of a column without the other parts of the data in that same column. In the list mentioned earlier—1, 2, 3, 6, 7—if the list is always treated as a single value in SQL, it might be acceptable to store the value in a single column. However, if you might need to deal with the value 3 individually, then the list is definitely not in First Normal Form. It is also important to note that even if there is not a plan to use the list elements individually, you should consider whether it is still better to store each value individually to allow for future possible usage.

One variation on atomicity is for complex datatypes. Complex datatypes can contain more than one value, as long as:

- There are always the same number of values.
- The values are rarely, if ever, dealt with individually.
- The values make up some atomic thing/attribute that could not be fully expressed with a single value.

For example, consider geographic location. Two values are generally used to locate something on Earth, these being the longitude and the latitude. Most of the time, either of these, considered individually, has some (if incomplete) meaning, but taken together, they pinpoint an exact position on Earth. Implementing as a complex type can give us some ease of implementing data-protection schemes and can make using the types in formulas easier. I'll present an example of implementing complex types in the next chapter when I cover user-defined datatypes. (I should also note that SQL Server 2008 has its own spatial datatypes to store a point on a map or even a polygon. This will be covered in Appendix C, which will be available as bonus, downloadable content.)

When it comes to First Normal Form, the test of reasonability is left up to the designer (and other designers who inherit their work after they have left, of course), but generally speaking, the goal is that any data you ever need to deal with as a single value is modeled as its own attribute, so it's stored in a column of its own (for example, as a search argument or a join criterion).

As an example of taking First Normal Form to the full extreme, consider a text document with ten paragraphs. A table to store the document might easily be implemented that would require ten different rows (one for each paragraph), but there's little reason to do this, because you'll be unlikely to deal with a paragraph as a single value in the SQL database language (and more often than not if you find yourself doing it, you may need to alter your thinking).

As further examples, consider some of the common locations where violations of this rule of First Normal Form often can be found:

- E-mail addresses
- Telephone numbers
- Names
- Mailing addresses

Each of these gives us a slightly different kind of issue with atomicity that needs to be considered when designing attributes.

## E-mail Addresses

In an e-mail message, the e-mail address is typically stored in a format such as the following:

name1@domain1.com;name2@domain2.com;name3@domain3.com

This format is fine for the FROM: line of an e-mail, because that's the format in which the e-mail database (generally not relational in nature) uses it. However, if you need to store the values in a relational database, this is a clear violation of First Normal Form, because it represents more than one e-mail address in a single email attribute. Each e-mail address should be represented individually in a separate row.

It's arguable whether any given e-mail address is in First Normal Form as well. name1@domain1.com contains two or three obvious parts. A common way to break these values up is into the following parts:

- AccountName: name1
- Domain: domain1.com

Whether this is desirable will usually come down to whether you intend to access the individual parts separately in your code. For example, if all you'll ever do is send e-mail, then a single column is perfectly acceptable. On the other hand, if you need to consider what domains you have e-mail addresses stored for, then it's a completely different matter.

Finally, the domain consists of two parts: domain1 and com. These values are rarely stored in separate columns, but they could be. The decision is simple: if it's necessary to rely on a "substring" operation to access parts of the data in an attribute (such as to find how many of your e-mail users come from .com addresses versus other types), then it clearly isn't in First Normal Form.

## Names

Consider the name R. Lee Badezine. The first name, middle name, and last name are in a single attribute. Break the name into three parts into FirstName, MiddleName (or MiddleInitial, if that is all your client wants, but consider that in this case you couldn't store the sample name in that design), and LastName. This is usually the reasonable limit chosen in my part of the world, because a person's name in the United States is generally considered to have three parts. In some situations, this might not be enough, and the number of parts might not be known until the user enters the data. Knowing the data requirements is important in these kinds of situations.

## Telephone Numbers

American telephone numbers are of the form 423-555-1212, plus some possible extension number. From our previous examples, you can see that several attributes are probably in that telephone number. However, complicating matters is that frequently the need exists to store more than just American telephone numbers in a database. The decision on how to handle this situation might be based on how often the users store international phone numbers, because it would be a hard task to build a table or set of entities to handle every possible phone format.

So, for an American-style telephone number, you can represent the address with four different attributes for each of the following parts, AAA-EEE-NNNN (XXXX):

- *(AAA) Area code*: Indicates a calling area located within a state
- *(EEE) Exchange*: Indicates a set of numbers within an area code
- *(NNNN) Number:* Number used to make individual phone numbers unique
- *(XXXX) Extension*: Number that must be dialed after connecting using the previous numbers

One of the coding examples later in this chapter will cover the sorts of issues that come up when storing phone numbers.

## Mailing Addresses

It should be clear by now that an address has many attributes—certainly for street address, city, state, and postal code (from here on I'll ignore the internationalization factor and focus on American-style addresses, for brevity). However, you can break street addresses down, in most cases, into number, street name, suite number, apartment number, post-office box, and so on. Addresses can be a complex issue. Take the following example:

1818 Whoknows Lane

Box 12A

Somewhere, SM 21234-2123

Figure 4-1 shows a common solution to the Address entity.

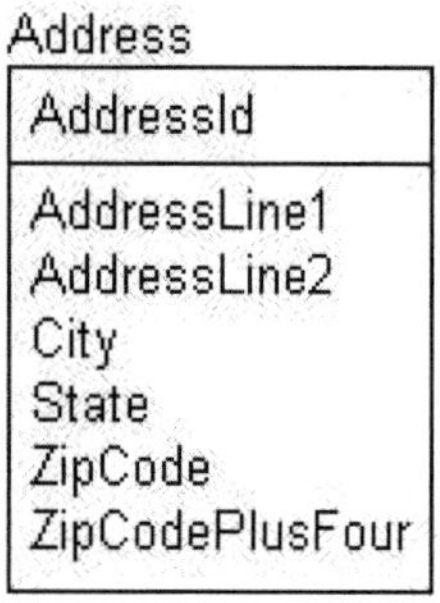

Address

| AddressId |
| --- |
| AddressLine1<br>AddressLine2<br>City<br>State<br>ZipCode<br>ZipCodePlusFour |

**Figure 4-1.** *The Address entity*

It's simple, to the point, and gets the job done. But this Address entity is far from perfect if you have more intense needs for using the parts of the AddressLine attributes to do proper postal service formatting. Consider the parts of the AddressLine1 attribute: 1818, Whoknows, and Lane. If you're doing serious mailing in your system, these values will be dealt with as three separate values (to format the address perfectly so mailing can be computerized). The same is true of the AddressLine2 value: Box 12a. This can be split up and re-formed, as shown in Figure 4-2.

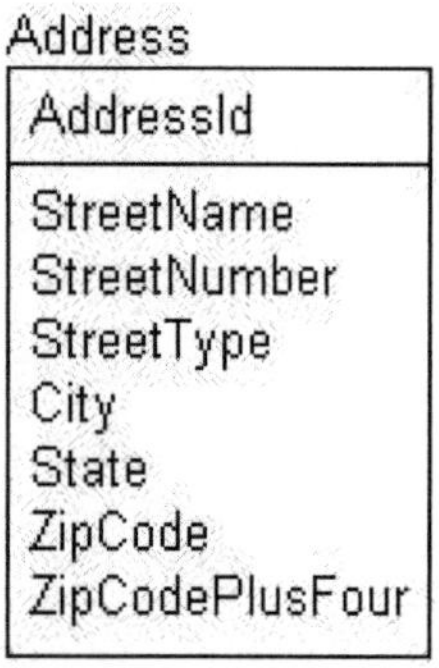

Address

| AddressId |
| --- |
| StreetName<br>StreetNumber<br>StreetType<br>City<br>State<br>ZipCode<br>ZipCodePlusFour |

**Figure 4-2.** *A refinement of the Address entity*

Fine, but what about the following address?

PO Box 12394

Somewhere Else, EL 32342

Well, it needs parts of the address used before—the City, State, ZipCode, and ZipCodePlusFour—but not others—the StreetNumber, StreetName, and StreetType. However, it does have a new attribute: PoBoxNumber. I'll use a subtype and add a type for a post-office box–style address, as shown in Figure 4-3.

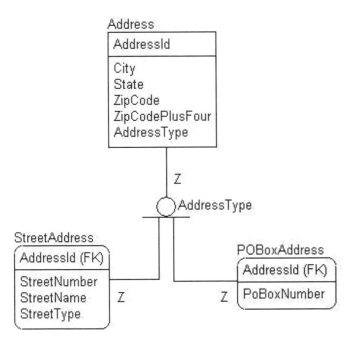

**Figure 4-3.** *Adding a subtype to the design*

There are a few other common address types, such as the rural route type that would also need to be modeled. Obviously, this form of an address model could get far too messy to deal with if it exhaustively modeled even most of the possible cases (rural routes, office buildings, apartments, and so on). The resulting model would end up being a great deal of work that the user interface developer would simply use to have you committed to "Uncle Maude's House of Waffles/Sanitarium" for being a raving loony. The truth is, if you're building a database from which you send thousands and thousands of pieces of mail, creating such an exhaustive model may not be a bad idea at all. Users will hate it if you give them ten choices for address type, but using a little bit of programming prowess (much the way Microsoft Outlook does for you when you enter a free-form address, though not down to this level), you can allow the user to look primarily at the following:

  1818 Whoknows Lane

  Somewhere, SM 21234-2123

while storing this data in the following style:

```
ColumnName     Value
-------------  ------------
StreetNumber   1818
StreetName     Whoknows
StreetType     Lane
City           Somewhere
State          SM
ZipCode        21234
ZipPlus4       2123
```

I should warn you, especially if you are part of the team that would have some part of the user interface (UI) design, the UI shouldn't always mimic the database structure, or in cases like addresses, the user will hate you. Addresses especially can turn out to be a difficult area when you try to go past the good old standard of attributes such as addressLine1, addressLine2, and addressLine3, or a single attribute to hold the whole street line, including carriage returns and line fees. You might not end up gaining much. It all goes back to the rule of thumb: "Break values down only as far as you will deal with the parts individually."

---

■**Tip** Every nation has its own idiosyncrasies when it comes to addresses. Things are compounded when it comes to dealing with addresses in multiple countries at the same time. However, the process and problems are the same. Break down parts of an address until you reach the point where you'll never need to deal with the pieces and parts separately (or at least the point where the cost to implement the solution outweighs the cost to deal with the pieces and parts).

---

## All Instances in an Entity Must Contain the Same Number of Values

This part of First Normal Form says that every instance has the same number of attributes. There are two interpretations of this:

- Entities have a fixed number of attributes (and tables have a fixed number of columns).
- Entities should be designed such that every attribute has a fixed number of values associated with it.

The first interpretation is simple. You cannot have an entity with a varying format with one instance such as {Name, Address, Haircolor}, and another with a different set of attributes such as {Name, Address, PhoneNumber, EyeColor}. This kind of implementation was common with record-based implementations but isn't possible with a relational database table.

The second is a more open interpretation. As an example, if you're building an entity that stores a person's name, then if one row has one name, all rows must have only one name. If they might have two, all instances must have precisely two (not one sometimes and certainly never three). If they may have a different number, it's inconvenient to deal with using SQL commands, which is the main reason a database is being built in an RDBMS! You must take some care with the concept of unknown values (NULLs) as well. The values aren't required, but there should always be the same number (even if the value isn't immediately known).

You can find an example of a violation of this rule of First Normal Form in entities that have several attributes with the same base name suffixed (or prefixed) with a number, such as Payment1, Payment2, and so on, as shown in Figure 4-4.

Customer

| Customerld |
| --- |
| Name (AK1) <br> <<other attributes>> <br> Payment1 <br> Payment2 |

**Figure 4-4.** *Violating First Normal Form with a variable number of attributes*

Usually, this is an attempt to allow multiple values for a single attribute in an entity. In the rare cases where there's always precisely the same number of values, then there's technically no violation of First Normal Form. In this case, you could state a business rule that "Each entity has exactly two payments." Even in such cases, allowing multiple values still isn't generally a good design decision. That's because users can change their minds frequently as to how many payments there are, such as if the person paid only a half payment—or some craziness that people always seem to do. To overcome all this, you should create a child entity to hold the values in the malformed entity, as shown in Figure 4-5.

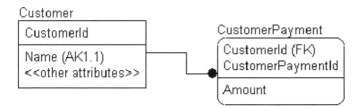

**Figure 4-5.** *A child entity holds the payments.*

This form also allows us to have virtually unlimited cardinality, whereas the previous solution had a finite (and small) number of possible configurations. One of the issues to deal with is that the child instances you create require sequencing information to get the rows properly organized for usage. You can use cardinality rules as described in the previous chapter to constrain the number of possible values. If need be, it's easy enough to choke things back, because our model states that we need a maximum of only two children and a minimum of one child. Relationship cardinality provides the mechanism for describing this.

---

■**Caution** Another common design uses attributes such as `UserDefined1`, `UserDefined2`, ..., `UserDefinedN`. This practice is wickedly heinous for many reasons, one of them related to the proper application of First Normal Form. Secondly, using such attributes is directly against the essence of Codd's fourth rule: dynamic online catalog based on the relational model. It states that the database description is represented at the logical level in the same way as ordinary data so that authorized users can apply the same relational language to its interrogation that they apply to regular data.

Putting data into the database into more or less nameless attributes requires extra knowledge about the system beyond what's included in the system catalogs. In Chapter 7, when I cover storing user-specified data (allowing user extensibility to your schema without changes in design), I will discuss methods of giving users the ability to extend the schema at will, and this will seldom be the preferred method.

---

## All Occurrences of an Entity Type in an Entity Must Be Different

This part of First Normal Form requires that every entity have a key defined (primary or unique). This is one of the most important things you must take care of when building a database. Having a key on a table that has some meaning, if at all possible, is tremendously important. It isn't reasonable 100 percent of the time to have a completely meaningful key, but it is nearly always the case that it is reasonable to do so. An example is a situation where you cannot tell the physical items apart, such as perhaps a small can of corn (or a large one, for that matter). Two cans cannot be told apart, so you might assign a value that has no meaning as part of the key, along with the things that differentiate the can from other similar objects, such as large cans of corn or small cans of spinach. You might also consider keeping just a count of the objects in a single row, depending on your needs (which will be dictated by your requirements).

Often, designers are keen to just add an artificial key value to their table, using a GUID or an integer, but as discussed in Chapter 1, adding an artificial key might technically make the entity comply with the letter of the rule, but it certainly won't comply with the purpose. The purpose is that no two instances represent the same thing. An artificial key by definition has no meaning, so it won't fix the problem. You could have two rows that represent the same thing because every meaningful value has the same value, with the only difference between rows being a system-generated value. Note that I am not against using an artificial key, just that it should rarely be the only defined key. As mentioned in Chapter 1, another term for such a key is a *surrogate key*, so named because it is a surrogate (or a stand in) for the real key.

Another common thing to do for a key is using a date and time value to differentiate between rows. If the date and time value is part of the row's logical identification, such as a calendar entry or a row that's recording/logging some event, this is not only acceptable but ideal. On the other hand, simply tossing on a date and time value to force uniqueness is no better than just adding a random number or GUID on the row.

---

■**Caution**  Key choice is one of the most important parts of your database design. Duplicated data causes tremendous and obvious issues to anyone who deals with it. It is particularly bad when you do not realize you have the problem and values can be associated with one instance one time and another the next.

---

# Programming Anomalies Avoided by First Normal Form

Violations of First Normal Form are often awkward if users frequently access the columns affected. The following examples will identify some of the situations we can avoid by putting our entities in First Normal Form.

Note that for these programming anomalies, I'll switch over into using tables, rather than entities. This is because the issues will eventually be manifested in our implemented table structures. Using tables also gives you some detail as to *why* this process is useful in tables and isn't just academic hooey. (You heard me . . . hooey.)

We will look at the following:

- Modifying lists in a single column

- Modifying multipart values

- Dealing with a variable number of facts in an instance

Each of these things can cause you far more work trying to manage them than it will to just design the database right.

## Modifying Lists in a Single Column

As I have probably stressed more than you can handle, SQL isn't set up to handle nonatomic values in a straightforward or consistent way. Consider our previous example of the e-mail addresses attribute. Suppose that the following table named Person exists with the following schema:

```
CREATE TABLE Person
(
    PersonId int NOT NULL PRIMARY KEY,
    Name varchar(100) NOT NULL,
    EmailAddress varchar(1000) NOT NULL
)
```

If users are allowed to have more than one e-mail address, the value of an email column might look like this: tay@bull.com; norma@liser.com. Also consider that several users in the database might use the tay@bull.com e-mail address (for example, if it were the family shared e-mail account). Consider the situation if one of the addresses changed—changing the e-mail address for all uses of tay@bull.com to family@bull.com. You could try to execute code such as the following for every person who uses this e-mail address:

```
UPDATE dbo.person
SET    EmailAddress = replace(EmailAddresses,'tay@bull.com',
       'family@bull.com')
WHERE  ';' + emailAddress + ';' like '%;tay@bull.com;%'
```

This code might not seem like that much trouble, but what about the case where there is also the e-mail address bigtay@bull.com? This code invalidly replaces that value as well. How do you deal with this? Now you have to start messing with adding semicolons to make sure the data fits just right. And that approach is fraught with all sort of potential errors in making sure the format of the data stays the same. Data in the table should have meaning, not formatting. You format data for use, not for storage. It is easy to format data with the UI or even with SQL. Don't format data for storage.

The proper solution would be to have another table to hold each e-mail address in its own row, as shown in Figure 4-6. Now these rows can be related to the Person entity. You can take this one step further and note that each e-mail address includes two values before and after an @. The first value is the e-mail name, and the second is the domain, as shown in Figure 4-7.

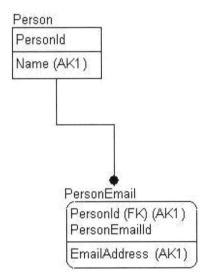

**Figure 4-6.** *A separate entity holds the e-mail details.*

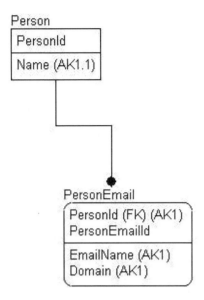

**Figure 4-7.** *We've split the e-mail address into the name and the domain.*

Frankly, you can legitimately go either way (and you can even break out the domain type if it makes sense). Because in many systems, the e-mail name and the domain are rarely, if ever, dealt with as separate things, it can be argued that there is little reason to break them up unless you analyze the places where you get or send e-mail. One good thing about breaking the e-mail name and domain into multiple pieces is that it ensures, with little doubt, that the resulting data will be a valid e-mail address as long as the characters in the names match.

---

■**Tip**  Honestly, the example in this section represents the type of situation in which you may have to balance user desires with your need to normalize. Sometimes it will be "too much" to have two columns to deal with, even if you encapsulate everything into database layer code.

---

## Modifying Multipart Values

The programming logic required to change part of the multipart value can be confusing. For example, take the case of telephone area codes. In the United States, people have more phones, pagers, cell phones, and so on, than the creators of the area code system ever thought of, so they frequently change or introduce new area codes.

I could start to model the phone number as shown in Figure 4-8.

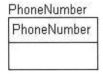

**Figure 4-8.** *Initial phone number model*

The code to modify existing area codes to a new area code is pretty messy, and certainly not the best performer. Usually, when an area code splits, it's for only certain exchanges. Assuming a well-maintained format of AAA-EEE-NNNN where AAA equals area code, EEE equals exchange, and NNNN equals the phone number, then the code looks like this:

```
UPDATE dbo.PhoneNumber
SET PhoneNumber = '423' + substring(PhoneNumber,4,8)
WHERE substring(PhoneNumber,1,3) = '615'
   AND substring(PhoneNumber,5,3) IN ('232','323',...,'989')  --area codes generally
                                                              --change for certain
                                                              --exchanges
```

This code requires perfect formatting of the phone number data to work, and unless the formatting is forced upon the users, this is unlikely to be the case. If all values are stored in single atomic containers, as shown in Figure 4-9, updating the area code would take a single, easy-to-follow, one-line SQL statement.

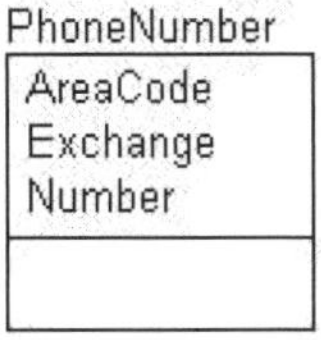

PhoneNumber

| AreaCode |
| Exchange |
| Number |
| |

**Figure 4-9.** *Splitting the phone number into atomic attributes*

Here's an example of the SQL:

```
UPDATE dbo.PhoneNumber
SET    AreaCode = '423'
WHERE  AreaCode = '615'
  AND  Exchange IN ('232','323',...,'989')
```

Again, this is one of those case-by-case decisions. Using three separate values is easier for these reasons and as a result will be the better performer in almost all cases. One value (with enforced formatting) has merit and will work, especially when you have to deal with multiple formats. You might even use a complex type to implement a phone number type. Sometimes I use a single column with a check constraint to make sure all the dashes are in there.

International telephone formats complicate matters greatly, since only a few other countries use the same format as we do. And they all have the same sorts of telephone number concerns as we do with the massive proliferation of telephone number–oriented devices. Much like addresses, how you model phone numbers is heavily influenced by how you will use them and especially how valuable they are to your organization. For example, a call center application might need far deeper control on the format of the numbers than would an application to provide simple phone functionality for an office. It might be legit to just leave it up to the user to fix numbers as they call them, rather than worry about programmability.

## Dealing with a Variable Number of Facts in an Instance

What I mean here is the situation where you have multiple columns in the table that hold the same kind of information, for example, Date1, Date2, Date3. All sorts of context-based questions arise: Is Date2 required to be before Date3, and what does it mean if Date1 is entered but not Date3? Does it matter?

Data entry into these columns is going to be the main issue that arises. For example, consider the case of a company that sells its products usually with two payments. A possible solution might be a basic structured table, such as Figure 4-10 shows.

Account

| AccountNumber |
| --- |
| <<other attributes>><br>Payment1<br>Payment2 |

**Figure 4-10.** *A simple representation of a bank account*

The first payment would go in the Payment1 column, but when the second payment is made, it would go in the Payment2 column. To do this, you'd have to do something such as the following:

```
UPDATE dbo.account
SET Payment1 = case WHEN Payment1 IS NULL THEN 1000.00 ELSE Payment1 END,
    Payment2 = case WHEN Payment1 IS NOT NULL AND Payment2 IS NULL THEN
    1000.00 ELSE Payment2 END
WHERE accountId = 1
```

What happens if on occasion there is a third payment or even a fourth? Would you add Payment3? Payment4? Where would this stop? And what happens when a payment is sent back because of insufficient funds? In reality, it's unlikely that this kludgy code would be using SQL to deal with values such as this, but even if this logic is done on the client side, the code is going to be problematic to deal with and very confusing to report on. (For example, when was a payment made? So, add Payment1Date? Payment2Date? No, please no . . .)

The more correct alternative is to have an entity structured as shown in Figure 4-11.

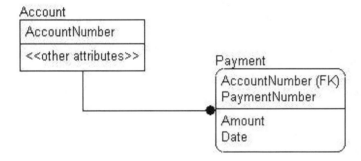

**Figure 4-11.** *The payments are now in a separate entity.*

Then, adding payments would be as simple as adding a new row to the Payment table:

```
INSERT dbo.Payment (AccountNumber, PaymentNumber, Amount, Date)
VALUES ('000002324', 1, $300.00, '20000612')
INSERT dbo.Payment (AccountNumber, PaymentNumber, Amount, Date)
VALUES ('000002324', 2, $100.00, '20000712')
```

You could calculate the payment number from previous payments, which is far easier to deal with using set-based SQL statements.

Not only is it easier to insert a new payment, but it clears up a host of annoyances, such as the following:

- *Deleting a payment*: Much like the update that had to determine what payment slot to fit the payment into, deleting anything other than the last payment requires shifting. For example, if you delete the payment in `Payment1`, then `Payment2` needs to be shifted to `Payment1`, `Payment3` to `Payment2`, and so on.

- *Updating a payment*: Say `Payment1` equals 10, and `Payment2` equals 10. Which one should you modify if you have to modify one of them because the amount was incorrect? Does it matter?

- *Lacking information about a value*: When was the payment made? Why was the payment changed? Because the "event" of the payment has additional interesting information, the `Payment` table offers a more natural place to record it.

# Clues That An Existing Design Is Not in First Normal Form

When you are looking at database design to evaluate it, there are a few basic things you can look at quickly to see whether the data is in First Normal Form. In this section, we'll look at some of these ways to recognize whether data in a given database is already likely to be in First Normal Form. Each of these clues isn't by any means a perfect test. Generally speaking, they're only clues that you can look for in data structures for places to dig deeper. Normalization is a moderately fluid set of rules somewhat based on the content and use of your data.

The following sections describe a couple of data characteristics that suggest that the data isn't in First Normal Form:

- String data that contains separator-type characters
- Attribute names with numbers at the end
- Tables with no or poorly defined keys

This is not an exhaustive list, of course, but these are a few places to start.

## String Data That Contains Separator-Type Characters

Separator-type characters include commas, brackets, parentheses, semicolons, pipe characters, and so on. These act as warning signs that the data is likely a multivalued attribute. Obviously, these same characters are often used in normal prose, so you need not go too far. For instance, if you're designing a solution to hold a block of text, you've probably normalized too much if you have a word entity, a sentence entity, and a paragraph entity (if you had been considering it, give yourself three points for thinking ahead, but don't go there). In essence, this clue is basically aligned to entities that have structured, delimited lists.

## Attribute Names with Numbers at the End

As noted, an obvious example would be finding entities with `Child1`, `Child2`, and similar attributes, or my favorite, `UserDefined1`, `UserDefined2`, and so on. These kinds of entities are usually messy to deal with and should be considered for a new, related table. They don't have to be wrong; for example, your entity might need exactly two values to always exist. In that case, it's perfectly allowable to have the numbered columns, but be careful that what's thought of as "always" is actually always. Too often, exceptions cause this solution to fail. "A person always has two forms of identification noted in fields `ID1` and `ID2`, *except when* . . ." In this case, *always* doesn't mean always.

These kinds of attributes are a common holdover from the days of flat-file databases. Multi-table data access was costly, so developers put many fields in a single file structure. Doing this in a relational database system is a waste of the power of the relational programming language.

Coordinate1, Coordinate2 might be acceptable in cases that always require two coordinates to find a point in a two-dimensional space, never any more or never any less (though CoordinateX and CoordinateY would likely be better attribute names). Also, when you have attributes such as these, which have no meaning without the other, you can design them as a complex datatype. For example, consider the attributes CoordinateX and CoordinateY. As mentioned previously, it would be perfectly acceptable to implement these attributes as a single complex datatype—call it point, perhaps—with two values, X and Y. Because these two values are part of the same attribute—the location of something—it can be reasonable to have them as a complex type, though not required.

### Tables with No or Poorly Defined Keys

As noted in the first chapters several times, key choice is very important. Almost every database will be implemented with some primary key (though this is not a given in many cases). However, all too often the key will simply be a GUID or an identity-based value. In Chapter 5, when I cover the T-SQL version of creating key, I will present several queries to run on your database (and others that you are evaluating) to get an idea of how well the indexes are created, looking for the following:

- Tables with no primary key

- Primary key on identity or GUID column with no other indexes

- Primary or unique constraints that include an identity or GUID

- Indexes that include a date value

It might seem like I am picking on identity and GUIDs, and frankly I am. You must be careful when using them as keys, and too often people use them incorrectly. Keeping row values unique is a big part of First Normal Form compliance and is something that should be high on your list of important activities.

# Relationships Between Attributes

The next set of normal forms to look at is concerned with the relationships between attributes in an entity and, most important, the key(s) of that entity. These normal forms deal with minimizing functional dependencies between the attributes. As discussed in Chapter 1, being functionally dependent implies that when running a function on one value (call it Value1), if the output of this function is *always* the same value (call it Value2), then Value2 is functionally dependent on Value1.

For example, consider the following situation. There are two values: Product Type and Serial Number. Because a product's Serial Number implies a particular product and a particular product will be a certain Product Type, they're functionally dependent. If you change the Product Type but fail to reflect this in the Serial Number, then your Serial Number and Product Type will no longer match, and the values will no longer be of any value. Because the two values are functionally dependent on each other, then they both must be modified at the same time.

In this section, I'll cover the following normal forms:

- *Second Normal Form*: Relationships between non-key attributes and part of the primary key

- *Third Normal Form*: Relationships between non-key attributes

- *BCNF*: Relationships between non-key attributes and any key

Each of these forms can be summarized by the following sentence:

*Non-key attributes must provide a detail about the key, the whole key, and nothing but the key.*

This means that non-key attributes have to further describe the key of the entity and not describe any other attributes. This will become clearer as I introduce each of the different normal forms throughout this section.

# Second Normal Form

Second Normal Form deals with the relationships and functional dependencies between non-key attributes. An entity complying with Second Normal Form has to have the following characteristics:

- The entity must be in First Normal Form.
- Each attribute must be a fact describing the entire key.

---

**■Note**  Second Normal Form is technically relevant only when a composite key (a key composed of two or more columns) exists in the entity.

---

## The Entity Must Be in First Normal Form

It's important that the entity be in First Normal Form; it's essential to consider each step of the normalization process to eliminate problems in data. It might be impossible to locate Second Normal Form problems if there are still First Normal Form problems. Otherwise, some of the problems identified that you're trying to fix by using this rule might show up in any misshapen attributes not dealt with in the previous rule.

## Each Non-Key Attribute Must Describe the Entire Key

Each non-key attribute must depict the entity described by *all* attributes in the key, and not simply parts. If this isn't true, and any of the non-key attributes are functionally dependent on a subset of the attributes in the key, then there will be data modification anomalies. For example, consider the structure in Figure 4-12.

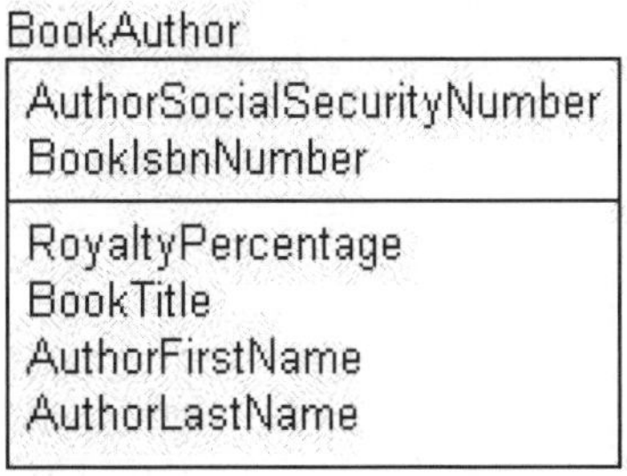

BookAuthor
```
AuthorSocialSecurityNumber
BookIsbnNumber

RoyaltyPercentage
BookTitle
AuthorFirstName
AuthorLastName
```

**Figure 4-12.** *An entity that contains information about a book's author*

The BookIsbnNumber attribute uniquely identifies the book, and AuthorSocialSecurityNumber uniquely identifies the author. Hence, these two columns create one key that uniquely identifies an author for a book. The problem is with the other attributes. The RoyaltyPercentage attribute defines the royalty that the author is receiving for the book, so this refers to the entire key. The BookTitle describes the book but doesn't describe the author at all. The same goes for the AuthorFirstName and AuthorLastName attributes. They describe the author, but not the book.

This is a prime example of a troublesome functional dependency that at first glance might not just pop out as a concern. For every distinct value in the BookIsbnNumber column, there must exist the same book title and author information, because it's the same book. But for every BookIsbnNumber, it isn't true that the same RoyaltyPercentage value will exist—this is dependent on *both* the author and the book, not one or the other. That's because when books are cowritten, the split might be based on many factors: celebrity, how much of the book each author produced, and so on.

Hence, there are problems, so I'll create three separate entities for this data, as shown in Figure 4-13.

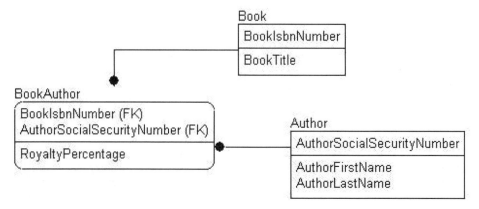

**Figure 4-13.** *The details are now in three separate entities.*

After splitting the entities, the RoyaltyPercentage attribute is still a fact describing the author writing the book, the BookTitle is now an attribute describing the entity defined by BookIsbnNumber, and the author's name attributes are attributes of the Author entity, identified by the AuthorSocialSecurityNumber.

Note that the Book to BookAuthor relationship is an identifying type of relationship. Second Normal Form violations are often remodeled in the conceptual model as identifying relationships in which the primary key of the new entity is migrated to the entity where the original problem occurred. In the corrected example, the functional dependencies are isolated such that attributes that are functionally dependent on another attribute are functionally dependent on the key.

Because all columns are now dependent on the entire key of the table, these entities are in Second Normal Form.

## Programming Problems Avoided by Second Normal Form

All the programming issues that arise with Second Normal Form (as well as the upcoming Third and Boyce-Codd Normal Forms) deal with functional dependencies that can end up corrupting data in ways that are not always easy to notice. Using the entities from the previous sections, consider the model that was originally proposed, how it would be affected if it were implemented, and what might happen if the following statement were executed:

```
UPDATE dbo.BookAuthor
SET    BookTitle = 'Database Design'
WHERE  BookIsbnNumber = '1234567890'
```

Here, you're updating an attribute that clearly represents a singular thing (in this case a book's title). If your update query in which you intend to change what seems like a single thing (such as a book) might modify more than one row, there's a problem with the structure of the design.

The crux of the problem is that many programmers don't have their database-design thinking caps on when they're churning out applications, so you end up with tables created with client screens such as the one shown in Figure 4-14.

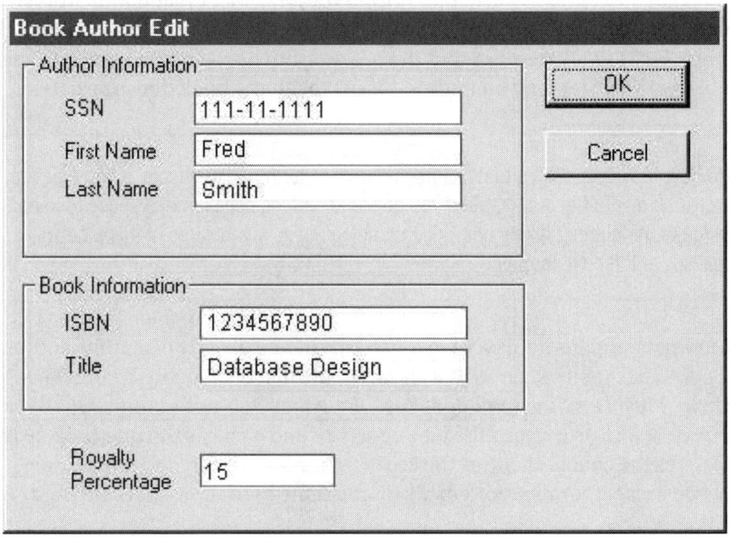

**Figure 4-14.** *A possible graphical front-end to our example*

The design of this screen looks reasonable, doesn't it? If this was in a prototype, I doubt anyone, including myself, would even notice the data issues (well, perhaps if I took the time to read it I'd notice, but it's rare that a DBA pays attention when the UI programmer is presenting a design).

You need to consider the cases where it's obvious that an entity models more than a single noun. In each of the issues identified, this is the problem. The BookAuthor entity isn't only the author of the book, but rather it's the book, the author, and their relationship to each other that presents the problem.

---

**■Tip** There was nothing *terrifyingly* wrong with the screen in Figure 4-14. If the design calls for this sort of data to be entered and the client wants this, fine. However, this is clearly a UI design issue, not a question of database structure. Don't let user interface dictate the database structure any more than the database structures should dictate the UI. When the user figures out the problem, you won't have to change your design. It might also be that this is the basic UI, and there is a button added to the form to implement the multiple cardinality situation of more than one author.

---

The problem is that you commonly need to deal with these independent things not in terms of their relationship but individually (Books or Authors rather than BookAuthors). It turns out that with the attributes in the same entity, it's impossible to do this in a reasonable way. For example, to delete the Author but leave the Book, you could nullify each of the Author's attribute values. To be honest, this will work if you only ever have one author for a book, but with one example of a multi-author book, the design fails. Of course, then the question centers on the author, as in, "What if one author writes more than one book?" The same author's information would have to be duplicated amongst all the books.

It's even more complicated when you start to insert or delete the data for one of the independent entities that are muddled in the BookAuthor table. You cannot delete only a book and keep the author around. And what if the author had written two different books, and they both are "deleted" and the book attributes nullified? Then two rows exist with the same author information and no book. In essence, a duplicated row would then exist. You could write functional routines to take care of such things, but a relational database, and in particular normalization, is set up to handle this situation by making every "thing" its own table. Back in the proper solution in Figure 4-13, deleting a book wouldn't affect the author, but it would require that the relationship between the book and the author be severed. Going the other way, deleting an author doesn't mean the book doesn't exist.

---

■**Tip** Business rules will dictate how to handle such situations as the book-to-author relationship. If you delete a book, it possibly doesn't make sense to delete the author, but if you delete an author, does it make sense to keep the book around without knowledge of the author? Likely not. Understanding needs and desires of this kind will help when implementing relationships in the next chapter.

---

As an aside, consider also what happens if this screen is used to change the title of a multi-author book in a database that has BookAuthor tables such as that shown in the first diagram in the previous section, "Each Non-Key Attribute Must Describe the Entire Key." If the book has two authors, this book would need two BookAuthor rows. Now a user opens the editing screen and changes the title, as shown back in Figure 4-14. When he saves the change, it alters the BookAuthor row only for Fred Smith, not the one for his coauthor. The two BookAuthor rows, originally for the same book, now show different titles.

This problem was rectified by applying Second Normal Form, as shown in the second diagram in that section. In this form, the Book table connects to two BookAuthor tables. Changing the title in this editor screen changes the BookTitle value for this single Book table. The two BookAuthor tables are linked to the Book table only by the BookIsbnNumber attribute, so the database still shows both authors as having coauthored the same book. Everything remains in sync.

---

■**Tip** The issue of multiple authors for a book is also related to Fourth Normal Form. The reason why will become clearer later in the chapter when covering that normal form.

---

## Clues That an Entity Is Not in Second Normal Form

The clues for detecting whether entities are in Second Normal Form aren't as straightforward as the clues for First Normal Form. In some cases, detection can take some careful thought and some thorough examination of your structures:

- Repeating key attribute name prefixes, indicating that the values are probably describing some additional entity

- Data in repeating groups, showing signs of functional dependencies between attributes

- Composite keys without a foreign key, which might be a sign you have key values that identify multiple things in the key, rather than a single thing

## Repeating Key Attribute Prefixes

The situation of repeating key attribute prefixes is one of the dead giveaways. Let's revisit our previous example, as shown in Figure 4-15.

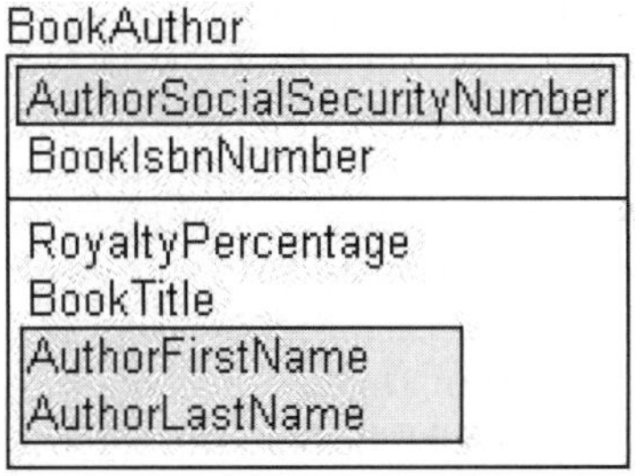

**Figure 4-15.** *The Author entity*

Here we have `AuthorFirstName` and `AuthorLastName`, which are functionally dependent on `AuthorSocialSecurityNumber`. We also have `BookTitle` and `BookIsbnNumber`, with the same situation.

Prefixes like this are a rather common tip-off, especially when designing new systems. Of course, having such an obvious prefix on attributes such as `Author%` or `Book%` is awfully convenient, but it isn't always the case.

## Repeating Groups of Data

More difficult to recognize are the repeating groups of data. Imagine executing multiple `SELECT` statements on a table, each time retrieving all rows (if possible), ordered by each of the important columns. If there's a functionally dependent attribute on one of the attributes—anywhere one of the values is equal to X—we'll see the dependent attribute, Y.

Take a look at some example entries for the tables we just used in the previous section:

```
AuthorSocialSecurityNumber     BookIsbnNumber      RoyaltyPercentage
-----------------------------  ------------------  -------------------
111-11-1111                    1111111111          2
111-11-1111                    2222222222          3
333-33-3333                    1111111111          3

BookTitle              AuthorFirstName       AuthorSecondName
---------------------  --------------------  ---------------------
Instant Tiddlywinks    Vervain               Delaware
Beginning Ludo         Vervain               Delaware
Instant Tiddlywinks    Gordon                Gibbon
```

`BookTitle` is, of course, dependent on `BookIsbnNumber`, so any time we see an ISBN number that equals 1111111111, we can be sure that the book title is *Instant Tiddlywinks*. If it isn't, then there's something wrong in the database (which is why we wouldn't leave the entity modeled in this manner).

The problem is also repeated for the `Author%` columns, as discussed in the previous section.

### Composite Keys Without a Foreign Key Reference

If there's more than one attribute in the key that isn't migrated from another table, consider the relationship between this attribute and the non-key attributes. There's a chance it may be violating Second Normal Form.

In our previous example of a key that was made up of the book ISBN number and author identification, consideration of the non-key attributes clearly gave us two keys that don't represent the same thing: in this case a book and an author.

Second Normal Form violations aren't always so cut and dried. Consider the example earlier of a phone number, in which each piece of the phone number made up the key. Because the three parts made up one thing (in this case a phone number), each part of the key might not relate on its own to the other possible attributes of the phone number, such as the local calling rate or type of phone number (for example, if it was a mobile number, landline, and so on). On the other hand, if information about the area code (like the state that it is part of, for example) were required, putting this attribute in the phone number table would be a violation, since this description wouldn't describe the whole phone number key.

For every table, carefully consider what the composite key values consist of. In the case of the phone number, the different parts of the phone number come together to identify a logically singular thing: a phone number.

## Existing Code That Maintains the Problem Data

Scouring any existing database code is one good way of discovering problems, based on the life span of the system being analyzed. Many times a programmer will simply write code to make sure that normal form violations aren't harmful to the data, rather than remodeling it into a proper structure (though often it won't even be noticed). At one time in the history of databases, this might have been the only way to handle this situation for performance reasons; however, now that technology has more than caught up with the relational theory, this is far less the case.

---

■**Caution**  I'm not trying to make the case that theory has changed a bit because of technology. The foundations of relational theory have been pretty much stable throughout the years, with the concepts maturing over the years. Ten years ago, we had quite a few problems making a normalized system operational in the hardware and operating system constraints we had to deal with (my first experience with a SQL Server machine had 16MB of RAM and 200MB of disk space), so corners were cut in our models for "performance" reasons.

Using modern server hardware, there's usually no need to begin to cut normalization corners for performance. It's best to resolve these issues with SQL joins instead of spaghetti code to maintain denormalized data. Of course, at this point in the design process, it's best not even to consider the topics of implementation, performance, or any subject where we are not simply working toward proper logical storage of data. This might not be 100 percent true when working with a mobile database, but this sort of exception is pretty rare.

---

# Third Normal Form

An entity that's in Third Normal Form has the following characteristics:

- The entity must be in Second Normal Form.
- Non-key attributes cannot describe other non-key attributes.

Third Normal Form differs from Second Normal Form in that it deals with the relationship of non-key data to non-key data, rather than to key data. The problems are similar, and many of the symptoms are the same, but it can be harder to locate the general kinds of violations that this form tends to deal with. The main difference is that data in one attribute, instead of being dependent on the key, is dependent on data in another non-key attribute. The requirements for Third Normal Form are as follows.

## The Entity Must Be in Second Normal Form

Once again, it's important that the entity be in Second Normal Form. It might be hard to locate Third Normal Form problems if Second Normal Form problems still remain.

## Non-Key Attributes Cannot Describe Other Non-Key Attributes

If any of the attributes are functionally dependent on an attribute other than the key, then we're again going to have data-modification anomalies. Because we're in Second Normal Form already, we've proven that all our attributes are reliant on the whole key, but we haven't looked at the relationship of the attributes to one another.

In the example shown in Figure 4-16, we take our Book entity and extend it to include the publisher and the city where the publisher is located.

Title defines the title for the book defined by the BookIsbnNumber, and Price indicates the price of the book. The case can clearly be made that PublisherName describes the book's publisher, and PublisherCity also sort of describes something about the book, in that it tells where the publisher was located (and hence the Second Normal Form compliance). However, it really doesn't make sense in this context, because the location of the publisher is directly dependent on what publisher is represented by PublisherName.

**Figure 4-16.** *The extended Book entity with publisher information added*

To correct this situation, we need to create a different entity to identify the publisher information, as shown in Figure 4-17.

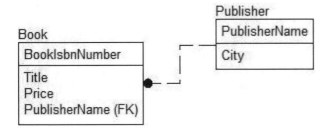

**Figure 4-17.** *The publisher information goes in a separate entity.*

Now the Publisher entity has data concerning only the publisher, and the Book entity has book information. An interesting offshoot of this is that now if we want to add information to our schema concerning the publisher—for instance, contact information or an address—it's obvious where we add that information. Now we have our City attribute clearly identifying the publisher, not the book. Once we get into physical modeling, we'll discuss the merits of having the PublisherName attribute as the primary key, but this is a reasonable key.

Note that the resolution of this problem was to create a *nonidentifying* relationship: Publisher publishes Book. Because the malevolent attributes weren't in the key to begin with, they don't go there now.

---

**■Tip** Third Normal Form can be summed up as follows:

All attributes must be a fact describing the key, the whole key, and nothing but the key.

If it sounds familiar, it should. This little saying is the backbone for the whole group of normal forms concerned with the relationship between the key and non-key attributes.

---

## Programming Problems Avoided by Third Normal Form

Although the methods of violating Third Normal Form are close to the violations of Second Normal Form, there are a few interesting differences. Because we aren't dealing with key values, every attribute's relationship to every non-key attribute needs to be considered, and so does every combination of attributes. In the book example, we structured the entity as shown in Figure 4-16.

You should consider every attribute against every other attribute. If entities are of reasonable size, then the process of weeding out Third Normal Form problems won't be too lengthy. (Ten to twenty attributes in an entity is probably as many columns that is reasonable to have without violating some normalization rule; however, of course this doesn't always hold true. It's just a clue to consider.)

In our example, doing a "perfect" job of comparing each attribute against each of the other attributes, we need to check each attribute against the other three attributes. Because there are four attributes, we need to consider the $(N* (N-1)) /2$ or $(4 * 3) / 2 = 6$ different permutations of attribute relations to be safe. In our example entity, we must check the following:

- Title against Price, PublisherName, and PublisherCity
- Price against Title, PublisherName, and PublisherCity
- PublisherName against Price, Title, and PublisherCity
- PublisherCity against Price, Title, and PublisherName

From this we notice that, when we check PublisherName against the other three attributes, it becomes clear that PublisherCity is functionally dependent on PublisherName and is hence a Third Normal Form violation.

After designing quite a few entities, common attributes will jump out as problems, and only a few attributes will have to be considered in routine normalization checks. Note that our example has tailored names to make it seem simple, but in reality, if you aren't starting from scratch, names can be far more cryptic. Take our example entity, and put it in terms that might exist in a client's legacy database, as shown in Figure 4-18.

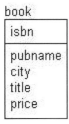

book

| isbn |
| --- |
| pubname |
| city |
| title |
| price |

**Figure 4-18.** *A legacy book entity*

These names are certainly less cryptic than those that exist in some legacy database entities; however, they're already ambiguous enough to cause problems. The `city` attribute seems almost fine here, unless we carefully consider that most books don't have a `city` attribute, but publishers might. The following example code shows what happens if we want to change the `city` attribute and keep it in sync.

---

**■Tip** Your first step in working with legacy systems ought to be to toss them in a data model and give them logical names that make it clear what each column is used for.

---

If we were in the logical design phase, we should have named things better, but we won't always be normalizing for design's sake. We might simply be normalizing a table to try to eliminate some problem areas in an existing system. Take, for example, the situation where we have the table as built previously:

```
CREATE TABLE book
(
    isbn varchar(20) NOT NULL,
    pubname varchar(60) NOT NULL,
    city varchar(30) NOT NULL,
    title varchar(60) NOT NULL
    price money NOT NULL
)
```

This has the Third Normal Form violations that we've identified. Consider the situation in which we want to update the `city` column for ISBN 3232380237, from a value of Virginia Beach to a value of Nashville. We first would update the single row:

```
UPDATE dbo.book
SET    city = 'Nashville'
WHERE  isbn = '23232380237'
```

But because we had the functional dependency of the `pubname` to `city` relationship, we now have to update all the books that have the same publisher name to the new value as well:

```
UPDATE dbo.book
SET    city = 'Nashville'
WHERE  city = 'Virginia Beach'
   AND pubname = 'Phantom Publishing' --publisher name
```

Although this is the proper way to ensure that the batch code updates the city properly, as well as the book, in most cases this code will be buried in the application, not tied together with a transaction—much less one in a batch. It's also easy to forget these types of relationships within the row when writing new processes that are required, because the system changes over time.

Make any errors in one UPDATE statement, and data can be compromised (clearly something we're trying to avoid by spending all this time designing our structures). For existing SQL Server applications that are being redesigned, employ the SQL Server Profiler to check what SQL the application is sending to SQL Server.

Even more troublesome than errors in the UPDATE statement is that you can't represent a publisher without identifying a book. Of course, nothing stops the user from creating a phony ISBN number (the primary key) and a bunch of nonsense column values so the publisher can be represented (face it, users will generally *always* find a way around a bad design, often in a way that will cause the support team more work). Now they will come up with some goofy way to eliminate the phony ISBN number when viewing only book data. It's horribly troublesome to keep all this in sync, so very often it won't be.

The point here is that although you *could* write code to keep the table in sync, it's a mess to maintain; the database is hard to modify; and it won't be faster, even if some folks will try to make you feel that denormalization performs better. Perhaps a join in a SELECT statement might be eliminated, but if the data isn't read-only, you'll pay the cost in modifications. If you want denormalized views of your data, consider indexed views, which are automaintaining.

## Clues That Entities Are Not in Third Normal Form

The clues for Third Normal Form are similar to those for Second Normal Form, because they try to solve the same sort of problem—making sure that all non-key attributes refer to the key of the entity:

- Multiple attributes with the same prefix, much like Second Normal Form, only this time not in the key
- Repeating groups of data
- Summary data that refers to data in a different entity altogether

### Multiple Attributes with the Same Prefix

Let's revisit our previous example, as shown in Figure 4-19.

**Figure 4-19.** *A revised Book entity*

It's obvious that PublisherName and PublisherCity are multiple attributes with the same prefix. In some cases, the prefix and context used might not be so obvious, such as PubName, PblishCity, or even LocationPub—all excellent reasons to establish a decent naming standard early in the process.

### Repeating Groups of Data

Repeating groups of data have much the same application as for Second Normal Form, but we need to consider more permutations of comparisons, because each attribute should be compared against the other non-key attributes.

### Summary Data

One of the common violations of Third Normal Form that might not seem obvious is *summary data*. This is where attributes are added to the parent entity that refer to the child rows and summarize them. Summary data has been one of the most frequently necessary evils that we've had to deal with throughout the history of the relational database server. There might be cases where calculated data needs to be stored in a table in violation of Third Normal Form, but in logical modeling there's *absolutely* no place for it. Not only is summary data not functionally dependent on non-key attributes, it's dependent on nonentity attributes. This causes all sorts of confusion, as I'll demonstrate. Summary data should be reserved either for physical design or for implementation in reporting/data warehousing databases.

Take the example of an auto dealer, as shown in Figure 4-20. The dealer has an entity listing all the automobiles it sells, and it has an entity recording each automobile sale.

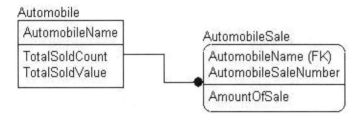

**Figure 4-20.** *The auto dealer has two entities.*

Summary data generally has no part in logical modeling, because the sales data is available in another entity. Instead of accepting that the total number of vehicles sold and their value is available, the designer has decided to add attributes in the parent entity that refer to the child rows and summarize them.

Is this required during the implementation? It's unlikely, but possible, depending on performance needs. (It could be that the total values are used millions of times a day, with very seldom changes to the data that makes up the total.) However, it's common that the complexity of the implemented system has most likely increased by an order of magnitude, because we'll have to have triggers on the AutomobileSale entity that calculate these values for any change in the AutomobileSale entity. If this is a highly active database with frequent rows added to the AutomobileSale entity, this tends to slow the database down considerably. On the other hand, if it's an often inactive database, then there will be few instances in the child entity, so the performance gains made by quickly being able to find the numbers of vehicles sold and their value will be small anyway.

The key is that in logical modeling, including summary data on the model isn't desirable, because the data modeled in the total attributes exists in the Sales entity. What you are actually modeling is usage, not the structure of the data. Data that we identify in our logical models should be modeled to exist in only one place, and any values that could be calculated from other values shouldn't be represented on the model. This aids in keeping the integrity of the design of the data at its highest level possible.

---

■**Tip** One way of dealing with summary data is to use a view. An automobile view might summarize the automobile sales. In many cases, you can index the view, and the data is automatically maintained for you. The summarized data is easier to maintain using the indexed view, though it can have negative performance repercussions on modifications but positive ones on reads. Only testing your actual situation will tell, but this is not the implementation part of the book! I'll discuss indexes in some detail in Chapter 8.

---

## Overnormalizing

The goal of normalization is to store only one piece of data in one place. However, you could reduce multiple values down to being stored in a single place, when more than one value is required. *Overnormalizing* is normalizing without considering all the consequences. Sometimes in the normalization process, we can lose important information because all the business rules are not considered. A common example of this is an invoice line item and the price that's being charged. Consider the model shown in Figure 4-21.

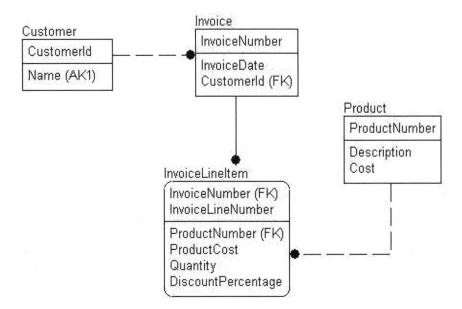

**Figure 4-21.** *An overnormalized design*

In particular, look at the `InvoiceLineItem.ProductCost` attribute. The product has a cost associated with it already, so do we need the product cost repeated for the `InvoiceLineItem`? At the time of the invoice being printed, we can get the cost from the product, and bam, we're done—right?

Will the price *always* be the same? And if not, what about the invoice information? We could no longer see the price that the customer was charged, losing some information in the process. When normalizing (and doing *any* logical data modeling), we must focus on making sure we deal with things that are always true. In this case, what happens if the cost of the product changes? Do we need to come up with an elaborate history of product costs, and how do we relate them to invoices during periods of time? Perhaps, but what if the manager that day says, "Yeah, that is my son-in-law, give it to 'em for half off"? Then even storing what the value was on a given day won't cover the price that the user paid. So in this case, it's better to have the data as it existed when the sale was made in the row with the sale (and you might want to keep up a table of values as the price changes as well). When faced with this sort of question, you will need to decide whether updating one value necessitates updating another.

You might also have noticed an absence of a total value for the `LineItem`. This value can be calculated by `ProductCost * Quantity * ( 1 - DiscountPercentage )` and shouldn't vary from that since there is no reason that the line total would not be functionally dependent on that formula (or one like it). Hence, adding a total value would most certainly violate Third Normal Form.

The most important thing to remember here is always to consider the possible side effects of removing/adding attributes to the entities you are designing, especially in consideration of the business rules. They can dictate whether a given attribute is functionally dependent on another attribute, based on usage and modifiability rules.

---

■**Tip**  The output of the conceptual/logical modeling phase of a design project is a very normalized model, even if you may have to step back from some of the normalizations for usability or performance reasons. Try not to mix design with implementation.

---

# Boyce-Codd Normal Form

The *Boyce-Codd Normal Form* (BCNF) is named after Ray Boyce, one of the creators of SQL, and Edgar Codd, who I introduced in the first chapter as the father of relational databases. It's a better-constructed replacement for both the Second and Third Normal Forms, and it takes the meaning of the Second and Third Normal Forms and restates it in a more general way. Note that, to be in BCNF, there's no mention of Second Normal Form or Third Normal Form. The BCNF encompasses them both and is defined as follows:

- The entity is in First Normal Form.
- All attributes are fully dependent on a key.
- An entity is in BCNF if every determinant is a key.

Let's look at the last two rules individually.

## All Attributes Are Fully Dependent on a Key

We can rephrase this like so: "All attributes must be a fact about *a* key and nothing but *a* key." This is a slight but important deviation from our previous rules for Second Normal Form and Third Normal Form. In this case, we don't specify *the entire* key or just *the* key—now it is *a* key. How does this differ? Well, it does, and it doesn't. It expands the meaning of Second Normal Form and Third Normal Form to deal with the typical situation in which we have more than one key. As mentioned before, a key can be *any* candidate key, whether the primary key or an alternate key.

---

■**Caution**  Depending on the choice of primary key, this can be a great distinction. There's a large group of database designers using meaningless surrogate keys (of which I am a big fan). If you don't deal with the case of more than one key, it's easy to forget that the important keys are the natural keys of the entity, and normalization should take them into consideration. Too often when answering forum posts, the problem of poor key choices for a table has to be solved before solving the problem at hand.

---

The attribute must be fully dependent on a key. Keys are defined as the unique identifier for an instance of the entity, regardless of whether we use a natural key or otherwise. Using the key, you're able to find the row within the set that makes up the entity. The entity is the logical representation of a single object, either real or imaginary. Think of the key in terms of being the entity's ID badge, Social Security number (SSN), or username. It's the way we tell it apart from other entities.

For example, let's take a person who works for a company and model that person. First we choose our key; let's say SSN, as shown in Figure 4-22.

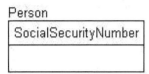

**Figure 4-22.** *Our Person entity has its SSN as the key.*

Then we start adding the other attributes we know about our employees—their name, their hair color, their eye color, the badge number they're given, their driver's license number, and so on. Now we have the entity shown in Figure 4-23.

Person

| SocialSecurityNumber |
| --- |
| FirstName<br>LastName<br>Height<br>Weight<br>BadgeNumber<br>EyeColor<br>DriversLicenseNumber<br>HairColor<br>ShoeSize |

**Figure 4-23.** *An enlarged Person entity*

Careful study of the entity shows that it's in Third Normal Form, because each of the attributes further describes the entity. The FirstName, Height, BadgeNumber, and others all refer to the entity. The same might be said for the SocialSecurityNumber. It has been chosen as the key, primarily because it was the first thing we came upon. In logical modeling, the choice of which attribute is a primary key isn't all that meaningful, and we can change the primary key at any time. (Chapter 5 will discuss the various choices of primary keys for a table.)

As I mentioned in the previous chapter as I built a sample conceptual data model, in practice I'll use a value that's simply the name of the table with "Id" appended to it for the primary key in the logical modeling phase. For example, in a previous example, we had Person and PersonEmail entities. For the key of the PersonEmail, the key was PersonId and EmailAddress. In a typical design, I choose to model this situation as shown in Figure 4-24.

In this book, I'll for the most part do examples of each style of modeling keys—sometimes using surrogates, sometimes using natural keys.

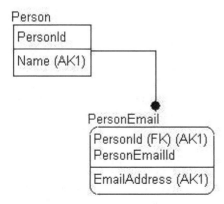

**Figure 4-24.** *Modeling a person's personal e-mail address*

### An Entity Is in Boyce-Codd Normal Form If Every Determinant Is a Key

The second part of the quest for BCNF is to make sure every determinant is a key or a unique identifier for the entity. I've adapted our definition of a determinant from Chapter 1 to include the following:

> *Any attribute or combination of attributes on which any other attribute or combination of attributes is functionally dependent.*

Based on our study of the Second and Third Normal Forms, we can see that this is nearly the same as the definition of a key. Because all attributes that aren't keys must be functionally dependent on a key, the definition of a determinant is close to the same as the definition of a key.

The BCNF simply extends the previous normal forms by saying that an entity might have many keys, and all attributes must be dependent on one of these keys. It's simplified a bit by noting that every key must uniquely identify the entity, and every non-key attribute must describe the entity.

One interesting thing that should be noted is that each key is a determinant for all other keys. This is because, in every place where one key value is seen, we can replace it with the other key value without losing the meaning of the entity. This is not to say that an alternate key cannot change values—not at all. The driver's license number is a good key, but if the Department of Motor Vehicles issues all new numbers, it's still a key, and it will still identify and describe the entity. If the value of any candidate key changes, this is perfectly acceptable.

With this definition in mind, consider the example entity shown in Figure 4-23 again.

Person

| SocialSecurityNumber |
| --- |
| FirstName |
| LastName |
| Height |
| Weight |
| BadgeNumber |
| EyeColor |
| DriversLicenseNumber |
| HairColor |
| ShoeSize |

What we're looking for now are attributes or groups of attributes that are dependent on the key and also that are unique to each instance of this entity.

FirstName isn't unique by itself, and it wouldn't be good to assume that FirstName and LastName are unique. (It all depends on the size of the target set as to whether the user would be willing to accept this. At least we would need to include middle initial and title, but still this isn't a good key.) Height describes the person but isn't unique. The same is true for Weight. BadgeNumber should be unique, so we'll make it a key. (Note that we don't have BadgeIssuedDate, because that would refer to the badge and doesn't help the BCNF example. However, if we did have a badge-issue date, we could easily have a Badge entity with a BadgeNumber primary key that's migrated to this table, and this table would not change in structure.)

The DriversLicenseNumber attribute is probably unique, but consider variations across localities. Two governments might have similar numbering schemes that might cause duplication. Taken with DriversLicenseState (which I'll add), this will be a key. HairColor and ShoeSize describe the person, but neither could be considered unique. Even taking the person's Height, Weight, EyeColor, HairColor, and ShoeSize together, you can't guarantee uniqueness between two random people. So, now we model the entity as shown in Figure 4-25.

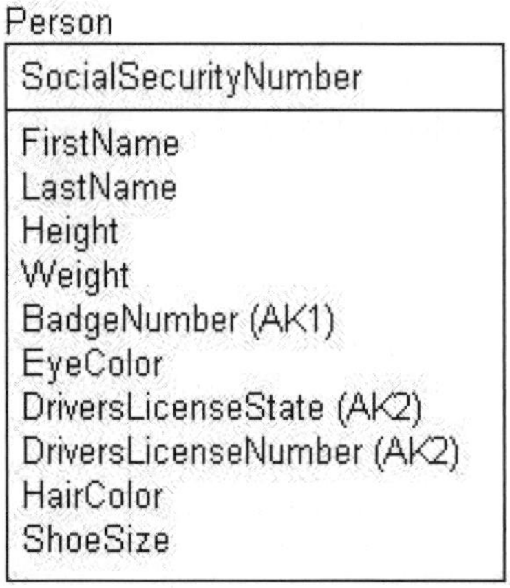

Person

```
SocialSecurityNumber

FirstName
LastName
Height
Weight
BadgeNumber (AK1)
EyeColor
DriversLicenseState (AK2)
DriversLicenseNumber (AK2)
HairColor
ShoeSize
```

**Figure 4-25.** *The license and badge number attributes are used as keys.*

We now have three keys for this object. When we do the modeling for the implementation, we'll choose the proper key from the keys we have defined or use an artificial key. As discussed in Chapter 1, an artificial key is simply a value that's used as a pointer to an object, much like BadgeNumber is a pointer that a company uses to identify an employee or like the government using SSNs to identify individuals in the United States. (The SSN is a smart key, because some digits identify where the number was issued, and it has an artificial element, probably a simple sequence number.)

It's also worth considering that an SSN isn't always a good key either. Even dealing with only those people in the United States, plenty of people don't have an SSN. And if we want to accommodate people from outside the United States, then the SSN will never work. It depends on the situation, because there are many circumstances where the user is required to have an SSN and some circumstances where an SSN or green card is required to identify the user as a valid resident of the United States. The situation always dictates the eventual solution, and this choice needs to be made during design to decide on the appropriate path.

Lastly, what about `DriversLicenseState` and `DriversLicenseNumber`? In all of our sections, having columns with the same prefix is a clue that there may be an issue. Well, in this case, you need to think, "If I know the state of the license, will I know the number?" and conversely, "If I know the number, will I know the state of the license?" In this case, the answer is probably that this is fine, since the key of a driver's license is actually the state and number. Hence, neither of these values is a determinant of any other attribute individually. Both parts do make up a determinant for the other attributes of the entity.

### Clues and Programming Anomalies

The clues for determining that an entity is in BCNF are the same as for Second Normal Form and Third Normal Form. The programming anomalies cured by the BCNF are the same too.

Once all the determinants are modeled during this phase of the design, implementing the determinants as unique keys will be far more likely of an occurrence. This prevents users from entering nonunique values in the columns that need to have unique values in them.

This completes our overview of the first four normal forms. I should probably state here that a great deal of people feel that this is "far" enough to take normalization. This is usually true, but only because there aren't often problems in data models that the Fourth and Fifth Normal Forms cover. I strongly suggest you don't ignore the next section, thinking that knowing the first three normal forms is good enough (and the lack of Fourth Normal Form coverage in many database books was my early impetus for writing the first version of this book). At the least, this section will put the idea in the back of your mind of what situation you might be getting into if your tables are of a certain type. What's that type? Sorry, you'll have to read on.

# Multivalued Dependencies in Entities

In this section, we'll take a look at the next level of normalization. It's definitely important, just like the previous sections have been, though it isn't commonly used because of perceived drawbacks in terms of both the time taken to implement the normalization and the cost in performance of the resulting database.

In the previous sections, we dealt with the structure of attributes and the relationship between non-key attributes and keys. The next two normal forms that I will discuss again deal with the relationship among the non-key attributes, but now we're dealing with the cardinality of the relationship and the kinds of problems that can arise when the cardinality is more than one.

While Third Normal Form is generally considered the pinnacle of proper database design, some serious problems might still remain in the logical design. To be more specific, the normal forms that this section will cover deal with the case of multivalued relationships and dependencies between attributes. For our purposes, we'll look at Fourth Normal Form in some detail and then simply introduce Fifth Normal Form.

## Fourth Normal Form

Our rules of normalization so far have resolved redundancies among columns in an entity but haven't resolved problems that arise from entities having composite primary keys while still possessing redundant data for one or more of the columns in the key. Normalizing entities to Fourth Normal Form addresses such problems. In a simple case, moving to Fourth Normal Form takes care of issues such as the modeling of an attribute that is stored as a single value but in reality the attribute needs multiple values. The second type of problem is more elusive, because it deals with ternary relationships and how to break them up into smaller tables that are easier to work with.

Briefly, consider the case of an entity that assigns students to a class. At the same time, we also want to represent the teacher of each student and each class, so we put teachers and students in a ClassAssignment entity as shown in Figure 4-26.

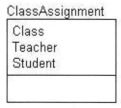

**Figure 4-26.** *A class assignment entity*

This seems right enough, and since all the attributes are necessary to represent a ClassAssignment instance, this may be an optimal solution. However, on further consideration, it turns out that this entity is unsatisfactory because now if we want to change the teacher for a class, we would have to modify instances for all the students in the class, since each ClassAssignment instance includes the class and teacher.

Clearly, this is not optimal because one of the main points of normalization is to eliminate redundant information, especially when modifying one piece of information requires modifying that single piece of information in multiple places. The simple solution can be found by noting that a class has multiple students and a student can be in multiple classes and have multiple teachers. (I will show another example along the same lines where I go through all of the steps of how you find the solution that isn't obvious to you immediately.)

To implement our new solution, we create three tables: one for class and two others to represent the relationship of a teacher and a student to the class. Figure 4-27 shows the modified design.

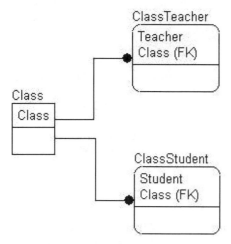

**Figure 4-27.** *The modified class model*

The key to this transformation was that the student to teacher relationship (as far as class assignments are concerned, at least) is fully centered around the class experience. Hence, we needn't represent a relationship between the Student and Teacher entities. A join through the Class entity will get you the information about which students are taught by which teacher.

This kind of transformation is a large part of what Fourth Normal Form is all about. We have to break up this ternary relationship into more useful forms without redundant information.

The following conditions must be met for an entity to be in Fourth Normal Form:

- *The entity must be in BCNF*: This condition ensures that all keys will be appropriately defined, and all values in an entity will be properly dependent on its key.

- *There must not be more than one multivalued dependency (MVD) between an attribute and the key of the entity*: No more than one attribute can store multiple values that relate to a key in any entity; otherwise, there will be data duplication. In addition, we should ensure that we don't repeat single-valued attributes for every multivalued one.

We'll look at a few examples to help make these ideas clearer. Let's first look at the three main forms that Fourth Normal Form violations take:

- Ternary relationships

- Lurking multivalued attributes

- Temporal data/value history

Fourth Normal Form, in my opinion, is critical to understand. The methods are easy enough to follow. There are some important misconceptions about the Normal Forms past the Third being meaningless, and they're wrong. Once you see what normalizing to the Fourth level means, you won't even consider ignoring what it stands for.

## Ternary Relationships

We briefly looked at ternary relationships in Chapter 1. Often in real life, relationships won't manifest themselves in simple binary-type relationships, and the ternary or greater relationships are common. Any place where we see three (or more) identifying or mandatory nonidentifying relationships in an entities key, we're likely to have trouble (consider also the case in which keys aren't perfectly chosen).

Take, as an example, a situation where we've designed a set of entities to support a conference planner, storing information concerning the session, presenter, and room where a session is to be given.

Let's also assume the following set of open business rules is to be enforced:

- More than one presenter can be listed to give a presentation.

- A presentation can span more than one room.

Figure 4-28 models the relationship presenter-*presents*-session-*in*-room.

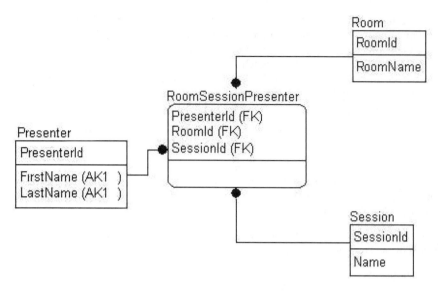

**Figure 4-28.** *The presenter-presents-session-in-room relationship*

Each of these entities is a BCNF entity; however, the relationship between the three is troublesome because of the three-column key, especially with all attributes being migrated from other entities. There might be nothing wrong with this at all, but any case in which this situation occurs bears some investigation to make sure that no multivalued dependencies will cause eventual problems in our data.

Consider the case that each of the sessions is going on at the same time. The table would require a session time, which would complicate matters even further. At this point, we're dealing with the case of one session time for all sessions. Let's look at a set of sample data (we've joined Room, Presenter, and Session to look at the natural keys):

| Session | Presenter | Room |
| ------- | --------- | ----------- |
| 101 | Davidson | River Room |
| 202 | Davidson | Stream Room |
| 202 | Hazel | Stream Room |
| 404 | Hawkins | Brook Room |
| 404 | Hawkins | Stream Room |

In the first row, there's no problem, because we have one row for session 101, which has one presenter, Davidson, and one room, the River Room. A problem becomes apparent in the next two rows, because one session, 202, has two different presenters and yet a single room. This forces us to repeat data unnecessarily in the Room attribute, because we now have stored in two places that session 202 is in the Stream Room. If the session moves, we have to change it in two places, and if we forget this property and update the room based on a value that we aren't currently displaying (for example, through the use of an artificial key), then we end up with the following values:

| Session | Presenter | Room |
| ------- | --------- | ---------------- |
| 202 | Davidson | Stream Room |
| 202 | Hazel | "Changed to Room" |

In this example, we have duplicated data in the Session and Room attributes, and the 404 session duplicates Session and Presenter data. The real problem with our scenario comes when adding to or changing our data. If we need to update the Session number that Davidson is giving with Hazel in the Stream Room, then two rows will require changes. Equally, if a Room assignment changes, then several rows will have to be changed.

When we implement entities in this fashion, we might not even see all the rows filled in as fully as this. Next, we see a set of rows that are functionally equivalent to the set in the previous entity:

| Session | Presenter | Room |
| ------- | --------- | ----------- |
| 101 | Davidson | <null> |
| 101 | <null> | River Room |
| 202 | Davidson | <null> |
| 202 | <null> | Stream Room |
| 202 | Hazel | <null> |
| 404 | <null> | Brook Room |
| 404 | Hawkins | <null> |
| 404 | <null> | Stream Room |

In this example, we have null values for some rooms, and we have some presenters. We have eliminated the duplicated data, but now all we have is some pretty strange-looking data with nulls everywhere. Furthermore, we aren't able to use nulls clearly to stand for the situation where we don't yet know the presenter for a session. We're storing an equivalent set of data to that in the previous example, but the data in this form is difficult to work with. Right or wrong, you can probably tell immediately just how annoying this data will be to work with.

To develop a solution to this problem, let's first make the Presenter entity primary, as shown in Figure 4-29.

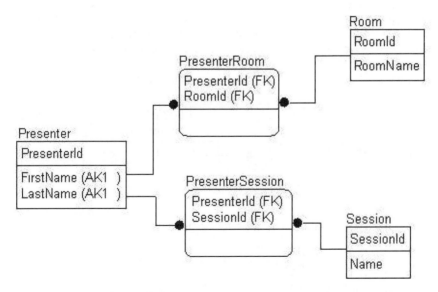

**Figure 4-29.** *The Presenter entity is primary.*

Then we take the data in the RoomSessionPresenter entity and break it into the entities in Figure 4-30.

| Presenter |
|-----------|
| Davidson |
| Hazel |
| Hawkins |

| Presenter | Room |
|-----------|------|
| Davidson | River Room |
| Davidson | Stream Room |
| Hazel | Stream Room |
| Hawkins | Stream Room |
| Hawkins | Brook Room |

| Presenter | Session |
|-----------|---------|
| Davidson | 101 |
| Davidson | 202 |
| Hazel | 404 |
| Hawkins | 404 |

**Figure 4-30.** *Data rearranged in a Presenter-centric way*

This is obviously not a proper solution, because we would never be able to determine what room a session is located in, unless a presenter had been assigned. Also, Davidson is doing a session in the River Room as well as the Stream Room, and there's no link back to the session that's being given in the room. When we decompose any relationship and we lose meaning to the data, the decomposition is referred to as a *lossy decomposition*. This is one such case and as such isn't a reasonable solution to our problem.

Next we try centering on the room where the sessions are held, as shown in Figure 4-31.

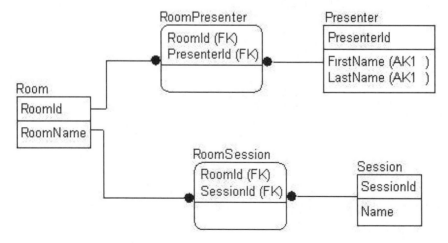

**Figure 4-31.** *The Room entity is now primary.*

Taking the data and fitting into the entities once again, see Figure 4-32.

| Room |
| --- |
| River Room |
| Brook Room |
| Stream Room |

| Room | Presenter |
| --- | --- |
| River Room | Davidson |
| Stream Room | Davidson |
| Stream Room | Hazel |
| Stream Room | Hawkins |
| Brook Room | Hawkins |

| Room | Session |
| --- | --- |
| River Room | 101 |
| Stream Room | 202 |
| Brook Room | 202 |
| Stream Room | 404 |

**Figure 4-32.** *Data rearranged in a Room-centric way*

Again, this is a lossy decomposition because we're unable to determine, for example, exactly who's presenting the 202 presentation. It's in the Stream Room, and Davidson, Hazel, and Hawkins are all presenting in the Stream Room; but they're not all presenting the 202 session. So once again we need to consider another design. This time we center our design on the sessions to be held, as shown in Figure 4-33.

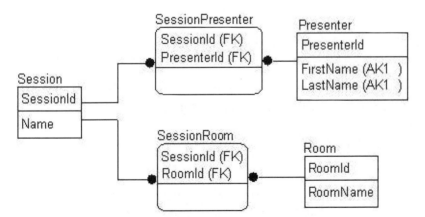

**Figure 4-33.** *The Session entity is now primary.*

Look at the data in Figure 4-34.

| Session |
|---------|
| 101 |
| 202 |
| 404 |

| Session | Room |
|---------|------|
| 101 | River Room |
| 202 | Stream Room |
| 404 | Brook Room |
| 404 | Stream Room |

| Session | Presenter |
|---------|-----------|
| 101 | Davidson |
| 202 | Davidson |
| 202 | Hazel |
| 404 | Hawkins |

**Figure 4-34.** *Data rearranged in a Session-centric way*

We have finally hit upon a solution to the problem that makes sense. From this data, we're able to determine precisely who is presenting what and where, and we'll have no problem adding or removing presenters, or even changing rooms. For example, take session 404. We have the data in the following sets of results in the sessionRoom and sessionPresenter entities for this session:

```
Session  Room
-------- -------------
404      Brook Room
404      Stream Room

Session  Presenter
-------- -------------
404      Hawkins
```

To add a presenter named Evans to the slate, we simply add another row:

```
Session  Presenter
-------  -------------
404      Hawkins
404      Evans
```

This is now a proper decomposition and won't have the problems we outlined in our original entity. Now that we've set the session separately from the presenter, the nulls are no longer required in the foreign key values, because if we want to show that a room hasn't been chosen, we don't create a sessionRoom instance. The same is true if we haven't yet chosen a presenter. More important, we can now set multiple rooms for a session without confusion.

If we need to have additional data that extends the concept of `SessionPresenter`, for example, to denote alternate presenter (or indeed primary and secondary presenter), we now have a clean and logical place to store this information. Note that if we had tried to store that information in the original entity, it would have violated BCNF because the `AlternatePresenter` attribute would be referring only to the `Session` and `Presenter`, not the `Room`.

The key to this process is to look for relationships between the attributes. In this case, there was a relationship between the session and who was presenting, as well as the session and where it was being given. On the other hand, there was no direct relationship between the presenter and where the session was located.

## Lurking Multivalued Attributes

I use the term *lurking* because the attributes I am discussing in this section don't always stand out as problems at first glance. The problem is that in many cases, it seems as if you need only a single value for an attribute, but upon additional consideration, there are cases where multiple values are required. To illustrate this idea, let's consider the design model shown in Figure 4-35.

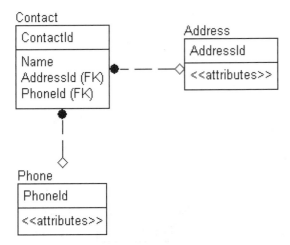

**Figure 4-35.** *A design that includes lurking multivalued attributes*

A problem arises here when we consider the `Contact` entity, because we have three attributes: the contact's name (assume that this name is in First Normal Form), the phone number, and the address. The name is fine, because all contacts have a single name by which we'll refer to them, but these days, many people have more than one address and phone number. We therefore have multivalued attributes that require further normalization to resolve them. To allow for such multiple addresses and phone numbers, we might modify our design as shown in Figure 4-36.

Although having multiple phone numbers isn't a First Normal Form violation (because they're all different types of phone numbers, rather than multiples of the same type), we do have a further problem. Because we have simply added the type of attribute to the name of the attribute (for example, `HomeAddressId`, `FaxPhoneId`), we'll have further multivalue attribute problems if, for example, the user has two fax phones or indeed two mobile phones. Furthermore, we're in the less than ideal situation of needing multiple nullable values for each of the attributes when the attribute doesn't exist, which technically states that the value is unknown, not that it doesn't exist.

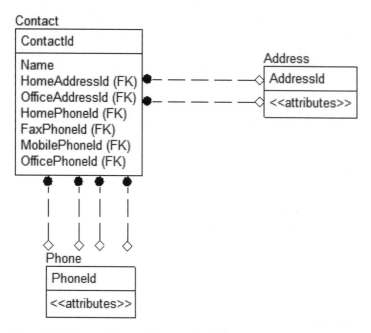

**Figure 4-36.** *The model now allows multiple addresses and phone numbers.*

This is a messy representation of the relationship. For example, if the client requires a spouse's office phone number attribute for a contact, we'll have to change the model, in all probability leading us to rewriting the application code.

Let's further modify the design, so as to have separate Contact and ContactInformation entities, as shown in Figure 4-37.

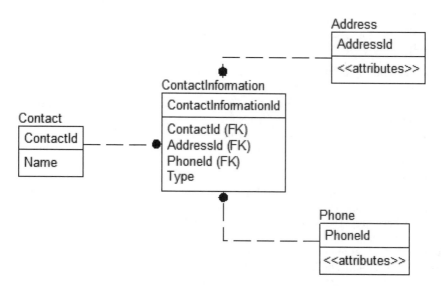

**Figure 4-37.** *Separate Contact and ContactInformation entities*

The Type attribute denotes the type of contact information that we're storing in an instance, so we can now have a ContactInformation instance with a Type of 'Home' and attach an address and phone number to it. This now allows us to add as many phone numbers and addresses as a user requires. However, because address and phone are held in the same table, we end up with null values where a contact has different numbers of home addresses and phone numbers.

At this stage, we need to decide how we want to proceed. We might want a phone number to be linked with an address (for example, linking a home address with a home phone number). In our case, we'll split the ContactInformation entity into ContactAddress and ContactPhone (though this isn't the only possible solution to the problem), as shown in Figure 4-38.

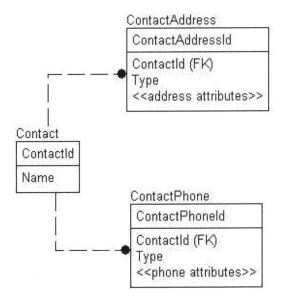

**Figure 4-38.** *ContactAddress and ContactPhone entities now represent the contact information.*

This modification has eliminated the remaining multivalued dependencies, because we can now have many addresses and many phone numbers independently of one another and are able to define as many types as desired without needing to modify our entity structures. However, we can take one further step by modeling the phone number and address as different entities in the logical model and adding domain entities for the Type column. In this way, we can prevent users from typing "Some," "Homer," "Hume," and so on, when they mean "Home." Modeling the phone number and address as different entities also gives us a user-configurable constraint so we can add types without having to change the model. We'll add a Description attribute to the domain entities, allowing us to describe the actual purpose of the type. This allows for situations such as where we have an address type of "Away" that's standard for a given organization but confusing to first-time users. We could then assign a description such as "Address for contact when traveling on extended sales trips." Figure 4-39 shows our final model.

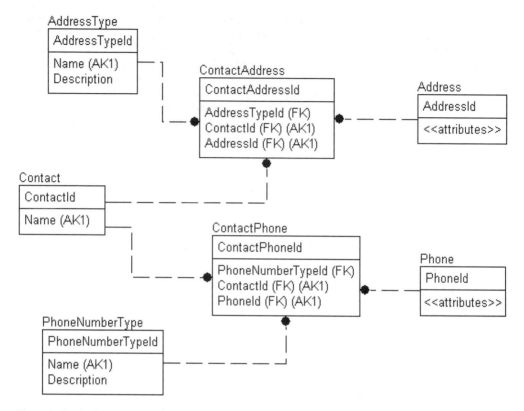

**Figure 4-39.** *The final model*

Note that I've made the additional attributes of Address and PhoneNumber alternate keys to avoid duplicating an address every time it's used in the system. This way, if we have five contacts that have the same address for their office, we have to change only one item. This might or might not be desirable in the final implementation, because it can increase complexity and might or might not be worth it from a business perspective.

The fact is, you'll tend to catch many of these types of issues during the First, Second, Third, or Boyce-Codd Normal Form checks. For example, think back to Payment1, Payment2, and so on, from First Normal Form. If the field had just read Payment, would it have been as noticeable? Maybe not. This is especially true if you're strict with your search for entities and realize that a payment is an independent thing from a customer.

---

■**Note**  This is one of the reasons why Fourth Normal Form is the most important normal form. It forces you to look deeper at the relationship between non-key and key attributes.

---

## Temporal Data/Value History

When I refer to temporal data in this context, what I mean is data where we want to know the value at a given time. Generally speaking, your data warehouse is where you should do most management of historical values (using Type 2 slowly changing dimensions), but there can be several reasons to store history of attribute values in your online transaction processing (OLTP) database.

A common example of temporal data is status-type information for an instance of some entity. For example, in Figure 4-40, we've built two entities that store the header of an order, as well as a domain entity for the order status.

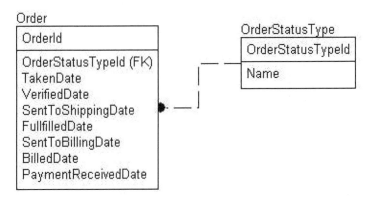

**Figure 4-40.** *A model of an Order entity*

The problem here is that the order status changes (and hence the value of the OrderStatusTypeId attribute) based both on the values of the other date attributes and on other external factors. For example, when the order is taken from the customer, the TakenDate attribute would be filled in with a date. The order then might be in 'Pending' status. After the customer's payment method has been verified, we'd then modify the VerifiedDate attribute with the date verified and set the status to 'InProcess'. 'InProcess' could mean more than one thing, such as "sent to shipping" or "bill sent."

Here, we're concerned with the OrderStatusTypeId attribute on the Order entity. It contains the current status for the Order instance. How do you answer questions about when an order got sent to the shipping department or when the order-verification department verified the order? The modeler of the data has added several attributes in the Order entity to store these bits of information, but what if it failed verification once? Do we care? And is the FulfilledDate the date when the order was either fully shipped or canceled or strictly when it was fully shipped? Do we need to add another attribute for CanceledDate?

To solve these problems, we'll have to change our model to allow the storing of multiple values for each of the attributes we've created, as shown in Figure 4-41.

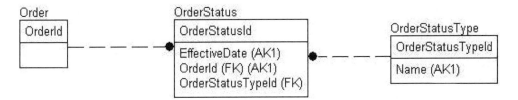

**Figure 4-41.** *We can now store multiple values for each attribute.*

Now whenever the order status changes, all we have to do is add an instance to the OrderStatus entity. Whatever instance has the latest EffectiveDate value is the current status. We could even extend our model to allow more than one status value at a time. For instance, not all statuses are fulfilled in a sequential fashion. In an Order type entity, for instance, you might send the invoice to be verified and then, once it's verified, send it to be processed by shipping and billing at the same time. With the new structure that we've created, when our order fails to be shipped, we can record that it failed to ship. We can also record that the client has paid. Note that, in this case, we want to model only the status of the overall order, and not the status of any items on the order.

Modeling and implementing this type of Fourth Normal Form solution sometimes requires a state diagram to determine in what order a status is achieved. For example, Figure 4-42 can be used to describe the process of an order being taken, from the time it was ordered to the time it was closed out. (We won't consider canceling or modifying an order, or indeed back orders, in this example. The solution to that problem would be much the same, however.)

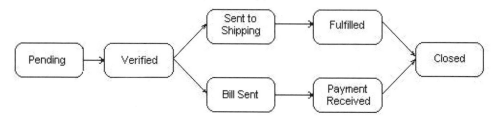

**Figure 4-42.** *The ordering process*

We can model this kind of simple state diagram fairly easily with one additional entity (the From relationship is optional), as shown in Figure 4-43.

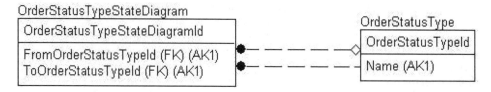

**Figure 4-43.** *Modeling the state diagram*

---

■**Note**  This is a type of recursive relationship, with the recursive structure split out in the OrderStatusType table. If a child can have only one parent, then it's a tree (and you can use a one-table recursive relationship for that). If you can have more than one parent (as is the case for the closed value), it is considered a graph.

---

Consider that we had our seven states in the OrderStatusType entity:

| OrderStatusTypeId | Name |
| --- | --- |
| 1 | Pending |
| 2 | Verified |
| 3 | Shipping |
| 4 | Bill Sent |
| 5 | Fulfilled |
| 6 | Paid |
| 7 | Closed |

To define our state diagram, we'd need the following instances for the OrderStatusType. StateDiagram entity (leaving off the key this time and including Name for clarity):

| fromOrderStatusTypeId | Name | toOrderStatusTypeId | Name |
|---|---|---|---|
| 1 | Pending | 2 | Verified |
| 2 | Verified | 3 | Shipping |
| 2 | Verified | 4 | Bill Sent |
| 3 | Shipping | 5 | Fulfilled |
| 4 | Bill Sent | 6 | Paid |
| 5 | Fulfilled | 7 | Closed |
| 6 | Paid | 7 | Closed |

In this manner, we can see whether we're in a particular state, what state we were previously in, and what state we can be in next. This state diagram also allows us to define the flow of our business rules in data, rather than hard-coding a bunch of fixed values.

In this case, our status might go through several values and in fact might have multiple statuses at any given time. You would have to document business rules outlining exactly how the process works in a given situation. In reality, the exception processing requires the most amount of time, with up to 80 percent of coding time generally spent on the exceptions to the rule.

■**Tip** Data warehousing technologies have eliminated much of the need for most historical information being stored in an OLTP-type system. The data warehouse receives a snapshot of the data at a given point of time and saves history in a useful manner for reporting. In practice, it's best to keep only as much history in the OLTP system as you need to support day-to-day operations. History is better kept in the dimensional model used in data warehousing.

## Fifth Normal Form

Not every ternary relationship can be broken down into two entities related to a third. The aim of Fifth Normal Form is to ensure that any ternary relationships that still exist in a Fourth Normal Form entity that can be decomposed into entities are decomposed. This eliminates problems with update anomalies due to multivalued dependencies, much like in Fourth Normal Form, only these are trickier to find.

The idea is that ternary relationships are safer to deal with if you break all ternary relationships down into binary relationships. We saw in Fourth Normal Form that some ternary relationships could be broken down into two binary relationships without losing information. When the breakdown into two binary relationships became a lossy one, it was declared that the relationship was in Fourth Normal Form.

At this point, Fifth Normal Form would suggest that it's best to break down any existing ternary relationship into three binary relationships. In some cases, you cannot break a ternary relationship down. For example, consider the case of the following Teacher, Student, and Class data:

| Teacher | Student | Class |
|---|---|---|
| Bob | Louis | Normalization |
| Bob | Fred | T-SQL |
| Larry | Fred | Normalization |

Break this down into three sets of data, TeacherStudent, TeacherClass, and StudentClass, respectively:

```
Teacher     Student
----------  -----------
Bob         Louis
Bob         Fred
Larry       Fred


Teacher     Class
----------  ---------------
Bob         Normalization
Bob         T-SQL
Larry       Normalization


Student     Class
----------  -----------
Louis       Normalization
Fred        T-SQL
Fred        Normalization
```

Now, the problem is that we can erroneously infer invalid data from looking at each set of data separately:

- Bob at one time taught Fred.

- Bob taught normalization.

- Fred took a class on normalization.

Hence, from this path through the data, Bob could have been Fred's teacher on normalization. Wrong answer! Larry did that. So, the StudentTeacherClass tables were in Fifth Normal Form already, because we needed all three pieces of information together to state a condition. One thing of note here is that the business rules play a part in our ability to break this table down further. If only one teacher could teach the normalization class, we wouldn't have had any problems with this entity. This is a large part of what makes Fifth Normal Form elusive and difficult to test for.

What can be gleaned from Fifth Normal Form, and indeed all the normal forms, is that when you think you can break down a table into smaller parts with different natural keys, it's likely better to do so. If you can join the parts together to represent the data in the original, less-broken-down form, your database will likely be better for it. Obviously, if you can't reconstruct the table from the joins, then leave it as it is.

# Denormalization

Denormalization is used primarily to improve performance in cases where overnormalized structures are causing overhead to the query processor, and in turn other processes in SQL Server, or to tone down some complexity to make things easier to implement. As I've tried to highlight in this chapter, although it can be argued that denormalizing to Third Normal Form might simplify queries by reducing the number of joins needed, this risks introducing data anomalies. Any additional code written to deal with these anomalies needs to be duplicated in every application that uses the database, thereby increasing the likelihood of human error. The judgment call that needs to be made in this situation is whether a slightly slower (but 100 percent accurate) application is preferable to a faster application of lower accuracy.

It's this book's contention that during logical modeling, we should never step back from our normalized structures to performance-tune our applications proactively. Because this book is centered on OLTP database structures, the most important part of our design is to make certain that our logical model represents all the entities and attributes that the resulting database will hold. Once you start the process of physical modeling (which should be analogous to performance tuning), there might well be valid reasons to denormalize the structures, either to improve performance or to reduce implementation complexity, but neither of these pertain to the *logical* model. We'll always have fewer problems if we implement physically what is true logically. For almost all cases, I always advocate waiting until the physical modeling phase to implement solutions, or at least until we find a compelling reason to do so (such as if some part of our system is failing), before we denormalize.

## Best Practices

The following are a few guiding principles that I use when normalizing a database. If you understand the fundamentals of why to normalize, these five points pretty much cover the entire process:

- *Follow the rules of normalization as closely as possible*: The chapter summary summarizes these rules. These rules are optimized for use with relational database management systems, such as SQL Server. Keep in mind that SQL Server now has, and will continue to add, tools that will not necessarily be of use for normalized structures, because the goal of SQL Server is to be all things to all people. The principles of normalization are 30-plus years old and are still valid today for properly utilizing the core relational engine.

- *All attributes must describe the essence of what's being modeled in the entity*: Be certain to know what that essence is. For example, when modeling a person, only things that describe or identify a person should be included. Anything that is not directly reflecting the essence of what the entity represents is trouble waiting to happen.

- *At least one key must uniquely identify and describe the essence of what the entity is modeling*: Uniqueness alone isn't a sufficient criterion for being an entity's only key. It isn't wrong to have a uniqueness-only key, but it shouldn't be the only key.

- *Choice of primary key isn't necessarily important at this point*: Keep in mind that the primary key is changeable at any time with any candidate key. I have taken a stance that only a surrogate or placeholder key is sufficient for logical modeling, because basically it represents any of the other keys (hence the name *surrogate*). This isn't a required practice; it's just a convenience that must not supplant choice of a proper key.

- *Normalize as far as possible during the logical phase*: There's little to lose by designing complex structures in the logical phase of the project; it's trivial to make changes at this stage of the process. The well-normalized structures, even if not implemented as such, will provide solid documentation on the actual "story" of the data.

## Summary

In this chapter, I've presented the criteria for normalizing our databases so they'll work properly with relational database management systems. At this stage, it's pertinent to summarize quickly the nature of the main normal forms we've outlined in this and the preceding chapter; see Table 4-1.

**Table 4-1.** *Normal Form Recap*

| Form | Rules |
|------|-------|
| First Normal Form | All attributes must be atomic—one value per attribute. All instances of an entity must contain the same number of values. All instances of an entity must be different from one another. |
| Second Normal Form | The entity must be in First Normal Form. All attributes must be a fact about the entire key and not a subset of the key. |
| Third Normal Form | The entity must be in Second Normal Form. An entity is in Third Normal Form if every non-key attribute is a fact about a key attribute. All attributes must be a fact about the key and nothing but the key. |
| BCNF | All attributes are fully dependent on a key; all attributes must be a fact about a key and nothing but a key. An entity is in BCNF if every determinant is a key. |
| Fourth Normal Form | The entity must be in BCNF. There must not be more than one multivalued dependency represented in the entity. |
| Fifth Normal Form | The entity must be in Fourth Normal Form. All relationships are broken down to binary relationships when the decomposition is lossless. |

So, is it always necessary to go through the steps one at a time in a linear fashion? Not exactly. Once you have done this a few times, you'll usually realize when your model is not quite right, and you'll work through the list of three things I mentioned originally:

- *Check attribute shape*: One attribute, one value.

- *Validate the relationships between attributes*: Attributes either are a key or describe something about the entity identified by the key.

- *Scrutinize multivalued dependencies*: Only one per entity. Make sure relationships between three values or tables are correct. Reduce all relationships to binary relationships if possible.

The goal is simple. Make sure that:

*All entities are relations and represent only a single thing!*

By making entities identify a single person, place, thing, or idea, we reduce all the modification anomalies on the data we have stored. In this way, any time we change an attribute of an entity, we're simply changing the description of that single entity and cannot effect an incidental change in the data.

There is also one truth that I feel the need to "slip" into the book right now. You are not done. You are just starting the process of design with the blueprints for the implementation. The blueprints can and almost with certainty will change because of any number of things. You may miss something the first time around or you may discover a technique for modeling something that you didn't know before (hopefully from reading this book!), but don't get too happy yet. It is time to do some real work and build what you have designed (well, after an extra example and a section that kind of recaps the first chapters of the book, but then we get rolling, I promise).

# Bonus Example

In this chapter, I felt that an extra example to fortify the material would be helpful to you to take in the material. Here, we'll work with a small example to tie all the material together. For this chapter, we'll take a cleared check and normalize it. We won't work with an entire check register, but the attributes of the single entity one might arrive at that is the check.

So, I've dummied up the sample document shown in Figure 4-44 (some of the handwriting is my wife's, but most everything else has been "rearranged" to protect the innocent, as well as me).

Note that for variety the names in this section are created using underscore characters between words, instead of Pascal cased.

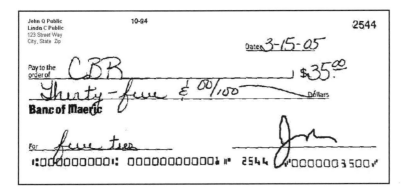

**Figure 4-44.** *Our sample document*

Now, let's create one entity that has all the attributes that we find on the check. First, we go through and identify all the fields on the check, as identified in Figure 4-45. If you wonder why I call them *fields*, it is because a field refers to a physical position of some sort, and a piece of paper has physical locations.

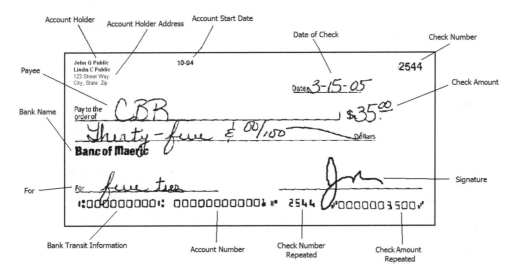

**Figure 4-45.** *The fields that make up the check*

Then, we take these fields and add them as attributes on a single check entity in a new data model, as shown in Figure 4-46.

check

| check_id |
| --- |
| check_number |
| date |
| account_holders |
| account_holders_address |
| payee |
| account_start_date |
| amount |
| bank_name |
| for |
| signed_by |
| bank_transit |
| account_number |

**Figure 4-46.** *Starting data model of the check entity*

First we start with checking these attributes against First Normal Form:

- All attributes must be atomic, one value per attribute.

- All instances of an entity must contain the same number of values.

- All instances of an entity must be different.

Any violations? There are three:

- `account_holders`: Because we can have one or more persons on the account, we ought to make this its own table.

- `account_holders_address`: In the `account_holder` entity, I'll break this down into the parts of an address.

- `bank_transit`: I didn't originally realize it, but this value consists of several values. The transit field is the routing number (four digits), bank number (four digits), and check digit.

I set the check number attribute to be unique, so all instances of the check entity will be unique (you probably realize that check numbers are unique only for a given account, but with the blinders on we pretend we don't know this yet).

We add an `account_holder` table and break down the transit field to two columns (leaving off the check digit, because we won't be using this value outside of this system).

From the information we have, I don't currently know how to make the `account_holder` unique, because people's names are hardly unique. So, I inquire with the client, and it uses its customer's `tax_identification_number` and `tax_identification_number_type`. This is either the `social_security_number` or a number that the person can use to keep his or her SSN private (see Figure 4-47).

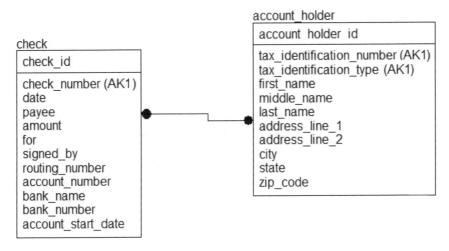

**Figure 4-47.** *The account_holder entity has been added to the model.*

Next, we look for Boyce-Codd violations, because they encompass Second and Third Normal Forms. As a refresher, in BCNF:

- All attributes are fully dependent on a key; all attributes must be a fact about a key and nothing but a key.

- An entity is in BCNF if every determinant is a key.

We determined that the key of the entity is the check_number. None of the other attributes will work as a key. So, we examine the other attributes of the check entity for violations:

- date: The check was produced on a date, so this is fine.

- payee: The check does have a payee, so this is fine.

- account_start_date: This is the date the account was started, not directly associated with the check. So, we add an account entity to the model. We also rearrange the account_holder entity such that it's associated with the account. We look also for any other account-related attributes, in this case, account_number, account_start_date, bank_name, and bank_number. I'll set the key to be the account_number and the bank information.

- bank_name *and* bank_number: These attributes describe a bank, so we create a bank entity. Both the number and the name are acceptable keys.

- amount: Checks have amounts, so this attribute is fine.

- for: The individual check is for a certain purpose, so this is fine.

- signed_by: Because the only person who can sign a check is an account holder, we add a relationship to the account_holder table.

- routing_number: This attribute pertains to the particular account, so I move it to the account.

The changes from our examination of the check entity are shown in the model in Figure 4-48.

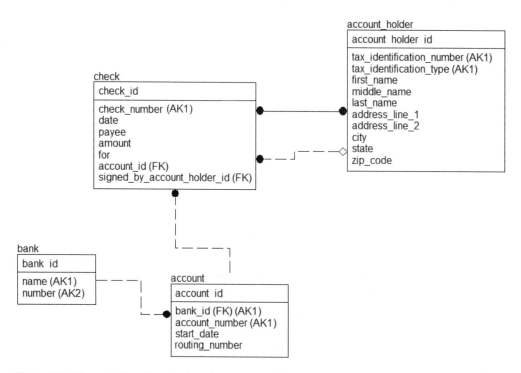

**Figure 4-48.** *The model now has bank and account entities.*

Next we move on to the account_holder entity. The account holder represents a person who has an account, so we change the relationship from being to the check entity to the account entity. We then add an associative entity named account_holder_association. The relationship from account_holder to check for the signed_by relationship is also changed to the account_holder_association entity because we want to record only that account holders sign checks (I don't mind if other people use my deposit slips, but not my checks!). These changes are reflected in Figure 4-49.

We'll look at the next attributes in groups:

- tax_identification_number, tax_identification_type: These values refer to the person who is the account_holder, and as such, belong here.

- first_name, middle_name, last_name: Just as with the identification number attributes, the name of the person certainly belongs here.

- address_line_1, address_line_2, city, state, zip_code: A case could be made that every person on an account might have a unique address, and it would be a correct one. However, we're modeling only a simple check, not a general banking system. The address information for the check goes in the account entity.

Finally, I look around the model again (and again) to validate that the choices I've made still stand. One additional thing I'll go ahead and do is change the unique key for the check to check_number and account_id. Now we're technically set up to record checks from multiple checking accounts. These changes are reflected in the final diagram of our example, shown in Figure 4-50.

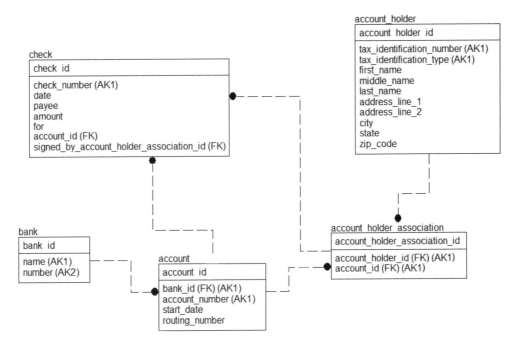

**Figure 4-49.** *Cleaning up the relationship between account_holder and check/account*

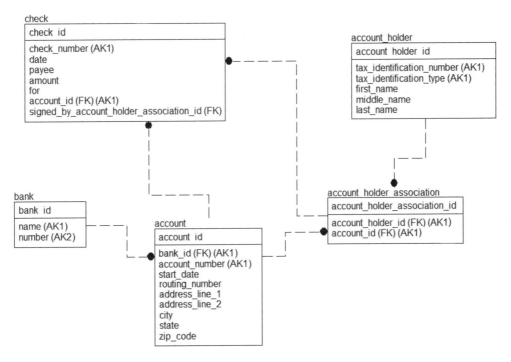

**Figure 4-50.** *Final model for the example*

The only obvious multivalued dependencies for this model revolve around addresses. Is there really only one address per account? (Doubtful.) I already mentioned that address information could be attached to an `account_holder`. Certainly, the `account_holder_association` table could have an address to tell the account holder's information based on the association. The bank has addresses for paying bills to, for corresponding with about problems, and a physical address for branches (branches could be another entity).

Needless to say, in a more complete model, attributes would be required for phone numbers, overdrafts, deposits, and so on. This example was simply to normalize the fields that we found on a check document. We could easily get carried away and end up with a complete model of a banking system that could take an entire chapter of its own, but it's time to get on with the process of implementation in Chapter 5.

# The Story of the Book So Far

This is the "middle" of the process of designing a database, so I want to take a page here and recap the process we have covered:

- You've spent time gathering information, doing your best to be thorough without going *Apocalypse Now* on your client. You know what the client wants, and the client knows that you know what they want.

- Then you looked for tables, columns, attributes, business rules, and so on, in this information and drew a picture, creating a model that gives an overview of the structures in a graphical manner. (The phrase "creating a model" always makes me think about a Frankenstein Cosmetics–sponsored beauty pageant.)

- Finally, these tables were broken down such that every table relayed a single meaning. One noun equals one table, pretty much. I'll bet if it's your first time normalizing, but not your first time working with SQL, you don't exactly love the process of normalization right now. I don't blame you; it's a startling change of mind that takes time to get used to. I know the first time I had to create ten tables instead of one I didn't like it (all those little tables look troublesome the first few times!). Do it a few times, implement a few systems with normalized databases, and it will not only make sense, but you will feel unclean when you have to work with tables that aren't normalized.

---

■**Caution** Also, be careful not to think that this is the end of your logical design process. There will be some solution patterns that may creep into your design later in the process, requiring some change to the model. It is also not rare at all to miss a thing or two in the logical design that does not become apparent until later in the implementation process. If you have done a decent job to this point, the damage will likely be minor (a new attribute here or there), but sometimes it can be quite major (particularly when employing some form of agile methodology done not quite right, leading to missed requirements).

---

If you're reading this book in one sitting (and I *hope* you aren't doing it in the bookstore without buying it), be aware that we're about to switch gears, and I don't want you to pull a muscle in your brain. We're turning away from the theory, and we're going to start working with SQL Server 2008 objects in reality. In all likelihood, it is probably what you thought you were getting when you first chunked down your hard-earned money for the book (or, hopefully your employer's money).

Well, it's here. We're heading off to statements to create and modify objects such as tables, procedures, triggers, and many others. If you aren't excited by this, then you just aren't doing something right.

If you haven't done so, go ahead and get access to a SQL Server, such as the free SQL Server Express from Microsoft. Or download a trial copy from http://www.microsoft.com/sql/. Everything done in this book will work on all versions of SQL Server other than the Compact Edition (or mobile edition, or baby edition, or whatever they have decided to call it by the time you get this book; in 2008 the name changed pretty frequently).

You will also need the AdventureWorks database installed for some of the examples. The version that ships with SQL Server will work fine, or if your server does not have AdventureWorks loaded, you can get it from http://www.microsoft.com/downloads and search for AdventureWorks. Current of this book being published, there is a case-sensitive and case-insensitive version. I assume that you are using the case-insensitive version. I do try my best to maintain proper casing of object names.

# CHAPTER 5

■ ■ ■

# Implementing the Base Table Structures

*The doctor of the future will give no medicine, but will interest her or his patients in the care of the human frame, in a proper diet, and in the cause and prevention of disease.*

—Thomas A. Edison

**M**uch like Thomas Edison expected doctors would be in the future, so must we be as data architects. In the logical design part of this book (the first four chapters), I discussed in quite some detail the process of defining the structure of the data the user needs to store. I did this not so you could solve problems as you observe them but rather so you can avoid problems by preventing them.

In this chapter, I'll take a logical model, convert it into a blueprint for the database implementation, and then create database objects from the model. In other words, I'll walk you through the process of converting a logical database model into an implementation model and in the process implement tables, keys, and relationships that comprise a relational database.

There is almost never a single "correct" design to a corresponding set of data storage and processing needs. In the same way, each person tasked with designing a relational database will take a subtly (or even dramatically) different approach to the design process. The final design will always be, to some extent, a reflection of the person who designed it, though usually all of the reasonable solutions "should" resemble one another. I present here the steps I follow when transforming a logical design into an implementation design. This approach is based on many years of experience and should guide you effectively through the process. Of course, it isn't the only possible approach, but the steps you take in your own designs will be somewhat close to these, if not in the same order (most of the time the steps are done in a nonlinear fashion).

Our logical model was essentially database agnostic and was unaffected by whether the final implementation would be on Microsoft SQL Server, Microsoft Access, Oracle, Sybase, or any relational database management system (heck, even MySQL). However, during this stage, in terms of the naming conventions that are defined, the datatypes chosen, and so on, the design is geared specifically for implementation on SQL Server 2008. Each of the relational engines has its own intricacies and quirks, so it is helpful to understand how to implement on the system you are tasked with. Most people don't have to worry about developing for cross platform, but if you do, the final chapter of this book covers the differences between many of the popular relational engine platforms.

■**Note** For this and subsequent chapters, I'll assume that you have SQL Server 2008 installed on your machine. For the purposes of this book, I recommend you use the Developer Edition, which is available for a small cost from `http://www.microsoft.com/sql/howtobuy/default.aspx`. The Developer Edition gives you all of the functionality of the Enterprise Edition of SQL Server for developing software. It also includes the fully functional Management Studio for developing queries and managing your databases. (The Enterprise Evaluation Edition will also work just fine if you don't have any money to spend.)

Another possibility is SQL Server Express Edition, which is free but doesn't come with the full complement of features that the Developer Edition has, though there is a limited (but complete enough for use with this book) user interface available along with the Express Edition. I won't make required use of any of the extended features, but if you're learning SQL Server, you'll probably want to have the full feature set to play around with. You can acquire the Express Edition at `http://www.microsoft.com/sql/`.

The process I'll take in this chapter is as follows:

- *Review the logical design*: I'll take one last chance to make zero-cost (at least low-cost) changes to the model.

- *Transform the logical model into an implementation model*: I'll look at some of the different design situations that are in (or not in) the logical model that are needed or that make implementing the database in SQL Server unnecessarily difficult.

- *Implement the design*: I'll take the design and build tables in SQL Server.

I'll work on a new example in this chapter, rather than continue with the example of the previous chapters. The reasons for this are twofold. First, it will introduce many different design scenarios in a model that is as simple as possible, and second, it will allow a higher degree of modularity. If you're specifically interested only in this logical-to-physical phase, I won't expect you to have read the previous chapter first to follow through this one.

The main example in this chapter is based on a movie-rental store database. Figure 5-1 shows the logical database design for this application on which I'll base the physical design. You can find larger, printable PDF versions of all large diagrams for this chapter in the Source Code/Download area of the Apress website (`http://www.apress.com`).

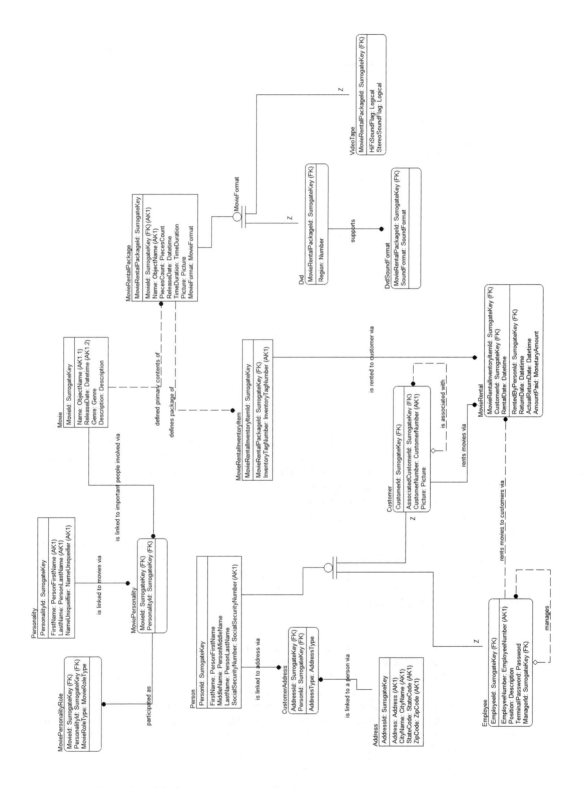

**Figure 5-1.** *Full logical model of movie-rental store database*

For the most part, it should, by this time in the book, be easy enough for you to read the data model, but I should point out a few things. Most important are the entities Movie, MovieRentalPackage, and MovieRentalInventoryItem (see Figure 5-2).

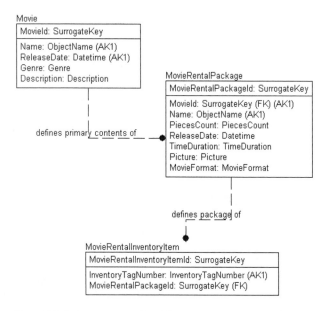

**Figure 5-2.** *Primary example tables*

The Movie table represents a general movie, regardless of how it's packaged. For example, take *The Good, The Bad, and the Ugly*. Several versions of this movie have been released in the United States (where our hypothetical movie store is located), but they're all basically the same film. The Movie table is used to record the fact that this movie may be available for rent at this store in some format. The MovieRentalPackage table documents the packaging of the movie, such as Special Edition, Extended Edition, and so on. It also notes in what format the movie is packaged: DVD or videotape (there could be a case for having another level of normalization for movie edition or packaging). The MovieRentalInventoryItem table represents the actual real-world item that's for rent. Each item for rent gets its own number or bar code that's affixed to the box so the movies can be tracked. These items are what will be tracked as the customer rents movies.

We occasionally diverge from this example to demonstrate specific physical design strategies and choices that cannot easily be illustrated within this model. However, the preceding design will largely drive the narrative of this chapter.

---

■**Note** All diagrams from now on will include the ordering part of the AK symbol to denote unique keys. This isn't, strictly speaking, a standard notation, but it's quite useful for seeing which columns will come first whenever we start to build the key or index. Usually the ordering should be from the most unique column to the least unique. For example, consider an invoiceLineItem table's keys. If you had InvoiceNumber and LineNumber, the InvoiceNumber would be the logical choice for the first column in the index because it's unique for each invoice's items. However, each invoice will have a line number 1, so this wouldn't be a great first column of the index. So the InvoiceNumber column would be AK-labeled 1.1, and the LineNumber column would be AK 1.2. I cover indexing in more detail in Chapter 9.

---

# Reviewing the Logical Design

This review stage is a crucial juncture. Once you start implementing SQL Server objects, it's going to be much harder to change things. (Each change can have a ripple effect, causing other objects to change and hence causing middle-tier and UI design to change, which makes the programming team far less happy than does waiting another afternoon for a final review.) Reviewing the logical design one more time with the users is certainly the prudent thing to do. Despite best efforts and asking the most insightful questions possible during the discovery phase, you'll often find that something is suddenly "remembered" that requires you to make small (or maybe not so small) amendments to your design. The only thing that can be predicted with 100 percent accuracy is that nothing can be predicted with 100 percent accuracy (and even that is probably grounds for a knock-down drag-out argument if you ask the wrong person). Try to describe the design in terms that the user will understand. Although 95 percent of all humans will give you that dog-staring-at-a-stop-sign look if you use the word *cardinality* in a sentence, those same people will have no problem with the concept of a person having between one and three active accounts (or whatever the case may be).

Finally, review your design with the DBAs and developers—they might well have alterations to suggest that will help the design best support the applications that must use it. These suggestions may affect how you approach the next section, "Transforming the Design." There might be architectural concerns as well, depending on the tools being used by the implementation teams.

Just as building engineers take an architect's blueprint and examine it to see what materials are needed and whether everything is realistic, I'll take the logical model and tweak those parts that might be unfeasible or too difficult to implement. Certain parts of an architect's original vision might have to be changed to fit what's realistic, based on factors that weren't known when the blueprint was first conceived, such as ground type, hills, material costs, and so on. We, too, are going to have to go through the process of translating things from raw concept to implementation.

---

■**Note** Every company will have its own set of rules, ideas, standards, and so on. The most important part of the rest of the book is the concepts I will try to share.

---

# Transforming the Design

Hardware and software advances, coupled with data warehousing methodologies, potentially allow you to implement the database almost exactly as it was logically designed. However, you must be careful when designing the physical database, because you should never try to implement something that's entirely too difficult to use in practice.

---

■**Caution** It can be too tempting to give in to the cries of the programmer who thinks so many tables are too "complex" to work with. Data integrity is almost always the most important thing for any corporate application. As with anything, there can be balance, especially when talking about more hobbyist-type applications.

---

In this section, I'll cover the following topics to transform the logical design into the implementation design from which to build the database:

- *Choosing names*: I'll mention naming concerns for tables and columns.
- *Dealing with subtypes*: You can implement subtypes in multiple tables or single tables. I'll cover why this might be done.

- *Determining tree implementation*: Determining what method to implement a tree structure with will be covered (such as an employee/manager structure in the same table).

- *Choosing key implementation*: Throughout the earlier bits of the book, you've made several types of key choices. In this section, you will go ahead and add all the keys to the model.

- *Determining domain implementation*: I'll cover the method to decide datatypes, nullability, and, also important, choosing between using a domain table or a column with a constraint for types of values where you want to have solid constraints on column values.

- *Setting up schemas*: Beginning in SQL Server 2005, you could set up groups of tables as schemas that provide groupings of tables for usage, as well as security.

- *Reviewing the "final" implementation model*: We'll conduct one final review before getting down to the business of producing DDL.

## Choosing Names

The target database for our model is SQL Server, so our table and column naming conventions must adhere to the rules imposed by this database and generally be consistent and logical.

In this section, I'll briefly cover some of the different concerns when naming tables and columns. All of these rules have been the same for the past few versions of SQL Server, certainly 2000, 2005, and now 2008.

### Table Naming

Object names in SQL Server are stored in a system datatype of sysname. The sysname datatype is defined as a 128-character (or less, of course) string using double-byte Unicode characters.

SQL Server's rules for the names of objects consist of two distinct naming methods:

- *Regular identifiers*: The preferred method, with the following rules:

  - The first character must be a letter as defined by Unicode Standard 3.2 (generally speaking, Roman letters A to Z, uppercase and lowercase, though this also includes other letters from other languages), or the underscore character (_). You can find the Unicode Standard at http://www.unicode.org.

  - Subsequent characters can be Unicode letters, numbers, the "at" sign (@), or the dollar sign ($).

  - The name must not be a SQL Server reserved word. There's a large list of reserved words in SQL Server 2008 Books Online (look in the "Reserved Keywords" section). Some of the keywords won't cause an error, but it's better to avoid all keywords if possible.

  - The name cannot contain spaces.

- *Delimited identifiers*: These should have either square brackets or double quotes around the name (though double quotes are allowed only when the SET QUOTED_IDENTIFIER option is set to on). By placing delimiters around an object's name, you can use *any* string as the name. For example, [Table Name] or [3232 fjfa*&(&^(] would both be legal (but really annoying) names. Delimited names are generally a bad idea when creating new tables and should be avoided if possible, because they make coding more difficult. However, they can be necessary for interacting with data tables in other environments.

Interestingly enough, if using quoted identifiers (or bracketed, as SQL Server allows), even a name like this could never harm the database. This sort of name is the kind of thing you have to be careful of when scripting objects, since leaving out the brackets and running your script could cause a table named Students to vanish . . . probably not a cool thing to do.

---

**■Note** If you need to put a ] or even a double quote character in the name, you have to include ]], just like when you need to include a single quote within a string. So, the name fred]olicious would have to be delimited as [fred]]olicious. However, if you find yourself *needing* to include special characters of any sort in your names, take a good long moment to consider whether you really do need this. If you determine after some thinking that you do, please ask someone else for help naming your objects. This is a pretty horrible thing to do and will make working with your objects very cumbersome. Even just including space characters is a bad enough practice that it should be avoided.

---

Although the rules for creating an object name are pretty straightforward, the more important question is, "What kind of names should be chosen?" The answer is predictable: "Whatever you feel is best, as long as others can read it." This might sound like a cop-out, but there are more naming standards than there are data architects (on the day we're writing this, I actually had two independent discussions about how to name several objects). The standard I generally go with is the standard that was used in the logical model, that being Pascal-cased names. With space for 128 characters, there's little reason to do much abbreviating.

---

**■Caution** Because most companies have existing systems, it's a must to know the shop standard for naming tables so that it matches existing systems and so that new developers on your project will be more likely to understand your database and get up to speed more quickly. The key thing to make sure of, though, is that you keep your full logical names intact for documentation purposes.

---

As an example, let's consider the name of the object that will be used in the sample model to store individual items for rental. The following list shows several different ways to build the name of this object:

- movie_rental_inventory_item (or sometimes, by some awful mandate, an all-caps version MOVIE_RENTAL_INVENTORY_ITEM): Use underscores to separate values. Most programmers aren't big friends of underscores, because they're cumbersome to type until you get used to them.

- [movie rental inventory item] *or* "movie rental inventory item": Delimited by brackets or quotes. This is not favored by anyone really, because it's impossible to use this name when building variables in code, and it's very easy to make mistakes with them. Being forced to use double quotes as delimiters (which is the ANSI standard) can be troublesome because many other languages use double quotes to denote strings (in SQL you should always uses single quotes!). On the other hand, the brackets [ and ] don't denote strings, though they aren't standard and are a Microsoft-only convention that will not port well if you need to do any kind of cross-platform programming.

- MovieRentalInventoryItemtelevisionScheduleItem *or* movieRentalInventoryItem: Pascal or camel case (respectively), using mixed case to delimit between words. I'll use Pascal style in the examples, because it's the style I like. (Hey, it's my book. You can choose whatever style you want!)

- mvRentlInvItem *or* mvrent_item *or* [mv rnt itm] *(something along these lines)*: Abbreviated forms. These are problematic because you must be careful always to abbreviate the same word in the same way in all your databases. You must maintain a dictionary of abbreviations, or you'll get multiple abbreviations for the same word; for example, getting "description" as "desc," "descr," "descrip," and/or "description."

Choosing names for objects is ultimately a personal choice but should never be made arbitrarily and should be based on existing corporate standards, existing software, and legibility. The most important thing to try to achieve is internal consistency. Naming, ownership, and datatypes are all things that will drive you nuts when not done consistently, because they keep everyone guessing what will be used next time. Your goal as an architect is that your users can use your objects easily and with as little thinking about structure as possible.

---

■**Note**  There is something to be said about the quality of corporate standards as well. If you have an archaic standard, like one that was based on the mainframe team's standard back in the 19th century, you really need to consider trying to change the standards so you don't end up with names like HWWG01_TAB_RENTALSTORE_MOVIE_T just because the shop standards say so (and yes, I do know when the 19th century was).

---

## Column Naming

The naming rules for columns are the same as for tables as far as SQL Server is concerned. As for how to choose a name for a column—again, it's one of those tasks for the individual architect, based on the same sorts of criteria as before (shop standards, best usage, and so on). This book follows this set of guidelines:

- Other than the primary key, my feeling is that the table name should rarely be included in the column name. For example, in an entity named Person, it isn't necessary to have columns called PersonName or PersonSocialSecurityNumber. No column should be prefixed with the table name other than with these two exceptions:

  - A surrogate key such as PersonId. This reduces the need for role naming (modifying names of attributes to adjust meaning, especially used in cases where multiple migrated foreign keys exist).

  - Columns that are naturally named with the entity name in them, such as PersonNumber, PurchaseOrderNumber, or something that's common in the language of the client and used as a domain-specific term.

- The name should be as descriptive as possible. Use few abbreviations in names. There are a couple notable exceptions:

  - *Extremely complex names*: Much like in table names, if you have a name that contains multiple parts, such as "Conglomerated Television Rating Scale," you might want to implement a name such as ConTvRatScale, even though it might take some training before your users become familiar with its meaning.

  - *Recognized abbreviations*: As an example, if you were writing a purchasing system and you needed a column for a purchase-order table, you could name the object PO, because this is widely understood. Often users will desire this, even if some abbreviations don't seem that obvious.

  - *Pronounced abbreviations:* If a value is read naturally as the abbreviation, then it can be better to use the abbreviation. For example, I always use id instead of identifier, first because it's a common abbreviation that's known to most people and second because the surrogate key of the Widget table is naturally pronounced Widget-Eye-Dee, not Widget-Identifier.

- Usually, the name should end in a "class" word that distinguishes the function of the column. This class word gives a general idea of the purpose of the attribute and general expectation of datatype. It should not *be* the datatype, necessarily. For example:

  - *name*: Denotes the column is a string of characters that names some item

  - *code*: Denotes the column is a string of characters that gives a short, human-readable value to know the row by

  - *id*: Used as an identifier, often a surrogate key

  - *time*: Represents a point in time, often a value with date and time values, but could be a time-only value.

  - *date*: Denotes the column would contain a date value, representing the entire day, and not just a point in time

**Note** There are many possible class words that are used, and this book is not about giving you all the standards to follow at that level. Too many variances from organization to organization make that too difficult. Spend 30 minutes on the newsgroups answering questions, and you will see that this is true.

I should point out that I didn't mention a Hungarian-style notation to denote the type of the column for a reason. I've never been a big fan of this style, and neither are a large number of the professional architects that I know. If you aren't familiar with Hungarian notation, it means prefixing the names of columns and variables with an indicator of the datatype and possible usage. For example, you might have a variable called `vc100_columnName` to indicate a `varchar(100)` datatype. Or you might have a Boolean or bit column named `bIsCar` or `bCarFlag`.

In my opinion, such prefixes are very much overkill, because it's easy to tell the type from other documentation you can get from SQL Server metadata. Class word usage indicators go at the end of the name and give you enough of an idea of what a column is used for without spelling out the exact implementation details. Consider what happens if you want to change the type of a column from `varchar(100)` to `varchar(200)` because the data is of a different size than was estimated. If you then have to change the name of the column, the user interface must change, the ETL to the data warehouse has to change, and all scripts and procedures have to change, even if there's no other reason to change. Otherwise, the change could be trivial, possibly needing to expand the size of only a few variables (and in some languages, this wouldn't be required).

A particularly hideous (in my opinion at least) practice that is common is to include something in the name to indicate that a column is a column, such as `colFirstName` or `columnCity`. Please don't do this (please?). It's clear by the context in which columns are used that a column is a column. It can be used only as a column. This practice, just like the other Hungarian-style notations, makes good sense in a functional programming language where the type of object isn't always clear just from context, but this practice is never needed with SQL tables.

By keeping the exact type out of the names, you avoid clouding the implementation interface that end users will be exposed to by adding bits and pieces of data in the names that are useless to many users. One of the beauties of using relational databases is that an abstraction layer hides the implementation details. To expose them via column naming is to set in concrete what changing requirements might make obsolete (for example, extending the size of a variable to accommodate a future business need).

■**Note** I'll use the same naming conventions for the implementation model as I did for the logical model: Pascal-cased names with a few abbreviations (mostly class words, like id for "identifier"). I'll also use a Hungarian-style notation for objects other than tables and columns, such as constraints, and for coded objects, such as procedures. This is mostly to keep the names unique and avoid clashes with the table and column names, plus it is easier to read in a list that contains multiple types of objects (the tables are the objects with no prefixes). Tables and columns are commonly used directly by users. They write queries and build reports directly using database object names and shouldn't need to change the displayed name of every column and table.

# Dealing with Subtypes

Dealing with categories and subtypes is one of the most important elements in determining how logical entities transform into tables. A category is a group of entities that can be divided into a number of different *types* of the whole. Each group has a supertype and one or more subtypes, and all members of the supertype are included in one or more of the subtypes.

For example, there might exist a person category, consisting of a person subtype, and subtypes that extend the meaning of "person"—for example, employee, teacher, customer, and so on. Subtypes are particularly significant in logical design, but don't be too quick to rush to a particular implementation, because there are also good reasons to keep them intact in our physical design too. I'll now present examples of cases where you *will* and *will not* want to transform the subtyped entities directly into tables.

One of the primary tests I use to decide whether to "roll" up the subtype into one table is how similar the subtypes are. If they share many characteristics but just have some small differences, roll them up. If there are major differences, it's generally best to leave them as different tables.

## Example 1: Rolling Up Subtypes

Consider from our model the MovieRentalPackage entity that represents the different configurations for rent. DVDs and videotapes have several different characteristics that customers will be interested in when they're choosing which package they want to rent. So, the logical model specifies two sub-types, VideoTape and Dvd, based on the discriminator MovieFormat, which can have values 'VideoTape' or 'Dvd' (see Figure 5-3).

■**Note** In the next edition of this book, I'm probably going to have to change this example to use different types of DVD (HD, BluRay, and so on), rather than videotapes. By then some of the younger readers may just furrow their brows when the term *videotape* is used.

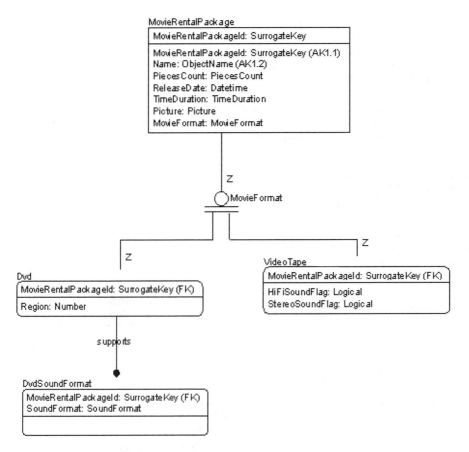

**Figure 5-3.** *MovieRentalPackage subtype*

The format is interesting from an informational standpoint because DVDs have many more features than videos, the most important of which are region encoding and the sound format. There's a special DvdSoundFormat entity for DVDs as a many-to-many relationship, because DVDs support multiple sound formats on the same discs. For the VideoTape type, there are columns only for hi-fi and stereo sound.

A few things about this implementation are interesting:

- To create a new media rental, you have to create rows in at least two tables (MovieRentalPackage and VideoTape or Dvd, and another in DvdSoundFormat for a DVD). This isn't a tremendous problem but can require some special handling.

- To see a list of all the items available for rental, including their sound properties, you have to write a moderately complex query that joins MovieRentalPackage with VideoTape and union this with another query between MovieRentalPackage and Dvd, which might be too slow or simply too cumbersome to deal with.

These are common issues with subtypes. You have to decide how valuable it is to keep a given set of tables implemented as a subtype. When considering what to do with a subtype relationship, one of the most important tasks is to determine how much each of the subtyped entities have in common and how many of their attributes they have in common.

A simple survey of the attributes of the subtyped tables in this example shows that they have much in common. In some cases, it's simply a matter of cardinality. Take the DVD: `RegionEncoding` is specific to this medium, but some videos have different versions, and technically every video product has an aspect ratio (the ratio of the height and width of the picture) that will be of interest to any enthusiast. Although it's true that you can specify the sound properties of a videotape using two simple checkboxes, you can use the same method of specifying the sound as you do for a DVD. You'd then have to enforce a limit on the cardinality of `SoundFormat` on a video, while `Dvd` might have up to eight different sound formats documented in the `MovieRentalPackageSoundFormat` table.

Redraw the subtype relationship as shown in Figure 5-4.

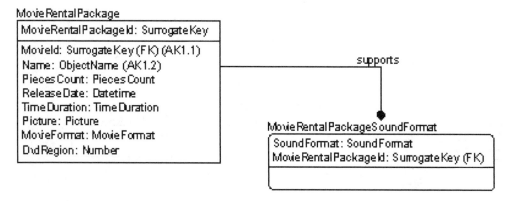

**Figure 5-4.** *Rolled up subtyped table*

The last point that has to be made is that, because the structure has changed and you're storing multiple types of information in the same entity, you must be careful not to allow improper data to be entered into the table. For example, when `MediaFormat` is `'VideoTape'`, the `DvdRegion` value doesn't apply and must be set to `NULL`. It's also true that some of the formats that will be used won't be applicable to `'VideoTape'` but would apply to `'Dvd'`. In this way, the structure becomes less and less self-documenting, requiring more code to keep everything straight and requiring constraints and triggers, because the values in one table are based on the values in another.

Rolling up (or combining) the subtype into a single table can seem to make implementation easier and more straightforward. The problem is that you're offloading the work of keeping things straight to triggers, rather than relying on the structure of the tables to dictate what values make sense. This in turn increases modification time and costs down the road.

---

■**Caution** Note also that `NULL` means something different than previously. Here, `NULL` means the inapplicability of a value, rather than a value that isn't known.

---

## Example 2: Leaving As Separate Tables

As a second example, let's look at a case where it certainly doesn't make sense to roll up the subtype. You generally have subtypes that shouldn't be rolled up when you have two (or more) objects that share a common ancestor, but, once subtyped, the subtypes of the items have little or no relationship to one another. Look at Figure 5-5.

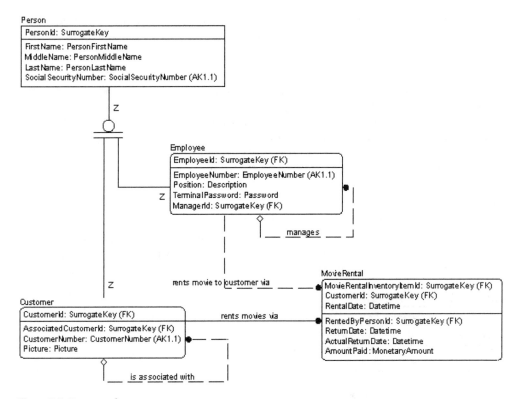

**Figure 5-5.** *Person subtype*

There's a Person table that has a name and other attributes, including some that are implemented as additional tables with relationships to the Person table (in our simplistic model, only address information has been included). In the example, employees and customers are both people, but the similarities in how the data is treated end there. So, in this case, it's best to leave the subtype as it is.

The only concern here is that, when someone wants to deal with the data, he or she has to touch multiple tables. Is this a problem? Not really, mostly because it's rare that you'd deal with a Customer and an Employee in the same query *as the same thing*. Even if a person is both things, an Employee and a Customer (which is an acceptable derivative of the subtype), you are not going to list employees and customers in the same list. You might want to indicate that a customer is also an employee (such as to give them higher late fees for wasting company money!), which can easily be done with a subquery.

So in this particular case, I'll leave the structures implemented exactly as they were designed using a subclassed architecture.

Determining when to roll up a table is one of those things that comes with time and experience. In most cases, the logical nature of the data is best preserved by implementing subtypes exactly how they're logically modeled, as follows:

- Consider rolling up when the subtyped tables are similar in characteristics to the parent table, especially when most columns will frequently be seen in a list together.

- Leave as subtypes when the data in the subtypes shares the common underpinnings but isn't logically related to the rest of the data in additional ways.

As you'll see later, in many cases, the primary features that make subtypes more reasonable to use revolve around creating views that make, for example, the Employee table look as if it contains the values for Person as well.

---

**Tip** A third alternative that I'll mention here only in passing is to have an Employee table and a Customer table that aren't implemented as subtypes. This can also be a valid way to deal with subtypes, but it does cause some things to be more difficult to implement, because now the same person has to have their information entered twice, which can cause confusion. This also makes the requirement inferred by the subtype (that a person cannot be a customer and an employee at the same time) difficult to implement.

---

# Determining Tree Implementation

Chapter 2 discussed tree structures as being rows in one table that are related to other rows in the same table. In our sample model, we will deal with the customer/associated customer using the tree structure as indicated in Figure 5-6.

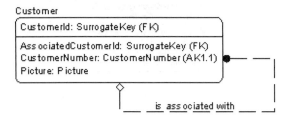

**Figure 5-6.** *Customer table example of a tree structure*

In this tree structure, the root nodes of each tree are the people who are the primary customers. The leaf nodes are customers who are on the same account. The main thing to understand about tree structures is that some people like to separate the structure from the data itself, and in many cases this can certainly make for a more descriptive structure. For example, in our Customer entity, the tree structure could be changed to the structure in Figure 5-7.

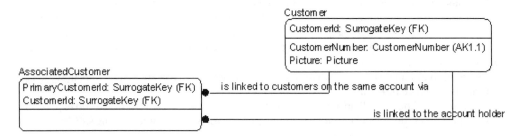

**Figure 5-7.** *Alternative modeling of a tree structure*

Unless there's a need for a row to have multiple parents, I usually just stick to the recursive relationship. It's easier to implement and just as valid. (I'll revert the Customer table to the original form it was in.)

Other methods that exist tend to include metadata about the tree in data, rather than just relying on the data in the tree. Metadata includes information such as the level in the tree, siblings, and so on. I won't delve deeper to cover these, but Adam Machanic includes a very nice chapter in his book *Expert SQL Server 2005 Development* (Apress, 2007), and the famed Joe Celko has a method called the Nested Sets and has written an entire book on the subject: *Joe Celko's Trees and Hierarchies in SQL for Smarties* (Morgan Kaufmann, 2004). There are also tons of resources on the Web giving various methods for implementing trees using various metadata formats. Most any way you want to implement trees will be fine, as long as it's equivalent in data to the logical model.

In 2008, Microsoft has added another method for dealing with hierarchies with the new `hierarchyId` datatype. Instead of putting the key of the customer as a relationship, the `hierarchyId` column maintains the hierarchy of values for you. So, you could model it as shown here.

Customer

| Customerld: SurrogateKey |
| --- |
| CustomerHierarchyId: HierarchyId<br>CustomerNumber: CustomerNumber<br>Picture: Picture |

Generally, I would use the parent/child version of the hierarchy when dealing with a situation like we have here, with a simple association of customers, because it is a very natural way to implement a relationship, particularly when it is informational in nature. However, the `hierarchyId` holds great promise to make implementing trees in SQL far easier. In Appendix C (which will be available as bonus, downloadable content), I will give an extended example of how the two different implementations can be done.

## Choosing Key Implementation

As discussed several times in the logical modeling chapters, defining keys is one of the most important tasks in database design. In this section, I won't look at why keys are defined but rather at how to implement them in the implementation model. I've already discussed two different types of unique keys:

- *Primary*: Contains the primary access to a row in the table
- *Alternate*: Contains alternate access to a row in the table; also protects any unique conditions that need to exist amongst one or more columns in the table

Primary and unique keys are hybrid objects—they are constraints, but physically they are implemented by applying a unique index. The distinction between an index and constraint should be understood. A constraint declares that some factor must be true, and for key constraints, this is declaring that the values in the selected columns must be unique. An index is a physical construct used specifically to speed up some operation (and in this case SQL Server is applying a unique index to speed up checking for duplicate values).

In the final subsection, I will add the keys to the example data model.

---

■**Tip** A basic understanding of how indexes work will give you a base level to determine what kinds of indexes to use. If you don't understand how SQL Server stores data and implements indexes in SQL Server 2008, read Chapter 9 where I give an overview of disk structures, which includes indexes. The most important thing to do is to make sure that primary key and unique constraints are applied on all the keys defined in the logical design phase.

---

## Primary Key

Choosing a primary key for implementation is an important choice. This value will be migrated to other tables as a reference, or *pointer*, to a particular value. Choosing a primary key style is also one of the most argued about topics on the newsgroups. In this book, I'll be reasonably agnostic about the whole thing, and I'll present several methods for choosing the implemented primary key (after reading the entire book, you'll no doubt know my personal style).

Presumably, during the logical phase you've identified all the different ways to uniquely identify a row. Hence, there should be several choices for the primary key:

- Using an existing column (or set of columns)
- Deriving a new surrogate column to represent the row

Each of these choices has pros and cons. I'll look at them in the following sections.

### Basing a Primary Key on Existing Columns

In many cases, a table will have an obvious, easy-to-use primary key. This is especially true when talking about independent entities. For example, take an entity such as a product. It would often have a productNumber defined. A person usually has some sort of identifier, either government issued or company issued. (For example, my company has an employeeNumber that I have to put on all documents, particularly when they need to write me a check.)

The primary keys for dependent entities then generally take the primary key of the independent entity, add one or more attributes, and—presto—primary key.

For example, I have a Ford SVT Focus, made by the Ford Motor Company, so to identify this particular model I might have a row in the Manufacturer table for Ford Motor Company (as opposed to GM or something). Then I'd have an automobileMake row with a key of manufacturerName = 'Ford Motor Company' and makeName = 'Ford' (instead of Lincoln, Mercury, Jaguar, and so on), style = 'SVT', and so on, for the other values. This gets messy to deal with, because the key of the automobileModelStyle table would be used in many places to describe which products are being shipped to which dealership. Note that this isn't about the size in terms of the performance of the key, just the number of values that make up the key. Performance will be better the smaller the key, as well, but this is true not only of the number of columns, but this also depends on the size of the values.

Note that the complexity in a real system such as this would be compounded by the realization that you have to be concerned with model year, possibly body style, different prebuilt packages, and so on.

### Basing a Primary Key on a New, Surrogate Value

A common thing to do is to use only a single column for the primary key, regardless of the size of the other keys. In this case, you'd specify that every table will have a single primary key and implement alternate keys in your tables, as shown in Figure 5-8.

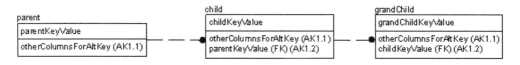

**Figure 5-8.** *Single-column key example*

Note that in this scenario, all of your relationships will be implemented as nonidentifying type relationships, though they will all be required values (no NULLs). Functionally this is the same as if the parentKeyValue was migrated from parent through child and down to grandChild, though it makes it harder to see in the model.

This method does have some useful advantages:

- *Every table has a single-column primary key*: It's much easier to develop applications that use this key, because every table will have a key that follows the same pattern. It also makes code generation easier to follow because it is always understood how the table will look, relieving you from having to deal with all the other possible permutations of key setups.

- *The primary key index will be small*: Thus, operations that use the index to access a row in the table will be faster. Most update and delete operations will likely modify the data by accessing the data based on primary keys that will use this index.

- *Joins between tables will be easier to code*: That's because all migrated keys will be a single column. Plus, if you use a surrogate key that is named TableName + Suffix, there will be less thinking to do when setting up the join.

There can be disadvantages to this method, such as always having to join to a table to find out what the value of the migrated key means, plus (in our example tables) you would have to join from the grandChild table through the child table to get values from parent. Because the goals of our OLTP system are to keep keys small, speed up modifications, and ensure data consistency, this strategy is not only acceptable but favorable.

Another issue is that some parts of the self-documenting nature of relationships are obviated because using only single-column keys eliminates all identifying relationships. The next choice is what data to use for the key. Let's look at two methods of implementing these keys, either by deriving the key from some other data or by using a meaningless surrogate value.

### Deriving a Key

By deriving a key, I'm referring to using some value from the data to use as the key, either in a stripped-down version or exactly as it is. For example, take the tables in Figure 5-9 from the model we're working with.

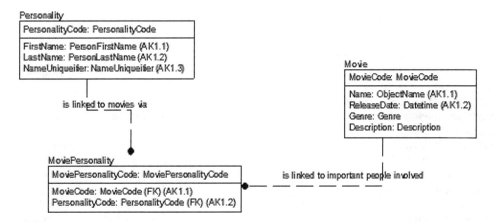

**Figure 5-9.** *Personality, Movie, and MoviePersonality tables*

If there were an actor `'John Smith (II)'` who worked in the movie *Blazing Adders*, you might have the following three key values:

- PersonalityCode: `'john-smith-ii'`
- MovieCode: `'blazing-adders'`
- MoviePersonalityCode: `'john-smith-ii--blazing-adders'`

(II is commonly called a *uniqueifier*, a meaningless value added to force uniqueness, because there have been other people named John Smith who were in the actor's union. SQL Server uses something like this internally to make clustered index keys unique, which will be discussed in Chapter 9.)

The first two seem reasonably natural, but the third is pretty clunky. You could use some other derivation, or you could use parts of the words or let the users come up with something whenever they create the row.

This sort of key strategy is seen quite often in the real world, for things such as model numbers of products, serial numbers, automotive VIN numbers, license numbers, and so on. Part of the key might not have any actual meaning or, like in an employeeId, it might be that the hiring department is part of the number. Social Security numbers (SSNs) have some information embedded in them, such as the state where they were issued. The key value need not be understandable to its user. Often keys like this will include some randomness to support uniqueness and just as often some form of check digit to make sure that not just any random string of characters can be used. This is common with account number key values.

For example, you could use a check digit. Say you've defined a key to be AANNNNC, where A equals any letter from A to Z (excluding O), N equals a numeric digit, and C is a check digit. You might calculate the value by taking the sum of digits together (for letters taking the position of the letters in the alphabet), except for the last digit. This last (check) digit is calculated from the one's-place sum of the other digits (so if it were 59, the check digit would be 9). For example, say the base key is `'AA1111'`:

A = 1, A = 1, so 1 + 1 + (1 + 1 + 1 + 1 ) = 6

`'AA11116'` would be the key value. `'AA11115'` would be an invalid value. Say the base value were QC1343:

Q = 17, C = 3, so 17 + 3 + (1 + 3 + 4 + 3) = 31

`'QC13431'` would be the key value. This is a good key strategy, if you can come up with random values such that you don't have collisions when you generate keys. This strategy also serves as a deterrent to guessing the value. Credit card numbers have this property, because not every 16-digit value could be used as a valid account number.

As alluded to earlier, sometimes a natural key cannot be 100 percent derived from data. For example, say you wanted to represent each can of food in a model for a grocery store. For the DVDs this is easy: slap a sticker on each box. Although we could do this for cans of food, there's little reason to do so. We might have hundreds of cans of corn, and who cares which is which? One solution is to have a single row that identifies the natural key of a can of corn (manufacturer, type of food, size of can, UPC barcode, and so on) and add a surrogate key. Then, when a customer purchases ten cans of corn, ten randomly chosen rows are tagged as being purchased.

The alternative would be to identify the same natural key but then have a single row with an accumulator column stating how many cans of corn are available, incrementing and decrementing it every time stock is accumulated or sold. Which method is right? It depends. In a data warehouse, it's important to have every row in a fact table have the same granularity (referred to as the *grain*). Hence, having a row for every item sold could easily be helpful. It would also make it easier to categorize sales. On the other hand, having just one row that gets modified all the time will take up much less space, and you can build the same kinds of rows for your data warehouse by getting information out of your sales tables or by taking a reading periodically and inferring the amount of sales based on the number that has changed (taking into mind the number of values that were added for the day too!). I don't think either idea is right or wrong, but they're certainly different.

One thing is for sure: a key of this nature should be memorable if a user will use it directly. The values should either be broken up into memorable chunks or the values should just be short enough. For example, SSNs are in the format XXX-XX-XXXX so users can remember them. People can generally remember about six to nine values, certainly if they're forced to reuse them often enough.

### Using Only a Meaningless Surrogate Key

Another popular way to define a primary key is to simply use a meaningless surrogate key like we've modeled previously, such as using a column with the IDENTITY property, which automatically generates a unique value. In this case, you rarely let the user have access to the value of the key but use it primarily for programming.

It's exactly what was done for most of the entities in the logical models worked on in previous chapters: simply employing the surrogate key while we didn't know what the actual value for the primary key would be. This method has one nice property:

*You never have to worry about what to do when the primary key value changes.*

Once the key is generated for a row, it never changes, even if all the data changes. This is an especially nice property when you need to do analysis over time. No matter what any of the other values in the table have been changed to, as long as the surrogate key value represents the same thing, you can still relate it to its usage in previous times. Consider the case of a row that identifies a company. If the company is named Bob's Car Parts and it's located in Topeka, Kansas, but then it hits it big, moves to Detroit, and changes the company name to Car Parts Amalgamated, only one row is touched: the row where the name is located. Just change the name, and it's done. Keys may change, but not primary keys. Also, if the method of determining uniqueness changes for the object, the structure of the database needn't change beyond dropping one UNIQUE constraint and adding another.

Over time, in a data warehouse this company would be the same company, and the name change would be reflected, as would the company's location and any other information that changed. This allows some neat historical queries to be done. Using surrogate keys makes the ETL to load this data far easier.

Using a surrogate key value doesn't in any way prevent you from creating additional single part keys, like we did in the previous section. In fact, for most tables, having a small code value is likely going to be a desired thing. Many clients hate long values, because they involve "too much typing." For example, say you have a value such as "Fred's Car Mart." You might want to have a code of "FREDS" for them as the shorthand value for their name. Some people are even so programmed by their experiences with ancient database systems that had arcane codes that they desire codes such as "XC10" to refer to "Fred's Car Mart."

In the demo model, all the keys are already set to a surrogate key, except the many-to-many resolution tables. So, you change all these to single-part keys and add alternate keys for the previous primary keys (see Figure 5-10).

MovieRental

| MovieRentalInventoryItemId: SurrogateKey (FK) |
| --- |
| CustomerId: SurrogateKey (FK) |
| RentalDate: Datetime |
| RentedByEmployeeId: SurrogateKey (FK) |
| ReturnDate: Datetime |
| ActualReturnDate: Datetime |
| AmountPaid: MonetaryAmount |

**Figure 5-10.** *MovieRental table with composite primary key*

This becomes the table in Figure 5-11. Notice too that the table is no longer modeled with rounded corners, because the primary key no longer is modeled with any migrated keys in the primary key.

MovieRental

| MovieRentalId: SurrogateKey |
|---|
| RentalDate: Datetime (AK1.1)<br>MovieRentalInventoryItemId: SurrogateKey (FK) (AK1.2)<br>CustomerId: SurrogateKey (FK) (AK1.3)<br>RentedByEmployeeId: SurrogateKey (FK)<br>ReturnDate: Datetime<br>ActualReturnDate: Datetime<br>AmountPaid: MonetaryAmount |

**Figure 5-11.** *MovieRental table with single-column surrogate primary key*

Having a common style for every table is valuable to have a common pattern for programming with the tables as well. Because every table has a single-column key that isn't updatable and is the same datatype, it's possible to exploit this in code, making code generation a far more straightforward process. Note once more that nothing should be lost when you use surrogate keys, because a surrogate of this style replaces an existing natural key.

By implementing tables using this pattern, I'm covered in two ways: I always have a single primary key value, but I always have a key that cannot be modified, which eases the difficulty for loading a warehouse. No matter the choice of human-accessible key, surrogate keys are the style of key that I use for all tables in databases I create, for every table.

## Don't Forget the Alternate Keys

If you use either of these approaches to a single part key, this is not the end of the key choice. You have to make sure you don't forget the values that make up the multipart keys in your table.

A primary key that's manufactured or even meaningless in the logical model shouldn't be your only defined key. One of the ultimate mistakes made by people using such keys is to ignore the fact that two rows whose only difference is a system-generated value are not different. That's because from the user's perspective, all the data that users will value is the same. At this point, it becomes more or less impossible to tell one row from another.

For example, take Table 5-1, a snippet Part table, where PartID is an IDENTITY column and is the primary key for the table.

**Table 5-1.** *Sample Data to Demonstrate How Surrogate Keys Don't Make Good Logical Keys*

| PartID | PartNumber | Description |
|---|---|---|
| 1 | XXXXXXXX | The X part |
| 2 | XXXXXXXX | The X part |
| 3 | YYYYYYYY | The Y part |

How many individual items are represented by the rows in this table? Well, there seem to be three, but are rows with PartIDs 1 and 2 actually the same row, duplicated? Or are they two different rows that should be unique but were keyed in incorrectly? You need to consider at every step along the way whether a human being could not pick which row they want from a table without knowledge

of the surrogate key. This is why there should be a key of some sort on the table to guarantee uniqueness, in this case likely on `PartNumber`.

---

■**Caution** As a rule, each of your tables should have a natural key that means something to the user and that
can uniquely identify each row in your table. In the very rare event that you cannot find a natural key (perhaps, for
example, a table that provides a log of events), then it is acceptable to make up some artificial key, but this is a
very rare occurrence, and you should really make sure you aren't just being lazy when you do this.

---

For each of the tables that don't already have a single-value surrogate key, I'll go through and
change the table to include the surrogate key (see Figure 5-12) and then make the previous primary
key an alternate key (*very important*).

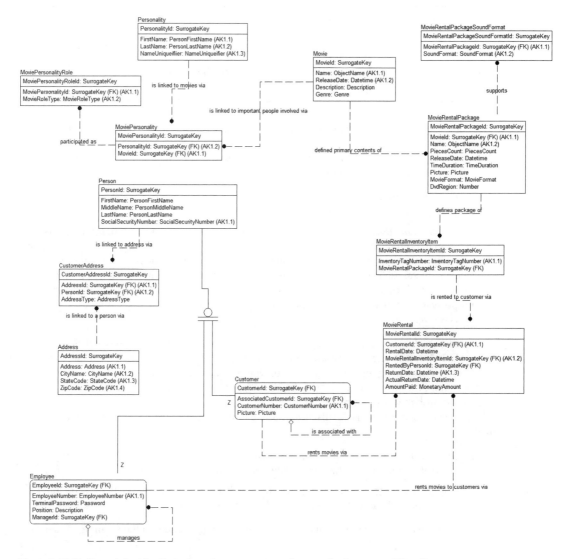

**Figure 5-12.** *Full model with all single-column surrogate keys and subtype modifications*

# Determining Domain Implementation

In logical modeling, the concept of domains involves specifying templates for datatypes and column types that are used over and over again. In physical modeling, domains are the same but with additional properties added for physical needs.

For example, in the logical modeling phase, domains are defined for such columns as name and description, which occur regularly across a database. The reason for defining domains might not have been completely obvious at the time of logical design, but it becomes clear during physical modeling. For example, for the ObjectName domain that's used often in the MovieRental model, you might specify the contents of Table 5-2.

**Table 5-2.** *Sample Domain*

| Property | Setting |
|---|---|
| Name | ObjectName |
| Nullability | NOT NULL |
| Datatype | varchar(100) |
| CHECK constraint | LEN(RTRIM(Name)) > 0 — may not be blank |
| DEFAULT | n/a |

I'll defer the CHECK constraint and DEFAULT bits to Chapter 6, where I discuss data protection using these objects.

Several tables will have a name column, and you'll use this template to build every one of them. This serves at least two purposes:

- *Consistency*: Define every name column in precisely the same manner; there will never be any question about how to treat the column.

- *Ease of implementation*: If the tool you use to model and implement databases supports the creation of domain and template columns, you can simply use the template to build similar columns with the same pattern, and you won't have to set the values over and over, which leads to mistakes! (Even using proper tools, I always miss some minor naming or typing issue that ends up in the final model that just irks me forever.) If you have tool support for property inheritance, when you change a property in the definition, the values change everywhere.

Domains aren't a requirement of logical or physical database design, nor does SQL Server use them precisely, but they enable easy and consistent design and are a great idea. Of course, consistent modeling is always a good idea regardless of whether you use a tool to do the work for you. As mentioned when we started out with domains, if you're doing modeling without a tool that supports it, you'd probably give this process a miss.

In the next two subsections, I'll discuss a couple topics concerning how to implement domains:

- *Implementing as a column or table*: You need to decide whether a value should simply be entered into a column or whether to implement a new table to manage the values.

- *Choosing the datatype*: SQL Server gives you a wide range of datatypes to work with, and I'll discuss some of the issues concerning making the right choice.

And finally, in the last section I will implement the datatype choices in the example model.

> ## NULLS
>
> As discussed in logical modeling, values for an attribute, now being translated to a physical column, may be optional or mandatory. Whether a column value is mandatory or optional is translated in the physical model as nullability. Before discussing how to implement NULLs, it's necessary to briefly discuss what NULL means. Although it can be inferred that a column defined as NULL means that the data is optional, this is an incomplete definition. A NULL value should be read as "unknown value." If you need to specify explicitly that a value doesn't apply, it's best to implement a value that explicitly states this. In this case, *optionality* means it's optional to specify the value.

## Implement as a Column or Table?

Although many domains have almost unlimited possible values (of course, all datatypes have a finite set of values), often a domain will specify a fixed set of values that a column might have that is less than can be fit into one of the base datatypes. For example, in the demonstration table Movie, a column Genre has a domain of Genre (see Figure 5-13).

Movie

| Movieid: SurrogateKey |
| --- |
| Name: ObjectName (AK1.1)<br>ReleaseDate: Datetime (AK1.1)<br>Genre: Genre<br>Description: Description |

**Figure 5-13.** *Movie table with domains modeled as columns*

You could specify this domain as in Table 5-3.

**Table 5-3.** *Genre Domain*

| Property | Setting |
| --- | --- |
| Name | Genre |
| Nullability | NOT NULL |
| Datatype | varchar(16) |
| CHECK constraint | IN ('Comedy', 'Drama', 'Family', 'Special Interest') |
| DEFAULT | n/a |

This is certainly an acceptable way to implement this domain and, in turn, the column. There are a couple of minor concerns with this form:

- *There is no place for table consumers to know the domain*: Unless you have a row with one of each of the values specified in the CHECK constraint (and you do the dreaded DISTINCT query on the column(s)), it isn't easy to know what the possible values are without either foreknowledge of the system or looking in the metadata. If you're doing rental activity reports by Genre, it won't be easy to find out what Genres had no activity, certainly not using a simple SQL query that has no hard-coded values.

- *Often, a value such as this could easily have additional information associated with it:* For example, this domain might have information about where the shelves are located. When a customer asks that familiar "Where is the comedy section?" question, where will that information be found? Ideally, if you define this sort of information in the location where you define the domain value, your implementation will be far easier to work with.

- *This form can be quite limiting:* What if the manager of the store decides that customers don't want to rent "Comedy" movies anymore, so he tries "Humor" (hey, this isn't a marketing book). Doing this would require a programming change, while if the value was in a table, it would be a simple data change.

So, I nearly always include tables for all domains that are essentially "lists" of items, again using a surrogate key for the actual primary key, for the same reasons mentioned previously. In fact, it's probably even more important to do this for domain tables because on a small scale (one rental store) the manager might change requirements and need new values. I'll change the Movie table to the format shown in Figure 5-14.

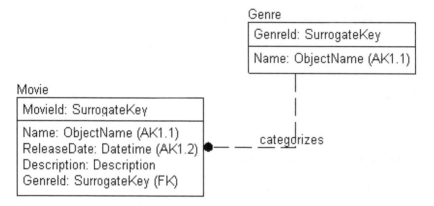

**Figure 5-14.** *Movie entity with Genre broken out as a domain table*

---

**Tip** I will rarely use an automatically generated value for the primary key of a domain table if the user cannot manage the values themselves. In our Genre table, if the system will allow users to add new genres, I might use an identity, whereas if they were fixed values created at install time (or service pack, for that matter), then a simple surrogate would suffice.

The main reason for this is that values that are not user editable can be coded with directly. For example, in your client code, it would be acceptable to code CONST genre_comedy = 1, genre_drama = 2, and so on, allowing for faster coding *and* easier "queriability."

---

## Choosing the Datatype

Choosing proper datatypes to match the domain chosen during logical modeling is an important task. One datatype might be more efficient than another of a similar type. For example, you can store integer data in an integer datatype, a numeric datatype, or even a floating-point datatype, but these datatypes are certainly not alike in implementation or performance.

■**Note** I have broken up the discussion of datatypes into several parts. First there is this and other sections in this chapter in which I provide some basic guidance on the types of datatypes that exist for SQL Server and some light discussion on what to use. In Chapter 7, I will introduce some advanced usages of datatypes and several patterns to follow for certain types of implementations, such as when working with date data, open schema data (when you need to allow your users to specify parts of their schema based on user needs that are beyond your control), and image/binary data. Finally, Appendixes B and C are dedicated to giving examples and example code snippets with all the types.

It's important to choose the best possible datatype when building the column. The following list contains the intrinsic datatypes and a brief explanation of each of them:

- *Precise numeric data*: Stores numeric data with no possible loss of precision.
    - bit: Stores either 1, 0, or NULL; frequently used for "Boolean"-like columns (1 = True, 0 = False, NULL = Unknown). (Up to 8-bit columns can fit in 1 byte.)
    - tinyint: Non-negative values between 0 and 255 (1 byte).
    - smallint: Integers between -32,768 and 32,767 (2 bytes).
    - int: Integers between 2,147,483,648 to 2,147,483,647 ($-2^{31}$ to $2^{31} - 1$). (4 bytes.)
    - bigint: Integers between 9,223,372,036,854,775,808 to 9,223,372,036,854,775,807 (that is, $-2^{63}$ to $2^{63} - 1$). (8 bytes.)
    - decimal *(*numeric *is a synonym)*: All numbers between $-10^{38} - 1$ through $10^{38} - 1$ (between 5 and 17 bytes, depending on precision).
- *Approximate numeric data*: Stores approximations of numbers, typically for scientific usage. Gives a large range of values with a high amount of precision but might lose precision of very large or very small numbers.
    - float(N): Values in the range from -1.79E + 308 through 1.79E + 308 (storage varies from 4 bytes for N between 1 and 24, and 8 for N between 25 and 53).
    - real: Values in the range from -3.40E + 38 through 3.40E + 38. real is a synonym for a float(24) datatype (4 bytes).
- *Date and time*: Stores date values, including time of day.
    - date: Date-only values from January 1, 0001, to December 31, 9999 (3 bytes).
    - time: Time-only values to 100 nanoseconds (3 to 5 bytes).
    - smalldatetime: Dates from January 1, 1900, through June 6, 2079, with accuracy to 1 minute (4 bytes).
    - datetime: Dates from January 1, 1753, to December 31, 9999, with accuracy to 3.33 milliseconds (8 bytes).
    - datetime2: Despite the hideous name, this type will store dates from January 1, 0001, to December 31, 9999, to 100-nanosecond accuracy (6 to 8 bytes).
    - datetimeoffset: Same as datetime2, but includes an offset for time zone (8 to 10 bytes).
- *Binary data*: Strings of bits, for example, files or images. Storage for these datatypes is based on the size of the data stored.
    - binary(N): Fixed-length binary data up to 8,000 bytes long.
    - varbinary(N): Variable-length binary data up to 8,000 bytes long.
    - varbinary(max): Variable-length binary data up to ($2^{31}$) – 1 bytes (2GB) long. All the typical functionality of the varbinary columns is allowed on these types.

- *Character (or string) data*:
  - char(N): Fixed-length character data up to 8,000 characters long.
  - varchar(N): Variable-length character data up to 8,000 characters long.
  - varchar(max): Variable-length character data up to ( $2^{31}$ ) – 1 bytes (2GB) long. All the typical functionality of the varchar columns is allowed on these types.
  - nchar, nvarchar, nvarchar(max): Unicode equivalents of char, varchar, and varchar(max).
- *Other datatypes*:
  - sql_variant: Stores any datatype. It's generally a bad idea to use this datatype, but it is handy in cases where you don't know the datatype of a value before storing. Best practice would be to describe the type in your own metadata when using this type.
  - rowversion (timestamp *is a synonym*): Used for optimistic locking to version-stamp a row. It changes on every modification. The name of this type was timestamp in all SQL Server versions before 2000, but in the ANSI SQL standards, the timestamp type is equivalent to the datetime datatype. I'll discuss the rowversion datatype in detail in Chapter 10, which is about concurrency.
  - uniqueidentifier: Stores a GUID value.
  - XML: Allows you to store an XML document in a column. The XML type gives you a rich set of functionality when dealing with structured data that cannot be easily managed using typical relational tables. You shouldn't use the XML type as a crutch to violate the First Normal Form by storing multiple values in a single column. I will not use XML in any of the designs in this book, but Appendix C has an introduction to the type.
  - geometry and geography: Used for storing spatial data, like for maps. I will not be using this type in this chapter but will introduce it in Appendix C.
  - heirarchyId: Used to store data about a hierarchy. I'll present examples in Appendix C.

## Deprecated or Bad Choice Types

Several datatypes weren't listed because they're very soon to be deprecated (I wouldn't be surprised if they were completely removed from the version after 2008, so be sure to stop using them as soon as possible). Their use was common in versions of SQL Server before 2008, but they're being replaced by types that are far easier to use:

- image: Replace with varbinary(max)
- text *or* ntext: Replace with varchar(max) and nvarchar(max)

Another few datatypes that weren't listed were the money datatypes:

- money: –922,337,203,685,477.5808 through +922,337,203,685,477.5807 (8 bytes)
- smallmoney: Money values from -214,748.3648 through +214,748.3647 (4 bytes)

In general, the money datatype sounds like a cool idea, but it has some confusing consequences from using it. In Appendix B, I spend a bit more time covering these consequences, but there are two problems:

- There are definite issues with round off because intermediate results for calculations are calculated using only four decimal places.
- Money data output includes formatting, including a monetary sign (such as $ or £).
- Inserting $100 and £100 results in the same value being represented in the variable or column.

Hence, it's generally accepted that it's best to store monetary data in decimal datatypes (for a more detailed discussion with examples, see Appendix B). This also gives you the ability to assign the types as are reasonable for the situation. For example, take the `MovieRental` table, as shown in Figure 5-15.

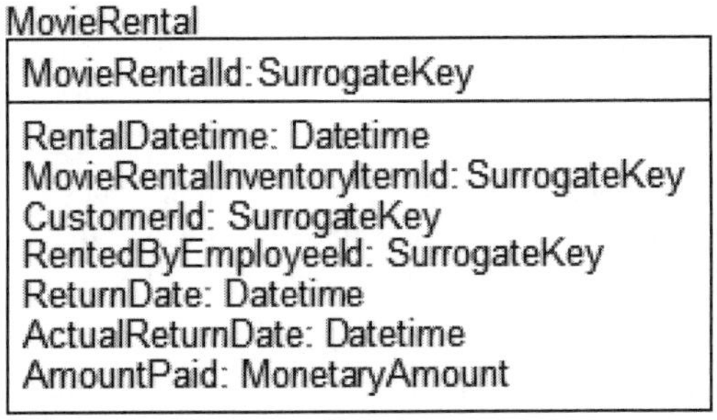

MovieRental

| MovieRentalId: SurrogateKey |
| --- |
| RentalDatetime: Datetime<br>MovieRentalInventoryItemId: SurrogateKey<br>CustomerId: SurrogateKey<br>RentedByEmployeeId: SurrogateKey<br>ReturnDate: Datetime<br>ActualReturnDate: Datetime<br>AmountPaid: MonetaryAmount |

**Figure 5-15.** *MovieRental table with domains listed*

For the `AmountPaid` column, I'll use a `decimal (4,2)` datatype, because a single rental will never cost more than $99.99, or business will be pitiful for sure (see Figure 5-16).

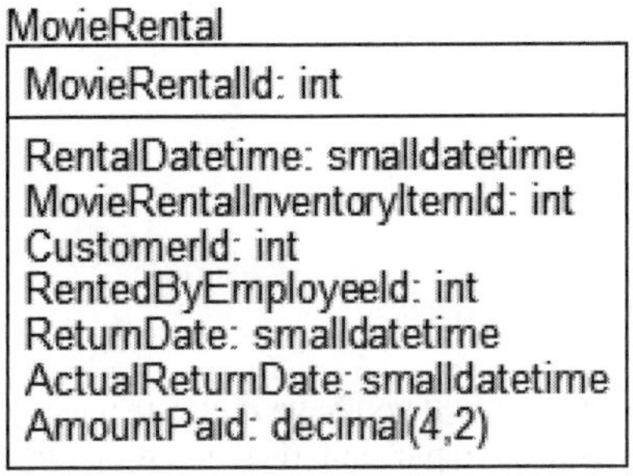

MovieRental

| MovieRentalId: int |
| --- |
| RentalDatetime: smalldatetime<br>MovieRentalInventoryItemId: int<br>CustomerId: int<br>RentedByEmployeeId: int<br>ReturnDate: smalldatetime<br>ActualReturnDate: smalldatetime<br>AmountPaid: decimal(4,2) |

**Figure 5-16.** *MovieRental table with datatype chosen for money amount*

---

■**Note** Appendix B covers the datatypes in more detail; I'll also discuss the situations and give examples of where datatypes are best used.

---

## Common Datatype Concerns

In this section, I will briefly cover concerns and issues relating to Boolean/logical values, large datatypes, and complex types and then summarize datatype concerns in order to discuss the most important thing you need to know about choosing a datatype.

### Boolean/Logical Values

Booleans are another of the hotly debated choices that are made for SQL Server data. There's no Boolean type in standard SQL, so a suitable datatype needs to be chosen through which to represent Boolean values. There are two common choices:

- There's the bit datatype -1 = True, 0 = False. This is by far the most common datatype because it works directly with programming languages such as VB .NET with no translation. The checkbox and option controls can directly connect to these values, even though VB uses -1 to indicate True.

- You could use a char(1) value as well, with a domain of 'Y', 'N', 'T', 'F', or other values. This is the easiest for ad hoc users who don't want to think about what 0 or 1 means, but it's generally the most difficult from a programming standpoint. Sometimes a char(3) is even better to go with 'yes' and 'no'.

To demonstrate this, I'll add a "flag" to the Customer table that tells whether people can rent movies meant for young people only or whether they can rent anything the store sells (see Figure 5-17).

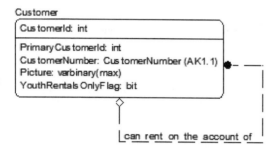

**Figure 5-17.** *Customer table with flag column for youth rentals*

Flag columns are used when you have a single yes or no condition. If you have multiple flag columns in a single table, there's sometimes a problem with the design, particularly when they are related to one another. For example, requirements might state that the user could choose the types of ratings the customer could rent. The table shown in Figure 5-18 would be a bad idea.

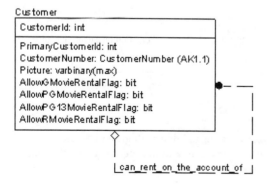

**Figure 5-18.** *Customer table with multiple columns for different levels of rentals*

If you notice this pattern in your tables, rebuild them as shown in Figure 5-19.

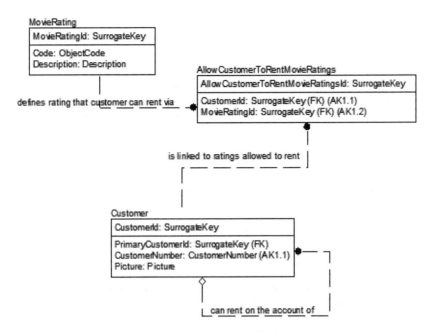

**Figure 5-19.** *Customer table with dynamic modifiable levels*

Another resolution would be to add an Ordering column to the MovieRating table and add a MaximumMovieRating column to the Customer table. This would be seemingly easier to do, and it would be. However, it would also mean you would have to make a decision about certain ratings that might not make sense in some situations. Should unrated films be placed into the upper rankings or the lower ones? The answer is probably the lower ones, but giving the flexibility to choose any combination of ratings might be the better way to go. From a UI standpoint, you could even mix the two solutions and automatically disallow ratings above the ratings you choose unless you override. (Rarely should the user interface dictate the data structure. It is the job of the different architects controlling the different layers of application logic to make the UI and the data structures both easy to use and rich enough to cover all possible needs.)

There are many ways to skin the cat (a concept that generally has my cat terrified as she reads over my arms just now) in a reasonable way, without resorting to multiple flag columns that have similar meanings. The key is that none of the columns should have a relationship to any other column, as stated in Third Normal Form. If multiple columns share a common meaning or theme, then this meaning may be able to stand on its own, just as in this case movie ratings are a thing in and of themselves that deserve a modeled table of their own.

To the actual model, I'll add the MovieRating table and relate it to the Movie table. It has a column AllowYouthRentalFlag to enable enforcement of the YouthRentalFlag.

---

■**Tip** When choosing a design, it is important to put the display out of your mind and model the data that needs to be stored. You can build stored procedures (or views) that model the display in most cases. The data has more value than the user interface and ought to represent what is being modeled, which will usually make working with the data far easier when it comes time to report on the data.

---

**Large-Value Datatype Columns**

As of SQL Server 2005, dealing with large datatypes changed quite a bit. By using the max specifier on varchar, nvarchar, and varbinary types, you can now store way more data than was possible in previous versions while still being able to deal with the data using "normal" methods.

As with all datatype questions, use the varchar(max) types only when they're required, and you should always use the smallest types possible. The larger the datatype, the more data possible, and the more trouble the row size can be to get optimal storage retrieval times. In cases where you know you need large data or in the case where you sometimes need greater than 8,000 bytes in a column, the max specifier is a fantastic thing.

Previously, using image and text datatypes, dealing with data that was greater than 8,000 characters (or 4,000 for Unicode types) was done in a different way than data that was less than or equal to 8,000 characters long. Now, you can deal with all character and binary data in the same way, regardless of size. There are two concerns, however:

- There's no automatic datatype conversion from the normal character types to the large-value types.

- Because of the possible large sizes of data, a special clause is added to the UPDATE statement.

The first issue is pretty simple, but it can be a bit confusing at times. For example, concatenate '12345' + '67890'. You've taken two varchar(5) values, and the result will be contained in a value that is automatically cast as a varchar(10). But if you concatenate two varchar(8000) values, you don't get a varchar(16000) value, and you don't get a varchar(max) value. The values get truncated to a varchar(8000) value. This isn't always intuitively obvious. For example, consider the following code:

```
SELECT   len(
             cast(replicate('a',8000) as varchar(8000))
             + cast(replicate('a',8000) as varchar(8000))
         )
```

It returns a value of type varchar(8,000). If you cast one of the varchar(8000) values to varchar(max), then the result will be 16,000:

```
SELECT   len(
             cast(replicate('a',8000) as varchar(max))
             + cast(replicate('a',8000) as varchar(8000))
         )
```

Second, because the size of columns stored using the varchar(max) datatype can be so huge, it wouldn't be favorable to always pass around these values just like you do with smaller values. Because the maximum size of a varchar(max) value is 2GB, imagine having to update a value of this size. Such an update would be pretty nasty, because the client would need to get the whole value, make its changes, and then send the value back to the server. Most client machines may not even have 2GB of physical RAM, so paging would occur, and the whole process would crawl and probably crash. Not good. So, you can do what are referred to as *chunked* updates. These are done using the .WRITE clause in the UPDATE statement. For example:

```
UPDATE TableName
SET    varcharMaxCol.WRITE('the value', <offset>, <expression>)
WHERE  . . .
```

One important thing to note is that varchar(max) values will easily cause the size of rows to go greater than the 8060-byte limit with the data placed on overflow pages. Overflow pages are not terribly efficient because SQL Server has to go fetch extra pages that will not be in line with other data pages. (Overflow pages are covered more in Chapter 9.)

I won't go over large types in any more detail at this point. Just understand that you might have to treat the data in the (max) columns differently if you're going to allow large quantities of data to be stored. In our model, we've used a varbinary(max) column in the Customer table to store the image of the customer.

The main point to understand here is that having a datatype with virtually unlimited storage comes at a price. SQL Server 2008 allows you some additional freedom when dealing with varbinary(max) data by placing it in the file system using what is called *filestream storage*. (I will discuss large object storage in Chapter 7 in more detail, including filestreams.)

### Complex Datatypes

As discussed in the previous chapters, it's acceptable to have complex datatypes in a normalized database. Complex types should follow the same rules as any other datatypes, in that you must always have the same number of values (no arrays) and such.

In SQL Server 2005, it was finally possible to create these types, but for the most part you should use them only in the cases where it makes a very compelling reason to do so. There are a few different possible scenarios where you could reasonably use user-defined types (UDTs) to extend the SQL Server type system with additional scalar types or different ranges of data of existing datatypes. Some examples include specialized datetime types for different countries, currency of various countries, a time- or date-only datatype, and unsigned integers. Here are some other potential uses of UDTs:

- Datatypes where you need specialized formatting, checks, or operations. For example, a coordinate, IP address, or SSN.

- Complex types that are provided by an owner of a particular format, such as a media format that could be used to interpret a varbinary(max) value as a movie or an audio clip. This type would have to be loaded on the client to get any value from the datatype.

- Complex types for a specialized application that has complex needs, when you're sure your application will be the only user.

Although the possibilities are virtually unlimited, I suggest that CLR UDTs be considered only for specialized circumstances that make the database design more robust and easy to work with. CLR UDTs are a nice addition to the DBA's and developer's toolkit, but they should be reserved for those times when adding a new scalar datatype solves a business problem.

In SQL Server 2008, Microsoft has provided several CLR user-defined types to implement hierarchies and spatial datatypes. I point this out here to note that if Microsoft is using the CLR to implement complex types (and the spatial types at the very least are pretty darn complex), the sky is the limit. I should note that the spatial and hierarchyId types push the limits of what should be in a type (in my opinion), and some of the data stored (like a polygon) is really an array of connected points.

Later in the chapter, I'll demonstrate creating an American Social Security domain, though I would never go through the trouble in a real system for such a simple type. Any actual usage would certainly need to be something far more complex, like the hierarchy or spatial types were (though both of those would be over my skill level in CLR programming!).

## The Most Important Thing for Choosing Datatypes . . .

When all is said and done, the most important thing when choosing a datatype is to keep things simple but to choose the right types for the job. SQL Server gives you a wide range of datatypes, and many of them can be declared in a wide variety of sizes. I never cease to be amazed by the number of databases around where every single column is either an integer or a varchar(N) (where N is the same for every single string column). One particular example I'm working with right now has everything, including GUID-based primary keys, *all stored* in NVARCHAR(200) columns! It is bad enough to store your GUIDs in a varchar column at all, since it is stored as a 16-byte binary value and as a varchar column it will take 36 bytes; however, store it in an nvarchar column, and now it takes 72 bytes! What a hideous waste of space. Even worse, now all data could be up to 200 characters wide, even if you plan to give entry space for only 30 characters. Now people using the data will feel like they need to allow for 200 characters on reports and such for the data. Time wasted, space wasted, money wasted.

As another example, say you want to store a person's name and date of birth. You could choose to store the name in a varchar(max) column and the date of birth in a sql_variant column. In all cases, these choices would certainly store the data that the user wanted, but they wouldn't be *good* choices. The name should be in something such as a varchar(30) column and the date of birth in a date column. Notice that I used a variable size type for the name. This is because you don't know the length and not all names are the same size. Because most names aren't nearly 30 bytes, using a variable-sized type will save space in your database.

Of course in reality, seldom would anyone make such poor choices of a datatype as putting a date value in a varchar(max) column. Most choices are reasonably easy. However, it's important keep in mind that the datatype is the first level of domain enforcement. A business rule states something like the following:

> *The name must be greater than or equal to 5 characters and less than or equal to 30 characters.*

You can enforce the first part of this at the database level by declaring the column as a varchar(30). This field won't allow a 31-character or longer value to be entered. It isn't possible to enforce the rule of greater than or equal to five characters using only a datatype. I'll discuss more about how to enforce these types of rules in Chapter 6 on integrity enforcement.

## Updating the Model

For each of the domains that have been set up in the model, go through and assign datatypes. For example, take the Person table in Figure 5-20.

```
Person
┌──────────────────────────────────────────────────────┐
│ PersonId: SurrogateKey                                 │
├──────────────────────────────────────────────────────┤
│ FirstName: PersonFirstName                             │
│ MiddleName: PersonMiddleName                           │
│ LastName: PersonLastName                               │
│ SocialSecurityNumber: SocialSecurityNumber (AK1.1)     │
└──────────────────────────────────────────────────────┘
```

**Figure 5-20.** *Choosing datatypes for the Person table*

- SurrogateKey: I generally use an integer for this. For larger databases, it can be useful to be specific and use one of the smaller datatypes for some of the surrogate key values, because most tables won't need the ability to have approximately 4 billion different values.

- PersonFirstName, PersonMiddleName, PersonLastName: All varchar(30). PersonMiddleName allows NULLs, but the others don't.

- SocialSecurityNumber: I'll use a CLR datatype, so this domain is left as the SocialSecurityNumber datatype. Would I do this in a production database? Probably not for something so simple. It would really need to be very complex and need special processing in the methods of the type to go to a user-defined type. This was chosen as a reasonably simple example that had enough realism coupled with some validation that many of the readers would know.

This table now looks like Figure 5-21.

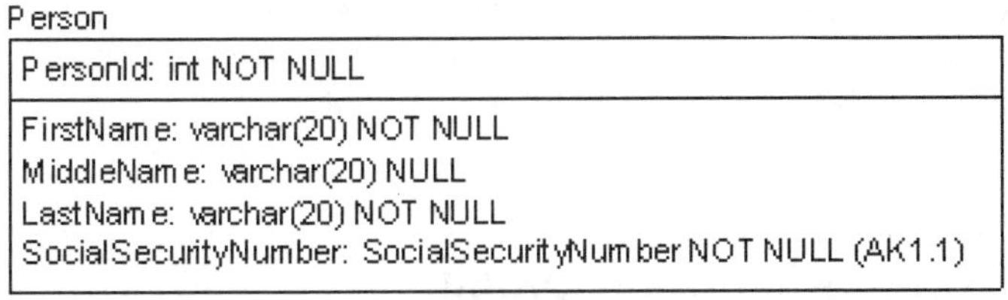

Person

| PersonId: int NOT NULL |
|---|
| FirstName: varchar(20) NOT NULL |
| MiddleName: varchar(20) NULL |
| LastName: varchar(20) NOT NULL |
| SocialSecurityNumber: SocialSecurityNumber NOT NULL (AK1.1) |

**Figure 5-21.** *Datatypes chosen for the Person table*

I'll then set up each of the other domains as SQL Server types. The entire model will be displayed in the next few pages, once schemas have been added.

## Setting Up Schemas

Starting with SQL Server 2005, you can use an additional level of organization to segregate the tables in a database. Between the database and table name, instead of owner, you can specify a schema. Schemas are great to segregate objects within a database for clarity of use.

For example, in the AdventureWorks2008 sample database that ships with SQL Server 2008, five schemas are present: HumanResources, Person, Production, Purchasing, and Sales. Use the following query:

```
SELECT  table_name
FROM    AdventureWorks2008.information_schema.tables
WHERE   table_schema = 'Purchasing'
ORDER   BY table_name
```

You can see the tables (including views) that make up the schema:

```
table_name
-------------------------
ProductVendor
PurchaseOrderDetail
PurchaseOrderHeader
ShipMethod
Vendor
vVendorWithAddresses
vVendorWithContacts
```

All of them are centered around purchasing. What makes schemas so nice is that you can deal with permissions on a schema level, rather than on an object-by-object level. Chapter 7 will discuss using schemas for security in more detail.

I'll segregate the MovieRental database model into three schemas:

- Inventory: Tables that pertain to the movies that will be stocked for rental
- People: Tables that pertain to the employees and customers that will be renting videos
- Rentals: Tables that pertain to recording the act of renting

The model in the next section will reflect this.

**Note**  No, we are not exactly done with the design process. However, we are done with our discussion of implementation needs for now. At this point, we are going to stop and build the database that we have so far. In Chapter 7 I will be showing you several ways you can work with an extended range of data by applying some common patterns that allow you to extend your designs and add a layer of polish to the implementation.

## Reviewing the "Final" Implementation Model

OK, I will just go ahead and tell you. Your database is unlikely to *ever* be "final," and I'll make changes later in this chapter to the model to illustrate this point (well, actually I thought of new material to illustrate another point, but you will never know that unless I tell you about it). If you do a good job of design up front, you can minimize the amount of changes required, but admittedly making changes is almost impossible to avoid.

The model in Figure 5-22 is the model I'll use for the rest of this chapter while turning the model into implemented tables and columns.

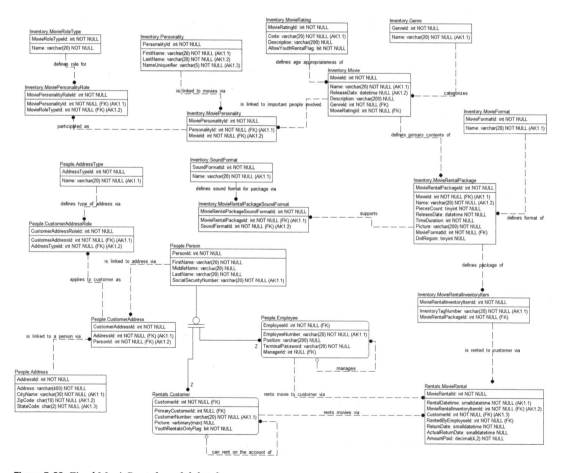

**Figure 5-22.** *Final MovieRental model database*

# Implementing the Design

This is the mechanical part of the chapter, in that all that's left is to implement the tables we have spent so much time designing. The blueprints have been drawn up, and now we can grab a hammer and start driving nails.

Just like in the rest of the book, I'll do this work manually, because it will help you understand what the tool is building for you. It's also a good exercise for any database architect or DBA to review the SQL Server syntax; I personally wouldn't suggest doing this on a database with 300 tables, but I definitely do know people who do this and wouldn't consider using a tool to create any of their database objects. On the other hand, the same data modeling tools that could be used to do the logical modeling can usually create the tables and often some of the associated code, saving your fingers from added wear and tear plus giving you more time to help Mario save the princess who always seems to get herself captured.

No matter how you do the work, you need to make sure that you save the scripts you use to create objects in some manner in the file system, because they're invaluable tools for the DBA to apply changes to production, test, development, QA, or whatever environments have been set up to allow developers, users, and DBAs to coexist throughout the process. It is not uncommon for DBAs to do all their work using scripts and never use a database design/generation tool (especially when they work for a company with smallish resources that they have already spent purchasing gold-plated laptops for all of the developers). Make sure that your scripts are in a source control system too, or at the very least backed up.

Before starting to build anything else, you'll need a database. I'll create this database using all default values, and my installation is totally generic on my laptop. I use the Developer Edition, and I used all the default settings when installing. I hate to state the completely obvious, but you'll need to do this with an account that has rights to create a database, especially if you're doing this on a shared server, such as your company dev server. Feel free to name your database anything you want, because what the database is named won't be important to the process.

The steps I'll take along the way are as follows:

- *Creating the basic table structures:* Building the base objects with columns.

- *Adding uniqueness constraints*: Using primary and unique constraints to enforce uniqueness between rows in the table.

- *Building default constraints*: Assisting users in choosing proper values when it isn't obvious.

- *Adding relationships*: Defining how tables relate to one another (foreign keys).

- *Dealing with collations*: How the collation of data can affect how it's used and how to use COLLATE to change the collation as needed temporarily.

- *Using computed columns*: How to use computed columns to avoid single-table denormalizations.

- *Considering the use of complex datatypes*: How the CLR types and datatype aliases can be used.

- *Documenting the database*: Including documentation directly in the SQL Server objects.

- *Validating the dependency information:* Using the catalog views and dynamic management views, you can validate that the objects you expect to depend on the existence of one another do in fact exist, keeping your database cleaner to manage.

The following statement creates a small database in your default directory:

```
CREATE DATABASE MovieRental
```

You can see where the database files were placed by running the following statement:

```
SELECT physical_name
FROM   sys.master_files
WHERE  database_id = db_id('MovieRental')
```

On my laptop, with an instance name of KATMAI, the data was created as C:\Program Files\ Microsoft SQL Server\MSSQL10.KATMAI\MSSQL\DATA\MovieRental.mdf and the log in C:\Program Files\Microsoft SQL Server\MSSQL10.KATMAI\MSSQL\DATA\MovieRental_log.LDF. You set the defaults when you installed SQL Server. On your production server, you will likely want to create your data files in some special folders on different drives than the default system drive.

The database is owned by the user who created the database, as you can see from the following query:

```
SELECT  name, suser_sname(sid) as [login]
FROM    sys.database_principals
WHERE   name = 'dbo'
```

This query returns the following result (though admittedly I'm not actually in the MYDOMAIN domain):

| name | login |
| --- | --- |
| dbo | MYDOMAIN\LBDAVI |

Again, on a production server I almost always will set the owner of the database to be the system administrator account so that all databases are owned by the same users. The only reason to not do this is when you are sharing databases or when you have implemented cross-database security. This will be covered more in Chapter 8 on security. You can change the owner of the database by using the ALTER AUTHORIZATION statement:

```
ALTER AUTHORIZATION ON Database::MovieRental to SA
```

Going back and checking the code, you will see that the owner is now SA.

## Creating the Basic Table Structures

The following is the basic syntax for the CREATE TABLE statement:

```
CREATE TABLE [<database>.][<schema>.]<tablename>
(
      <column specification>
)
```

If you look in Books Online, you will see that there are a lot of extra settings that allow you to place the table on a filegroup, partition the table onto multiple filegroups, control where max/over- flow data is placed, and so on. Where to place your data on different filegroups will be discussed in Chapter 9 on table structures and indexing.

The CREATE clause is straightforward:

```
CREATE TABLE [<database>.][<schema>.]<tablename>
```

I'll expand upon the items between the angle brackets (< and >). Anything in square brackets ([ and ]) is optional.

- `<database>`: It's seldom necessary to specify the database in the CREATE TABLE statements. If not specified, this defaults to the current database where the statement is being executed. Specifying the database means that the script will be executable only in a single database, which precludes us from using the script unchanged to build alternate databases on the same server, should the need arise.

- `<schema>`: This is the schema to which the table will belong.

- `<tablename>`: This is the name of the table. I'll briefly discuss how to name tables in the next section.

---

**Tip** If the first character of the table name is a single # symbol, the table is a temporary table. If the first two characters of the table name are ##, it's a global temporary table. Temporary tables are not so much a part of database design as a mechanism to hold intermediate results in complex queries, so don't use them in your database design.

---

The combination of `schema` and `tablename` must be unique in a database.

---

**Note** In versions of SQL Server prior to 2005, the second part of the name was the owner, and almost every best-practice guide would suggest that all tables were owned by the `dbo` (database user).

Also note that the word *schema* has two usages. One means a container of objects within a database, and the other simply refers to the tables within the schema. I'll try to be clear as to which meaning I'm using.

---

## Schema

Back in the first main section of the book, schemas were set up for each of the tables in the implemented databases. In SQL Server 2005, the owner part of an object name was changed to the more proper schema. A *schema* is a namespace: a container where database objects are contained, within a database. One thing that is nice is that because the schema isn't tightly tied to a user, you can drop the user without changing the exposed name of the object. Changing owners of the schema changes owners of the table. (This is done using the ALTER AUTHORIZATION statement.)

In SQL Server 2000 and earlier, the table was owned by a user; starting with SQL Server 2005, a schema is owned by a user, and tables are contained in a schema. Just as in 2000, the generally suggested best practice was that all tables were owned by the dbo user. Now, this is done by having the schema *owned* by the dbo, but this doesn't mean you have to have every schema *named* dbo.

Not just tables are bound to a given schema; just about every object is schema bound. You can access objects using the following naming method:

`[<databaseName>.][<schemaName>.]objectName`

The `<databaseName>` defaults to the current database. The `<schemaName>` defaults to the user's default schema. In general, it is best to always specify the schema in any and all SQL statements because it saves SQL the work of having to decide which schema to use (when the schema is not specified, the call is considered to be *caller dependent*).

Schemas are of great use to segregate objects within a database for clarity of use. If you look at the AdventureWorks database, you'll see that instead of all the tables still being "owned" by dbo, they're now members of various schemas. For example, using the new sys.schemas system view, you can list the schemas in the database:

```
SELECT name,
       SCHEMA_NAME(schema_id) as schemaName,
       USER_NAME(principal_id) as principal
FROM   AdventureWorks2008.sys.schemas
```

Cutting out all the system schemas (run the query for yourself!), the AdventureWorks database has the following schemas:

| name | schemaName | principal |
| --- | --- | --- |
| HumanResources | HumanResources | dbo |
| Person | Person | dbo |
| Production | Production | dbo |
| Purchasing | Purchasing | dbo |
| Sales | Sales | dbo |

For example, now let's look at the different tables owned by the Purchasing schema:

```
SELECT  table_name
FROM    AdventureWorks2008.information_schema.tables
WHERE   table_schema = 'Purchasing'
ORDER   BY table_name
```

You see the following tables:

```
table_name
--------------------
ProductVendor
PurchaseOrderDetail
PurchaseOrderHeader
ShipMethod
Vendor
vVendorWithAddresses
vVendorWithContacts
```

When you access an object using a single part name, in editions of SQL Server before 2005, it always defaulted to dbo. In 2005 and later you can specify a default schema, other than the dbo schema (which mimics earlier versions for easier backward compatibility). Then when you execute SELECT columnName FROM tableName, instead of defaulting to dbo.tablename, it would use the defaultSchemaName.tablename.

This is done using the following code:

```
CREATE USER <schemaUser>
       FOR LOGIN <schemaUser>
       WITH DEFAULT SCHEMA = schemaname
```

There's also an ALTER USER command that allows the changing of default schema for existing users (it unfortunately does not work on Windows Group–based users, just basic users). What makes schemas so nice is that you can deal with permissions on a schema level, rather than on an object-by-object level. Schemas also give you a logical grouping of objects when you view them within a list, such as in Management Studio.

I'm not going to go any further into the security aspects of using schemas at this point in the book, but I'll just mention that they're a good idea. Throughout the book, I'll always name the schema that a table is in when doing examples. Schemas will be part of any system I design in this book, simply because it's going to be best practice to do so going further. On a brief trip back to the land of reality, I would expect that beginning to use schemas in production systems will be a slow process, because it hasn't been the normal method in years past. Chapter 8 will discuss using schemas for security in more detail.

For all the tables in the MovieRental database, we'll create the following three schemas. We'll do this and all operations while logged in as the user who created the database:

```
CREATE SCHEMA Inventory --tables pertaining to the videos to be rented
GO
CREATE SCHEMA People --tables pertaining to people (nonspecific)
GO
CREATE SCHEMA Rentals --tables pertaining to rentals to customers
GO
```

Note that CREATE SCHEMA must be the first statement in the batch. We'll also create another schema for tables that are for demonstration of some concept that isn't part of the MovieRental "experience":

```
CREATE SCHEMA Alt
GO
```

## Columns and Base Datatypes

The lines with the arrows are the ones used to define a column:

```
CREATE TABLE [<database>.][<schema>.]<tablename>
(
    <columnName> <datatype> [<NULL specification>]
                                [IDENTITY [(seed,increment)]]
     --or
    <columnName> AS <computed definition>
)
```

The <columnName> placeholder is where you specify the name of the column.
There are two types of columns:

- *Implemented*: This is an ordinary column, in which physical storage is allocated and data is stored for the value.

- *Computed (or virtual)*: These columns are made up by a calculation derived from any of the physical columns in the table.

Most of the columns in any database will be implemented columns, but computed columns have some pretty cool uses, so don't think they're of no use just because they aren't talked about much. You can avoid plenty of code-based denormalizations by using computed columns. (I'll demonstrate them later in this chapter.)

## Nullability

In the column-create phrase, simply change the <NULL specification> in your physical model to NULL to allow NULLs, or NOT NULL not to allow NULLs:

```
<columnName> <data type> [<NULL specification>]
```

For example:

```
CREATE TABLE Alt.NullTest
(
   NullColumn varchar(10) NULL,
   NotNullColumn varchar(10) NOT NULL
)
```

There's nothing particularly surprising there. Leaving off the NULL specification altogether, the SQL Server default is used. To determine the current default property for a database, execute the following statement:

```
SELECT   name, is_ansi_null_default_on
FROM     sys.databases
WHERE    name = 'MovieRental'
```

This has the following results:

| name | is_ansi_null_default_on |
| --- | --- |
| MovieRental | 0 |

To set the default for the database, you can use ALTER DATABASE. The syntax to change the setting is as follows:

```
ALTER DATABASE MovieRental
    SET ANSI_NULL_DEFAULT OFF
```

---

■**Tip** We recommend having this setting always OFF so that if you forget to set it explicitly, you won't be stuck with nullable columns that quickly fill up with NULL data you'll have to clean up.

---

To set the default for a session, use the following command:

```
SET ANSI_NULL_DFLT_ON OFF
```

Or use ON if you want the default to be NULL. Yes, it is confusing to be setting an option to OFF. Here's an example:

```
--turn off default NULLs
SET ANSI_NULL_DFLT_ON OFF

--create test table
CREATE TABLE Alt.testNULL
(
    id    int
)

--check the values
EXEC sp_help 'Alt.testNULL'
```

This code returns the following:

| Column_name | [...] | Nullable |
| --- | --- | --- |
| Id | ... | no |

---

■**Note** Considerable stuff has been removed from the sp_help output here for space reasons. sp_help returns information about the tables, columns, and constraints.

---

Let's take the `Inventory.Movie` table from the model and demonstrate the syntax (see Figure 5-23). Create the table using the following DDL:

```
CREATE TABLE Inventory.Movie
(
        MovieId              int NOT NULL,
        Name                 varchar(20) NOT NULL,
        ReleaseDate          date NULL,
        Description          varchar(200) NULL,
        GenreId              int NOT NULL,
        MovieRatingId        int NOT NULL
)
```

Inventory.Movie

| MovieId: int NOT NULL |
|---|
| Name: varchar(20) NOT NULL (AK1.1) |
| ReleaseDate: datetime NULL (AK1.2) |
| Description: varchar(200) NULL |
| GenreId: int NOT NULL (FK) |
| MovieRatingId: int NOT NULL (FK) |

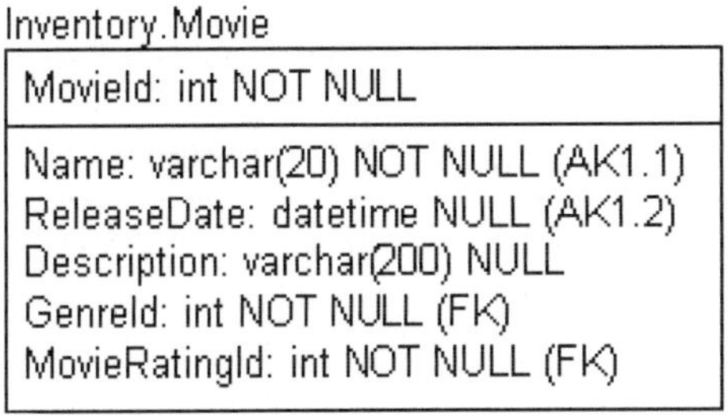

**Figure 5-23.** *Inventory.Movie table to be created*

This builds the table, though this isn't "good enough," because nothing prevents the user from creating duplicate rows. In the next section, you'll implement the surrogate key (in this case `MovieId`), followed by key constraints to prevent duplication.

## Surrogate Keys

Finally, before getting too excited and starting to build a lot of tables, there's one more thing to discuss. In the first section of this chapter, I discussed how to implement a surrogate key. In this section, I'll present the method that I typically use. I break down surrogate key values into two types that I use:

- Manually managed:
  - Letting the client choose the surrogate value. This could mean using GUIDs or some hash function to create a value. I won't cover this topic any more than to say that it's up to the client to build such values and include them in the `INSERT` statements when creating new rows.
  - Manually created by the DBA during load (for tables that are read-only to the client, to present a domain table to the client).
- Automatically generated using the `IDENTITY` property. For tables where data is created by users, the `IDENTITY` property is employed.

An acceptable cross between the two would be to manually load some values to give programmers direct access to the surrogate value and use the `IDENTITY SEED` to set a range for automatically generated values in a different range. I have rarely needed this, but it is available and would be useful in cases where there are some key values that need to be programmed against but the user needs to be able to add to the list.

## Manually Managed (Read-Only Tables)

A couple good examples of tables where there's no need to allow users access to create new rows manually are the Genre and MovieRating tables (values from these two tables are part of the next example as well). The way these values are used, adding a new value could require changes to the code of the system and probably changes in the physical realm of the rental store. Hence, instead of building tables that require code to manage, as well as user interfaces, we simply choose a permanent value for each of the surrogate values. This gives you control over the values in the key (which you pretty much won't have when using the IDENTITY property) and allows usage of the surrogate key directly in code if desired (likely as a constant construct in the host language). It also allows a user interface to cache values from this table (or even implement them as constants), with confidence that they won't change without the knowledge of the programmer who is using them (see Figure 5-24).

Inventory.MovieRating

| MovieRatingId: int NOT NULL |
| --- |
| Code: varchar(20) NOT NULL (AK1.1)<br>Description: varchar(200) NULL<br>AllowYouthRentalFlag: bit NOT NULL |

Inventory.Genre

| GenreId: int NOT NULL |
| --- |
| Name: varchar(20) NOT NULL (AK1.1) |

**Figure 5-24.** *Manually managed domain tables*

Create these tables and load some data:

```
CREATE TABLE Inventory.MovieRating (
        MovieRatingId        int NOT NULL,
        Code                 varchar(20) NOT NULL,
        Description          varchar(200) NULL,
        AllowYouthRentalFlag bit NOT NULL
)
```

Then load data into the table, manually creating the key values (this kind of code would be something that you could keep in source control with the database creation code, because it is never planned to change):

```
INSERT INTO Inventory.MovieRating
            (MovieRatingId, Code, Description, AllowYouthRentalFlag)
VALUES    (0, 'UR','Unrated',1),
        (1, 'G','General Audiences',1),
        (2, 'PG','Parental Guidance',1),
        (3, 'PG-13','Parental Guidance for Children Under 13',1),
        (4, 'R','Restricted, No Children Under 17 without Parent',0)
```

Note that there is a row with an ID value of 0. This is a common shorthand I often used in place of NULL values to indicate no value (rather than unknown value) is to have a row with a 0 as a surrogate key that explicitly states this value. Then load the Genre table:

```
CREATE TABLE Inventory.Genre (
        GenreId        int NOT NULL,
        Name           varchar(20) NOT NULL
)
GO
INSERT INTO Inventory.Genre (GenreId, Name)
VALUES (1,'Comedy'),
       (2,'Drama'),
       (3,'Thriller'),
       (4,'Documentary')
```

I don't include a 0 value here because there isn't a case where the Genre of a movie doesn't exist. I didn't allow NULLs for the Genre in the Movie table because in this sort of database, the genre of a movie will have been chosen so the movie can be sorted on shelves.

Note that it's generally expected that once you manually create a value, the meaning of this value will never change. For example, if you had a row (1, STOP), it would be fine to change it to (1, HALT), but not to (1, GO). This consistency allows you to cache values with little concern for how long (does it matter if one user chooses STOP and the other HALT?). Also, the key you choose will be excellent for ETL to a data warehouse.

---

**■Tip** If you are confused by the syntax of the VALUES clause of my insert statements, don't be. This is a new feature of 2008 that allows you to use row/table constructors to build a set of data in a simple string, rather than needing multiple statements.

---

### Generation Using the IDENTITY Property

Most of the time, tables are created to allow users to create new rows. Implementing a surrogate key on these tables is commonly done using (what are commonly referred to as) IDENTITY columns. For any of the precise numeric datatypes (the numeric type and any of the integer types other than bit), there's an option to create an automatically incrementing (or decrementing, depending on the increment value) column. The column that implements this IDENTITY column must also be defined as NOT NULL. From our initial section on columns, I had this for the column specification:

```
<columnName> <data type> [<NULL specification>] IDENTITY [(seed,increment)]
```

The seed portion specifies the number that the column values will start with, and the increment is how much the next value will increase. For example, take the Movie table created earlier, this time implementing the IDENTITY-based surrogate key:

```
DROP TABLE Inventory.Movie
GO
CREATE TABLE Inventory.Movie
(
        MovieId              int NOT NULL IDENTITY(1,2),
        Name                 varchar(20) NOT NULL,
        ReleaseDate          date NULL,
        Description          varchar(200) NULL,
        GenreId              int NOT NULL,
        MovieRatingId        int NOT NULL
)
```

In this CREATE TABLE statement, I've added the IDENTITY property for the MovieId column. The seed of 1 indicates that the values will start at 1, and the increment says that the second value will be 2 greater, in this case 3, the next 5, and so on. (Note that I'm doing this just as a demonstration of what can be done with the IDENTITY property, not as a common best practice to use only odd numbers.)

The following script inserts two new rows into the Movie table:

```
--Genre and Ratings values create as literal values because
--they are built with explicit values
INSERT INTO Inventory.Movie (Name, ReleaseDate,
                             Description, GenreId, MovieRatingId)
VALUES ('The Maltese Falcon','19411003',
        'A private detective finds himself surrounded by strange people ' +
        'looking for a statue filled with jewels',2,0),
```

```
('Arsenic and Old Lace','19440923',
 'A man learns a disturbing secret about his aunt''s methods ' +
 'for treating gentlemen callers',1,0)
```

---

■**Tip** To insert a single quote value into a string, you need to escape the value with two single quotes. In the previous statement, I entered aunt''s, but aunt's would be saved. To actually enter '', you need to type ''''.

---

Now view the new values with the following code:

```
SELECT  MovieId, Name, ReleaseDate
FROM    Inventory.Movie
```

This produces the following result:

```
MovieId   Name                  ReleaseDate
-------   --------------------  -----------------------
1         The Maltese Falcon    1941-10-03
3         Arsenic and Old Lace  1944-09-23
```

The IDENTITY property is useful for creating a surrogate primary key that's small and fast. The int datatype requires only 4 bytes and is good, because most tables will have fewer than 2 billion rows (you should hope so, unless you have incredible hardware!). I'll discuss primary keys in some detail later in this chapter.

There are a couple of *major* caveats that you have to understand about IDENTITY values:

- IDENTITY values are apt to have holes in the sequence. If an error occurs when creating a new row, the IDENTITY value that was going to be used will be lost to the identity sequence. (This is one of the things that allows them to be good performers when you have heavy concurrency needs. Because IDENTITY values aren't affected by transactions, other connections don't have to wait until another's transaction completes.)

- If a row gets deleted, the deleted value won't be reused. Hence, you shouldn't use IDENTITY columns if you cannot accept this constraint on the values in your table.

- The value of a column with the IDENTITY property cannot be updated. You can insert your own value by using SET IDENTITY_INSERT <tablename> ON, but for the most part you should use this only when starting a table using values from another table.

- You cannot alter a column to turn on the IDENTITY property, but you can add an IDENTITY column to an existing table.

Keep in mind the fact (I hope I've said this enough) that the surrogate key should not be the only key on the table or that the only uniqueness is a more or less random value! For example, executing the INSERT again now for the *Arsenic and Old Lace* row would end up with the following:

```
MovieId  Name                  ReleaseDate
-------  --------------------  -----------------------
1        The Maltese Falcon    1941-10-03 00:00:00.000
3        Arsenic and Old Lace  1944-09-23 00:00:00.000
5        Arsenic and Old Lace  1944-09-23 00:00:00.000
```

There could be two movies with the same name but never (based on the database we've designed) released on the same day. Could you imagine the fight between the two directors?

Now we need to clean up the little mess we made. We could manually go in and delete this one row, but just for kicks, I will write the statement that we would need to clean this mess up en masse when we mess this up and get duplicates like this. We have all had to do it at one time or another. I know I have missed a key or two in my life.

```
--add a numbering column to the set, partitioned by the duplicate names.
--order by the MovieId, to keep the lowest key (not that it really matters)
WITH numberedRows as (
SELECT ROW_NUMBER() OVER (PARTITION BY Name ORDER BY MovieId) AS RowNumber,
       MovieId
FROM   Inventory.Movie )
--only keep one row per unique name
DELETE FROM numberedRows
WHERE  RowNumber <> 1
```

One thing I generally caution about when using identity columns is that you shouldn't rely on the values to be monotonically increasing in your code. In a simple duplication routine like this, where it isn't important which one you keep, it is fine. But if the order of the row's creation means anything, then you should add data to the row to indicate that order. In Chapter 6, I will introduce triggers to maintain automatically maintained values.

■**Note** The IDENTITY property is not a magic bullet. It does not guarantee uniqueness; it's just that the seed and increment you set at create time, or the reseed you set with DBCC CHECKIDENT ('table_name', RESEED, new_reseed_value), will increment as you add data to the table.

## Adding Uniqueness Constraints

As we've mentioned several times, it's important that every table have at least one constraint that prevents duplicate rows from being created. In this section, I'll introduce the following tasks, plus a topic (indexes) that inevitably comes to mind when I start talking keys that are implemented with indexes:

- Adding primary key constraints
- Adding alternate (UNIQUE) key constraints
- Implementing selective uniqueness
- Viewing uniqueness constraints
- Where other indexes fit in

Both types of constraints are implemented on top of unique indexes to enforce the uniqueness. It's conceivable that you could use unique indexes instead of constraints, but using a constraint is the favored method of implementing a key and enforcing uniqueness.

Constraints are intended to semantically represent and enforce constraints on data, and indexes (which are covered in detail in Chapter 9) are intended to speed access to data. In actuality, it doesn't matter how the uniqueness is implemented, but it is necessary to have either unique indexes or unique constraints in place. In some cases, other RDBMSs don't always use indexes to enforce uniqueness by default. They can use hash tables that are good only to see whether the values exist but not to look up values. By and large, when you need to enforce uniqueness, it's also the case that a user or process will be searching for values in the table and often for a single row (which indexes are perfect for).

## Adding Primary Key Constraints

The syntax of the primary key declaration is straightforward:

```
[CONSTRAINT constraintname] PRIMARY KEY [CLUSTERED | NONCLUSTERED]
```

I'll talk more about the index options in Chapter 9. Note that the constraint name is optional, but you should never treat it as such. I'll name primary key constraints using a name such as PK<schema>_<tablename>.

For a single column implemented with a clustered index (the default), you can specify it when creating the table, such as the domain table in Figure 5-25. 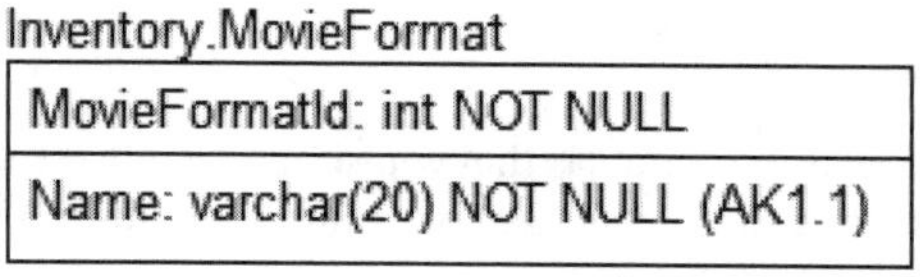

**Inventory.MovieFormat**

| MovieFormatId: int NOT NULL |
| --- |
| Name: varchar(20) NOT NULL (AK1.1) |

**Figure 5-25.** *Primary key generation sample table*

```
CREATE TABLE Inventory.MovieFormat (
      MovieFormatId        int NOT NULL
         CONSTRAINT PKInventory_MovieFormat PRIMARY KEY CLUSTERED,
      Name                 varchar(20) NOT NULL
)
```

Then you load the data:

```
INSERT INTO Inventory.MovieFormat(MovieFormatId, Name)
VALUES  (1,'Video Tape')
        ,(1,'DVD')
```

Whoops. Well, looky there, I accidentally tried to create duplicate values:

```
Msg 2627, Level 14, State 1, Line 3
Violation of PRIMARY KEY constraint ' PKInventory_MovieFormat'. Cannot insert
duplicate key in object 'Inventory.MovieFormat'.
The statement has been terminated.
```

Then you can fix the data and resubmit:

```
INSERT INTO Inventory.MovieFormat(MovieFormatId, Name)
VALUES  (1,'Video Tape')
        ,(2,'DVD')
```

**Tip** The primary key and other constraints of the table will be members of the table's schema, so you don't need to name your constraints for uniqueness over all objects, just those in the schema.

If you're using natural keys for your primary keys, then when dealing with multiple column keys, you need to specify the column names:

```
CREATE TABLE Alt.Product
(
    Manufacturer varchar(30) NOT NULL,
    ModelNumber varchar(30) NOT NULL,
    CONSTRAINT PKAlt_Product PRIMARY KEY NONCLUSTERED (Manufacturer, ModelNumber)
)
DROP TABLE Alt.Product
```

You can also add a PRIMARY KEY constraint to a table with no primary key by using ALTER TABLE, which I'll do to all the other tables already created:

```
ALTER TABLE Inventory.MovieRating
    ADD CONSTRAINT PKInventory_MovieRating PRIMARY KEY CLUSTERED (MovieRatingId)

ALTER TABLE Inventory.Genre
    ADD CONSTRAINT PKInventory_Genre PRIMARY KEY CLUSTERED (GenreId)

ALTER TABLE Inventory.Movie
    ADD CONSTRAINT PKInventory_Movie PRIMARY KEY CLUSTERED (MovieId)
```

Note that you might not have any NULL columns in a primary key, even though you might have NULL columns in a unique index. The reason for this is simple. The primary key is the row identifier, and a NULL provides no form of row identification.

Chapter 9 addresses the choice of clustered or nonclustered indexes on the primary key, but typically when using an integer-based primary key column, the primary key is set as the clustered index for performance reasons.

---

■**Tip** Although the CONSTRAINT <constraintName> part of any constraint declaration isn't required, it's a very good idea always to name constraint declarations using some name. Otherwise, SQL Server will assign a name for you, and it will be ugly. For example, create the following object in tempdb:

```
CREATE TABLE Test (TestId int PRIMARY KEY)
```

Look at the object name with this query:

```
SELECT constraint_name
FROM   information_schema.table_constraints
WHERE  table_schema = 'dbo'
  and  table_name = 'test'
```

You see the name chosen is something like PK__Test__8CC331600EA330E9.

---

## Adding Alternate Key Constraints

Alternate key creation is an important task of implementation modeling. Enforcing these keys is just as important. When implementing alternate keys, it's best to use a UNIQUE constraint. These are pretty much the same thing as primary key constraints and can even be used as the target of a relationship (relationships are covered later in the chapter).

The syntax for their creation is as follows:

```
[CONSTRAINT constraintname] UNIQUE [CLUSTERED | NONCLUSTERED]
```

For example, take the `Personality` table from the `MovieRental` model (see Figure 5-26).

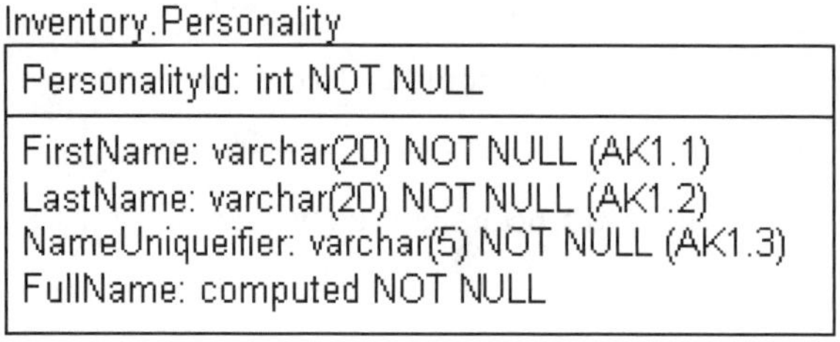

Inventory.Personality

| PersonalityId: int NOT NULL |
|---|
| FirstName: varchar(20) NOT NULL (AK1.1)<br>LastName: varchar(20) NOT NULL (AK1.2)<br>NameUniqueifier: varchar(5) NOT NULL (AK1.3)<br>FullName: computed NOT NULL |

**Figure 5-26.** *Alternate key generation sample table*

You can create this table using the following code:

```
CREATE TABLE Inventory.Personality
(
        PersonalityId           int NOT NULL IDENTITY(1,1)
            CONSTRAINT PKInventory_Personality PRIMARY KEY,
        FirstName               varchar(20) NOT NULL,
        LastName                varchar(20) NOT NULL,
        NameUniqueifier         varchar(5) NOT NULL,
            CONSTRAINT AKInventory_Personality_PersonalityName
                UNIQUE NONCLUSTERED (FirstName, LastName, NameUniqueifier)
)
```

Alternately, you can add the constraint to existing tables using `ALTER TABLE`. For example, these tables were already created with primary keys:

```
ALTER TABLE Inventory.Genre
  ADD CONSTRAINT AKInventory_Genre_Name UNIQUE NONCLUSTERED (Name)

ALTER TABLE Inventory.MovieRating
  ADD CONSTRAINT AKInventory_MovieRating_Code UNIQUE NONCLUSTERED (Code)

ALTER TABLE Inventory.Movie
  ADD CONSTRAINT AKInventory_Movie_NameAndDate
      UNIQUE NONCLUSTERED (Name, ReleaseDate)
```

When you have a relationship that is of the required one-to-one cardinality type (for example, a table assigning one employee to a given office), you can use a `UNIQUE CONSTRAINT` on the column that must have only one value in it. If the column is nullable, then see the following "Implementing Selective Uniqueness" section for more information on how to implement this.

## Implementing Selective Uniqueness

We previously discussed `PRIMARY KEY` and `UNIQUE` constraints, but in some situations neither of these will exactly fit the situation. For example, you may need to make sure some subset of the data is unique, rather than every row. An example of this is a one-to-one relationship where you need to allow nulls, for example, a `customerSettings` table that lets you add a row for optional settings for a customer. If a user has settings, a row is created, but you want to ensure that only one row is created.

For example, say you have an employee table, and each employee can possibly have an insurance policy. The policy numbers must be unique, but the user might not have a policy.

There are two solutions to this problem that are common:

- *Filtered indexes:* New for SQL Server 2008, the CREATE INDEX command syntax now has a WHERE clause so that the index pertains only to certain rows in the table.

- *Indexed view:* In recent versions prior to 2008, the way to implement this is to create a view that has a WHERE clause and then index the view.

First, create the table:

```
CREATE TABLE alt.employee
(
    EmployeeId int identity(1,1) constraint PKalt_employee primary key,
    EmployeeNumber char(5) not null
            CONSTRAINT AKalt_employee_employeeNummer UNIQUE,
    --skipping other columns you would likely have
    InsurancePolicyNumber char(10) null
)
```

In SQL Server 2008, one of the lesser discussed but pretty interesting features is filtered indexes. Everything about the index is the same, save for the WHERE clause. So, you add an index like this:

```
--Filtered Alternate Key (AKF)
CREATE UNIQUE INDEX AKFalt_employee_InsurancePolicyNumber ON
                                alt.employee(InsurancePolicyNumber)
WHERE InsurancePolicyNumber is not null
```

Then create an initial sample row:

```
INSERT INTO Alt.Employee (EmployeeNumber, InsurancePolicyNumber)
VALUES ('A0001','1111111111')
```

Upon attempting to give another employee the same insurancePolicyNumber:

```
INSERT INTO Alt.Employee (EmployeeNumber, InsurancePolicyNumber)
VALUES ('A0002','1111111111')
```

this fails:

```
Msg 2601, Level 14, State 1, Line 1
Cannot insert duplicate key row in object 'alt.employee' with unique index
'AKFalt_employee_InsurancePolicyNumber'.
```

However, adding two rows with null will work fine:

```
INSERT INTO Alt.Employee (EmployeeNumber, InsurancePolicyNumber)
VALUES ('A0003','2222222222'),
       ('A0004',NULL),
       ('A0005',NULL)
```

You can see that this:

```
SELECT *
FROM    Alt.Employee
```

returns the following:

```
EmployeeId   EmployeeNumber InsurancePolicyNumber
-----------  -------------- ---------------------
1            A0001          1111111111
3            A0003          2222222222
4            A0004          NULL
5            A0005          NULL
```

The NULL example is the classic example, because it is common to desire this functionality. However, this technique can be used for more than just NULL exclusion. As another example, consider the case where you want to ensure that only a single row is set as primary for a group of rows, such as a primary contact for an account:

```
CREATE TABLE Alt.AccountContact
(
    ContactId   varchar(10) not null,
    AccountNumber    char(5) not null, --would be FK
    PrimaryContactFlag bit not null,
    CONSTRAINT PKalt_accountContact
        PRIMARY KEY(ContactId, AccountNumber)
)
```

Again, create an index, but this time choose only those rows with primaryContactFlag = 1. The other values in the table could have as many other values as you want (of course, in this case, since it is a bit, the values could be only 0 or 1):

```
CREATE UNIQUE INDEX
    AKFAlt_AccountContact_PrimaryContact
            ON Alt.AccountContact(AccountNumber)
            WHERE PrimaryContactFlag = 1
```

So if you try to insert two rows that are primary, as in the following statements that will set both contacts 'fred' and 'bob' as the primary contact for the account with account number '11111':

```
INSERT INTO Alt.AccountContact
SELECT 'bob','11111',1
go
INSERT INTO Alt.AccountContact
SELECT 'fred','11111',1
```

then the following error is returned:

```
Msg 2601, Level 14, State 1, Line 1
Cannot insert duplicate key row in object 'alt.AccountContact' with unique
index 'AKFAlt_AccountContact_PrimaryContact'.
```

So to insert the row with 'fred' as the name and set it as primary (assuming the 'bob' row was inserted previously), you will need to update the other row to be not primary and then insert the new primary row:

```
BEGIN TRANSACTION

UPDATE Alt.AccountContact
SET primaryContactFlag = 0
WHERE   accountNumber = '11111'

INSERT Alt.AccountContact
SELECT 'fred','11111',1

COMMIT TRANSACTION
```

Note that in cases like this you would definitely want to use a transaction in your code so you don't end up without a primary contact if the insert fails for some reason.

Prior to SQL Server 2008, where there were no filtered indexes, the preferred method of implementing this was to create an indexed view. There are a couple of other ways to do this (such as in a trigger or stored procedure using an EXISTS query, or even using a user-defined function in a CHECK constraint), but the indexed view is the easiest. Then when the insert does its cascade operation to the indexed view, if there are duplicate values, the operation will fail. You can use indexed views in all versions of SQL Server though only Enterprise Edition will make special use of the indexes for performance purposes. (In other versions, you have to specifically reference the indexed view to realize the performance gains.)

Returning to the `InsurancePolicyNumber` uniqueness example, you can create a view that returns all rows other than null `insurancePolicyNumber` values. Note that it has to be schema bound to allow for indexing:

```
CREATE VIEW Alt.Employee_InsurancePolicyNumberUniqueness
WITH SCHEMABINDING
AS
    SELECT  InsurancePolicyNumber
    FROM    Alt.Employee
    WHERE   InsurancePolicyNumber is not null
```

Now, you can index the view by creating a unique, clustered index on the view:

```
CREATE UNIQUE CLUSTERED INDEX
    AKalt_Employee_InsurancePolicyNumberUniqueness
    ON alt.Employee_InsurancePolicyNumberUniqueness(InsurancePolicyNumber)
```

Now, attempts to insert duplicate values will be met with (assuming you drop the existing filtered index) the following:

```
Cannot insert duplicate key row in object
'alt.Employee_InsurancePolicyNumberUniqueness' with unique index
'AKalt_Employee_InsurancePolicyNumberUniqueness'
```

Both of these techniques are really quite fast and easy to implement, so it is really just a question of education for the programming staff members who might come up against the slightly confusing error messages in their UI or SSIS packages, for example. Pretty much no constraint error should be bubbled up to the end user, unless they are a very advanced group of users, so the UI should be smart enough to either prevent the error from occurring or at least translate it into words that the end user can understand.

## Viewing the Constraints

You can see information about the indexes and constraints using the `information` and `sys` schema views:

- `information_schema.table_constraints`
- `information_schema.key_column_usage`
- `sys.key_constraints`
- `sys.indexes`

■**Tip** It is generally best to use the `information_schema` views for system information when they're available. There are a plethora of `sys` schema objects. However, they can be a bit messier to use and aren't based on standards, so they're apt to change in future versions of SQL Server, just as these views replaced the system tables from versions of SQL Server before 2005.

For example, use this code to see the constraints that you've created in the MovieRental database you've been building throughout this chapter:

```
SELECT TABLE_NAME, CONSTRAINT_NAME, CONSTRAINT_TYPE
FROM   INFORMATION_SCHEMA.table_constraints
WHERE  CONSTRAINT_SCHEMA = 'Inventory'
ORDER  BY  CONSTRAINT_SCHEMA, TABLE_NAME
```

This returns the following results:

```
TABLE_NAME    CONSTRAINT_NAME                          CONSTRAINT_TYPE
-----------   --------------------------------------   ---------------
Genre         PKInventory_Genre                        PRIMARY KEY
Genre         AKInventory_Genre_Name                   UNIQUE
Movie         PKInventory_Movie                        PRIMARY KEY
Movie         AKInventory_Movie_NameAndDate            UNIQUE
MovieFormat   PKInventory_MovieFormat                  PRIMARY KEY
MovieRating   PKInventory_MovieRating                  PRIMARY KEY
MovieRating   AKInventory_MovieRating_Code             UNIQUE
Personality   PKInventory_Personality                  PRIMARY KEY
Personality   AKInventory_Personality_PersonalityName  UNIQUE
```

> **■Tip** The INFORMATION_SCHEMA and catalog views are important resources for the DBA to find out what is in the database. Throughout the book, I will try to give insight into some of them, but there is another book's worth of information out there on the metadata of SQL Server.

## Where Other Indexes Fit In

When you look at the INFORMATION_SCHEMA, you will notice that there is not a view for indexes. The reason for this is that indexes are physical database structures, whereas constraints are part of the logical implementation of the database. It is true that constraints are built with indexes (and need upkeep like indexes), but you shouldn't think of them in the same way as indexes. Indexes have a singular responsibility for increasing performance. (At the same time, they have to be maintained, so they decrease performance too, though hopefully considerably less than they increase it. This conundrum is the foundation of the "science" of performance tuning.)

In an OLTP system, it's usually a bad practice to do performance "guessing"—adding indexes before a need is shown—versus performance "tuning," where you respond to *known* performance problems. Only at that time is it reasonable to decide how a performance "tune" will affect the rest of the database. I'll discuss more about non-constraint-based indexes in Chapter 9.

# Building Default Constraints

If a user doesn't know what value to enter into a table, the value can be omitted, and the default constraint sets it to a valid predetermined value. This helps, in that you help users avoid having to make up illogical, inappropriate values if they don't know what they want to put in a column yet they need to create a row. (Any user interface would have to honor this default and not pass in a NULL value for a default constraint to matter; you'll learn more about that later.)

For example, consider that an experienced SQL Server user must enter a value into a column called barnDoogleFlag, which is a bit column (barnDoogleFlag was chosen because it has just as much meaning to you as some of the columns that make sense for other users). Not knowing what barnDoogleFlag represents but forced to create a new row, the user might choose to enter a 1 (hopefully barnDoogle isn't shorthand for blowing up the world!). Using default values gives the users an example of a likely value for the column. There's no question that setting default values for columns is convenient for the user.

The statement to add a default follows this structure:

```
ALTER TABLE <tableName>
    ADD [ CONSTRAINT <DefaultName> ]
    DEFAULT <constantExpression>
    FOR <columnName>
```

I'll use a simple naming standard for constraints:

```
Dflt<schema>_<tableName>_<columnName>
```

The <constantExpression> is a scalar expression that can be either a literal value, a NULL, or a function. You'll look at several different scenarios for constant expressions in the following section.

You'll look at two styles of defaults:

- *Literals*: A single value that will always be the same value.

- *Rich expressions*: These use functions to set a default value based on a situation.

## Literal Defaults

A literal is a simple single value in the same datatype that requires no translation by SQL Server. For example, Table 5-4 has sample literal values that can be used as defaults for a few datatypes.

**Table 5-4.** *Sample Default Values*

| Datatype | Possible Default Value |
|---|---|
| Int | 1 |
| varchar(10) | 'Value' |
| binary(2) | 0x0000 |
| datetime | '20080101' |

As an example in our sample database, I'll set the default in the YouthRentalsOnlyFlag column in the Customer table to 0. (First, I need to create the Person table and the Customer table.) I include the relationship between the tables as well (relationships are discussed in more detail later); see Figure 5-27.

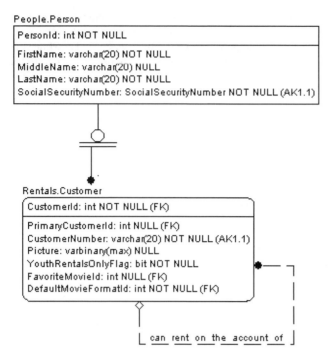

**Figure 5-27.** *Subtype implementation*

You can create the tables using the following DDL:

```
CREATE TABLE People.Person (
     PersonId              int NOT NULL IDENTITY(1,1)
        CONSTRAINT PKPerson PRIMARY KEY,
     FirstName             varchar(20) NOT NULL,
     MiddleName            varchar(20) NULL,
     LastName              varchar(20) NOT NULL,
     SocialSecurityNumber char(11) --will be redefined using CLR later
        CONSTRAINT AKPerson_SSN UNIQUE
)

CREATE TABLE Rentals.Customer (
     CustomerId            int NOT NULL
        CONSTRAINT PKRentals_Customer PRIMARY KEY,
     CustomerNumber        char(10)
        CONSTRAINT AKRentals_Customer_CustomerNumber UNIQUE,
     PrimaryCustomerId     int NULL,
     Picture               varbinary(max) NULL,
     YouthRentalsOnlyFlag  bit NOT NULL
        CONSTRAINT People_Person$can_be_a$Rentals_Customer
           FOREIGN KEY (CustomerId)
                        REFERENCES People.Person  (PersonId)
                        ON DELETE CASCADE   --cascade delete on SubType
                        ON UPDATE NO ACTION,
```

```
        CONSTRAINT
            Rentals_Customer$can_rent_on_the_account_of$Rentals_Customer
                FOREIGN KEY (PrimaryCustomerId)
                            REFERENCES Rentals.Customer  (CustomerId)
                            ON DELETE NO ACTION
                            ON UPDATE NO ACTION
)
```

The part that is of interest for this section follows:

```
ALTER TABLE Rentals.Customer
    ADD CONSTRAINT DfltRentals_Customer_YouthRentalsOnlyFlag DEFAULT (0)
        FOR YouthRentalsOnlyFlag
```

Now, when a customer is created without specifying this column, 0 is set:

```
INSERT INTO People.Person(FirstName, MiddleName, LastName, SocialSecurityNumber)
VALUES ('Doe','','Maign','111-11-1111')

--skipping several of the columns that are either nullable or have defaults
INSERT INTO Rentals.Customer(CustomerId, CustomerNumber)
SELECT Person.PersonId, '1111111111'
FROM    People.Person
WHERE   SocialSecurityNumber = '111-11-1111'
```

Then view the data:

```
SELECT CustomerNumber, YouthRentalsOnlyFlag
FROM    Rentals.Customer
```

The data returns the following result:

| CustomerNumber | YouthRentalsOnlyFlag |
| -------------- | -------------------- |
| 1111111111     | 0                    |

As another example, consider a table to store URLs. (I could have forced this into the example schema, but it didn't fit. It's a pretty good example for using defaults, however.)

```
--Using the Alt schema for alternative examples
CREATE TABLE Alt.url
(
        scheme          varchar(10) NOT NULL, --http, ftp
        computerName    varchar(50) NOT NULL, --www, or whatever
                        --base domain name (microsoft, amazon, etc.)
        domainName varchar(50) NOT NULL,
        siteType varchar(5) NOT NULL, --net, com, org
        filePath varchar(255) NOT NULL,
        fileName varchar(20) NOT NULL,
        parameter varchar(255) NOT NULL,
            CONSTRAINT PKAlt_Url  PRIMARY KEY (scheme, computerName,
                                               domainName, siteType,
                                               filePath, fileName, parameter)
)
```

Entering data into this particular table would be a pain, especially by hand. For example, say you wanted to enter http://www.microsoft.com:

```
INSERT INTO alt.url (scheme, computerName, domainName, siteType,
                         filePath, filename, parameter)
VALUES ('http','www','microsoft','com','','','')

--then display the data
SELECT   scheme + '://' + computerName +
                case when len(rtrim(computerName)) > 0 then '.' else '' end +
                domainName + '.'
        + siteType
        + case when len(filePath) > 0 then '/' else '' end + filePath
        + case when len(fileName) > 0 then '/' else '' end + fileName
        + parameter as display
FROM alt.url
```

This code returns the following result:

```
display
---------------------------
http://www.microsoft.com
```

Most of these parts are common, so it isn't unreasonable to default all the common parts of the table. For example, most URLs entered start with http, most then have www, and most are com-type sites. Execute the following:

```
ALTER TABLE Alt.url
    ADD CONSTRAINT DFLTAlt_Url_scheme
    DEFAULT ('http') FOR scheme

ALTER TABLE alt.url
    ADD CONSTRAINT DFLTAlt_Url_computerName
    DEFAULT ('www') FOR computerName

ALTER TABLE alt.url
    ADD CONSTRAINT DFLTAlt_Url_siteType
    DEFAULT ('com') FOR siteType

ALTER TABLE alt.url
    ADD CONSTRAINT DFLTAlt_Url_filePath
    DEFAULT ('') FOR filePath

ALTER TABLE alt.url
    ADD CONSTRAINT DFLTAlt_Url_fileName
    DEFAULT ('') FOR fileName

ALTER TABLE alt.url
    ADD CONSTRAINT DFLTAlt_Url_parameter
    DEFAULT ('') FOR parameter
```

Now, to insert a simple URL, such as http://www.usatoday.com, simply use the following code:

```
INSERT INTO alt.url (domainName)
VALUES ('usatoday')
```

Running the SELECT again, you'll see that you now have two rows:

```
display
---------------------------
http://www.microsoft.com
http://www.usatoday.com
```

Defaults are useful for systems in which a lot of hand-coding is required. If you want to see the defaults for a given table, you can check the INFORMATION_SCHEMA.columns table:

```
SELECT cast(column_name as varchaR(20)) as column_name, column_default
FROM   information_schema.columns
WHERE  table_schema = 'Alt'
  AND  table_name   = 'url'
```

In this case, it returns the following:

```
column_name          column_default
-------------------- ----------------
scheme               ('http')
computerName         ('www')
domainName           NULL
siteType             ('com')
filePath             ('')
fileName             ('')
parameter            ('')
```

**Tip** The expression needed to "build" the legal web address used in this section is far too messy to have to code over and over again. In the section "Computed Columns" later in this chapter, I will demonstrate how to make this calculation part of the table so that it is automatically maintained for you.

## Rich Expressions

An alternative to hard-coding a default value is to use an expression to return the default value. This expression can include any scalar function (system or user defined). You may not reference any other column in the table or have any SELECT statements, even if they return scalars (though you *can* include statements that reference other tables in a user-defined function). A common example is a physical-only column that tells you when the row was created. For example, take the MovieRental table in Figure 5-28.

```
Rentals.MovieRental
┌────────────────────────────────────────────────────────────┐
│ MovieRentalId: int NOT NULL                                   │
├────────────────────────────────────────────────────────────┤
│ RentalDatetime: smalldatetime NOT NULL (AK1.1)                │
│ MovieRentalInventoryItemId: int NOT NULL (FK) (AK1.2)         │
│ CustomerId: int NOT NULL (FK) (AK1.3)                         │
│ RentedByEmployeeId: int NOT NULL (FK)                         │
│ ReturnDate: smalldatetime NOT NULL                            │
│ ActualReturnDate: smalldatetime NULL                          │
│ AmountPaid: decimal(4,2) NOT NULL                             │
└────────────────────────────────────────────────────────────┘
```

**Figure 5-28.** *Rentals.MovieRental table for applying a complex default statement*

```
CREATE TABLE Rentals.MovieRental (
      MovieRentalId        int NOT NULL IDENTITY(1,1)
          CONSTRAINT PKRentals_MovieRental PRIMARY KEY,
      ReturnDate           date NOT NULL,
      ActualReturnDate     date NULL,
      MovieRentalInventoryItemId int NOT NULL,
      CustomerId           int NOT NULL,
      RentalTime           smalldatetime NOT NULL,
      RentedByEmployeeId   int NOT NULL,
      AmountPaid           decimal(4,2) NOT NULL,
      CONSTRAINT AKRentals_MovieRental_RentalItemCustomer UNIQUE
          (RentalTime, MovieRentalInventoryItemId, CustomerId)
)
```

A default could make sense in two columns: the `RentalDatetime` and the `ReturnDate`. For the `RentalDatetime`, the default is just the date and time that the row is created. For the `ReturnDate`, build a constraint that sets it to 10 p.m. on the fourth day after the rental occurs:

```
ALTER TABLE Rentals.MovieRental
    ADD CONSTRAINT DFLTMovieRental_RentalTime
        DEFAULT (GETDATE()) FOR RentalTime

ALTER TABLE Rentals.MovieRental
    ADD CONSTRAINT DFLTMovieRental_ReturnDate
        --Default to fourth days later
        DEFAULT (DATEADD(Day,4,GETDATE()))
            FOR ReturnDate
```

Then create a row (leaving all the other columns as 0, because they aren't germane to the example):

```
INSERT  Rentals.MovieRental (MovieRentalInventoryItemId, CustomerId,
        RentedByEmployeeId, AmountPaid)
VALUES (0,0,0,0.00)
```

Then look at the data in the defaulted columns:

```
SELECT  RentalTime, ReturnDate
FROM    Rentals.MovieRental
```

You can see the resulting values:

```
RentalTime               ReturnDate
----------------------   ----------
2007-12-16 15:22:00.000  2007-12-20
```

This is not the limit of how rich you can build defaults. You can also use other system-defined and user-defined functions as well. I will say this, however: quite often it is not the best idea to go nuts and use database logic to implement fancy defaults to implement business rules. In the `MovieRental` database, an example could be created to use a user-defined function to access some data to decide how long to set the rental date for. However, usually business rules that surround this sort of operation are more complex and should be put into the application logic. For example, you could have new rentals with a two-day rental and others with four. But most rules that have variances like this are also going to be overridable by someone (for example, if the manager wants to allow you three days, if a sale is on, or if the customer has purchased a plan that lets them keep the movie indefinitely . . .).

For scalar expressions or simple system functions, functions can make sense, such as in this example. However, more complex defaults that use other data are usually done using a trigger or more commonly using the client objects. I will cover triggers in detail in the next chapter.

---

■**Note** The most common use of defaults is to set system-managed values such as creation dates and who created a row.

---

## Adding Relationships (Foreign Keys)

I've covered relationships in previous chapters already, so I'll try to avoid saying too much more about why to use them. In this section, I'll simply discuss how to implement relationships. It's common to add constraints using the ALTER TABLE statement, but you can also do this using the CREATE TABLE statement. However, because tables are frequently created all at once, it's usually more likely that the ALTER TABLE command will be used, because parent tables needn't be created before dependent child tables in scripts.

The typical foreign key is implemented as a unique key of one table migrated to the child table that represents the entity from which it comes. Almost all the time, the unique key will be the primary key of the table, but it can be another unique key as well. (An example is a table with an identity key and a textual code. You could migrate the textual code to a table to make it easier to read, if user requirements required that.) There are several issues to consider and work through when creating relationships:

- Validating data being entered into a column against the values in a foreign key

- Cascading operations

- Relationships that span different databases or servers

The syntax of the statement for adding foreign key constraints is pretty simple:

```
[CONSTRAINT <constraintName>]
   FOREIGN KEY REFERENCES <referenceTable> (<referenceColumns>)
   [ON DELETE <NO ACTION | CASCADE | SET NULL | SET DEFAULT> ]
   [ON UPDATE <NO ACTION | CASCADE | SET NULL | SET DEFAULT> ]
```

where

- <referenceTable> is the parent table in the relationship.

- <referenceColumns> is a comma-delimited list of columns in the child table in the same order as the columns in the primary key of the parent table.

- ON DELETE or ON UPDATE clauses specify what to do in case of an invalid value. Each of these cases is covered in detail later in this section. For this section, I'll use the NO ACTION option, which causes "no action" to take place and an error to be raised.

You might need to implement an optional relationship (where the migrated key is nullable), such as the one in Figure 5-29.

**Figure 5-29.** *Optional parent-to-child relationship requires NULL on the migrated key*

The `child.parentId` column needs to allow NULLs. This is all you need to do, because SQL Server knows that when the referencing key allows a NULL, the relationship value is optional. You don't need to have a NULL primary key value for the relationship because, as discussed, it's impossible to have a NULL attribute in a primary key.

Let's go back to the tables that have been central to the examples so far (see Figure 5-30).

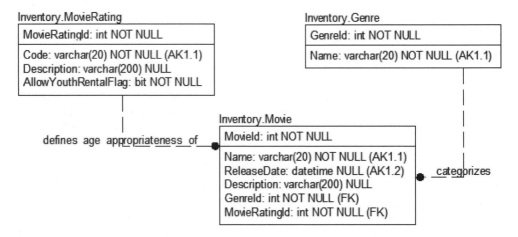

**Figure 5-30.** *Tables for implementing relationships*

Now create the relationships between these tables as follows:

```
ALTER TABLE Inventory.Movie
     ADD CONSTRAINT
         Inventory_MovieRating$defines_age_appropriateness_of$Inventory_Movie
           FOREIGN KEY (MovieRatingId)
                          REFERENCES Inventory.MovieRating  (MovieRatingId)
                          ON DELETE NO ACTION
                          ON UPDATE NO ACTION
ALTER TABLE Inventory.Movie
     ADD CONSTRAINT Inventory_Genre$categorizes$Inventory_Movie
            FOREIGN KEY (GenreId)
                          REFERENCES Inventory.Genre (GenreId)
                          ON DELETE NO ACTION
                          ON UPDATE NO ACTION
```

It's as simple as this to protect the parent/child relationships that have been set up in the design. I'll present examples of relationships and cascading deletes, as well as briefly discuss cross-database relationships in a moment. Let's try to create a Movie without a valid Genre:

```
INSERT INTO Inventory.Movie (Name, ReleaseDate,
                              Description, GenreId, MovieRatingId)
VALUES ('Stripes','19810626',
        'A loser joins the Army, though the Army is not really '+
        'ready for him',-1,-1)
```

This causes the following error:

```
Msg 547, Level 16, State 0, Line 1
The INSERT statement conflicted with the FOREIGN KEY constraint
"Inventory_MovieRating$defines_age_appropriateness_of$Inventory_Movie". The
conflict occurred in database "MovieRental", table "Inventory.MovieRating",
column 'MovieRatingId'.
```

■**Note** Note that SQL Server returns only one error from constraints. In this case, I made two errors, one with ratings and the other with the genre, but only the rating one was returned. If I fixed the rating and left the genre in error, I would just get the genre error.

In this query, look up the correct values for the INSERT:

```
INSERT INTO Inventory.Movie (Name, ReleaseDate,
                              Description, GenreId, MovieRatingId)
SELECT 'Stripes','19810626',
       'A loser joins the Army, though the Army is not really '+
       'ready for him',
       (SELECT Genre.GenreId
        FROM   Inventory.Genre as Genre
        WHERE  Genre.Name = 'Comedy') as GenreId,
       (SELECT MovieRating.MovieRatingId
        FROM   Inventory.MovieRating as MovieRating
        WHERE  MovieRating.Code = 'R') as MovieRatingId
```

■**Note** Although this query gets you what you want, if you put in a wrong value for the rating or genre values, you would get a slightly confusing error that a NULL cannot be inserted for the value. For example, if you put 'T' in for the rating, the error would read as follows:

```
Msg 515, Level 16, State 2, Line 1
Cannot insert the value NULL into column 'MovieRatingId', table
'MovieRental.Inventory.Movie'; column does not allow nulls. INSERT fails.
```

When naming foreign key constraints, you use the following convention:

```
<parentTableSchema>_<parentTable>$<verbPhrase>$<childTableSchema>_<childTable>
```

This makes any system messages that pertain to the constraints easier to trace. Any naming convention will suffice. I realize that sometimes these names seem almost comically long and a little bizarre. However, they work great in action and will generally keep you from automatically coming up with duplicate names. Frankly, as long as you don't let SQL Server generate a name for you, whatever naming convention you decide on is perfectly fine. Just make sure that it makes sense to the other people who need to be able to figure it out.

Because the relationship is defined using NO ACTION, see what happens if you now try to delete the row from the Genre table for comedy:

```
DELETE FROM Inventory.Genre
WHERE  Name = 'Comedy'
```

The following error is raised:

```
Msg 547, Level 16, State 0, Line 2
The DELETE statement conflicted with the REFERENCE constraint
"Inventory_Genre$categorizes$Inventory_Movie". The conflict occurred in
database "MovieRental", table "Inventory.Movie", column 'GenreId'.
```

To delete this row, all rows in the child table (Inventory.Movie) that used the GenreId value that corresponds to 'Comedy' would need to be deleted. The next section covers ways around this.

There are a few subtopics to consider when building relationships. The first includes the options that can automate handling some relationship options, and the other is how to deal with relationships that go outside the primary database container.

## Automated Relationship Options

In the previous example, the database prevented you from deleting the parent row if a child row existed with a reference to the parent. This is the desired action in most cases, but there are cases where the data in the child table is so integrated with the data of the parent table that, when the parent table is changed or deleted, SQL Server would always seek to modify or delete the child record without any further interaction with the user.

In this section, I'll talk more about the two clauses that were glossed over when the FOREIGN KEY constraint was first introduced—ON DELETE and ON UPDATE:

```
ALTER TABLE <tablename>
    ADD [CONSTRAINT <constraintName>]
    FOREIGN KEY REFERENCES <referenceTable> (<referenceColumns>)
    [ON DELETE <NO ACTION | CASCADE | SET NULL | SET DEFAULT> ]
    [ON UPDATE <NO ACTION | CASCADE | SET NULL | SET DEFAULT> ]
```

The default (as underlined) is the action demonstrated earlier. If the action violates referential integrity by deleting a child row, or changing a key value to something other than a value that matches a child row, just fail the operation. There are three other options:

- CASCADE: ON DELETE, delete child rows; ON UPDATE, change child rows to match updated values.

- SET NULL: ON DELETE or UPDATE of key values, set child row values to NULL, even if the value is updated to a valid value. This is useful in cases where changing the value of a key changes the meaning of the row, so you don't want to just automatically change the values.

- SET DEFAULT: ON DELETE or UPDATE, set child values to a default value. Much like SET NULL, but this is useful for columns that cannot be set to NULL.

In each of the following sections, I'll introduce the cascading types in pairs on the UPDATE and DELETE operations together. In reality, you can apply them in any combination (UPDATE CASCADE, DELETE SET NULL, and so on).

### CASCADE

When a child table implements a has-a relationship for a parent table, it's often desired to delete all the rows in the child as part of the delete of the parent. The litmus test I use is to consider whether the child is either of the following:

- *A part of the parent, such as an invoice and an invoice line item*: In this case, it usually makes sense to clean up the items on the invoice automatically because they exist only to be part of the invoice. Many-to-many resolution tables are often places where cascading makes sense.

- *Just related, like a customer and an invoice*: Deleting a customer shouldn't automatically, with no warning, delete all of that customer's invoices in the system. This kind of thing likely needs a user interface to warn the user and delete the child rows ("Like, whoa, are you sure?"). For this, leave the constraint set to `ON DELETE NO ACTION`.

For example, consider the `Personality` and `Movie` tables' relationships to the `MoviePersonality` table (see Figure 5-31).

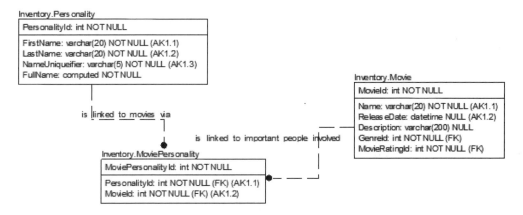

**Figure 5-31.** *Sample tables for implementing cascading relationships*

We haven't created the `MoviePersonality` table yet, so let's create it:

```
CREATE TABLE Inventory.MoviePersonality (
     MoviePersonalityId    int NOT NULL IDENTITY (1,1)
     CONSTRAINT PKInventory_MoviePersonality PRIMARY KEY,
     MovieId            int NOT NULL,
     PersonalityId      int NOT NULL,
     CONSTRAINT AKInventory_MoviePersonality_MoviePersonality
          UNIQUE (PersonalityId,MovieId)
)
```

Next, create the relationships to the `Movie` and `Personality` tables, in both cases setting the `ON DELETE CASCADE` option. If a `Movie` is deleted, go ahead and delete the connection between the movie and the `People` in it, and vice versa:

```
ALTER TABLE Inventory.MoviePersonality
     ADD CONSTRAINT
        Inventory_Personality$is_linked_to_movies_via$Inventory_MoviePersonality
           FOREIGN KEY (MovieId)
                    REFERENCES Inventory.Movie  (MovieId)
                    ON DELETE CASCADE
                    ON UPDATE NO ACTION
```

```
ALTER TABLE Inventory.MoviePersonality
     ADD CONSTRAINT
      Inventory_Movie$is_linked_to_important_people_via$Inventory_MoviePersonality
            FOREIGN KEY (PersonalityId)
                        REFERENCES Inventory.Personality  (PersonalityId)
                        ON DELETE CASCADE
                        ON UPDATE NO ACTION
```

UPDATE is left at NO ACTION because there's no need to update a surrogate primary key. Now, because we haven't yet added personalities, we'll add a couple:

```
INSERT INTO Inventory.Personality (FirstName, LastName, NameUniqueifier)
VALUES ('Cary','Grant',''),
       ('Humphrey','Bogart','')
```

Then, load some data into the MoviePersonality table:

```
INSERT INTO Inventory.MoviePersonality (MovieId, PersonalityId)
SELECT  (SELECT  Movie.MovieId
          FROM    Inventory.Movie as Movie
          WHERE   Movie.Name = 'The Maltese Falcon') as MovieId,
         (SELECT  Personality.PersonalityId
          FROM    Inventory.Personality as Personality
          WHERE   Personality.FirstName = 'Humphrey'
            AND   Personality.LastName = 'Bogart'
            AND   Personality.NameUniqueifier = '')
                                        as PersonalityId
UNION ALL
SELECT  (SELECT  Movie.MovieId
          FROM    Inventory.Movie as Movie
          WHERE   Movie.Name = 'Arsenic and Old Lace') as MovieId,
         (SELECT  Personality.PersonalityId
          FROM    Inventory.Personality as Personality
          WHERE   Personality.FirstName = 'Cary'
            AND   Personality.LastName = 'Grant'
            AND   Personality.NameUniqueifier = '')
                                        as PersonalityId
```

Then use the following code to see the data in the tables:

```
SELECT Movie.Name as Movie,
       Personality.FirstName + ' '+ Personality.LastName as Personality
FROM   Inventory.MoviePersonality as MoviePersonality
         JOIN Inventory.Personality as Personality
             On MoviePersonality.PersonalityId = Personality.PersonalityId
         JOIN Inventory.Movie as Movie
             ON Movie.MovieId = MoviePersonality.MovieId
```

This code returns the following results:

```
Movie                  Personality
-------------------    ----------------------------------------
The Maltese Falcon     Humphrey Bogart
Arsenic and Old Lace   Cary Grant
```

See what happens if you delete a row from the Movie table:

```
DELETE FROM Inventory.Movie
WHERE  Name = 'Arsenic and Old Lace'
```

Reexecuting the SELECT statement from earlier, this returns only one row:

```
Movie              Personality
------------------ -----------------------------------------
The Maltese Falcon Humphrey Bogart
```

If you're using editable keys, you can use the UPDATE CASCADE option to cascade changes from the primary key values to the child table. As an example, I'll build an alternate couple of tables, much like the tables already created (again using the Alt schema for tables that aren't part of the actual solution):

```
CREATE TABLE Alt.Movie
(
    MovieCode   varchar(20)
        CONSTRAINT PKAlt_Movie PRIMARY KEY,
    MovieName   varchar(200)
)
CREATE TABLE Alt.MovieRentalPackage
(
    MovieRentalPackageCode varchar(25)
        CONSTRAINT PKAlt_MovieRentalPackage PRIMARY KEY,
    MovieCode   varchar(20)
        CONSTRAINT Alt_Movie$is_rented_as$Alt_MovieRentalPackage
                FOREIGN KEY References Alt.Movie(MovieCode)
                ON DELETE CASCADE
                ON UPDATE CASCADE
)
```

Now, insert one of the movies with a user-defined key, as well as a rental package that uses this key:

```
INSERT INTO Alt.Movie (MovieCode, MovieName)
VALUES ('ArseOldLace','Arsenic and Old Lace')
INSERT INTO Alt.MovieRentalPackage (MovieRentalPackageCode, MovieCode)
VALUES ('ArsenicOldLaceDVD','ArseOldLace')
```

Then, once you realize that the key you've chosen sounds kind of weird, you update the primary key of the Movie row:

```
UPDATE Alt.Movie
SET    MovieCode = 'ArsenicOldLace'
WHERE  MovieCode = 'ArseOldLace'
```

---

■**Note** Note that if you have not used SET NOCOUNT OFF to turn off the rows' affected messages, only one message will be returned, with no indication that any ancillary rows were affected by the cascading constraint.

---

Then, check the rows in the tables:

```
SELECT *
FROM   Alt.Movie

SELECT *
FROM   Alt.MovieRentalPackage
```

The following rows are in the table:

```
MovieCode        MovieName
--------------   ----------------------------
ArsenicOldLace   Arsenic and Old Lace

MovieRentalPackageCode    MovieCode
----------------------    -------------------
ArsenicOldLaceDVD         ArsenicOldLace
```

## SET NULL

The SET NULL functionality on a constraint was new to SQL Server 2005, but it isn't new to the relational database. Prior to 2005, SET NULL relationship types were implemented using triggers. The idea is that instead of deleting child rows, you set the foreign key value to NULL, in essence invalidating the value. For example, say in our Person table we have the person's default media format (this is a video-store customer, perhaps).

To use the SET NULL relationship type, the relationship must be defined as optional and the migrated foreign key columns set to allow NULLs. To demonstrate this, add a relationship between the Movie table and the Customer table.

Now, let's add a new column to support the user's favorite movie choice (see Figure 5-32).

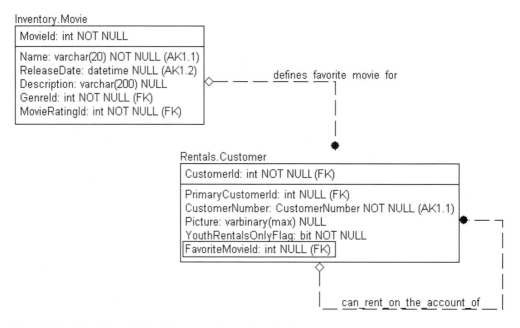

**Figure 5-32.** *Added FavoriteMovie relationship to Rentals.Customer*

```
ALTER TABLE Rentals.Customer
    ADD FavoriteMovieId INT NULL --allow nulls or SET NULL will be invalid
```

```
--Next define the foreign key constraint with SET NULL:
ALTER TABLE Rentals.Customer
    ADD CONSTRAINT Inventory_Movie$DefinesFavoriteFor$Rentals_Customer
        FOREIGN KEY (FavoriteMovieId)
                    REFERENCES Inventory.Movie  (MovieId)
                    ON DELETE SET NULL
                    ON UPDATE NO ACTION
```

Now, create a new person and make them a customer:

```
INSERT INTO People.Person(FirstName, MiddleName, LastName, SocialSecurityNumber)
VALUES ('Doe','M','Aigne','222-22-2222')

INSERT INTO Rentals.Customer(CustomerId, CustomerNumber,
                             PrimaryCustomerId, Picture, YouthRentalsOnlyFlag,
                             FavoriteMovieId)
SELECT Person.PersonId, '2222222222',NULL, NULL, 0, NULL
FROM   People.Person
WHERE  SocialSecurityNumber = '222-22-2222'
```

This person does the search for his favorite movie, *Stripes*:

```
SELECT MovieId, ReleaseDate
FROM   Inventory.Movie
WHERE   Name  = 'Stripes'
```

The list is returned with the release date, which is part of the natural key of the table:

```
MovieId     ReleaseDate
----------- ----------------------
7           1981-06-26
```

Now set the FavoriteMovieId for this customer to 7 (your value for this might be different for the key, because this is an identity key):

```
UPDATE  Rentals.Customer
SET     FavoriteMovieId = 7
WHERE   CustomerNumber = '2222222222'
```

■**Note** I used the identity key for this example because this is the way this operation would normally occur using a user interface. The "better" way to do this in a single set-based statement would be as follows:

```
UPDATE  Rentals.Customer
SET     FavoriteMovieId =  (SELECT MovieId
                            FROM   Inventory.Movie
                            WHERE   Name  = 'Stripes')
WHERE   CustomerNumber = '2222222222'
```

Then view the data:

```
SELECT  Customer.CustomerNumber, Movie.Name AS FavoriteMovie
FROM    Rentals.Customer AS Customer
            LEFT OUTER JOIN Inventory.Movie AS Movie
             ON Movie.MovieId = Customer.FavoriteMovieId
WHERE   Customer.CustomerNumber = '2222222222'
```

This returns the following result:

| CustomerNumber | FavoriteMovie |
| --- | --- |
| 2222222222 | Stripes |

Say the movie gets deleted:

```
DELETE   Inventory.Movie
WHERE    Name = 'Stripes'
  AND    ReleaseDate = '19810626'
```

You can run the SELECT again to show that the favorite movie is now NULL:

| CustomerNumber | FavoriteMovie |
| --- | --- |
| 2222222222 | NULL |

■**Note** I won't demonstrate the UPDATE SET NULL capability, because it's of limited use and it would be more or less redundant to what you have seen with SET DEFAULT (only with nothing instead of something). Any change to the value of the key in the parent causes the value in the child table to change to NULL. This would be used whenever the change to the key indicates that the row means something different from what it did before, not just a tweak to the value of the key.

**SET DEFAULT**

The example for SET DEFAULT is quite similar to SET NULL. However, in this case you don't want the value to become unknown; you also need to set it to a common value to use as a default value. Because it isn't necessary to define the column as NOT NULL, this can be better than SET NULL. A common usage could be to have a domain value of 'None', 'Not Applicable', and so on, to tell the user that the value is known, and it's just nothing.

For the example, I'll use the default example previously created using the Customer table. I created a default such that a new customer who didn't choose a default movie format was initially set to 'Dvd'. In this example, consider that a new format is added (see Figure 5-33). (I won't be adding a new subtype table for this type, because I'll be deleting the format quickly just for this example.)

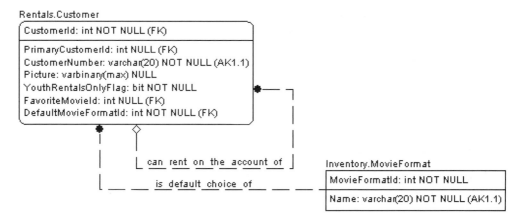

**Figure 5-33.** *Adding a relationship to allow customers their default MovieFormat*

First create the new format:

```
INSERT INTO Inventory.MovieFormat(MovieFormatId, Name)
VALUES (3, 'Playstation Portable')
```

Next, add the new column and constraint:

```
ALTER TABLE Rentals.Customer
    ADD DefaultMovieFormatId INT NOT NULL
            CONSTRAINT DFLTRentals_Customer_DefaultMovieFormatId
                DEFAULT (2) --DVD (Can hard code because surrogate key
                            --hand created, just make sure to document
                            --usage)
```

Add the referential integrity (RI) constraint:

```
ALTER TABLE Rentals.Customer
    ADD CONSTRAINT
        Inventory_MovieFormat$DefinesDefaultFormatFor$Rentals_Customer
          FOREIGN KEY (DefaultMovieFormatId)
            REFERENCES Inventory.MovieFormat  (MovieFormatId)
              ON DELETE SET DEFAULT
              ON UPDATE NO ACTION
```

Using the customer that was previously created, set the DefaultMovieFormat to 3 (PlaystationPortable):

```
UPDATE Rentals.Customer
SET    DefaultMovieFormatId = 3
WHERE  CustomerNumber = '2222222222'
```

You can check this value with the following query:

```
SELECT  MovieFormat.Name
FROM    Inventory.MovieFormat as MovieFormat
          JOIN Rentals.Customer
              ON MovieFormat.MovieFormatId = Customer.DefaultMovieFormatId
WHERE   Customer.CustomerNumber = '2222222222'
```

This returns the following result:

```
Name
--------------------
Playstation Portable
```

Once this "fad" disappears and the rental store stops renting these movies, the store deletes
PlaystationPortable as a possible MovieFormat:

```
DELETE FROM Inventory.MovieFormat
WHERE  Name = 'Playstation Portable'
```

Reexecuting the SELECT, you can see the value has reverted to the default value:

```
Name
--------------------
DVD
```

■**Note** Just like with SET NULL, I won't demonstrate the UPDATE SET DEFAULT capability because it's of limited
use, for the same reasons as stated in the previous section.

### Extra-Database Relationships

The primary limitation on constraint-based foreign keys is that the tables participating in the relationship cannot span different databases. When this situation occurs, these relationship types need
to be implemented via triggers.

It's generally a bad idea to design databases with cross-database relationships. A database
should be considered a unit of related tables that are always kept in sync. When designing solutions
that extend over different databases or even servers, carefully consider how spreading around
references to data that isn't within the scope of the database will affect your solution. You need to
understand that SQL Server cannot guarantee the existence of the value, because SQL Server uses
databases as its "container," and another user could restore a database with improper values, even
an empty database, and the cross-database RI would be invalidated. Of course, as is almost always
the case with anything that isn't "best-practice material," there are times when cross-database relationships are unavoidable, and I'll demonstrate building triggers to support this need in the next
chapter on data protection.

## Dealing with Collations and Sorting

The collation sequence shows how data is sorted when needed and how data is compared. SQL
Server and Windows provide a tremendous number of collation types from which to choose.

It's somewhat uncommon to need to change the collation from the default, which is usually
chosen to be the most generally useful. The default collation is *usually* a case-insensitive collation
that sorts 'A' = 'a'. We've used an alternative collation only a few times for columns where case
sensitivity was desired (one time was so that a client could force more four-character codes than a
case-insensitive collation would allow!).

## Viewing the Current Collation Type

To see the current collation type for the server and database, you can execute the following commands:

```
SELECT serverproperty('collation')
SELECT databasepropertyex('MovieRental','collation')
```

On most systems installed in English-speaking countries, the default collation type is
SQL_Latin1_General_CP1_CI_AS, where Latin1_General represents the normal Latin alphabet, CP1
refers to code page 1252 (the SQL Server default Latin 1 ANSI character set), and the last parts
represent case insensitive and accent sensitive, respectively. You can find full coverage of all
collation types in the SQL Server documentation

## Listing Available Collations

To list all the sort orders installed in a given SQL Server instance, you can execute the following
statement:

```
SELECT *
FROM ::fn_helpcollations()
```

On the computer on which I do testing, this query returned more than 1,000 rows, but usually
you don't need to change from the default that the database administrator initially chooses.

## Specifying a Collation Sequence

To set the collation sequence for a char, varchar, text, nchar, nvarchar, or ntext column when creating a column, you specify it using the COLLATE clause of the column definition, like so:

```
CREATE TABLE alt.OtherCollate
(
    OtherCollateId integer IDENTITY
        CONSTRAINT PKAlt_OtherCollate PRIMARY KEY ,
    Name nvarchar(30) NOT NULL,
    FrenchName nvarchar(30) COLLATE French_CI_AS_WS NULL,
    SpanishName nvarchar(30) COLLATE Modern_Spanish_CI_AS_WS NULL
)
```

Now, when you sort output by FrenchName, it's case insensitive but arranges the rows according
to the order of the French character set. The same applies with Spanish, regarding the SpanishName
column.

## Overriding an Assigned Collation

In the next example, I'll briefly show another cool use of the COLLATE keyword that can come in
handy if you need to do case-sensitive searches on a column created as case insensitive. You can use
this to affect the comparisons made in an expression. You do this by changing one or both the values on either side of the expression to a binary collation. Let's create a table, called collateTest:

```
CREATE TABLE alt.collateTest
(
    name    VARCHAR(20) COLLATE SQL_Latin1_General_CP1_CI_AS NOT NULL
)
```

```
INSERT INTO alt.collateTest(name)
VALUES ('BOB')
INSERT INTO alt.collateTest(name)
VALUES ('bob')
```

Note that for demonstration purposes, the COLLATE statement that I've included is the default for my server. This is likely to be your collation also if you have taken the default (I'll assume this collation for the rest of the book). Then execute the following against the database:

```
SELECT name
FROM alt.collateTest
WHERE name = 'BOB'
```

This returns both rows:

```
name
-------
bob
BOB
```

However, try changing the collation on the BOB literal to a binary collation and executing it:

```
SELECT name
FROM    alt.collateTest
WHERE   name = 'BOB' COLLATE Latin1_General_BIN
```

You get back only the single row that matches BOB character for character:

```
name
-------
BOB
```

You should have noticed that you cast only the scalar value 'BOB' to a binary collation. Determining collation precedence can be a tricky matter, and it's one that won't be covered here (for more information, check SQL Server Books Online). In general, it's best to add the COLLATE function to both sides of the expression when performing such an operation to avoid any ambiguity.

In our case, instead of the COLLATE on just the scalar value, you should write the statement this way, explicitly putting COLLATE on both sides of the equality operator:

```
SELECT name
FROM    alt.collateTest
WHERE name COLLATE Latin1_General_BIN = 'BOB' COLLATE Latin1_General_BIN
```

## Searching and Sorting

One of the more confusing parts of dealing with different collations is how they affect the ordering of data when sorted and how that can affect other operations such as using the LIKE operator for pattern-matching searches. When it comes to case-insensitive collations, it is pretty clear—data is treated as if 'A' and 'a' were the same character. The other common situation is accent insensitivity where 'a' and 'á' are treated as the same character. When you are using a case- and accent-insensitive collation, there will be no guarantee when sorting data that either of these characters would come first in the list. The great part about this is that when you search for a pattern such as '%A%', you know that you will get back aardvark, Abel, and Pená with no worries.

In some situations, the case and accent insensitivity that we've just described is not desirable, and you set up a column, table, or database to be case sensitive and/or accent sensitive. This is where sometimes you can get confused when using BETWEEN, LIKE, or other range type queries on characters. As an example, we'll create the following table and seed it with some single-character values:

```
CREATE TABLE alt.TestSorting
(
        value nvarchar(1) collate Latin1_General_CI_AI --case and accent
                                                        --insensitive
)
INSERT into alt.TestSorting
VALUES ('A'),('a'),(nchar(256)) /*Ā*/,('b'),('B')
```

Doing a normal case-insensitive search using the base collation (looking for all values that start with a letter) yields the results shown in the following example:

```
SELECT value
FROM alt.TestSorting
WHERE value like '[A-Z]%'
```

```
value
-----
A
a
Ā
b
B
```

Things get more interesting when you want to do a case-sensitive search. You choose a case-sensitive collation and specify it either in the WHERE clause or in your table declaration. I will specify my collation in a COLLATE condition on the search:

```
SELECT value
FROM alt.TestSorting
WHERE value collate Latin1_General_CS_AI
          like '[A-Z]%' collate Latin1_General_CS_AI   --case sensitive and
                                                        --accent insensitive
```

This query returns what seems at first a very confusing result set:

```
value
-----
A
Ā
b
B
```

Almost everyone who sees these results the first time will likely think "What the heck, why is the little b in there?" This is not an uncommon question in online forums. (In fact, that is why I added this section to the book!) The key is to look at how the values sort in the collation you are working with. Looking at the results of the following query that returns all the data in the table sorted case sensitively:

```
SELECT value
FROM    alt.TestSorting
ORDER  BY value collate Latin1_General_CS_AI
```

this query returns the following:

```
value
-----
a
Ā
A
b
B
```

You can see that A-Z, in case-sensitive terms, does not include the little a, but it does include the Ā value, since the collation is accent insensitive, and the little b because the little a is earlier than the Ā value. The little b falls within the range, since case-sensitive sorts (with Latin character sets) sort things as aAbBcC, and not as ABCabc. Logically, many expect an ABCabc sort because of the ASCII character chart that is ordered: ABCabc. In fact, a binary collation will give such an ABCabc sort, because sorting with a binary collation is based on the ASCII or Unicode values of the characters being sorted.

An alternative way of performing a case-sensitive search would be to use a LIKE operation such as the following:

```
SELECT value
FROM   alt.TestSorting
WHERE  value collate Latin1_General_CS_AI
           --Doing case sensitive search by looking for a value that has any of
           --the capital letters in it.
           like '[ABCDEFGHIJKLMNOPQRSTUVWXYZ]%' collate Latin1_General_CS_AI
```

This query returns only the capital letters including the accented capital letter Ā. For example:

```
value
-----
A
Ā
B
```

The key to understanding how searches work with different collations is to take a look at the sorting of data when you choose a collation to make sure it is clear to you how data will be sorted. The following query is a utility query I use to generate the characters I'm interested in, to see how they sort:

```
;WITH
digits (i) as(--set up a set of numbers from 0-9
        SELECT i
        FROM   (VALUES (0),(1),(2),(3),(4),(5),(6),(7),(8),(9)) as digits (i))
--builds a table FROM 0 to 99999
,sequence (i) as (
        SELECT D1.i + (10*D2.i) + (100*D3.i) + (1000*D4.i) + (10000*D5.i)
        FROM digits AS D1 CROSS JOIN digits AS D2 CROSS JOIN digits AS D3
             CROSS JOIN digits AS D4 CROSS JOIN digits AS D5)
SELECT i, nchar(i) as character
FROM sequence
WHERE i between 48 and 122 --vary to include any characters
                           --in the character set of choice
ORDER BY nchar(i) collate Latin1_General_bin --change to the collation you
                                             --are trying
```

By examining this output, you can get a feeling for how data will be sorted.

I won't delve any deeper into the subject of collation. In the SQL Server documentation, there's a large amount of information about collations, including the rules for collation precedence.

---

**■Caution** If you are building a corporate application, collation is usually no big deal. One collation is good enough for all your databases, and you don't have to care about the case where the database might be installed with a different collation. However, if you are building a product to ship to other clients, you need to be careful so that if you have to join across database boundaries or to system views, you will not have a collation mismatch. When collations clash, you may get errors telling you that operations cannot be done because of collation mismatches.

And once you have set the collation for a server/database, changing it is very difficult. The collation chosen is used for system objects and all columns where it is not set. You cannot alter a column's collation if it has any constraints or indexes referring to it.

---

## Computed Columns

Computed columns are a cool feature that was added in SQL Server 7.0 that allow you to make "virtual" columns from stored expressions to be output as part of SELECT statements without requiring a view to be created. They are perfect to implement "in-row denormalizations" without having to use "tricky" code.

The syntax is as follows:

```
<columnName> AS <computed definition> [PERSISTED]
```

A significant improvement in SQL Server 2005 was the ability to persist the data in the column automatically, so you don't have to do the calculation every time you fetch the row. This is limited to formulas that use deterministic functions (meaning they always return the same output for the same input). GETDATE() is nondeterministic since it returns a different date value based on what time it is, while UPPER is deterministic because it will return the same value when it is run with the same parameter, every time.

As an example in our system, let's add a FullName column to the Personality table so you can avoid having to do the calculation every time:

```
ALTER TABLE Inventory.Personality
    ADD FullName as
            FirstName + ' ' + LastName + RTRIM(' ' + NameUniqueifier) PERSISTED
```

Let's add a couple personalities with the same names (based on http://www.imdb.com, there are about 40 different John Smiths registered):

```
INSERT INTO Inventory.Personality (FirstName, LastName, NameUniqueifier)
VALUES ('John','Smith','I'),
       ('John','Smith','II')
```

Then you can see the data by doing a SELECT:

```
SELECT *
FROM Inventory.Personality
```

This returns the following results:

| PersonalityId | FirstName | LastName | NameUniqueifier | FullName |
| --- | --- | --- | --- | --- |
| 1 | Cary | Grant | | Cary Grant |
| 2 | Humphrey | Bogart | | Humphrey Bogart |
| 3 | John | Smith | I | John Smith (I) |
| 4 | John | Smith | II | John Smith (II) |

An example where computed columns came in handy in a database system I created was for building a grouping on the day, month, and year. In the following code, we have an example that's close to this. It groups on the second column to make the example easier to test:

```
CREATE TABLE alt.calcColumns
(
    dateColumn    datetime2(7),
    dateSecond    AS datepart(second,dateColumn) PERSISTED -- calculated column
)
SET NOCOUNT ON
DECLARE @i int
SET @i = 1
WHILE (@i < 200)
BEGIN
    INSERT INTO alt.calcColumns (dateColumn) VALUES (sysdatetime())
    WAITFOR DELAY '00:00:00.01' --or the query runs too fast
                               --and you get duplicates
    SET @i = @i + 1
END

SELECT dateSecond, max(dateColumn) as dateColumn, count(*) AS countStar
FROM alt.calcColumns
GROUP BY dateSecond
ORDER BY dateSecond
```

This returns the following results (at least it did when we were writing this book; your mileage will vary a bit):

| dateSecond | dateColumn | countStar |
| --- | --- | --- |
| 21 | 2008-06-11 17:37:21.98 | 20 |
| 22 | 2008-06-11 17:37:22.55 | 28 |
| 23 | 2008-06-11 17:37:23.96 | 53 |
| 24 | 2008-06-11 17:37:24.99 | 65 |

An almost dangerous feature with calculated columns is that they're ignored when you're inserting data if you omit the insert-field list. SQL Server ignores any calculated columns and matches the fields up as if they don't exist. For example, create the following table:

```
CREATE TABLE alt.testCalc
(
    value varchar(10),
    valueCalc AS UPPER(value),
    value2 varchar(10)
)
```

Then create some new values without the list of columns to affect:

```
INSERT INTO alt.testCalc
VALUES ('test','test2')
```

No error occurs. Execute the code:

```
SELECT *
FROM  alt.testCalc
```

You get back the following results:

| value | valueCalc | value2 |
| --------- | --------- | --------- |
| test | TEST | test2 |

■**Caution** Regardless of calculated columns, it's poor practice to code INSERT statements with no insert list. The insert should have been INSERT INTO designBook.testCalc (value, value2) VALUES ('test','test2').

As promised in the earlier section on DEFAULT constraints, I want to add a bit to the example in that section. We had coded a statement that looked like this:

```
SELECT   scheme + '://' + computerName +
                case when len(rtrim(computerName)) > 0 then '.' else '' end +
                domainName + '.'
         + siteType
         + case when len(filePath) > 0 then '/' else '' end + filePath
         + case when len(fileName) > 0 then '/' else '' end + fileName
         + parameter as display
FROM alt.url
```

Since users will rarely want to view the data in its individual bits and pieces (though they will likely want to search on them, which is why you would break up a column like this into separate columns), we would almost certainly add the following:

```
ALTER TABLE alt.url
   ADD formattedUrl AS
           scheme + '://' + computerName +
                case when len(rtrim(computerName)) > 0 then '.' else '' end +
                domainName + '.'
         + siteType
         + case when len(filePath) > 0 then '/' else '' end + filePath
         + case when len(fileName) > 0 then '/' else '' end + fileName
         + parameter PERSISTED
```

Now you can simply type this:

```
SELECT formattedUrl
FROM   Alt.url
```

And the output will be as follows:

```
formattedUrl
--------------------------------
http://www.microsoft.com
http://www.usatoday.com
```

Once you have created the computed column, you can use a couple of catalog views to see the metadata about them. The first is sys.columns, and the second is sys.computed_columns. As an example, using the tables that have already been created, you can see when a column is computed in sys.columns in the is_computed column.

```
SELECT cast(name as varchar(20)) as name, is_computed
FROM   sys.columns
WHERE  object_id('alt.testCalc') = object_id
```

This returns the following:

```
name                 is_computed
-------------------- ------------
value                0
valueCalc            1
value2               0
```

If you want to see the specific metadata about the computed column, you can use the sys.computed_columns view, which will give you several pieces of information, including whether or not the column is persisted and the definition of the computed column:

```
SELECT name, is_persisted, definition
FROM   sys.computed_columns
WHERE  object_id('alt.testCalc') = object_id
```

which in our case is as follows:

```
name                 is_persisted    definition
-------------------- --------------- ----------------------------------------
valueCalc            0               (upper([value]))
```

# Implementing User-Defined Datatypes

Complex datatypes build upon the intrinsic datatypes and allow you to shape the type to some exact need. In SQL Server 2005 and later, UDTs can be in the following categories:

- *Datatype aliases*: Allow you to predefine a datatype based on the intrinsic types.
- *CLR-based datatypes*: Allow you to base a datatype on a CLR assembly. Allow for complex datatypes.

Generally speaking, user-defined types should be used minimally because they increase the complexity of the implemented system, particularly when upgrading the system. However, there are definite uses for them, particularly the CLR-based datatypes. For example, Microsoft implemented the spatial types using CLR-based datatypes.

■**Caution**  Several features are going to be removed in the version of SQL Server that follows 2008, so you should stop using them immediately. These features are as follows:

- `sp_addtype`: Added a user-defined type
- `CREATE RULE`: Created a rule that could be bound to columns
- `sp_bindrule`: Bound a rule to a column
- `CREATE DEFAULT`: Created a default that could be bound to columns
- `sp_binddefault`: Bound a default to a column

Also deprecated are any of the functions that are used to manage rules and default objects.

## Datatype Aliases

You can use the datatype alias to specify a commonly used datatype configuration that's used in multiple places. The syntax is as follows:

```
CREATE TYPE <typeName>
        FROM <intrinsic type> --any type that can be used as a column of a
                              --table, with precision and scale or length,
                              --as required by the intrinsic type
        [NULL | NOT NULL]
```

When declaring a table, if nullability isn't specified, then `NULL` or `NOT NULL` will be based on this setting, not on the setting of `ANSI_NULL_DFLT_ON` (as discussed in an earlier section, "Nullability").

For example, let's create a type for an American Social Security number. We'll do this example using an alternate `Person` table in the `alt` schema; then we'll build the same thing in the CLR section and implement it in the `People.Person` table from the main example as follows:

```
CREATE TYPE SSN
        FROM char(11)
              NOT NULL
```

Then build the example table with it:

```
CREATE TABLE alt.Person
(
    PersonId     int NOT NULL,
    FirstName    varchar(30) NOT NULL,
    LastName     varchar(30) NOT NULL,
    SSN          SSN              --no null specification to make a point
                                  --generally it is a better idea to
                                  --include a null spec.
)
```

Then create a new row:

```
INSERT Alt.Person
VALUES (1,'rie',' lationship','234-43-3432')

SELECT PersonId, FirstName, LastName, SSN
FROM    Alt.Person
```

This returns the following result:

| personId | firstName | lastName | SSN |
| --- | --- | --- | --- |
| 1 | rie | lationship | 234-43-3432 |

Then, let's try to enter a row with a NULL SSN:

```
INSERT  Alt.Person
VALUES  (2,'dee','pendency',NULL)
```

You get the following error:

```
Msg 515, Level 16, State 2, Line 1
Cannot insert the value NULL into column 'SSN', table
'tempdb.designBook.person';column does not allow nulls. INSERT fails.
The statement has been terminated.
```

I have never really used these kinds of types, because you cannot do anything with these other than simply alias a type. For example, take the SSN type. It's char(11), so you cannot put a 12-character value in, sure. But what if the user had entered 234433432 instead of including the dashes? The datatype would have allowed it, but it isn't what's desired. The data will still have to be checked in other methods (such as CHECK constraints, which is covered in Chapter 6).

In practice, datatype aliases aren't all that useful in practice, but they're available in cases where they make sense, such as if a tool expects a certain datatype name, other than one of the SQL Server ones. My advice is to shy away from them unless they make sense in your particular situation.

## CLR-Based Datatypes

SQL Server 2005 introduced a new way to extend the type system by allowing DBAs and developers the ability to use .NET and the CLR to create user-defined datatypes. Chapter 11 discusses more details on all the database objects that you can create with the CLR integration and how it works and performs.

We simply want to say "avoid them," because several quirks make these UDTs complex to use. For example, the CLR class they're based on has to be registered on any client that uses them. On the other hand, CLR-based UDTs allow for an interesting tool and can provide more flexibility than simply aliasing intrinsic datatypes. You can add properties and methods to the datatypes to extend their functionality, as well as include complex validation and manipulation logic for modifications and extensive formatting when returning values.

There are several rules to follow when creating your own UDTs with .NET. Your .NET class or structure must be serializable, support NULL values, allow for conversion to and from a string type, and follow the specific .NET "contract" for creating a UDT. Let's look at an example of creating a datatype for an American Social Security number again, this time as a CLR datatype coded in VB .NET. I want to give you the complete code required for a simple example. I won't go into the specifics of the code too much. For a deeper understanding of the code and all the details for coding CLR-based objects, consider the book *Pro SQL Server 2005 Assemblies* by Robin Dewson and Julian Skinner (Apress, 2005) or Books Online.

To use CLR objects such as our UDT inside SQL Server, you must first enable the CLR for the server. By default, running code in .NET assemblies inside SQL Server is disabled. Note that the option to enable the CLR is a server-wide option and cannot be enabled per database. To enable the loading of .NET assemblies for the server, run the following commands:

```
EXEC sp_configure 'clr enabled', 1
go
RECONFIGURE
```

To finish the sample database that has been built throughout the chapter, I'll build a CLR datatype to implement an SSN type. You can use the following code to create a `SocialSecurity` datatype in VB .NET. (You can use any version of Visual Studio, even the command line if you aren't faint of heart, though the Professional Team System version comes with project templates to make building datatypes easier. There are resources on the Web to help you build CLR objects for SQL Server if you're using other versions.)

```vbnet
Option Strict On

Imports System
Imports System.Data
Imports System.Data.Sql
Imports System.Data.SqlTypes
Imports Microsoft.SqlServer.Server
Imports System.Text.RegularExpressions


'-------------------------------------------------
' Purpose: Social Security number user-defined type
' Written: 12/17/2005
' Comment:
'
' SqlUserDefinedType attribute contains data used by SQL Server 2005
' at runtime and by the Professional version of Visual Studio
' and above at deployment time. UDT's must be serializable and implement
' INullable.
'
' Format.Native - indicates SQL server can Serialize the type for us
' Name - Name of UDT when created in SQL Server (used by VS at deployment)
' IsByteOrdered - indicates if type can be ordered (used by SQL Server at
' runtime)
' IsFixedLength - indicates if length of type is fixed (used by SQL Server
' at runtime)
'-------------------------------------------------
<Serializable()> _
<Microsoft.SqlServer.Server.SqlUserDefinedType(Format.Native, _
     IsByteOrdered:=True, IsFixedLength:=True, Name:="CLRSSN")> _
Public Structure SsnUdt
    Implements INullable

    ' Private member
    Private m_Null As Boolean
    Private m_ssn As Integer

    Public Overrides Function ToString() As String
        ' format SSN for output
        Return Me.Ssn.ToString("000-00-0000")
    End Function
```

```vbnet
    ' private property to set/get ssn stored as integer
    Private Property Ssn() As Integer
        Get
            Return m_ssn
        End Get
        Set(ByVal value As Integer)
            m_ssn = value
        End Set
    End Property

    Public ReadOnly Property IsNull() As Boolean Implements INullable.IsNull
        Get
            Return m_Null
        End Get
    End Property

    ' return our UDT as a null value
    Public Shared ReadOnly Property Null() As SsnUDT
        Get
            Dim h As SsnUDT = New SsnUDT
            h.m_Null = True
            Return h
        End Get
    End Property

    ' get data from SQL Server as string and parse to return our UDT
    Public Shared Function Parse(ByVal s As SqlString) As SsnUDT
        If s.IsNull Then
            Return Null
        End If

        ' validate value being passed in as a valid SSN
        If IsSsnValid(s.ToString()) Then
            Dim u As SsnUDT = New SsnUDT
            u.Ssn = ConvertSSNToInt(s.ToString())
            Return u
        Else
            Throw New ArgumentException("SSN is not valid.")
        End If
    End Function

    ' validate ssn using regex matching - returns true if valid, false if not
    Private Shared Function IsSsnValid(ByVal ssn As String) As Boolean
        Return Regex.IsMatch(ssn, _
                "^(?!000)([0-6]\d{2}|7([0-6]\d|7[012]))([ -
]?)(?!00)\d\d\3(?!0000)\d{4}$", _
                RegexOptions.None)
    End Function

    ' private function to convert SSN as a string to an integer
    Private Shared Function ConvertSSNToInt(ByVal ssn As String) As Integer
        Dim ssnNumbers As Integer
        Try
            ' try a simple conversion
            ssnNumbers = Convert.ToInt32(ssn)
```

```
        Catch ex As Exception
            ' if simple conversion fails, strip out everything
            ' but numbers and convert to integer
            Dim ssnString As String = ""
            For i As Integer = 0 To ssn.Length - 1
                If "0123456789".IndexOf(ssn.Chars(i)) >= 0 Then
                    ssnString += ssn.Chars(i)
                End If
            Next
            ssnNumbers = Convert.ToInt32(ssnString)
        End Try
        Return ssnNumbers
    End Function

End Structure
```

After the UDT is coded, you must compile and deploy it to SQL Server. You can do this automatically using Visual Studio 2005 or manually using the .NET 2.0 SDK and T-SQL. To deploy our new UDT using Visual Studio 2005, I'll create a new project and select the SQL Server Project template from the database project type. Visual Studio then asks you to add a database reference. In the Solution Explorer, right-click your new project, and select Add ➤ User-Defined Type. Name the file, and click Add. Enter the code for the UDT and then select Build ➤ Deploy *Projectname*. This compiles the project, loads the assembly to the database specified when you added the database reference, and creates the UDT with the name you used for the structure in your code.

To create the UDT manually, you must first compile the UDT code using the appropriate compiler for your language: `csc.exe` for C#, `vbc.exe` for VB, and so on. Please see the .NET SDK help for the command syntax. After compiling the code into a .NET DLL assembly, you deploy the code to SQL Server using the `CREATE ASSEMBLY` statement:

```
CREATE ASSEMBLY UDTSsn from 'D:\Projects\udtSSN.dll' WITH PERMISSION_SET = SAFE
```

Once the assembly that contains your UDT is deployed to SQL Server, you must register the class in the assembly as a UDT type using the `CREATE TYPE` statement. Note that this is the same statement you use to create an alias datatype with a slightly different syntax.

For deploying the CLR type (and any CLR objects) to different environments, you can also script the assembly from Management Studio, and it will include the binary files so you can create the object without the source files (it will include `CREATE ASSEMBLY` and `ALTER ASSEMBLY` commands):

```
CREATE ASSEMBLY [Apress]
AUTHORIZATION [dbo]
FROM 0x4D5A900003000000040000 --lots of hex code removed
WITH PERMISSION_SET = SAFE
```

---

■**Note** In the code download, I have included the binary code for the SSN type in the T-SQL code for your usage, if you don't want to build the type from the CLR code provided (also in the download). There are a few `ALTER ASSEMBLY` statements that add more stuff from other files that have binary representations also.

---

In the following statement, `CLRSSN` is the name of the type, `Apress` is the name of the assembly that was loaded with the `CREATE ASSEMBLY` statement, and `Apress.ProSqlServerDatabaseDesign.SsnUdt` is the namespace followed by the UDT structure name, as defined in the .NET code and project settings:

```
CREATE TYPE [dbo].[CLRSSN]
EXTERNAL NAME [Apress].[ProSqlServerDatabaseDesign.SsnUdt]
```

Now you can use this new UDT just like you would any intrinsic SQL Server datatype such as int or datetime. It's even in the datatype drop-down when designing tables using SQL Server Management Studio.

There are some interesting things to note about the example. First, the class is tagged with the Serializable() attribute and a special SQL Server attribute for UDTs called SqlUserDefinedType(). These two attributes are required for CLR-based UDTs. The SqlUserDefinedType() attribute also requires a Format property. This property can either be Format.Native or Format.UserDefined.

Format.Native uses standard SQL Server binary serialization to store the data for the UDT column. IsByteOrdered defines that the values this datatype represents can be ordered, and it's sorted on the binary representation when the value is serialized. The good part is that you don't have to write any of the serialization yourself. The disadvantage is that it can be used only if all the public properties of the class are fixed-length and value-type datatypes. This includes a majority of .NET datatypes, such as numbers and dates. If your UDT uses reference types such as .NET strings, or you need more flexibility when serializing your data, you need to use the Format.UserDefined property and implement IBinarySerialize. Implementing IBinarySerialize requires writing your own Read and Write functions to serialize the UDT as binary data, a task that's beyond what we need to put in a section such as this.

An important optional parameter on the SqlUserDefined() attribute is the IsByteOrdered parameter. When this value is TRUE, this informs SQL Server that the stored data for columns that use this datatype is in binary order. The column can therefore be used in comparison operations, in ORDER BY and GROUP BY clauses, can be indexed, and can be used in primary and foreign key relationships. This means that the physical serialization of the value is sortable using the value. SQL Server can sort and compare the values *without* instantiating the CLR object.

There are two required conversion functions for UDTs: a Parse() function and a ToString() function. The Parse() function allows data to be inserted into a UDT column as a string, similar to the way you insert data into a column of type DateTime.

Let's add the new datatype to our Person table, which has already been established in this chapter:

```
/* --table was created earlier.  Included as a reminder of the structure
CREATE TABLE People.Person (
        PersonId              int NOT NULL IDENTITY(1,1)
            CONSTRAINT PKPerson PRIMARY KEY,
        FirstName             varchar(20) NOT NULL,
        MiddleName            varchar(20) NULL,
        LastName              varchar(20) NOT NULL,
        SocialSecurityNumber char(11) --will be redefined using CLR later
            CONSTRAINT AKPeople_Person_SSN UNIQUE
)
*/
```

You'll change the datatype to the new type just created. Start out by adding it as a NULL type:

```
ALTER TABLE People.Person
   ADD SocialSecurityNumberCLR CLRSSN NULL
```

Then update the new column to the existing values:

```
UPDATE People.Person
SET    SocialSecurityNumberCLR = SocialSecurityNumber
```

Then drop the column (and constraint) and rename the column to the original name:

```
ALTER TABLE People.Person
  DROP CONSTRAINT AKPeople_Person_SSN
ALTER TABLE People.Person
  DROP COLUMN SocialSecurityNumber
EXEC sp_rename 'People.Person.SocialSecurityNumberCLR',
  'SocialSecurityNumber', 'COLUMN';
```

Put back the constraints:

```
ALTER TABLE People.Person
  ALTER COLUMN SocialSecurityNumber CLRSSN NOT NULL
ALTER TABLE People.Person
  ADD CONSTRAINT AKPeople_Person_SSN UNIQUE (SocialSecurityNumber)
```

Next, let's look at the data. If the type isn't registered on the client machine, simply using a type such as a normal SQL Server type will return the binary version of the data. To get the textual version, you can use the ToString() method:

```
SELECT SocialSecurityNumber, socialSecurityNumber.ToString() as CastedVersion
FROM  People.Person
```

This returns the following results:

| SocialSecurityNumber | CastedVersion |
| --- | --- |
| 0x00869F6BC7 | 111-11-1111 |
| 0x008D3ED78E | 222-22-2222 |

If you try to insert invalid data, the CLR object will throw an error that was coded in the Parse method, stating that the SSN isn't valid:

```
Msg 6522, Level 16, State 2, Line 2
A .NET Framework error occurred during execution of user defined routine or
aggregate 'SSN':
System.ArgumentException: SSN is not valid.
System.ArgumentException:
  at APress.udtSsn.Parse(SqlString s)
```

Note that there was the following validation logic in the Parse() function to verify that what's being entered is a valid SSN:

```
If Regex.IsMatch(s.ToString(), _
    "^(?!000)([0-6]\d{2}|7([0-6]\d|7[012]))([ -]?)(?!00)\d\d\3(?!0000)\d{4}$" _
    , _
```

Here I chose to use the RegEx .NET class with a regular expression pattern for SSNs. It accepts the SSN as nine numbers, in the format 999-99-9999 or in the format 999 99 9999. It also checks against some published rules of SSNs, such as that the first three digits cannot be 000. (This pattern was found at http://www.regexlib.com/REDetails.aspx?regexp_id=535.) This is something that would certainly be more complex to do using only T-SQL code. It's a benefit of CLR UDTs over alias datatypes and allows us to keep complex field-level validation close to the SQL Server engine.

Internally, I'll store the SSN as an Int32, but then format the output NNN-NN-NNNN by overriding the ToString() function:

```
Public Overrides Function ToString() As String
    ' format SSN for output
    Return Me.SSN.ToString("000-00-0000")
End Function
```

Note that the UDT assembly that's created must be registered in SQL Server and must also be available in the client application to be functional. When accessing a column defined with the SSN datatype from a client application, either you have to use the ToString() method to get a "pretty" version of the data or you must have the UDT assembly registered on the client machine, which has the rather large downside of coupling your database to your application far more than any of the intrinsic types will. You can then make use of any UDT properties or methods and can serialize and deserialize the column as necessary.

---

■**Note**  When SELECTing a UDT column using SQL Server Management Studio, Management Studio returns the byte representation of the UDT. To see the string representation of the UDT column, you must use the ToString() method of the UDT column.

---

### Visual Studio

The preceding code for the Social Security CLR UDT can look a little bit daunting at first. When creating a CLR UDT, it's easiest to use a version of Visual Studio 2005 that includes the SQL Server project templates. A large portion of the code for the SSN UDT was created by the template inside the new SQL Server project type within Visual Studio 2005. The template provides a shell that handles most of the "rules" necessary for coding a CLR UDT and example properties and methods that can be used as starting points for your own projects. Visual Studio also includes the ability to debug UDTs on the server and automatically deploys the assembly and creates the UDT on the database specified when creating the UDT. I'll discuss a bit more about creating CLR database objects using Visual Studio 2005 in Chapter 11.

### Uses for CLR UDTs

CLR UDTs are best used to extend the SQL Server type system with additional scalar types or different ranges of data. Some examples include specialized currency of various countries and unsigned integers. Here are some other potential uses of UDTs:

- *IP addresses*: Has properties for each of the four octets and validates each IP address. It might also include a property for the class of IP address, such as whether it's a Class A, Class B, or Class C address. An interesting benefit of this datatype is that you could serialize it such that it would sort correctly, unlike what happens if you store an IP address as varchar or char datatypes.

- *A URL/URN/URI datatype*: It would include validation logic and perhaps some special serialization that allows for sorting by domain name.

Although the possibilities are unlimited, we'd suggest that CLR UDTs be considered only for very specialized circumstances that make the database design far more robust and easy to work with. CLR UDTs are a nice addition to the DBA's and developer's toolkit, but they should be reserved for those times when adding a new scalar datatype solves a business problem.

### Challenges with UDTs

With all the power of creating our own UDTs with .NET code, it might seem logical to want to create business objects inside of SQL Server as UDTs. After all, you can add properties and methods to your UDTs much the same way you would create an Employee business object. The ADO.NET code that's written to access the UDTs from SQL Server automatically marshals the binary data between client and server. Is there still a need for a middle tier that houses our custom business objects? Absolutely. Let's look at some of the drawbacks to using UDTs as business objects. It's more difficult to index individual properties of UDTs. For example, an employee business object might have a first name, last name, employee number, address, phone number, and so on. In a normalized table, each of these entities would have its own column. Any of these columns might have an index for optimized performance. It takes a lot more effort to persist a calculated column of a single property of a UDT to serve as an indexed column.

---

■**Note** It's possible to use the ALTER ASSEMBLY statement to update CLR UDTs without dropping them first. You can use this feature to update UDTs with fixes in the code. If the public properties change at all, the existing columns using this UDT will have to be updated, or some special versioning code in the UDT will have to be used and persisted in the serialized data so you know which version of the UDT was used for the data.

---

For both types of UDTs, once the type is bound and used by any columns, you cannot change the type. This can be a real problem when you're developing, if you don't do a good enough job designing your datatypes.

---

■**Tip** Complex datatypes of either type have limited uses. Use them only in cases where they're absolutely necessary and provide a great benefit.

---

# Documenting Your Database

In your modeling, you've created descriptions, notes, and various pieces of data that will be extremely useful in helping the developer understand the whys and wherefores of using the tables you've created. In previous versions of SQL Server, it was difficult to make any use of this data directly in the server. In SQL Server 2000, Microsoft introduced extended properties that allow you to store specific information about objects. This is great, because it allows you to extend the metadata of your tables in ways that can be used by your applications using simple SQL statements.

By creating these properties, you can build a repository of information that the application developers can use to do the following:

- Understand what the data in the columns is used for
- Store information to use in applications, such as the following:
  - Captions to show on a form when a column is displayed
  - Error messages to display when a constraint is violated
  - Formatting rules for displaying or entering data

To maintain extended properties, you're given the following functions and stored procedures:

- `sys.sp_addextendedproperty`: Used to add a new extended property.
- `sys.sp_dropextendedproperty`: Used to delete an existing extended property.
- `sys.sp_updateextendedproperty`: Used to modify an existing extended property.
- `fn_listextendedproperty`: A system-defined function that can be used to list extended properties.
- `sys.extendedproperties`: Can be used to list all extended properties in a database. Less friendly than `fn_listextendedproperty`.

Each (other than `sys.extendedproperties`) has the following parameters:

- `@name`: The name of the user-defined property.
- `@value`: What to set the value to when creating or modifying a property.
- `@level0type`: Top-level object type, often schema, especially for most objects that users will use (tables, procedures, and so on).
- `@level0name`: The name of the object of the type that's identified in the `@level0type` parameter.
- `@level1type`: The name of the type of object such as `Table`, `View`, and so on.
- `@level1name`: The name of the object of the type that's identified in the `@level1type` parameter.
- `@level2type`: The name of the type of object that's on the level 2 branch of the tree under the value in the `@level1Type` value. For example, if `@level1type` is `Table`, then `@level2type` might be `Column`, `Index`, `Constraint`, or `Trigger`.
- `@level2name`: The name of the object of the type that's identified in the `@level2type` parameter.

For example, let's go back to the `Inventory.Movie` table (and schema) created a while back:

```
/*
CREATE SCHEMA Inventory --tables pertaining to the videos to be rented

CREATE TABLE Inventory.Movie
(
        MovieId              int NOT NULL,
        Name                 varchar(20) NOT NULL,
        ReleaseDate          datetime NULL,
        Description          varchar(200) NULL,
        GenreId              int NOT NULL,
        MovieRatingId        int NOT NULL
)
*/
```

To document this table, let's add a property to the table and columns named `Description` (or whatever you want to name it). You execute the following script after creating the table:

```
--dbo.person table description
EXEC sp_addextendedproperty @name = 'Description',
   @value = 'tables pertaining to the videos to be rented',
   @level0type = 'Schema', @level0name = 'Inventory'

--dbo.person table description
EXEC sp_addextendedproperty @name = 'Description',
   @value = 'Defines movies that will be rentable in the store',
   @level0type = 'Schema', @level0name = 'Inventory',
   @level1type = 'Table', @level1name = 'Movie'
```

```
--dbo.person.personId description
EXEC sp_addextendedproperty @name = 'Description',
   @value = 'Surrogate key of a movie instance',
   @level0type = 'Schema', @level0name = 'Inventory',
   @level1type = 'Table', @level1name = 'Movie',
   @level2type = 'Column', @level2name = 'MovieId'

--dbo.person.firstName description
EXEC sp_addextendedproperty @name = 'Description',
   @value = 'The known name of the movie',
   @level0type = 'Schema', @level0name = 'Inventory',
   @level1type = 'Table', @level1name = 'Movie',
   @level2type = 'Column', @level2name = 'Name'

--dbo.person.lastName description
EXEC sp_addextendedproperty @name = 'Description',
   @value = 'The date the movie was originally released',
   @level0type = 'Schema', @level0name = 'Inventory',
   @level1type = 'Table', @level1name = 'Movie',
   @level2type = 'Column', @level2name = 'ReleaseDate'
```

. . . and so on.

Now, when you go into Management Studio, right-click your table and select Properties. Choose Extended Properties, and you see your description, as shown in Figure 5-34.

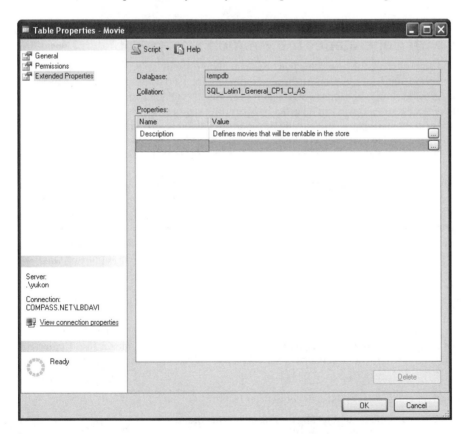

**Figure 5-34.** *Reward for hard work done. Descriptions in Management Studio.*

The `fn_listExtendedProperty` object is a system-defined function you can use to fetch the extended properties (the parameters are as discussed earlier—the name of the property and then each level of the hierarchy):

```
SELECT objname, value
FROM   fn_listExtendedProperty ('Description',
                                'Schema','Inventory',
                                'Table','Movie',
                                'Column',null)
```

This code returns the following results:

```
objname              value
-------------------  -----------------------------------------
MovieId              Surrogate key of a movie instance
Name                 The known name of the movie
ReleaseDate          The date the movie was originally released
```

There's some pretty cool stuff in there using extended properties, and not just for documentation. Because the property value is a `sql_variant`, you can put just about anything in there (with a 7,500-character limitation, that is). A possible use could be to store data entry masks and other information that the client could read in once and use to make the client experience richer.

For more information, check the SQL Server 2008 Books Online section "Using Extended Properties on Database Objects."

## Working with Dependency Information

Once you build your objects, the next thing will be to use them (otherwise, why on Earth did you spend all of this time, right?). Documenting how your objects are used by other objects can be a pretty tedious process, and in versions of SQL Server previous to 2008, figuring out what object uses which using the system objects was not a particularly fruitful task, because dependency information was stored only when objects were created. If you dropped and re-created a table, then the dependency information for that table was lost because it was not re-created once it was gone. (This is one of the reasons I did not even mention dependency information in the previous editions of the book.)

The problem was that dependency information was stored by object ID. When you dropped and re-created an object, its object ID changed, invalidating the dependency information. Worse yet, you had to drop and re-create all of your subordinate objects to fix dependencies, and even that would not guarantee that your dependencies were re-created, because you might have circular references where one object refers to another object that refers to it. And to make matters yet again worse, stored procedures didn't need to refer to an existing object, because they supported deferred name resolution, in case you want to create the object at a later time. And if you were interested in dependencies across database or server boundaries, then you could forget it. Convinced yet? Dependency information was horribly maintained in the manner that it had been implemented since the early days of SQL Server.

In SQL Server 2008, Microsoft has implemented functionality to track dependencies by name, rather than by numeric identifiers (seems logical, huh?). This will allow dependency information to be far more useful than in previous versions of SQL Server. It will allow you to determine things like this:

- Cross-server and cross-database dependencies by name

- The impact of dropping an object by finding all objects that use it

- What dependent objects you will need to execute an object

- Entities that have caller-dependent references (objects that have schema parts left unknown, such as database.objectName, so it could change depending on the caller)

- What tables use a given object to determine the impact of dropping the object (such as a UDT used by numerous columns)

The objects you can use to get dependency information are as follows:

- sys.sql_expression_dependencies: Dependencies based on names. Shows column dependencies only for schema-bound objects

- sys.dm_sql_referenced_entities: Dynamic management object that lists objects that depend on a given object (passed as a parameter). This will also get column references where sys.sql_expression_dependencies would not.

- sys.dm_sql_referencing_entities: Dynamic management object that lists objects that depend on a given object (passed as a parameter). This will also get column references where sys.dm_sql_referenced_entities would not.

---

■**Caution** There is also a catalog view called `sys.sql_dependencies` that returned dependencies based solely on the ID values that were stored. It is being deprecated, and you should use `sys.sql_expression_dependencies` in all current and future work.

---

First, we have the `Sys.sql_expression_dependencies` catalog view. This object will give you dependencies from one object to another (does not include constraints, because they have dependency information documented elsewhere). In our current database, we have a few dependencies already with several computed columns we have created so far:

```
SELECT  objects.type_desc as object_type,
        OBJECT_SCHEMA_NAME(referencing_id) + '.' +
                    OBJECT_NAME(referencing_id) AS object_name,
        COL_NAME(referencing_id, referencing_minor_id) as
                    column_name,
        CASE WHEN referenced_id IS NOT NULL THEN 'Does Exist'
                ELSE 'May Not Exist' END
            AS referencedObjectExistance,
        referenced_class_desc,
        coalesce(referenced_server_name,'<>') + '.'
            + coalesce(referenced_database_name,'<>') + '.'
            + coalesce(referenced_schema_name,'<>') + '.'
            + coalesce(referenced_entity_name,'<>') as
                                    referenced_object_name,
        COL_NAME(referenced_id, referenced_minor_id) as
                            referenced_column_name,
        is_caller_dependent,
        is_ambiguous
FROM  sys.sql_expression_dependencies
        join sys.objects
            on objects.object_id = sql_expression_dependencies.referencing_id
```

This query returns the following result set:

- object_type: type_desc from sys.objects tells the type of object that references some other item.

- object_name: This specifies the schema and name of the object that references some other item.

- `column_name`: If the object is a column, this specifies the name of it (for example, a computed column).

- `referenced_object_existance`: If the object being referenced no longer exists, the `referenced_id` will be null.

- `referenced_class`: This indicates the type of thing that is being referenced.

- `referenced_object_name`: This specifies the name of the object being referenced, with `<>` filling in any of the pieces that are not in the name.

- `is_caller_dependent`: This specifies whether the reference depends on who is calling the object. It indicates that the schema is left out of the call, so it is decided based on the user's default schema and then the database's default schema (dbo).

In our database, running the query will show you that the `USER_TABLE` Inventory.Personality's column `FullName` is dependent on `<>.<>.`Inventory.Personality's `FirstName`, `LastName`, and `NameUniqueifier` columns.

Where things get really nice are in other, coded objects like stored procedures, since sometimes tables get dropped and procedures hang around, even though they could not be executed. So as an example, I will create the following two objects:

```
CREATE TABLE Alt.DependencyTest
(
    DependencyTestId    int
        CONSTRAINT PKAlt_DependencyTest PRIMARY KEY,
    Value   varchar(20)
)
GO
CREATE PROCEDURE Alt.DependencyTest$Proc
(
        @DependencyTestId int
) AS
   BEGIN
        SELECT DependencyTest.DependencyTestId, DependencyTest.Value
        FROM Alt.DependencyTest
        WHERE DependencyTest.DependencyTestId = @DependencyTestId
   END
```

Now, if you re-execute this, you will see that the stored procedure shows up in the list, with a reference to `<>.<>.`Alt.DependencyTest, but the column does not. The column will not show up in this view but will in the dynamic management views.

If you drop the table:

```
DROP TABLE Alt.DependencyTest
```

you will now see that the stored procedure still shows a dependency on `<>.<>.`Alt.DependencyTest, but it says that it may not exist (yay!). This is the kind of check you will want to run after creating a new procedure where you expect all references to be complete.

The catalog view does a good job of getting dependency information, but when you want a more complete picture for an object, you can use the two dynamic management objects (both functions) that Microsoft has provided. They dig into the actual code that was parsed and return all dependencies. For example, the `sys.dm_sql_referenced_entities` dynamic management object lets you see what the Alt.DependencyTest$Proc references, and you can run the following (re-create the Alt.DependencyTest table, because it will give you all of the references):

```
SELECT    coalesce(referenced_server_name,'<>') + '.'
            + coalesce(referenced_database_name,'<>') + '.'
            + coalesce(referenced_schema_name,'<>') + '.'
            + coalesce(referenced_entity_name,'<>') as referenced_object_name,
        referenced_minor_name
FROM    sys.dm_sql_referenced_entities ('Alt.DependencyTest$Proc','OBJECT')
```

This returns the following:

| referenced_object_name | referenced_minor_name |
| --- | --- |
| <>.<>.Alt.DependencyTest | DependencyTestId |

```
Msg 2020, Level 16, State 1, Line 1
The dependencies reported for entity "Alt.DependencyTest$Proc" do not include
references to columns. This is either because the entity references an object that
does not exist or because of an error in one or more statements in the entity.
Before rerunning the query, ensure that there are no errors in the entity and that
all objects referenced by the entity exist.
```

It returns this because in the procedure the table is referenced, and the two columns are also. This is excellent information, because now you can see what might be locked when using this procedure. The opposite procedure, sys.dm_sql_referencing_entities, gives you, at a table level, what objects are referring to the object, in this case, the Alt.DependencyTest table. Re-create the table:

```
CREATE TABLE Alt.DependencyTest
(
    DependencyTestId    int
        CONSTRAINT PKAlt_DependencyTest PRIMARY KEY,
    Value   varchar(20)
)
```

Then execute the following query:

```
SELECT coalesce(referencing_schema_name,'<>') + '.'
        + coalesce(referencing_entity_name,'<>') as referenced_object_name,
            referencing_class_desc as referencing_class
FROM    sys.dm_sql_referencing_entities ('Alt.DependencyTest','OBJECT')
```

This will return the following:

| referenced_object_name | referencing_class |
| --- | --- |
| Alt.DependencyTest$Proc | OBJECT_OR_COLUMN |

This is just a brief overview of the new functionality in 2008 to get dependency information for the common objects you should be interested in when managing your databases. There are deeper uses of the objects, such as seeing objects using XML, Service Broker objects, and so on. This is beyond the scope of this section as well as this book.

# Best Practices

The following are a set of some of the most important best practices when implementing your database structures. Pay particular attention to the advice about UNIQUE constraints. Just having a surrogate key on a table is one of the worst mistakes made when implementing a database.

- *Make sure you've invested in proper database generation tools*: Do this after you know what the tool should be doing (not before). Implementing tables, columns, relationships, and so on is a tedious and painful task when done by hand. There are many great tools that double as logical data modeling tools and also generate these objects, as well as sometimes the objects and code to be covered in the upcoming three chapters.

- *Maintain normalization*: As much as possible, try to maintain the normalizations that were designed in Chapter 4. It will help keep the data better protected and will be more resilient to change.

- *Be careful when implementing subtypes*: Carefully consider whether leaving subtypes as multiple tables makes more sense than rolling them up into a single table. The single-table solution always *seems* the easiest idea (because it is always easier to use!), but it can end up causing more trouble because you end up with tables that have complex logic to determine which fields are valuable in a given situation or not. Implementing subtypes makes coding the other application layers more troublesome, because it isn't overly apparent which fields fit in which situation, whereas it's clear when the objects are subtyped. (Remember, data integrity always comes first!)

- *Develop a real strategy for naming objects*: Keep the basics in mind:
  - *Give all objects reasonably user-friendly names*: Make sure that it's obvious—at least to support personnel—what the purpose of every object, column, and so on is without digging into documentation, if at all possible.
  - *Have either all plural or all singular names for tables*: Consistency is the key.
  - *Have all singular names for columns*.
  - *I use only singular names for tables or columns*.

- *Develop template domains*: Reuse in every case where a similar datatype is needed. This cuts down on time spent implementing and makes users of the data happy, because every time they see a column called Description, it's likely that it will have the same characteristics of other like columns.

- *Carefully choose the datatype and nullability for each column*: These are the first level of data protection to keep your data clean and pure. Also, improper datatypes can cause precision difficulties with numbers and even performance issues.

- *Make certain that every table has at least one UNIQUE constraint that doesn't include an artificial value*: It's a good idea to consider using an IDENTITY column as the primary key. However, if that is the only UNIQUE constraint on the table, then there can (and usually will) be duplication in the *real* columns of the table—a bad idea.

- *Be cautious with user-defined datatypes*:
  - Use CLR-based types only when needed to implement something special such as a complex datatype, such as a point (x,y). Intrinsic types are faster and more standard to work with.
  - Generally avoid the use of datatype aliases. They're generally more trouble than they're worth.

- *Implement foreign keys using foreign key constraints*: They're fast, and no matter what kind of gaffes a client makes, the relationship between tables cannot be gotten wrong if a foreign key constraint is in place.

- *Document and script everything*: Using extended properties to document your objects can be extremely valuable. Most of all, when you create objects in the database, keep scripts of the T-SQL code for later use when moving to the QA and Production environments. A further step of keeping your scripts in a source control repository is a definite good next step as well so you can see where you are, where you are going, and where you have been in one neat location.

# Summary

This has been a long chapter covering a large amount of ground. Understanding how to build tables, and how they're implemented, is the backbone of every database designer's knowledge.

We've taken our logical model and examined each entity to determine how feasible it is to implement. Then we dealt specifically with subtypes, because they can be problematic. In some cases, consider possible deviations from the strict normalization rules in extreme cases (though fight this as much as possible).

After getting satisfied that a model was ready to implement, I took a deep look at SQL Server tables, walking through limits on tables and the CREATE TABLE and ALTER TABLE syntax for adding constraints and modifying columns. General guidelines were given for naming tables, columns, indexes, and foreign key constraints. The key to good naming is consistency, and if the naming standards I suggested here seem too ugly, messy, or just plain weird to you, choose your own. Consistency is the most important thing for any naming convention. This is something I learn every day when I work with people who are so set in their ways that a value such as 'X-100' means more to them than the full description that says exactly what the code means, which rarely bears any resemblance to the code. But it's what they're used to and have been doing since the days when a code could be only five characters.

The two most important sections of this chapter were on choosing datatypes and implementing unique keys. I completed this chapter by discussing the process of choosing primary keys and at least one natural key per table. In the next chapter, I'll show how to finish the task of implementing the base OLTP system by implementing the rest of the business rules required to keep the data in your database as clean as possible.

CHAPTER 6

■■■

# Protecting the Integrity of Your Data

*What person would spend hundreds of hours outfitting their home with the perfect furnishings to keep the occupants comfortable, only to neglect to erect a roof and walls to keep out the bugs, the burglars, and even the weather?*

—Me

**Y**es, it does seem pretty silly, but the fact is, many people spend tremendous amounts of time designing the correct database storage (or at least what seems like tremendous amounts of time to them) and then just leave the data unprotected. To be honest, I know what some people are thinking. "This is what the data access layer is for." I couldn't agree more . . . and less. Do you stop protecting your home with a few walls? That depends on where you live, I suppose, but most of us lock our doors, have a community watch group, and possibly even have armed guards if we are wealthy and have expensive belongings, right? In most companies, the data that is stored in the database is worth far more than even the belongings of the richest rock stars (well, other than their families, of course). So, keeping the data from becoming an untrustable calamity of random bits is in everyone's best interest.

The point of the chapter is simple: protect the data. So many people think that just building tables to hold data is the stopping point for the usefulness of SQL Server's part in the solution, but I submit to you that at the heart of a great database implementation is the ability to maintain that database in a state whereby the data conforms to your original design specifications. Perhaps in an ideal world you could control all data input carefully, but in reality the database is designed and then turned over to the programmers and users to "do their thing." Those pesky users immediately exploit any weakness in your design to meet the requirements that they "*thought* they gave you in the *first* place." No matter how many times I've forgotten to apply a UNIQUE constraint in a place where one was natural to be (yeah, I am preaching to myself along with the choir in this book sometimes), it's amazing to me how quickly the data duplications start to occur. Ultimately, user perception is governed by the reliability and integrity of the data users retrieve from your database. If they detect data anomalies in their data sets (usually in skewed report values), their faith in the whole application plummets faster than a skydiving elephant who packed lunch instead of a parachute. After all, your future reputation is somewhat based on the perceptions of those who use the data on a daily basis.

The foundations of strong data integrity lie in well-defined and normalized sets of tables, correctly defined relationships (PKs, FKs), and precise datatype specifications—all of which I covered in previous chapters. In this chapter, we add the final layer of protection, in the form of the constraints and logic that control and validate data input and manipulation. With this in place, we hope we'll protect our database from "bad" data, no matter what the end users do. To this end, in this chapter I will discuss the topic of data protection in two major groups:

- *Automatic data protection:* This type of protection includes methods that protect data without any intervention from the client. They simply occur based on normal DML actions, regardless of the user interface used.

- *Manual data protection:* This type of protection requires the client to specifically use some object for the data to be protected. Using a different object may or may not validate the data in the same way (which is a major problem of many applications).

Nearly every application will have some amount of each of these buckets, but in my opinion, the more protection you can place in the "automatic protection" category, the easier it will be on the database administrator over the years of life of your application.

One of the things I hope you will feel as you read this chapter (and keeping the earlier ones in mind) is that, if at all possible, use the data storage layer to protect the fundamental integrity of the data. Not that the other code shouldn't play a part: I don't want to have to wait for the database layer to tell me that a value is required, but at the same time, I don't want a back-end loading process to have to use application code to validate that the data is fundamentally correct either. The point is that the application layers do a good job of making it easy for the user, but the data layer can realistically be made nearly 100 percent trustable, whereas the application layers cannot.

The hard part is deciding how much to use the database and how much to use the application. This is a good part of the goal of this chapter. The basic rule of thumb I use is that the database should protect data at a fundamental level. The rules implemented in database code are rarely changing, and even more rarely can these rules be overridden. At a basic level, you expect keys to be validated, data to be reasonably formatted and fall within acceptable ranges, and required values to always exist, just to name a few. When those criteria can be assured, the rest won't be so difficult, since the application layers can trust that the data they fetch from the database meets them, rather than having to revalidate.

# Best Practices

*Applications come and applications go, but the data must always be protected.*

Up to this point in the book, I don't consider the design principles I've covered to be open to much debate. There are levels of compliance to be sure, but in general they're all good guiding principles that should be followed as closely as possible.

At this point, however, opinions and strategies all too often diverge. Many people think they achieve optimum flexibility by placing most data protection and validation logic outside the database. In this way, they avoid using database-specific code (such as triggers, procedures, and even sometimes constraints) as far as possible. Others take a much more database-centric approach, placing as much of the data logic as possible right in the database, as close to the data as possible. Others (with saner heads) adopt an approach that's "somewhere in between." When I talk of "best practices," these are the practices I adopt, and I definitely take a reasonably database-centric approach where the database is responsible for protecting the basic, fundamental integrity of the data, regardless of what validations occur outside the database.

The reason I like to have the data validation and protection logic as close as possible to the data it guards is that it has the advantage that you *have* to write this logic only once. It's all stored in the same place, and it takes forethought to bypass.

At the same time, I believe you should put most validation code in the database *and* in the client, mostly for software usability sake. No user wants to have to wait for the round-trip to the server to find out that a column value is required. You build these simple validations into the client so they get immediate feedback. Putting code in multiple locations like this bothers a lot of people because they think it's:

- Bad for performance
- More work

Well, these are true statements. It is a bit worse on performance, in a minor way, but done right, it will help the overall performance of the system rather than hinder it. Is it more work? Well, yeah, it is. I certainly can't try to make it seem like it's less work to do something in multiple places other than to say that it is completely worth it. In a good user interface, you will likely code even simple rules in multiple places, such as having the color of a column indicate that a value is required and having a check in the submit button that looks for a reasonable value instantly before trying to save the value.

Even though it is a little bit bad for performance and more work, the main reason it is worth it to implement data protection in the database is that even if you have to do it in other places, many different clients can access your data. I tend to group them into four broad classifications:

- Users using custom front-end tools
- Users using generic data manipulation tools, such as Microsoft Access
- Routines that import data from external sources
- Raw queries executed by data administrators to fix problems caused by user error

Each of these poses different issues for your integrity scheme. What's more important is that each of these scenarios (with the possible exception of the second) forms part of nearly every database system developed. To best handle each scenario, the data must be safeguarded, using mechanisms that work without the responsibility of the user.

If you decide to implement your data logic in a different tier other than directly in the database, then you have to make sure that you implement it—and far more importantly, implement it *correctly*—in every single one of those clients. If you update the logic, you have to update it in multiple locations anyhow. If a client is "retired" and a new one introduced, then the logic must be replicated in that new client. You're much more susceptible to coding errors if you have to write the code in more than one place. Having your data protected in a single location helps prevent programmers from forgetting to enforce a rule in one situation, even if they remember *everywhere* else.

With that in mind, the following are my recommended best practices for implementing data protection and validation logic. Throughout the remainder of the chapter, I'll describe each methodology outlined, as follows:

- *Use CHECK constraints as often as possible to manage single row requirements*: CHECK constraints are fast and easy to apply and can even access other tables' data using functions.

- *Use triggers to perform data validations that CHECK constraints cannot handle*: The work of some trigger functionality may be moved off into middle-tier objects, though triggers do often have performance benefits over external objects. Use triggers when the following types of validations need to be made:

  - *Cross-database referential integrity (RI)*: Just basic RI, but SQL Server doesn't manage declarative constraints across database boundaries.

  - *Intra-table, inter-row constraints*: For example, when you need to see that the sum of a column value over multiple rows is less than some value (possibly in another table).

  - *Inter-table constraints*: For example, if a value in one table relies on the value in another. This might also be written as a functions-based CHECK constraint, but it is often more maintainable to use a trigger.

  - *Introducing desired side effects to your queries*: For example, cascading inserts, maintaining denormalized data, and so on.

- *Make sure that triggers are able to handle multirow operations*: Although most modifications are in terms of a single row, if a user enters data in more than one row, there's a possibility of invalid data being entered.

- *Consider using stored procedures to encapsulate SQL used to enforce additional rules*: When several SQL statements are involved in data modification, use stored procedures to batch statements together, usually using a transaction (covered in Chapter 9 in more detail).

- *Use client code for primary rule enforcement sparingly*: When constraints and triggers won't cover a need, then you will not be able to implicitly trust that the data in the table will meet the requirements. This is because you can't get around triggers and constraints unless you make a conscious effort by dropping or disabling them.

In moving down this list, the solutions become less desirable (from an ease of use and maintenance point of view), yet each one has specific benefits that are appropriate in certain situations, so you need to understand them all.

---

■**Note**  In this chapter, I'll present various examples that aren't tied to previous chapters. I'll be building these objects in a new sample database I'll create called `ProtectionChapter`. You can use whatever database you wish. Also, some of the stand-alone examples use a different format for the example code. I did this to drive home the point that any standard is fine.

---

# Automatic Data Protection

The first type of protection I will discuss is automatic, in that once it has been installed, there is very little concern that it won't do its job. You want to use automatic data protection when it is absolutely necessary that the data is validated to meet certain criteria. When the data is cleaned and checked, no further process (like an ETL process) needs to check to see whether criteria are met. Whenever you perform a DML operation (INSERT, UPDATE, or DELETE), the database engine will protect the data from invalid values. There are two types of automatic data protection:

- *Declarative data protection:* Mechanisms used to declare some condition must be true. This group includes the constraint types I have already discussed (NULL, PRIMARY KEY, UNIQUE, FOREIGN KEY, and DEFAULT) and the one I will cover in this chapter, the CHECK constraint. CHECK constraints are used to validate data at a row level in a declarative manner. They are natural to implement and are often useful to the optimizer to improve query-processing performance.

- *DML triggers:* Special procedures that automatically execute whenever a row is inserted, updated, or deleted from a table.

Of course, nothing is perfect, and each of these can be disabled. However, the fact is that normal users will not (and most certainly should not) have access to disable triggers and must follow these rules, no matter if they are using an application or manually writing DML statements.

---

■**Note**  I built in several types of protection into a database I was developing, and the programmer in charge of the application was doing it with DBO rights in the database. My error messages were annoying him, so he executed the code to disable the triggers before doing a DML statement. This is one of the reasons why you never let the application behave as the DBO, since the programmers can do whatever they want along these lines (this was not malicious, but sometimes the actions are). In the end, I rewrote my triggers to work with his code better, but it was kind of a touchy situation. True story.

---

# Declarative Data Protection

Constraints are SQL Server devices that are used to enforce data integrity automatically on a single column or row. You should use constraints as extensively as possible to protect your data, because they're simple, they're declarative, and they have minimal overhead.

One of the greatest aspects of constraints is that the query optimizer can use them to optimize queries. For example, say you place a constraint on a column that requires that all values for that column must fall between 5 and 10. If a query is executed that asks for all rows with a value greater than 100 for that column, the optimizer will know without even looking at the data that no rows meet the criteria.

SQL Server has five kinds of constraints:

- NULL: Though NULL constraints aren't technically constraints, they behave like constraints.
- PRIMARY KEY *and* UNIQUE *constraints*: Used to make sure your keys contain only unique combinations of values.
- FOREIGN KEY: Used to make sure that any migrated keys have only valid values that match the keys they reference.
- DEFAULT: Used to set an acceptable default value for a column when the user doesn't provide one. (Some people don't count defaults as constraints, because they don't constrain updates.)
- CHECK: Used to limit the values that can be entered into a single column or an entire row.

Having previously considered the first four of these in Chapter 5, I'll now focus attention on the final one, the CHECK constraint. You use CHECK constraints to disallow improper data from being entered into columns of a table. CHECK constraints are executed after DEFAULT constraints (so you cannot specify a default value that would contradict a CHECK constraint) and INSTEAD OF triggers (which I'll cover later in this chapter). CHECK constraints cannot affect the values being inserted or deleted but are used to verify the validity of the supplied values.

There are two flavors of CHECK constraint: column and table. Column constraints reference a single column and are used only when the individual column is referenced in a modification. CHECK constraints are considered table constraints when more than one column is referenced in the criteria. Fortunately, you don't have to worry about declaring a constraint as either a column constraint or a table constraint. When SQL Server compiles the constraint, it verifies whether it needs to check more than one column and sets the proper internal values.

We'll be looking at building CHECK constraints using two methods:

- Simple expressions
- Expressions using user-defined functions

The two methods are similar, but you can build more complex constraints using functions, though the code in a function can be more complex and difficult to manage. In this section, we'll take a look at some examples of constraints built using each of these methods; then we'll take a look at a scheme for dealing with errors from constraints. First, though, let's build the simple schema that will form the basis of the examples in this section.

## Example Schema

All the examples in this section on creating CHECK constraints use the sample tables shown in Figure 6-1.

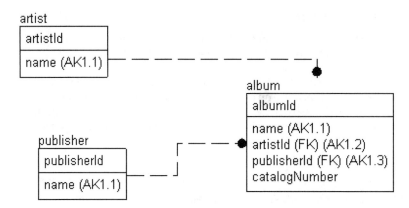

**Figure 6-1.** *The example schema*

To create and populate the tables, execute the following code:

```
CREATE SCHEMA Music
GO
CREATE TABLE Music.Artist
(
   ArtistId int NOT NULL,
   Name varchar(60) NOT NULL,

   CONSTRAINT PKMusic_Artist PRIMARY KEY CLUSTERED (ArtistId),
   CONSTRAINT PKMusic_Artist_Name UNIQUE NONCLUSTERED (Name)
)
CREATE TABLE Music.Publisher
(
        PublisherId               int primary key,
        Name                      varchar(20),
        CatalogNumberMask varchar(100)
        CONSTRAINT DfltMusic_Publisher_CatalogNumberMask default ('%'),
        CONSTRAINT AKMusic_Publisher_Name UNIQUE NONCLUSTERED (Name),
)

CREATE TABLE Music.Album
(
   AlbumId int NOT NULL,
   Name varchar(60) NOT NULL,
   ArtistId int NOT NULL,
   CatalogNumber varchar(20) NOT NULL,
   PublisherId int NOT null --not requiring this information

   CONSTRAINT PKMusic_Album PRIMARY KEY CLUSTERED(AlbumId),
   CONSTRAINT AKMusic_Album_Name UNIQUE NONCLUSTERED (Name),
   CONSTRAINT FKMusic_Artist$records$Music_Album
           FOREIGN KEY (ArtistId) REFERENCES Music.Artist(ArtistId),
   CONSTRAINT FKMusic_Publisher$published$Music_Album
           FOREIGN KEY (PublisherId) REFERENCES Music.Publisher(PublisherId)
)
```

Then seed the data with the following:

```
INSERT  INTO Music.Publisher (PublisherId, Name, CatalogNumberMask)
VALUES (1,'Capitol',
        '[0-9][0-9][0-9]-[0-9][0-9][0-9a-z][0-9a-z][0-9a-z]-[0-9][0-9]'),
        (2,'MCA', '[a-z][a-z][0-9][0-9][0-9][0-9][0-9]')

INSERT  INTO Music.Artist(ArtistId, Name)
VALUES (1, 'The Beatles'),(2, 'The Who')

INSERT INTO Music.Album (AlbumId, Name, ArtistId, PublisherId, CatalogNumber)
VALUES (1, 'The White Album',1,1,'433-43ASD-33'),
        (2, 'Revolver',1,1,'111-11111-11'),
        (3, 'Quadrophenia',2,2,'CD12345')
```

# Basic Syntax

The basic syntax of the ALTER TABLE statement that concerns CHECK constraints is as follows:

```
ALTER TABLE <tableName> [WITH CHECK | WITH NOCHECK]
    ADD [CONSTRAINT <constraintName>]
    CHECK <BooleanExpression>
```

Most of this is the same as presented in the previous chapter when I built DEFAULT constraints. However, two particular parts of this declaration need to be discussed:

- <BooleanExpression>
- [WITH CHECK | WITH NOCHECK]

Note also that you can include CHECK constraint declarations in the CREATE TABLE statements, just like you can for DEFAULT and FOREIGN KEY constraints.

## <BooleanExpression>

The <BooleanExpression> component is similar to the WHERE clause of a typical SELECT statement, but with the caveat that no subqueries are allowed. (They are allowed in standard SQL, but not in T-SQL. In T-SQL you must use a function to access other tables, something I cover later in the chapter.) It can access system and user-defined functions and use the name or names of any columns in the table. However, it cannot access any other table, and it cannot access any row other than the current row being modified (except through a function, as I'll discuss in the next section). If multiple rows are modified, each row is checked against this expression individually.

The interesting thing about this expression is that unlike a WHERE clause, the condition is checked for falseness rather than truth. Without going completely into a discussion of NULL (a trip worth taking on your own), it's important to understand that CHECK constraints fail only on rows that are explicitly False. If the result of a comparison is UNKNOWN because of a NULL comparison, then the row will succeed.

Even if this isn't immediately confusing, it is often confusing when figuring out why an operation on a row did or did not work as you might have expected. For example, consider the Boolean expression value <> 'fred'. If value is NULL, then this is accepted, because NULL <> 'fred' is UNKNOWN. If value is 'fred', it fails because 'fred' <> 'fred' is False. You can look for NULL values by explicitly checking for them using IS NULL or IS NOT NULL.

For example, if you wanted to implement a rule that no artist with a name that contains the word *Duran* is allowed, you could code the following:

```
ALTER TABLE Music.Artist WITH CHECK
    ADD CONSTRAINT chkMusic_Artist$Name$NoDuranNames
            CHECK (Name not like '%Duran%')
```

Then test by trying to insert a new row with an offending value:

```
INSERT INTO Music.Artist(ArtistId, Name)
VALUES (3, 'Duran Duran')
```

This returns the following result:

```
Msg 547, Level 16, State 0, Line 1
The INSERT statement conflicted with the CHECK constraint
"chkMusic_Artist$Name$noDuranNames". The conflict occurred in database
"ProtectionChapter", table "Music.Artist", column 'Name'.
```

thereby keeping my music collection safe from at least one band from the '80s.

## [WITH CHECK | WITH NOCHECK]

When you create a CHECK constraint, the WITH CHECK setting (the default) gives you the opportunity to decide whether to check the existing data in the table.

Let's add a row for another musician who I don't necessarily want in my table:

```
INSERT INTO Music.Artist(ArtistId, Name)
VALUES (3, 'Madonna')
```

You might specify the constraint using WITH NOCHECK because you now want to allow this new constraint, but there's data in the table that conflicts (usually more difficult to clean up):

```
ALTER TABLE Music.Artist WITH NOCHECK
    ADD CONSTRAINT chkMusic_Artist$Name$noMadonnaNames
            CHECK (Name not like '%Madonna%')
```

The statement is added to the table definition, though the NOCHECK means that the bad value is retained in the table. However, any time a modification statement references the column, the CHECK constraint is fired. The next time you try to set the value of the table to the same bad value, an error occurs. In the following statement, I simply set every row of the table to the same name it has stored in it:

```
UPDATE Music.Artist
SET Name = Name
```

This gives you the following error message:

```
Msg 547, Level 16, State 0, Line 1
The UPDATE statement conflicted with the CHECK constraint
"chkMusic_Artist$Name$noMadonnaNames". The conflict occurred in database
"ProtectionChapter", table "Music.Artist", column 'Name'.
```

"What?" most users would exclaim. If the value was in the table, shouldn't it already be good? The user is correct (how often do you get to say that!?!). This kind of thing will confuse the heck out of everyone and cost you greatly in support, unless the data in question is *never* used. But if it's never used, then just delete it, or include a time range for the values. CHECK Name not like %Madonna% OR rowCreateDate < '20050101' is a reasonable compromise.

Using NOCHECK and leaving the values unchecked is a pretty bad thing to do, in my opinion. If the constraint is built WITH CHECK, the optimizer could possibly make use of this fact when building plans if the constraint didn't use any functions and just used simple comparisons such as less than, greater than, and so on. For example, imagine you have a constraint that says that a value must be less than 10. If in a query you look for all values 11 and greater, the optimizer can use this fact and immediately return zero rows, rather than having to scan the table to see whether any value matches.

If a constraint is built with WITH CHECK, it's considered trusted, because the optimizer can trust that all values conform to the CHECK constraint. You can determine whether a constraint is trusted by using the INFORMATION_SCHEMA and the object_property function:

```
SELECT CHECK_CLAUSE,
        objectproperty(object_id(CONSTRAINT_SCHEMA + '.' +
                            CONSTRAINT_NAME),'CnstIsNotTrusted') AS NotTrusted
FROM INFORMATION_SCHEMA.CHECK_CONSTRAINTS
WHERE CONSTRAINT_SCHEMA = 'Music'
  And CONSTRAINT_NAME = 'chkMusic_Artist$Name$noMadonnaNames'
```

This returns the following results (with some minor formatting, of course):

```
CHECK_CLAUSE                         NotTrusted
---------------------------------    ----------------------
(NOT [Name] like '%Madonna%')        1
```

Make sure that the system trusts all your CHECK constraints so that the optimizer can use the information when building plans.

---

■**Caution** Adding constraints with NOCHECK to save time hits upon one of the odd realities of dealing with very large systems. They take forever to modify, so often you'll feel like you need to cut corners to get it done fast. The problem is that the shortcut on design or implementation often costs way more in later maintenance costs or, even worse, in the user experience. If at all possible, it's best to try to get everything set up properly in production.

---

There is a method to disable and reenable a constraint using ALTER TABLE tableName NOCHECK | CHECK CONSTRAINT constraintName. However, this method suffers from the same issues that creating the constraint with NOCHECK in the first place does. The constraint will not be trusted, not to mention it is too easy to forget to reenable the constraint.

## CHECK Constraints Based on Simple Expressions

By far, most CHECK constraints are simple expressions that just test some characteristic of a value in a column or columns. These constraints don't reference any data other than the single column.

As a few examples, consider the following:

- *Empty strings*: Prevent users from inserting a space character to avoid any real input into a column—CHECK (LEN(ColumnName) > 0).

- *Date range checks*: Make sure a reasonable date is entered. For example:

  - Movie rental return date (as we had in the previous chapter) should be greater than one day after the RentalDate—CHECK (ReturnDate > dateadd(day,1,RentalDate)).

  - Date of some event that's supposed to have occurred already in the past—CHECK (EventDate <= GETDATE()).

- *Value reasonableness*: Make sure some value, typically a number of some sort, is reasonable for the situation. Reasonable, of course, does not imply that the value is necessarily correct for the given situation—just that it is within a reasonable domain of values. For example:

  - *Values must be non-negative integers*: This is common, because there are often columns where negative values don't make sense (hours worked, miles driven, and so on)—CHECK (MilesDriven >= 0).

  - *Royalty rate for an author that's less than or equal to 30 percent*: If this rate ever could be greater, then it isn't a CHECK constraint. So if 15 percent is the typical rate, the UI might warn that it isn't normal, but if 30 percent is the absolute ceiling, it would be a good CHECK constraint—CHECK (RoyaltyRate <= .3).

CHECK constraints of this variety are always a good idea when you have situations where there are data conditions that *must* always be true. Another way to put this is that the very definition of the data is being constrained, not just a user-specified convention that could change fairly often. These CHECK constraints are generally extremely fast and won't negatively affect performance except in extreme situations. As an example, I'll just show the code for the first, empty string check, because simple CHECK constraints are easy to code once you have the syntax. A common CHECK constraint that I add to many string type columns (varchar, char, and so on) prevents blank data from being entered. This is because most of the time if a value is required, it isn't desired that the value for a column be blank, unless it makes sense to have no value for the column (as opposed to a NULL value, meaning that the value is not currently known).

For example, in the Album table, a Name column doesn't allow NULLs. The user has to enter something, but what about a single space character or empty string?

```
INSERT INTO Music.Album ( AlbumId, Name, ArtistId, PublisherId, CatalogNumber )
VALUES ( 4, '', 1, 1,'dummy value' )
```

If you allowed this in your database, you'd certainly end up with a blank row, because there would likely be one occasion for which a user would enter a row prematurely after having failed to input his name. The second time a space is entered instead of a name:

```
INSERT INTO Music.Album ( AlbumId, Name, ArtistId, PublisherId, CatalogNumber )
VALUES ( 5, '', 1, 1,'dummy value' )
```

an error would be returned:

```
Msg 2627, Level 14, State 1, Line 1
Violation of UNIQUE KEY constraint 'AKAlbum_Name'. Cannot insert duplicate
key in object 'Music.Album'.
```

Alternatively, you might have a nonunique, constraint-bound column, such as a description or notes column, where you might have many blank entries. You might add the following constraint to prevent this from ever happening again (after deleting the two blank rows). It works by trimming the value in Name, eliminating any space characters, and checking the length:

```
DELETE FROM Music.Album
WHERE   Name = ''
GO
ALTER TABLE Music.Album WITH CHECK
    ADD CONSTRAINT chkMusic_Album$Name$noEmptyString
          CHECK (LEN(RTRIM(Name)) > 0)
```

The CHECK expression here uses the LEN function on an RTRIMed column to ensure that if there are no characters other than space characters, then a zero-length string is returned (or a NULL if your table allowed it). Of course, you know you already entered a value that will clash with your constraint, so you get the following error message:

```
Msg 547, Level 16, State 0, Line 1
The ALTER TABLE statement conflicted with the CHECK constraint
'chkMusic_Album$Name$noEmptyString'. The conflict occurred in database 'tempdb',
 table 'Music.Album'.
```

When data that violates this constraint is entered, it should signal the user interface to provide a warning so that the user can add data for the column. (All too often nonsensical data is entered just to get around your warning, but that is more of a UI/managerial oversight problem than a database design concern because the check to see whether 'ASDFASDF' is a reasonable name value is definitely not of the definite true/false variety. Have you seen what some people name their kids?) What's generally the case is that the user interface will then prevent such data from being created via the UI, but the CHECK constraint is there to prevent other processes from putting in completely invalid data as well.

# CHECK Constraints Based on Functions

Far less typical, but far more powerful and in many ways more useful, can be to build CHECK constraints on conditions that use user-defined functions (UDFs). For the most part, CHECK constraints usually consist of the simple task of checking a stable format or value of a single column, and for these tasks a standard CHECK constraint using the simple <BooleanExpression> is perfectly adequate.

However, a CHECK constraint need not be so simple. A UDF can be complex and might touch several tables in the server. For what reasons might you build a UDF and use a CHECK constraint? The following are some uses for function-based CHECK constraints:

- *Complex scalar validations*: For example, in a situation where a regular expression would be easier to use than a LIKE comparison.

- *Validations that access other tables*: For example, to check a domain that is based on values in several tables, rather than a simple foreign key. In the example I will implement an entry mask that is table-based, so it changes based on a related table's value.

- *Validations that access other rows in the same table*: For example, if you can have only a certain number of a value in a column or set of columns and a unique index will not work.

I should warn you that calling a UDF to do a simple scalar CHECK constraint incurs overhead that will not be incurred with a simple Boolean expression. I realize that this can be counterintuitive to a person who is a good programmer thinking that encapsulation is one of the most important goals of programming, but it is true. SQL code does best when it is working with code that it can compile into direct SQL commands. Hence, it's best to try to express your Boolean expression without a UDF unless it's entirely necessary to access additional tables or do something more complex than a simple expression can. In the following examples, I'll employ UDFs to provide generic range-checking functionality and powerful rule checking, which can implement complex rules that would prove difficult to code using a simple Boolean expression.

You can implement the UDFs in either T-SQL or in VB .NET (or in C#, or any .NET language that lets you exploit the capabilities of SQL Server 2005 or 2008 to write CLR-based objects in the database). In many cases, and especially if you aren't doing any kind of table access in the code of the function, the CLR will perform much better than the T-SQL version.

## Example Constraint That Accesses Other Tables (Entry Mask)

For this example, I need to access values in a different table, so I'm going to build an example that implements an entry mask that varies based on the parent of a row. Consider that it's desirable to validate that catalog numbers for albums are of the proper format. However, different publishers have different catalog number masks for their clients' albums.

For this example, I will continue to use the tables from the previous section. Note that the mask column, `Publisher.CatalogNumberMask`, needs to be considerably larger (five times larger in my example code) than the actual `CatalogNumber` column, because some of the possible masks use multiple characters to indicate a single character. You should also note that it's a `varchar`, even though the column is stored as a `char` value, because using `char` variables as `LIKE` masks can be problematic because of the space padding at the end of such columns (the comparison thinks that the extra space characters that are padded on the end of the fixed-length string need to match in the target string, which is rarely what's desired).

To do this, I build a T-SQL function that accesses this column to check that the value matches the mask, as shown (note that we'd likely build this constraint using T-SQL rather than by using the CLR, because it accesses a table in the body of the function):

```
CREATE FUNCTION Music.Publisher$CatalogNumberValidate
(
    @CatalogNumber char(12),
    @PublisherId int --now based on the Artist ID
)

RETURNS bit
AS
BEGIN
    DECLARE @LogicalValue bit, @CatalogNumberMask varchar(100)

    SELECT @LogicalValue = CASE WHEN @CatalogNumber LIKE CatalogNumberMask
                                    THEN 1
                             ELSE 0   END
    FROM    Music.Publisher
    WHERE   PublisherId = @PublisherId

    RETURN @LogicalValue
END
```

When I loaded the data in the start of this section, I preloaded the data with valid values for the `CatalogNumber` and `CatalogNumberMask` columns:

```
SELECT Album.CatalogNumber, Publisher.CatalogNumberMask
FROM    Music.Album as Album
        JOIN Music.Publisher as Publisher
            ON Album.PublisherId = Publisher.PublisherId
```

This returns the following results:

```
CatalogNumber CatalogNumberMask
------------- ----------------------------------------------------------------------
433-43ASD-33  [0-9][0-9][0-9]-[0-9][0-9][0-9a-z][0-9a-z][0-9a-z]-[0-9][0-9]
111-11111-11  [0-9][0-9][0-9]-[0-9][0-9][0-9a-z][0-9a-z][0-9a-z]-[0-9][0-9]
CD12345       [a-z][a-z][0-9][0-9][0-9][0-9][0-9]
```

Now you can add the constraint to the table, as shown here:

```
ALTER TABLE Music.Album
    WITH CHECK ADD CONSTRAINT
        chkMusic_Album$CatalogNumber$CatalogNumberValidate
        CHECK (Music.Publisher$CatalogNumbervalidate
                        (CatalogNumber,PublisherId) = 1)
```

If the constraint gives you errors because of invalid data existing in the table (in real development, this often occurs with test data from trying out the UI that someone is building), you can use a query like the following to find them:

```
--to find where your data is not ready for the constraint,
--you run the following query
SELECT Album.Name, Album.CatalogNumber, Publisher.CatalogNumberMask
FROM Music.Album AS Album
        JOIN Music.Publisher AS Publisher
          on Publisher.PublisherId = Album.PublisherId
WHERE Music.Publisher$CatalogNumbervalidate
                       (Album.CatalogNumber,Album.PublisherId) <> 1
```

Now, let's add a new row with an invalid value:

```
INSERT  Music.Album(AlbumId, Name, ArtistId, PublisherId, CatalogNumber)
VALUES  (4,'who''s next',2,2,'1')
```

This causes the error, because the catalog number of '1' doesn't match the mask:

```
Msg 547, Level 16, State 0, Line 2
The INSERT statement conflicted with the CHECK constraint
"chkMusic_Album$CatalogNumber$CatalogNumberValidate". The conflict occurred
in database "ProtectionChapter", table "Music.Album".
```

Now we change the number to something that matches our constraint:

```
INSERT  Music.Album(AlbumId, Name, ArtistId, CatalogNumber, PublisherId)
VALUES  (4,'who''s next',2,'AC12345',2)

SELECT * FROM Music.Album
```

This returns the following results:

| AlbumId | Name | ArtistId | CatalogNumber | PublisherId |
| --- | --- | --- | --- | --- |
| 1 | the white album | 1 | 433-43ASD-33 | 1 |
| 2 | revolver | 1 | 111-11111-11 | 1 |
| 3 | quadrophenia | 2 | CD12345 | 2 |
| 4 | who's next | 2 | AC12345 | 2 |

Using this kind of approach, you can build any single-row validation code for your tables. As described previously, each UDF will fire once for each row and each column that was modified in the update. If you are making large numbers of inserts, performance might suffer, but it is worth it to have data that you can trust.

Alternatively, you could create a trigger that checks for the existence of any rows returned by a query, based on the query used earlier to find improper data in the table:

```
SELECT *
FROM   Music.Album AS Album
          JOIN Music.Publisher AS Publisher
                on Publisher.PublisherId = Album.PublisherId
WHERE  Music.Publisher$CatalogNumbervalidate
                       (Album.CatalogNumber,Album.PublisherId) <> 1
```

There's one drawback to this type of constraint, whether implemented in a constraint or trigger. As it stands right now, the Album table is protected from invalid values being entered into the CatalogNumber column, but it doesn't say anything about what happens if a user changes the

CatalogEntryMask on the Publisher table. If this is a concern, then you'd need to add a CHECK constraint to the Publisher table that validates changes to the mask against any existing data.

---

**Tip** A likely problem with this design is that it isn't normalized to the Fourth Normal Form. Publishers do usually have a mask that's valid at a point in time (or you can just set the mask to '%'), but everything changes. If the publishers lengthen the size of their catalog numbers or change to a new format, what happens to the older data? For a functioning system, it would likely be valuable to have a release-date column and catalog number mask that was valid for a given range of dates. Of course, the enterprising user, to get around your lack of proper design, would then create publisher rows such as 'MCA 1989-1990', 'MCA 1991-1994', and so on, and mess up the data for future reporting needs since now you have work to do to correlate values from the MCA company (and your table is now not even technically in First Normal Form!). It's harder to design and implement (and way messier for an example on using CHECK constraints), but it's something to keep in mind nevertheless.

---

## Example Constraint That Accesses Other Rows (Cardinality Enforcement)

Sometimes, a business rule states that for some entity you may have no more than N related entities of some sort. This rule will require you to access not only the current row being inserted but other rows that are related to some value in this row.

There are a few possibilities that you can use for the task of implementing this in the database. In Chapter 5, I mentioned that you can enforce part of the one-to-one relationship using a unique constraint. However, for a cardinality greater than 1, it gets trickier. You can't create an index that allows two unique values. The most natural place that programmers think of implementing this rule is a trigger, but a trigger has more overhead than a check constraint.

An example of this type of cardinality enforcement problem might be of employee to office assignments. In our scenario, the client makes the claim that an employee can be assigned to one and only one office and that an office can have no more than two people occupying it. So, I will build tables for each of these needs (in a schema called alt, just like in other chapters, since this problem type does not go along directly with our main example):

```
CREATE TABLE alt.employee
(
    employeeId    int NOT NULL CONSTRAINT PKalt_employee PRIMARY KEY,
    employeeNumber char(4) NOT NULL
                    CONSTRAINT AKalt_employee_employeeNumber UNIQUE
)
CREATE TABLE alt.office
(
    officeId int NOT NULL CONSTRAINT PKalt_office PRIMARY KEY,
    officeNumber char(4) NOT NULL
                    CONSTRAINT AKalt_office_officeNumber UNIQUE,
)
```

I also need a table for the assignment of offices to employees. This will allow us to assign more than one person to an office (and in fact, the point of this example is that we want to be able to assign no more than some amount of employees to an office). Here is the code to create that table:

```
CREATE TABLE alt.employeeOfficeAssignment
(
    employeeId int,
    officeId   int,
    CONSTRAINT PKalt_employeeOfficeAssignment
            PRIMARY KEY (employeeId, officeId),
```

```
        CONSTRAINT FKemployeeOfficeAssignment$assignsAnOfficeTo$employee
                FOREIGN KEY (employeeId) REFERENCES alt.employee(employeeId),
        CONSTRAINT FKemployeeOfficeAssignment$assignsAnOfficeTo$officeId
                FOREIGN KEY (officeId) REFERENCES alt.office(officeId)
)
```

Then we apply a UNIQUE constraint to the employeeId column to allow one employee to be assigned to one office:

```
ALTER TABLE alt.employeeOfficeAssignment
    ADD CONSTRAINT AKalt_employeeOfficeAssignment_employee UNIQUE (employeeId)
```

Then set up several employees and offices:

```
INSERT employee(employeeId, employeeNumber)
VALUES (1,'A001'),
       (2,'A002'),
       (3,'A003')

INSERT INTO office(officeId,officeNumber)
VALUES (1,'3001'),
       (2,'3002'),
       (3,'3003')
```

Now, to implement the business rule that no more than two people are allowed to be assigned to an office, I will create a function to count the number of people in an office:

```
CREATE FUNCTION alt.employeeOfficeAssignment$officeEmployeeCount
( @officeId int)
RETURNS int AS
 BEGIN
    RETURN (SELECT count(*)
            FROM    employeeOfficeAssignment
            WHERE   officeId = @officeId
            )
  END
GO
```

Now, we create our constraint to check to see whether the number of office occupants is greater than desired by passing the value of officeId from the row that has been inserted to the function:

```
ALTER TABLE alt.employeeOfficeAssignment
    ADD CONSTRAINT CHKalt_employeeOfficeAssignment_employeesInOfficeTwoOrLess
        CHECK (alt.employeeOfficeAssignment$officeEmployeeCount(officeId) <= 2)
```

This works because the constraint fires after the row has been created, so when you insert the third row, it will fail. To test, I will add, individually, some new employees to the officeId = 1:

```
INSERT alt.employeeOfficeAssignment(officeId, employeeId)
VALUES (1,1)
GO
INSERT alt.employeeOfficeAssignment(officeId, employeeId)
VALUES (1,2)
```

On the third row:

```
INSERT alt.employeeOfficeAssignment(officeId, employeeId)
VALUES (1,3)
```

we see the following error:

```
Msg 547, Level 16, State 0, Line 1
The INSERT statement conflicted with the CHECK constraint
"CHKalt_employeeOfficeAssignment_employeesInOfficeTwoOrLess".
 The conflict occurred in database "ProtectionChapter",
table "alt.employeeOfficeAssignment", column 'officeId'.
```

But putting employee 3 into office 2 is fine:

```
INSERT alt.employeeOfficeAssignment(officeId, employeeId)
VALUES (2,3)
```

You could easily extend this example to be parameter-driven (in case the user changes their mind) or even data-driven from a table so when they change their mind, they can fix it. One last concern is that you will want to be sure and performance tune for the check that your functions are doing; in our example, you would likely add an index to the officeId column so that SQL Server can execute this statement quickly to get the count. Otherwise, when the table gets large, it could become very slow to do the check.

## Errors Caused by Constraints

The real downside to using check constraints is error messages. The error messages are certainly things you don't want to show to a user, if for no other reason other than it will generate a help-desk call every time it is seen. Dealing with these errors is one of the more annoying parts of using constraints in SQL Server.

Whenever a statement fails a constraint requirement, SQL Server provides you with an ugly message and with no real method for displaying a clean message automatically. Luckily, SQL Server 2005 implemented vastly improved error-handling capabilities in T-SQL over previous versions. In this section, I'll briefly detail a way to take the ugly messages you get from a constraint error message, much like the error from the previous statement:

```
Msg 547, Level 16, State 0, Line 1
The INSERT statement conflicted with the CHECK constraint
'chkAlbum$CatalogNumber$CatalogNumberValidate'. The conflict occurred in
database 'tempdb', table 'Music.Album'.
```

I'll show you how to map this to an error message that at least makes some level of sense. First, the parts of the error message are as follows:

- *Error number*—Msg 547: The error number that's passed back to the calling program. In some cases, this error number is significant; however, in most cases it's enough to say that the error number is nonzero.

- *Level*—Level 16: A severity level for the message. 0 through 18 are generally considered to be user messages, with 16 being the default. Levels 19–25 are severe errors that cause the connection to be severed (with a message written to the log) and typically involve data corruption issues.

- *State*—State 0: A value from 0–127 that represents the state of the process when the error was raised. This value is rarely used by any process.

- *Line*—Line 1: The line in the batch or object where the error is occurring. However, this value is useful for debugging purposes.

- *Error description*: A text explanation of the error that has occurred.

Unhandled, this is the exact error that will be sent to the client. Using the new TRY-CATCH error handling, we can build a simple error handler and a scheme for mapping constraints to error messages. Part of the reason we name constraints is to determine what the intent was in creating the constraint in the first place. In the following code, we'll implement a very rudimentary error-mapping scheme by parsing the text of the name of the constraint from the message, and then we'll look this value up in a mapping table. It isn't a "perfect" scheme, but it does the trick when using constraints as the only data protection for a situation.

First, let's create a mapping table where we put the name of the constraint that we've defined and a message that explains what the constraint means:

```
CREATE SCHEMA utility
CREATE TABLE utility.ErrorMap
(
    ConstraintName sysname primary key,
    Message          varchar(2000)
)
go
INSERT dbo.ErrorMap(constraintName, message)
VALUES ('chkAlbum$CatalogNumber$CatalogNumberValidate',
        'The catalog number does not match the format set up by the Publisher')
```

Then we create a procedure to do the actual mapping by taking the values that can be retrieved from the ERROR_%() procedures that are accessible in a CATCH block and using them to look up the value in the ErrorMap table:

```
CREATE PROCEDURE utility.ErrorMap$MapError
(
    @ErrorNumber  int = NULL,
    @ErrorMessage nvarchar(2000) = NULL,
    @ErrorSeverity INT= NULL,
    @ErrorState INT = NULL
) AS
  BEGIN
    --use values in ERROR_ functions unless the user passes in values
    SET @ErrorNumber = Coalesce(@ErrorNumber, ERROR_NUMBER())
    SET @ErrorMessage = Coalesce(@ErrorMessage, ERROR_MESSAGE())
    SET @ErrorSeverity = Coalesce(@ErrorSeverity, ERROR_SEVERITY())
    SET @ErrorState = Coalesce(@ErrorState,ERROR_STATE())

    DECLARE @originalMessage nvarchar(2000)
    SET @originalMessage = ERROR_MESSAGE()


    IF @ErrorNumber = 547
      BEGIN
        SET @ErrorMessage =
                      (SELECT message
                       FROM   dbo.ErrorMap
                       WHERE  constraintName =
        --this substring pulls the constraint name from the message
        substring( @ErrorMessage,CHARINDEX('constraint "',@ErrorMessage) + 12,
                        charindex('"',substring(@ErrorMessage,
                        CHARINDEX('constraint "',@ErrorMessage) +
                                                    12,2000))-1)
                      )      END
```

```
    ELSE
        SET @ErrorMessage = @ErrorMessage

    SET @ErrorState = CASE when @ErrorState = 0 THEN 1 ELSE @ErrorState END

    --if the error was not found, get the original message
    SET @ErrorMessage = isNull(@ErrorMessage, @originalMessage)
    RAISERROR (@ErrorMessage, @ErrorSeverity,@ErrorState )
  END
```

Now, see what happens when we enter an invalid value for an album catalog number:

```
BEGIN TRY
    INSERT  Music.Album(AlbumId, Name, ArtistId, CatalogNumber, PublisherId)
    VALUES  (5,'who are you',2,'badnumber',2)
END TRY
BEGIN CATCH
    EXEC dbo.ErrorMap$MapError
END CATCH
```

The error message is as follows:

```
Msg 50000, Level 16, State 1, Procedure ErrorMap$mapError, Line 24
The catalog number does not match the format set up by the Publisher
```

instead of the following:

```
Msg 547, Level 16, State 0, Line 1
The INSERT statement conflicted with the CHECK constraint
'chkAlbum$CatalogNumber$CatalogNumberValidate'. The conflict occurred in
database 'tempdb', table 'Music.Album'.
The statement has been terminated.
```

This is far more pleasing, even if it was a bit of a workout getting to this new message. This isn't a programming book, so we won't go any deeper into programming error handling right now (I'll cover it a bit more in the next section on triggers).

# DML Triggers

Triggers are a type of stored procedure attached to a table or view that is executed automatically when the contents of a table are changed. You can use them to enforce almost any business rule, and they're especially important for dealing with situations that are too complex for a CHECK constraint to handle. As a simple case, consider a situation in which you want to ensure that an update of a value is performed on both the tables where that value occurs. You can write a trigger that disallows the update unless it occurs in both tables.

Triggers often get a bad name because they can be troublesome. For example, if you have a trigger on a table and try to update a million rows, you are likely to have issues. However, for most OLTP operations in a relational database, operations shouldn't be touching more than a handful of rows at a time. The fact is, triggers are wonderful for what they are good for, because mostly they are used for stuff that the application really can't do. Trigger usage does need careful consideration, but where they are needed, they are terribly useful. My recommendation is to use triggers when you need to do the following:

- Perform cross-database referential integrity
- Check inter-row rules, where just looking at the current row isn't enough for the constraints
- Check inter-table constraints, when rules require access to data in a different table
- Introduce desired side effects to your data-modification queries, such as maintaining required denormalizations

Most of these operations could also be done in an application layer, but for the most part, these operations are far easier and safer when done using triggers. The main advantage that triggers have over constraints is the ability to access other tables seamlessly and to operate on multiple rows at once. In a trigger, you can run almost every T-SQL command, except for the following ones:

- ALTER DATABASE
- CREATE DATABASE
- DROP DATABASE
- RESTORE LOG

- RECONFIGURE
- RESTORE DATABASE
- LOAD LOG
- LOAD DATABASE

Also, you cannot use the following commands on the table that the trigger protects:

- CREATE INDEX
- ALTER INDEX
- DROP INDEX
- DBCC REINDEX

- ALTER PARTITION FUNCTION
- DROP TABLE
- ALTER TABLE

---

**Note** You can't use ALTER TABLE to add or modify columns, switch partitions, or add or drop primary key columns.

---

Truthfully, it isn't good design to change the schema of *any* table or do any of the things in this list in a trigger, much less the one that the trigger is built on, so these aren't overly restrictive requirements at all.

One of the most important tips that I can give you about using triggers is to keep them as lean as possible. Avoid using cursors, calling stored procedures, or doing any sort of looping operation, and instead get the job done fast. If you need to do some extra processing (a common example is sending an e-mail for every row affected by the trigger), create a table that can be used as a queue for another process to work on. When your code is executing in a trigger, you can be holding locks, unnecessarily forcing other users to wait, and you cannot be completely certain that the rows that were modified to fire the trigger will actually be committed. If you send e-mail directly via the trigger, it may have already sent the e-mail. (Note, in SQL Server 2005, the SQL-based mail object was changed to use SQL Server queues to implement mail, so if you roll back the transaction, it will roll back the mail command.)

---

**Tip** SQL Server 2005 included two new types of triggers called Data Definition Language (DDL) and Login triggers. These are considered to be security tools, which Chapter 8 covers. They can also be coded in T-SQL or the CLR languages.

---

## Types of DML Triggers

There are two different types of DML triggers:

- AFTER: These triggers fire after the DML statement (INSERT/UPDATE/DELETE) has affected the table. AFTER triggers are usually used for handling rules that won't fit into the mold of a constraint, for example, rules that require data to be stored, such as a logging mechanism. You may have a virtually unlimited number of AFTER triggers that fire on INSERT, UPDATE, and DELETE, or any combination of them.

- INSTEAD OF: These triggers operate "instead of" the built-in command (INSERT, UPDATE, or DELETE) affecting the table or view. In this way, you can do whatever you want with the data, either doing exactly what was requested by the user or doing something completely different (you can even just ignore the operation altogether). You can have a maximum of one INSTEAD OF INSERT, UPDATE, and DELETE trigger of each type per table. It is allowed (but not a generally good idea) to combine all three into one and have a single trigger that fires for all three operations.

## Coding DML Triggers

Coding DML triggers is very much like coding a stored procedure, but there are some important differences. Instead of having data passed in to the stored procedure, you use two special in-memory tables that are instantiated for the life of the operation and are scoped specifically to code executing directly in the trigger. These tables are called inserted and deleted. The inserted table contains new or updated rows for an INSERT or UPDATE operation, and the deleted table contains the original rows that have been deleted for a DELETE statement execution or that have been modified by an UPDATE statement. It is important to note that these tables can have multiple rows in them, if you modify more than one row in your DML statement. Also, since they are scoped to the executing trigger, if you call a stored procedure, the tables will not be accessible, and if your trigger causes another trigger to fire, the contents of the tables will be for the currently executing trigger.

The following list contains some of the most important aspects of trigger coding:

- *Determining modified columns*: For performance reasons, you usually don't want to validate data that's in a column that isn't affected by a DML statement. You can tell which columns were part of the INSERT or UPDATE statement by using the UPDATE(<columnName>) function to check the column to see whether it was involved in the DML operation. Note that this does not indicate that a value has *changed*, just that the column was referenced. For example, given the simple statement UPDATE tableName SET column1=column1, the values would not change, but UPDATE(column1) would return true. (There is also another method using the function COLUMNS_UPDATED(columnBitmask) to check the columns by their position in the table. 1+2+4 = 7 would mean the first three columns were updated, but it's generally a bad practice to address columns in a table positionally, for future maintenance purposes.)

- *Error handling and triggers*: Handling errors that occur in a trigger is somewhat different than in any other T-SQL code. I'll demonstrate the differences and implement an error handler for T-SQL triggers in the upcoming sections.

- *Nesting triggers*: Take care when building `AFTER` triggers that modify data (the same table or other tables) because these updates could in turn cause other triggers to fire. `INSTEAD OF` triggers always cause other triggers to fire. There are two important settings to be concerned with:

  - *Database option*—`ALTER DATABASE`–`RECURSIVE_TRIGGERS`: When set to `ON`, when an `AFTER` trigger modifies the data in the same table, the triggers for that table execute again. This setting is usually set to `OFF`. Because it's common practice to modify the same table in the trigger, it's assumed that any modifications done in a trigger will meet all business rules for the same table.

  - *Server option*—`sp_serveroption`–`nested triggers`: When this setting is set to 1, it indicates that if you modify a different table, that table's trigger will be fired. This setting is usually set to 1, because it allows for data validations to occur in the other tables without coding every business rule again.

- *Having multiple* `AFTER` *triggers for the same action*: It's possible to have many different triggers on a table. This is a blessing and a curse. It does give you the ability to add triggers to third-party systems without touching triggers that the third-party created. However, often the order of triggers can be important, especially when you have to deal with validating data that another trigger might modify. You do get some minor control over the order in which triggers fire. Using the `sp_settriggerorder` system stored procedure, you can choose the first and the last trigger to fire. Usually this is all you need, because there are places where you want to set the first trigger (often the third-party trigger) and the last trigger (such as a trigger to implement an audit trail, as we do in a later section).

- *Writing multirow validations*: Because triggers fire once for a multirow operation, statements within triggers have to be coded with multiple rows in mind. This can be confusing, because unlike what seems to be natural, trigger code for validations typically needs to look for rows that don't meet your criteria, instead of those that do. Unless you want to force users into entering one row at a time, you have to code your triggers in a way that recognizes that more than one row in the table might be being modified.

- *Performance*: When few rows are dealt with in a trigger, they are usually quite fast, but as the number of modified rows increases, triggers can become tremendous performance drains. This is largely because the `inserted` and `deleted` tables aren't "real" tables. Because they don't have indexes and because the optimizer cannot guess how many rows will be modified each time, the plans chosen for the queries can be fairly optimistic about the number of rows in `inserted` and `deleted` tables. Because OLTP systems usually deal with small numbers of rows at a time, there's rarely a major performance hit because of using triggers, but it is something you have to be cognizant of anytime you create a new trigger.

Because multirow operations are the most frequently messed up aspect of trigger writing, it's worth discussing this aspect in more detail. If you insert a thousand rows, the `inserted` table will have a thousand rows. The `deleted` table will remain empty on an insert. When you delete rows, the `deleted` table is filled, and the `inserted` table remains empty. For an `UPDATE`, both tables are filled with the rows in the updated table that had been modified as they appeared before and after the update.

Because of this, writing validations must take this into consideration. For example, the following all-too-typical approach wouldn't be a good idea:

```
SELECT @column1 = column1 FROM inserted
IF @column1 < 0
   BEGIN
        --handle the error
```

This is wrong because only a single row would be checked—in this case, the last row that the SELECT statement came to (there's no order, but @column1 would be set to every value in the inserted table, and would end up with the last value it came upon). Instead, the proper way to code this would be as follows:

```
If EXISTS (SELECT  *
          FROM    inserted
          WHERE   column1 < 0)
   BEGIN
          --handle the error
```

This does work because each row in the inserted table is checked against the criteria. If any rows do match the criteria, the EXISTS Boolean expression returns True, and the error block is started.

You'll see this more in the example triggers. However, you need to make a conscious effort as you start to code triggers to consider what the effect of modifying more than one row would be on your code, because you certainly don't want to miss an invalid value because of coding like the first wrong example.

If you need a full reference on the many details of triggers, refer to SQL Server Books Online. In the following section, we'll look at the different types of triggers, the basics of coding them, and how to use them to handle the common tasks for which we use triggers. Luckily, for the most part triggers are straightforward, and the basic settings will work just fine.

---

■**Note**  I don't think I could stress nearly enough about the need to understand multirow operations in triggers. Almost every time a question is raised on the forums about triggers, the code that gets posted contains code that will handle only one row.

---

## AFTER Triggers

AFTER triggers fire after all the constraints pass all constraint requirements. For instance, it wouldn't be proper to insert rows in a child table (thereby causing its entire trigger/constraint chain to fire) when the parent's data hasn't been validated. Equally, you wouldn't want to check the status of all the rows in your table until you've completed all your changes to them; the same could be said for cascading delete operations. The five examples that follow are but a small subset of all the possible uses for triggers, but they're representative of the common usages of AFTER triggers.

Before the examples, however, I need to set up the basic structure of the triggers. I use a basic template for all triggers I create, either using a code generator or, when I have to break down and code a procedure, using nothing but the ends of my eight fingers and two thumbs. Each of the examples fits into a trigger (of any type) that is of the following format:

```
CREATE TRIGGER <schema>.<tablename>$<actions>[<purpose>]Trigger
ON <schema>.<tablename>
AFTER <comma delimited actions> AS
BEGIN

    DECLARE @rowsAffected int,    --stores the number of rows affected
            @msg varchar(2000)    --used to hold the error message

    SET @rowsAffected = @@rowcount

    --no need to continue on if no rows affected
    IF @rowsAffected = 0 return
```

```
SET NOCOUNT ON --to avoid the rowcount messages
SET ROWCOUNT 0 --in case the client has modified the rowcount

BEGIN TRY
        --[validation section]
        --[modification section]
END TRY
BEGIN CATCH
            IF @@trancount > 0
                ROLLBACK TRANSACTION

            EXECUTE utility.ErrorLog$insert

            DECLARE @ERROR_MESSAGE nvarchar(4000)
            SET @ERROR_MESSAGE = ERROR_MESSAGE()
            RAISERROR (@ERROR_MESSAGE,16,1)

    END CATCH
END
```

---

■**Tip**  The AFTER keyword was introduced in the 2000 version of SQL Server when INSTEAD OF triggers were introduced. Prior to this, the keyword was FOR, since the trigger was *for* certain actions. Both are still quite common, but it is best to use AFTER in all new code.

---

I generally write triggers so that when the first error occurs, an error will be raised, and I roll back the transaction to halt any further commands. In the trigger template, there were two comments: --[validation section] and --[modification section]. The [validation section] denotes where you will start adding validation logic that will be executed after the DML has been performed on the table. This would be used instead of a constraint when you need to code some complex validation that doesn't fit the mold of a constraint well. The [modification section] will contain DML statements to modify the contents of tables or to *do* something. In this section, you might modify the same table as the triggering table or any other table.

The form I use for [validation section] is something like the following code. Note that I will try usually to code different messages for the case when one row was affected by the DML operation (the @rowsAffected variable is set earlier in the trigger, by a code block found back in the main template, to the number of rows that were affected by the DML operation) and when many rows were changed:

```
IF EXISTS (<some condition, commonly using inserted and/or deleted tables>)
    BEGIN
        IF @rowsAffected = 1 --custom error message for single row
            SELECT @msg = '<reason>' + inserted.value
            FROM   inserted -and/or deleted, depending on action
        ELSE
            SELECT @msg = '<more generic reason>'

        --in the TRY . . . CATCH block, this will redirect to the CATCH
        RAISERROR (@msg, 16, 1)
    END
```

The [modification section] section in SQL Server 2005 and later is just a simple INSERT, UPDATE, or DELETE statement thanks to the TRY-CATCH block. Any errors raised because of the DML (such as from a constraint or another trigger) will be caught and sent to a TRY-CATCH block. In the CATCH block, I use a procedure called utility.ErrorLog$insert to log the error for later debugging.

The utility.ErrorLog$insert procedure is used to log the errors that occur in a table to give you a history of errors that have occurred. I do this because, in almost every case, an error that occurs in a trigger is a bad thing. The fact that the client sends data that might cause the trigger to fail should be fixed and treated as a bug. In stored procedures, this may or may not be the case, because stored procedures can be written to do things that may work or may fail in some situations. This is a very broad statement and in some cases may not be true, so you can adjust the code as fits your desires.

The DML for the table and the code for the procedure are as follows:

```
CREATE TABLE utility.ErrorLog(
        ERROR_NUMBER int NOT NULL,
        ERROR_LOCATION sysname NOT NULL,
        ERROR_MESSAGE varchar(4000),
        ERROR_DATE datetime NULL
            CONSTRAINT dfltErrorLog_error_date  DEFAULT (getdate()),
        ERROR_USER sysname NOT NULL
            --use original_login to capture the user name of the actual user
            --not a user they have impersonated
            CONSTRAINT dfltErrorLog_error_user_name DEFAULT (original_login())
)
GO
CREATE PROCEDURE utility.ErrorLog$insert
(
        @ERROR_NUMBER int = NULL,
        @ERROR_LOCATION sysname = NULL,
        @ERROR_MESSAGE varchar(4000) = NULL
) as
 BEGIN
        BEGIN TRY
           INSERT INTO utility.ErrorLog(ERROR_NUMBER,
                                        ERROR_LOCATION, ERROR_MESSAGE)
           SELECT isnull(@ERROR_NUMBER,ERROR_NUMBER()),
                  isnull(@ERROR_LOCATION,ERROR_MESSAGE()),
                  isnull(@ERROR_MESSAGE,ERROR_MESSAGE())
        END TRY
        BEGIN CATCH
           INSERT INTO utility.ErrorLog(ERROR_NUMBER,
                                        ERROR_LOCATION, ERROR_MESSAGE)
           VALUES (-100, 'utility.ErrorLog$insert',
                       'An invalid call was made to the error log procedure')
        END CATCH
END
```

This basic error logging procedure can make it much easier to understand what has gone wrong when a user has an error. Expand your own system to meet your organization's needs, but having an audit trail will prove invaluable when you find out that certain types of errors have been going on for weeks and your users "assumed" you knew about it!

---

**Tip** To log errors to the Windows Event Log (which isn't affected by transactions), you can use the xp_logevent extended stored procedure in the error handler. Using this method can be handy if you have deeply nested errors, in which all the utility.ErrorLog rows get rolled back because of external transactions.

---

For the rest of this section on DML triggers, I will present examples that demonstrate several common forms of triggers that I use to solve problems that are similar to most of the typical uses for AFTER triggers I have seen. I'll give examples of the following types of triggers:

- Range checks on multiple rows
- Maintaining summary values (only as necessary)
- Cascading inserts
- Child-to-parent cascades
- Relationships that span databases and servers
- Maintaining an audit trail

## Range Checks on Multiple Rows

The first type of check we'll look at is the range check, in which we want to make sure that a column is within some specific range of values. You can do range checks using a CHECK constraint to validate the data in a single row (for example that column > 10) quite easily, but you wouldn't want to use them to validate conditions based on aggregates of multiple rows (sum(column) > 10) since if you updated 100 rows, you would have to do 100 validations where one statement could do the same work.

If you need to check that a row or set of rows doesn't violate a given condition, usually based on an aggregate like a maximum sum, you should use a trigger. As an example, I'll look at a simple accounting system. As users deposit and withdraw money from an account, you want to make sure that the balance never dips below zero. All transactions for a given account have to be considered.

First, we create a schema for the accounting groups:

```
CREATE SCHEMA Accounting
```

Then we create a table for an account  and then one to contain the activity for the account:

```
CREATE TABLE Accounting.Account
(
        AccountNumber        char(10)
                constraint PKAccounting_Account primary key
        --would have other columns
)

CREATE TABLE Accounting.AccountActivity
(
        AccountNumber                char(10)
            constraint Accounting_Account$has$Accounting_AccountActivity
                    foreign key references Accounting.Account(AccountNumber),
        --this might be a value that each ATM/Teller generates
        TransactionNumber            char(20),
        Date                         datetime,
        TransactionAmount            numeric(12,2),
        constraint PKAccounting_AccountActivity
                PRIMARY KEY (AccountNumber, TransactionNumber)
)
```

Now we add a trigger to the Accounting.AccountActivity table that checks to make sure that when you sum together the transaction amounts for an Account, that the sum is greater than zero:

```
CREATE TRIGGER Accounting.AccountActivity$insertUpdateTrigger
ON Accounting.AccountActivity
AFTER INSERT,UPDATE AS
```

```
BEGIN
    DECLARE @rowsAffected int,      --stores the number of rows affected
            @msg varchar(2000)      --used to hold the error message

    SET @rowsAffected = @@rowcount

    --no need to continue on if no rows affected
    IF @rowsAffected = 0 return

    SET NOCOUNT ON
    SET ROWCOUNT 0 --in case the client has modified the rowcount

    BEGIN TRY

    --[validation section]
    --disallow Transactions that would put balance into negatives
    IF EXISTS ( SELECT AccountNumber
                FROM Accounting.AccountActivity as AccountActivity
                WHERE EXISTS (SELECT *
                              FROM    inserted
                              WHERE   inserted.AccountNumber =
                                      AccountActivity.AccountNumber)
                    GROUP BY AccountNumber
                    HAVING sum(TransactionAmount) < 0)
      BEGIN
         IF @rowsAffected = 1
            SELECT @msg = 'Account: ' + AccountNumber +
                    ' TransactionNumber:' +
                    cast(TransactionNumber as varchar(36)) +
                    ' for amount: ' + cast(TransactionAmount as varchar(10))+
                    ' cannot be processed as it will cause a negative balance'
            FROM    inserted
         ELSE
           SELECT @msg = 'One of the rows caused a negative balance'
         RAISERROR (@msg, 16, 1)
      END

    --[modification section]
    END TRY
    BEGIN CATCH
            IF @@trancount > 0
                ROLLBACK TRANSACTION

            EXECUTE utility.ErrorLog$insert

            DECLARE @ERROR_MESSAGE varchar(4000)
            SET @ERROR_MESSAGE = ERROR_MESSAGE()
            RAISERROR (@ERROR_MESSAGE,16,1)

    END CATCH
END
```

The key to using this type of trigger is to look for the existence of rows in the base table, not the rows in the inserted table, because the concern is how the inserted rows affect the overall status for an Account. Take this query, which we'll use to determine whether there are rows that fail the criteria:

```
SELECT AccountNumber
FROM Accounting.AccountActivity as AccountActivity
WHERE EXISTS (SELECT *
              FROM   inserted
              WHERE  inserted.AccountNumber = AccountActivity.AccountNumber)
GROUP BY AccountNumber
HAVING sum(TransactionAmount) < 0
```

The key here is that we could remove the bold part of the query, and it would check all rows in the table. The WHERE clause simply makes sure that the only rows we consider are for accounts that have new data inserted. This way, we don't end up checking all rows that we know our query hasn't touched. Note too that I don't use a JOIN operation. By using an EXISTS criteria in the WHERE clause, we don't affect the cardinality of the set being returned in the FROM clause, no matter how many rows in the inserted table have the same AccountNumber.

To see it in action, use this code:

```
--create some set up test data
INSERT into Accounting.Account(AccountNumber)
VALUES ('1111111111')

INSERT  into Accounting.AccountActivity(AccountNumber, TransactionNumber,
                                        Date, TransactionAmount)
VALUES ('1111111111','A0000000000000000001','20050712',100),
 ('1111111111','A0000000000000000002','20050713',100)
```

Now, let's see what happens when we violate this rule:

```
INSERT  into Accounting.AccountActivity(AccountNumber, TransactionNumber,
                                        Date, TransactionAmount)
VALUES ('1111111111','A0000000000000000003','20050713',-300)
```

Here's the result:

```
Msg 50000, Level 16, State 1, Procedure AccountActivity$insertTrigger, Line 47
Account: 1111111111 TransactionNumber:A0000000000000000002 for amount: -300.00
cannot be processed as it will cause a negative balance

Msg 3609, Level 16, State 1, Line 1
The transaction ended in the trigger. The batch has been aborted.
```

The first error message is the custom error message that we coded in the case where a single row was modified. The second is a message that SQL Server raises, starting in SQL Server 2005, when the batch is halted for a transaction rollback in a trigger. Now, let's make sure that the trigger works when we have greater than one row in the INSERT statement:

```
--create new Account
INSERT  into Accounting.Account(AccountNumber)
VALUES ('2222222222')
GO
--Now, this data will violate the constraint for the new Account:
INSERT  into Accounting.AccountActivity(AccountNumber, TransactionNumber,
                                        Date, TransactionAmount)
VALUES ('1111111111','A0000000000000000004','20050714',100),
       ('2222222222','A0000000000000000005','20050715',100),
       ('2222222222','A0000000000000000006','20050715',100),
       ('2222222222','A0000000000000000007','20050715',-201)
```

This causes the following error:

```
Msg 50000, Level 16, State 1, Procedure AccountActivity$insertTrigger, Line 51
One of the rows in the operation caused a negative balance
Msg 3609, Level 16, State 1, Line 6
The transaction ended in the trigger. The batch has been aborted.
```

The multirow error message is much less informative, though you could expand it to include information about a row (or all the rows) that caused the violation with some more text, even showing the multiple failed values. Usually a simple message is sufficient to deal with, because generally if multiple rows are being modified in a single statement, it's a batch process, and the complexity of building error messages is way more than it's worth. Processes would likely be established on how to deal with certain errors being returned.

**Tip** In the error message, note that the first error states it's from line 51. This is line 51 of the trigger where the error message was raised. This can be valuable information when debugging triggers. Note also that because the ROLLBACK command was used in the trigger, the batch was terminated, this being on line 6 of the batch you're in.

## VIEWING TRIGGER EVENTS

To see the events for which a trigger fires, you can use the following query:

```
SELECT sys.trigger_events.type_desc
FROM sys.trigger_events
        JOIN sys.triggers
                ON sys.triggers.object_id = sys.trigger_events.object_id
WHERE sys.triggers.name = 'AccountActivity$insertUpdateTrigger'
```

This returns INSERT and UPDATE in two rows, because we declared the Accounting.AccountActivity$insertUpdateTrigger trigger to fire on INSERT and UPDATE operations.

### Maintaining Summary Values

It was hard for me to decide whether to include this section, because most of the time when people decide to include summary values in their tables (aka denormalizations), it is more an act of laziness to avoid having to build proper indexes and tune queries. (Keep in mind the title of the book is about relational database design, so this statement does not include databases built for reporting purposes, like dimensional structures. For static data, it is perfectly acceptable to go nuts and denormalize, since the principles of normalization do not really apply.) However, there are places where this is actually the best way to go when you have to tune some section of code, and:

- There is no other reasonable method available.
- The amount of data to be summarized is large.
- The amount of reads of the summary values is far greater than the activity on the lower values.

As an example, let's extend the previous example of the Account and AccountActivity tables from the "Range Checks on Multiple Rows" section. To the Account table, I will add a Balance column:

```
ALTER TABLE Accounting.Account
   ADD Balance numeric(12,2)
      CONSTRAINT DfltAccounting_Account_Balance (0.00)
```

Then, we will update the `Balance` column to have the current value of the data in the `AccountActivity` rows. First, running this query to view the expected values:

```
SELECT  Account.AccountNumber,
        SUM(coalesce(TransactionAmount,0.00)) AS NewBalance
FROM    Accounting.Account
          LEFT OUTER JOIN Accounting.AccountActivity
              ON Account.AccountNumber = AccountActivity.AccountNumber
GROUP   BY Account.AccountNumber
```

returns the following:

```
AccountNumber NewBalance
------------- ------------------------------
1111111111    200.00
2222222222    0.00
```

Now update the `Balance` column values to the existing rows using the following statement:

```
WITH  Updater as (
SELECT  Account.AccountNumber,
        SUM(coalesce(TransactionAmount,0.00)) as NewBalance
FROM    Accounting.Account
          LEFT OUTER JOIN Accounting.AccountActivity
              On Account.AccountNumber = AccountActivity.AccountNumber
GROUP   BY Account.AccountNumber, Account.Balance)
UPDATE Account
SET    Balance = Updater.NewBalance
FROM   Accounting.Account
           JOIN Updater
               on Account.AccountNumber = Updater.AccountNumber
```

That statement will make the basis of our changes to the trigger that we added in the previous section (the changes appear in bold). The only change that needs to be made is to filter the `Account` set down to the accounts that were affected by the DML that cause the trigger to fire. Using an `EXISTS` filter lets you not have to worry about whether one new row was created for the account or 100.

```
ALTER TRIGGER Accounting.AccountActivity$insertUpdateTrigger
ON Accounting.AccountActivity
AFTER INSERT,UPDATE AS
BEGIN
    DECLARE @rowsAffected int,    --stores the number of rows affected
            @msg varchar(2000)    --used to hold the error message

    SET @rowsAffected = @@rowcount

    --no need to continue on if no rows affected
    IF @rowsAffected = 0 return

    SET NOCOUNT ON
    SET ROWCOUNT 0 --in case the client has modified the rowcount

    BEGIN TRY
```

```
    --[validation section]
    --disallow Transactions that would put balance into negatives
    IF EXISTS ( SELECT AccountNumber
                FROM Accounting.AccountActivity as AccountActivity
                WHERE EXISTS (SELECT *
                              FROM   inserted
                              WHERE  inserted.AccountNumber =
                                  AccountActivity.AccountNumber)
                GROUP BY AccountNumber
                HAVING sum(TransactionAmount) < 0)
       BEGIN
         IF @rowsAffected = 1
             SELECT @msg = 'Account: ' + AccountNumber +
                 ' TransactionNumber:' +
                 cast(TransactionNumber as varchar(36)) +
                 ' for amount: ' + cast(TransactionAmount as varchar(10))+
                 ' cannot be processed as it will cause a negative balance'
            FROM   inserted
         ELSE
           SELECT @msg = 'One of the rows caused a negative balance'
         RAISERROR (@msg, 16, 1)
       END

    --[modification section]
    IF UPDATE (TransactionAmount)
       ;WITH  Updater as (
       SELECT  Account.AccountNumber,
               SUM(coalesce(TransactionAmount,0.00)) as NewBalance
       FROM    Accounting.Account
                LEFT OUTER JOIN Accounting.AccountActivity
                    On Account.AccountNumber = AccountActivity.AccountNumber
                --This where clause limits the summarizations to those rows
                --that were modified by the DML statement that caused
                --this trigger to fire.
       WHERE  EXISTS (SELECT *
                      FROM   Inserted
                      WHERE  Account.AccountNumber = Inserted.AccountNumber)
       GROUP  BY Account.AccountNumber, Account.Balance)
       UPDATE Account
       SET    Balance = Updater.NewBalance
       FROM   Accounting.Account
                 JOIN Updater
                    on Account.AccountNumber = Updater.AccountNumber

END TRY
BEGIN CATCH
            IF @@trancount > 0
                ROLLBACK TRANSACTION

            EXECUTE utility.ErrorLog$insert

            DECLARE @ERROR_MESSAGE varchar(4000)
            SET @ERROR_MESSAGE = ERROR_MESSAGE()
            RAISERROR (@ERROR_MESSAGE,16,1)

    END CATCH
END
```

Now, insert a new row into `AccountActivity`:

```
INSERT  into Accounting.AccountActivity(AccountNumber, TransactionNumber,
                            Date, TransactionAmount)
VALUES ('1111111111','A0000000000000000004','20050714',100)
```

Then examine the state of the `Account` table, comparing it to the query used previously to check what the balances should be. Both queries should return the following:

```
AccountNumber NewBalance
------------- ------------------------------
1111111111    300.00
2222222222    0.00
```

The next step is very important when building a trigger such as this: the multirow test. You need to be sure that if a user inserts more than one row at a time, it will work. Be sure also to test boundaries. In our example, we will insert rows for both accounts in the same DML statement and two rows for one of the accounts. This is not a sufficient test necessarily, but it's enough for demonstration purposes at least:

```
INSERT  into Accounting.AccountActivity(AccountNumber, TransactionNumber,
                            Date, TransactionAmount)
VALUES ('1111111111','A0000000000000000005','20050714',100),
       ('2222222222','A0000000000000000006','20050715',100),
       ('2222222222','A0000000000000000007','20050715',100)
```

Again, both queries on the `AccountActivity` and `Account` should show the same balances:

```
AccountNumber NewBalance
------------- ------------------------------
1111111111    400.00
2222222222    200.00
```

If you wanted a `DELETE` trigger (and in the case of a ledger like this, you generally do not want to actually delete rows but rather insert offsetting values, so to delete a $100 insert, you would insert a –100), the only difference is that instead of the `EXISTS` condition referring to the `inserted` table, it needs to refer to the `deleted` table:

```
;WITH  Updater as (
SELECT  Account.AccountNumber,
        SUM(coalesce(TransactionAmount,0.00)) as NewBalance
FROM    Accounting.Account
          LEFT OUTER JOIN Accounting.AccountActivity
             On Account.AccountNumber = AccountActivity.AccountNumber
WHERE   EXISTS (SELECT *
               FROM    deleted
               WHERE   Account.AccountNumber = deleted.AccountNumber)
GROUP  BY Account.AccountNumber, Account.Balance)
UPDATE Account
SET     Balance = Updater.NewBalance
FROM    Accounting.Account
          JOIN Updater
               on Account.AccountNumber = Updater.AccountNumber
```

I can't stress enough that this type of strategy should be the exception, not the rule. But when you have to implement summary data, this is the way to go in most cases. One of the more frustrating things to have to deal with is summary data that is out of whack, because it takes time away from making progress with creating new software.

---

■**Caution**  I want to reiterate to be extremely careful to test your code extra thoroughly when you include denormalizations like this. If you have other DML in triggers that insert or update into the same table, there is a chance that the trigger will not fire again, based on how you have the nested triggers and recursive triggers options set that I discussed previously. Good testing strategies are important in all cases really, but the point here is to be extra careful when using triggers to modify data.

---

### Cascading Inserts

A cascading insert refers to the situation whereby after a row is inserted into a table, one or more other new rows are automatically inserted into other tables. This is frequently done when you need to initialize a row in another table, quite often a status of some sort.

For this example, we're going to build a small system to store URLs for a website-linking system. During low-usage periods, an automated browser connects to the URLs so that they can be verified (hopefully limiting broken links on web pages).

To implement this, I'll use the set of tables in Figure 6-2.

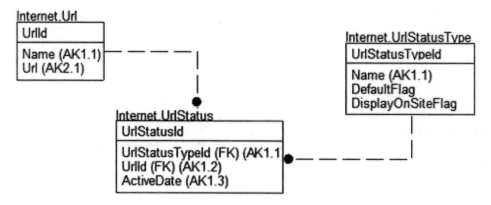

**Figure 6-2.** *Storing URLs for a website-linking system*

```
CREATE SCHEMA Internet
go
CREATE TABLE Internet.Url
(
    UrlId int not null identity(1,1) constraint PKUrl primary key,
    Name  varchar(60) not null constraint AKInternet_Url_Name UNIQUE,
    Url   varchar(200) not null constraint AKInternet_Url_Url UNIQUE
)

--Not a user manageable table, so not using identity key (as discussed in
--Chapter 5 when I discussed choosing keys) in this one table.  Others are
--using identity-based keys in this example.
CREATE TABLE Internet.UrlStatusType
```

```
(
        UrlStatusTypeId  int not null
                        CONSTRAINT PKInternet_UrlStatusType PRIMARY KEY,
        Name varchar(20) NOT NULL
                        CONSTRAINT AKInternet_UrlStatusType UNIQUE,
        DefaultFlag bit NOT NULL,
        DisplayOnSiteFlag bit NOT NULL
)

CREATE TABLE Internet.UrlStatus
(
        UrlStatusId int not null identity(1,1)
                        CONSTRAINT PKInternet_UrlStatus PRIMARY KEY,
        UrlStatusTypeId int NOT NULL
                        CONSTRAINT
            Internet_UrlStatusType$defines_status_type_of$Internet_UrlStatus
                        REFERENCES Internet.UrlStatusType(UrlStatusTypeId),
        UrlId int NOT NULL
          CONSTRAINT Internet_Url$has_status_history_in$Internet_UrlStatus
                        REFERENCES Internet.Url(UrlId),
        ActiveTime          datetime,
        CONSTRAINT AKInternet_UrlStatus_statusUrlDate
                        UNIQUE (UrlStatusTypeId, UrlId, ActiveTime)
)
--set up status types
INSERT  Internet.UrlStatusType (UrlStatusTypeId, Name,
                                    DefaultFlag, DisplayOnSiteFlag)
VALUES (1, 'Unverified',1,0),
       (2, 'Verified',0,1),
       (3, 'Unable to locate',0,0)
```

The Url table holds URLs to different sites on the Web. When someone enters a URL, we initialize the status to 'Unverified'. A process should be in place in which the site is checked often to make sure nothing has changed (particularly the unverified ones!).

You begin by building a trigger that inserts a row into the UrlStatus table on an insert that creates a new row with the UrlId and the default UrlStatusType based on DefaultFlag having the value of 1.

```
CREATE TRIGGER Internet.Url$afterInsertTrigger
ON Internet.Url
AFTER INSERT AS
BEGIN

    DECLARE @rowsAffected int,     --stores the number of rows affected
            @msg varchar(2000)     --used to hold the error message

    SET @rowsAffected = @@rowcount

    --no need to continue on if no rows affected
    IF @rowsAffected = 0 return

    SET NOCOUNT ON --to avoid the rowcount messages
    SET ROWCOUNT 0 --in case the client has modified the rowcount

    BEGIN TRY
            --[validation section]
```

```
                    --[modification section]

                    --add a row to the UrlStatus table to tell it that the new row
                    --should start out as the default status
                    INSERT INTO Internet.UrlStatus (UrlId, UrlStatusTypeId, ActiveTime)
                    SELECT inserted.UrlId, UrlStatusType.UrlStatusTypeId,
                            current_timestamp
                    FROM inserted
                        CROSS JOIN (SELECT UrlStatusTypeId
                                    FROM    UrlStatusType
                                    WHERE   DefaultFlag = 1)  as UrlStatusType
                                                    --use cross join with a WHERE clause
                                                    --as this is not technically a join
                                                    --between inserted and UrlType
        END TRY
        BEGIN CATCH
                    IF @@trancount > 0
                        ROLLBACK TRANSACTION

                    --or this will not get rolled back
                    EXECUTE utility.ErrorLog$insert

                    DECLARE @ERROR_MESSAGE varchar(4000)
                    SET @ERROR_MESSAGE = ERROR_MESSAGE()
                    RAISERROR (@ERROR_MESSAGE,16,1)


            END CATCH
    END
```

The idea here is that for every row in the inserted table, we'll get the single row from the UrlStatusType table that has DefaultFlag equal to 1. So, let's try it:

```
INSERT  INTO Internet.Url(Name, Url)
VALUES ('More info can be found here',
        'http://sqlblog.com/blogs/louis_davidson/default.aspx')

SELECT * FROM Internet.Url
SELECT * FROM Internet.UrlStatus
```

This returns the following results:

```
UrlId      Name
---------- -----------------------------------
1          More info can be found here

Url
------------------------------------------------------
http://sqlblog.com/blogs/louis_davidson/default.aspx

UrlStatusId UrlStatusTypeId UrlId       activeDate
----------- --------------- ----------- ------------
1           1               1           2005-07-13
```

■**Tip** It's easier if users can't modify tables such as the UrlStatusType table, so there cannot be a case where there's no status set as the default (or too many rows). If there were no default status, then the URL would never get used, because the processes wouldn't see it. You could also create a trigger to check to see whether more than one row is set to the default, but the trigger still doesn't protect you against there being zero rows that are set to the default.

### Cascading from Child to Parent

All the cascade operations that you can do with constraints (CASCADE or SET NULL) are strictly from parent to child. Sometimes you want to go the other way around and delete the parents of a row when you delete the child. Typically you do this when the child is what you're interested in and the parent is simply maintained as an attribute of the child. Also typical of this type of situation is that you want to delete the parent only if all children are deleted.

A common (though non–SQL Server database) application of this sort of operation is DLLs registered on a computer. When the last program that refers to the object is uninstalled, the DLL is unregistered and deleted (with a warning message, of course).

In our example, we have a small model of my game collection. I have several game systems and quite a few games. Often, I have the same game on multiple platforms, so I want to track this fact, especially if I want to go and trade a game that I have on multiple platforms for something else. So, we have a table for the GamePlatform (the system) and another for the actual game itself. This is a many-to-many relationship, so we have an associative entity called GameInstance to record ownership, as well as when the game was purchased for the given platform. Each of these tables has a delete-cascade relationship, so all instances are removed. What about the games, though? If all GameInstance rows are removed for a given game, then we want to delete the game from the database. The tables are shown in Figure 6-3.

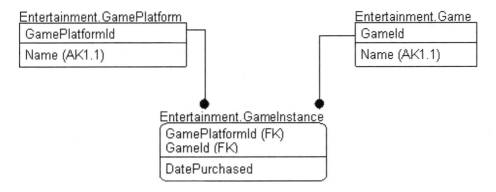

**Figure 6-3.** *The game tables*

```
--start a schema for entertainment-related tables
CREATE SCHEMA Entertainment
go
CREATE TABLE Entertainment.GamePlatform
(
    GamePlatformId int CONSTRAINT PKGamePlatform PRIMARY KEY,
    Name  varchar(20) CONSTRAINT AKGamePlatform_Name UNIQUE
)
```

```
CREATE TABLE Entertainment.Game
(
    GameId  int CONSTRAINT PKGame PRIMARY KEY,
    Name    varchar(20) CONSTRAINT AKGame_Name UNIQUE
    --more details that are common to all platforms
)

--associative entity with cascade relationships back to Game and GamePlatform
CREATE TABLE Entertainment.GameInstance
(
    GamePlatformId int,
    GameId int,
    PurchaseDate date,
    CONSTRAINT PKGameInstance PRIMARY KEY (GamePlatformId, GameId),
    CONSTRAINT
    Entertainment_Game$is_owned_on_platform_by$Entertainment_GameInstance
      FOREIGN KEY (GameId)REFERENCES Entertainment.Game(GameId)
                                          ON DELETE CASCADE,
      CONSTRAINT
        Entertainment_GamePlatform$is_linked_to$Entertainment_GameInstance
      FOREIGN KEY (GamePlatformId)
          REFERENCES Entertainment.GamePlatform(GamePlatformId)
              ON DELETE CASCADE
)
```

Then I insert a sampling of data:

```
INSERT  into Entertainment.Game (GameId, Name)
VALUES (1,'Super Mario Bros').
       (2,'Legend Of Zelda')

INSERT  into Entertainment.GamePlatform(GamePlatformId, Name)
VALUES (1,'Nintendo Wii'),    --Yes, as a matter of fact I am a
       (2,'Nintendo DS')      --Nintendo Fanboy, why do you ask?

INSERT  into Entertainment.GameInstance(GamePlatformId, GameId, PurchaseDate)
VALUES (1,1,'20060404'),
       (1,2,'20070510'),
       (2,2,'20070404')

--the full outer joins ensure that all rows are returned from all sets, leaving
--nulls where data is missing
SELECT  GamePlatform.Name as Platform, Game.Name as Game, GameInstance. PurchaseDate
FROM    Entertainment.Game as Game
            FULL OUTER JOIN Entertainment.GameInstance as GameInstance
                on Game.GameId = GameInstance.GameId
            FULL OUTER JOIN Entertainment.GamePlatform
                on GamePlatform.GamePlatformId = GameInstance.GamePlatformId
```

As you can see, I have two games for Nintendo 64 and only a single one for GameCube:

```
Platform               Game                   PurchaseDate
--------------------   --------------------   -----------------------
Nintendo Wii           Super Mario Bros       2006-04-04
Nintendo Wii           Legend Of Zelda        2007-05-10
Nintendo DS            Legend Of Zelda        2007-04-04
```

So, we create a trigger on the table to do the "reverse" cascade operation (*note that nontemplate code is in bold*):

```
CREATE TRIGGER Entertainment.GameInstance$afterDeleteTrigger
ON Entertainment.GameInstance
AFTER delete AS
BEGIN

   DECLARE @rowsAffected int,    --stores the number of rows affected
           @msg varchar(2000)    --used to hold the error message

   SET @rowsAffected = @@rowcount

   --no need to continue on if no rows affected
   IF @rowsAffected = 0 return

   SET NOCOUNT ON --to avoid the rowcount messages
   SET ROWCOUNT 0 --in case the client has modified the rowcount

   BEGIN TRY
        --[validation section]

        --[modification section]
        --delete all Games
        DELETE Game         --where the GameInstance was delete
        WHERE  GameId in (SELECT deleted.GameId
                          FROM    deleted      --and there are no GameInstances
                          WHERE  not exists (SELECT *         --left
                                             FROM    GameInstance
                                             WHERE   GameInstance.GameId =
                                                            deleted.GameId))
   END TRY
   BEGIN CATCH
            IF @@trancount > 0
                ROLLBACK TRANSACTION

            EXECUTE utility.ErrorLog$insert

            DECLARE @ERROR_MESSAGE varchar(4000)
            SET @ERROR_MESSAGE = ERROR_MESSAGE()
            RAISERROR (@ERROR_MESSAGE,16,1)

      END CATCH
END
```

It's as straightforward as that. Just delete the games, and let the error handler cover the rest. Delete the row for the GameCube:

```
DELETE  Entertainment.GamePlatform
WHERE   GamePlatformId = 1
go
SELECT  GamePlatform.Name as platform, Game.Name as Game, GameInstance. PurchaseDate
FROM    Entertainment.Game as Game
            FULL OUTER JOIN Entertainment.GameInstance as GameInstance
                 on Game.GameId = GameInstance.GameId
            FULL OUTER JOIN Entertainment.GamePlatform
                 on GamePlatform.GamePlatformId = GameInstance.GamePlatformId
```

You can see that now we have only a single row in the Game table:

| platform | Game | PurchaseDate |
| --- | --- | --- |
| Nintendo DS | Legend Of Zelda | 2007-04-04 00:00:00 |

### Relationships That Span Databases and Servers

Prior to constraints, all relationships were enforced by triggers (for you young 'uns out there, that was back in SQL Server 6.0 and earlier!). Thankfully, when it comes to relationships, triggers are now relegated to enforcing special cases of relationships, such as when you have relationships between tables that are on different databases. I have used this sort of thing when I had a common demographics database that many different systems used.

To implement a relationship using triggers, you need several triggers:

- Parent:
  - UPDATE: Disallow the changing of keys if child values exist, or cascade the update.
  - DELETE: Prevent or cascade the deletion of rows that have associated parent rows.
- Child:
  - INSERT: Check to make sure the key exists in the parent table.
  - UPDATE: Check to make sure the "possibly" changed key exists in the parent table.

Instead of coding full triggers for this example, I'm going to present a few templates to use to build these triggers. For these snippets of code, I refer to the tables as *parent* and *child*, with no schema or database named. Replacing the bits that are inside these greater-than and less-than symbols with appropriate code and table names that include the database and schema gives you the desired result when plugged into the trigger templates we've been using throughout this chapter.

#### Parent Update

Note that you can omit the parent update step if using surrogate keys based on identity property columns, because they aren't editable and hence cannot be changed.

There are a few possibilities you might want to implement:

- Cascading operations to child rows
- Preventing updating parent if child rows exist

Cascading operations is not possible from a proper generic trigger coding standpoint. The problem is that if you modify the key of one or more parent rows in a statement that fires the trigger, there is not necessarily any way to correlate rows in the inserted table with the rows in the deleted table, leaving you not able to know which row in the inserted table is supposed to match which row in the deleted table. So, I would not implement the cascading of a parent key change in a trigger; I would do this in your external code (though frankly I rarely see the need for modifiable keys anyhow).

Preventing an update of parent rows where child rows exist is very straightforward. The idea here is that you want to take the same restrictive action as the NO ACTION clause on a relationship. For example:

```
IF update(<parent_key_columns>)
   BEGIN
        IF EXISTS ( SELECT  *
                      FROM    deleted
                              JOIN <child>
                                on <child>.<parent_keys> =
                                            deleted.<parent_keys>
                  )
        BEGIN
           IF @rowsAffected = 1
                 SELECT @msg = 'one row message' + inserted.somedata
                 FROM   inserted
             ELSE
                 SELECT @msg = 'multi-row message'
           RAISERROR (@msg, 16, 1)
        END
   END
END
```

**Parent Delete**

Like the update possibilities, when a parent table row is deleted, we can either:

- Cascade the delete to child rows

- Prevent deleting parent rows if child rows exist

Cascading is very simple. For the delete, you simply use a correlated EXISTS subquery to get matching rows in the child table to the parent table:

```
DELETE from <child>
WHERE   EXISTS ( SELECT *
            FROM    <parent>
            WHERE <child>.<parent_key> = <parent>.<parent_key> )
```

To prevent the delete from happening when a child row exists, here's the basis of code to prevent deleting rows that have associated parent rows:

```
IF EXISTS  ( SELECT   *
          FROM    deleted
                  JOIN <child>
                     ON <child>.<parent_key> = deleted.<parent_key>
          )
   BEGIN
       IF @rowsAffected = 1
           SELECT @msg = 'one row message' + inserted.somedata
           FROM   inserted
       ELSE
           SELECT @msg = 'multi-row message'
       RAISERROR (@msg, 16, 1)
   END
END
```

### Child Insert and Child Update

On the child table, the goal will basically be to make sure that for every value you create in the child table, there exists a corresponding row in the parent table. The following snippet does this and takes into consideration the case where null values are allowed as well:

```
--@numrows is part of the standard template
DECLARE @nullcount int,
        @validcount int

IF UPDATE(<parent_key>)
 BEGIN
    --you can omit this check if nulls are not allowed
    SELECT  @nullcount = count(*)
    FROM    inserted
    WHERE   inserted.<parent_key> is null

    --does not count null values
    SELECT  @validcount = count(*)
    FROM    inserted
                JOIN <parent> as Parent
                    ON  inserted.<parent_keys> = Parent.<parent_keys>

    if @validcount + @nullcount != @numrows
      BEGIN
          IF @rowsAffected = 1
            SELECT @msg = 'The inserted <parent_key_name>: '
                            + cast(parent_key as varchar(10))
                            + ' is not valid in the parent table.'
               FROM    INSERTED
          ELSE
               SELECT @msg = 'Invalid <parent key> in the inserted rows.'
            RAISERROR (@msg, 16, 1)
      END
  END
```

Using basic blocks of code such as these, you can validate most any foreign key relationship using triggers. For example, say you have a table in your PhoneData database called Logs.Call, with a primary key of CallId. In the CRM database, you have a Contacts.Journal table that stores contacts made to a person. To implement the child update and insert a trigger, just fill in the blanks. (I've put the parts of the code in bold where I've replaced the tags with the text specific to this trigger.)

```
CREATE TRIGGER Contacts.Journal$afterInsertUpdateTrigger
ON Contacts.Journal
AFTER INSERT, UPDATE AS
BEGIN

    DECLARE @rowsAffected int,    --stores the number of rows affected
            @msg varchar(2000)    --used to hold the error message

    SET @rowsAffected = @@rowcount

    --no need to continue on if no rows affected
    IF @rowsAffected = 0 return

    SET NOCOUNT ON --to avoid the rowcount messages
    SET ROWCOUNT 0 --in case the client has modified the rowcount
```

```
BEGIN TRY
   --[validation section]
   --@numrows is part of the standard template
   DECLARE @nullcount int,
           @validcount int

   IF update(CallId)
    BEGIN
       --omit this check if nulls are not allowed
       --(left in here for an example)
       SELECT  @nullcount = count(*)
       FROM    inserted
       WHERE   inserted.CallId is null

       --does not include null values
       SELECT  @validcount = count(*)
       FROM    inserted
                   join PhoneData.Logs.Call as Parent
                       on  inserted.CallId = Parent.CallId

       if @validcount + @nullcount <> @numrows
          BEGIN
             IF @rowsAffected = 1
                SELECT @msg = 'The inserted CallId: '
                                + cast(CallId as varchar(10))
                                + ' is not valid in the'
                                + ' PhoneData.Logs.Call table.'
                 FROM    INSERTED
             ELSE
                 SELECT @msg = 'Invalid CallId in the inserted rows.'
               RAISERROR (@msg, 16, 1)
          END
     END
   --[modification section]

END TRY
BEGIN CATCH
         IF @@trancount > 0
             ROLLBACK TRANSACTION

         EXECUTE utility.ErrorLog$insert

         DECLARE @ERROR_MESSAGE varchar(4000)
         SET @ERROR_MESSAGE = ERROR_MESSAGE()
         RAISERROR (@ERROR_MESSAGE,16,1)

    END CATCH
END
```

## Maintaining an Audit Trail

A common task that's implemented using triggers is the audit trail or audit log. You use it to record previous versions of rows or columns so you can determine who changed a given row. Often an audit trail is simply for documentation purposes, so we can go back to other users and ask why they made a change.

■**Note** In SQL Server 2008, the new SQL Server Audit feature may eliminate the need for many audit trails in triggers, and two other features called Change Tracking and Change Data Capture may obviate the necessity to use triggers to implement tracking of database changes in triggers. However, using triggers is still a possible tool for building an audit trail depending on your requirements and version/edition of SQL Server. Auditing is covered in Chapter 8 in the "Server and Database Audit" section. I will not cover Change Tracking and Change Data Capture because they are more of a programming/ETL building tool, and they don't include information about the user who made the change.

An audit trail is straightforward to implement using triggers. In our example, we'll build an employee table and audit any change to the table. I'll keep it simple and have a copy of the table that has a few extra columns for the date and time of the change, plus the user who made the change and what the change was.

We implement an employee table (using names with underscores just to add variety) and then a replica to store changes into:

```
CREATE SCHEMA hr
go
CREATE TABLE hr.employee
(
    employee_id char(6) CONSTRAINT PKhr_employee PRIMARY KEY,
    first_name  varchar(20),
    last_name   varchar(20),
    salary      money
)
CREATE TABLE hr.employee_auditTrail
(
    employee_id         char(6),
    date_changed        datetime not null --default so we don't have to
                                          --code for it
        CONSTRAINT DfltHr_employee_date_changed DEFAULT (current_timestamp),
    first_name          varchar(20),
    last_name           varchar(20),
    salary              decimal(12,2),
    --the following are the added columns to the original
    --structure of hr.employee
    action              char(6)
        CONSTRAINT ChkHr_employee_action --we don't log inserts, only changes
                                    CHECK(action in ('delete','update')),
    changed_by_user_name sysname
                CONSTRAINT DfltHr_employee_changed_by_user_name
                                    DEFAULT (original_login_id()),
    CONSTRAINT PKemployee_auditTrail PRIMARY KEY (employee_id, date_changed)
)
```

Now we create a trigger with code to determine whether it's an UPDATE or a DELETE, based on how many rows are in the inserted table:

```
CREATE TRIGGER hr.employee$insertAndDeleteAuditTrailTrigger
ON hr.employee
AFTER UPDATE, DELETE AS
BEGIN

    DECLARE @rowsAffected int,    --stores the number of rows affected
            @msg varchar(2000)    --used to hold the error message
```

```
        SET @rowsAffected = @@rowcount

        --no need to continue on if no rows affected
        IF @rowsAffected = 0 return

        SET NOCOUNT ON --to avoid the rowcount messages
        SET ROWCOUNT 0 --in case the client has modified the rowcount
        BEGIN TRY
                --[validation section]
                --[modification section]
                --since we are only doing update and delete, we just
                --need to see if there are any rows
                --inserted to determine what action is being done.
                DECLARE @action char(6)
                SET @action = case when (SELECT count(*) from inserted) > 0
                                  then 'update' else 'delete' end

                --since the deleted table contains all changes, we just insert all
                --of the rows in the deleted table and we are done.
                INSERT employee_auditTrail (employee_id, first_name, last_name,
                                          salary, action)
                SELECT employee_id, first_name, last_name, salary, @action
                FROM    deleted

        END TRY
        BEGIN CATCH
                IF @@trancount > 0
                    ROLLBACK TRANSACTION

                EXECUTE utility.ErrorLog$insert

                DECLARE @ERROR_MESSAGE varchar(4000)
                SET @ERROR_MESSAGE = ERROR_MESSAGE()
                RAISERROR (@ERROR_MESSAGE,16,1)

        END CATCH
END
```

We create some data:

```
INSERT hr.employee (employee_id, first_name, last_name, salary)
VALUES (1, 'Phillip','Taibul',10000)
```

Now, much unlike the real world in which we live, the person gets a raise immediately (though a salary of 11,000 American dollars is still not exactly an invitation to dance any sort of dance of joy, even if you are just starting out!):

```
UPDATE hr.employee
SET salary = salary * 1.10 --ten percent raise!
WHERE employee_id = 1

SELECT *
FROM    hr.employee
```

This returns the data with the new values:

| employee_id | first_name | last_name | salary |
|---|---|---|---|
| 1 | Phillip | Taibul | 11000.00 |

Check the audit trail table:

```
SELECT *
FROM   hr.employee_auditTrail
```

You can see that the previous values for the row are stored here:

| employee_id | first_name | last_name | salary | action |
| --- | --- | --- | --- | --- |
| 1 | Phillip | Taibul | 10000.00 | update |

| date_changed | changed_by_user_name |
| --- | --- |
| 2008-01-19 10:47:06.077 | MYDOMAIN\LBDAVI |

This can be a cheap and effective auditing system for many smaller systems. If you have a lot of columns, it can be better to check and see which columns have changed and implement a table that has `tablename`, `columnname`, and previous value columns, but often this simple strategy works quite well when the volume is low and the number of tables to audit isn't large. Keeping only recent history in the audit trail table helps as well.

## INSTEAD OF Triggers

As introduced at the beginning of this fairly long section, INSTEAD OF triggers happen prior to the DML action being affected by the SQL engine, rather than after it for AFTER triggers. In fact, when you have an INSTEAD OF trigger on a table, it's the first thing that's done when you INSERT, UPDATE, or DELETE from a table. These triggers are named INSTEAD OF because they fire *instead of* the native action the user executed. Inside the trigger, you perform the action—either the action that the user performed or some other action. One thing that makes these triggers useful is that you can use them on views to make noneditable views editable. Doing this, you encapsulate calls to all the affected tables in the trigger, much like you would a stored procedure, except now this view has all the properties of a physical table, hiding the actual implementation from users.

Probably the most obvious limitation of INSTEAD OF triggers is that you can have only one for each action (INSERT, UPDATE, and DELETE) on the table, or you can combine them just like you can for AFTER triggers (something I strongly suggest against for INSTEAD OF triggers). We'll use the same trigger template that we used for the T-SQL AFTER triggers, with only the modification that now you have to add a step to perform the action that the user was trying to do (in **bold** for your reading pleasure):

```
CREATE TRIGGER <schema>.<tablename>$InsteadOf<actions>[<purpose>]Trigger
ON <schema>.<tablename>
INSTEAD OF <comma delimited actions> AS
BEGIN

    DECLARE @rowsAffected int,    --stores the number of rows affected
            @msg varchar(2000)    --used to hold the error message

    SET @rowsAffected = @@rowcount

    --no need to continue on if no rows affected
    IF @rowsAffected = 0 return

    SET NOCOUNT ON --to avoid the rowcount messages
    SET ROWCOUNT 0 --in case the client has modified the rowcount
```

```
BEGIN TRY
        --[validation section]
        --[modification section]
        --<perform action>
END TRY
BEGIN CATCH
            IF @@trancount > 0
                ROLLBACK TRANSACTION

            EXECUTE utility.ErrorLog$insert

            DECLARE @ERROR_MESSAGE nvarchar(4000)
            SET @ERROR_MESSAGE = ERROR_MESSAGE()
            RAISERROR (@ERROR_MESSAGE,16,1)

    END CATCH
END
```

The most annoying part of the INSTEAD OF trigger is that you have to perform the operation yourself. This is the purpose of the <perform action> addition. Technically, *performing the action* is optional, because in one of our examples we'll demonstrate how to use INSTEAD OF triggers to prevent a DML operation from occurring altogether, but generally speaking, the point of the INSTEAD OF trigger is to control how a DML action is processed.

I most often use INSTEAD OF triggers to set or modify values in my statements automatically so that the values are set to what I want, no matter what the client sends in a statement. A good example is a column to record the last time the row was modified. If you record last update times through client calls, it can be problematic if one of the client's clock is a minute, a day, or even a year off. (You see this all the time in applications. My favorite example was in one system where phone calls appeared to be taking negative amounts of time because the client was reporting when something started and the server was recording when it stopped.) It's generally a best practice not to use INSTEAD OF triggers to do validations and to use them only to shape the way the data is seen by the time it's stored in the DBMS. There's one slight alteration to this. You can use INSTEAD OF triggers to prevalidate data so that it's never subject to constraints or AFTER triggers.

I'll demonstrate four ways you can use INSTEAD OF triggers:

- Automatically maintained columns
- Formatting user input
- Redirecting invalid data to an exception table
- Forcing no action to be performed on a table, even by someone who technically has proper rights

### Automatically Maintaining Columns

An INSTEAD OF trigger is an ideal way to handle "implementation-only" columns—those that aren't strictly part of the data model but that are there to track database usage. Good examples of this are columns to indicate when a row was created, and by whom, as shown in Figure 6-4. In the following example code, we'll use an INSTEAD OF trigger to capture the time and user who originally created the row.

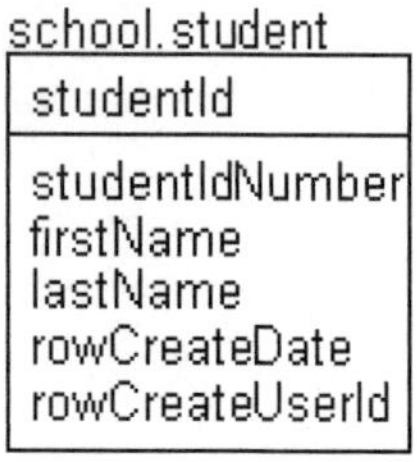

**Figure 6-4.** *A table that tracks database usage*

```
CREATE SCHEMA school
Go
CREATE TABLE school.student
(
      studentId          int identity not null
          CONSTRAINT PKschool_student PRIMARY KEY,
      studentIdNumber char(8) not null
          CONSTRAINT AKschool_student_studentIdNumber UNIQUE,
      firstName          varchar(20) not null,
      lastName           varchar(20) not null,
--Note that we add these columns to the implementation model, not to the logical
--model. These columns do not actually refer to the student being modeled, they are
--required simply to help with programming and tracking.
      rowCreateDate      datetime not null
          CONSTRAINT dfltSchool_student_rowCreateDate
                              DEFAULT (current_timestamp),
      rowCreateUser    sysname not null
          CONSTRAINT dfltSchool_student_rowCreateUser DEFAULT (current_user)
)
```

Note that we include default values so the consumer of this table doesn't need to include the columns in INSERT or UPDATE statements. Next we code the trigger to set these values automatically for us:

```
CREATE TRIGGER school.student$insteadOfInsert
ON school.student
INSTEAD OF INSERT AS
BEGIN

    DECLARE @rowsAffected int,    --stores the number of rows affected
            @msg varchar(2000)    --used to hold the error message

    SET @rowsAffected = @@rowcount

    --no need to continue on if no rows affected
    IF @rowsAffected = 0 return

    SET ROWCOUNT 0 --in case the client has modified the rowcount
    SET NOCOUNT ON --to avoid the rowcount messages

    BEGIN TRY
            --[validation section]
            --[modification section]
            --<perform action>
```

```
        INSERT INTO school.student(studentIdNumber, firstName, lastName,
                            rowCreateDate, rowCreateUser)
        SELECT studentIdNumber, firstName, lastName,
                            current_timestamp, suser_sname()
        FROM  inserted   --no matter what the user put in the inserted row
END TRY          --when the row was created, these values will be inserted
BEGIN CATCH
        IF @@trancount > 0
            ROLLBACK TRANSACTION

        EXECUTE utility.ErrorLog$insert

        DECLARE @ERROR_MESSAGE nvarchar(4000)
        SET @ERROR_MESSAGE = ERROR_MESSAGE()
        RAISERROR (@ERROR_MESSAGE,16,1)

    END CATCH
END
```

Next, we try inserting some data:

```
INSERT  into school.student(studentIdNumber, firstName, lastName)
VALUES ( '0000001',' Gray', ' Tezine' )
```

---

■**Tip** If we were to run SELECT scope_identity(), it would return NULL (because the actual insert was out of scope). Instead of scope_identity(), use the alternate key, in this case the studentIdNumber that equals '0000001'. You might also want to forgo using an IDENTITY value for a surrogate key in the case where another suitable candidate key can be found for that table.

---

Next, we can look at the values:

```
SELECT * FROM school.student
```

You can see that the rowCreateDate and rowCreateUser have been set automatically:

| studentId | studentIdNumber | firstName | lastName |
| --------- | --------------- | --------- | -------- |
| 1 | 0000001 | Gray | Tezine |

| rowCreateDate | rowCreateUser |
| ------------- | ------------- |
| 2008-01-19 13:38:42.480 | DOMAIN\username |

This, you say, would have been the result without us adding the trigger, right? Yes, but what if the newbie programmer didn't realize that the default would take care of this for you and just put whatever value into the INSERT for the rowCreateDate and rowCreateUser?

```
INSERT  school.student(studentIdNumber, firstName, lastName, rowCreateDate,
                    rowCreateUser)
VALUES ( '000002','Norm', 'Ull','99990101','some user' )
```

Without the trigger, horrible dates would be inserted, but because we have the INSTEAD OF trigger, the correct creation information is stored as follows:

| studentId | studentIdNumber | firstName | lastName |
|---|---|---|---|
| 1 | 0000001 | Gray | Tezine |
| 2 | 0000002 | Norm | Ull |

| rowCreateDate | rowCreateUser |
|---|---|
| 2008-01-19 13:38:42.480 | DOMAIN\username |
| 2008-01-19 14:06:34.290 | DOMAIN\username |

It put the actual date when I was working on the book, rather than allowing the obscenely wrong data that was entered by the client. This is especially useful when you have users working in multiple time zones, because allowing the client to send the creation information would then require each client to translate the time to some time zone, possibly using Coordinated Universal Time (UTC).

From here, it's pretty easy to see that we could also add an UPDATE INSTEAD OF trigger that would fire on every UPDATE to keep up with the last user to modify the values in the table. Some people prefer to use columns like this for all of their optimistic locking needs, instead of using a column of the type rowversion. I almost always end up having both pieces of information in most implemented tables. I generally prefer the rowversion mechanism for optimistic locking because it is completely automated by SQL Server and is guaranteed to work, regardless of any code I (or another programmer) might write. However, knowing the last user to modify the row and when that person modified it are often handy pieces of information.

### Formatting User Input

Consider the columns firstName and lastName. What if the users who were entering this were heads-down, paid-by-the-keystroke kinds of users? Would we want them to go back and futz around with "joHnson" and make sure that it was formatted as "Johnson"? Or what about data received from services that still use mainframes, in which lowercase letters are still considered a work of the underlord? We don't want to have to make anyone go in and reformat the data by hand (even the newbie intern who doesn't know any better).

One good place for this kind of operation is an INSTEAD OF trigger, often using a function to handle the formatting. Here I'll present them both in their basic state, generally capitalizing the first letter of each word. (This way, we can handle names that have two parts, such as Von Smith, or other more reasonable names that are found in reality.) The crux of the function is that I'm simply capitalizing the first character of every letter after a space. The function needs to be updated to handle special cases, such as McDonald.

I am going to simply code this function in T-SQL. The syntax for functions hasn't changed much since SQL Server 2000, though in 2005 Microsoft did get a bit more lenient on what you're allowed to call from a function, such as CURRENT_TIMESTAMP—the standard version of GETDATE()—which was one of the most requested changes to functions in SQL Server 2000.

If this were going to be heavily used by many different systems, it would probably behoove you to build a proper CLR edition of this function, and you would probably also want versions to use for address formatting, and so on.

```
CREATE FUNCTION Utility.TitleCase
(
    @inputString varchar(2000)
)
RETURNS varchar(2000) AS
```

```
BEGIN
   -- set the whole string to lower
   SET @inputString = LOWER(@inputstring)
   -- then use stuff to replace the first character
   SET @inputString =
   --STUFF in the uppercased character in to the next character,
   --replacing the lowercased letter
   STUFF(@inputString,1,1,UPPER(SUBSTRING(@inputString,1,1)))

   --@i is for the loop counter, initialized to 2
   DECLARE @i int
   SET @i = 1

   --loop from the second character to the end of the string
   WHILE @i < LEN(@inputString)
   BEGIN
      --if the character is a space
      IF SUBSTRING(@inputString,@i,1) = ' '
      BEGIN
         --STUFF in the uppercased character into the next character
         SET @inputString = STUFF(@inputString,@i +
         1,1,UPPER(SUBSTRING(@inputString,@i + 1,1)))
      END
      --increment the loop counter
      SET @i = @i + 1
   END
   RETURN @inputString
END
```

### The Example Trigger

Now we can alter our trigger from the previous section, which was used to set the rowCreateDate rowCreate user for the school.student table. This time you'll modify the trigger to title-case the name of the student. The changes are in **bold**:

```
ALTER TRIGGER school.student$insteadOfInsertTrigger
ON school.student
INSTEAD OF INSERT AS
BEGIN

   DECLARE @rowsAffected int,    --stores the number of rows affected
           @msg varchar(2000)    --used to hold the error message

   SET @rowsAffected = @@rowcount

   --no need to continue on if no rows affected
   IF @rowsAffected = 0 return

   SET ROWCOUNT 0 --in case the client has modified the rowcount
   SET NOCOUNT ON --to avoid the rowcount messages

   BEGIN TRY
         --[validation section]
         --[modification section]
         --<perform action>
         INSERT INTO school.student(studentIdNumber, firstName, lastName,
                                   rowCreateDate, rowCreateUser)
```

```
            SELECT studentIdNumber,
                   Utility.titleCase(firstName),
                   Utility.titleCase(lastName),
                   current_timestamp, suser_sname()
            FROM   inserted   --no matter what the user put in the inserted row
    END TRY                   --when the row was created, these values will be inserted
    BEGIN CATCH
            IF @@trancount > 0
                ROLLBACK TRANSACTION

            EXECUTE utility.ErrorLog$insert

            DECLARE @ERROR_MESSAGE nvarchar(4000)
            SET @ERROR_MESSAGE = ERROR_MESSAGE()
            RAISERROR (@ERROR_MESSAGE,16,1)

    END CATCH
END
```

Then insert a new row with funky formatted data:

```
INSERT school.student(studentIdNumber, firstName, lastName)
VALUES ( '0000007','CaPtain', 'von nuLLY')

SELECT *
FROM school.student
```

Now you see that this data has been formatted:

| studentId | studentIdNumber | firstName | lastName |
| --- | --- | --- | --- |
| 1 | 0000001 | Gray | Tezine |
| 2 | 0000002 | Norm | Ull |
| 3 | 0000003 | Captain | Von Nully |

| rowCreateDate | rowCreateUser |
| --- | --- |
| 2008-01-19 13:38:42.480 | DOMAIN\username |
| 2008-01-19 14:06:34.290 | DOMAIN\username |
| 2008-01-19 14:38:05.977 | DOMAIN\username |

I'll leave it to you to modify this trigger for the UPDATE version, because there are few differences, other than updating the row rather than INSERTing it.

■**Note** It is not uncommon for this kind of formatting to be done at the client to allow for overriding as needed. Just as I have said many times, T-SQL code could (and possibly *should*) be used to manage formatting when it is *always* done. If there are options to override, then you cannot exclusively use a trigger for sure. In our example, you could just use the INSERT trigger to format the name columns initially and then not have an UPDATE trigger to allow for overrides.

### Redirecting Invalid Data to an Exception Table

On some occasions, instead of returning an error when an invalid value is set for a column, you simply want to ignore it and log that an error had occurred. Generally, this wouldn't be used for bulk loading data (using SSIS's facilities to do this is a much better idea), but some examples of why you might do this are as follows:

- *Heads-down key entry*: In many shops where customer feedback or payments are received by the hundreds or thousands, there are people who open the mail, read it, and key in what's on the page. These people become incredibly skilled in rapid entry and generally make few mistakes. The mistakes they do make don't raise an error on their screen; rather, it falls to other people—exception handlers—to fix. You could use an INSTEAD OF trigger to redirect the wrong data to an exception table to be handled later.

- *Values that are read in from devices*: An example of this is on an assembly line, where a reading is taken but is so far out of range it couldn't be true, because of the malfunction of a device or just a human moving a sensor. Too many exception rows would require a look at the equipment, but only a few might be normal and acceptable. Another possibility is when someone scans a printed page using a scanner and inserts the data. Often the values read are not right and have to be checked manually.

For our example, I'll design a table to take weather readings from a single thermometer. Sometimes this thermometer sends back bad values that are impossible. We need to be able to put in readings, sometimes many at a time, because the device can cache results for some time if there is signal loss, but it tosses off the unlikely rows.

We build the following table, initially using a constraint to implement the simple sanity check. In the analysis of the data, we might find anomalies, but in this process all we're going to do is look for the "impossible" cases:

```
CREATE SCHEMA Measurements
go
CREATE TABLE Measurements.WeatherReading
(
    WeatherReadingId int identity
        CONSTRAINT PKWeatherReading PRIMARY KEY,
    ReadingTime    datetime
        CONSTRAINT AKMeasurements_WeatherReading_Date UNIQUE,
    Temperature        float
        CONSTRAINT chkMeasurements_WeatherReading_Temperature
                CHECK(Temperature between -80 and 150)
                --raised from last edition for global warming
)
```

Then we go to load the data, simulating what we might do when importing the data all at once:

```
INSERT  into Measurements.WeatherReading (ReadingTime, Temperature)
VALUES ('20080101 0:00',82.00), ('20080101 0:01',89.22),
       ('20080101 0:02',600.32),('20080101 0:03',88.22)
       ('20080101 0:04',99.01)
```

As we know with CHECK constraints, this isn't going to fly:

```
Msg 547, Level 16, State 0, Line 5
The INSERT statement conflicted with the CHECK constraint
"chkMeasurements_WeatherReading_Temperature". The conflict occurred in database
"ProtectionChapter", table "WeatherReading", column 'Temperature'.
The statement has been terminated.
```

Select all the data in the table, and you'll see that this data never gets entered. Does this mean we have to dig through every row individually? Yes, in the current scheme. Or you could insert each row individually (which would take a lot more work for the server), but if you've been following along, you know we're going to write an INSTEAD OF trigger to do this for us. First we add a table to hold the exceptions to the Temperature rule:

```
CREATE TABLE Measurements.WeatherReading_exception
(
    WeatherReadingId  int identity
          CONSTRAINT PKMeasurements_WeatherReading_exception PRIMARY KEY,
    ReadingTime       datetime,
    Temperature       float
)
```

Then we create the trigger:

```
CREATE TRIGGER Measurements.WeatherReading$InsteadOfInsertTrigger
ON Measurements.WeatherReading
INSTEAD OF INSERT AS
BEGIN

    DECLARE @rowsAffected int,    --stores the number of rows affected
            @msg varchar(2000)    --used to hold the error message

    SET @rowsAffected = @@rowcount

    --no need to continue on if no rows affected
    IF @rowsAffected = 0 return

    SET NOCOUNT ON --to avoid the rowcount messages
    SET ROWCOUNT 0 --in case the client has modified the rowcount

    BEGIN TRY
          --[validation section]
          --[modification section]

          --<perform action>

           --BAD data
          INSERT Measurements.WeatherReading_exception
                                    (ReadingTime, Temperature)
          SELECT ReadingTime, Temperature
          FROM   inserted
          WHERE  NOT(Temperature between -80 and 120)

           --GOOD data
          INSERT Measurements.WeatherReading (ReadingTime, Temperature)
          SELECT ReadingTime, Temperature
          FROM   inserted
          WHERE  (Temperature between -80 and 120)
    END TRY
    BEGIN CATCH
            IF @@trancount > 0
                ROLLBACK TRANSACTION

            EXECUTE utility.ErrorLog$insert
```

```
DECLARE @ERROR_MESSAGE nvarchar(4000)
SET @ERROR_MESSAGE = ERROR_MESSAGE()
RAISERROR (@ERROR_MESSAGE,16,1)

   END CATCH
END
```

Now we try to insert the rows with the bad data still in there:

```
INSERT  into Measurements.WeatherReading (ReadingTime, Temperature)
VALUES ('20080101 0:00',82.00), ('20080101 0:01',89.22),
    ('20080101 0:02',600.32),('20080101 0:03',88.22),
    ('20080101 0:04',99.01)

SELECT *
FROM Measurements.WeatherReading
```

The good data is in the following output:

| WeatherReading | ReadingTime | Temperature |
| --- | --- | --- |
| 6 | 2005-01-01 00:00:00.000 | 88 |
| 7 | 2005-01-01 00:01:00.000 | 88.22 |
| 8 | 2005-01-01 00:03:00.000 | 89.22 |
| 9 | 2005-01-01 00:04:00.000 | 90.01 |

The nonconforming (if you want to impress someone, otherwise "bad") data can be seen by viewing the data in the exception table:

```
SELECT *
FROM   Measurements.WeatherReading_exception
```

This returns the following result:

| WeatherReading | ReadingTime | Temperature |
| --- | --- | --- |
| 1 | 2005-01-01 00:02:00.000 | 600.32 |

Now, it might be possible to go back and work on the exceptions, perhaps extrapolating the value it should have been, based on the previous and the next measurements taken:

```
(88.22 + 89.22) /2 = 88.72?
```

Of course, if we did that, we would probably want to include another attribute that indicated that a reading was extrapolated rather than an actual reading from the device.

### Forcing No Action to Be Performed on a Table

Our final INSTEAD OF trigger example deals with what's almost a security issue. Often users have *too* much access, and this includes administrators who generally use sysadmin privileges to look for problems with systems. (Admit it, you know you have way too much access, don't you?) Some tables we simply don't ever want to be modified. We might implement triggers to keep any user—even a system administrator—from changing the data. We'll again look at something along these lines when we get to Chapter 7, because we can implement row-level security using this method as well.

In this example, we're going to implement a table to hold the version of the database. It's a single-row "table" that behaves more like a global variable. It's here to tell the application which version of the schema to expect, so it can tell the user to upgrade or lose functionality:

```
CREATE SCHEMA System
go
CREATE TABLE System.Version
(
    DatabaseVersion varchar(10)
)
INSERT  into System.Version (DatabaseVersion)
VALUES ('1.0.12')
```

Our application always looks to this value to see what objects it expects to be there when it uses them. We clearly don't want this value to get modified, even if someone has db_owner rights in the database. So, we might apply an INSTEAD OF trigger:

```
CREATE TRIGGER System.Version$InsteadOfInsertUpdateDeleteTrigger
ON System.Version
INSTEAD OF INSERT, UPDATE, DELETE AS
BEGIN

    DECLARE @rowsAffected int,    --stores the number of rows affected
            @msg varchar(2000)    --used to hold the error message

    SET @rowsAffected = @@rowcount
    --no need to complain if no rows affected
    IF @rowsAffected = 0 return

    --No error handling necessary, just the message.
    --We just put the kibosh on the action.
    RAISERROR
        ('The System.Version table may not be modified in production',
        16,1)
END
```

Attempts to delete the value, like so:

```
DELETE system.version
```

will result in the following:

```
Msg 50000, Level 16, State 1, Procedure version$InsteadOfInsertUpdateDelete, Line 15
The system.version table may not be modified in production
```

The users, if they had permissions, would then have to take the conscious step of running the following code:

```
ALTER TABLE system.version
    DISABLE TRIGGER version$InsteadOfInsertUpdateDelete
```

Using a trigger like this (not disabled, of course, which is something you can catch with a DDL trigger) enables you to "close the gate," keeping the data safely in the table, even from accidental changes.

# Handling Errors from Triggers and Constraints

One important thing to consider about triggers and constraints is how you need to deal with the error-handling errors caused by constraints or triggers. One of the drawbacks to using triggers is that the state of the database after a trigger error is different from when you have a constraint error. This is further complicated by the changes that were in SQL Server 2005 to support TRY-CATCH.

In previous versions of SQL Server, doing error handling for triggers was easy—error in trigger, everything stops in its tracks. Now this has changed. We need to consider two situations when we do a ROLLBACK in a trigger, using an error handler such as we have in this chapter:

- *You aren't using a* TRY-CATCH *block*: This situation is simple. The batch stops processing in its tracks. SQL Server handles cleanup for any transaction you were in.

- *You* are *using a* TRY-CATCH *block*: This situation can be a bit tricky.

Take a TRY-CATCH block, such as this one:

```
BEGIN TRY
        <DML STATEMENT>
END TRY
BEGIN CATCH
        <handle it>
END CATCH
```

If the T-SQL trigger rolls back and an error is raised, when you get to the <handle it> block, you won't be in a transaction. For CLR triggers, you're in charge of whether the connection ends. When a CHECK constraint causes the error or executes a simple RAISERROR, then you'll be in a transaction. Generically, here's the CATCH block that I use (making use of the objects we've already been using in the triggers):

```
BEGIN CATCH
        IF @@trancount > 0
            ROLLBACK TRANSACTION

        EXECUTE utility.ErrorLog$insert

        DECLARE @ERROR_MESSAGE nvarchar(4000)
        SET @ERROR_MESSAGE = ERROR_MESSAGE()
        RAISERROR (@ERROR_MESSAGE,16,1)

END CATCH
```

In almost every case, I roll back any transaction, log the error, and then reraise the error. As an example, I will build the following abstract tables for demonstrating trigger and constraint error handling:

```
CREATE SCHEMA alt
GO
CREATE TABLE alt.errorHandlingTest
(
    errorHandlingTestId   int CONSTRAINT PKerrorHandlingTest PRIMARY KEY,
    CONSTRAINT ChkAlt_errorHandlingTest_errorHandlingTestId_greaterThanZero
        CHECK (errorHandlingTestId > 0)
)
GO
```

Note that if you try to put a value greater than 0 into the errorHandlingTestId, it will cause a constraint error. In the trigger, we will force a RAISERROR immediately and then a ROLLBACK to end the transaction:

```
CREATE TRIGGER alt.errorHandlingTest$afterInsertTrigger
ON alt.errorHandlingTest
AFTER INSERT
AS

    RAISERROR ('Test Error',16,1)
    ROLLBACK TRANSACTION
```

The first thing to understand is that when a constraint causes the DML operation to fail, the batch will continue to operate:

```
--NO Transaction, Constraint Error
INSERT alt.errorHandlingTest
VALUES (-1)
SELECT 'continues'
```

You will see that the error is raised, and then the SELECT statement is executed:

```
Msg 547, Level 16, State 0, Line 2
The INSERT statement conflicted with the CHECK constraint
"ChkAlt_errorHandlingTest_errorHandlingTestId_greaterThanZero". The conflict
occurred in database "tempdb", table "alt.errorHandlingTest", column
'errorHandlingTestId'.
The statement has been terminated.


---------
continues
```

However, do this with a trigger error:

```
INSERT alt.errorHandlingTest
VALUES (1)
SELECT 'continues'
```

This returns the following:

```
Msg 50000, Level 16, State 1, Procedure errorHandlingTest$afterInsertTrigger,
Line 7
Test Error
Msg 3609, Level 16, State 1, Line 1
The transaction ended in the trigger. The batch has been aborted.
```

There are also differences in dealing with errors from constraints and triggers when you are using TRY-CATCH and transactions. Take the following batch. The error will be a constraint type. The big thing to cover here is the state of a transaction after the error. This is definitely an issue that you have to be careful with.

```
BEGIN TRANSACTION
BEGIN TRY
    INSERT alt.errorHandlingTest
    VALUES (-1)
    COMMIT
END TRY
```

```
BEGIN CATCH
    SELECT  CASE XACT_STATE()
                WHEN 1 THEN 'Committable'
                WHEN 0 THEN 'No transaction'
                ELSE 'Uncommitable tran' END as XACT_STATE
            ,ERROR_NUMBER() AS ErrorNumber
            ,ERROR_MESSAGE() as ErrorMessage
    ROLLBACK TRANSACTION
END CATCH
```

This returns the following:

| XACT_STATE | ErrorNumber | ErrorMessage |
| --- | --- | --- |
| Committable | 547 | The INSERT statement conflicted with the .... |

However, for the trigger error:

```
BEGIN TRANSACTION
BEGIN TRY
    INSERT alt.errorHandlingTest
    VALUES (1)
    COMMIT
END TRY
BEGIN CATCH
    SELECT  CASE XACT_STATE()
                WHEN 1 THEN 'Committable'
                WHEN 0 THEN 'No transaction'
                ELSE 'Uncommitable tran' END as XACT_STATE
            ,ERROR_NUMBER() AS ErrorNumber
            ,ERROR_MESSAGE() as ErrorMessage
    ROLLBACK TRANSACTION
END CATCH
```

this returns the following:

| XACT_STATE | ErrorNumber | ErrorMessage |
| --- | --- | --- |
| Uncommitable tran | 50000 | Test Error |

In the error handler, the session is still in a transaction, but we had a rollback in the trigger, right? Unfortunately, the RAISERROR in the trigger was bubbled up into this CATCH statement and the ROLLBACK never occurred, but the RAISERROR of a normal error in the trigger caused this to become uncommittable. The point to all of this is that you need to be careful when you code your error handling to do a few things:

- *Keep it simple:* Do only as much handling as you need. The key is to deal with the errors and get back out to a steady state.

- *Keep it standard:* Set a standard and follow it. Always use the same handler for all your code.

- *Test it well:* The most important bit of information is to test and test again all the possible paths your code can take.

For a standard handler, I almost always simply use a pattern like this in all my code:

```
BEGIN TRY
    DECLARE @errorMessage nvarchar(4000)
    SET @errorMessage = 'Error inserting data into alt.errorHandlingTest'
    INSERT alt.errorHandlingTest
    VALUES (1)
    COMMIT TRANSACTION
END TRY
BEGIN CATCH
    IF @@TRANCOUNT > 0
        ROLLBACK TRANSACTION

    --I also add in the stored procedure or trigger where the error
    --occurred also when in a coded object
    SET @errorMessage = Coalesce(@errorMessage,'') +
          ' ( System Error: ' + CAST(ERROR_NUMBER() as varchar(10)) +
          ':' + ERROR_MESSAGE() + ': Line Number:' +
          CAST(ERROR_LINE() as varchar(10)) + ')'
    RAISERROR (@errorMessage,16,1)
END CATCH
```

Executing that code gives you an error like this:

```
Msg 50000, Level 16, State 1, Line 15
Error attempting to insert data into alt.errorHandlingTest
( System Error: 547:The INSERT statement conflicted with the CHECK constraint
"ChkAlt_errorHandlingTest_errorHandlingTestId_greaterThanZero". The conflict
occurred in database "tempdb", table "alt.errorHandlingTest", column
'errorHandlingTestId'.: Line Number:5)
```

This returns the manually created message and the system message, as well as where the error occurred. I might also include the call to the utility.ErrorLog$insert object, depending on whether the error was something that you expected to occur on occasion or whether it is something (as I said about triggers) that really shouldn't happen. If I was implementing the code in such a way that I expected errors to occur, I might also include a call to something like the utility.ErrorMap$ MapError procedure that was discussed earlier to beautify the error message value for the system error.

Error handling did take a leap of improvement in 2005, but it is still not perfect or straightforward. As always, the most important part of writing error handing code is the testing you do to make sure that it works!

# Manual Data Protection

The rules I have discussed in this and the previous chapter on datatypes, constraints, and triggers are rules that I feel strongly should be applied to any database that's implemented in SQL Server (or any RDBMS, really). Even if the UI or middle tier duplicates some of the work, it's still pretty much essential to have these rules implemented as close to the data as possible so that no matter what tool is used to put data into tables, the data is still protected from cruddy data.

Beyond what you can implement in triggers and constraints, it is really a personal choice where to implement rules. The rules that can be implemented using stored procedures or client code aren't necessarily requirements that are 100 percent of the time enforced for the data, meaning that there's no reasonable way to implement them using triggers or constraints, because they generally are hard to code and can require a user to do something.

From a data integrity standpoint, it can almost be stated that these rules don't "matter." The static rules that have already been implemented have placed a hedge of protection around the data in the tables, and these rules make sure that data that isn't "possible" cannot be stored.

Many business rules that will be implemented will be there to make sure that the data is "reasonable." For example, consider a column named `salary` that has been declared as `INT NOT NULL` with a `CHECK` constraint (`salary between 10000 and 30000`). When writing queries, you won't need to be concerned that a value might be `NULL`; or if you were summing 1,000 values, you don't have to worry about arithmetic overflow of the `integer` datatype, because `30000 * 1000 = 30,000,000`, far short of the approximately two billion maximum value for an integer.

However, if the rule was that `salary` *should* be between `10000` and `30000` and it was declared as allowing `NULL`s, then things aren't quite so straightforward. All comparisons with this column would require you to consider `NULL` comparisons, and there easily could be negative values. It is also possible that the salary could be outside of reasonable boundaries, so you have to allow any value to be entered and consider the possibility of arithmetic overflow in your summarizations. The user will need to make the decision if the value being entered is actually reasonable if it is outside of the expected domain.

The best litmus test for whether a rule is "optional" is to consider whether the user is ever able to bypass it. As an example, most personal finance programs give you the option of entering a category for a transaction, but they don't force it. They only open a dialog box saying, "Are you sure you want to be careless and not enter a category? A good person would enter a category." (Yeah, I hate those kinds of warnings too!)

Another example is that of a `Customer` table where the status of the customer needs to be recorded. For example, say we have the tables shown in Figure 6-5.

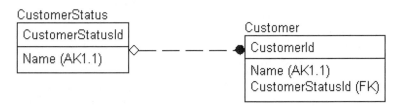

**Figure 6-5.** *A customer status table links to the customer details*

The business rules might state this: "When a new customer is created, the user should assign a status." "Should" cannot be Booleanized. Every rule that we could implement in triggers or constraints must say "will." In this case, we might need to determine what "should" means. We generally have two options:

- *Make the `CustomerStatusId` in the `Customer` table nullable and hence optional*: In other words, allow the user to create a new `Customer` without supplying a status. To follow the rule "should," the front-end would then likely open a dialog box asking the user, "Are you sure you don't want to assign a status to the customer?"

- *Allow any value to be entered*: This brings up the question of validity and whether an invalid status value will be saved. This would mean that the database could allow any value for the `CustomerStatusId` and indeed lets the client application handle the validation by checking the value to see whether it's correct. The client application then sends a dialog box stating the following: "Are you sure you don't want to assign a status to this customer?" Worse still: "You have entered an invalid `CustomerStatusId`; you should enter a valid one." You would then have to drop the database validations in case the user says, "Nah, let me enter the invalid value." (Not a good idea! *Note that this is an `Id` value that should have a valid domain, unlike a reading that might be out of normal bounds where you might want to allow it.*)

The point is that SQL Server automatic data protection mechanisms do not converse with the user in an interactive manner. The hard-and-fast trigger and constraint validations still depend largely on the process of submitting a request and waiting to see whether it completes successfully.

To implement more optional types of rules, we will use either of the following:

- *Stored procedures:* You can place data protection code in a procedure, but it will be effective only when using that one procedure. Using procedures is useful when rules need to be executed on the server yet parameterized in some manner to be executed only situationally.

- *Client code that runs outside the database:* From a database coder's point of view, code that is outside the database is very much the least desirable place for data protection code to go. Using client code can be best for rules that can be overridden and are not necessarily followed. For example, if a manager can override a rule, putting it into SQL code may not be the best place.

When rules are coded in stored procedures, there can be no points in the code where you code `MessageBox("Are you sure?")`. Instead, you have to provide parameters or multiple procedures that enforce rules as if they were not optional. It's up to the client interface to use such rules as it needs.

---

**Tip** For the most part, I suggest most optional rules be implemented in the client code. Stored procedures should almost always be used to encapsulate the SQL for your application but generally should have very few parameters that make business rule–type decisions.

In Chapter 11 on architecture, I will strongly make the case that all your queries should be encapsulated into stored procedures. However, understand that there is a major difference between implementing your SQL code in stored procedures and implementing optional business rules in stored procedures. T-SQL is not a rich language and provides no dialogue between the user and the interface. Even worse, stored procedures become less and less efficient the more control of flow language you need to implement them.

---

In the following examples, I will present a few rules that you can't realistically implement via triggers and constraints. Admittedly, where there's a will, there's a way. It's possible, using temporary tables as messaging mechanisms, to "pass" values to a trigger or constraint. In this manner, you can optionally override functionality. However, triggers and constraints aren't generally considered suitable places to implement optional business rules.

## Stored Procedures

Stored procedures are batches of SQL that can be optimized outside the client code, in a way that is optimal for the optimizer and for you as a programmer. There are two types of rules that people commonly think about implementing in stored procedures:

- Data formatting
- Optional rules based on user input gathered in the UI.

Data formatting is a sticky point in many discussions about how to use stored procedures. For example, say you need to format all dates in the output of your code as YYYY#MM#DD (or any weird nonstandard format that your crazy users will ask for). In every stored procedure, you could code this format into the procedure, and if you were an enterprising coder, you are no doubt going to start building functions. This is not really a good idea. The client has all the facilities to implement this sort of formatting in the place where you are going to need to present the data anyhow. You already need an object to display a date, so just use that code to format the data the way you need it. This code on the client will execute fast, and changing that code will take a change to one place.

Optional business rules are the next thing to discuss. A common example of a rule that might be implemented using a procedure is an optional cascading delete. Cascading deletes are a great resource, but as I covered in Chapter 5, you should use them with care. As discussed, they automatically remove child rows that are dependent on the content of the deleted parent row. However, when tables are just associated to one another (for example `Customer–Invoice`) and not part of the entity (like `Invoice–Invoice Line Item`), you probably don't want to delete all associated data when you delete a row in an associated table. Most likely, in the case of a customer and invoices, you wouldn't want to delete the customer if he or she had made purchases, but if you wanted to delete a `Customer` and all references, a cascade operation would be ideal.

However, this wouldn't be ideal in the case of a bank account. Let's say you have the tables in Figure 6-6. In this case, it makes sense to cascade deletions of `AccountOption` rows automatically if you delete a row from the `Account` table. However, if an account has entries in the `Xaction` table, you need to ensure that the users are aware of them and thus warn them if a cascading delete is requested. This increases complexity, because you won't be able to delete an account, as well as its properties and transactions, in a single statement.

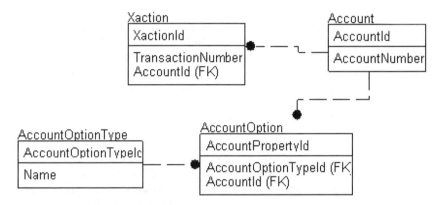

**Figure 6-6.** *A basic account model*

Instead of a single statement, you have to execute the following steps:

1. Run a `SELECT` statement for each child table that you optionally want to cascade-delete to so you can show the user what exists.

2. If the user accepts, execute a `DELETE` statement for each child table that has rows related to your primary table, and in the same atomic operation, delete the row you're interested in.

This code could be built into a single stored procedure that checks for the children and, if they exist, returns a result set of rows for the user to see what needs to be deleted. It also includes a parameter to allow the user to ignore the existence of rows and go ahead and delete them. The following code shows you an example of how you might handle this situation (note that for clarity I've removed transactions and error handling):

```
CREATE PROCEDURE Accounting.Account$delete
(
    @AccountId int,
    @RemoveChildTransactionsFl bit = 0
) as
--error handling and transaction code skipped for clarity of example
-- if they asked to delete them, just delete them
```

```
IF @RemoveChildTransactionsFl = 1
   DELETE Accounting.Xaction --transaction
   WHERE  AccountId = @AccountId
ELSE --check for existence
  BEGIN
     IF EXISTS (SELECT *
                FROM   Accounting.Xaction
                WHERE  AccountId = @AccountId)
        BEGIN
           RAISERROR ('Child transactions exist that must be deleted before the
                       account can be deleted.',16,1)
           RETURN -100
        END
  END
```

```
Delete Accounting.Account
WHERE  AccountId = @AccountId
```

Now the user could try to execute the stored procedure with the flag equal to 0, and if any children existed, the user would get a notification. If not, the account would be deleted, and presumably the properties would be removed as well via a cascading relationship.

It is important to remember that there's no way to solicit answers to questions between the server and client for stored procedures. Ideally, when stored procedures are written to handle business-rule needs, they're written such that there's a way to make one call to the server to handle as many operations as possible, using transactions (which are covered in Chapter 10 on concurrency) to make sure that commands that need to succeed as one don't do part of the job they were sent to do but not others.

A most important thing to consider is to keep your SQL as very straightforward as possible with as few optional steps as are required. T-SQL is by no means a good place for a lot of branching and optional steps. When you have optional steps, you should make sure that the SQL is very simple (like in our case, there should be indexes in place on the foreign key that will definitely get used to do this query to delete transactions). Stored procedures should, in most cases, just be a replacement for DML that you would call if you were just sending queries from the user interface (like is the norm for many simple systems, though not generally a best practice, even if it is easier to code).

The real thing that determines whether you should batch together operations is the need for transactions. In Chapter 10 on concurrency, I will discuss transactions in more detail, but the basic thing to note is that if you didn't want to delete the transactions if the account could not be deleted, you would probably want to put both deletes into a single stored procedure call and wrap that with a transaction. Keeping transactions at a procedure level is generally good for concurrency.

## Client Code

For quite a while, there has been a groundswell of support to move much of the business-rule implementation and data-protection code out of SQL Server and into a middle-tier set of interface objects. In this way, the database, client, and business rules exist in three units that can be implemented independently. Thus, business rules that the database professional would have implemented via constraints and triggers get moved out of this "data" layer and into client-based code, such as a .NET object and stored procedures. In this scenario, SQL Server is relegated to more or less a data storage device with some rudimentary indexing mechanisms.

Such a multitier design also attempts to make the users' lives easier, because users edit data using custom front-end tools using the same objects that the middle-tier services maintain and protect data that passes through them. Doing the majority of coding in a functional language protects the programmer from having to write and maintain all the required SQL code. Not only that, but these services can also directly handle any errors that occur and present the user with meaningful error messages. Because application users primarily edit rows one at a time, rather than a large number of rows, this works great.

The other point is that, in most enterprise applications (for instance, situations with hundreds of thousands of users on a website), the database is usually considered as the "system bottleneck." Though it's possible to distribute the load on multiple servers, in many cases it can be easier to spread the load across many application servers and use the database as a data storage device.

However, almost any data protection mechanism that's enforced without the use of constraints or triggers will almost inevitably prove problematic from a data integrity standpoint. Let's consider the list of possible users that I introduced at the beginning of the chapter, namely, the following:

- *Users using custom front-end tools*: When users all use the custom front-end tools that are developed for the interface, there's less problem with employing the middle tier. In fact, it can have some great benefits, because as discussed, the object methods used to enforce the rules can be tuned for maximum performance. The only problem is this coordination of objects and user interfaces will often prove too much of a burden for all but the best-managed organizations.

- *Users using generic data manipulation tools such as Microsoft Access*: Let's consider a case in which a user needs to modify a set of "live" data but needs it only for a week or a weekend, and there's no time to write a full-blown application. You won't be able to let the user directly access the data because it's in a raw unprotected state. Hence, you either have to code a relevant business rule into the Access database or deny the user and make him or her wait until an application is created. This type of thing is relatively rare, and you can usually stop this kind of activity with strict policies against such data access.

- *Data import routines that acquire data from external sources*: Almost every system of any magnitude includes some import facilities to take data in a raw format from external systems, maybe from another part of your company, or another company altogether, and place this data in a table on the database server. This can be in as simple a form as a user application to import a spreadsheet or as complex as an interface between all the schools in a state and the respective state's Department of Education. The tools range from user applications, SQL Server Integration Services (SSIS), or even BCP (a bulk copy program that comes with SQL Server). When the middle tier owns all the business rules and data-integrity checks, you either have to go in through the middle tier one row at a time or extract all the business rules and recode checks into your import routines.

- *Raw queries executed by data administrators to fix problems caused by user error*: Almost anybody with administration experience has had to remove a few rows from a database that users have erroneously created but cannot easily remove and in so doing might have mistakenly deleted the wrong rows (for example, active account rows rather than inactive ones). In this situation, if you had business rules built into a trigger that allowed the deletion of inactive accounts only, an error message would have been returned to the user warning that active accounts couldn't be deleted. Obviously, you cannot protect against a bad action, such as systematically deleting every row in a table, but when a fully featured database is implemented and the data protected using constraints and triggers, it's next to impossible to make even small mistakes in data integrity.

I very much desire the possibilities offered by the multitier architecture. However, the load of business-rule and data-integrity–rule implementation should at worst be "shared" between the middle tier and database server as appropriate. In the previous version of SQL Server, Microsoft started blurring this sort of tiering of data access with CLR-based objects. Things can be coded in the CLR almost the same way in SQL Server as out of it. Hence, the CLR tier of code could be shifted from the client to a middle tier to the database server using the same language. Theoretically, this is a great idea, but it bears repeating that we must be careful that we aren't misusing technology and avoiding the tool that's most appropriate for data-access queries: T-SQL. I discuss when to use the CLR versus T-SQL in Chapter 11.

Two specific types of such rules that are far better implemented in the database are as follows:

- *Any rule that can be covered by a datatype,* NULL, *foreign key, or* CHECK *constraint:* This is because, when building additional external interfaces, this kind of check will generally make up quite a bit of the coding effort. Furthermore, base data integrity should be guaranteed at the lowest level possible, which allows as many programs as possible to code to the database. As a final point, the optimizer uses these constraints to make queries run faster.

- *Rules that require much inter-table validations:* For example, whenever you save a value, you must check to see whether a value exists in a different table. You have to access the additional table automatically to make certain that the state that was expected still exists. In some cases, the middle tier tries to cache the data on the database to use in validation, but there's no way to spread this cached data to multiple servers in a manner that ensures that the value you're entering has proper data integrity.

Now that I have restated what I don't like about client code, let's discuss what ought to be implemented using client code. Rules that certainly should never be implemented in the database are *mutable rules*: rules that can and frequently do change over time. Although a good number of rules in a system might be hard and fast rules at any given time, many rules change over time. For example:

- Today we give a customer a 20-percent discount, tomorrow a 10-percent discount.

- The maximum age that we offer this discount to is 35; next week we'll change it to 30.

- Send out the red toy with the meal, until the red toys run out; then send out the blue.

Mutable rules differ a great deal from optional rules, because these rules are hard and fast at a given point in time. The problem is that tomorrow the rule changes based on the changing realities of business. Much like optional rules, the RDBMS tables and queries on those tables cannot make any assumptions about data in the tables based on these ever-changing requirements. If rules are frequently changing, it is troublesome to implement them in constraints, even if they are always hard and fast at the time of implementing. Why? If you have to go back and make changes to older rows, they will no longer actually match the rules. Remember what I said earlier about nontrusted constraints where you save a row and an error occurs with data you didn't touch. That really sucks for the user.

Optional rules are also always to be implemented in the client code. And unfortunately, you have to be really careful to discern what is optional and what is hard and fast. Often rules seem *very* stable but aren't when they reach the actual end users who start using the code. Take the following:

- All customers must pay a 10-percent deposit at the time of rental.

- Before the product is shipped, payment must be processed.

- Customer Y requires quality level X for his product and won't accept anything less.

Sounds perfect for constraints, right? Maybe, but dig a bit deeper, and you will probably find out that that is not exactly the case:

- Well, all customers except Bob. We always let him pay 5 percent, though we'd prefer it if he would pay full price. Don't let him know about the discount.

- Customer Z is in a big need, so we accepted a PO from him this time instead of requiring payment up front.

- Customer Y has a big order, so for this week, quality level X * .85 will be fine.

All? Except? This time? Sometimes different? Aughhh! Exceptions should come up in design, but often don't. This is what I often refer to as "rules based on how a person feels." (It's kind of like when you were a kid and Dad had football to watch; he didn't care about your chores, but when he wasn't happy, out came the white glove on the basement floor—or was that just me?) These rules make it tricky for SQL programmers because we tend to think in terms of the business, not the semantic model on which we've based the tables. If a payment is optional, all SQL must assume that there's a possibility that there will be no payment row, so an `OUTER JOIN` might have to be used instead of an `INNER JOIN` in queries to the `Payment` table if the query isn't centered on payments.

Mutable rules such as this certainly may have data stored for them, such as the current discount percentage, toy style, and minimum quality level, but this data is often as transitory as the rules. Rules in the database generally should center around the core data that's stored for later analysis, because it pertains to all instances of a particular activity. Non-data-tier code is best for this type of operation because it can be changed much more easily. The database's job is to maintain data integrity over the long run in a relatively unchanging manner.

---

■**Note** Determining where to implement rules is not an easy thing to do. You have to be sure to carefully consider what the user wants before you implement, or you can end up with a mess. In the end, it is best to be too restrictive initially and catch it in user acceptance testing, but beware even there. Users don't think about some stuff until they are trying to get an order out the door and your software is too restrictive to let them.

---

# More Best Practices

The main best practice is to use the right tool for the job. There are many tools in (and around) SQL to use to protect the data. Picking the right tool for a given situation is essential. For example, every column in every table could be defined as `nvarchar(max)`. Using `CHECK` constraints, you could then constrain the values to look like almost any datatype. It sounds silly perhaps, but it is possible. But you know better after reading Chapter 5 and now this chapter, right?

When choosing your method of protecting data, it's best to apply the following types of objects, in this order:

- *Datatypes*: Choosing the right type is the first line of defense. If all your values need to be integers between 1 and 10,000, just using an `integer` datatype takes care of one part of the rule immediately.

- *Defaults*: Though you might not think defaults can be considered data-protection resources, you should know that you can use them to set columns automatically where the purpose of the column might not be apparent to the user (and the database adds a suitable value for the column).

- `CHECK` *constraints*: These are important in ensuring that your data is within specifications. You can use almost any scalar functions (user-defined or system), as long as you end up with a single logical expression.

- *Triggers*: These are used to enforce rules that are too complex for `CHECK` constraints. Triggers allow you to build pieces of code that fire automatically on any `INSERT`, `UPDATE`, and `DELETE` operation that's executed against a single table.

- *User code*: This is important for enforcing rules that are optional or frequently changing. The major difference between user code and the previous three methods is that the other three are automatic and cannot (accidentally) be overridden. On the other hand, rules implemented using stored procedures or .NET objects cannot be considered as required rules. A simple `UPDATE` statement can be executed from Management Studio that violates rules enforced in a stored procedure.

Don't be afraid to enforce rules in more than one location, either. Although having rules as close to the data storage as possible is essential to trusting the integrity of the data when you use the data, there's no reason why the user needs to suffer through a poor user interface with a bunch of simple textboxes with no validation. If the tables are designed and implemented properly, you *could* do it this way, but the user should get a nice rich interface as well.

# Summary

Now you've finished the task of developing the data storage for your databases. If you've planned out your data storage, the only bad data that can get into your system has nothing to do with the design (if a user wants to type the name John as "Jahn" or even "Bill"—stranger things have happened!—there's nothing that can be done in the database server to prevent it). As architects and programmers, it isn't possible to stop users from putting the names of pieces of equipment in a table named `Employee`. There's no semantic checking built in, and it would be impossible to do so without tremendous work and tremendous computing power. Only education can take care of this. Of course, it helps if you've given the users tables to store all their data, but still, users will be users.

In the previous chapter, you built the physical storage for the data by creating the tables. In this chapter, you took the next step and completed your scheme to safeguard it. During this process, you looked at the resources that SQL Server gives you to protect your data from having invalid values.

Once you've built and implemented a set of appropriate data-safeguarding resources, you can then trust that the data in your database has been validated. You should never need to revalidate keys or values in your data once it's stored in your database, but it's a good idea to do random sampling so you know that no integrity gaps have slipped by you, especially during the testing process.

---

■**Note** You might have noticed that I didn't write any triggers using the CLR. I see great use in coding UDFs in the CLR for use in T-SQL triggers, but there are no great use cases, as of the writing of this book, for CLR triggers. Over the lifetime of the product, this might change, perhaps based on changes in a service pack release of SQL Server 2005. Check the Source Code/Download area of the Apress website (`http://www.apress.com`) for updated information about each of the service packs as they come out, or check my website (`http://drsql.org/ProSQLServerDatabaseDesign.aspx`).

---

■ ■ ■

# Patterns and Query Techniques

*A thousand monkeys with a thousand typewriters given enough time would stumble upon the greatest works in literature.*

—Unknown

**B**ecause a tiny part of me is a math guy, reluctantly and against my better judgment I have to agree that it's true: a thousand monkeys with infinite time could possibly write anything, even this book (though they wouldn't format it as nicely). Frankly, any random set of characters is *possible*, but I have to also say that this is very unlikely, and any mathematician would heartily agree. On the other hand, what the heck is the point? One person wrote *War and Peace*, and another wrote the *Hitchhiker's Guide to the Galaxy*. If you want to hear the exact same story, you buy a duplication of that book. If you want to do something new, like a book on super monkeys with laser typewriters, well, please don't.

The reason I bring this up is that from my experience in the newsgroups and forums, a thousand programmers with a thousand keyboards will all try to solve the same problem . . . in different ways. And the problem is, although there are different ways to solve the same problem, most of the ways are not as good as the one or two ideal ways. The goal of a software programmer should be to first try understanding existing techniques and then either use or improve upon them. Solving the same problem over and over without any knowledge of the past is nuts.

In this chapter, I will present a couple of common solutions to problems that can easily be used to enhance the design you have already made or can be used to implement "challenging" situations. This is a new chapter for this edition of the book and one that I hope will grow in future editions to provide you with extensions to the designs you have already created naturally from the steps I have gone through so far. The patterns and solutions that I will present are as follows:

- Precalculated values
- Large valued objects
- Storing user-specified data
- Commonly implemented objects

In the "Anti-patterns" section, I will demonstrate a couple of ways to do things that exemplify things you really *shouldn't* do but that are common problems I see in people's designs that make my teeth hurt to have to deal with them.

Several of the examples of this chapter will extend the example database from Chapter 5. I will include scripts to create the tables again here as necessary.

This chapter will at times walk the line between implementation and query techniques. The primary distinction I will make is that I will try to encroach only on those techniques that require storing additional data in the database (thereby making them design issues rather than query techniques). The code I will include is truly not intended to be a complete coverage of the topic but rather be a subset of the possible uses for each technique to make it clear *why* it is useful.

If you want to learn more about writing challenging queries, consider purchasing the book *Inside Microsoft SQL Server 2005: T-SQL Querying* by Itzik Ben Gan, Lubor Kollar, and Dejan Sarka (or the next edition when it arrives). Dejan was a tech reviewer on the previous edition of this book, and all three of these folks know their stuff in spades.

---

■**Note** I desire feedback from you at my e-mail address `louis@drsql.org`, because I am always looking for other patterns that can solve common issues and enhance your designs (as well as mine).

---

# Precalculated Values

When I hear the term *precalculated*, I immediately start to think of improper normalization or possibly a denormalization for performance. In some ways, the solutions that I will mention in this chapter (and any that you may come up with as a result) are a sort of denormalization. If I have a table that has the two columns `integerValue` and `evenFlag`, is the column `evenFlag` a denormalized value? In one way, the answer is yes. I can calculate that a value is even, so there's no need to store it. On the other hand, the answer is no, since the fact that the value is even describes the integer value.

The example I will introduce is a calendar table. The natural key of the table is the date value. With a date value, you can easily calculate the month, the year, what day of the week it is, whether this is Christmas, and so on. Each of these values is functionally dependent on the value of the date. However, it turns out that placing these values in a single row in a table will save you a tremendous amount of functional programming. And where it would seem silly to have a table of dates with one column where you calculated the other values on the fly would be interesting, but it would be nowhere near as useful and fast as the calendar table/solution we will explore as a subsection of this section. We will build several static tables of data that can be used without having to burn the CPU by recalculating the values over and over to obtain these values.

Let's take the tack that it is denormalization. Might denormalization still be the best thing in a case like a calendar table? Oh no, you may be thinking, he has gone off the deep end. When Chapter 6 was finished, he finally cracked and said, "To heck with it, just denormalize . . ." That cracked business might just be true, but there is one very prominent place where almost any database architect will tell you that denormalization is the best policy for performance.

The principle that allows this seemingly evil concept of denormalization to be acceptable is when the data will *never, ever* change. But be careful that the definition of *never* is not driven by a user. I have this saying about users that mimics that of one of my favorite TV characters, a doctor named House, played by Hugh Laurie. "Everybody lies." I mean asking whether a patient has ever cheated on his spouse is completely useless. "Of course I did, sir. Now, please, give her half my stuff."

I am not quite that cynical, because I don't think they do it on purpose, but I just don't think people think about all of the angles. Most users get about as involved with the process of creating a system as I do when my wife starts making all sorts of plans during a football game. I agree to almost any sort of process she describes, just so we can get the conversation over with. Most users feel the same way because they want to get back to their "real" work. And who blames them? But for your design, knowing what is always true is an important thing to know. And just like I do when the time comes around to do the real work, the users are mad when you listened to them and got it wrong.

In the example of a calendar table, there will never be a reason to change the fact that October 12, 2006, is a Thursday. It will always be a Thursday, unless our country is invaded and taken over by some other culture that uses different names for days. (And at that point, it won't matter, will it?) And although you can make the point that Thursday does describe the entity that represents a day, you are certainly welcome to put redundant data galore in this table if you want: THURSDAY, TH, OCT, October, and so on. The goal is to enhance the usage of the data in SQL by making standardized data available via a join condition rather than a function (joins are a natural part of how SQL Server works; functions, not so much).

In this section, I will present two particular solutions of tables where we will use precalculated values to enhance the way SQL can be used to access, aggregate, and summarize data:

- Using a tables of numbers
- Using dates and calendars

And you probably have others in your organization where this is the case. Many of the domain tables we discussed in Chapter 5 were just tables of values for our convenience. Here we are taking it to a different logical level.

## Sequence Tables

A *sequence table* is just a precalculated table of values (usually numbers, primarily non-negative integers, but they can be anything you want) that you can use for some purpose. (The name *sequence* may seem kind of odd, but the point is that it is an ordered set of values used to do range calculations.) You might also call it a *numbers table*, but that name is sort of ambiguous. Naming the table *integers* is too open-ended, and getting so specific as *nonNegativeIntegers* is going to get you ridiculed by the other programmers on the playground. I figure that the person who came up with the name *sequence* finally just gave up and called it that to save a few years of this kind of circular arguments about what to name it.

Often, the sequence table is just a simple table of non-negative integers from 0 to some reasonable limit, where *reasonable* is more or less how many you find you need. I generally load mine up to 99999 (99999 just because the load tool works in powers of 10 from 0 up), because I haven't really found much need for anything bigger than that, and to be honest I am not sure why I go to that level. With the algorithm I will present, you can easily expand to create a sequence of numbers that is larger than you can store in SQL Server.

There are two really beautiful things behind this concept. First, the table of non-negative integers has some great uses dealing with text data, as well as doing all sorts of math with. Second, you can create additional attributes or even other sequence tables that you can use to represent other sets of numbers that you find useful or interesting. For example:

- Even or odd, prime, squares, cubes, and so on
- Other ranges or even other grains of values, for example, (-1, -.5, 0, .5, 1)
- Letters of the alphabet
- Or whatever really

The point of this is that once you calculate them and the values are stored, you never have to recalculate the values again; you just use them. So if you need to count the number of prime numbers between 1 and 100,000, you could do it or even join to a set of prime numbers; the value is there and ready to use. On the practical side, if you want to break up a comma-delimited list into rows of data (so you can work with the data relationally rather than iteratively), there is an easy solution, which I will present later in the section.

The code to generate a sequence of numbers is pretty simple, though it looks a bit daunting the first time you see it:

```
;WITH
digits (i) as(--set up a set of numbers from 0-9
            SELECT i
            FROM  (VALUES (0),(1),(2),(3),(4),
                          (5),(6),(7),(8),(9)) as digits (i))
,sequence (i) as (
        SELECT D1.i + (10*D2.i) + (100*D3.i) + (1000*D4.i)
            --+ (10000*D5.i) + (100000*D6.i)
        FROM digits AS D1 CROSS JOIN digits AS D2 CROSS JOIN digits AS D3
            CROSS JOIN digits AS D4
            --CROSS JOIN digits AS D5 CROSS JOIN digits AS D6
            )
SELECT *
FROM   sequence
ORDER  BY i
```

This code will generate a sequence of numbers from 0 to 9,999 as is. Uncommenting the D5 and D6 tables will give you an order of magnitude increase for each, up to 999,999. Breaking the code down, you get the following:

```
;WITH
digits (i) as(--set up a set of numbers from 0-9
            SELECT i
            FROM  (VALUES (0),(1),(2),(3),(4),
                          (5),(6),(7),(8),(9)) as digits (i))
```

This is just simply a set of 10 rows from 0–9. The next bit is where the true brilliance begins. (No, I am not claiming I came up with this. I first saw it on Erland Sommarskog's website, using a technique I will show you in a few pages to split a comma-delimited string.) You cross-join the first set over and over, multiplying each level by a greater power of 10. The result is that you get one permutation for each number. For example, since 0 is in each set, you get one permutation that results in 0. You can see this better in the following smallish set:

```
;WITH digits (i) as(--set up a set of numbers from 0-9
        SELECT i
        FROM  (VALUES (0),(1),(2),(3),(4),(5),(6),(7),(8),(9)) as digits (i))
SELECT D1.i as D1i, D2.i as D2i, D1.i + (10*D2.i) as [Sum]
FROM digits AS D1 CROSS JOIN digits AS D2
ORDER BY 1, 2
```

This returns the following, keeping in mind that the SUM column is the sum of D1i + 10 * D2i, not just added together (rows removed and replaced with . . . for clarity):

| D1i | D2i | SUM |
| --- | --- | --- |
| 0 | 0 | 0 |
| 0 | 1 | 10 |
| 0 | 2 | 20 |
| 0 | 3 | 30 |
| 0 | 4 | 40 |
| 0 | 5 | 50 |
| ... | | |

| 3 | 0 | 3 |
| 3 | 1 | 13 |
| 3 | 2 | 23 |
| ... | | |
| 8 | 7 | 78 |
| 8 | 8 | 88 |
| ... | | |
| 9 | 7 | 79 |
| 9 | 8 | 89 |
| 9 | 9 | 99 |

This kind of combination of sets is a very useful technique in relational coding. Like I said earlier, this isn't a query book, but I feel it necessary to show you the basics of why this code works, because it is a very good mental exercise. Using the full sequence query, you can create a sequence of numbers that you can use in a query.

So, initially create a simple table. You can create this table in any database. I again will just use tempdb for this exercise, but I will still create a schema for my tables/functions/procs that can be used as tools by any user (in reality I would grant EXECUTE and SELECT on this schema to public):

```
CREATE SCHEMA tools
go
CREATE TABLE tools.sequence
(
    i    int CONSTRAINT PKtools_sequence PRIMARY KEY
)
```

Then I will load it, up to 99999:

```
;WITH DIGITS (i) as(--set up a set of numbers from 0-9
        SELECT i
        FROM    (VALUES (0),(1),(2),(3),(4),(5),(6),(7),(8),(9)) as digits (i))
--builds a table from 0 to 99999
,sequence (i) as (
        SELECT D1.i + (10*D2.i) + (100*D3.i) + (1000*D4.i) + (10000*D5.i)
                --+ (100000*D6.i)
        FROM digits AS D1 CROSS JOIN digits AS D2 CROSS JOIN digits AS D3
                CROSS JOIN digits AS D4 CROSS JOIN digits AS D5
                /* CROSS JOIN digits AS D6 */)
INSERT INTO tools.sequence(i)
SELECT i
FROM    sequence
```

As an example usage, a reasonably common thing that occurs is that a value in a string you are dealing with is giving your code fits, but it isn't easy to find it. If you want to look at the Unicode (or ASCII) value for every character in a string, you can do something like this:

```
DECLARE @string varchar(21) = 'This is my test value'

SELECT SUBSTRING(split.value,sequence.i,1) as [char],
        UNICODE(SUBSTRING(split.value,sequence.i,1)) as [Unicode]
FROM    tools.sequence
            cross join (select @string as value) as split
WHERE   sequence.i > 0
  AND   sequence.i <= len(@string)
```

This returns the following:

```
char Unicode
---- -----------
T    84
h    104
i    105
s    115
     32
i    105
s    115
     32
m    109
y    121
     32
t    116
e    101
s    115
t    116
     32
v    118
a    97
l    108
u    117
e    101
```

This in and of itself is interesting, since you can easily do this for a large number of rows at once, this time joining to a table in the AdventureWorks2008 database:

```
SELECT LastName, sequence.i as position,
          SUBSTRING(Person.LastName,sequence.i,1) as [char],
          UNICODE(SUBSTRING(Person.LastName,sequence.i,1)) as [Unicode]
FROM   AdventureWorks2008.Person.Person
        JOIN tools.sequence
            ON sequence.i <= LEN(Person.LastName )
  And  UNICODE(SUBSTRING(Person.LastName,sequence.i,1)) is not null
ORDER BY 1
```

This returns 111,969 rows (one for each character in a last name) in only around 3 seconds on my laptop:

| LastName | position | | Unicode |
| --- | --- | --- | --- |
| Abbas | 1 | A | 65 |
| Abbas | 2 | b | 98 |
| Abbas | 3 | b | 98 |
| Abbas | 4 | a | 97 |
| Abbas | 5 | s | 115 |
| Abel | 1 | A | 65 |
| Abel | 2 | b | 98 |
| Abel | 3 | e | 101 |
| Abel | 4 | l | 108 |
| Abercrombie | 1 | A | 65 |
| ... | | | |

With that set, you could easily start eliminating known safe Unicode values and find your evil outlier that is causing some issue with some process. My last immediately useful example comes from Erland Sommarskag's website (http://www.sommarskog.se/) on arrays in SQL Server, as well as Aaron Bertrand's old ASPFAQ website (the last example is more thought provoking than useful in any immediate manner). Using this code, you can take a comma-delimited list to return it as a table of values (which is the most desirable form for data in SQL Server):

```
DECLARE @delimitedList VARCHAR(100) = '1,2,3,4,5'

SELECT word = SUBSTRING(',' + @delimitedList + ',',i + 1,
                CHARINDEX(',',',' + @delimitedList + ',',i + 1) - i - 1)
FROM tools.sequence
WHERE i >= 1
  AND i < LEN(',' + @delimitedList + ',') - 1
  AND SUBSTRING(',' + @delimitedList + ',', i, 1) = ','
ORDER BY i
```

The way this code works is pretty interesting in and of itself. It works by doing a substring on each row. The key is in the WHERE clause:

```
WHERE i >= 1
  AND i < LEN(',' + @delimitedList + ',') - 1
  AND SUBSTRING(',' + @delimitedList + ',', i, 1) = ','
```

The first line is there because SUBSTRING starts with position 1. The second limits the rows in tools.sequence to more than the length of the @delimitedList variable. The third includes rows only where the SUBSTRING of the value at the position returns the delimiter, in this case, a comma. So, take this query:

```
DECLARE @delimitedList VARCHAR(100) = '1,2,3,4,5'

SELECT i
FROM tools.sequence
WHERE i >= 1
  AND i < LEN(',' + @delimitedList + ',') - 1
  AND SUBSTRING(',' + @delimitedList + ',', i, 1) = ','
ORDER BY i
```

Executing this, you will see the following results:

```
i
-----------
1
3
5
7
9
```

Since the list has a comma added to the beginning and end of it in the query, you can see now that the positions of the commas are represented in the list. The SUBSTRING in the SELECT clause simply fetches all of the @delimitedList value up to the next comma. This sort of use of the sequence table will allow you to do what at first seems like it would require a massive iterating algorithm in order to touch each position in the string individually (which would be slow in T-SQL, though you might get away with it in the CLR) and does it all at once in a set-based manner that is actually very fast.

Finally, I have expanded on this technique to allow you to do this for every row in a table that needs it by joining the tools.sequence table and joining on the values between 1 and the length of the string (and delimiters). The best use for this code is to normalize a set of data where some programmer thought it was a good idea to store data in a comma-delimited list (it rarely is) so that you can use proper relational techniques to work with this data:

```
CREATE TABLE poorDesign
(
    poorDesignId    int,
    badValue        varchar(20)
)
INSERT INTO poorDesign
VALUES (1,'1,3,56,7,3,6'),
       (2,'22,3'),
       (3,'1')
```

The code just takes the stuff in the WHERE clause of the previous query and moves it into JOIN criteria:

```
SELECT poorDesign.poorDesignId as betterDesignId,
       SUBSTRING(',' + poorDesign.badValue + ',',i + 1,
              CHARINDEX(',',',' + poorDesign.badValue + ',',i + 1) - i - 1)
                              as betterScalarValue
FROM   poorDesign
         JOIN tools.sequence
           on i >= 1
             AND i < LEN(',' + poorDesign.badValue + ',') - 1
             AND SUBSTRING(',' + + poorDesign.badValue  + ',', i, 1) = ','
```

This returns the following:

```
betterDesignId betterScalarValue
-------------- ----------------------
1              1
1              3
1              56
1              7
1              3
1              6
2              22
2              3
3              1
```

That's much better. Each row of the output represents only a single value, not an array of values. As I have said many times throughout the book, SQL works with atomic values great, but try to get individual values out of a single column, and you get ugly code like I have just presented. It is an excellent solution for the problem; in fact, it is the fault of the problem that makes it ugly.

Finally, I want to give you a last entertaining and esoteric usage of the sequence table to get your mind working on the possibilities. I recently (well, when I was writing this the first time anyways) watched the *Futurama* video "Bender's Big Score," and they have a little math lesson section on the video that was very interesting, but the thing that stuck in my mind was this reference to a previous episode called the "Lesser of Two Evils." Bender and the Bender look-alike named Flexo (they are both Bender units) start talking and have the following exchange:

Bender: Hey, brobot, what's your serial number?

Flexo: 3370318.

Bender: No way! Mine's 2716057!

Fry (a human): I don't get it.

Bender: We're both expressible as the sum of two cubes!

So, I figured, the sum of two cubes would be an interesting and pretty easy abstract utilization of the sequence table. Then I found a reference to "taxicab" numbers on the ScienceNews.org website (July 27, 2002; Vol. 162, No. 4), where the goal is to discover the smallest value that can be expressed as the sum of three cubes in N different ways.

---

■**Note** My example here harks back to an old story in which one mathematician remarked to another mathematician that the number on a taxicab was "dull," to which the other one remarked that it was very interesting, because it was the smallest number that could be expressed as the sum of two cubes. (You can judge your own nerdiness by whether you think: A. This is stupid, B. This is cool, or C. You have done it yourself.)

---

How hard is the query? It turns out that once you have a sequence table with numbers from 1 to 100,000 or so, you can calculate that Taxicab(2) = 1729 very easily (and all of the other numbers that are the sum of two cubes too) and the sum of two cubes in three different ways also pretty easily (it took three seconds on my laptop, and that value is 87539319).

But, instead of calculating the value of each integer cubed (power(i,3)) for each iteration, you can add a computed column to the table, this time as a bigint to give the later calculations room to store the very large intermediate values when you start to multiply the two cube values together. You can do something like this:

```
ALTER TABLE tools.sequence
  ADD i3 as cast( power(cast(i as bigint),3) as bigint) PERSISTED
  --Note that I had to cast i as bigint first to let the power function
  --return a bigint
```

Now, here is the code:

```
DECLARE @level int = 2 --sum of two cubes

;WITH cubes as
(SELECT i3
FROM   tools.sequence
WHERE  i >= 1 and i < 500) --<<<Vary for performance, and for cheating reasons,
                     --<<<max needed value

SELECT c1.i3 + c2.i3 as [sum of 2 cubes in N Ways]
FROM   cubes as c1
         cross join cubes as c2
WHERE c1.i3 <= c2.i3
GROUP by (c1.i3 + c2.i3)
HAVING count(*) = @level
ORDER BY 1
```

This will return 559 rows in a few seconds. The first row is 1729, which is the smallest number that is the sum of two cubes in two different ways. OK, breaking this down the cube's CTE, the code is pretty simple:

```
(SELECT i3
FROM   tools.sequence  --the table holds 100000 values
WHERE  i >= 1 and i < 500)
```

This limits the values to a table of cubes, but only the first 500 of them. The next query is a bit more interesting. I sum the two cube values, which I get from cross-joining the CTE twice:

```
SELECT c1.i3 + c2.i3 as [sum of 2 cubes in N Ways]
FROM    cubes as c1
              cross join cubes as c2
WHERE c1.i3 <= c2.i3 --this gets rid of the "duplicate" value pairs
```

The WHERE condition of c1.i3 <= c2.i3 gets rid of the "duplicate" value pairs since c1 and c2 have the same values, so without this, for 1729 you would get the following:

| c1.i3 | c2.i3 |
|-------|-------|
| 1     | 1728  |
| 729   | 1000  |
| 1000  | 729   |
| 1728  | 1     |

These pairs are the same. I don't eliminate equality to allow for the case where both numbers are equal, because they won't be doubled up. With these values:

| c1.i3 | c2.i3 |
|-------|-------|
| 1     | 1728  |
| 729   | 1000  |

you can see that 1729 is the sum of two cubes in two different ways. So, lastly, the question of performance must come up. Reading the articles, it is clear that this is not a terribly easy problem to solve. Values for the sum of three cubes are fairly simple. Leaving the sequence values bounded at 500, I get two values in about one second:

```
[sum of 2 cubes in N Ways]
--------------------------------
87539319
119824488
```

Four, however, was a "bit" more challenging. Knowing the answer from the article, I knew I could set a boundary for my numbers using 20000 and get the answer. Using this "cheat" on my laptop, I was able to calculate that the value of taxicab(4) was 6963472309248 (yes, it found only the one) in just 1 hour and 33 minutes; this was on a 2.2GHz Pentium M laptop with 2GB of RAM. I tried calculating taxicab(5), but alas, I ran out of space for tempdb (and I had 50GB available). For that you had to go up to i being greater than something like 350000 . . .

Clearly, the main value of T-SQL isn't in tricks like this but that using a sequence table can give you the immediate jumping-off point to solve some problems that initially seem difficult.

## Calculations with Dates

It is a common task for a person to want to know how to do groupings and calculations with date values. For example, you might want sales grouped by month, week, year, or any other grouping. You can usually do this using the SQL Server date functions, but often it is costly in performance, and always it is uncomfortable. Using a calendar table is commonplace in OLAP implementations, but it certainly can be useful in OLTP databases when you get stuck doing a confusing date range query.

Using the same form of precalculated data that we applied to the sequence table, we can create a table that contains date values. I will set the date as the primary key and then have data related to the date as columns. The following is the basic date table that I currently use. (You can extend it as you want to include working days, holidays, special events, and so on, to filter/group by in the same manner as you do with these columns, along with the others I will add later in the section.)

```
CREATE TABLE tools.calendar
(
        dateValue datetime NOT NULL CONSTRAINT PKtools_calendar PRIMARY KEY,
        dayName varchar(10) NOT NULL,
        monthName varchar(10) NOT NULL,
        year varchar(60) NOT NULL,
        day tinyint NOT NULL,
        dayOfTheYear smallint NOT NULL,
        month smallint NOT NULL,
        quarter tinyint NOT NULL
)
```

The next step is to load the table with values, which is pretty much a straightforward task using the sequence table that we just finished creating in the previous section. Using the datename and datepart functions and a few simple case expressions, you load the different values. I will make use of many of the functions in the examples, but most are very easy to understand.

**Note** I wanted to make this into a bunch of persisted computed columns, but it turns out that datename and datepart are not deterministic functions in 2008.

```
WITH dates (newDateValue) as (
        select dateadd(day,i,'17530101') as newDateValue
        from tools.sequence
)
INSERT tools.calendar
        (dateValue ,dayName
        ,monthName ,year ,day
        ,dayOfTheYear ,month ,quarter
)
SELECT
        dates.newDateValue as dateValue,
        datename (dw,dates.newDateValue) as dayName,
        datename (mm,dates.newDateValue) as monthName,
        datename (yy,dates.newDateValue) as year,
        datepart(day,dates.newDateValue) as day,
        datepart(dy,dates.newDateValue) as dayOfTheYear,
        datepart(m,dates.newDateValue) as month,
        datepart(qq,dates.newDateValue) as quarter

FROM    dates
WHERE   dates.newDateValue between '20000101' and '20100101' --set the date range
ORDER   BY datevalue
```

Just like the sequence examples, there are several ways to use the calendar table. The first I will demonstrate is general grouping types of queries, and the second is calculating ranges. As an example of grouping, say you want to know how many sales had been made during each year in Sales.SalesOrderHeader in the AdventureWorks2008 database. This is why there is a year column in the table:

```
SELECT calendar.year, COUNT(*) as orderCount
FROM   AdventureWorks2008.Sales.SalesOrderHeader
          JOIN tools.calendar
                  --note, the cast here could be a real performance killer
                  --consider using date columns where
              ON CAST(SalesOrderHeader.OrderDate as date) = calendar.dateValue
GROUP BY calendar.year
ORDER BY calendar.year
```

This returns the following:

| year | orderCount |
| ---- | ---------- |
| 2001 | 1379 |
| 2002 | 3692 |
| 2003 | 12443 |
| 2004 | 13951 |

And of course, you can do it by month, week of the year, and so on. One thing you can do that is really interesting is query the calendar table to get some information that is pretty hard to do with just the date functions. For example, what is the last day of each month? Easy. The following:

```
SELECT MAX(dateValue)
FROM   tools.calendar
WHERE  year = '2008'
GROUP  BY year, month
```

returns this:

```
----------------------
2008-01-31 00:00:00.000
2008-02-29 00:00:00.000
2008-03-31 00:00:00.000
2008-04-30 00:00:00.000
2008-05-31 00:00:00.000
2008-06-30 00:00:00.000
2008-07-31 00:00:00.000
2008-08-31 00:00:00.000
2008-09-30 00:00:00.000
2008-10-31 00:00:00.000
2008-11-30 00:00:00.000
2008-12-31 00:00:00.000
```

The beauty of the calendar table isn't just finding values; it is getting these values and grouping them. For example, sales on Tuesdays and Thursdays?

```
SELECT calendar.dayName, COUNT(*) as orderCount
FROM   AdventureWorks2008.Sales.SalesOrderHeader
          JOIN tools.calendar
                  --note, the cast here could be a real performance killer
                  --consider using date columns where
              ON CAST(SalesOrderHeader.OrderDate as date) = calendar.dateValue
WHERE calendar.dayName in ('Tuesday','Thursday')
GROUP BY calendar.dayName
ORDER BY calendar.dayName
```

This returns the following:

| dayName | orderCount |
| --- | --- |
| Thursday | 4483 |
| Tuesday | 4346 |

OK, I see you are possibly still skeptical. What if I throw in the first Tuesday after the second Wednesday? How? Well, it is really a simple matter of building the set step by step:

```
WITH onlyWednesdays as --get all wednesdays
(
    SELECT *,
           ROW_NUMBER()  over (partition by calendar.year, calendar.month
                                    order by calendar.day) as wedRowNbr
    FROM   tools.calendar
    WHERE  dayName = 'Wednesday'
),
secondWednesdays as --limit to second Wednesdays of the month
(
    SELECT *
    FROM   onlyWednesdays
    WHERE  wedRowNbr = 2
)
,finallyTuesdays as --finally limit to the Tuesdays after the second wed
(
    SELECT calendar.*,
           ROW_NUMBER() OVER (partition by calendar.year, calendar.month
                                   order by calendar.day) as rowNbr
    FROM   secondWednesdays
             JOIN tools.calendar
               ON secondWednesdays.year = calendar.year
                  AND secondWednesdays.month = calendar.month
    WHERE  calendar.dayName = 'Tuesday'
      AND  calendar.day > secondWednesdays.day
)
--and in the final query, just get the one month
SELECT year, monthName, day
FROM   finallyTuesdays
WHERE  year = 2008
  AND  rowNbr = 1
```

This returns the following:

| year | monthName | day |
| --- | --- | --- |
| 2008 | January | 15 |
| 2008 | February | 19 |
| 2008 | March | 18 |
| 2008 | April | 15 |
| 2008 | May | 20 |
| 2008 | June | 17 |
| 2008 | July | 15 |
| 2008 | August | 19 |
| 2008 | September | 16 |
| 2008 | October | 14 |
| 2008 | November | 18 |
| 2008 | December | 16 |

Now, utilizing another CTE, you could use this to join to the Sales.SalesOrderHeader table and find out sales on the first Tuesday after the second Wednesday. And that is exactly what I would do if this requirement were the idea of a madman (hmm, should this be mad person? Or perhaps the term is *marketing analyst*?) and would be done one time. But if this were something regular for this client, I would add a column to the calendar table (maybe called firstTuesdayAfterSecondWednesdayFlag) and set it to 1 for every date that it matches. For example, the company sale could start on this day every month, so the report needs to know how sales were for four days after. So, perhaps the column would be bigSaleDaysFlag, or whatever works.

In the standard calendar table, it is common to have, at a minimum, the following generic events/time ranges:

```
--Saturday or Sunday set to 1, else 0
weekendFlag bit not null,

fiscalYear smallint NOT NULL,
fiscalMonth tinyint NULL,
fiscalQuarter tinyint NOT NULL
```

Almost every company has a fiscal year that it uses for its business calendar. This technique allows you to treat the fiscal time periods more or less like regular calendar dates in your code, with no modification at all. (I will demonstrate this after we load the data in just a few paragraphs.)

This covers the basics; now I'll discuss one last thing you can add to the calendar table to solve the problem that really shifts this into "must-have" territory: floating windows of time.

---

**■Note** This is actually one of the few techniques that I created on my own. I am not actually claiming that I am the owner of the technique per se, but I have not read about it anywhere else, and I built this myself when trying to solve a particular type of problem using the system functions to no avail.

---

The idea is to add a relative positioning value to the table. Years are already contiguous, increasing numbers, so it is easy to do math with them. But it is not particularly comfortable to do math with months. I found myself often having to get the past 12 months of activity, sometimes including the current month and sometimes not. Doing math that wraps around a 12-month calendar was a pain, so to the calendar, I add the following columns that I will load with increasing values with no gaps:

```
relativeDayCount int NOT NULL,
relativeWeekCount int NOT NULL,
relativeMonthCount int NOT NULL
```

Using these columns I will store sequence numbers that start at an arbitrary point in time. (I will use '20000101' here, but it is really unimportant, and negative values are not a problem either. You should never refer to the value itself, just the value's relative position to some point in time you choose.) And days are numbered from that point (negative before, positive before), months, and again weeks. This returns the following "final" calendar table (the final one for this book at the very least):

```
CREATE TABLE tools.calendar
(
        dateValue date NOT NULL CONSTRAINT PKdate_dim PRIMARY KEY,
        dayName varchar(10) NOT NULL,
        monthName varchar(10) NOT NULL,
        year varchar(60) NOT NULL,
        day tinyint NOT NULL,
        dayOfTheYear smallint NOT NULL,
```

```
        month smallint NOT NULL,
        quarter tinyint NOT NULL,
        weekendFlag bit not null,

        --start of fiscal year configurable in the load process, currently
        --only supports fiscal months that match the calendar months.
        fiscalYear smallint NOT NULL,
        fiscalMonth tinyint NULL,
        fiscalQuarter tinyint NOT NULL,

        --used to give relative positioning, such as the previous 10 months
        --which can be annoying due to month boundaries
        relativeDayCount int NOT NULL,
        relativeWeekCount int NOT NULL,
        relativeMonthCount int NOT NULL
)
```

Last I will reload the table with the following code:

```
WITH dates (newDateValue) as (
        select dateadd(day,i,'17530101') as newDateValue
        from tools.sequence
)
INSERT tools.calendar
        (dateValue ,dayName
        ,monthName ,year ,day
        ,dayOfTheYear ,month ,quarter
        ,weekendFlag ,fiscalYear ,fiscalMonth
        ,fiscalQuarter ,relativeDayCount,relativeWeekCount
        ,relativeMonthCount)
SELECT
        dates.newDateValue as dateValue,
        datename (dw,dates.newDateValue) as dayName,
        datename (mm,dates.newDateValue) as monthName,
        datename (yy,dates.newDateValue) as year,
        datepart(day,dates.newDateValue) as day,
        datepart(dy,dates.newDateValue) as dayOfTheYear,
        datepart(m,dates.newDateValue) as month,
        case
                when month ( dates.newDateValue) <= 3 then 1
                when month ( dates.newDateValue) <= 6 then 2
                when month ( dates.newDateValue) <= 9 then 3
        else 4 end as quarter,

        case when datename (dw,dates.newDateValue) in ('Saturday','Sunday')
                then 1
                else 0
        end as weekendFlag,

        ------------------------------------------------
        --the next three blocks assume a fiscal year starting in July.
        --change if your fiscal periods are different
        ------------------------------------------------
        case
                when month(dates.newDateValue) <= 6
                then year(dates.newDateValue)
                else year (dates.newDateValue) + 1
        end as fiscalYear,
```

```
        case
                when month(dates.newDateValue) <= 6
                then month(dates.newDateValue) + 6
                else month(dates.newDateValue) - 6
         end as fiscalMonth,

        case
                when month(dates.newDateValue) <= 3 then 3
                when month(dates.newDateValue) <= 6 then 4
                when month(dates.newDateValue) <= 9 then 1
         else 2 end as fiscalQuarter,

        -----------------------------------------------
        --end of fiscal quarter = july
        -----------------------------------------------

        --these values can be anything, as long as they
        --provide contiguous values on year, month, and week boundaries
        datediff(day,'20000101',dates.newDateValue) as relativeDayCount,
        datediff(week,'20000101',dates.newDateValue) as relativeWeekCount,
        datediff(month,'20000101',dates.newDateValue) as relativeMonthCount

FROM    dates
WHERE   dates.newDateValue between '20000101' and '20100101' --set the date range
```

Now we can build a query to get only weekends, grouped by fiscalYear like this:

```
SELECT calendar.fiscalYear, COUNT(*) as orderCount
FROM   AdventureWorks2008.Sales.SalesOrderHeader
        JOIN tools.calendar
                --note, the cast here could be a real performance killer
                --consider using date columns where
            ON CAST(SalesOrderHeader.OrderDate as date) = calendar.dateValue
WHERE    weekendFlag = 1
GROUP BY calendar.fiscalYear
ORDER BY calendar.fiscalYear
```

This returns the following:

| fiscalYear | orderCount |
| --- | --- |
| 2002 | 881 |
| 2003 | 1478 |
| 2004 | 6707 |
| 2005 | 291 |

To demonstrate the floating windows of time using the relative_____Count columns, consider that you want to count the sales for the previous two weeks. It's not impossible to do this using the date functions perhaps, but it's simple to do with a calendar table:

```
DECLARE @interestingDate date = '20080107'

SELECT calendar.dateValue as previousTwoWeeks, currentDate.dateValue as today,
        calendar.relativeWeekCount
FROM    tools.calendar
            JOIN (SELECT *
                FROM tools.calendar
                WHERE dateValue = @interestingDate) as currentDate
```

```
on   calendar.relativeWeekCount < (currentDate.relativeWeekCount)
     and calendar.relativeWeekCount >=
                                (currentDate.relativeWeekCount -2)
```

This returns the following:

| previousFourWeeks | today | relativeWeekCount |
| --- | --- | --- |
| 2007-12-23 00:00:00.000 | 2008-01-07 00:00:00.000 | 417 |
| 2007-12-24 00:00:00.000 | 2008-01-07 00:00:00.000 | 417 |
| 2007-12-25 00:00:00.000 | 2008-01-07 00:00:00.000 | 417 |
| 2007-12-26 00:00:00.000 | 2008-01-07 00:00:00.000 | 417 |
| 2007-12-27 00:00:00.000 | 2008-01-07 00:00:00.000 | 417 |
| 2007-12-28 00:00:00.000 | 2008-01-07 00:00:00.000 | 417 |
| 2007-12-29 00:00:00.000 | 2008-01-07 00:00:00.000 | 417 |
| 2007-12-30 00:00:00.000 | 2008-01-07 00:00:00.000 | 418 |
| 2007-12-31 00:00:00.000 | 2008-01-07 00:00:00.000 | 418 |
| 2008-01-01 00:00:00.000 | 2008-01-07 00:00:00.000 | 418 |
| 2008-01-02 00:00:00.000 | 2008-01-07 00:00:00.000 | 418 |
| 2008-01-03 00:00:00.000 | 2008-01-07 00:00:00.000 | 418 |
| 2008-01-04 00:00:00.000 | 2008-01-07 00:00:00.000 | 418 |
| 2008-01-05 00:00:00.000 | 2008-01-07 00:00:00.000 | 418 |

The basics of the query is simply to take a derived table that fetches the calendar row for the "interesting" date and then join that to the full calendar table using a range of dates in the join. In the previous week example, I used the following:

```
calendar.relativeWeekCount < (currentDate.relativeWeekCount)
   and calendar.relativeWeekCount >= (currentDate.relativeWeekCount -2)
```

This was because I wanted the weeks that are previous to the current week and weeks two weeks back. Weeks aren't the sweet spot of this technique exactly, because weeks are of fixed length (but they are easier to get a full result set in print, since I don't get paid by the page). Now, join the values in previousFourWeeks to your sales table, and you can see sales for the past two weeks. Want to see it broken down by week? Use relative week count. If you wanted the previous 12 months:

```
DECLARE @interestingDate date = '20080315'

SELECT MIN(calendar.dateValue) as MinDate, MAX(calendar.dateValue) as MaxDate
FROM   tools.calendar
          JOIN (SELECT *
                FROM tools.calendar
                WHERE dateValue = @interestingDate) as currentDate
          ON   calendar.relativeMonthCount < (currentDate.relativeMonthCount)
               AND calendar.relativeMonthCount >=
                                  (currentDate.relativeMonthCount -12)
```

this returns the following:

| MinDate | MaxDate |
| --- | --- |
| 2007-03-01 00:00:00.000 | 2008-02-29 00:00:00.000 |

This query includes all earlier months, but not the one loaded into @interestingDate. Notice that the results did not include the current month. Change the < to <=, and it will include the current month. If you want to get a 24-month window, get the 12 months plus or minus the current month, like this:

```
ON  calendar.relativeMonthCount < (currentDate.relativeMonthCount + 12)
     and calendar.relativeMonthCount >=
                                    (currentDate.relativeMonthCount -12)
```

Using that ON clause results in the following:

```
MinDate                 MaxDate
----------------------  ----------------------
2007-03-01 00:00:00.000 2009-02-28 00:00:00.000
```

Now you can use these dates in other criteria either by assigning these values to a variable or (if you are one of the cool kids) by using the tables in a join to other tables. As a real example, let's hop in the Wayback machine and go to the Adventureworks2008 database where it is still 2004. (Keep in mind that the sample databases could change in the future to get more up-to-date data. This data was current as of the release of the book.)

```
DECLARE @interestingDate date = '20040927'

SELECT calendar.year, calendar.month, COUNT(*) as orderCount
FROM   AdventureWorks2008.Sales.SalesOrderHeader
        JOIN tools.calendar
          JOIN (select *
                 from tools.calendar
                 where dateValue = @interestingDate) as currentDate
             on  calendar.relativeMonthCount <=
                                        (currentDate.relativeMonthCount )
                 and calendar.relativeMonthCount >=
                                        (currentDate.relativeMonthCount -10)
           on cast(salesOrderHeader.shipDate as date)= calendar.dateValue
GROUP BY calendar.year, calendar.month
ORDER BY calendar.year, calendar.month
```

This query will give you items that shipped in the previous ten months and in August and group them by month:

```
year                 month  orderCount
-------------------- ------ -----------
2003                 10     1763
2003                 11     1825
2003                 12     2228
2004                 1      1998
2004                 2      2034
2004                 3      2100
2004                 4      2058
2004                 5      2395
2004                 6      2360
2004                 7      1271
2004                 8      211
```

I included the current month by changing the first condition to <=. So, you should be able to see that the calendar table and sequence table are two excellent tables to add to almost any database. They give you the ability to take a functional problem like getting the last day of the month or the previous time periods and turn it into a relational question that SQL Server can chew up and spit out using the relational techniques it is built for.

Keep in mind too that creating more fiscal calendars, reporting calendars, corporate holiday calendars, sales calendars, and so forth, is easily done by adding more columns to this very same calendar table. For instance, you may have multiple business units, each with their own fiscal calendar (why keep things simple when you can keep them complicated? I always say). With the one normal calendar, you can add any variation of the fiscal calendar multiple times. It's easy to just add those columns, since they all relate back to a normal calendar date.

# Binary Large Valued Objects (BLOB)

Storing large binary objects, such PDFs, images, and really any kind of object you might find in your Windows file system, is generally not the domain of SQL Server. However, when such data needs to be related to data in your tables, you have no choice but to find some manner of associating the file-based data to the data in your SQL Server database.

When discussing how to store large objects in SQL Server, generally speaking this would be in reference to data that is (obviously) large but usually is some form of binary format, such as a picture, a formatted document, and so on. Most of the time, this is not considering simple text data or even formatted or semistructured text, such as XML. SQL Server has an XML type (covered in Appendix B in some detail), and it has a `varchar(max)`/`nvarchar(max)` type for storing "plain" text data. The techniques outlined in this chapter *can* be used to store text data, and there may be places where this is the best thing (such as *very* large textual data). But generally speaking, the text storage is (better than) adequate using the internal storage of text data.

When deciding a way to store binary data in SQL Server, there are typically two ways that are available:

- Storing a path reference to the file data
- Storing the binaries using SQL Server's storage engine

---

**■Note**  There is one other type of storage using the Remote Blob Store API. It allows you to use an external storage device to store and manage the images via an API that is not in T-SQL. It is not a typical case, but it will definitely be of interest to people building high-end solutions needing to store blobs on an external device. I will focus on the very common uses of binary values.

---

Prior to 2008, this kind of question was very simple indeed. Almost always the most reasonable solution was to store files in the file system and just store a reference to the data in a `varchar` column. In SQL Server 2008, Microsoft has implemented a new type of binary storage called a *filestream*, which allows binary data to be stored in the file system as actual files, which makes accessing this data from a client much faster than if it were stored in a binary column in SQL Server. You still deal with the data in T-SQL as before, and even that may be improved, though you cannot do partial writes to the values like you can in a `varbinary(max)` column.

---

**■Tip**  You cannot use filestream data in a database that also needs to use snapshot isolation level or that implements the `READ_COMMITTED_SNAPSHOT` database option.

---

Now, before you get too excited, note that you cannot directly access this data in the file system in a natural manner; you can get access to the file data only through an ADO.NET interface, which allows the data to be used in a transactionally safe manner. As Zach Owens said on his blog (http://blogs.msdn.com/zowens) about filestream data, "It ain't rocket science, but there are a few tricks." I won't cover filestreams in any great depth in the book. In this section, I simply want to point out some of the basic factors that go into deciding to use it or not. There are some good examples in Books Online that will get you to the point of using it from a code standpoint, but the most important thing is to understand that in T-SQL it looks and feels pretty much like a normal binary value. You should also know that even though you can get the virtual path and filename through T-SQL, you cannot just type it into the Run entry on your server and get the file. An ADO.NET application is required to use the file access in Windows applications.

In the 2005 edition of the book, I separated the choice between the two possible ways to store binaries into one main simple reason to choose one or the other: transactional integrity. If you required transaction integrity, you use SQL Server's storage engine, regardless of the cost you would incur. If transaction integrity isn't tremendously important, use the file system. For example, if you were just storing an image that a user could go out and edit, leaving it with the same name, then the file system is perfectly natural. Performance was a consideration, but if you needed performance, you could write the data to the storage engine first and then regularly refresh the image to the file system and use it from a cache.

In SQL Server 2008, the choice is expanded to need some basic understanding of the following topics:

- *Transactional integrity*: It's far easier to guarantee that the image is stored and remains stored if it is managed by the storage engine, either as a filestream or as a binary value, than it is if you store the filename and path and have an external application manage the files.

- *Consistent backup of image and data*: Knowing that the files and the data are in sync is related to transactional integrity. Storing the data in the database, either as a binary columnar value or as a filestream, ensures that the binary values are backed up with the other database objects.

- *Size*: For typical object size less than 1MB, Books Online suggests using storage in a varchar(max). If objects are going to be less than 2GB, then you must use filestream storage.

- *API*: Which API is the client using? If the API does not support filestreams, then you should definitely give it a pass.

- *Utilization*: How will the data be used? If it is used very frequently, then you would choose either filestream or file system storage.

- *Location of files:* Filestream filegroups are located on the same server as the relational files. You cannot specify a UNC path to store the data in. The data, just like a normal filegroup, must be transactionally safe for utilization.

- *Encryption*: Encryption is not supported on the data store in filestream filegroups.

- *Security*: If the image's integrity is important to the business process (such as the picture on a security badge that's displayed to a security guard when a badge is swiped), then it's worth it to pay the extra price for storing the data in the database, where it's much harder to make a change. (Modifying an image manually in T-SQL is a tremendous chore indeed.)

In the sample model in Chapter 5, there were two examples of images, with two different needs. First, there's the Picture column on the MovieRentalItem table. Because this is just the picture of a movie, I'm going to choose to store a path to the data. This data will be used to present electronic browsing of the store's stock on an in-store kiosk, as well as on a web page for the customer to rent online and pick up at the store. So, I'll change the column from a domain of Picture to UncFileName, which will be a varchar(200) to allow for the filename as well as the UNC file path (see Figure 7-1).

```
MovieRentalPackage
┌─────────────────────────────────┐
│ MovieRentalPackageId: int       │
├─────────────────────────────────┤
│ MovieId: int (AK1.1)            │
│ Name: varchar(20) (AK1.2)       │
│ PiecesCount: tinyint            │
│ ReleaseDate: datetime           │
│ TimeDuration: TimeDuration      │
│ Picture: varchar(200)           │
│ MovieFormatId: int              │
│ DvdRegion: tinyint              │
└─────────────────────────────────┘
```

**Figure 7-1.** *MovieRentalPackage table with Picture datatype set as a path to a file*

This file location will likely be on some web server's image cache and could be replicated to other web servers. The path may or may not be stored as a full UNC location; it really would depend on your infrastructure needs. The goal will be when the page is fetching data from the server to be able to build a bit of HTML such as this:

```sql
SELECT '<img src = "' + MovieRentalPackage.Picture + '">', ...
FROM    MovieRentalPackage.Picture
WHERE   MovieId = @MovieId
```

If this data were stored in the database as a binary format, it would have needed to be materialized onto disk as a file first and then used in the page, which is going to be far slower than doing it this way, no matter what your architecture. This is probably not a case where you would want to do this or go through the hoops necessary for filestream access, since transactionally speaking, if the picture link is broken, it would not invalidate the other data, and it is probably not very important. Plus, you will probably want to access this file directly, making the main web screens very fast and easy to code.

An alternative example is found in the Customer table (see Figure 7-2). To fight fraud, this particular movie rental chain decided to start taking customer pictures and comparing them whenever customers rented an item. This data is far more important from a security standpoint and has privacy implications. For this, I'll use a varbinary(max).

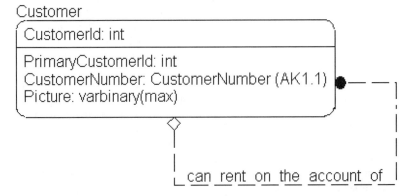

**Figure 7-2.** *Customer table with picture stored as data in the table*

At this point, you have definitely decided that transactional integrity is necessary and that you want to retrieve the data directly from the server. The next thing to decide will be whether to employ filestreams. The big questions here would be if your API will support filestreams. If so, then it would likely be a very good place to make use of them for sure.

Overall, speed probably isn't a big deal, and even if you needed to take the binary bits and stream them from SQL Server's normal storage into a file, it would probably still perform well enough since only one image needs to be fetched at a time, and performance will be adequate as long as the image displays before the rental transaction is completed. Don't get me wrong; the varbinary(max) types aren't that slow, but performance would be acceptable for these purposes even if they were.

Using FILESTREAM will give you nearly the same performance of saving it to a file, with the transactional integrity of storing it in the database. Using/allowing FILESTREAM is easy from a database developer/architect's point of view. There are articles in Books Online that will walk you through the process of enabling it. Filestream data can have its own filegroup that is just a directory reference that you will add to your database when you create it or alter it. Then you simply use the following syntax in your table create statement:

```
CREATE TABLE <tableName>
(
    ...
    <columnName> varbinary(max) filestream null
)
```

From this point onward, from a T-SQL standpoint, it is more or less a normal varbinary value. I won't go any deeper into filestreams because all of the more interesting bits of the technology are external to SQL Server in API, which I have been careful to avoid for my entire career.

# Storing User-Specified Data

One of the common problems that has no comfortable solution is giving users a method to expand the catalog of values they can store without losing control of the database and (most important) the integrity of the data that they want to store in this database. In this section, I will explore a couple of the common methods for doing this, including one that is based on SQL Server 2008's new sparse column feature.

As I have tried to make clear throughout the rest of the book so far, relational tables are not meant to be flexible. SQL Server code is not really meant to be overly flexible. In Chapter 11, I will again try to hammer home that not only are tables not meant to be flexible, but T-SQL as a language is not made for flexibility (at least not from the standpoint of producing reliable databases that produce expected results and producing good performance while protecting the quality of the data, which I have said many times is almost always the most important thing).

Unfortunately, reality is that users want flexibility, and frankly you can't tell users that they can't get what they want, when they want it, and in the form they want it. As an architect I want to give the users what they want, within the confines of reality and sensibility, so it is necessary to ascertain some method of giving the user the flexibility they demand, along with methods to deal with this data in a manner that feels good to them. The technique used to solve this problem is pretty simple. It requires the design to be flexible enough to morph to the needs of the user, without the intervention of a database programmer manually changing the catalog. But with all problems, there are generally a couple of solutions that can be used to improve them.

■**Note** I will specifically speak only of methods that are T-SQL methods. Dejan Sarka, at the PASS 2007 conference, presented material about "open schema" (as this need is often called), and he gave a nice presentation on the subject (the slides are accessible via a web search). One of his methods used a CLR object to serialize the user's values to a binary value, as well as an XML example. The CLR version was interesting, but I don't think many folks would implement it like that, since each individual value in the CLR representation could not be indexed (it is there on his presentation if you are intrigued), and the XML example is also a possibility if you are in 2005 or earlier, but the sparse table solution is also XML based in a way that will please XMLophiles and relational folks alike. (Plus, I am sure that the editor would prefer the book not be the longest book ever, even if it nearly has the longest title . . .)

The methods I will demonstrate are as follows:

- Big old list of generic columns
- Entity-attribute-value (EAV)
- Adding columns to the table, likely using sparse columns

The last time I had this type of need was to gather the properties on networking equipment. Each router, modem, and so on, on a network has various properties (and hundreds or thousands of them at that). For this section, I will present this example as three different examples.

The basis of this example will be a simple table called `Equipment`. It will have a surrogate key and a tag that will identify it, as shown in Figure 7-3.

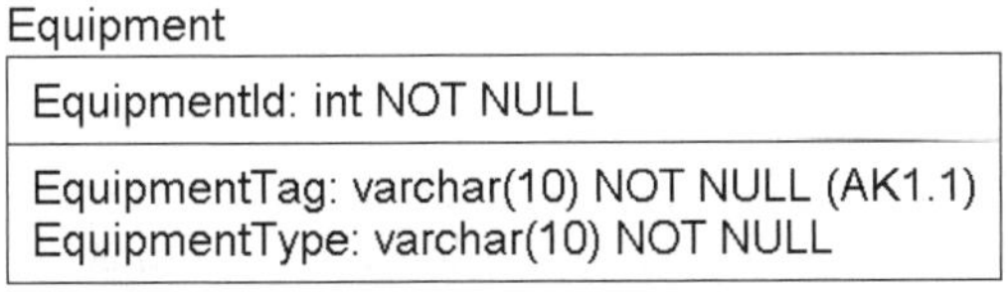

Equipment

| EquipmentId: int NOT NULL |
| --- |
| EquipmentTag: varchar(10) NOT NULL (AK1.1)<br>EquipmentType: varchar(10) NOT NULL |

**Figure 7-3.** *Equipment table for storing user-specified data sections*

It can be created using the following code:

```
CREATE TABLE Equipment
(
    EquipmentId int NOT NULL
        CONSTRAINT PKEquipment PRIMARY KEY,
    EquipmentTag varchar(10) NOT NULL
        CONSTRAINT AKEquipment UNIQUE,
    EquipmentType varchar(10)
)
GO
INSERT INTO Equipment
VALUES (1,'CLAWHAMMER','Hammer'),
       (2,'HANDSAW','Saw'),
       (3,'POWERDRILL','PowerTool')
```

By this point in the book you should know that this is not how the whole table would look in the actual solutions, but these three columns will give you enough to build an example from.

# Big Old List of Generic Columns

Yes, the title of this section *is* in fact meant to be read with a little whiff of disdain. This method is generally not a good way to go, but I figured I had to mention it here since it is probably the most often used, particularly going back to the days of the record management databases (like FoxPro or many mainframe databases that were very tied to their physical storage). If this were a website, it would be linked in this section and the "Anti-patterns" section later in this chapter.

The basics of this plan is to create your normalized tables, make sure you have everything nicely normalized, and then, just in case the user wants to store "additional" information, create a bunch of generic columns. This sort of tactic is quite common in "product-offering" databases, where the people who are building the database are trying to make sure that the end users have some "space" in the tool for their custom application. For our example, adjusting the Equipment table, someone might implement a set of columns as shown in Figure 7-4.

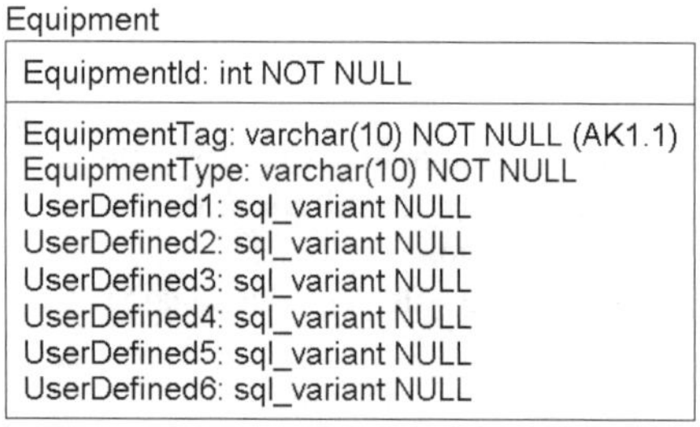

Equipment

| EquipmentId: int NOT NULL |
| --- |
| EquipmentTag: varchar(10) NOT NULL (AK1.1)<br>EquipmentType: varchar(10) NOT NULL<br>UserDefined1: sql_variant NULL<br>UserDefined2: sql_variant NULL<br>UserDefined3: sql_variant NULL<br>UserDefined4: sql_variant NULL<br>UserDefined5: sql_variant NULL<br>UserDefined6: sql_variant NULL |

**Figure 7-4.** *Using generic columns to implement user-specified data*

On the good hand, the end user has a place to store some values that they might need. On the not so good, without some corporate policy, these columns will just be used in any manner that each user decides. This is often the case, and this leads to chaos when using this data in SQL. Best case, userDefined1 is where they *always* put the schmeglin number, and the second the cooflin diameter or some other value. If the programmer building the user interface is "clever," he could give names to these columns in some metadata that he defines so that they show up on the screen with usable names.

The next problem, though, comes for the person who is trying to query the data, because knowing what each column means is too often a mystery. If you are lucky, there will be metadata you can query and then build views, and so on. The problem is, you have put the impetus on the end user to know this before using the data, whereas in the other methods, the definition will be part of even creating storage points, and the usage of them will be slightly more natural, if sometimes a bit more troublesome.

From a physical modeling point of view, the problem with this is that by adding these sql_variant columns, you are potentially bloating your base table, making any scans of the table take longer, increasing page splits, and so on. I won't produce sample code for this because it would be my goal to dissuade you from using this pattern of implementing user-defined data, but it is a technique that is commonly done.

# Entity-Attribute-Value (EAV)

The next method of implementing user-specified data is using the entity-attribute-value method. These are also known by a few different names, such as property tables, loose schemas, or open schema. In 2005 and earlier, this technique was generally considered the best/easiest method of implementing a table to allow users to configure their own storage.

The basic idea behind this method is to have another related table associated with the table you want to add information about. This table will hold the values that you want to store. Then you can either include the name of the attribute in the property table or (as I will do) have a table that defines the basic properties of a property.

Considering our needs with equipment, I will use the model shown in Figure 7-5.

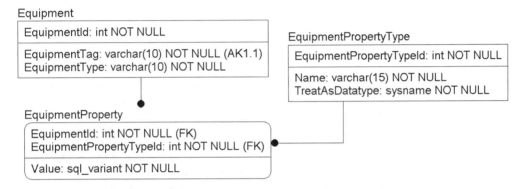

**Figure 7-5.** *Property schema for storing equipment properties with unknown attributes*

Using these values in queries isn't a "natural" task at all, and as such, you should avoid loose schemas like this unless absolutely necessary. The main reason is that you should rarely, if ever, have a limit to the types of data that the user can store. For example, if you as the architect know that you want to allow only three types of properties, then you should almost never use this technique because it is almost certainly better to add the three known columns, possibly using the techniques for subtyped entities presented earlier in the book to implement the different tables to hold the values that pertain to only one type or another. The goal here is to build loose objects that can be expanded for some reason or another. In our example, it is possible that the people who develop the equipment you are working with will add a property that you want to then keep up with. In my real-life usage of this technique, there were hundreds of properties added as different equipment was brought online and each device was interrogated for its properties.

To do this, I will create an `EquipmentPropertyType` table and add a few types of properties:

```
CREATE TABLE EquipmentPropertyType
(
    EquipmentPropertyTypeId int NOT NULL
        CONSTRAINT PKEquipmentPropertyType PRIMARY KEY,
    Name varchar(15)
        CONSTRAINT AKEquipmentPropertyType UNIQUE,
    TreatAsDatatype sysname NOT NULL
)
```

```
INSERT INTO EquipmentPropertyType
VALUES(1,'Width','numeric(10,2)'),
      (2,'Length','numeric(10,2)'),
      (3,'HammerHeadStyle','varchar(30)')
```

Then I create an EquipmentProperty table:

```
CREATE TABLE EquipmentProperty
(
    EquipmentId int NOT NULL
        CONSTRAINT Equipment$hasExtendedPropertiesIn$EquipmentProperty
            REFERENCES Equipment(EquipmentId),
    EquipmentPropertyTypeId int
        CONSTRAINT EquipmentPropertyTypeId$definesTypesFor$EquipmentProperty
            REFERENCES EquipmentPropertyType(EquipmentPropertyTypeId),
    Value sql_variant,
    CONSTRAINT PKEquipmentProperty PRIMARY KEY
                    (EquipmentId, EquipmentPropertyTypeId)
)
```

Then I need to load some data. For this task, I will build a procedure that can be used to insert the data by name and at the same time will validate that the datatype is right. That is a bit tricky because of the sql_variant type, and it is one reason that property tables are sometimes built using character values. Since everything has a textual representation and it is easier to work with in code, it just makes things simpler for the code but often far worse for the storage engine to maintain.

In the procedure, I will insert the row into the table and then use dynamic SQL to validate the value by casting the value as the datatype the user passed in. (Note that the procedure follows the standards that I will establish in later chapters for transactions and error handling. I don't always do this in this chapter to keep the samples clean, but this procedure deals with validations.)

```
CREATE PROCEDURE EquipmentProperty$Insert
(
    @EquipmentId int,
    @EquipmentPropertyName varchar(15),
    @Value sql_variant
)
AS
    SET NOCOUNT ON
    DECLARE @entryTrancount int = @@trancount

    BEGIN TRY
        DECLARE @EquipmentPropertyTypeId int,
                @TreatASDatatype sysname

        SELECT @TreatASDatatype = TreatAsDatatype,
               @EquipmentPropertyTypeId = EquipmentPropertyTypeId
        FROM   EquipmentPropertyType
        WHERE  EquipmentPropertyType.Name = @EquipmentPropertyName

      BEGIN TRANSACTION
        --insert the value
        INSERT INTO EquipmentProperty(EquipmentId, EquipmentPropertyTypeId,
                    Value)
        VALUES (@EquipmentId, @EquipmentPropertyTypeId, @Value)
```

```
      --Then get that value from the table and cast it in a dynamic SQL
      -- call.  This will raise a trappable error if the type is incompatible
      DECLARE @validationQuery  varchar(max) =
              ' DECLARE @value sql_variant
                SELECT  @value = cast(value as ' + @TreatASDatatype + ')
                FROM    EquipmentProperty
                WHERE   EquipmentId = ' + cast (@EquipmentId as varchar(10)) + '
                  and   EquipmentPropertyTypeId = ' +
                        cast(@EquipmentPropertyTypeId as varchar(10)) + ' '

       EXECUTE (@validationQuery)
    COMMIT TRANSACTION
  END TRY
  BEGIN CATCH

      --if the tran is doomed, and the entryTrancount was 0
      --we have to rollback
      IF xact_state()= -1 and @entryTrancount = 0
           rollback transaction

    DECLARE @ERRORmessage nvarchar(4000)
    SET @ERRORmessage = 'Error occurred in procedure ''' +
                object_name(@@procid) + ''', Original Message: '''
                + ERROR_MESSAGE() + ''''
    RAISERROR (@ERRORmessage,16,1)
    RETURN -100

  END CATCH
```

So, if you try to put in an invalid piece of data:

```
EXEC EquipmentProperty$Insert 1,'Width','Claw' --width is numeric(10,2)
```

you will get the following error:

```
Msg 50000, Level 16, State 1, Procedure EquipmentProperty$Insert, Line 45
Error occurred in procedure 'EquipmentProperty$Insert', Original Message:
'Error converting data type varchar to numeric.'
```

Now I create some proper demo data:

```
EXEC EquipmentProperty$Insert @EquipmentId =1 ,
     @EquipmentPropertyName = 'Width', @Value = 2
EXEC EquipmentProperty$Insert @EquipmentId =1 ,
     @EquipmentPropertyName = 'Length',@Value = 8.4
EXEC EquipmentProperty$Insert @EquipmentId =1 ,
     @EquipmentPropertyName = 'HammerHeadStyle',@Value = 'Claw'
EXEC EquipmentProperty$Insert @EquipmentId =2 ,
     @EquipmentPropertyName = 'Width',@Value = 1
EXEC EquipmentProperty$Insert @EquipmentId =2 ,
     @EquipmentPropertyName = 'Length',@Value = 7
EXEC EquipmentProperty$Insert @EquipmentId =3 ,
     @EquipmentPropertyName = 'Width',@Value = 6
EXEC EquipmentProperty$Insert @EquipmentId =3 ,
     @EquipmentPropertyName = 'Length',@Value = 12.1
```

To view the data in a "raw" manner, I can simply query the data as such:

```
SELECT Equipment.EquipmentTag,Equipment.EquipmentType,
       EquipmentPropertyType.name, EquipmentProperty.Value
FROM   EquipmentProperty
          JOIN Equipment
             on Equipment.EquipmentId = EquipmentProperty.EquipmentId
          JOIN EquipmentPropertyType
             on EquipmentPropertyType.EquipmentPropertyTypeId =
                                  EquipmentProperty.EquipmentPropertyTypeId
```

This is usable but not very natural as results:

```
EquipmentTag EquipmentType name            Value
------------ ------------- --------------- ---------------------
CLAWHAMMER   Hammer        Width           2
CLAWHAMMER   Hammer        Length          8.4
CLAWHAMMER   Hammer        HammerHeadStyle Claw
HANDSAW      Saw           Width           1
HANDSAW      Saw           Length          7
POWERDRILL   PowerTool     Width           6
POWERDRILL   PowerTool     Length          12.1
```

To view this in a natural, tabular format along with the other columns of the table, I could use PIVOT, but the "old" style method to perform a pivot, using MAX() aggregates, works better here because I can fairly easily make the statement dynamic (which is the next query sample):

```
SET ANSI_WARNINGS OFF --eliminates the NULL warning on aggregates.
SELECT  Equipment.EquipmentTag,Equipment.EquipmentType,
    MAX(CASE WHEN EquipmentPropertyType.name = 'Width' THEN Value END) AS Width,
    MAX(CASE WHEN EquipmentPropertyType.name = 'Length'THEN Value END) AS Length,
    MAX(CASE WHEN EquipmentPropertyType.name = 'HammerHeadStyle' THEN Value END)
                                                     AS 'HammerHeadStyle'
FROM   EquipmentProperty
          JOIN Equipment
             on Equipment.EquipmentId = EquipmentProperty.EquipmentId
          JOIN EquipmentPropertyType
             on EquipmentPropertyType.EquipmentPropertyTypeId =
                                  EquipmentProperty.EquipmentPropertyTypeId
GROUP BY Equipment.EquipmentTag,Equipment.EquipmentType
```

This returns the following:

```
EquipmentTag EquipmentType Width     Length  HammerHeadStyle
------------ ------------- --------- ------- ----------------
CLAWHAMMER   Hammer        2         8.4     Claw
HANDSAW      Saw           1         7       NULL
POWERDRILL   PowerTool     6         12.1    NULL
```

If you execute this on your own in the text mode, what you will quickly notice is how much editing I had to do to the data. Each sql_variant column will be formatted for a huge amount of data. And, you had to manually set up the values. In the following extension, I have used XML PATH to output the different properties to different columns, starting with MAX. (This is a common SQL Server 2005 and later technique for turning rows into columns. Do a search for turning rows into columns in SQL Server, and you will find the details.)

```
SET ANSI_WARNINGS OFF
DECLARE @query varchar(8000)
SELECT  @query = 'select Equipment.EquipmentTag,Equipment.EquipmentType ' + (
               SELECT distinct
                   ',MAX(CASE WHEN EquipmentPropertyType.name = ''' +
                      EquipmentPropertyType.name + ''' THEN cast(Value as ' +
                      EquipmentPropertyType.TreatAsDatatype + ') END) AS [' +
                      EquipmentPropertyType.name + ']' AS [text()]
               FROM
                   EquipmentPropertyType
               FOR XML PATH('') ) + '
               FROM  EquipmentProperty
                         JOIN Equipment
                            on Equipment.EquipmentId =
                                EquipmentProperty.EquipmentId
                         JOIN EquipmentPropertyType
                            on EquipmentPropertyType.EquipmentPropertyTypeId
                                = EquipmentProperty.EquipmentPropertyTypeId
          GROUP BY Equipment.EquipmentTag,Equipment.EquipmentType  '
EXEC (@query)
```

Executing this will get you the following:

| EquipmentTag | EquipmentType | HammerHeadStyle | Length | Width |
| --- | --- | --- | --- | --- |
| CLAWHAMMER | Hammer | Claw | 8.40 | 2.00 |
| HANDSAW | Saw | NULL | 7.00 | 1.00 |
| POWERDRILL | PowerTool | NULL | 12.10 | 6.00 |

I won't pretend that I didn't have to edit the results to get them to fit, but each of these columns was formatted as the datatype that you specified in the EquipmentPropertyType table, not as 8,000-character values (that is a lot of little minus signs under each heading . . . ).

One thing I won't go any further into in this example is the EquipmentType column and how you might use it to limit certain properties to apply only to certain types of equipment. It would require adding a table for type and relating it to the Equipment and EquipmentPropertyType tables. Then you could build even smarter display procedures by asking only for columns of type HandTool; then the display routine would get back only those properties that are for the type you want.

## Adding Columns to a Table

For the final choice that I will demonstrate, consider the idea of using the facilities that SQL Server gives us for implementing columns, rather than implementing your own metadata system. In the previous examples, it was impossible to use the table structures in a natural way, meaning that if you wanted to query the data, you had to know what they meant by interrogating the metadata. In the EAV solution, a normal SELECT statement was almost impossible. One could be simulated with a dynamic stored procedure, or you could possibly create a hard-coded view, but it certainly would not be easy for the typical end user without the aid of a programmer.

Note that the columns you create do not need to be on the base tables. You could easily build a separate table, just like the EAV solution in the previous section, but instead of building your own method of storing data, add columns to the new property table. Using the primary key of the existing table to implement it as a one- to zero-on-one cardinality relationship will keep users from needing to modify the main table.

---

■**Tip** Always have a way to validate the schema of your database. If this is a corporate situation, then a simple copy of the database structure might be good enough. If you ship a product to a customer, then you should produce an application to validate the structures against before applying a patch or upgrade or even allowing your tech support to help out with a problem. Although you cannot stop a customer from making a change (like a new column, index, trigger, or whatever), you don't want the change to cause an issue that your tech support won't immediately recognize.

---

The key to this method is to use SQL Server more or less naturally (there may still be some metadata required to manage data rules, but it is possible to use native SQL commands with the data). Instead of all the stuff we went through in the previous section to save and view the data, just use ALTER TABLE and add the column. Of course, it isn't necessarily as easy as making changes to the tables and granting control of the tables to the user, especially if you are going to allow non-admin users to add their own columns ad hoc. However, building a stored procedure or two would allow the user to add columns to the table (and possibly remove), but you might want to allow only those columns with a certain prefix to be added, or you could use extended properties. This would just be to prevent "whoops" events from occurring, not to prevent an administrator from dropping a column. You really can't prevent an admin user of an instance from dropping anything in the database unless you lock things down far too much from your customers. If the app doesn't work because they have removed columns from the application that are necessary, well, that is going to be the DBA's fault.

A possible downside of using this method on the base table is that you can really affect the performance of a system if you just allow users to randomly add large amounts of data to your tables. In some cases, the user who is extending the database will have a need for a column that is very important to their usage of the system, like a key value to an external system. For those needs you might want to add a column to the base table. But if the user wants to store just a piece of data on a few rows, it may not make any sense to add this column to the base physical table (more on the physical aspects of storing data in Chapter 9), especially if it will not be used on many rows.

In versions prior to SQL Server 2008, to use this method I would have likely built another table to hold these additional columns and then joined to the table to fetch the values or possibly built an XML column.

In SQL Server 2008, we get the best of both solutions with sparse columns. A *sparse column* is a type of column storage where a column that is NULL takes no storage at all (normal NULL columns require space to indicate that they are NULL). Basically, the data is stored internally as a form of EAV solution that is associated with each row in the table. Sparse columns are added and dropped from the table using the same DDL statements as normal columns (with the added keyword of SPARSE on the column create statement). You can also use the same DML operations on the data as you can for regular tables. However, since the purpose of having sparse columns is to allow you to add many columns to the table (the max is 30,000!), you can also work with sparse columns using a *column set*, which gives you the ability to retrieve and work with only the sparse columns that you desire to or that have values in the row.

Sparse columns are slightly less efficient in many ways when compared to normal columns, so the idea would be to add nonsparse columns to your tables when they will be used quite often, and if they will pertain only to rare or certain types of rows, then you could use a sparse column. Several types cannot be stored as sparse. These are as follows:

- geography
- geometry
- timestamp
- User-defined datatypes
- text, ntext, image (*Note: You shouldn't use these anyway; use* varchar(max), nvarchar(max), *and* varbinary(max) *instead.*)

Returning to the Equipment example, all I'm going to use this time is the single table. Note that the data I want to produce looks like this:

| EquipmentTag | EquipmentType | HammerHeadStyle | Length | Width |
| --- | --- | --- | --- | --- |
| HAMMER | Hammer | Claw | 8.40 | 2.00 |
| HANDSAW | Saw | NULL | 7.00 | 1.00 |
| POWERDRILL | PowerTool | NULL | 12.10 | 6.00 |

To add the Length column to the Equipment table, use this:

```
ALTER TABLE Equipment
    ADD Length numeric(10,2) SPARSE NULL
```

If you were building an application to add a column, you could use a procedure like the following to give the user rights to add a column without getting all the other control types over the table. Note that if you are going to allow users to drop columns, you will want to use some mechanism to prevent them from dropping primary system columns, such as a naming standard or extended property. You also may want to employ some manner of control to prevent them from doing this at just any time they want.

```
CREATE PROCEDURE equipment$addProperty
(
    @propertyName    sysname, --the column to add
    @datatype        sysname, --the datatype as it appears in a column creation
    @sparselyPopulatedFlag bit = 1 --Add column as sparse or not
)
WITH EXECUTE AS SELF
AS
  --note: I did not include full error handling for clarity
  DECLARE @query nvarchar(max)

 --check for column existance
 IF NOT EXISTS (select *
                from    sys.columns
                where   name = @propertyName
                  and   OBJECT_NAME(object_id) = 'equipment')
  BEGIN
    --build the ALTER statement, then execute it
    SET @query = 'ALTER TABLE equipment ADD ' + quotename(@propertyName) + ' '
               + @datatype
               + case when @sparselyPopulatedFlag = 1 then ' SPARSE ' end
               + ' NULL '
    EXEC (@query)
  END
ELSE
    RAISERROR ('The property you are adding already exists',16,1)
```

Now any user you give rights to run this procedure can add a column to the table:

```
--EXEC equipment$addProperty 'Length','numeric(10,2)',1 -- added manually
EXEC equipment$addProperty 'Width','numeric(10,2)',1
EXEC equipment$addProperty 'HammerHeadStyle','varchar(30)',1
```

Viewing the table, you see the following:

```
SELECT EquipmentTag, EquipmentType, HammerHeadStyle
     ,Length,Width
FROM   Equipment
```

which returns the following (I will use this SELECT statement several times):

| EquipmentTag | EquipmentType | HammerHeadStyle | Length | Width |
| --- | --- | --- | --- | --- |
| CLAWHAMMER | Hammer | NULL | NULL | NULL |
| HANDSAW | Saw | NULL | NULL | NULL |
| POWERDRILL | PowerTool | NULL | NULL | NULL |

Now you can treat the new columns just like they were normal columns. You can update them using a normal UPDATE statement:

```
UPDATE Equipment
SET    Length = 7,
       Width =  1
WHERE  EquipmentTag = 'HANDSAW'
```

Checking the data, you can see that the data was updated:

| EquipmentTag | EquipmentType | HammerHeadStyle | Length | Width |
| --- | --- | --- | --- | --- |
| HAMMER | Hammer | NULL | NULL | NULL |
| HANDSAW | Saw | NULL | 7.00 | 1.00 |
| POWERDRILL | PowerTool | NULL | NULL | NULL |

One thing that is so much easier using this method of doing user-specified columns is validation. Because the columns behave just like columns should, you can use a CHECK constraint to validate row-based constraints:

```
ALTER TABLE Equipment
 ADD CONSTRAINT CHKEquipment$HammerHeadStyle CHECK
        ((HammerHeadStyle is NULL AND EquipmentType <> 'Hammer')
         OR EquipmentType = 'Hammer')
```

■**Note** You could easily create a procedure to manage a user-defined check constraint on the data just like I created the columns.

Now, if you try to set an invalid value, like a saw with a HammerHeadStyle, you get an error:

```
UPDATE Equipment
SET    Length = 12.1,
       Width =  6,
       HammerHeadStyle = 'Wrong!'
WHERE  EquipmentTag = 'HANDSAW'
```

This returns the following:

```
Msg 547, Level 16, State 0, Line 2
The UPDATE statement conflicted with the CHECK constraint
"CHKEquipment$HammerHeadStyle". The conflict occurred in database "tempdb",
table "dbo.Equipment".
```

Setting the rest of the values, I return to where I was in the previous section's data, only this time the SELECT statement could have been written by a novice:

```
UPDATE Equipment
SET    Length = 12.1,
       Width =  6
WHERE  EquipmentTag = 'POWERDRILL'

UPDATE Equipment
SET    Length = 8.4,
       Width =  2,
       HammerHeadStyle = 'Claw'
WHERE  EquipmentTag = 'CLAWHAMMER'

GO
SELECT EquipmentTag, EquipmentType, HammerHeadStyle
       ,Length,Width
FROM   Equipment
```

which returns that result set I was shooting for:

| EquipmentTag | EquipmentType | HammerHeadStyle | Length | Width |
| --- | --- | --- | --- | --- |
| HAMMER | Hammer | Claw | 8.40 | 2.00 |
| HANDSAW | Saw | NULL | 7.00 | 1.00 |
| POWERDRILL | PowerTool | NULL | 12.10 | 6.0 |

Now, up to this point, it really did not make any difference if this was a SPARSE column or not. Even if I just used a SELECT * from the table, it would look just like a normal set of data. Pretty much the only way you can tell is by looking at the metadata:

```
SELECT name, is_sparse
FROM   sys.columns
WHERE  OBJECT_NAME(object_id) = 'Equipment'
```

This returns the following:

| name | is_sparse |
| --- | --- |
| EquipmentId | 0 |
| EquipmentTag | 0 |
| EquipmentType | 0 |
| Length | 1 |
| Width | 1 |
| HammerHeadStyle | 1 |

There is a different way of working with this data that can be much easier to deal with if you have many sparse columns with only a few of them filled in. You can define a column that defines a *column set*, which is the XML representation of the set of columns that are stored for the sparse column. With a column set defined, you can access the XML that manages the sparse columns and work with it directly. This is handy for dealing with tables that have a lot of empty sparse columns because NULL sparse columns do not show up in the XML, allowing you to pass very small amounts of data to the user interface, though it will have to deal with it as XML rather than in a tabular data stream.

---

**Tip** You cannot add or drop the column set once there are sparse columns in the table, so decide which to use carefully.

For our table, I will drop the check constraint and sparse columns and add a column set (you cannot modify the column set when any sparse columns exist, presumably because this is something new that they have not added yet in 2008, and in addition, you may have only one):

```
ALTER TABLE Equipment
    DROP CONSTRAINT CHKEquipment$HammerHeadStyle
ALTER TABLE Equipment
    DROP COLUMN HammerHeadStyle, Length, Width
```

Now I add a column set, which I will name SparseColumns:

```
ALTER TABLE Equipment
  ADD SparseColumns xml column_set FOR ALL_SPARSE_COLUMNS
```

Now I add back the sparse columns and constraints using my existing procedure:

```
EXEC equipment$addProperty 'Length','numeric(10,2)',1
EXEC equipment$addProperty 'Width','numeric(10,2)',1
EXEC equipment$addProperty 'HammerHeadStyle','varchar(30)',1
GO
ALTER TABLE Equipment
  ADD CONSTRAINT CHKEquipment$HammerHeadStyle CHECK
        ((HammerHeadStyle is NULL AND EquipmentType <> 'Hammer')
        OR EquipmentType = 'Hammer')
```

Now, I can still update the columns individually using the UPDATE statement:

```
UPDATE Equipment
SET    Length = 7,
       Width =  1
WHERE  EquipmentTag = 'HANDSAW'
```

But this time, using SELECT * does not return the sparse columns as normal SQL columns; it returns them as XML:

```
SELECT *
FROM   Equipment
```

This returns the following:

| EquipmentId | EquipmentTag | EquipmentType | SparseColumns |
| --- | --- | --- | --- |
| 1 | CLAWHAMMER | Hammer | NULL |
| 2 | HANDSAW | Saw | <Length>7.00</Length><Width>1.00</Width> |
| 3 | POWERDRILL | PowerTool | NULL |

You can also update the SparseColumns column directly using the XML representation:

```
UPDATE Equipment
SET    SparseColumns = '<Length>12.10</Length><Width>6.00</Width>'
WHERE  EquipmentTag = 'POWERDRILL'

UPDATE Equipment
SET    SparseColumns = '<Length>8.40</Length><Width>2.00</Width>
                        <HammerHeadStyle>Claw</HammerHeadStyle>'
WHERE  EquipmentTag = 'CLAWHAMMER'
```

Enumerating the columns gives us the output that matches what we expect:

```
SELECT EquipmentTag, EquipmentType, HammerHeadStyle
      ,Length,Width
FROM   Equipment
```

Finally, we're back to the same results as before:

```
EquipmentTag EquipmentType HammerHeadStyle     Length             Width
------------ ------------- ------------------  -----------------  ----------------
CLAWHAMMER    ClawHammer    Claw                8.40               2.00
HANDSAW       Saw           NULL                7.00               1.00
POWERDRILL    PowerTool     NULL                12.10              6.00
```

Sparse columns can be indexed, but you will likely want to create a filtered index (discussed in Chapter 5 for selective uniqueness and mentioned again in Chapter 9 in the index structure sections) on such columns. The WHERE clause of the filtered index could possibly be used either to associate the index with the type of row that makes sense (like in our HAMMER example's CHECK constraint, you would likely want to include EquipmentTag and HammerHeadStyle) or to simply ignore NULL.

In comparison to the methods used with property tables, this method is going to be tremendously easier to implement, and if you are able to use sparse columns, it's faster and far more natural to work with in comparison to the entity-attribute-value method. It is going to feel strange allowing users to change the table structures of your main data tables, but with proper coding/testing/security practices, you will end up with a far better-performing and more flexible system.

# Commonly Implemented Objects

Consistency is one of the major desired properties of any application, and this is definitely true for the databases you will design. In every database, there is generally a set of things that you will always need in order to get the job done. For example, in Chapter 6, I implemented a utility schema, with one initial table in it called ErrorLog with the following structure:

```
CREATE TABLE utility.ErrorLog(
       ERROR_NUMBER int NOT NULL,
       ERROR_LOCATION sysname NOT NULL,
       ERROR_MESSAGE varchar(4000),
       ERROR_DATE datetime NULL
            CONSTRAINT dfltErrorLog_error_date  DEFAULT (getdate()),
       ERROR_USER sysname NOT NULL
            --use original_login to capture the user name of the actual user
            --not a user they have impersonated
            CONSTRAINT dfltErrorLog_error_user_name DEFAULT (original_login())
)
```

I also created a stored procedure named utility.ErrorLog$insert for inserting data in this table. Presumably, if you do something like this for one of your databases, you are going to want to do it for every database. Not only is it a good idea to have a table to store the errors that have occurred, but it is a good idea that every database developer in your organization use the same objects/API. There are quite a few little things that you could use and hence standardize on. For example:

- *Security objects*: For example, a function that reads security information from a table, from the logged-in user, or from the contextInfo for a connection, depending on your security needs.

- *Schema management functions*: Functions to manage indexes (such as disabling all indexes), drop all constraints, and so on. These would be objects that you would want to be very careful with.

- *DBA tool tables*: Table rowcount history, logs, and so on. Other examples could center around performance tuning tools.

- *Common libraries of functionality*: For example, if you have a date function that gives you time zone–corrected times.

- *Configuration values/constants*: Since SQL Server doesn't have global constants, it is a common task to create a table to hold configuration properties. Usually a common EAV-style solution (as presented earlier) will suffice nicely, with a function that takes the name of the constant as a parameter and returns the value.

There are three main considerations for how to manage these types of objects. The first is where to put them. In the days of yore, it was commonplace to add many objects to the master database. I am very much against this practice today, because it causes versioning issues galore (which is part of the second consideration). I think the best idea is to create most of your objects in every database individually (some of the history tools could be an exception, because you might use a tool to provide that sort of monitoring that has its own database). I always use a schema that is appropriate (and not the same as the data) for these things that you can lock down (which requires the nonuse of db_owner roles as well as dbdatareader, which is something I will discuss more in Chapter 8).

---

**Note** The code downloads for this book include examples of some of the just-mentioned APIs. For example, in Chapter 6, I implemented a standard utility.errorLog table and procedure, as well as an object to map constraints to error messages called utility.errorMap.

---

The second consideration is versioning. By keeping objects in your local database rather than some database you create (or even master, which was a common practice in much earlier versions of SQL Server), you can change them out at an interval that is right for your other database code. By putting common code in a central location, you start your own version of DLL hell that makes it necessary to be very backward compatible with all your code.

Lastly, distribution is a question. You can place your objects in the model database or keep a script to create those objects in other databases. The main goal is that you have version information for what version a database is currently running and methods to upgrade from version to version as time passes. For this reason, I suggest having two classes of common objects that you will implement: client facing (meaning the programmers/users have the rights to use these objects and the right to expect them not to fall apart on them) and internal. Internal objects can be dropped and added with no business impact, whereas the client-facing ones must be treated like first-class citizens of the database.

# Anti-patterns

In many ways, you, as a reader so far in the book, probably think that I worship Codd and all of his rules with such reverence that I would get together an army of vacuuming robots and start a crusade in his name (and if you are still looking for pictures of hot "models" in this book, you now are probably concerned that this is a secret fish worship book), and in a way, you would be correct (other than the worship thing, of course). He was the theorist who got the relational model rolling and put the theories into action for years and years. It has to be noted that his theories have held up for 30 years now and are just now being realized in full as hardware is getting more and more powerful. His goals of an invisible physical layer for the relational user is getting closer and closer, though we still need physical understanding of the data for performance tuning purposes, which is why I reluctantly included Chapter 9 on physical database structures.

That having been said, I am equally open to new ideas. Things like identity columns are offensive to many "purists," and I am very much a big fan of them. For every good idea that comes out to challenge solid theory, there come many that fail to work (can't blame folks for trying). In this section, I will outline three of these practices and explain why I think they are such bad ideas:

- One-size-fits-all domain

- Generic key references

- Overusing unstructured data

There are a few others I need to reiterate (with chapter references), in case you have read only this chapter so far. My goal in this section is to hit upon some patterns that would not come up in the "right" manner of designing a database but are common ideas that designers get when they haven't gone through the heartache of these patterns:

- *Poor normalization practices*: Normalization is an essential part of the process of database design, and it is far easier to achieve than it will seem when you first start. And don't be fooled by people who say that Third Normal Form is the ultimate level; Fourth Normal Form is very important and common as well. (Chapter 4 covers normalization in depth.)

- *Poor domain choices:* Lots of databases just use varchar(50) for every nonkey column, rather than taking the time to determine proper domains for their data. Sometimes this is even true of columns that are related via foreign key and primary key columns, which makes the optimizer work harder. (See Chapter 5.)

- *No standardization of datatypes:* It is a good idea to make sure you use the same sized/typed column whenever you encounter like typed "things." For example, if your company's account number is char(9), just don't have it 20 different ways: varchar(10), varchar(20), char(15), and so on. All of these will store the data lossless, but only char(9) will be best and will help your users to not need to think about how to deal with the data. (See Chapter 5.)

And yes, there are many more things you probably shouldn't do, but these are some of the bigger design-oriented issues that really drive you crazy when you have to deal with the aftermath of them being used.

The most important issue to understand (if Star Trek has taught us nothing) is that if you use one of these anti-patterns along with the other patterns discussed in this chapter, the result will likely be mutual annihilation.

## One-Size-Fits-All Key Domain

Relational databases are based on the fundamental idea that every object represents one and only one thing. There should never be any doubt as to what a piece of data refers to. By tracing through the relationships, from column name to table name to primary key, it should be easy to examine the relationships and know exactly what a piece of data means.

However, oftentimes it will seem reasonable that since domain type data looks the same in almost every table, wouldn't creating just one such table and reusing it in multiple locations be a great idea? This is an idea from people who are architecting a relational database who don't really understand relational database architecture (me included early in my career)—that the more tables there are, the more complex the design will be. So, conversely, condensing multiple tables into a single "catchall" table should simplify the design, right? That sounds logical . . . but at one time giving Pauly Shore the lead in a movie sounded like a good idea.

As an example, consider I am building a database to store customers and orders. I need domain values for the following:

- Customer credit status
- Customer type
- Invoice status
- Invoice line item back order status
- Invoice line item ship via carrier

Why not just use one generic table to hold these domains, as shown in Figure 7-6?

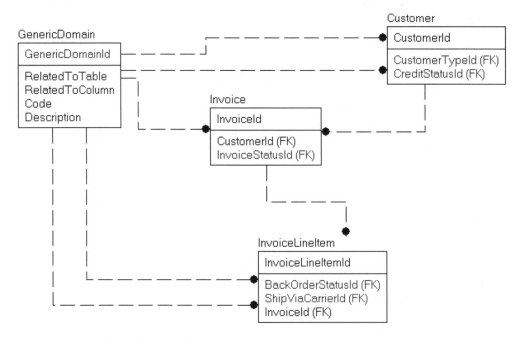

**Figure 7-6.** *One multiuse domain table*

I agree with you if you are thinking that this seems like a very clean way to implement this. In an object-oriented system, you might do something very much like this, but the problem is that it is just not natural to work with in SQL. In many cases, the person who does this does not even think about SQL access. The data in GenericDomain is most likely read into cache in the application and never queried again. Unfortunately, however, this data will need to be used when the data is reported on. For example, say the report writer wants to get the domain values for the Customer table:

```
SELECT *
FROM Customer
  JOIN GenericDomain as CustomerType
    ON Customer.CustomerTypeId = CustomerType.GenericDomainId
      and CustomerType.RelatedToTable = 'Customer'
      and  CustomerType.RelatedToColumn = 'CustomerTypeId'
```

```
JOIN GenericDomain as CreditStatus
  ON  Customer.CreditStatusId = CreditStatus.GenericDomainId
    and CreditStatus.RelatedToTable = 'Customer'
    and CreditStatus.RelatedToColumn = ' CreditStatusId'
```

As you can see, this is far from being a "natural" operation in SQL. It comes down to the problem of mixing apples with oranges. In every usage you will have to identify the apples or oranges so they don't get mixed together. At first glance, domain tables are just an abstract concept of a container that holds text. And from an implementation-centric standpoint, this is quite true, but it is not the correct way to build a database because we never want to mix the rows together as the same thing ever in a query.

Possibly the worst problem is the case of the domain that is used by multiple tables. As an example, consider a domain of countries. If you used this to store the countries of the world and you needed it in multiple places, you would have to duplicate the data. (I used this example because I have actually seen it occur.)

In a database, the process of normalization as a means of breaking down and isolating data takes every table to the point where one table represents one type of thing and one row represents the existence of one of those things. Each domain of values is a distinctly different thing from all the other domains (unless it is not, in which case one table will suffice). So, what you do, in essence, is normalize the data over and over on each usage, spreading the work out over time, rather than doing the task once and getting it over with.

Instead of a single table for all domains, you should model it as shown in Figure 7-7.

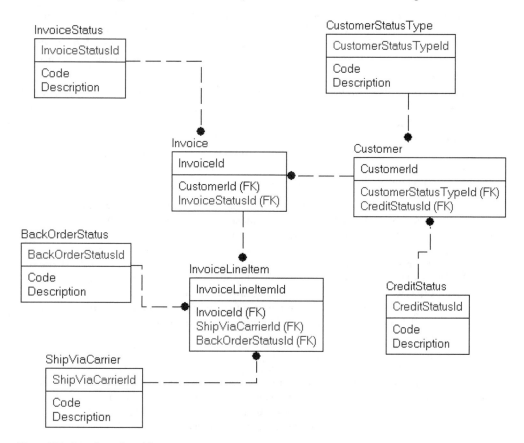

**Figure 7-7.** *One domain table per purpose*

That looks harder to do, right? Well, it is initially (like for the 5 or 10 minutes it takes to create a few tables). Frankly, it took me longer to flesh out the example tables. The fact is, there are quite a few tremendous gains to be had:

- *Using the data in a query is much easier:*

```
SELECT *
FROM   Customer
  JOIN CustomerType
    ON Customer.CustomerTypeId = CustomerType.CustomerTypeId
  JOIN CreditStatus
    ON  Customer.CreditStatusId = CreditStatus.CreditStatusId
```

- *Data can be validated using foreign key constraints:* This was something not feasible for the one-table solution. Now, validation needs to be in triggers or just managed solely by the application.

- *Expandability and control:* If it turns out that you need to keep more information in your domain row, then it is as simple as adding a column or two. For example, if you have a domain of shipping carriers, you might define a `ShipViaCarrier` in your master domain table. In its basic form, you would get only one column for a value for the user to choose. But if you wanted to have more information—such as a long name for reports, as in "United Parcel Service"; a description; and some form of indication when to use this carrier—then you would be forced to implement a table and change all the references to the domain values.

- *Performance considerations:* All of the smaller domain tables will fit on a single page or disk. This ensures a single read (and likely a single page in cache). If the other case, you might have your domain table spread across many pages, unless you cluster on the referring table name, which then could cause it to be more costly to use a nonclustered index if you have many values.

- *You can still make the data look like one table for the application:* There is nothing precluding the developer from building a caching mechanism that melds together all the individual tables to populate the cache and use the data however you want. With some clever use of extended properties, this could be as simple as adding a value to a property and letting a dynamic SQL procedure return all the data. A common concern that developers have is that now they will need 50 editors instead of 1. You can still have one editor for all rows, because most domain tables will likely have the same base structure/usage.

Returning to the logical design, every table should represent one and only one thing. When you see a column in a table by itself, there should be no question as to what it means, and you certainly shouldn't need to go to the table and figure out what the meaning of a value is.

Some tools that implement an "object-oriented" view of a design tend to use this frequently, because it's easy to implement tables such as this and use a cached object. One table means one set of methods instead of hundreds of different methods for hundreds of different objects—er, tables. (The fact that it stinks when you go to use it in the database for queries is of little consequence, because generally systems like this don't intend for you to go into the database and do queries, except through special interfaces that take care of this situation for you.)

## Generic Key References

In an ideal situation, one table is related to another via a key. However, because the structures in SQL Server don't require constraints or any enforcement, this can lead to interesting relationships occurring. What I am referring to here is the case where you have a table that has a primary key that can actually be a value from several different tables, instead of just one.

For example, consider the case where you have several objects, all of which need a reference to one table. In our sample, say you have a customer relationship management system with SalesOrders and TroubleTickets (just these two to keep it simple, but in reality you might have many objects in your database that will fit this scenario). Each of these objects has the need to store journal items, outlining the user's contact with the customer (for example, in the case where you want to make sure not to overcommunicate with a customer!). You might logically draw it up like in Figure 7-8.

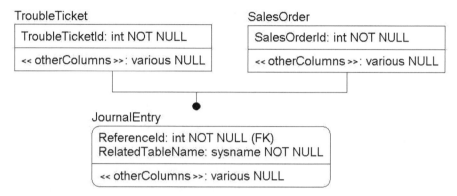

**Figure 7-8.** *Multiple tables related to the same key*

You might initially consider modeling it like a classic subtype relationship, but it really doesn't fit that mold because you probably can have greater than one journal entry per sales order and trouble ticket. Fair enough, each of these relationships is 1–N, where N is between 0 and infinity (though the customer with infinite journal entries must really hate you). Having all parents relate to the same column is a possible solution to the problem, but not really a very favorable one. For our table in this scenario, we build something like this:

```
CREATE TABLE SalesOrder
(
    SalesOrderId <int or uniqueidentifier> PRIMARY KEY,
    <other columns>
)
CREATE TABLE TroubleTicket
(
    TroubleTicketId <int or uniqueidentifier> PRIMARY KEY,
    <other columns>
)
CREATE TABLE JournalEntry
(
    JournalEntryId  <int or uniqueidentifier>,
    RelatedTableName sysname,
    PRIMARY KEY (JournalEntryId, RelatedTableName)
    <other columns>
)
```

Now, to use this data, you have to indicate the table you want to join to, which is very much a non-natural way to do a join. You can use a universally unique GUID key so that all references to the data in the table are unique, eliminating the need for the specifically specified related table name. However, I find when this method is employed if the RelatedTableName is actually used, it is far clearer to the user what is happening.

A major concern with this method is that you cannot use constraints to enforce the relationships; you need either to use triggers or to trust the middle layers to validate data values, which definitely increases the costs of implementation/testing since you have to verify that it works in all cases, which is something we trust for constraints; even triggers are implemented in one single location.

One reason this method is employed is that it is very easy to add references to the one table. You just put the key value and table name in there, and you are done. Unfortunately, for the people who have to use this for years and years to come, well, it would have just been easier to spend a bit longer and do some more work because the generic relationship means that using a constraint is not possible to validate keys, leaving open the possibility of orphaned data.

A second way to do this that is marginally better is to just include keys from all tables, like this:

```
CREATE TABLE JournalEntry
(
    JournalEntryId  <int or uniqueidentifier> PRIMARY KEY,
    SalesOrderId <int or uniqueidentifier> NULL REFERERENCES
                                        SalesOrder(SalesOrderId),
    TroubleTicketId <int or uniqueidentifier> NULL REFERERENCES
                                        TroubleTicket(TroubleTicketId),
    <other columns>
)
```

This is better in that now joins are clearer and the values are enforced by constraints, but now you have one more problem (that I conveniently left out of the initial description). What if you need to store some information about the reason for the journal entry? For example, for an order, are you commenting in the journal for a cancelation notice?

There is also the matter of Fourth Normal Form concerns, since each of the related values doesn't exactly relate to the key in the same way. It seems like a decent idea that one JournalEntry might relate to more than one SalesOrder or JournalEntry. So, the better idea is to model it more like Figure 7-9.

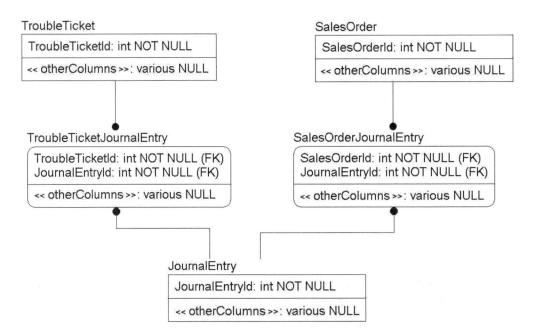

**Figure 7-9.** *Objects linked for maximum usability/flexibility*

```
CREATE TABLE JournalEntry
(
    JournalEntryId  <int or uniqueidentifier> PRIMARY KEY,
    <other columns>
)
CREATE TABLE SalesOrderJournalEntry
(
    JournalEntryId <int or uniqueidentifier>
                    REFERENCES JournalEntry(JournalId),
    SalesOrderId <int or uniqueidentifier>,
                    REFERENCES SalesOrder(SalesOrderId),
    <SalesOrderSpecificColumns>
    PRIMARY KEY (JournalEntryId, SalesOrderId)
)
CREATE TABLE TroubleTicketJournalEntry
(
    JournalEntryId <int or uniqueidentifier>
                    REFERENCES JournalEntry(JournalId),
    TroubleTicketId <int or uniqueidentifier>,
                    REFERENCES TroubleTicket (TroubleTicketId),
    <TroubleTicketSpecificColumns>
    PRIMARY KEY (JournalEntryId, SalesOrderId)
)
```

Yes, this takes longer to code and build. I will not dispute that; in fact, unless this is the first section of the book you have read, you know that some extra up-front work is pretty much a theme of this book. Just like any job done well, if you know what you are doing, it takes a bit longer than if you just blindly do whatever seems right initially. There are very often twists and turns in the road that you would have never thought of. For example, when painting a house, you can paint over the cracked dead paint very quickly, but then you have to repaint. Do it right, and it will last for years and years.

Note that this database is far more self-documented as well. You can easily find the relationships between the tables and join on them. Yes, there are a few more tables, but that can play to your benefit as well in some scenarios, but most important, you can represent any data you need to represent, in any cardinality or combination of cardinalities needed. This is the goal in almost any design.

## Overusing Unstructured Data

As much as I would like to deny it, or at least find some way to avoid it, people need to have unstructured notes to store various bits and pieces of information about their data. I will confess that a large number of the tables I have created in my career included some column that allowed users to insert whatever into. In the early days, it was a varchar(256) column, then varchar(8000) or text, and now varchar(max). It is not something that you can get away from because users need this scratchpad just slightly more than Linus needs his security blanket. And it is not such a terrible practice, to be honest. What is the harm in letting the user have a place to note that the person has special requirements when you go out to lunch?

Nothing much, except that far too often what happens is that notes become a replacement for the types of stuff that I mentioned in the "User-Specified Data" section or, when this is a corporate application, the types of columns that you could go in and create in 10 minutes or about 2 days including testing and deployment. Once the user does something once and particularly finds it useful, they will do it again. And they tell their buddies, "Hey, I have started using notes to indicate that the order needs processing. Saved me an hour yesterday . . ." Don't get me wrong, I have nothing against users saving time, but in the end everyone needs to work together.

See, if storing some value unstructured in a notes column saves the user any time at all (considering that most likely it will require a non-indexed search or a one-at-a-time manual search), just think what having a column in the database could do that can be easily manipulated, indexed, searched on, and oblivious to the spelling habits of the average human being. And what happens when a user decides that they can come up with a "better" way and practices change, or, worse, everyone has their own practices?

Probably the most common use of this I have seen that concerns me is contact notes. I have done this myself in the past, where you have a column that contains formatted text something like the following on a `Customer` table. Users can add new notes but usually are not allowed to go back and change the notes.

```
ContactNotes
---------------------------------------------------------------------------
2008-01-11 - Stuart Pidd -Spoke to Fred on the phone.  Said that his wangle was
broken, referencing Invoice 20001.  Told him I would check and call back
tomorrow.
2008-02-15 - Stuart Pidd - Fred called back, stating his wangle was still
broken, and now it had started to dangle.  Will call back tomorrow.
2008-04-12 - Norm Oliser - Stu was fired for not taking care of one of our best
customers.
```

I could almost write another full section on why this is horrible (I won't, but I could), but what a terrible waste of data. The proper solution would be to take this data that is being stored into this text column and apply the rigors of normalization to it. Clearly, in this example, you can see three "rows" of data, with at least three "columns." So instead of having a `Customer` table with a `ContactNotes` column, implement the tables like this:

```
CREATE TABLE Customer
(
      CustomerId    int    CONSTRAINT PKCustomer PRIMARY KEY
      <other columns>
)
CREATE TABLE CustomerContactNotes
(
      CustomerId  int,
      NoteTime    datetime,
      PRIMARY KEY (CustomerId, NoteTime),
      UserId  datatype, --references the User table
      Notes varchar(max)
)
```

You might even stretch this to the model we discussed earlier with the journal entries where the notes are a generic part of the system and can refer to the customer, multiple customers, and other objects in the database. This might even link to a reminder system to remind Stu to get back to Fred, and he would not now be jobless. Though one probably should have expected such out of a guy named Stu Pidd (ba boom ching).

Even using XML to store the notes in this structured manner would be an amazing improvement. You could then determine who entered the notes, what the day was, and what the notes were, and you could fashion a UI that allowed the users to add new fields to the XML, right on the fly. What a tremendous benefit to your users and, let's face it, to the people who have to go in and answer questions like this: "How many times have we talked to this client by phone?"

The point of this section is simply this: educate your users. Give them a place to write the random note, but teach them that when they start to use notes to store the same sorts of things over and over, their jobs could be easier if you gave them a place to store their values that would be searchable, repeatable, and so on. Plus, never again would you have to write queries to "mine" information from notes.

# Summary

This chapter was dedicated to expanding the way you think about tables and to giving you some common solutions to problems that are themselves common. I was careful not to get too esoteric with my topics in this chapter. The point was simply to cover some solutions that are a bit beyond the basic table structures I covered in Chapter 6, but not so beyond them that the average reader would say "Bah!" to the whole chapter as a waste of time.

There are many uses for a sequence table, but the most commonly used is breaking a comma-delimited list into rows. Try as we may, comma-delimited lists are just too prevalent and will just not go away, even with the table type now allowed for parameters of objects. Having a technique to work with them is no excuse to make more use of comma-delimited lists, of course, but even if Sheriff Taylor didn't carry a gun, he always had one in the gun case if he needed one. Having a technique in your repertoire doesn't make it right, but it makes it available for use if needed.

It is rare that a system won't need reports broken down by time, so we looked at how to build and use a calendar table. Calendar tables are an amazingly valuable part of your toolkit and will give you access to ranges and groupings that were next to impossible just using the system functions.

Then came techniques for storing large binary objects, because the choice of where to store binary objects gets more interesting in SQL Server 2008. SQL Server 2008 will really change the landscape of how binary objects can be dealt with in your relational data. It isn't as perfect as getting Windows directory level access to the data, but if you are using the right API, you can get that kind of performance. Also, storing a filename reference directly in SQL Server is still available and useful.

The last technique I covered in a positive light was dealing with user-specified data. Open schema, loose schema, property tables, whatever you call it, the goal is to let Joe User tweak your schema and store what they want. It isn't always what you want to let happen, but in the end nearly every user is going to need somewhere to store data that you didn't think about, and if you cannot react quickly enough to their needs, they will find somewhere to store it (that you may not like).

This brings me to the last section on anti-patterns. One of the bad practices outlined was over-using unstructured data. This isn't always the fault of the architect at design time to give the users a place to enter whatever they want. More often, it is the users finding a place to stuff data that they need to store into some place where it doesn't go because it was more convenient to ask the dev staff for help. If you have ever found weird data in a tech column, particularly if there was a pattern to the values you found, you might be looking at one such situation. The users didn't need a middle name column, but they did need to hold their widget number references. Bam, problem solved, for them.

We also looked at a few structural possibilities that make working with relational data more challenging, including one domain table to cover all domains and having many parents relating to the same child by the same key. Regardless of how you feel about children, it definitely doesn't take a village to manage a single key.

# The Continuing Story of the Book So Far

Wow, you're awesome to have made it this far, unless you're still flipping around for the pictures of models, or possibly you're wondering why there is only one Dilbert cartoon in this book. (That's because I could afford one only; perhaps if you bought a thousand copies of my book, next time I will put in two or maybe even three.)

If you're at this point in the process, you should celebrate, because essentially you're largely done with the implementation of the database (yes, you will almost certainly have to go back and make changes as the project progresses, but if not, you could be let go and have to break in new programmers to the idea of normalization).

Let's recap:

- In the first part of the book, we defined data needs and formed a logical model.

- This logical model was taken and fitted for implementation in the RDBMS as follows:

  - We added columns to assist in using the data.

  - We chose datatypes to match up with our data needs.

  - We implemented keys by which to identify our data.

  - We added foreign keys to make sure that relationship data always has proper matches, so our joins don't give us spurious results.

  - We added default constraints to make data entry easier.

  - We used CHECK constraints to make sure that the data in each row meets basic row-level criteria.

  - We added triggers to do the heavy lifting for validations across rows, tables, databases, or even servers.

- We briefly discussed how non-database code is used to make sure that our data meets the ever-changing rule set that dynamic businesses often require.

- Finally, we looked at some additional tweaks to the design that you could make to ease in querying and storing certain types of data, along with some patterns to avoid.

One word of caution: I know this database design stuff can get pretty compelling, but if your spouse is yelling at you to put down the darn book and come to the bedroom, put the book down. I can't promise it isn't a trap to get you to clean the bathroom, but I also can't promise it isn't something else entirely. All I can promise is that the book will still be there tomorrow, and your spouse may not (besides, your bathroom may need cleaning! I also refuse to testify on your behalf at the divorce hearings; you are on your own).

That being done, it is time to switch gears one more time (consider this little section the clutch) and start putting the finishing touches on the system, such as the following:

- Securing access to the data

- Working with the physical model and looking at the optimum ways to work with SQL Server data (the "optimization" part of the book title), including table structures and indexing

- Discussing how to maximize the number of users who can concurrently access the system, particularly working with the same data all at once

- Talking a bit about the finer points of structuring SQL code to access the data

- Finally, priming you on some of the things you should think about if you're going to be using your same design on multiple database server platforms

So hang on, we are really close to the end of the process, though not really to the end of the book.

# CHAPTER 8

■ ■ ■

# Securing Access to the Data

*"Today you can go to a gas station and find the cash register open and the toilets locked. They must think toilet paper is worth more than money."*

—Joey Bishop

Look at the quote at the beginning of this chapter. True, isn't it? In the average office building it is harder for the average person to get office supplies than it is to access important, even damaging, personal information. In my home city of Nashville, Tennessee, thieves broke into the Election Commission and stole laptops with all the names of the voters for the city. What the devil were the people thinking who allowed this data to reside on a portable device? The election administrator was quoted as saying "Thank goodness they didn't get the whole Social Security number." All they got was the name, address, phone number, and last four digits of our Social Security numbers. Golly, wasn't that enough?

So, why do I tell this sordid story? If you are the architect of a database system that holds personal and private information, it could be you who is jobless on a fairly permanent basis if it turns out to be your fault that data leaks out into the hands of some junkie looking for stuff to hock.

Security is on the minds of everyone today, as evidenced by the constant stream of privacy policies that we come across these days. They're *everywhere*, and if your company does business with anyone, it likely has one too. And let's be clear, for too many organizations, security is implemented by hoping users aren't adventurous enough to click a button or two. Of course, fear of joblessness is a good motivator, and luckily most average users aren't that adventurous or they'd find that they probably have incredible power to see more than they probably need to see.

At this point, we need to agree on one term, and that is *average user*. This is the user for whom the system in question was built, be it an employee or a customer. It's reasonably beyond the scope of this chapter to consider measures for protecting data from superusers with high-privilege accounts (db_owner or higher), such as DBAs or programming staff. I will discuss some strategies, but since a user with high privileges has to set up these measures, they could also unset them for a time being if they wanted. Further, because our focus is on the database, I'll avoid any in-depth discussion of exactly how data access applications will use the security, such as whether to use trusted connections (Windows Authentication) or SQL Server Standard security. That isn't to say that if the database were secured in a proper manner structurally, that the election administrator's job in Tennessee wouldn't have been easier. His quote could have said, "Yes, our database was taken, but it is encrypted with . . . and it would take (on average) 17.8 years to crack the encryption without the key, which was not stored on the same media as the encrypted data." Then it would just be the guy who runs the physical security for the office building's head in the guillotine.

In this chapter, I will focus on database-level security, so I won't cover many security precautions that are implemented outside the database (such as firewalls). It also assumes that certain measures have been put in place to protect your system from malicious hackers. For example, I assume the following:

- Strong passwords have been applied to all accounts—certainly all known system accounts (such as sa, if you haven't changed the name). *Certainly there are no blank passwords for any accounts!*

- SQL Server isn't just sitting unguarded on the Web, with no firewall and no logging of failed login attempts.

- The guest user has been removed from all databases where it isn't necessary.

- You've guarded against SQL injection accounts by avoiding query strings whereby a user could simply inject SELECT * FROM sys.sql_logins and get a list of all your logins in a textbox in your application. (Chapter 11 mentions SQL injection again, where I contrast ad hoc SQL with stored procedures.)

- You've secured access to your application passwords and put them where only the necessary people can see them (such as the DBA and the application programmers who use them in their code) and have encrypted the password into application code modules when using application logins.

- You've made certain that few people have file-level access to the server where the data is stored and, probably more important, where the backups are stored. If one malicious user has access to your backup file or tape, then that person has access to your data by simply attaching that file to a different server, and you can't stop him or her from accessing the data (even encryption isn't 100 percent secure if the hacker has unlimited time).

---

■**Note**  To make SQL Server as secure as possible "out of the box," many features are disabled by default and have to be enabled explicitly before you can use them. For example, remote admin connections, Database Mail, CLR programming, and others are all "off by default." You can enable these features and others using the sp_configure stored procedure.

---

Because this is a database design and implementation book, this chapter focuses squarely on security from the *database* perspective. We'll consider the security features that we might need to design into our physical schema, to control and monitor what data can be accessed by certain users, what data can be seen, and so on. I'll cover some of the common SQL Server security techniques you can use to protect your data from unauthorized viewing and access, including the following:

- *Controlling data access*: I demonstrate how to do this using permissions and by giving users access to coded objects rather than the underlying database tables.

- *Obfuscating sensitive data*: You can use encryption to do this so that if a user does somehow gain "rogue" access to the database, this data remains protected.

- *Monitoring and auditing user actions*: You can watch users, so you can go back after the fact and identify any improper usage.

---

■**Note**  You can place the code in this chapter in any database. I include a CREATE DATABASE SecurityChapter statement in the downloadable code for this book (in the Source Code/Downloads area of the Apress website at http://www.apress.com). I also include a script to clean up the many users that will be created. I suggest that you not execute the scripts from this chapter on a production server, because you'll be creating many system-level logins, which might make the DBA mad (unless you're the DBA, and then you'd simply be mad at me).

---

I should also note that not everyone will use many, if any, of the guidelines in this chapter in their security implementations. Often it's left to the application layer to do the security, showing or hiding functionality from the user. This is a common approach, but it can leave gaps in security, especially when you have to give users ad hoc access to the database or you have multiple user interfaces that have to implement different methods of security. My advice is to make use of the permissions in the database server as much as possible. However, having the application layer control security isn't a tremendous hole in the security, as long as the passwords used are seriously complex and well guarded. Later in the chapter, the "Application Roles" section presents an approach to this sort of security. This approach can be useful for implementing database-server permissions without having to lose the identity of the user.

# Principals and Securables

The SQL Server 2005 security model relies on the concepts of *principals* and *securables*. Principals are those objects that may be granted permission to access particular database objects, while *securables* are those objects to which access can be controlled.

Principals can represent a *specific user*, a *role* that may be adopted by multiple users, or an *application*. SQL Server divides principals into three classes:

- *Windows principals*: These represent Windows user accounts or groups, authenticated using Windows security.

- *SQL Server principals*: These are server-level logins or groups that are authenticated using SQL Server security.

- *Database principals*: These include database users, groups, and roles, as well as application roles.

In this chapter, I'll focus on what you can do to secure the data in the database. I won't cover how the user gets access to the server via some Windows or SQL Server principal in any depth, other than to create test logins to support the examples. SQL Server 2005 gives you a rich set of ways for a user to connect, including using certificates to connect with.

On the other hand, the important aspects relevant to database design are pretty straightforward. Database principals are users who are members of roles. You can map database principals to server principals, so when setting up security on a database server, most security is applied to database roles. For most normal, non-DBA, non-programmer–type users, at a system level the only thing granted to a user is access to databases.

Inside the database, database roles (groups of users and other roles) and users are granted rights to use database objects. Best practice is to set up roles to grant rights to, putting database users in the roles. I talk more about roles and users in the "Permissions" section.

---

■**Caution** Most of the examples in this book grant rights to users, only to keep the examples reasonable to follow. Use roles for almost every right you grant in the database, except where it makes sense for exceptions (for example, if you want to give rights to one user only as a very special case, possibly even temporarily).

---

*Securables* are the database objects to which you can control access and to which you can grant principals permissions. SQL Server 2005 distinguishes between three scopes at which different objects can be secured:

- *Server scope*: Server-scoped securables include logins, HTTP endpoints, event notifications, and databases. These are objects that exist at the server level, outside of any individual database, and to which access is controlled on a server-wide basis.

- *Database scope*: Securables with database scope are objects such as schemas, users, roles, and CLR assemblies, which exist inside a particular database but not within a schema.

- *Schema scope*: This group includes those objects that reside within a schema in a database, such as tables, views, and stored procedures. A SQL Server 2005 schema corresponds roughly to the owner of a set of objects (such as dbo) in SQL Server 2000.

In this chapter, I'll focus on objects at the database and schema scope, focusing more on schema scope objects, because this is generally what you need to know in terms of database implementation.

# Database Security Overview

Permissions are the rights, granted (or denied) to a principal, to access some securable. I'll cover the basics of database permissions for a foundation of best practices. Taken to the full extreme there is an extensive set of things that are considered securable, especially at the server level, but 90+ percent of security for the average DBA (and certainly a data architect, as is the main focus of this book) is securing tables, views, and procedures, and this is what's primarily interesting from a database-design standpoint.

At the database level, there are two main types of principals, the *user* and the *role*. A user represents the mapping from either a Windows Authenticated User or Group or a SQL Server Standard Login (which has a username and password managed by SQL Server). It is best to use Windows Authenticated principals as much as possible, since they are more secure than are standard logins, but as far as we are concerned, it is not important which method you use. The database implementation will be essentially the same.

The next principal is a role. The role is a way to set up different functional roles and then assign a user or group (the name it used to have) of users to it. The very best practice for assigning security to database principals is to nearly always use roles, even if you have only a single user in a role. It may sound like more work, but in the end the practice makes keeping rights straight between your development and production environments (and all environments in between) coordinated. The roles will be the same in all areas; the users who are associated with the roles need not change.

I'll cover the following topics, which revolve around giving users permissions to use securables:

- *User impersonation*: This allows one user to impersonate another user temporarily. User impersonation is used often in testing security but can also be used in an object to give a user enhanced security for the life of the procedures.

- *Grantable permissions*: This section covers the different sorts of database permissions and how to grant and revoke permission on securables.

- *Roles and schemas*: You'll learn how to use roles and schemas to grant rights efficiently to database securables.

These three topics will give you most of the information you need to know about setting up your database-level security.

# Impersonation

Ideally, this section on impersonation would not be the first section in this chapter with real examples. However, the ability to pretend to be another user is fairly important when it comes to testing security. Impersonation is in fact one of the most important tools you will need when you are testing your security configuration. It is common to get a call from a client after some code has been migrated to production who claims that they cannot do something that you think they really ought to be able to do. Since all system problems are inevitably blamed on the database first, it is a useful trick to impersonate the user and then try the questioned code in Management Studio to see whether it is a security problem. If the code works in Management Studio, your job is almost certainly done from a database standpoint, and you can point your index finger at some other part of the system.

To demonstrate security in a reasonable manner on a single SQL Server connection, I will use a feature that was new to SQL Server 2005. In 2000 and earlier, if the person with admin rights wanted to impersonate another user, he used SETUSER. For our examples, SETUSER would have been sufficient, but SETUSER was never a good tool to use in your production code. Instead, you should impersonate another user using the EXECUTE AS statement. You can impersonate any server login or a database user principal, and you get all rights that user has (and consequently lose the rights you previously had). You can go back to the previous security context by executing REVERT.

---

■**Note** For a non-dbo or sa user to use EXECUTE AS, the user must have IMPERSONATE permissions on the specified login name or username that they are trying to impersonate.

---

As an example, I'll show a way that you can have a user impersonating a member of the server-system sysadmin role. Using impersonation in such a way takes some getting used to, but it certainly makes it easier to have full sysadmin power only when it's needed. As said previously, there are lots of server privileges, so you can mete out rights that are needed on a day-to-day basis and reserve the "dangerous" ones like DROP DATABASE only for logins that you have to impersonate.

As an example (and this is the kind of example that I'll have throughout this chapter), we first create a login that we never expect to be logged into directly. I use a standard login, but you could map it to a certificate, a key, a Windows user, or whatever. Standard logins make it much easier to test situations and learn from them because they're self-contained. Then we add the login to the sysadmin role. You probably also want to use a name that isn't so obviously associated with system administration. If a hacker got into your list of users somehow, the name 'itchy' wouldn't so obviously be able to do serious damage to your database server as would a name like 'godlikelogin'.

---

■**Caution** You might not want to execute this code on your server.

---

```
CREATE LOGIN system_admin WITH PASSWORD = 'tooHardToEnterAndNoOneKnowsIt'
EXEC sp_addsrvrolemember 'system_admin','sysadmin'
```

Then we create a regular login (again standard, but whenever possible a normal user's login should use integrated security) and give rights to impersonate the system_admin user:

```
CREATE LOGIN louis with PASSWORD = 'reasonable', DEFAULT_DATABASE=tempdb

--Must execute in Master Database
USE MASTER
GRANT IMPERSONATE ON LOGIN::system_admin TO louis;
```

> **Tip** Defaulting the database to the `tempdb` for system administrator–type users is useful because it requires a conscious effort to go to a user database and start building objects, or even dropping them. However, any work done in `tempdb` is deleted when the server is stopped. This is actually one of those things that will save you more times than you might imagine. Often a script gets created and the database is not specified, and I have built more test objects on my local SQL Server in `master` than I care to admit. Avoid that trouble by specifying `tempdb` as your default database.

We log in as the user, `louis`, and try to run the following code (in Management Studio, you can just right-click in the query window to use the Connection ➤ Change Connection context menu and use a standard login):

```
USE AdventureWorks2008
```

The following error is raised:

```
Msg 916, Level 14, State 1, Line 1
The server principal "louis" is not able to access the database "AdventureWorks2008"
under the current security context.
```

Now, we change security context to the `system_admin` user:

```
EXECUTE AS LOGIN = 'system_admin'
```

We now have control of the server in that window as the `system_admin` user! To look at the security context, you can use several variables/functions. The following code:

```
USE     AdventureWorks2008
SELECT user as [user], system_user as [system_user],
       original_login() as [original_login]
```

will return the following:

- user: Gives the name of context for the user in the database
- system_user: Specifies the name of context for the login
- original_login(): Gives the login name of the user who actually logged in to start the connection (this is an important function that you should use when logging which login performed an action)

This returns the following result:

```
user                 system_user          original_login
-----------------    -----------------    -----------------
dbo                  system_admin         louis
```

Then you execute the following code:

```
REVERT --go back to previous context
```

We see the following result:

```
Msg 15447, Level 16, State 1, Line 1
The current security context cannot be reverted. Please switch to the original
database where 'Execute As' was called and try it again.
```

You started in `tempdb`, so you use the following code:

```
USE tempdb

REVERT
SELECT user
```

This returns the following result:

```
----------------
guest
```

Impersonation gives you a lot of control over what a user can do and allows you to situationally play one role or another, such as creating a new database. I'll use impersonation for many situations to change security context to demonstrate security concepts.

■**Note** The user here is `guest`, which is a user I recommend that you consider disabling in every non-system database unless it is specifically needed. Disable `guest` by executing `REVOKE CONNECT FROM GUEST`. You cannot disable the `guest` user in the `tempdb` or `master` database, because users must have access to these databases to do any work. Trying to disable `guest` in these databases will result in the following message: "`Cannot disable access to the guest user in master or tempdb`".

Using impersonation, you can execute your code as a member of the `sysadmin` server or `db_owner` database role and then test your code as a typical user without opening multiple connections (and making the sample code considerably easier to follow).

# Permissions

Using SQL Server security, you can easily build a security plan that prevents unwanted usage of your objects by any user. You can control rights to almost every object type, and in SQL Server 2005 you can secure a tremendous number of object types. For our purposes here, I'll cover data-oriented security specifically, limited to the objects and the actions you can give or take away access to (see Table 8-1).

**Table 8-1.** *Database Objects and Permissions*

| Object Type | Permission Type |
|---|---|
| Tables | SELECT, INSERT, UPDATE, DELETE, REFERENCES |
| Views | SELECT, INSERT, UPDATE, DELETE |
| Columns (view and table) | SELECT, INSERT, UPDATE, DELETE |
| Functions | EXECUTE (scalar) SELECT (table valued) |
| Stored procedures | EXECUTE |

Most of these are straightforward and probably are familiar if you've done any SQL Server administration, although perhaps REFERENCES isn't familiar. This is for the situation in which tables are owned by schemas that are then owned by different principals. If you wanted to apply a foreign key between the tables, you'd be required to give the child table REFERENCES permissions.

You can then grant or deny usage of these objects to the roles that have been created. SQL Server uses three different commands to give or take away rights from each of your roles:

- GRANT: Gives the privilege to use an object.

- DENY: Denies access to an object, regardless of whether the user has been granted the privilege from any other role.

- REVOKE: Used to remove any GRANT or DENY permissions statements that have been applied to an object. This behaves like a delete of an applied permission.

Typically, you'll simply give permissions to a role to perform tasks that are specific to the role. You should use the DENY command only as an "extreme" type of command, because no matter how many other times the user has been granted privileges to an object, the user won't have access to it while there's one DENY.

As an example, consider that you have an Invoice table. If you wanted to remove access to this table from user Steve because of a job change, you'd execute a REVOKE. If Steve was in another group that had rights to the Invoice table, he could still access it. If you used DENY, Steve would lose rights to the object completely, even if another manager GRANTed rights.

Once you've built all your objects—including tables, stored procedures, views, and so on—you can grant rights to them. For stored procedures, views, and functions, as long as the owner of the object is the same, you don't have to grant rights to the underlying objects that are used in these objects.

For example, to give a privilege on a table or stored procedure to a user, the command would be as follows:

```
GRANT <privilege> ON <object> to <userName>
```

Next, if you want to remove the privilege, you have two choices. You can either REVOKE the permission, which just deletes the granted permission, or you can DENY the permission. Execute the following:

```
REVOKE <privilege> ON <object> to <userName>
```

I haven't covered role membership yet (it's covered later in the chapter), but if the user were a member of a role that had access to this object, the user would still have access. However, execute the following code:

```
DENY <privilege> ON <object> to <userName>
```

Because of the DENY command, the users will not be able to access the object, regardless of any right granted to them. To remove the DENY, you again use the REVOKE command. This will all become clearer when I cover roles later in the chapter, but in our experience, DENY isn't a typical thing to use on a principal's privilege set. It's punitive in nature and is confusing to the average user. More commonly, users are given rights and not denied access.

To see the user's rights in the database, you can use the sys.database_permissions catalog view. For example, use the following code to see all the rights that have been granted in the database:

```
SELECT object_name(major_id), permission_name, state_desc,
       user_name(grantee_principal_id) as Grantee
FROM   sys.database_permissions
WHERE  objectproperty(major_id,'isTable') = 1
  AND  objectproperty(major_id,'isMsShipped') = 0
```

For more information on the security catalog views, check Books Online.

# Controlling Access to Objects

One of the worst things that can happen in an organization is for a user to see data out of context and start a worry- or gossip-fest. Creating roles and associating users with them is a fairly easy task and is usually worth the effort. Once you've set up the security for a database using sufficient object groupings (as specific as need be, of course), management can be relatively straightforward.

Your goal is to allow the users to perform whatever tasks they need to but to prohibit any other tasks and not to let them see any data that they shouldn't. You can control access at several levels. At a high level, you might want to grant (or deny) a principal access to all invoices—in which case you might control access at the level of a table. At a more granular level, you might want to control access to certain columns or rows within that table. In a more functional approach, you might give rights only to use stored procedures to access data. All these approaches are commonly used in the same database in some way, shape, or form.

In this section, I'll cover table and column security as it's done using the built-in vanilla security, before moving on to the more complex strategies I'll outline during the rest of the book.

> **Note** In this chapter, you'll be creating a lot of logins that are based on the Standard security type. In general, it's best to create your logins using Windows Authentication mode, but in an example space, it's far too difficult to pull off, because we would need to create local or domain groups and logins. Database security is not significantly affected by using either the Standard or Windows Authentication mode. You may substitute any Windows Authentication login in lieu of the standard users if your server doesn't allow standard authentication.

## Table Security

As already mentioned, for tables at an object level, you can grant a principal rights to INSERT, UPDATE, DELETE, or SELECT data from a table. This is the most basic form of security when dealing with data. The goal when using table-based security is to keep users looking at, or modifying, the entire set of data, rather than specific rows. We'll progress to the specific security types as we move through the chapter.

> **Note** As mentioned in the introduction to this section, all objects should be owned by the same user for most normal databases (not to be confused with the owner from the previous versions of SQL Server), so we won't deal with the REFERENCES permission type.

As an example of table security, you'll create a new table, and I'll demonstrate, through the use of a new user, what the user can and cannot do.

```
--start with a new schema for this test
CREATE SCHEMA TestPerms
GO

CREATE TABLE TestPerms.TableExample
(
    TableExampleId int identity(1,1)
                CONSTRAINT PKTableExample PRIMARY KEY,
    Value   varchar(10)
)
```

Then create a new user, not associating it with a login. You won't need a login for many of the examples, because you'll use impersonation to pretend to be the user without logging in.

---

■**Note** The ability to have a user without login privileges allows you to have objects in the database that aren't actually owned by a particular login, making managing objects cleaner, particularly when you drop a login.

---

```
CREATE USER Tony WITHOUT LOGIN
```

You change to impersonate user Tony and try to create a new row:

```
EXECUTE AS USER = 'Tony'
INSERT INTO TestPerms.TableExample(Value)
VALUES ('a row')
```

Well, as you would expect, here's the result:

---

```
Msg 229, Level 14, State 5, Line 2
INSERT permission denied on object 'TableExample', database 'SecurityChapter',
schema 'TestPerms'.
```

---

You then go back to being the dbo using the REVERT command, give the user rights, return to being Tony, and try to insert again:

```
REVERT
GRANT INSERT on TestPerms.TableExample to Tony

EXECUTE AS USER = 'Tony'
INSERT INTO TestPerms.TableExample(Value)
VALUES ('a row')
```

No errors here. Now, because Tony just created the row, the user should be able to select the row, right?

```
SELECT TableExampleId, value
FROM   TestPerms.TableExample
```

No, the user had rights only to INSERT data, not to view it:

---

```
Msg 229, Level 14, State 5, Line 1
SELECT permission denied on object 'tableExample', database 'SecurityChapter',
schema 'TestPerms'.
```

---

Now, you can give the user Tony rights to SELECT data from the table using the following GRANT statement:

```
REVERT
GRANT SELECT on TestPerms.TableExample to Tony
```

The SELECT statement does return data. At a table level, you can do this for the four DML statements: INSERT, UPDATE, DELETE, and SELECT.

## Column-Level Security

For the most part, it's enough simply to limit a user's access to data at a table or view level, but as the next two major sections will discuss, sometimes the security needs to be more granular. Sometimes you need to restrict users to using merely part of a table. In this section, I'll look at the security syntax that SQL Server provides at a basic level to grant rights at a column level. Later in the chapter, I'll present other methods that use views or stored procedures.

For our example, we'll create a couple database users:

```
CREATE USER Employee WITHOUT LOGIN
CREATE USER Manager WITHOUT LOGIN
```

Then we'll create a table to use for our column-level security examples for a Product table. This Product table has the company's products, including the current price and the cost to produce this product:

```
CREATE SCHEMA Products
go
CREATE TABLE Products.Product
(
    ProductId   int identity CONSTRAINT PKProduct PRIMARY KEY,
    ProductCode varchar(10) CONSTRAINT AKProduct_ProductCode UNIQUE,
    Description varchar(20),
    UnitPrice   decimal(10,4),
    ActualCost  decimal(10,4)
)
INSERT INTO Products.Product(ProductCode, Description, UnitPrice, ActualCost)
VALUES ('widget12','widget number 12',10.50,8.50),
       ('snurf98','Snurfulator',99.99,2.50)
```

Now, we want our employees (as a reminder, in your real system you ought to create an employee role and associate Bob user with the role rather than having an employee user, but it's just a cleaner example to use two users) to be able to see all the products, but we don't want them to see what the product costs to manufacture. The syntax is the same as the GRANT on a table, but we include in parentheses the columns, comma delimited, to which the user is being denied access. In the next code block, we grant SELECT rights to both users but take away these rights on the ActualCost column:

```
GRANT SELECT on Products.Product to employee,manager
DENY SELECT on Products.Product (ActualCost) to employee
```

To test our security, we impersonate the manager:

```
EXECUTE AS USER = 'manager'
SELECT  *
FROM    Products.Product
```

This returns all columns with no errors:

| ProductId | ProductCode | Description | UnitPrice | ActualCost |
| --- | --- | --- | --- | --- |
| 1 | widget12 | widget number 12 | 10.5000 | 8.5000 |
| 3 | snurf98 | Snurfulator | 99.9900 | 2.5000 |

■**Tip** I know you are probably thinking that it's bad practice to use SELECT * in a query. It's true that using SELECT * in your permanent code is a bad idea, but generally speaking, when writing ad hoc queries, most users use the * shorthand for all columns.

The manager worked fine; what about the employee?

```
REVERT --revert back to SA level user or you will get an error that the
       --user cannot do this operation because it is unclear if the employee
       --user actually exists
GO
EXECUTE AS USER = 'employee'
GO
SELECT *
FROM    Products.Product
```

This returns the following result:

```
Msg 230, Level 14, State 1, Line 1
SELECT permission denied on column 'ActualCost' of object 'Product',
database 'SecurityChapter', schema 'Products'.
```

"Why did I get this error?" the user first asks; then (and this is harder to explain): "How do I correct it?"

You might try to explain to the user, "Well, just list all the columns you *do* have access to, without the columns you cannot see, like this":

```
SELECT ProductId, ProductCode, Description, UnitPrice
FROM    Products.Product
```

This returns the following results for user employee:

```
ProductId   ProductCode Description        UnitPrice
----------- ----------- ----------------- ----------------
1           widget12    widget number 12  10.5000
3           snurf98     Snurfulator       99.9900
```

The answer, although technically correct, isn't even vaguely what the user wants to hear. "So every time I want to build an ad hoc query on the Product table (which has 87 columns instead of the 5 we've generously mocked up for your learning ease), I have to type out all the columns?"

This is why, for the most part, column-level security is rarely used as a primary security mechanism, because of how it's implemented. You don't want users getting error messages when they try to run a query on a table. You might add column-level security to the table "just in case," but for the most part, use coded objects such as stored procedures or views to control access to certain columns. I'll discuss these solutions in the next section.

One last tidbit about column security syntax: once you've applied the DENY option on a column, to give the user rights you need to REVOKE the DENY to restore the ability to access the column and then GRANT access to the column option. Using REVOKE alone would only delete the DENY.

# Roles

Core to the process of granting rights is who to grant rights to. I've introduced the database user, commonly referred to as just *user*. The user is the lowest level of security principal in the database and can be mapped to logins, certificates, and asymmetrical keys, or even not mapped to a login at all. In this section, I will expand a bit more on just what a role is.

Roles are groups of users and other roles that allow you to grant object access to multiple users at once. Every user in a database is a member of at least the public role, which will be mentioned again in the "Built-in Database Roles" section, but may be a member of multiple roles. In fact, roles may be members of other roles. I'll discuss a couple types of roles:

- *Built-in database roles*: Roles that are provided by Microsoft as part of the system
- *User-defined database roles*: Roles that, defined by you, group Windows users together in a user-defined package of rights
- *Application roles*: Roles that are used to give an application specific rights, rather than to a group or individual user

Each of these types of roles is used to give rights to objects in a more convenient manner than granting them directly to an individual user. Many of these possible ways to implement roles (and all security really) are based on the politics of how you get to set up security in your organization. There are many different ways to get it done, and a lot of it is determined by who will do the actual work. End users may need to give another user rights to do some things, as a security team, network admins, DBAs, and so on, also dole out rights. The whole idea of setting up roles to group users is to lower the amount of work required to get things done and managed right.

## Built-in Database Roles

As part of the basic structure of the database, Microsoft provides a set of nine built-in roles that give a user a special set of rights at a database level:

- db_owner: Users associated with this role can perform any activity in the database.
- db_accessadmin: Users associated with this role can add or remove users from the database.
- db_backupoperator: Users associated with this role are allowed to back up the database.
- db_datareader: Users associated with this role are allowed to read any data in any table.
- db_datawriter: Users associated with this role are allowed to write any data in any table.
- db_ddladmin: Users associated with this role are allowed to add, modify, or drop any objects in the database (in other words, execute any DDL statements).
- db_denydatareader: Users associated with this role are denied the ability to see any data in the database, though they may still see the data through stored procedures.
- db_denydatawriter: Much like the db_denydatareader role, users associated with this role are denied the ability to modify any data in the database, though they still may modify data through stored procedures.
- db_securityadmin: Users associated with this role can modify and change permissions and roles in the database.

Of particular interest in these groups to many DBAs and developers are the db_datareader and db_datawriter roles. All too often these roles (or unfortunately the db_owner role) are the only permissions ever used in the database. For most any database, this should rarely be the case. Even when the bulk of the security is being managed by the user interface, there are going to be tables that you may not want users to be able to access. As an example, in my databases, I almost always have a utility schema that I place objects in to implement certain database-level utility tasks. If I wanted to keep up with the counts of rows in tables on a daily basis, I would create a row in the table each day with the row count of each table.

The point is, security should be well thought out and managed in a thoughtful manner and not just managed by giving full access and hoping for the best from the user interface standpoint. As I will introduce in the "Schemas" section, instead of using the db_datareader fixed role, consider granting SELECT permissions at a schema level. Then any new schema added for some purpose will not automatically be accessible to everyone by the db_datareader membership.

## Standard Database Roles

In addition to the fixed database roles, you can create your own database roles to grant rights to database objects. A feature that was new to SQL Server 2005 was the ability to grant database-level rights such as ALTER, ALTER ANY USER, DELETE (from any table), CREATE ROLE, and so on, to a role. (There are also new server-level rights too, but I won't cover this topic because it relates more to database administration than to design.) You can control rights to database management and data usage together in the same package, rather than needing to grant users ownership of the database where they have unlimited power to make your day busy restoring from backups and fixing the database.

Roles should be used to create a set of database rights for each job description. Take, for example, any typical human resources system that has employee information such as name, address, position, manager, pay grade, and so on. We'll likely need several roles, such as the following:

- HRManagers: Can do any task in the system.

- HRWorkers: Can maintain any attribute in the system, but approval rows are required to modify salary information.

- Managers: All managers in the company might be in a role like this, which might give them rights to high-level corporate information. You can then limit them to only the ability to see the details for their own workers, using further techniques I'll present in the section "Implementing Configurable Row-Level Security with Views" later in this chapter.

- Employees: Can see only their own information and can modify only their own personal address information.

and so on to cover all the common roles that individuals and some processes need to do their job. Setting up a tight security system isn't an easy task, and it takes lots of thought, planning, and hard work to get it done right.

Each of the roles would then be granted access to all the resources that they need. A member of the Managers role would likely also be a member of the Employees role. Then, as stated, the managers could see the information for their employees and also for themselves. Users can be members of multiple roles, and roles can be members of other roles. Permissions are additive, so if a user is a member of three roles, the user has an effective set of permissions that's the union of all permissions of the groups. For example:

- Managers: Can view the Employees table

- Employees: Can view the Product table

- HRWorkers: Can see employment history

If the Managers role were a member of the Employees role, a member of the Managers role could also do activities that were enabled by either role. If a user were a member of the HRWorkers group and the Employees role, then the user could see employment history and the Product table (it might seem logical that users could see the Employees table, but this hasn't been explicitly set in our tiny example). If a manager decides that making the lives of others miserable is no longer their thing, as part of their demotion they would be removed from the Managers role.

Programmatically, you can determine some basic information about a user's security information in the database:

- IS_MEMBER ('<role>'): Tells you whether the current user is the member of a given role. This is useful for building security-based views.

- USER: Tells you the current user's name in the database.

- HAS_PERMS_BY_NAME: Lets you interrogate the security system to see what rights a user has. This function has a complex public interface, but it's powerful and useful.

You can use these functions in applications and T-SQL code to determine at runtime what the user can do. For example, if you wanted only `HRManager` members to execute a procedure, you could check this:

```
SELECT is_member('HRManager')
```

A return value of 1 means the user is a member; 0 means not a member of the role. A procedure might start out like the following:

```
IF (SELECT is_member('HRManager')) = 0 or (SELECT is_member('HRManager')) is null
      SELECT 'I..DON''T THINK SO!'
```

This prevents even the database owner from executing the procedure, though this user can get the code for the procedure and execute the procedure if they're desirous enough (the "Monitoring and Auditing" section of this chapter covers some security precautions to handle nosy DBA types, though this is generally a hard task).

---

■**Tip** If there isn't an `HRManager` role configured, `is_member` will return `NULL`, which won't return anything. If this is a consideration, be certain and code for it, or add another block of code to warn/log that the setup is invalid.

---

As an example, take the HR system I was just discussing. If you wanted to remove access to the `salaryHistory` table just from the `Employees` role, you wouldn't deny access to the `Employees` role, because managers are employees also and would need to have rights to the `salaryHistory` table. To deal with this sort of change, you might have to revoke rights to the `Employees` role and then give rights to the other groups, rather than deny rights to a group that has lots of members.

For example, consider that you have three users in the database:

```
CREATE USER Frank WITHOUT LOGIN
CREATE USER Julie WITHOUT LOGIN
CREATE USER Rie WITHOUT LOGIN
```

Julie and Rie are members of the `HRWorkers` role:

```
CREATE ROLE HRWorkers

EXECUTE sp_addrolemember 'HRWorkers','Julie'
EXECUTE sp_addrolemember 'HRWorkers','Rie'
```

Next you have a `Payroll` schema, and in this is (at the least) an `EmployeeSalary` table:

```
CREATE SCHEMA Payroll

CREATE TABLE Payroll.EmployeeSalary
(
    EmployeeId  int,
    SalaryAmount decimal(12,2)

)
GRANT SELECT ON Payroll.EmployeeSalary to HRWorkers
```

Next, test the users:

```
EXECUTE AS USER = 'Frank'

SELECT *
FROM   Payroll.EmployeeSalary
```

This returns the following error, because Frank isn't a member of this group:

```
Msg 229, Level 14, State 5, Line 1
SELECT permission denied on object 'EmployeeSalary', database 'SecurityChapter',
schema 'Payroll'.
```

However, change over to Julie:

```
REVERT
EXECUTE AS USER = 'Julie'

SELECT *
FROM    Payroll.EmployeeSalary
```

She can view the data of tables in the Payroll schema because she's a member of the role that was granted EXECUTE permissions to the table:

```
EmployeeId   SalaryAmount
-----------  ---------------------------------------
```

Roles are always the best way to apply security in a database. Instead of giving individual users specific rights, develop roles that match job positions. Not that granting rights to an individual is not necessarily bad. To keep this section reasonable, I won't extend the example to include multiple roles, but a user can be a member of many roles, and the user gets the cumulative effect of the chosen rights. So if there was an HRManagers role and Julie were a member of this group as well as the HRWorkers role, the rights of the two groups would effectively be UNIONed. This would be the user's rights.

There's one notable exception. As mentioned earlier in the chapter, one DENY prevents another's GRANTs from applying. Say Rie had her rights to the EmployeeSalary table denied:

```
REVERT
DENY SELECT ON payroll.employeeSalary TO Rie
```

Say she tried to select from the table:

```
EXECUTE AS USER = 'Rie'
SELECT *
FROM    payroll.employeeSalary
```

She would be denied:

```
Msg 229, Level 14, State 5, Line 1
SELECT permission denied on object 'EmployeeSalary',
database 'SecurityChapter', schema 'Payroll'.
```

This is true even though she was granted rights via the HRWorkers group. This is why DENY is generally not used much. Rarely will you punish users via rights, if for no other reason than it can be too difficult to keep up with. You might apply a DENY to a sensitive table or procedure to be certain it wasn't used, but only in limited cases.

■**Note** For most examples in this chapter, I'll apply rights to users to keep examples as simple as possible.

If you want to know from which tables the user can SELECT, you can use a query such as the following:

```
--note, this query only returns rows for tables where the user has SOME rights
SELECT  table_schema + '.' + table_name as tableName,
        has_perms_by_name(table_schema + '.' + table_name, 'object', 'SELECT')

                                                                    as allowSelect
FROM    information_schema.tables
```

## Application Roles

Developers commonly like to set up applications using a single login and then manage security in the application. This can be an adequate way to implement security, but it requires you to re-create all the login stuff, when you could use simple Windows Authentication to check whether a user can execute an application. Application roles let you use the SQL Server login facilities to manage who a person is and if that person has rights to the database and then let the application perform the finer points of security.

To be honest, this can be a nice mix, because the hardest part of implementing security isn't restricting a person's ability to do an activity; it's nicely letting them know by hiding actions they cannot do. I've shown you a few of the security catalog views already, and there are more in Books Online. Using them, you can query the database to see what a user can do to help facilitate this process. However, it isn't a trivial task and is often considered too much trouble, especially for homegrown apps.

An application role is almost analogous to using EXECUTE AS to set rights to another user, but instead of a user, it's clearer in its use that the user is an application. You change to the context of the application role using sp_setapprole. You grant the application role permissions just like any other role, by using the GRANT statement.

As an example of using an application role, you'll create both a user named Bob and an application role and give them totally different rights. The TestPerms schema was created earlier, so if you didn't create it before, go ahead and create it.

```
CREATE TABLE TestPerms.BobCan
(
    BobCanId int identity(1,1) CONSTRAINT PKBobCan PRIMARY KEY,
    Value varchar(10)
)
CREATE TABLE TestPerms.AppCan
(
    AppCanId int identity(1,1) CONSTRAINT PKAppCan PRIMARY KEY,
    Value varchar(10)
)
```

Now create the new login and give it rights to the database:

```
CREATE USER Bob WITHOUT LOGIN
```

Next, give Bob SELECT rights to his table:

```
GRANT SELECT on TestPerms.BobCan to Bob
GO
```

Finally, create a new application role, and give it rights to its table:

```
CREATE APPLICATION ROLE AppCan_application with password = '392921jasll23'
GO
GRANT SELECT on TestPerms.AppCan to AppCan_application
```

You probably note that one of the drawbacks to using an application role is that it requires a password. This password is passed around in clear text to the application, so make sure that, first, the password is complex and, second, that you encrypt any connections that might be using these when there's a threat of impropriety. Look up Secure Sockets Layer (SSL) in Books Online for more information on encrypting connections. Then, set the user you're working as to Bob:

```
EXECUTE AS USER = 'Bob'
```

Now, select from the BobCan table:

```
SELECT * FROM TestPerms.BobCan
```

It works with no error:

```
BobCanId      Value
------------- -----------
```

However, try selecting from the AppCan table:

```
SELECT * FROM TestPerms.AppCan
```

The following error is returned:

```
Msg 229, Level 14, State 5, Line 1
SELECT permission denied on object 'AppCan', database 'SecurityChapter',
schema 'TestPerms'.
```

This isn't surprising, because Bob has no permissions on the AppCan table. Next, still logged in as Bob, use the sp_setapprole procedure to change the security context of the user to the application role, and the security is reversed:

```
REVERT
GO
EXECUTE sp_setapprole 'AppCan_application', '39292ljasll23'
GO
SELECT * FROM TestPerms.BobCan
```

This returns the following error:

```
Msg 229, Level 14, State 5, Line 1
SELECT permission denied on object 'BobCan', database 'SecurityChapter',
schema 'TestPerms'.
```

That's because you're now in context of the application role, and the application role doesn't have rights to the table. Finally, the application role can read from the AppCan table:

```
SELECT * from TestPerms.AppCan
```

This doesn't return an error:

```
AppCanId      Value
------------- -----------
```

When you're in the application role context, you look to the database as if you're the application, not your user, as evidenced by the following code:

```
SELECT user as userName, system_user as login
```

This returns the following result:

```
userName                login
--------------------    --------------------
AppCan_application       DOMAIN\USER
```

The login returns whatever login name you're logged in as, without regard to the impersonation you're doing, because the user is database level and the login is server level. Once you've executed sp_setapprole, the security stays as this role until you disconnect from the SQL server or you execute sp_unsetapprole. However, sp_unsetapprole doesn't work nearly as elegantly as REVERT. For example:

```
--Note that this must be executed as a single batch because of the variable
--for the cookie
DECLARE @cookie varbinary(8000);
EXECUTE sp_setapprole 'AppCan_application', '39292ljasll23'
            , @fCreateCookie = true, @cookie = @cookie OUTPUT

SELECT @cookie as cookie
SELECT USER as beforeUnsetApprole

EXEC sp_unsetapprole @cookie

SELECT USER as afterUnsetApprole

REVERT --done with this user
```

This returns the following results:

```
cookie
-------------------------------------------------------------------------------
0x2242652073375726520746F206472696E6B20796F7572204F76616C74696E652E20220000

beforeUnsetApprole
---------------------------------
AppCan_application

afterUnsetApprole
---------------------------------
dbo
```

The cookie is an interesting value, much larger than a GUID—it was declared as varbinary(8000) in Books Online, so I used that as well. It does change for each execution of the batch.

# Schemas

Schemas were introduced and used heavily in the past two chapters, and up to this point, they've been used merely as a method to group like objects. The were first introduced in the "Setting Up Schemas" section of Chapter 5 to group that chapter's example tables together, and you listed the schemas in the AdventureWorks2008 sample database if you installed it. (I'd suggest you install it on any development box. Although it isn't perfect, AdventureWorks2008 contains some workable data for example code, much like the `Northwind` database for SQL Server 2000 is an upgrade from `AdventureWorks` in SQL Server 2005 to support some of the new features.)

Logical grouping is an important usage of schemas, but it is only the first step. Using these logical groups to apply security is where they really pay off. A user owns a schema, and a user can also own multiple schemas. For most any database that you'll develop for a system, the best practice is to let all schemas be owned by the `dbo` system user. You might remember from versions before 2005 that the `dbo` owned all objects, and although this hasn't technically changed, it is the schema that is owned by `dbo`, and the table in the schema. Hence, instead of the reasonably useless `dbo.` prefix being attached to all objects representing the owner, you can nicely group together objects of a common higher purpose and then (because this is a security chapter) grant rights to users at a schema level, rather than at an individual object level.

For our database-design purposes, we will assign rights for users to use the following:

- Tables and (seldomly) individual columns

- Views

- Synonyms (which can represent any of these things and more)

- Functions

- Procedures

You can grant rights to other types of objects, including user-defined aggregates, queues, and XML schema collections, but I won't cover them here. As an example, in the `AdventureWorks` database, there's a `HumanResources` schema. Use the following query of the `sys.objects` catalog view (which reflects schema-scoped objects):

```
USE AdventureWorks
GO
SELECT  type_desc, count(*)
FROM    sys.objects
WHERE   schema_name(schema_id) = 'HumanResources'
  AND   type_desc in ('SQL_STORED_PROCEDURE','CLR_STORED_PROCEDURE',
                      'SQL_SCALAR_FUNCTION','CLR_SCALAR_FUNCTION',
                      'CLR_TABLE_VALUED_FUNCTION','SYNONYM',
                      'SQL_INLINE_TABLE_VALUED_FUNCTION',
                      'SQL_TABLE_VALUED_FUNCTION','USER_TABLE','VIEW')
GROUP BY type_desc
GO
USE SecurityChapter --or your own db if you are not using mine
```

This query shows how many of each object can be found in the version of the `HumanResources` schema I have on my writing laptop:

```
type_desc
----------------------------------------------------------- -----------
SQL_STORED_PROCEDURE                                        3
USER_TABLE                                                  6
VIEW                                                        6
```

Although I'll introduce permissions in the next section, I should note here that to grant permissions to a schema to a role or user, you use `::` between `SCHEMA` and the schema name. To give the users full usage rights to all these, you can use the following command:

```
GRANT EXECUTE, SELECT, INSERT, UPDATE, DELETE ON
                         SCHEMA::<schemaname> to <username>
```

By using schemas and roles liberally, the complexity of granting rights to users on database objects can be pretty straightforward. That's because, instead of having to make sure rights are granted to 10 or even 100 stored procedures to support your application's `Customer` section, you need just a single line of code:

```
GRANT EXECUTE on SCHEMA::Customer to CustomerSupport
```

Bam! Every user in the `CustomerSupport` role now has access to the stored procedures in this schema. Be prudent by not going so far down this path that you forget any special cases, but certainly this is a good technique for many cases. Nicer still is that even new objects added to the schema at a later date will be automatically accessible to people with rights at a schema level. For example, create a user named Tom; then grant Tom `SELECT` rights on the `TestPerms` schema created in the previous section:

```
CREATE USER Tom WITHOUT LOGIN
GRANT SELECT ON SCHEMA::TestPerms To Tom
```

Immediately, Tom has rights to select from the tables that have been created:

```
EXECUTE AS USER = 'Tom'
GO
SELECT * FROM TestPerms.AppCan
GO
REVERT
```

But also Tom gets rights to the new table that we create here:

```
CREATE TABLE TestPerms.SchemaGrant
(
    SchemaGrantId int primary key
)
GO
EXECUTE AS USER = 'Tom'
GO
SELECT * FROM TestPerms.schemaGrant
GO
REVERT
```

Essentially, a statement like `GRANT SELECT ON SCHEMA::` is a much better way to give a user read rights to the database, rather than using the db_datareader fixed database role, especially if you use schemas. This assures that if a new schema is created and the user shouldn't have access, they will not automatically get access.

# Controlling Object Access Via T-SQL Coded Objects

Just using the database-level security in SQL Server allows you to give a user rights to access only certain objects, but as you've seen, the database-level security doesn't work in an altogether user-friendly manner, nor does it give you a great amount of specific control. You can control access to the entire table or at the most restrict access at a column level. In many cases, you might want to let a user join to a table to get a value, but not to browse the entire table using a `SELECT` statement. Using table/object-level security alone, this is not possible, but using T-SQL coded objects it is very much possible.

In this chapter, we get down to the business of taking complete control over database access by using the following types of objects:

- *Stored procedures and scalar functions*: These objects give users an API to the database, and then the DBA can control security based on what the procedure does.

- *Views and table-valued functions*: In cases where the tools being used can't use stored procedures, you can still use views to present an interface to the data that appears to the user as a normal table would. In terms of security, views and table-valued functions can be used for partitioning data vertically by hiding columns or even horizontally by providing row-level security.

Coded objects let you take control of the data in ways that not only give you security over the data from a visibility or modifiability standpoint but let you control everything the user can do. (No, modifiability is probably not technically a word, but it will be if you just start using it. Then Webster's will cite this book as the origin, and I will sell a million copies to curious English professors! Yeah, that'll work . . .)

Controlling security with coded objects requires an understanding of how ownership affects rights to objects. For example, if a user owns a stored procedure and that stored procedure uses other objects it owns, the user who executes the procedure doesn't need direct rights to the other objects. The name for the way rights are allowed on owned objects in coded objects is *ownership chaining*.

Just because a user can use a stored procedure or function doesn't necessarily mean that he or she will need to have rights to every object to which the stored procedure refers. As long as the owner or the object owns all the schemas for all the objects that are referenced, the ownership chain isn't broken, and any user granted rights to use the object can see any referenced data. If you break the ownership chain and reference data in a schema not owned by the same user, the user will require rights granted directly to the object, instead of the object being created. This concept of the ownership chain is at the heart of why controlling object access via coded objects is so nice.

I put these both together in a section because whichever option you choose, you will still have accomplished the separation of interface from implementation. As long as the contract between the stored procedure or view is what the developer/application is coding/being coded to, the decision of which option to select will offer different sorts of benefits.

## Stored Procedures and Scalar Functions

Security in stored procedures and functions is always at the object level. This is nice because you can give the user rights to do many things without the user knowing how it's done. Also, the user needn't have the ability to do any of the actions without the stored procedures.

In some companies, stored procedures are used as the primary security mechanism, by requiring that all access to the server be done without executing a single "raw" DML statement against the tables. By building code that encapsulates all functionality, you then can apply permissions to the stored procedures to restrict what the user can do.

In security terms only, this allows you to have *situational control* on access to a table. This means that you might have two different procedures that functionally do the same operation, but giving a user rights to one procedure doesn't imply that he or she has rights to the other. (I will summarize the other benefits of stored procedures in Chapter 11.)

Take, for example, the case where a screen is built using one procedure; the user might be able to do an action, such as deleting a row from a specific table. But when the user goes to a different screen that allows deleting 100 rows, they might be denied that ability. What makes this even nicer is that with decent naming of your objects, you can give end users or managers rights to dole out security based on actions they want their employees to have, without needing the IT staff to handle it.

As an example, I will create a new user for the demonstration:

```
CREATE USER procUser WITHOUT LOGIN
```

Then (as dbo), create a new schema and table:

```
CREATE SCHEMA procTest
CREATE TABLE procTest.misc
(
    Value varchar(20),
    Value2 varchar(20)
)
GO
INSERT INTO procTest.misc
VALUES ('somevalue','secret'),
       ('anothervalue','secret')
```

Next, create a new procedure to return the values from the value column in the table, not the value2 column:

```
CREATE PROCEDURE procTest.misc$select
AS
    SELECT Value
    FROM   procTest.misc
GO
GRANT EXECUTE on procTest.misc$select to procUser
```

Then change the context to the procUser user and try to SELECT from the table:

```
EXECUTE AS USER = 'procUser'
GO
SELECT Value, Value2
FROM   procTest.misc
```

You get the following error message, because the user hasn't been given rights to access this table:

```
Msg 229, Level 14, State 5, Line 1
SELECT permission denied on object 'misc', database 'SecurityChapter',
schema 'procTest'.
```

However, execute the following procedure:

```
EXECUTE procTest.misc$select
```

The user does have access to execute the procedure, so you get the results expected:

```
Value
--------------------
somevalue
anothervalue
```

In the eyes of most database architects, this is the best way to architect a database solution. It leaves a manageable surface area, gives you a lot of control over what SQL is executed in the database, and lets you control data security nicely.

You can see what kinds of access a user has to stored procedures by executing the following statement (this is an alternate method to the sys.database_permissions catalog view used earlier):

```
SELECT  routine_schema + '.' + routine_name as procedureName,
        has_perms_by_name(routine_schema + '.' + routine_name, 'object',
                          'EXECUTE') as allowExecute
FROM    information_schema.routines
WHERE   routine_type = 'PROCEDURE'

REVERT
```

If you were only using stored procedures to access the data, this query could be executed by the application programmer to know everything the user can do in the database.

---

■**Tip** If you don't like using stored procedures as your access layer, I know you can make a list of reasons why you disagree with this practice. However, as I mentioned, this is largely considered a best practice in the SQL Server architect community because of not only the security aspects of stored procedures but also the other reasons I will discuss in Chapter 11.

---

## Impersonation Within Objects

I already talked about the EXECUTE AS statement, and it has some great applications, but the WITH EXECUTE clause on a procedure/function declaration can give you some incredible flexibility to give the executor greater powers than might have been possible otherwise, certainly not without granting additional rights. Instead of changing context before doing an operation, you can change context while executing a stored procedure, function, or DML trigger (plus queues for Service Broker, but I won't be covering that topic). Unfortunately, the WITH EXECUTE clause is not available for views, because they are not executable objects.

By adding the following code, you can change the security context of a procedure to a different server or database principal when the execution begins:

```
CREATE PROCEDURE <schemaName>.<procedureName>
WITH EXECUTE AS <'loginName' | caller | self | owner>
```

The different options for whom to execute as are as follows:

- 'userName': A specific user principal in the database.

- caller: The context of the user who called the procedure. This is the default security context you get when executing an object.

- self: It's in the context of the user who created the procedure.

- owner: It's executed in the context of the owner of the module or schema.

Note that using EXECUTE AS doesn't affect the ownership chaining of the call. The security of the statements in the object is still based on the security of the schema owner. Only when the ownership chain is broken will the ownership chaining come into play. The following statements go along with the EXECUTE AS clause:

- EXECUTE AS CALLER: You can execute this in your code to go back to the default, where access is as the user who actually executed the object.

- REVERT: This reverts security back to the security specified in the WITH EXECUTE AS clause.

As an example (and this example does get a little bit messy with all the changes in security), I'll show how to build a situation where one schema owner has a table and where the next schema owner has a table and a procedure that the schema owner wants to use to access the first user's table. Finally, you have an average user who wants to do his or her job by executing the stored procedure.

First, you create a few users and give them rights to create objects in the database. The three users are named as follows:

- schemaOwner: This user owns the primary schema where one of the objects resides.
- procedureOwner: This user owns the owner of an object and a stored procedure.
- aveSchlub: This is the average user who finally wants to use procedureOwner's stored procedure.

```
USE SecurityChapter
GO
--this will be the owner of the primary schema
CREATE USER schemaOwner WITHOUT LOGIN
GRANT CREATE SCHEMA to schemaOwner
GRANT CREATE TABLE to schemaOwner

--this will be the procedure creator
CREATE USER procedureOwner WITHOUT LOGIN
GRANT CREATE SCHEMA to procedureOwner
GRANT CREATE PROCEDURE to procedureOwner
GRANT CREATE TABLE to procedureOwner
GO


--this will be the average user who needs to access data
CREATE USER aveSchlub WITHOUT LOGIN
```

Then, you change to the context of the main object owner, create a new schema, and create a table with some rows:

```
EXECUTE AS USER = 'schemaOwner'
GO
CREATE SCHEMA schemaOwnersSchema
GO
CREATE TABLE schemaOwnersSchema.Person
(
    PersonId    int constraint PKtestAccess_Person primary key,
    FirstName   varchar(20),
    LastName    varchar(20)
)
Go
INSERT INTO schemaOwnersSchema.Person
VALUES (1, 'Phil','Mutayblin'),
       (2, 'Del','Eets')
```

Next, this user gives SELECT permissions to the procedureOwner user:

```
GRANT SELECT on schemaOwnersSchema.Person to procedureOwner
```

Then you set context to the secondary user to create the procedure:

```
REVERT --we can step back on the stack of principals,
        --but we can't change directly
        --to procedureOwner. Here I step back to the db_owner user you have
        --used throughout the chapter
GO
EXECUTE AS USER = 'procedureOwner'
```

Then you create a schema and another table:

```
CREATE SCHEMA procedureOwnerSchema
GO
```

```
CREATE TABLE procedureOwnerSchema.OtherPerson
(
    personId    int constraint PKtestAccess_person primary key,
    FirstName   varchar(20),
    LastName    varchar(20)
)
go
INSERT INTO procedureOwnerSchema.OtherPerson
VALUES (1, 'DB','Smith')
INSERT INTO procedureOwnerSchema.OtherPerson
VALUES (2, 'Dee','Leater')
```

You can see the owners of the objects and their schema using the following query of the catalog views:

```
REVERT
SELECT tables.name as [table], schemas.name as [schema],
       database_principals.name as [owner]
FROM   sys.tables
         join sys.schemas
            on tables.schema_id = schemas.schema_id
         join sys.database_principals
            on database_principals.principal_id = schemas.principal_id
WHERE  tables.name in ('Person','OtherPerson')
```

This returns the following:

| table | schema | owner |
| --- | --- | --- |
| Person | schemaOwnersSchema | schemaOwner |
| otherPerson | procedureOwnerSchema | procedureOwner |

Next you create two procedures as the secondary users, one for the WITH EXECUTE AS as CALLER, which is the default, and then SELF, which puts it in the context of the creator, in this case procedureOwner:

```
EXECUTE AS USER = 'procedureOwner'
GO
CREATE PROCEDURE  procedureOwnerSchema.person$asCaller
WITH EXECUTE AS CALLER --this is the default
AS
SELECT  personId, FirstName, LastName
FROM    procedureOwnerSchema.OtherPerson --<-- ownership same as proc

SELECT  personId, FirstName, LastName
FROM    schemaOwnersSchema.person  --<-- breaks ownership chain
GO

CREATE PROCEDURE procedureOwnerSchema.person$asSelf
WITH EXECUTE AS SELF --now this runs in context of procedureOwner,
                     --since it created it
AS
SELECT  personId, FirstName, LastName
FROM    procedureOwnerSchema.OtherPerson --<-- ownership same as proc

SELECT  personId, FirstName, LastName
FROM    schemaOwnersSchema.person  --<-- breaks ownership chain
```

Next you grant rights on the proc to the aveSchlub user:

```
GRANT EXECUTE ON procedureOwnerSchema.person$asCaller to aveSchlub
GRANT EXECUTE ON procedureOwnerSchema.person$asSelf to aveSchlub
```

Then you change to the context of the aveSchlub:

```
REVERT; EXECUTE AS USER = 'aveSchlub'
```

You then execute the procedure:

```
--this proc is in context of the caller, in this case, aveSchlub
EXECUTE procedureOwnerSchema.person$asCaller
```

This produces the following output, because the ownership chain is fine for the procedureOwnerSchema object, but not for the schemaOwnerSchema:

```
personId     FirstName           LastName
-----------  ------------------  --------------------
1            DB                  Smith
2            Dee                 Leater

Msg 229, Level 14, State 5, Procedure person$asCaller, Line 4
The SELECT permission was denied on object 'Person', database 'SecurityChapter',
schema 'schemaOwnerSchema'.
```

Next you execute the asSelf variant:

```
--procedureOwner, so it works
EXECUTE procedureOwnerSchema.person$asSelf
```

This returns two result sets:

```
personId     FirstName           LastName
-----------  ------------------  --------------------
1            DB                  Smith
2            Dee                 Leater

personId     FirstName           LastName
-----------  ------------------  --------------------
1            Phil                Mutayblin
2            Del                 Eets
```

What makes this different is that when the ownership chain is broken, the security context you're in is the secondaryUser, not the context of the caller, aveSchlub. Using EXECUTE AS to change security context is a cool feature. Now you can give a user temporary rights that won't even be apparent to him or her and won't require granting any permissions.

However, EXECUTE AS isn't a feature that should be overused, and its use should definitely be monitored by code reviews! It can be all too easy just to build your procs in the context of the dbo and forget about doing decent security altogether. And that is the "nice" reason for taking care in using the feature. Another reason to take care is that a malicious programmer could (if they were devious or stupid) include dangerous code that would run as if it were the database owner, which could certainly cause undesired effects.

For example, using impersonation is a great way to implement dynamic SQL calls (I will discuss more in Chapter 11 when I discuss code-level design), but if you aren't careful to secure your code against an injection attack, the attack might just be in the context of the database owner rather than the basic application user that *should* have only limited rights if you have listened to anything I have said in the rest of this chapter.

One thing that you can do with this EXECUTE AS technique is to give a user super rights temporarily in a database. For example, consider the following procedure:

```
REVERT
GO
CREATE PROCEDURE dbo.testDboRights
AS
 BEGIN
    CREATE TABLE dbo.test
    (
        testId int
    )
 END
```

This procedure isn't executable by any user other than one who has rights in the database. Say we have the following user:

```
CREATE USER leroy WITHOUT LOGIN
```

You give him rights (presuming Leroy is a male name and not just some horrible naming humor that a female had to live with) to execute the procedure:

```
GRANT EXECUTE on dbo.testDboRights to leroy
```

Note that you grant *only* rights to the dbo.testDboRights procedure. The user leroy can run only one stored procedure. Now, you execute the procedure:

```
EXECUTE AS USER = 'leroy'
EXECUTE dbo.testDboRights
```

The result is predictably bad, because leroy isn't a member of the db_owner's role. Here's the output:

```
Msg 262, Level 14, State 1, Procedure testDboRights, Line 5
CREATE TABLE permission denied in database 'SecurityChapter'.
```

**Tip** If I had a nickel for every time I have seen security issues come up when new changes were moved to a production server, I would be rich. In fact, if I just had the nickels from my own mistakes, I wouldn't exactly die a pauper.

If you alter the procedure with EXECUTE AS 'dbo', the result is that the table is created, if there isn't already a table with that name:

```
REVERT
GO
ALTER PROCEDURE dbo.testDboRights
WITH EXECUTE AS 'dbo'
AS
 BEGIN
    CREATE TABLE dbo.test
    (
        testId int
    )
 END
```

Now you can execute this procedure and have it create the table. Run the procedure twice, and you will get an error about already having a table called `dbo.test` in the database. For more detailed information about `EXECUTE AS`, check the "Extending Database Impersonation by Using EXECUTE AS" topic in Books Online.

---

**■Tip** As will be discussed in the next sections, to use external resources (like a table in a different database) using impersonation, you need to set `TRUSTWORTHY` to `ON` using the `ALTER DATABASE` command.

---

In Chapter 11, a rather large section discusses the value of ad hoc SQL versus stored procedures, and we use the `EXECUTE AS` functionality to provide security when it comes to executing dynamic SQL in stored procedures. This is a great new feature that will bring stored procedure development—including stored procedures that are CLR-based—to new heights because dynamic SQL-based stored procedures were a security issue in earlier versions of SQL Server.

## Crossing Database Lines

So far, all the code and issues we've discussed have been concerned with everything owned by a single owner in a single database. When our code and/or relationships must go outside the database limits, the complexity is greatly increased. This is because in SQL Server architecture, databases are generally thought of as independent containers of data (more on the architecture of SQL Server databases in the next chapter). However, often you need to share data from one database to another, often for some object that's located in a third-party system your company has purchased.

This can be a real annoyance for the following reasons:

- Foreign key constraints cannot be used to handle referential integrity needs (I covered in Chapter 6 how you implement relationships using triggers to support this).

- Backups must be coordinated. You lose some of the protection from a single database-backup scenario. This is because when, heaven forbid, a database restore is needed, it isn't possible to make certain that the data in the two databases is in sync.

Although accessing data in outside databases is not optimal, sometimes it's unavoidable. A typical example might be linking an off-the-shelf system into a homegrown system. Beyond the coding and maintenance aspects, which aren't necessarily trivial, a very important consideration is security. As mentioned in the first paragraph of this section, databases are generally considered independent in the security theme of how SQL Server works. This causes issues when you need to include data outside the database, because users are scoped to a database. That's why `userA` in `database1` is never the same as `userA` in `database2`, even if they're mapped to the same login.

The ownership chain inside the boundaries of a database is relatively simple. If the owner of the object refers only to other objects he owns, then the chain isn't broken. Any user to whom he grants rights can use the object. However, when leaving the confines of a single database, things get murky. Even if a database is owned by the same system login, the ownership chain is broken when an object references data outside the database. So, not only does the object creator need to have access to the objects outside the database, the caller needs rights also.

There are three reasonable ways to handle this:

- Using cross-database chaining
- Impersonation
- Certificate-based trusts

I'll briefly explain and demonstrate each type of solution.

## Using Cross-Database Chaining

The cross-database chaining solution is to tell the database to recognize that indeed the owners of database1 and database2 are the same. Then, if you as system administrator want to allow users to use your objects seamlessly across databases, then it's fine. However, a few steps and requirements need to be met:

- Each database that participates in the chaining relationship must be owned by the same system login.

- The DB_CHAINING database option (set using ALTER DATABASE) must be set to ON for each database involved in the relationship. It's OFF by default.

- The database where the object uses external resources must have the TRUSTWORTHY database option set to ON; it's OFF by default. (Again, set this using ALTER DATABASE.)

- The users who use the objects need to have a user in the database where the external resources reside.

I often will use the database chaining approach to support a reporting solution. For example, we have several databases that make up a complete reporting solution in our production system. We have a single database with views of each system to provide a single database for reporting from the OLTP databases (for real-time reporting needs only; other reporting comes from a copy of the database and a data warehouse). Users have access to the views in the reporting database, but not rights to the base database tables.

---

**■Caution** If I could put this caution in a flashing font, I would, but my editor would probably say it wasn't cost effective or something silly like that. It's important to understand the implications of the database chaining scenario. You're effectively opening up the external database resources completely to the users in the database who are members of the db_owner database role, even if they have no rights in the external database. Because of the last two criteria in the bulleted list, chaining isn't necessarily a bad thing to do for most corporate situations where you simply have to retrieve data from another database. However, opening access to the external database resources can be especially bad for shared database systems, because this can be used to get access to the data in a chaining-enabled database. All that may need to be known is the username and login name of a user in the other database.

---

Note that if you need to turn chaining on or off for all databases, you can use sp_configure to set 'Cross DB Ownership Chaining' to '1'; but this is not considered a best practice. Use ALTER DATABASE to set chaining *only* where absolutely required.

As an example, consider the following scenario where I'll create two databases with a table in each database and then a procedure. First, I'll create the new database and add a simple table. I won't add any rows or keys, because this isn't important to this demo. Note that you have to create a login for this demo, because the user must be based on the same login in both databases:

```
CREATE DATABASE externalDb
GO
USE externalDb
GO
                            --smurf theme song :)
CREATE LOGIN smurf WITH PASSWORD = 'La la, la la la la, la, la la la la'
CREATE USER smurf FROM LOGIN smurf
CREATE TABLE dbo.table1 ( value int )
```

Next, you create a local database, the one where you'll be executing your queries. You add the login you created as a new user and again create a table:

```
CREATE DATABASE localDb
GO
USE localDb
GO
CREATE USER smurf FROM LOGIN smurf
```

Next, you create a simple procedure, selecting data from both databases, with the objects being owned by the same owner. You then give rights to our new user:

```
CREATE PROCEDURE dbo.externalDb$testCrossDatabase
AS
SELECT Value
FROM    externalDb.dbo.table1
GO
GRANT execute on dbo.externalDb$testCrossDatabase to smurf
```

Now try it:

```
EXECUTE AS USER = 'smurf'
go
EXECUTE dbo.externalDb$testCrossDatabase
GO
REVERT
```

This will give you the following error:

```
Msg 916, Level 14, State 1, Procedure externalDb$testCrossDatabase, Line 3
The server principal "smurf" is not able to access the database "externalDb"
under the current security context.
```

You then set the chaining and trustworthy attributes for the `localDb` and chaining for the `externalDb`. (Making these settings requires sysadmin rights.)

```
ALTER DATABASE localDb
    SET DB_CHAINING ON
ALTER DATABASE localDb
    SET TRUSTWORTHY ON

ALTER DATABASE externalDb
    SET DB_CHAINING ON
```

Now if you execute it, you will see that the procedure returns a valid result. This is because now the owner of the objects/databases are the same, and the user has access to the external database via the user you created in that database (you can also use the guest login to achieve this as well).

You can validate the metadata for these databases using the `sys.databases` catalog view:

```
SELECT cast(name as varchar(10)) as name,
       cast(suser_sname(owner_sid) as varchar(10)) as owner,
       is_trustworthy_on, is_db_chaining_on
FROM   sys.databases where name in ('localdb','externaldb')
```

This returns the following results:

| name | owner | is_trustworthy_on | is_db_chaining_on |
| --- | --- | --- | --- |
| externalDb | DOMAIN\Username | 0 | 1 |
| localDb | DOMAIN\Username | 1 | 1 |

I find that the biggest issue when setting up cross database chaining is the question of owner-ship of the databases involved. The owner changes sometimes because users create databases and leave them owned by their security principals. In most cases on my corporate database servers, I will set the owner for all databases to be sa as a rule. I do that because it is a good practice not to have databases owned by the login of the person who happened to create them.

## Using Impersonation to Cross Database Lines

As mentioned in the earlier section introducing impersonation, impersonation can be an alterna-tive to using the DB_CHAINING setting. Now you no longer need to set the chaining on; all you need is to set it to TRUSTWORTHY:

```
ALTER DATABASE localDb
    SET DB_CHAINING OFF
ALTER DATABASE localDb
    SET TRUSTWORTHY ON

ALTER DATABASE externalDb
    SET DB_CHAINING OFF
```

Now you can rewrite the procedure like this, which lets the person execute in the context of the owner of the schema that the procedure is in:

```
CREATE PROCEDURE dbo.externalDb$testCrossDatabase_Impersonation
WITH EXECUTE AS SELF --as procedure creator
AS
SELECT Value
FROM    externalDb.dbo.table1
GO
GRANT execute on dbo.externalDb$testCrossDatabase_impersonation to smurf
```

If the login of the owner of the dbo schema (in this case my login, because I created both data-bases) has access to the other database, then you can impersonate the dbo in this manner. In fact, you can access the external resources seamlessly. This is probably the simplest method of handling cross-database chaining for most corporate needs. However, impersonation should raise a big flag if you're working on a database server that's shared among many different companies.

Because it requires sysadmin privileges to set TRUSTWORTHY on, using impersonation isn't a tremendous hole, but note that the members of the sysadmin role aren't required to understand the implications if one of their users calls up and asks for TRUSTWORTHY to be turned on for them.

If TRUSTWORTHY is set to OFF, you'll receive the following error:

```
Msg 916, Level 14, State 1,
Procedure externalDb$testCrossDatabase_Impersonation, Line 4
The server principal "COMPASS.NET\lbdavi" is not able to access the database
"externalDb" under the current security context.
```

## Using a Certificate-Based User

The final thing I'll demonstrate is using a single certificate installed in both databases. We'll use it to sign the stored procedure and map a user to this certificate in the target database. This is a straight-forward technique and is the best way to do cross-database security chaining when the system isn't a dedicated corporate resource. It takes a bit of setup, but it isn't overwhelmingly difficult. What makes using a certificate nice is that you don't need to open the hole left in the system's security by setting the database to TRUSTWORTHY. This is because the user who will be executing the procedure is a user in the database, just as if the target login or user were given rights in the externalDB. Because the certificate matches, SQL Server knows that this cross-database access is acceptable.

First turn off the TRUSTWORTHY setting:

```
REVERT
GO
USE localDb
GO
ALTER DATABASE localDb
  SET TRUSTWORTHY OFF
```

Check the status of your databases using this:

```
SELECT cast(name as varchar(10)) as name,
       cast(suser_sname(owner_sid) as varchar(10)) as owner,
       is_trustworthy_on, is_db_chaining_on
FROM   sys.databases where name in ('localdb','externaldb')
```

This should return the following results (if not, go back and turn off trustworthy and chaining for the databases where necessary):

| name | owner | is_trustworthy_on | is_db_chaining_on |
| --- | --- | --- | --- |
| externalDb | DOMAIN\Username | 0 | 0 |
| localDb | DOMAIN\Username | 0 | 0 |

Now we will create another procedure and give the user smurf rights to execute it, just like the others (which won't work now because TRUSTWORTHY is turned off):

```
CREATE PROCEDURE dbo.externalDb$testCrossDatabase_Certificate
AS
SELECT Value
FROM   externalDb.dbo.table1
GO
GRANT EXECUTE on dbo.externalDb$testCrossDatabase_Certificate to smurf
```

Then create a certificate:

```
CREATE CERTIFICATE procedureExecution ENCRYPTION BY PASSWORD = 'Cert Password'
WITH SUBJECT =
       'Used to sign procedure:externalDb$testCrossDatabase_Certificate'
```

Then add this certificate as a signature on the procedure:

```
ADD SIGNATURE TO dbo.externalDb$testCrossDatabase_Certificate
   BY CERTIFICATE procedureExecution WITH PASSWORD = 'Cert Password'
```

Finally, make an OS file out of the certificate so a certificate object can be created in the externalDb based on the same certificate (choose a directory that works best for you):

```
BACKUP CERTIFICATE procedureExecution TO FILE = 'c:\temp\procedureExecution.cer'
```

This completes the setup of the localDb. Next, you have to apply the certificate to the externalDb:

```
USE externalDb
GO
CREATE CERTIFICATE procedureExecution FROM FILE = 'c:\temp\procedureExecution.cer'
```

Next, map the certificate to a user, and give this user rights to the table1 that the user in the other database is trying to access:

```
CREATE USER procCertificate FOR CERTIFICATE procedureExecution
GO
GRANT SELECT on dbo.table1 TO procCertificate
```

Now you're good to go. Change back to the localDb and execute the procedure:

```
USE localDb
GO
EXECUTE AS LOGIN = 'smurf'
EXECUTE dbo.externalDb$testCrossDatabase_Certificate
```

The stored procedure has a signature that identifies it with the certificate, and in the external database, it connects with this certificate to get the rights that the certificate-based user has. So, since the certificate user can view data in the table, your procedure can use the data.

The certificate-based approach isn't as simple as the other possibilities, but it's more secure, for certain. Pretty much the major downside to this is that it works only with procedures and not with views, and I didn't really cover any of the intricacies of using certificates. However, now you have a safe way of crossing database boundaries that doesn't require giving the user direct object access and doesn't open up a hole in your security. Hence, you could use this solution on any server in any situation. Make sure to secure/destroy the certificate file once you've used it so no other user can use it to gain access to your system. Then we can clean up the databases used for the example.

```
REVERT
GO
USE MASTER
GO
DROP DATABASE externalDb
DROP DATABASE localDb
GO
USE SecurityChapter
```

# Different Server (Distributed Queries)

I want to make brief mention of distributed queries and introduce the functions that can be used to establish a relationship between two SQL Servers, or a SQL Server and an OLE DB or ODBC data source. You can use two methods:

- *Linked servers*: You can build a connection between two servers by registering a "server" name that you then access via a four-part name (<linkedServerName>.<database>.<schema>. <objectName>) or through the OPENQUERY interface. The linked server name is the name you specify using sp_addlinkedserver. This could be a SQL Server or anything that can be connected to via OLE DB.

- *Ad hoc connections*: Using the OPENROWSET or OPENDATASOURCE interfaces, you can return a table of data from any OLE DB source.

In either case, the security chain will be broken when crossing SQL Server instance connections and certainly when using any data source that isn't SQL Server–based. Whether or not this is a problem is based on the connection properties and/or connection string used to create the linked server or ad hoc connection. Using linked servers, you could be in the context of the Windows login you are logged in with, a SQL Server Standard login on the target machine, or even a single login that everyone uses to "cross over" to the other server. The best practice is to use the Windows login where possible.

As I mentioned briefly in the previous section, one use for EXECUTE AS could be to deal with the case where you're working with distributed databases. One user might be delegated to have rights to access the distributed server, and then you execute the procedure as this user to give access to the linked server objects.

# Views and Table-Valued Functions

In this section, I'll talk about using views and table-valued functions to encapsulate the views of the data in ways that leave the data in table-like structures. You might use views and table-valued functions in concert with, or in lieu of, a full stored procedure approach to application architecture. Views, as discussed in previous chapters, allow you to form pseudotables from other table sources, sometimes by adding tables together and sometimes by splitting a table up into smaller chunks. In this section, the goal is to "hide" data, like a column, from users or hide certain rows in a table, providing data security by keeping the data out of the view of the user in question.

As an overall architecture, I will always suggest that you should use stored procedures to access data in your applications, if for no other reason than you can encapsulate many data-oriented tasks in the background, giving you easy access to tweak the performance of an activity with practically zero impact to the application. (In Chapter 11, I will give some basic coverage of application architecture.)

In this section, I'll look at the following:

- *General usage*: Basic use of views to implement security.

- *Configurable row-level security*: You can use views to implement security at the row level, and this can be extended to provide user-manageable security.

Instead of the more up-front programming-heavy stored procedure methods from the previous section, simply accessing views and table-valued functions allows for more straightforward usage. Sometimes, because of the oft-repeated mantra of "just get it done," sometimes the concept of stored procedures is an impossible sale. You will lose a bit of control, and certain concepts won't be available to you (for example, you cannot use EXECUTE AS in a view definition), but it will be better in some cases when you don't want to dole out access to the tables directly.

## General Usage

We'll use two properties of views to build a more secure database. The first is assigning privileges to a user such that he can use a view, though not the underlying tables. For example, let's go back to the Products.Product table used earlier in this chapter. As a reminder, execute this statement (after executing REVERT, if you haven't already, from the previous example):

```
SELECT *
FROM   Products.Product
```

The following data is returned:

| ProductId | ProductCode | Description | UnitPrice | ActualCost |
| --- | --- | --- | --- | --- |
| 1 | widget12 | widget number 12 | 10.5000 | 8.5000 |
| 2 | snurf98 | Snurfulator | 99.9900 | 2.5000 |

We could construct a view on this:

```
CREATE VIEW Products.allProducts
AS
SELECT ProductId,ProductCode, Description, UnitPrice, ActualCost
FROM   Products.Product
```

Selecting data from either the table or the view returns the same data. However, they're two separate structures to which you can separately assign access privileges and deal with separately. If you need to tweak the table, you might not have to modify the view. Of course in practice, the view won't usually include the same columns and rows as the base table, but as an example it is interesting to realize that if you build the view in this manner, there would be little if any difference with using the two objects, other than how the security was set up.

One of the most important things that makes views useful as a security mechanism is the ability to partition a table structure, by limiting the rows or columns visible to the user. First, you'll look at using views to implement *column-level security*, which is also known as *projection* or *vertical partitioning* of the data, because you'll be dividing the view's columns. (In the next section, I will cover horizontal partitioning, or row-level security.) For example, consider that the users in a warehouseUsers role need only to see a list of products, not how much they cost and certainly not how much they cost to produce. You might create a view like the following to partition the columns accordingly:

```
CREATE VIEW Products.WarehouseProducts
AS
SELECT ProductId,ProductCode, Description
FROM   Products.Product
```

By the same token, you can use table-valued functions in much the same way, though you can do more using them, including forcing some form of filter on the results. For example, you might code the following function to list all products that are less than some price:

```
CREATE FUNCTION Products.ProductsLessThanPrice
(
    @UnitPrice  decimal(10,4)
)
RETURNS table
AS
    RETURN ( SELECT ProductId, ProductCode, Description, UnitPrice
             FROM   Products.Product
             WHERE  UnitPrice <= @UnitPrice)
```

This can be executed like the following:

```
SELECT * FROM Products.ProductsLessThanPrice(20)
```

This returns the following result:

| ProductId | ProductCode | Description | UnitPrice |
|-----------|-------------|-------------|-----------|
| 1 | widget12 | widget number 12 | 10.5000 |

**Tip** One of the most painful downfalls of using views for security is that you cannot "overload" the name of the object with several different objects. One might see products as having `ProductId`, `ProductCode`, and `Description`, although a different user might see the `Product` row with all columns. By using row-level security, you can hide rows based on security but not columns. Hence, you have to come up with "coy" names for your views, such as `allProducts`, `ProductSimple`, and so on, which can be kind of annoying.

Using a multistatement table-valued function (say that three times fast), you could force the condition that only users of a given security group can look at items with a price greater than some amount. Here's an example of such a function:

```
CREATE FUNCTION Products.ProductsLessThanPrice_GroupEnforced
(
    @UnitPrice  decimal(10,4)
)
RETURNS @output table (ProductId int,
                       ProductCode varchar(10),
                       Description varchar(20),
                       UnitPrice decimal(10,4))
AS
 BEGIN
    --cannot raise an error, so you have to implement your own
    --signal, or perhaps simply return no data.
    IF @UnitPrice > 100 and (
                            IS_MEMBER('HighPriceProductViewer') = 0
                            or IS_MEMBER('HighPriceProductViewer') is null)
        INSERT @output
        SELECT -1,'ERROR','',-1
    ELSE
        INSERT @output
        SELECT ProductId, ProductCode, Description, UnitPrice
        FROM   Products.Product
        WHERE  UnitPrice <= @UnitPrice
    RETURN
 END
```

Note too that the hard-coded roles could just as easily be changed to a SELECT from a table that you create to table-drive your security like this from. I'm a big proponent of driving as many of the settings in your application as possible from data. The more you do so, the easier it is to make changes. Once you have tested an infrastructure, just adding values to a table should not need rigorous testing.

To test, I will create a couple of roles and add users (with what I hope are obvious enough names):

```
CREATE ROLE HighPriceProductViewer
CREATE ROLE ProductViewer

CREATE USER HighGuy WITHOUT LOGIN
CREATE USER LowGuy WITHOUT LOGIN

EXEC sp_addrolemember 'HighPriceProductViewer','HighGuy'
EXEC sp_addrolemember 'ProductViewer','HighGuy'
EXEC sp_addrolemember 'ProductViewer','LowGuy'
```

Then I will grant rights to the procedure to the ProductViewer group *only*. This gives them rights to execute the procedure, but the checks in the procedure still have to be passed.

```
GRANT SELECT ON Products.ProductsLessThanPrice_GroupEnforced TO ProductViewer
```

Then, executing as the high-limit user, look for products up to $10,000:

```
EXECUTE AS USER = 'HighGuy'
SELECT * FROM Products.ProductsLessThanPrice_GroupEnforced(10000)
REVERT
```

You get these results:

```
ProductId    ProductCode Description           UnitPrice
-----------  ----------- --------------------  ----------------------------------
1            widget12    widget number 12      10.5000
2            snurf98     Snurfulator           99.9900
```

But execute as the low-limit user with too large of a parameter value:

```
EXECUTE AS USER = 'LowGuy'
SELECT * FROM Products.ProductsLessThanPrice_GroupEnforced(10000)
REVERT
```

and you get the following error output:

```
ProductId    ProductCode Description          UnitPrice
-----------  ----------- -------------------- ----------------------------------
-1           ERROR                            -1.0000
```

> ■**Note** The lack of error reporting from table-valued functions is annoying at times. I chose to output some form of error output to give the example some flashiness, but just returning no values could be an acceptable output too.

Using the same GRANT syntax as in the "Table Security" section, you can give a user rights to use the view for SELECT, INSERT, UPDATE, or DELETE to a view such that it will look and act to the user just like a table. If the view is a view of multiple tables, the view might not support modifications or deletions, but you can implement INSTEAD OF triggers (as discussed in a previous chapter) to allow these operations on a view to do nearly anything you need.

What makes this grand is that if you aren't able to use stored procedures, because of some technical or political reason (or personal choice, I suppose), you can do most of the things that you need to do in code using INSTEAD OF triggers or, at worst, user-defined functions, and the client programmers needn't know that they exist. The only concern here is that if you change any data that the client might have cached, you might have to work this out so the data and cached copies aren't significantly out of sync.

## Implementing Configurable Row-Level Security with Views

I've covered vertical partitioning, which is pretty easy. Row-level security, or *horizontally partitioning* data, isn't quite so elegant, especially if you can't use stored procedures in your applications. Using stored procedures, you could have a procedure that fixes certain operations, such as modifying active customers, or just certain products of a specific type, and so on.

With some planning, the same kind of partitioning can be done with views, and you could implement views that included all of a given type of product, another view for a different type, and yet another for other types. This scheme can work, but it isn't altogether flexible, and it's generally unnatural for a UI to have to view different objects to do ostensibly the same operation, just with a slightly different filter of data based on the security context of a user. It makes the objects tightly coupled with the data in the table. For some fixed domain tables that never change, this isn't a problem. But for many situations, users don't want to have to go back to the programming staff and ask for an implementation for which they have to jump through hoops, because the change will cost money for planning, programming, testing, and such.

In this section, I'll demonstrate a way to implement runtime configurable row-level security: using views. Views let you cut the table in sections that include all the columns, but not all the rows, based on some criteria. To the example table, you're going to add a productType column that you'll use to partition on:

```
ALTER TABLE Products.Product
   ADD ProductType varchar(20) NULL
GO
UPDATE Products.Product
SET    ProductType = 'widget'
WHERE  ProductCode = 'widget12'
GO
UPDATE Products.Product
SET    ProductType = 'snurf'
WHERE  ProductCode = 'snurf98'
```

Looking at the data in the table, you can see the following results:

| ProductId | ProductCode | Description | UnitPrice | ActualCost | ProductType |
|-----------|-------------|-------------|-----------|------------|-------------|
| 1 | widget12 | widget number 12 | 10.5000 | 8.5000 | widget |
| 2 | snurf98 | Snurfulator | 99.9900 | 2.5000 | snurf |

As discussed, the simplest version of row-level security is just building views to partition the data. For example, suppose you want to share the widgets only with a certain group in a company, mapped to a role. You can build the following view:

```
CREATE VIEW Products.WidgetProducts
AS
SELECT ProductId, ProductCode, Description, UnitPrice, ActualCost
FROM    Products.Product
WHERE   ProductType = 'widget'
WITH CHECK OPTION --This prevents the user from entering data that would not
                  --match the view's criteria
```

Now, you can select data from this table and never know that other products exist:

```
SELECT *
FROM    Products.WidgetProducts
```

This returns the following result:

| ProductId | ProductCode | Description | UnitPrice | ActualCost |
|-----------|-------------|-------------|-----------|------------|
| 1 | widget12 | widget number 12 | 10.5000 | 8.5000 |

---

**■Note** You can grant INSERT, UPDATE, and DELETE rights to the user to modify the view as well, because it's based on one table and we set the WITH CHECK OPTION. This option ensures that the rows after modification remain visible through the view after the change, or in this case, that the user couldn't change the ProductType if it were in the SELECT list. The only rows a user of this view would be able to modify would be the ones WHERE ProductType = 'widget'. Using INSTEAD OF triggers as discussed in Chapter 6, you can code almost any security you want to for modifications on your views. For simple views, the CHECK OPTION might work fine; otherwise, use triggers or stored procedures as needed.

---

This view can then have permissions granted to let only certain people use it. This is a decent technique when you have an easily described set, or possibly few types to work with, but can become a maintenance headache.

In the next step, ramping up row-level security, you build the following view to let users see snurfs only if they're members of the snurfViewer role, using the is_member function:

```
CREATE VIEW Products.ProductsSelective
AS
SELECT ProductId, ProductCode, Description, UnitPrice, ActualCost
FROM    Products.Product
WHERE   ProductType <> 'snurf'
   or   (is_member('snurfViewer') = 1)
   or   (is_member('db_owner') = 1) --can't add db_owner to a role
WITH CHECK OPTION
GO
GRANT SELECT ON Products.ProductsSelective to public
```

Then you create a principal named chrissy and the snurfViewer role. Note that you don't add this user to the group yet; you'll do that later in the example:

```
CREATE USER chrissy WITHOUT LOGIN
CREATE ROLE snurfViewer
```

Then you change security context to chrissy and select from the view:

```
EXECUTE AS USER = 'chrissy'
SELECT * from Products.ProductsSelective
REVERT
```

This returns the one row to which she has access:

| ProductId | ProductCode | Description      | UnitPrice | ActualCost | ProductType |
|-----------|-------------|------------------|-----------|------------|-------------|
| 1         | widget12    | widget number 12 | 10.5000   | 8.5000     | widget      |

Next, you add Chrissy to the snurfViewer group, go back to context as this user, and run the statement again:

```
EXECUTE sp_addrolemember 'snurfViewer', 'chrissy'
GO
EXECUTE AS USER = 'chrissy'
SELECT * from Products.ProductsSelective
REVERT
```

Now you see all the rows:

| ProductId | ProductCode | Description      | UnitPrice | ActualCost | ProductType |
|-----------|-------------|------------------|-----------|------------|-------------|
| 1         | widget12    | widget number 12 | 10.5000   | 8.5000     | widget      |
| 2         | snurf98     | Snurfulator      | 99.9900   | 2.5000     | snurf       |

This is even better, but still rigid, and requires foreknowledge of the data during the design phase. Instead, you'll create a table that maps database role principals with different types of products. Now this gives you total control. You create the following solution:

```
CREATE TABLE Products.ProductSecurity
(
    ProductsSecurityId int identity(1,1)
                CONSTRAINT PKProducts_ProductsSecurity PRIMARY KEY,
    ProductType varchar(20), --at this point you probably will create a
                            --ProductType domain table, but this keeps the
                            --example a bit simpler
```

```
DatabaseRole    sysname,
            CONSTRAINT AKProducts_ProductsSecurity_typeRoleMapping
                    UNIQUE (ProductType, DatabaseRole)
)
```

Then you insert a row that will be used to give everyone with database rights the ability to see widget-type products:

```
INSERT INTO Products.ProductSecurity(ProductType, DatabaseRole)
VALUES ('widget','public')
```

Then we alter the ProductsSelective view to show only rows to which the user has rights, based on row security:

```
ALTER VIEW Products.ProductsSelective
AS
SELECT Product.ProductId, Product.ProductCode, Product.Description,
      Product.UnitPrice, Product.ActualCost, Product.ProductType
FROM   Products.Product as Product
          JOIN Products.ProductSecurity as ProductSecurity
          on  (Product.ProductType = ProductSecurity.ProductType
              and is_member(ProductSecurity.DatabaseRole) = 1)
              or is_member('db_owner') = 1 --don't leave out the dbo!
```

This view joins the Product table to the ProductSecurity table and checks the matching roles against the role membership of the principal. Now you test it:

```
EXECUTE AS USER = 'chrissy'
SELECT *
FROM   Products.ProductsSelective
REVERT
```

This returns the following result:

| ProductId | ProductCode | Description | UnitPrice | ActualCost | ProductType |
|-----------|-------------|-------------|-----------|------------|-------------|
| 1 | widget12 | widget number 12 | 10.5000 | 8.5000 | widget |

Then you add the snurfViewer role to the ProductSecurity table and try again:

```
INSERT INTO Products.ProductSecurity(ProductType, databaseRole)
VALUES ('snurf','snurfViewer')
go
EXECUTE AS USER = 'chrissy'
SELECT * from ProductsSelective
REVERT
```

Now you see it returns all data:

| ProductId | ProductCode | Description | UnitPrice | ActualCost | ProductType |
|-----------|-------------|-------------|-----------|------------|-------------|
| 1 | widget12 | widget number 12 | 10.5000 | 8.5000 | widget |
| 2 | snurf98 | Snurfulator | 99.9900 | 2.5000 | snurf |

This causes a bit of overhead, but then again, all solutions for row-level security will. If you need it, you need it, and not much more can be said. The important aspect of this solution is that we can now use this view in a stored procedure, and regardless of who owns the stored procedure, we can restrict column usage in a generic manner that uses only SQL Server security.

---

**■Tip** You can take this type of thing to another level and get really specific with the security. You can even selectively hide and show columns to the user (replacing values with NULLs, or securevalue, or something). What's better is that once you have set it up, it's a no-brainer to add a principal to a group, and bam, that person has everything he or she needs, without costly setup.

---

# Obfuscating Data

It isn't always possible to keep users from accessing data. We database administrator types too often have unfettered access to entire production systems with way too much access. Even with the far-improved security granularity starting with SQL Server 2005, a few users will still have rights to run as a member of the sys_admin server role, giving them access to *all* data.

Also, technically, once a person has access to unencrypted backups of the system, he or she can technically, and with great ease, access any data in the database by simply restoring it to a different server where they are an admin. And don't forget that if you can attach the database, the data is also going to be viewable, in some fashion. If you're dealing with sensitive data—and who isn't these days—you need to be wary of how you deal with this data:

- Do you back the database up? Where are these backups?

- Do you send the backups to an offsite safe location? Who takes them there?

- Who has access to the servers where data is stored? Do you trust the fate of your company in their hands? Could these servers be hacked?

On one hand, SQL Server has definitely improved in this respect for the 2008 version in terms of the DBA job of protecting data by implementing *Transparent Data Encryption*. Basically, this will encrypt the data and log files during I/O so that you don't have to change your code, but anytime the data is at rest, it will stay encrypted (including when it is backed up). You can also use several third-party tools to encrypt backups.

When data is at rest in the database and users have access to the data, it is also important that we obfuscate the data such that a user cannot tell what it is exactly. This is one of the main ways that we can protect data from casual observers, especially ones like we DBA types who generally have full control over the database (in other words,way too much power in the database).

The biggest key to encryption is that you don't include all the information needed to decrypt the data easily available to the user. SQL Server has a rich set of encryption features, featuring a key and certificate management system. You can use this system to encrypt data from each user and from people who might get access to the data outside of the server.

In the following example, I'll use the simplest encryption that SQL Server gives us, using the encryptByPassPhrase. (You can also use keys, asymmetric keys, and certificates.) The encryptByPassPhrase function lets you specify your key as a string value that SQL Server uses to "munge" the data, such that you must have this key to reconstitute the data. Passphrase encryption can be one of the most useful forms of encryption, because you can let each row have its own password. So, let's say we have a column of very personal information, such as a vault of information that an end user might be able to save securely. Using the password in the application, the data could become visible, but it would not be available to anyone else who did not know the password. Of course, passphrase encryption does suffer from the problem that if the password is lost, the data is lost for good.

As an example, we'll build an incredibly simple encryption scheme that you could use to secure a column in your database. First, as a quick demonstration of how the function works, consider the following:

```
SELECT encryptByPassPhrase('hi', 'Secure data')
```

'Secure data' is the value to be encrypted, and 'hi' is the passphrase that's required to get this value back later. Executing this statement returns the following result:

```
--------------------------------------------------------------------
0x010000004D2B87C6725612388F8BA4DA082495E8C836FF76F32BCB642B36476594B4F014
```

This is a clearly unreadable binary string, and even cooler, the value is different every time you execute it, so no one can come behind and decrypt it with any ease. To decrypt it, just use the following:

```
SELECT decryptByPassPhrase('hi',
    0x010000004D2B87C6725612388F8BA4DA082495E8C836FF76F32BCB642B36476594B4F014)
```

This returns the following result:

```
-----------------------
0x5365637572652064617461
```

This is the binary representation of our original string, which makes it easy to represent most any datatype. To use the value, you have to cast it back to the original varchar type:

```
SELECT cast(decryptByPassPhrase('hi',
    0x010000004D2B87C6725612388F8BA4DA082495E8C836FF76F32BCB642B36476594B4F014)
                                    as varchar(30))
```

This returns the following result:

```
-----------------------------
Secure data
```

**■Tip** The data is different each time because the encryption scheme uses various nonencrypted data, such as the time value, to encrypt the data (this is generally known as the *salt value* of the encryption). You cannot infer the decryption of all values based on breaking a single value.

Let's take this to the next level. In this example, we'll encrypt a credit card number in the database, a common need in many databases. Such personal and financial information needs to be kept where it can be used only by the correct people or processes.

The first step is to create a database that no one has rights to, other than the owner of the database. This database should be as isolated as possible from any of the staff, because if the value is known, the encryption is easy pickings.

This database has a single table with the password for encrypting and decrypting data (which is credit cards, in our example):

```
CREATE DATABASE EncryptionMaster
go
USE EncryptionMaster
go
CREATE SCHEMA Security
CREATE TABLE Security.passphrase
(
    passphrase nvarchar(4000) --the max size of the passphrase
)
```

This is the passphrase that all encryption and decryption will use for our solution:

```
INSERT  into Security.passphrase
VALUES ('ljlOIUEojljljieo#*JlLjlIu*o7G8i&t87*&Yh[pOO') --the more unobvious the
                                                       --better!
```

Then we create the application database to hold `Customer` rows, including our encrypted `CreditCardNumber`:

```
CREATE DATABASE CreditInfo
GO
ALTER DATABASE EncryptionMaster   -- we will be using impersonation to keep the
    SET TRUSTWORTHY ON            -- example simple, in practice I would
                                  -- probably use certificates
GO
USE CreditInfo
GO

CREATE SCHEMA Sales
GO
CREATE TABLE Sales.Customer
(
    CustomerId  char(10),
    FirstName   varchar(30),
    LastName    varchar(30),
    CreditCardLastFour char(4),
    CreditCardNumber varbinary(44)
)
```

Now, the key here is to build the procedure without enabling database security chaining on the server or enabling it on the `encryptionMaster` database. No user should have direct access to the passphrase table. We use the `WITH EXECUTE AS` setting we discussed earlier in this chapter. This allows us not to give the caller any rights to the encryption database, but the user can still get values out:

```
CREATE PROCEDURE Customer$insert
(
    @CustomerId  char(10),
    @FirstName   varchar(10),
    @LastName    varchar(10),
    @CreditCardNumber char(16)
)
WITH EXECUTE AS 'dbo'
as

INSERT INTO Sales.Customer (CustomerId,FirstName, LastName, CreditCardLastFour,
                            CreditCardNumber)
SELECT  @CustomerId, @FirstName,@LastName,substring(@CreditCardNumber,13,4),
        encryptByPassPhrase(pass.passPhrase, @CreditCardNumber)
FROM    encryptionMaster.Security.passphrase as pass
```

Now we can test the procedure using the following code:

```
EXEC Customer$insert 'cust1','Bob','jones','0000111122223333'
```

To view the data, we use a stored procedure:

```
CREATE PROCEDURE Sales.CustomerWithCreditCard
WITH EXECUTE AS 'dbo'
AS
 BEGIN
```

```
SELECT  Customer.CustomerId, FirstName, LastName,
        CreditCardLastFour,
        cast(decryptByPassPhrase(pass.passPhrase,CreditCardNumber)
                as char(16)) as CreditCardNumber
FROM    Sales.Customer
            CROSS JOIN encryptionMaster.Security.passphrase as pass
END
```

Then we execute as follows:

```
EXEC Sales.CustomerWithCreditCard
```

This returns the row with decrypted values:

| CustomerId | FirstName | LastName | CreditCardLastFour | CreditCardNumber |
| --- | --- | --- | --- | --- |
| 1 | Bob | Jones | 3333 | 0000111122223333 |

Now granting rights to this procedure and giving access to it gives the user rights to view credit card numbers, but not to see how they're encrypted or decrypted. Also note that the procedure would likely be used only by a computer process to send the credit card to the authorization authority.

Now, here's the most important part. *Don't back up the encryptionMaster database* to the same media as the CreditInfo database, because if someone gets both databases, it's child's play to steal your data. It's good policy to back up this database to a CD (or two), write down the key (it might take a day to enter, but that would be better than losing all your data), and store it in a cool, dry place where no one can get access to it.

Now, say your backup tape is pocketed by an employee who's changing jobs from legit IT worker to a credit-card-number salesperson. The data is worthless, and all your press release need say is "Company X regrets to say that some financial data tapes were stolen from our vaults. All data was encrypted; hence, there is little chance any usable data was acquired." And you, as DBA, will be worshipped!

# Monitoring and Auditing

Often a client won't care too much about security, so he or she doesn't want to limit what a user can do in the database. However, many times there's a hidden subtext: "I don't want to be restrictive, but how can we keep up with what users have done?"

An alternative to implementing a full-blown security system can be simply to watch what users do, in case they do something they shouldn't. To implement our Big Brother security scenario, I'll demonstrate three possible techniques:

- *Server and database audit:* In SQL Server 2008, you can define audit specifications that will watch and log all the activity as you define.

- *Watching table changes using DML triggers*: Keep up with a history of previous values for rows in a table.

- *DDL triggers*: Use these to log any DDL events, such as creating users, creating or modifying tables, and so on.

- *Using Profiler*: Profiler catches everything, so you can use it to watch user activity.

In some cases, these techniques are used to augment the security of a system, for example, to make sure system administrators keep out of certain parts of the system.

■**Note** In SQL Server 2008, Microsoft introduced two other new features that are interesting for watching changes to the database, but they are not of value for a security purpose. Change Data Capture is an Enterprise Edition–only feature that allows you to do full tracking of every change in data, and Change Tracking is available to other editions to capture that a change has occurred since the last time you checked the Change Tracking system. However, neither of those new features will tell you the user who made a given change; thus, they don't have security applications. They are, however, amazingly useful for implementing an reporting/data warehouse system, because finding the rows that changed for ETL has always been always the hardest thing. These new features have less overhead (and certainly less setup) than do triggers that you might write to accomplish the same goal.

## Server and Database Audit

For the 2008 release, Microsoft has added a very nice feature for auditing the activities of your users. It is called SQL Server Audit, and it allows you to define server and database-level audits that you can use to monitor almost everything your logins and users do to your server and/or databases. It is, however, a feature that is included only in the Enterprise Edition.

In previous versions, such monitoring would have required a web of DML and DDL triggers, plus the use of Profiler to watch everyone's moves. Now you can implement detailed monitoring in a declarative manner. SQL Server Audit is a tremendously cool feature and will make the process of meeting auditing requirements *much* easier than ever before. Instead of lots of code to pore through, you can just print the audits that you are enforcing, and you are done. Note that SQL Server Audit does not obviate the use of DML or DDL triggers as a tool for watching what users are doing, mostly because in a trigger you can react to what a user is doing and alter their path. Using SQL Server Audit, you will simply be able to watch what the user is doing.

■**Note** As usual, there are graphical user interface (GUI) versions of everything I discuss, and I imagine that many DBAs (even some hardcore ones) will probably use the use the GUI for the most part, but as with everything else in this book, I want to show the syntax because it will make using the GUI easier, and if you have to apply these settings to more than one server, you will quickly learn to write scripts, or at least to use the GUI and right-click.

The auditing is file based, in that you don't do your logging to a database; rather, you specify a directory on your server (or off your server if you so desire). You will want to make sure that the directory is a very fast access location to write to, because writing to it will be part of the transactions you execute. When auditing is turned on, each operation will be audited or not executed. However, it doesn't write directly to the file; rather, for maximum performance, SQL Server Audit uses Service Broker queues under the covers, so it doesn't have to write audit data to the file as part of each transaction. Instead, queue mechanisms make sure that the data is written asynchronously (there is a setting to force an audit trail to be written in some amount of time or synchronously if you need it to be guaranteed 100 percent up-to-date).

The audit structures consist of three basic objects:

- *Server audit*: Top-level object that defines where the audit file will be written to and other essential settings

- *Server audit specification*: Defines the actions at the server level that will be audited

- *Database audit specification*: Defines the actions at the database level that will be audited

## Defining an Audit Specification

As an example, I will set up an audit on our test server/security database to watch for logins to be changed (such as a new login created or one changed/dropped) as well as watching for the employee or manager user to execute a SELECT statement against the Products.Product table and SELECTs by anyone on Sales.Invoice. First, you define the SERVER AUDIT:

```
USE master
GO
CREATE SERVER AUDIT ProSQLServerDatabaseDesign_Audit
TO FILE                        --choose your own directory, I expect most people
(    FILEPATH = N'c:\temp\' --have a temp directory on their system drive
    ,MAXSIZE = 15 MB
    ,MAX_ROLLOVER_FILES = 0 --unlimited
)
WITH
(
    ON_FAILURE = SHUTDOWN --if the file cannot be written to,
                          --shut down the server
)
```

---

■**Note**  The audit is created in a disabled state. You need to start it once you have added audit specifications.

---

The next step is to define an audit specification to set up the container to hold a list of related items to audit. This container-based approach lets you easily enable or disable auditing for the entire group of related features. Create the container by defining a SERVER AUDIT SPECIFICATION:

```
CREATE SERVER AUDIT SPECIFICATION ProSQLServerDatabaseDesign_Server_Audit
    FOR SERVER AUDIT ProSQLServerDatabaseDesign_Audit
    WITH (STATE = OFF) --disabled. I will enable it later
```

The next step is to add things to the specification to audit. There are lots of different things you can audit. You can find the list under "SQL Server Audit Action Groups and Actions" in Books Online. In our sample, we are going to watch for server principals to change:

```
ALTER SERVER AUDIT SPECIFICATION ProSQLServerDatabaseDesign_Server_Audit
    ADD (SERVER_PRINCIPAL_CHANGE_GROUP)
```

Next, I will go through the same process for the database that I did for the server, setting up the container for the audit using the DATABASE AUDIT SPECIFICATION command:

```
USE SecurityChapter
GO
CREATE DATABASE AUDIT SPECIFICATION
                ProSQLServerDatabaseDesign_Database_Audit
    FOR SERVER AUDIT ProSQLServerDatabaseDesign_Audit
    WITH (STATE = OFF)
```

This time, we will audit the employee and manager database principals use of the Products.Product table and the Sales.Invoice table by any user. Here is how we add those items to the specification:

```
ALTER DATABASE AUDIT SPECIFICATION
ProSQLServerDatabaseDesign_ Database_Audit
    ADD (SELECT ON Products.Product BY employee,manager),
    ADD (SELECT ON Sales.Invoice BY public)
```

## Enabling an Audit Specification

Finally, we enable the two audit specifications that we've just created. Remember, to enable a specification is to enable all the audits defined in that container. For example:

```
USE master
GO
ALTER SERVER AUDIT ProSQLServerDatabaseDesign_Audit
    WITH (STATE = ON)
ALTER SERVER AUDIT SPECIFICATION ProSQLServerDatabaseDesign_Server_Audit
    WITH (STATE = ON)
GO
USE SecurityChapter
GO
ALTER DATABASE AUDIT SPECIFICATION ProSQLServerDatabaseDesign_Database_Audit
    WITH (STATE = ON)
```

## Viewing the Audit Trail

Now that our audits are enabled, we can monitor the usage of the features and functionality that we're auditing. The following code executes some actions that will be audited as a result the specifications we've just created. The following script will do a few actions that will be audited by the audit objects we have set up in the previous sections:

```
CREATE LOGIN MrSmith WITH PASSWORD = 'Not a good password'
GO
EXECUTE AS USER = 'manager'
GO
SELECT *
FROM    Products.Product
GO
SELECT  *
FROM    Products.AllProducts--Permissions will fail
REVERT
GO
SELECT  *
FROM    Products.AllProducts
```

The following query will let us view the log that was set up with the CREATE SERVER AUDIT command in the first step of the process. By executing this:

```
SELECT event_time, succeeded,
    database_principal_name,statement
FROM sys.fn_get_audit_file ('c:\temp\*',default,default);
```

we can see the different statements that were executed:

| event_time | succeeded | database_principal_name | statement |
| --- | --- | --- | --- |
| 2008-02-19 04:11:00.183 | 1 | dbo | CREATE LOGIN MrSmith WITH PASSWORD = '***' |
| 2008-02-19 04:11:07.246 | 1 | Manager | SELECT * FROM  Products.Product |
| 2008-02-19 04:11:23.825 | 0 | Manager | SELECT  * FROM  Products.AllProducts |
| 2008-02-19 04:11:26.950 | 1 | dbo | SELECT  * FROM  Products.AllProducts |

There are lots of other pieces of information returned by the sys.fn_get_audit_file function that are very useful, especially including the server principal information. Using a few of the catalog views, you can get a picture of what the audits do. Note that the query I built works only at an object level. It could be extended if you wanted to do column-level audits.

## Viewing the Audit Configuration

Finally, once you have set up the audit trail, it is often important to find out what is being audited. You can do this using several of the catalog views:

- sys.server_audits: One row per server audit
- sys.server_audit_specifications: Details about the audits that have been configured for this server, such as when it was started, the last time it was modified, and so on
- sys.server_audit_specification_details: Links the objects being audited and actions being audited

The following query, using these views, will get you the definition of what is being audited at a server level:

```
SELECT  sas.name as audit_specification_name,
        audit_action_name
FROM    sys.server_audits as sa
           join sys.server_audit_specifications as sas
              on sa.audit_guid = sas.audit_guid
           join sys.server_audit_specification_details as sasd
              on sas.server_specification_id = sasd.server_specification_id
WHERE   sa.name = 'ProSQLServerDatabaseDesign_Audit'
```

By executing this, given all of the audit stuff we had set up, will return the following:

| audit_specification_name | audit_action_name |
| --- | --- |
| ProSQLServerDatabaseDesign_Server_Audit | SERVER_PRINCIPAL_CHANGE_GROUP |

Digging deeper, to get the objects and actions, the following query will get you the database-level actions that are being audited:

```
SELECT --sas.name  as audit_specification_name,
       audit_action_name,dp.name as [principal],
       SCHEMA_NAME(o.schema_id) + '.' + o.name as object
FROM   sys.server_audits as sa
          join sys.database_audit_specifications as sas
             on sa.audit_guid = sas.audit_guid
          join sys.database_audit_specification_details as sasd
             on sas.database_specification_id = sasd.database_specification_id
          join sys.database_principals as dp
             on dp.principal_id = sasd.audited_principal_id
          join sys.objects as o
             on o.object_id = sasd.major_id
WHERE  sa.name = 'ProSQLServerDatabaseDesign_Audit'
  and  sasd.minor_id = 0 --need another query for column level audits
```

This query returns the following:

```
audit_action_name    principal        object
-------------------   --------------   --------------------------
SELECT                public           Sales.invoice
SELECT                Employee         Products.Product
SELECT                Manager          Products.Product
```

Quite a few more catalog views pertain to the server and database facilities of SQL Server 2008, certainly more than is necessary in this chapter for me to cover. The basic setup of auditing is really quite straightforward, and auditing is a nice new feature of SQL Server 2008 that is going to be a welcome tool for users who have the need to audit the activities of their users and especially administrators.

# Watching Table History Using DML Triggers

Even in addition to the kind of logging you can do with SQL Server Audit, you will still find uses for trigger-based logging of table history. And in previous versions of SQL Server, trigger-based logging is very much the way to watch what your users do with your data.

As discussed in Chapter 6, you can run code whenever a user executes an INSERT, UPDATE, or DELETE DML statement on a table or view. We already constructed an auditing trigger in Chapter 6 in the section "DML Triggers" that audited change, and we'll create another one here. When finished, a history of the previous values for a column in a table will be maintained, in case some user changes the data improperly.

The scenario is that we have a slice of the Sales and Inventory sections of the database for products and invoices (see Figure 8-1).

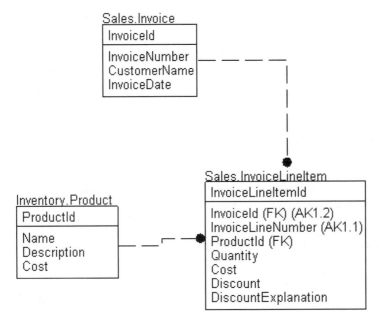

**Figure 8-1.** *Sample tables for table history example*

On each invoice line item, there's a cost and a discount percentage. If the cost value doesn't match the current value in the Product table and the discount percentage isn't zero, we want to log the difference. A report of differences will be built and sent to the manager to let the values be checked to make sure everything is within reason.

First we build the tables, going back to the SecurityChapter database:

```
USE SecurityChapter
GO
CREATE SCHEMA Sales
GO
CREATE SCHEMA Inventory
GO
CREATE TABLE Sales.invoice
(
    InvoiceId   int not null identity(1,1) CONSTRAINT PKInvoice PRIMARY KEY,
    InvoiceNumber char(10) not null
                    CONSTRAINT AKInvoice_InvoiceNumber UNIQUE,
    CustomerName varchar(60) not null , --should be normalized in real database
    InvoiceDate smalldatetime not null
)
CREATE TABLE Inventory.Product
(
    ProductId int identity(1,1) CONSTRAINT PKProduct PRIMARY KEY,
    name varchar(30) not null CONSTRAINT AKProduct_name UNIQUE,
    Description varchar(60) not null ,
    Cost numeric(12,4) not null
)
CREATE TABLE Sales.InvoiceLineItem
(
    InvoiceLineItemId int identity(1,1)
                    CONSTRAINT PKInvoiceLineItem PRIMARY KEY,
    InvoiceId int not null,
    ProductId int not null,
    Quantity numeric(6,2) not null,
    Cost numeric(12,4) not null,
    discount numeric(3,2) not null,
    discountExplanation varchar(200) not null,
    CONSTRAINT AKInvoiceLineItem_InvoiceAndProduct
            UNIQUE (InvoiceId, ProductId),
    CONSTRAINT FKSales_Invoice$listsSoldProductsIn$Sales_InvoiceLineItem
            FOREIGN KEY (InvoiceId) REFERENCES Sales.Invoice(InvoiceId),
    CONSTRAINT FKSales_Product$isSoldVia$Sales_InvoiceLineItem
            FOREIGN KEY (InvoiceId) REFERENCES Sales.Invoice(InvoiceId)
    --more constraints should be in place for full implementation
)
```

Now, we create another table to hold the audit of the line item of an invoice:

```
CREATE TABLE Sales.InvoiceLineItemDiscountAudit
(
    InvoiceLineItemDiscountAudit  int identity(1,1)
        CONSTRAINT PKInvoiceLineItemDiscountAudit PRIMARY KEY,
    InvoiceId    int,
    InvoiceLineItemId int,
    AuditTime    datetime,
    SetByUserId sysname,
```

```
    Quantity numeric(6,2) not null,
    Cost numeric(12,4) not null,
    Discount numeric(3,2) not null,
    DiscountExplanation varchar(300) not null
)
```

I used a surrogate primary key with no other uniqueness criteria here because you just cannot predict whether two users could change the same row at the same point in time (heck, even the same user could change the row twice at the same time on two different connections!) In this case, we settle on the surrogate to simply represent the order of events, rather than their existing logical uniqueness.

Then we code a trigger, using the same trigger template as in the previous chapter. The trigger will cascade the change from the primary table to the audit table behind the scenes:

```
CREATE TRIGGER Sales.InvoiceLineItem$insertAndUpdateAuditTrail
ON Sales.InvoiceLineItem
AFTER INSERT,UPDATE AS
BEGIN

    DECLARE @rowsAffected int,    --stores the number of rows affected
            @msg varchar(2000)    --used to hold the error message

    SET @rowsAffected = @@rowcount

    --no need to continue on if no rows affected
    IF @rowsAffected = 0 return

    SET NOCOUNT ON --to avoid the rowcount messages
    SET ROWCOUNT 0 --in case the client has modified the rowcount
    BEGIN TRY
        --[validation blocks]
        --[modification blocks]
        IF UPDATE(Cost)
            INSERT INTO Sales.InvoiceLineItemDiscountAudit (InvoiceId,
                        InvoiceLineItemId, AuditTime, SetByUserId, Quantity,
                        Cost, Discount, DiscountExplanation)
            SELECT inserted.InvoiceId, inserted.InvoiceLineItemId,
                   current_timestamp, suser_sname(), inserted.Quantity,
                   inserted.Cost, inserted.Discount,
                   inserted.DiscountExplanation

            FROM   inserted
                     join Inventory.Product as Product
                       on inserted.ProductId = Product.ProductId
            --if the Discount is more than 0, or the cost supplied is less than the
            --current value
            WHERE  inserted.Discount > 0
               or  inserted.Cost < Product.Cost
                            -- if it was the same or greater, that is good!
                            -- this keeps us from logging if the cost didn't actually
                            -- change
    END TRY
    BEGIN CATCH
                IF @@trancount > 0
                    ROLLBACK TRANSACTION
```

```
                --This object created in CH 6
                --EXECUTE dbo.errorLog$insert

                DECLARE @ERROR_MESSAGE varchar(8000)
                SET @ERROR_MESSAGE = ERROR_MESSAGE()
                RAISERROR (@ERROR_MESSAGE,16,1)

       END CATCH
END
```

We then test the code by creating a few products:

```
INSERT INTO Inventory.Product(name, Description,Cost)
VALUES ('Duck Picture','Picture on the wall in my hotelRoom',200.00),
       ('Cow Picture','Picture on the other wall in my hotelRoom',150.00)
```

Then we start an invoice:

```
INSERT INTO Sales.Invoice(InvoiceNumber, CustomerName, InvoiceDate)
VALUES ('IE00000001','The Hotel Picture Company','1/1/2005')
```

Then we add an `InvoiceLineItem` that's clean, has the same price, and has no discount:

```
INSERT INTO Sales.InvoiceLineItem(InvoiceId, ProductId, Quantity,
                                  Cost, Discount, DiscountExplanation)
SELECT  (SELECT InvoiceId
         FROM   Sales.Invoice
         WHERE  InvoiceNumber = 'IE00000001'),
        (SELECT ProductId
         FROM   Inventory.Product
         WHERE  Name = 'Duck Picture'),  1,200,0,''
```

We check our log:

```
SELECT * FROM Sales.InvoiceLineItemDiscountAudit
```

Nothing is returned on insert:

| InvoiceId | InvoiceLineItemId | AuditDate | SetByUserId | Quantity |
| --- | --- | --- | --- | --- |

| Cost | Discount | DiscountExplanation |
| --- | --- | --- |

Then we create a row with a discount percentage:

```
INSERT INTO Sales.InvoiceLineItem(InvoiceId, ProductId, Quantity,
                                  Cost, Discount, DiscountExplanation)
SELECT  (SELECT InvoiceId
         FROM Sales.Invoice
         WHERE InvoiceNumber = 'IE00000001'),
        (SELECT ProductId
         FROM Inventory.Product
         WHERE name = 'Cow Picture'),
        1,150,.45,'Customer purchased two, so I gave 45% off'

SELECT * FROM Sales.InvoiceLineItemDiscountAudit
```

Now we see that a result has been logged:

| InvoiceId | InvoiceLineItemId | AuditDate | SetByUserId | Quantity |
| --- | --- | --- | --- | --- |
| 1 | 4 | 2008-02-13 17:49:35.437 | DOMAIN\USER | 1.00 |

| Cost | Discount | DiscountExplanation |
| --- | --- | --- |
| 150.0000 | 0.45 | Customer purchased two, so I gave 45% off |

DML triggers make wonderful security devices for keeping an eye on what users do, because those triggers can be completely transparent to users *and* to programmers. The only catch is when an application layer isn't passing the security context through to the application. Sometimes the application uses one common login, and there isn't any automatic way for the database code to determine which user is actually doing the DML operation. Most of the time when that is the case, you'll have already dealt with the problem using some method (such as just passing the username to the stored procedure, adding a column to the table to hold the user that is doing the operation, and so on).

# DDL Triggers

DDL triggers let you watch what users do, but instead of watching what they do to data, you can watch what they do to the system. They let us protect and monitor changes to the server or database structure by firing when a user executes any DDL statement. The list of DDL statements you can monitor is quite long. (There are server-level events, such as creating and altering logins, as well as for the database, including creating and modifying tables, indexes, views, procedures, and so on. For a full list, check SQL Server 2008 Books Online in the "DDL Events Groups" topic.)

DDL triggers are of no value in protecting data values, because they don't fire for operations where data is changed or manipulated. They are, however, good for monitoring and preventing changes to the system, even by users who have the rights to do so. For example, consider the all-too-frequent case where the manager of the IT group has system administration powers on the database, though he can barely spell SQL (if this power wasn't granted, it would seem like a slight to the abilities/power of this manager). Now, let's assume that this manager is just pointing and clicking his way around the UI, and one click is to the wrong place and all of a sudden, your customer table joins the choir invisible. Now you have to restore from a backup and waste a day cleaning up the mess, while trying to figure out who dropped the table. (OK, so if you have constraints on your table, you can't actually drop it that easily. And yes, to be honest most every DBA has dropped some object in a production database. That ends the honest part of this section.)

## Preventing a DDL Action

With a simple DDL trigger, we can prevent the accidental drop of the table by trapping for the event and stopping it, or we can log who it was who dropped the table. In the first example, I will create a DDL trigger that will prevent any alterations to the schema without the user going in and manually disabling this trigger. It is a great safeguard to secure your objects from accidental change.

```
CREATE TRIGGER tr_server$allTableDDL_prevent --note, not a schema owned object
ON DATABASE
AFTER CREATE_TABLE, DROP_TABLE, ALTER_TABLE
AS
 BEGIN
   BEGIN TRY  --note the following line will not wrap
       RAISERROR ('The trigger: tr_server$allTableDDL_prevent must be disabled
                before making any table modifications',16,1)
```

```
      END TRY
      --using the same old error handling
      BEGIN CATCH
                IF @@trancount > 0
                     ROLLBACK TRANSACTION

                --commented out, build from Chapter 6 if desired
                --EXECUTE dbo.errorLog$insert

                DECLARE @ERROR_MESSAGE varchar(8000)
                SET @ERROR_MESSAGE = ERROR_MESSAGE()
                RAISERROR (@ERROR_MESSAGE,16,1)

        END CATCH
END
```

Now we try to create a simple table:

```
CREATE TABLE dbo.test  --dbo for simplicity of example
(
    testId int identity CONSTRAINT PKtest PRIMARY KEY
)
```

We get the following error message:

```
Msg 50000, Level 16, State 1, Procedure tr_server$allTableDDL_prevent, Line 19
The trigger: tr_server$allTableDDL_prevent must be disabled before making any
table modifications
```

No harm, no foul. We could log the error message so we can see whether this happens often.

**■Note** I wouldn't put the name of the trigger in the error message if this were a production application that had any external exposure. Otherwise, the hackers get everything they need to disable the trigger right in the error message.

## Recording a DDL Action

The second case, and just as useful, is to log DDL that is executed in a database so you can see what has been done. Although stopping DDL is something I usually do in a production database, logging changes is something I often do in a development environment. Not that logging is never useful in a production environment; it is just that it shouldn't be as necessary, since tables in the production system should be very stable and changed only in an organized manner, not just randomly by a user or a DBA. Sometimes I will use DDL logging to catch things that are routine such as index changes so I will know to watch the new indexes especially closely for a while to see whether they are valuable.

Let's look at creating a trigger similar to the one created in the preceding section. The difference is that this time we will have the trigger monitor DDL changes, not prevent them. First, let's drop the trigger created previously:

```
--Note: Slight change in syntax to drop DDL trigger, requires clause indicating
--where the objects are
DROP TRIGGER tr_server$allTableDDL_prevent ON DATABASE
```

Now, we create a table to contain the history of changes to our table:

```
--first create a table to log to
CREATE TABLE dbo.TableChangeLog
(
    TableChangeLogId int identity
        CONSTRAINT pkTableChangeLog PRIMARY KEY (TableChangeLogId),
    ChangeTime        datetime,
    UserName          sysname,
    Ddl               varchar(max)--so we can get as much of the batch as possible
)
```

And we build another trigger to fire when a user creates, alters, or drops a table:

```
--not a schema bound object
CREATE TRIGGER tr_server$allTableDDL
ON DATABASE
AFTER CREATE_TABLE, DROP_TABLE, ALTER_TABLE
AS
 BEGIN
   SET NOCOUNT ON --to avoid the rowcount messages
   SET ROWCOUNT 0 --in case the client has modified the rowcount

   BEGIN TRY

       --we get our data from the EVENT_INSTANCE XML stream
       INSERT INTO dbo.TableChangeLog (ChangeTime, userName, Ddl)
       SELECT getdate(), user,
           EVENTDATA().value('(/EVENT_INSTANCE/TSQLCommand/CommandText)[1]',
           'nvarchar(max)')

   END TRY
   --using the same old error handling
   BEGIN CATCH
               IF @@trancount > 0
                   ROLLBACK TRANSACTION

               --From Ch6, get code if you want to enable
               --EXECUTE dbo.errorLog$insert

               DECLARE @ERROR_MESSAGE varchar(8000)
               SET @ERROR_MESSAGE = ERROR_MESSAGE()
               RAISERROR (@ERROR_MESSAGE,16,1)

      END CATCH
END
```

Now we run this to create the dbo.test table:

```
CREATE TABLE dbo.test
(
    id int
)
GO
DROP TABLE dbo.test
```

We check out the TableChangeLog data to see what has changed:

```
SELECT * FROM dbo.TableChangeLog
```

This shows us our commands:

```
TableChangeLogId DateOfChange            UserName           Ddl
---------------- ----------------------- ------------------ ----------------------
1                2008-02-13 20:11:48.707 dbo                CREATE TABLE dbo.test
                                                            (
                                                                 id int
                                                            )
2                2008-02-13 20:11:48.720 dbo                DROP TABLE dbo.test
```

Now we can see what users have been up to in the database without them having to do anything special to cause it to happen (or without them even knowing, either).

---

■**Tip** It's usually best when building production-quality applications not to have users dropping and creating tables, even with a good set of schema structures with which to work. DDL triggers give us the power to see what kind of activity is occurring. You can also use DDL triggers to prevent unwanted DDL from occurring, as I demonstrated earlier in this section as well.

---

# Logging with Profiler

The last line of defense is the "security camera" approach. Just watch the activity on your server and make sure it looks legit. This is probably the only approach that has a chance to work with malicious (or stupid) programmers and DBAs. I include DBAs in here because there's often no way to avoid giving a few of them system-administration powers. Hence, they might have access to parts of the data that they should never go to, unless there's a problem. They might stumble into data they shouldn't see, though as we discussed previously, we can use encryption to obfuscate this data. Unfortunately, even encryption won't necessarily stop a user with sys_admin rights.

Using Profiler, we can set up filters to look at certain events that we know shouldn't be happening, even when a DBA has access. For example, think back to our encryption example, where we stored the encryption password in the table. We could formulate a Profiler task to log only usage of this object. This log might be pretty small, especially if we filter out users who *should* be regularly accessing encrypted data. None of this is perfect, because any users who have admin rights to the Windows server and the database server could hide their activity with enough effort.

---

■**Note** Profiler is far more than a security tool, and in fact I would go so far as to say that is very much a secondary utilization of the tool. The number-one usage of Profiler is to watch what users are doing for debugging and tuning your server, in development, in production, and in all phases of a project. On my website (http://drsql.org/presentations.aspx), there is a link to a presentation I did on performance tuning where I cover some of these types of uses of Profiler.

---

An expedient and fairly cheap way to set up the tracing is using a startup stored procedure and the sp_trace% procedures. The following procedure starts up a simple trace each time you start SQL Server. I use this script on my test box on my laptop to capture every change and every script I run on my 2005 server in case I have a crash. Or say I press the wrong button when the dialog box "Do you want to save file: 'big_query_you_worked_on_for_five_hours.sql'?" comes up, and I hit No because I want to go home and start a night job. This procedure logs up to 10MB in each file, and it creates up to 20 files (incrementing the filenames as it goes up).

```
CREATE PROCEDURE dbo.Server$Watch
as

--note that we have to do some things because these procedures are very picky
--about datatypes.
declare @traceId int, @retval int,
        @stoptime datetime, @maxfilesize bigint, @filecount int
set @maxfilesize = 10 --MB
set @filecount = 20

--creates a trace, placing the file in the root of the server (clearly you should
--change this location to something that fits your own server standards other than
--the root of the c: drive)
exec @retval =  sp_trace_create @traceId = @traceId output,
                     @options = 2, --rollover to a different file
                                   --once max is reached
                     @tracefile = N'c:\trace.trc',
                     @maxfilesize = @maxfilesize,
                     @stoptime = @stoptime,
                     @filecount = 20

--this is because the fourth parameter must be a bit, and the literal 1 thinks it is
--an integer
declare @true bit
set @true = 1

--then we manually add events
exec sp_trace_setevent @traceID, 12, 1, @true
exec sp_trace_setevent @traceID, 12, 6, @true  --12 = sql:batchstarting
                                               --6 = NTUserName
exec sp_trace_setevent @traceID, 12, 7, @true  --12 = sql:batchstarting
                                               --7=NTDomainName
exec sp_trace_setevent @traceID, 12, 11, @true --12 = sql:batchstarting
                                               --11=LoginName
exec sp_trace_setevent @traceID, 12, 14, @true --12 = sql:batchstarting
                                               --14=StartTime

exec sp_trace_setevent @traceID, 13, 1, @true --13 = sql:batchending
                                              -- 1 = textdata
exec sp_trace_setevent @traceID, 13, 6, @true --13 = sql:batchending
                                              -- 6=NTUserName
exec sp_trace_setevent @traceID, 13, 7, @true --13 = sql:batchending
                                              -- 7=NTDomainName
exec sp_trace_setevent @traceID, 13, 11, @true --13 = sql:batchending
                                               --11=LoginName
exec sp_trace_setevent @traceID, 13, 14, @true --13 = sql:batchending
                                               --14=StartTime

--and start the trace
exec sp_trace_setstatus @traceId = @traceId, @status = 1 --1 starts it

--this logs that we started the trace to the event viewer
declare @msg varchar(2000)
set @msg = 'logging under trace:' + cast(@traceId as varchar(10)) + ' started'
exec xp_logevent 60000, @msg, 'informational'
```

Now, you can set this procedure to execute every time the server starts by setting its procedure property (you have to create the procedure in the master database to make that work):

```
exec master..sp_procoption 'dbo.Server$Watch','startup','true'
```

You can view the trace data by opening the file it creates in Profiler, the latest being c:\trace.trc. (There will be others as the tool cycles through the generations you tell it to create. We set it to rotate at 20 in our procedure.) See Figure 8-2.

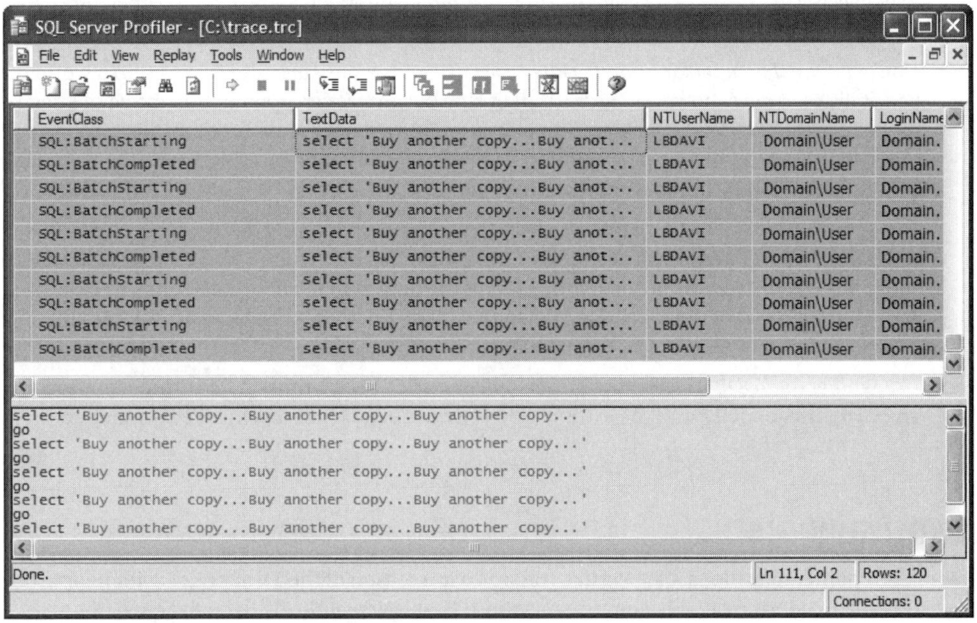

**Figure 8-2.** *Viewing a trace in Profiler*

This is an effective device to diagnose security issues after they occur, which is sometimes the only kind of security we can get.

---

■**Tip**  I often keep a trace like this running locally on my test box in case I accidentally forget to save my code when I'm testing (though that almost ~~always~~ never happens).

---

# Best Practices

Security is always one of the most important tasks to consider when implementing a system. Storing data could be worse than not storing it, if it can be used for improper purposes.

- *Secure the server first*: Although this topic is outside the scope of this book, be certain that the server is secure. If a user can get access to your backup files and take them home, all the database security in the world won't help.

- *Grant rights to roles rather than users*: People come and people go, but the roles that they fulfill will be around for a long time. By defining common roles, you can make adding a new user easy (possibly to replace another user). Just make the users a member of the same role, rather than adding rights directly to the user.

- *Use schemas to simplify security*: Because you can grant rights at a schema level, you can grant rights to SELECT, INSERT, UPDATE, DELETE, and even EXECUTE everything within a schema. Even new objects that are added to the schema after the rights are granted are usable by the grantees.

- *Consider security using stored procedures*: Using stored procedures as the only way for a user to get access to the data presents the user with a nice interface to the data. If procedures are well named, you can also easily apply security to match up with the interfaces that use them.

- *Don't overuse the impersonation features*: EXECUTE AS is a blessing, and it opens up a world of possibilities. It does, however, have a darker side because it can open up too much of a security hole without careful consideration of its use. Add a database with TRUSTWORTHY access set to on, and a procedure can be written to do anything on the server, which could be exploited as a big security hole by a devious programmer.

- *Encrypt sensitive data*: SQL Server has several means of encrypting data, and there are other methods available to do it off of the SQL Server box. Use it as much as necessary, but make sure not to store everything needed to decrypt the data with the encrypted data, in case someone gets hold of the data. Use Transparent Data Encryption to secure important files from exploit if they fall into the wrong hands.

- *Use Profiler and DDL triggers to monitor system activity*: Sometimes it's advantageous to keep an eye on user activity, and these tools give you the ability to do this in an easy manner.

# Summary

Parts of this chapter may make it sound like the world is a season of the TV show *24*, with people out to get you from inside and outside your organization. That is very unlikely to be the case, but . . . what . . . if it isn't? Darn it, if you have any sensitive data out there, you have to consider that someone might get to it. You can't just ignore the risk because it is unlikely. You have to protect your data as much as is reasonably possible.

Security is a large topic, and understanding all the implications is way more than we covered in this chapter. I discussed some of the ways to secure your data inside a single SQL Server database. This isn't an easy subject, but it's far easier than dealing with securing the SQL Server. Luckily, usually in the database we're looking to protect ourselves from ordinary users, though doing a good job of encryption is a good barricade to keep most thieves at bay.

Working in your favor is the consideration that ordinary users won't go to long lengths to hack your database because getting caught can cause loss of employment. Hence, just setting up basic security is generally good enough for all but the really sensitive/valuable data (such as a database of credit card numbers linked with names and addresses of the card holders . . . not a good idea). A good example of this kind of security in the real world is locker-room doors. Just putting a picture of a man or a woman on the door is enough to keep reasonable people of the opposite sex from going in the door. There's nothing to stop you from walking right in, other than good taste and the promise of spending a few years sharing a room with a psychopath and sleeping on an uncomfortable bed that is way too close to the restroom facilities. Usually when bad people break rules of this sort, they don't go through obvious ways.

The same is true about most business users. They'll peruse data to which they have access, but if you put up even a paper barrier saying "Do Not Enter," they usually won't. If they do, they won't go through the paper barrier, they'll go around it. This outside access is why the DBA and network engineers are there: to put locks on the outside doors and secure hallways and corridors those users shouldn't go into.

To provide this security, I discussed several topics for which we need to design security into our database usage:

- Permissions-based security using SQL Server 2005 DDL statements:
    - *Basics of SQL Server security*: How security works on SQL Server objects, including using principals of several types: users, roles, and application roles.
    - *Table security*: Keeping users out of tables they shouldn't be in.
    - *Column security*: Restricting access to only parts of tables.
- Using coded objects:
    - *Stored procedures and scalar functions*: Giving advanced usages to users without letting them know *how* they're doing it. Included in this section was how security works across database lines and server lines.
    - *Views and table-valued functions*: Used to break tables up in a simple manner, either row-wise or column-wise. The goal is to make security seamless, such that the users feel that only this database has the data to which they have rights.
- Obfuscating data is about making it too darn hard to access the data, by using encryption to make the data unreadable without a key.
- Watching users with something that's analogous to a store security camera:
    - *Using an audit trail*: Giving the user an audit of what goes on in given rows and columns in the database. This is the typical method when it comes to most data, because it's easy to give the users access to the lists of what has changed (and why, if the application asks for a reason with certain types of changes).
    - *DDL triggers*: Auditing users who have rights to create new objects in your databases or server to make sure they aren't doing anything out of the ordinary.
    - *Logging with a profiler*: The most silent of devices; it can be used to capture all moves made on the server.

The fact is, if you can build an outer shell of protective devices such as firewalls, proper domain security, and so on, building the inside security will be a snap. It will be the most tedious and time-consuming part of database development, there's no question about that, and it will fall off the radar slightly faster than testing will in many projects. There's no way to combat the problem of schedule slippage, because it's a management issue, not a technical issue, but if planned for ahead of time, security isn't a difficult thing to put in the application.

# CHAPTER 9

■■■

# Table Structures and Indexing

*To the optimist, the glass is half full. To the pessimist, the glass is half empty. To the engineer, the glass is twice as big as it needs to be.*

—Unknown, http://www.boardofwisdom.com

When it comes to tuning your database structures, you must maintain a balance between doing too much and doing too little. Indexing strategies are a great example of this. If you don't use indexes enough, searches will be slow, as the query processor could have to read every row of every table for every query. Use too many indexes, and modifying data could take too long, as indexes have to be maintained. Balance is the key, kind of like matching the amount of fluid to the size of the glass.

Everything we have done so far has been centered on the idea that the quality of the data (as far as we can help that with our database structures) is the number one concern. Although this is still true, in this chapter, we are going to assume that we've done our job in the logical and implementation phases and that the data quality is covered. Slow and right is always better than fast and wrong (how would you like to get paid a week early, but only get half your money?), but the obvious goal of building a computer system is to do things right *and* fast. Nothing we do in this chapter should affect data quality in the least.

We have added indexes in previous chapters, but they were just a side effect of adding primary key and unique constraints (in that a unique index is built by SQL Server to implement the uniqueness condition). In many cases, those indexes will turn out to be most of what you need to make queries run nicely. Of course, you will likely discover that some of the operations you are trying to achieve won't be nearly as fast as you hope. This is where physical tuning comes in, and at this point, you need to understand how tables are structured and consider organizing the physical structures.

The goal of this chapter is to provide an understanding of the types of things you can do with the physical database implementation, including the indexes that are available to you, how they work, and how to use them in an effective physical database strategy. This understanding relies on a base knowledge of the physical data structures on which we based these indexes—in other words, of how the data is structured in the physical SQL Server storage engine. In this chapter, I'll cover the following:

- *Physical database structure overview*: An overview of how the database and tables are stored. This acts mainly as foundation material for subsequent indexing discussion, but the discussion also highlights the importance of choosing and sizing your datatypes carefully.

- *Indexing overview*: A survey of the different types of indexes and their structure. I'll demonstrate many of the index settings and how these might be useful when developing your strategy, to correct any performance problems identified during optimization testing.

- *Index usage scenarios*: I'll discuss a few cases of how to apply and use indexes.

Once you understand the physical data structures, you can optimize data storage and access without affecting the correctness of the data. It's essential to the goals of database design and implementation that the physical model not affect the logical model. This is what Codd's eighth rule, also known as the Physical Data Independence rule—is about. It states that the physical storage can be implemented in any manner as long as the users don't know about it. It also implies that if you change the physical storage, the users shouldn't be affected. Indexes should change the physical model but not the implemented or logical models. All we want to do with the physical model is enhance performance, and understanding the way SQL Server stores data is an important step.

---

**■Note** I am generally happy to treat most of the deeper internals of SQL Server as a mystery, and I will leave deeper explanation to Kalen Delaney's books, where I go whenever I feel the pressing need to figure out why something that seems bizarre is occurring. The purpose of this chapter is to give you a basic feeling for what the structures are like, so you can visualize the solution to some problems and understand the basics of how to lay out your physical structures.

Some of the samples may not work 100 percent the same way on your computer, depending on our hardware situations, or changes to the optimizer.

---

# Physical Database Structure

In SQL Server, databases are physically structured as several layers of "containers" that allow you to move parts of the data around to different disk drives for optimum access. As discussed in Chapter 1, a database is a collection of related data. At the logical level, it contains tables that have columns that contain data. At the physical level, databases contain *files*, where the data is physically stored. These files are basically just typical Microsoft Windows files. These different files can be logically grouped into *filegroups* that control where they are stored on a disk. Each file contains a number of *extents*, which are a 64K allocation in a database file that's made up of eight individual contiguous 8K *pages*. Finally, the page is the basic unit of data storage in SQL Server databases. Everything that's stored in SQL Server is stored on pages of several types: data, index, and overflow (and others, but these are the ones that are most important to you. I will list the others later in the section on "Extents and Pages.") The following sections describe each of these "containers" in more detail, so you understand the basics of how data is laid out on disk.

---

**■Note** Because of the extreme variety of hardware possibilities and needs, it's impossible in a book on design to go into serious depth about how and where to place all your files in physical storage. I'll leave this task to the DBA-oriented books. For detailed information about choosing and setting up your hardware, check out `http://msdn.microsoft.com` or `http://www.sql-server-performance.com`.

---

## Files and Filegroups

Figure 9-1 provides a high-level depiction of the objects used to organize the files (I'm ignoring logs in this chapter, because you don't have direct access to them).

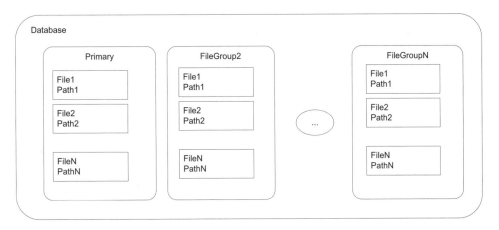

**Figure 9-1.** *Database storage organization*

At the top level of a SQL Server instance we have the database. The database is comprised of one or more filegroups, which are a logical grouping of one or more files. We can place different filegroups on different disk drives (hopefully on a different disk drive controller) to distribute the I/O load evenly across the available hardware. It's possible to have multiple files in the filegroup, in which case SQL Server allocates space across each file in the filegroup. For best performance, it's best to have no more files in a filegroup than you have physical CPUs (not including hyperthreading).

---

■ **Note** There's usually very little, if any, performance benefit to using multiple filegroups if they're all on the same physical drive. The benefit of having multiple filegroups is getting data spread about to maximize I/O across different controllers. There can be some benefit to having multiple files in a filegroup on the same drive, but no more than available physical CPUs.

---

A filegroup contains one or more files, which are actual operating system files. Each database has at least one primary filegroup, whose files are called *primary files* (commonly suffixed as .mdf, although there's no requirement to give the files any particular names or extension). Each database can possibly have other secondary filegroups containing the secondary files (commonly suffixed as .ndf), which are in any other filegroups. Files may only be a part of a single filegroup. SQL Server proportionally fills files by allocating extents in each filegroup equally. (There is also a file type for full-text indexing that I will largely ignore as well. I will focus only on the core file types that you will use for implementing your structures.)

You control the placement of objects that store physical data pages at the filegroup level (code and metadata is always stored on the primary filegroup, along with all the system objects). New objects created are placed in the *default* filegroup, which is the primary filegroup unless another filegroup is specified in any CREATE <object> commands. For example, to place an object in a filegroup other than the default, you need to specify the name of the filegroup using the ON clause of the table- or index-creation statement, for example:

```
CREATE TABLE <tableName>
(...) ON <fileGroupName>
```

This command assigns the table to the filegroup, but not to any particular file. Where in the files the object is created is strictly out of your control.

---

**■Tip** If you want to move a table to a different filegroup, you can use the MOVE TO option on ALTER TABLE/DROP CONSTRAINT if a constraint is clustered, or just drop or create a clustered index on the object (like for a heap).

---

Use code like the following to create indexes:

```
CREATE INDEX <indexName> ON <tableName> (<columnList>) ON <filegroup>
```

Use the following type of command (or use ALTER TABLE) to create constraints that in turn create indexes (UNIQUE, PRIMARY KEY):

```
CREATE TABLE <tableName>
(
    ...
    <primaryKeyColumn> int CONSTRAINT PKTableName ON <fileGroup>
    ...
)
```

For the most part, having just one filegroup and one file is the best practice for a large number of databases. If you are unsure if you need multiple filegroups, my advice is to build your database on a single filegroup and see if the data channel provided can handle the I/O volume (for the most part, I will avoid making too many such generalizations, as tuning is very much an art that requires knowledge of the actual load the server will be under). As activity increases and you build better hardware with multiple CPUs and multiple drive channels, you might place indexes on their own filegroup, or even place files of the same filegroup across different controllers.

In the following example, I create a sample database with two filegroups, with the secondary filegroup having two files in it (I put this sample database in the root of the C drive to keep the example simple, but it is rarely a good practice to place your files in the root of the drive, let alone the root of the system drive):

```
CREATE DATABASE demonstrateFilegroups ON
PRIMARY ( NAME = Primary1, FILENAME = 'c:\demonstrateFilegroups_primary.mdf',
          SIZE = 10MB),
FILEGROUP SECONDARY
         ( NAME = Secondary1,FILENAME =
                               'c:\demonstrateFilegroups_secondary1.ndf',
           SIZE = 10MB),
         ( NAME = Secondary2,FILENAME =
                               'c:\demonstrateFilegroups_secondary2.ndf',
           SIZE = 10MB)
LOG ON ( NAME = Log1,FILENAME = 'c:\demonstrateFilegroups_log.ldf', SIZE = 10MB)
```

You can define other file settings, such as minimum and maximum sizes, and growth. The values you assign depend on what hardware you have. For growth, you can set a FILEGROWTH parameter that allows you to grow the file by a certain size or percentage of the current size, and a MAXSIZE, so the file cannot just fill up existing disk space. For example, if you wanted the file to start at 1GB and grow in chunks of 100MB up to 2GB, you could specify the following:

```
CREATE DATABASE demonstrateFileGrowth ON
PRIMARY ( NAME = Primary1,FILENAME = 'c:\demonstrateFileGrowth_primary.mdf',
                          SIZE = 1GB, FILEGROWTH=100MB, MAXSIZE=2GB)
LOG ON ( NAME = Log1,FILENAME = 'c:\demonstrateFileGrowth_log.ldf', SIZE = 10MB)
```

The growth settings are fine for smaller systems, but it's usually better to make the files large enough so there's no need for them to grow. File growth can be slow and cause ugly bottlenecks when OLTP traffic is trying to use a file that's growing. When running on a desktop operating system like Windows XP or greater, or on a server operating system such as Windows Server 2003 or greater, you can improve things by using "instant" file allocation (though only for data files.) Instead of initializing the files, the space on disk can simply be allocated and not written to immediately. To use this capability, the system account cannot be LocalSystem, and the user account that the SQL Server runs under must have SE_MANAGE_VOLUME_NAME Windows permissions. Even with the existence of instant file allocation, it's still better to have the space allocated beforehand, as you then have cordoned off the space ahead of time: no one else can take it from you, and you won't fail when the file tries to grow and there isn't enough space. In either event, the DBA staff should be on top of the situation and make sure that you don't run out of space.

You can query the sys.filegroups catalog view to view the files in the newly created database:

```
USE demonstrateFilegroups
GO
SELECT fg.name as file_group,
       df.name as file_logical_name,
       df.physical_name as physical_file_name
FROM   sys.filegroups fg
         join sys.database_files df
            on fg.data_space_id = df.data_space_id
```

This returns the following results:

| file_group | file_logical_name | physical_file_name |
| --- | --- | --- |
| PRIMARY | Primary1 | c:\demonstrateFilegroups_primary.mdf |
| SECONDARY | Secondary1 | c:\demonstrateFilegroups_secondary1.ndf |
| SECONDARY | Secondary2 | c:\demonstrateFilegroups_secondary2.ndf |

**Note** The LOG file isn't part of a filegroup, so it isn't shown in the results.

There's a lot more information than just names in the catalog views I've referenced in this chapter. If you are new to the catalog views, dig in and learn them. There is a wealth of information in those views that will be invaluable to you when looking at systems to see how they are set up and to determine how to tune them.

**Tip** An interesting feature of filegroups is that you can back them up and restore them individually. If you need to restore and back up a single table for any reason, placing it on its own filegroup can achieve this.

These databases won't be used anymore, so if you created them, just drop them if you desire (also a good idea since these files were placed in the root of the c drive.):

```
USE MASTER
GO
DROP DATABASE demonstrateFileGroups
DROP DATABASE demonstrateFileGrowth
```

## Extents and Pages

As shown in Figure 9-2, files are further broken down into a number of *extents*, each consisting of eight separate 8K pages where tables, indexes, and so on are physically stored. SQL Server only allocates space in a database to extents. When files grow, you will notice that the size of files will be incremented only in 64K increments.

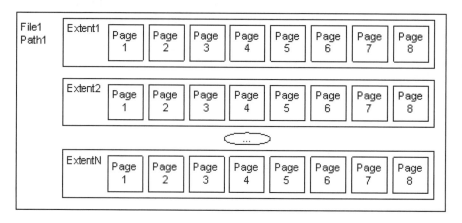

**Figure 9-2.** *Files and extents*

Each extent in turn has eight pages that hold one specific type of data each:

- *Data*: Table data.
- *Index*: Index data.
- *Overflow data*: Used when a row is greater than 8,060 bytes, or for varchar(max), varbinary(max), text, or image values.
- *Allocation map*: Information about the allocation of extents.
- *Page free space*: Information about what different pages are allocated for.
- *Index allocation*: Information about extents used for table or index data.
- *Bulk changed map*: Extents modified by a bulk INSERT operation.
- *Differential changed map*: Extents that have changed since the last database backup command. This is used to support differential backups.

In larger databases, most every extent will contain just one type of page, but in smaller databases, SQL Server can place any kind of page in the same extent. When all data is of the same type, it's known as a *uniform* extent. When pages are of various types, it's referred to as a *mixed* extent.

SQL Server places all table data in pages, with a header that contains metadata about the page (object ID of the owner, type of page, and so on), as well as the rows of data (which I'll cover later in this chapter). At the end of the page are the offset values that tell the relational engine where the rows start.

Figure 9-3 shows a typical data page from a table. The header of the page contains identification values such as the page number, the object ID of the object the data is for, compression information, and so on. The data rows hold the actual data, which I'll discuss more in a moment. Finally, there's an allocation block that has the offsets/pointers to the row data.

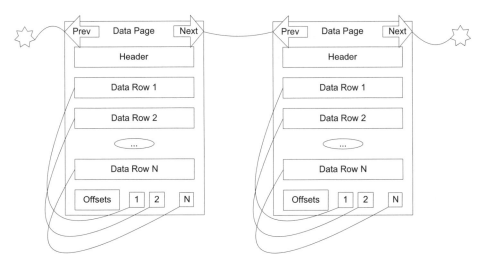

**Figure 9-3.** *Data pages*

Figure 9-3 showed that there are pointers from the next to the previous rows. These pointers are only used when pages are ordered, such as in the pages of an index. Heap objects (tables with no clustered index) are not ordered. I will cover this a bit later in the "Index Types" section.

The other kind of page that is frequently used that you need to understand is the overflow page. It is used to hold row data that won't fit on the basic 8,060-byte page. There are two reasons an overflow page is used:

1. The combined length of all data in a row grows beyond 8,060 bytes. In versions of SQL Server prior to 2000, this would cause an error. In versions after this, data goes on an overflow page automatically, allowing you to have virtually unlimited page sizes.

2. By setting the sp_tableoption setting on a table for large value types out of row to 1, all the (max) and XML datatype values are immediately stored out of row on an overflow page. If you set it to 0, then SQL Server places all data on the main row, as long as it fits into the 8,060-byte row.

For example, Figure 9-4 depicts the type of situation that might occur for a table that has the large value types out of row set to 1. Here, Data Row 1 has two pointers to a varbinary(max) columns: one that spans two pages, and another that spans only a single page. Using all of the data in Data Row 1 will now require up to four reads (depending on where the actual page gets stored in the physical structures), making data access far slower than if all of the data were on a single page. This kind of performance problem can be easy to overlook, but on occasion, overflow pages will really drag down your performance, especially when other programmers use SELECT * on tables where they don't really need all of the data.

The overflow pages are linked lists that can accommodate up to 2GB of storage in a single column. Generally speaking, it isn't a good idea to store 2GB in a single column (or even a row), but the ability to do so is available if needed.

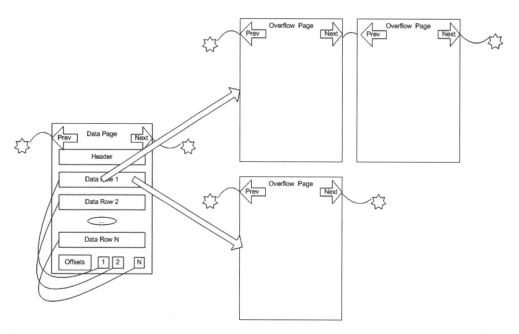

**Figure 9-4.** *Sample overflow pages*

Understand that storing large values that are placed off of the main page will be far more costly when you need these values than if all of the data can be placed in the same data page. On the other hand, if you seldom use the data in your queries, placing them off the page can give you a much smaller footprint for the "important" data, requiring far less disk access on average. It is a balance that you need to take care with, as you can imagine how costly a table scan of columns that are on the overflow pages is going to be. Not only will you have to read extra pages, you have to be redirected to the overflow page for every row that's overflowed.

Be careful when allowing data to overflow the page. It's guaranteed to make your processing more costly, especially if you include the data that's stored on the overflow page in your queries (like if you use the dreaded SELECT * regularly in production code!). It's important to choose your datatypes correctly to minimize the size of the data row to include only frequently needed values. If you frequently need a large value, keep it in row; otherwise, place it off row or even create two tables and join them together as needed.

---

**■Tip** The need to access overflow pages is just one of the reasons to avoid using SELECT * FROM <tablename>–type queries in your production code, but it is an important one. Too often, you get data that you don't intend to use, and when that data is located off the main data page, performance could suffer tremendously, and in most cases needlessly.

---

## Data on Pages

When you get down to the row level, the data is laid out with metadata, fixed length fields, and variable length fields, as shown in Figure 9-5 (note that this is a generalization, and the storage engine does a lot of stuff to the data for optimization, including compression).

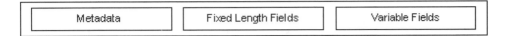

**Figure 9-5.** *Data row*

The metadata describes the row, gives information about the variable length fields, and so on. Generally speaking, since data is dealt with by the query processor at the page level, even if only a single page is needed, data can be accessed very rapidly no matter the exact physical representation.

---

**▪Note** I use the term *column* when discussing logical SQL objects such as tables and indexes, but when discussing the physical table implementation, *field* is the proper term. Remember from Chapter 1 that a field is a physical location within a record.

---

The maximum amount of data that can be placed on a single page (including overhead from variable fields) is 8,060 bytes. As illustrated back in Figure 9-4, when a data row grows larger than 8,060 bytes, the data in variable length columns can spill out onto an overflow page. A 16-byte pointer is left on the original page and points to the page where the overflow data is placed.

## Page Splits

When inserting or updating rows, SQL Server might have to rearrange the data on the pages due to the pages being filled up. Such rearranging can be a particularly costly operation. Consider the situation from our example shown in Figure 9-6, assuming that only three values can fit on a page.

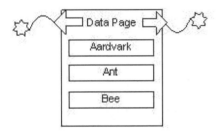

**Figure 9-6.** *Sample data page before page split*

Say we want to add a value of Bear onto the page. Because that value won't fit onto the page, the page needs to be reorganized. Pages that need to be split are split into two, generally with 50 percent of the data on one page, and 50 percent on the other (there are usually more than three values on a real page!). Once the page is split, and its values are reinserted, the new pages would end up looking something like Figure 9-7.

Page splits are awfully costly operations and can be terrible for performance, because after the page split, data won't be located on successive physical pages. This condition is commonly known as *fragmentation*. Page splits occur in a normal system and are simply a part of adding data to your table. However, they can occur extremely rapidly and seriously degrade performance if you are not careful. Understanding the effect that page splits can have on your data and indexes is important as you tune performance on tables that have large numbers of inserts or updates.

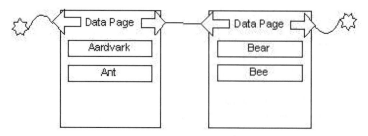

**Figure 9-7.** *Sample data page after page split*

To tune your tables and indexes to help minimize page splits, you can use the FILL FACTOR of the index. When you build or rebuild an index or a table (using ALTER TABLE <tablename> REBUILD, a command new in SQL Server 2008), the fill factor indicates how much space is left on each page for future data. If you are inserting random values all over the structures, you will want to leave adequate space on each page to cover the expected numbers of rows that will be created in the future. During a page split, the data page is always split fifty-fifty, and it is left half empty on each page, and even worse, the structure is becoming, as mentioned, fragmented.

Let's jump ahead a bit: one of the good things about using a monotonously increasing value for a clustered index is that page splits over the entire index are greatly decreased. The table grows only on one end of the index, and while the index does need to be rebuilt occasionally using ALTER INDEX REORGANIZE or ALTER INDEX REBUILD, you don't end up with page splits all over the table.

You can decide whether to reorganize or to rebuild using the criteria stated by SQL Server Books Online. With the following query using the dynamic management view sys.dm_db_index_physical_stats, you can check the FragPercent column and REBUILD indexes with greater than 30 percent fragmentation, and REORGANIZE those that are just lightly fragmented.

```
SELECT   s.[name] AS SchemaName,
         o.[name] AS TableName,
         i.[name] AS IndexName,
         f.[avg_fragmentation_in_percent] AS FragPercent,
         f.fragment_count
FROM sys.dm_db_index_physical_stats(DB_ID(), NULL, NULL, NULL, DEFAULT) f
         JOIN sys.indexes i
             ON f.[object_id] = i.[object_id] AND f.[index_id] = i.[index_id]
         JOIN sys.objects o
             ON i.[object_id] = o.[object_id]
         JOIN sys.schemas s
             ON o.[schema_id] = s.[schema_id]
WHERE o.[is_ms_shipped] = 0
  AND i.[is_disabled] = 0 -- skip disabled indexes
```

This book's downloads include a version of this query that will formulate the query and execute it.

## Compression

The reason that the formats for pages and rows are generalized in the previous sections is that in SQL Server 2008, Microsoft has implemented compression of data at the row and page levels. In versions prior to SQL Server 2005 SP2, all data was stored on a page in the raw format that we talked about in Chapter 5. However, in SQL Server 2005 SP2, Microsoft introduced datatype-level compression, which allowed data of the decimal datatype to be stored in a variable length field, also referred to as vardecimal. Datatype compression was set using the sp_tableoption procedure with a setting of 'vardecimal storage format'.

In SQL Server 2008, the concept of compression is extended even further to all of the fixed length datatypes, including int, char, and float data types. Basically, you can allow SQL Server to save space by storing your data like it was a variable-sized type, yet in usage, the data will appear and behave like a fixed length type.

For example, if you stored the value of 100 in an int column, SQL Server needn't use all 32 bits; this can be done in the same size as a tinyint. So instead of taking a full 32 bits, SQL Server can simply use 8 bits (1 byte). Another case is when you use a char(30) column but store only two characters; 28 characters could be saved. There is an overhead of 2 bytes per variable-length column (or 4 bits if the size of the column is less than 8 bytes). Note that compression is only available in the Enterprise Edition.

This datatype-level compression is referred to as *row compression*. In Appendix B, I will indicate for each of the datatypes how it is affected by row compression, or for a list (which may show any changes since RTM), check SQL Server Books Online for the topic of "Row Compression Implementation." Row compression is a very interesting thing for many databases that use lots of fixed length data (for example, integers, especially for surrogate keys).

SQL Server 2008 also includes an additional compression capability called *page compression*. With page compression (which includes row compression), the storage engine does a couple of interesting things to compress the data on a page:

- *Prefix compression:* Looks for repeated values in a value (like '0000001' and compresses the prefix to something like 6-0 (six zeros)

- *Dictionary compression:* For all values on the page, the storage engine looks for duplication and stores the duplicated value once and then stores pointers on the data pages where the duplicated values originally resided.

You can apply data compression to your tables and indexes with the CREATE TABLE, ALTER TABLE, CREATE INDEX, and ALTER INDEX syntaxes. As an example, I will create a simple table, called test, and enable page compression on the table, row compression on a clustered index, and page compression on another index:

```
CREATE TABLE test
(
    testId int,
    value  int
)
WITH (DATA_COMPRESSION = ROW) -- PAGE or NONE
    ALTER TABLE test REBUILD WITH (DATA_COMPRESSION = PAGE) ;

CREATE CLUSTERED INDEX XTest_value
   ON test (value) WITH ( DATA_COMPRESSION = ROW ) ;

ALTER INDEX XTest_value
   ON test REBUILD WITH ( DATA_COMPRESSION = PAGE )
GO
```

---

■**Note** The syntax of the CREATE INDEX command allows for compression of the partitions of an index in different manners. I mention partitioning later in the chapter. For full syntax, check SQL Server Books Online.

---

Giving advice on whether to use compression is not really possible without knowing the factors that surround your actual situation. One tool you can use is the system procedure— sp_estimate_data_compression_savings—to check existing data to see just how compressed the data in the table or index would be after applying compression, but it won't tell you how the compression will positively or negatively affect your performance. There are trade-offs to any sorts of compression. CPU utilization will certainly go up, because instead of directly using the data right from the page, the query processor will have to translate the values from the compressed format into the uncompressed format that SQL Server will use. On the other hand, if you have a lot of data that would benefit from compression, you could possibly lower your I/O enough to make doing so worth the cost. Frankly, with CPU power growing by leaps and bounds with multiple-core scenarios these days and I/O still the most difficult to tune, compression could definitely be a great thing for many systems. However, I suggest testing both ways, if you can spare the time to do that.

## Partitioning

The last physical structure topic that will be covered is *partitioning*. Partitioning allows you to break a table (or index) into multiple physical structures by breaking them into more manageable chunks. Partitioning can allow SQL Server to scan data from different processes, enhancing opportunities for parallelism. SQL Server 7.0 and 2000 had partitioned views (2005 and 2008 allow them also), where you define a view and a set of tables, with each serving as a partition. If you have properly defined (and trusted) constraints, SQL Server would use the WHERE clause to know which of the tables referenced in the view would have to be scanned in response to a given query. One thing you still can do with partitioned views is to build distributed partitioned views, which reference tables on different servers.

In SQL Server 2005, you could begin to define partitioning as part of the table structure. Instead of making a physical table for each partition, you define, at a DDL level, the different partitions of the table, and internally, the table is broken into the partitions based on a scheme that you set up. Note too that this feature is only included in the Enterprise Edition.

At query time, SQL Server can then dynamically scan only the partitions that need to be searched, based on the criteria in the WHERE clause of the query being executed. I am not going to describe partitioning too much, but I felt that it needed a mention in this edition of the book as a tool at your disposal with which to tune your databases, particularly if they are very large or very active. For deeper coverage, I would suggest you consider *Inside Microsoft SQL Server 2005: The Storage Engine* by Kalen Delaney (Microsoft Press, 2006) or her forthcoming book, *SQL Server 2008 Internals*.

I will, however, present the following basic example of partitioning. Use whatever database you desire. I used tempdb for the data and AdventureWorks2008 for the sample data on my test machine and included the USE statement in the code download. The example is that of a sales order table. I will partition the sales into three regions based on the order date. One region is for sales before 2002, another for sales between 2002 and 2003, and the last for 2003 and later. The first step is to create a partitioning function. You must base the function on a list of values, where the VALUES clause sets up partitions that the rows will fall into based on the smalldatetime values that are presented to it, for example:

```
CREATE PARTITION FUNCTION PartitionFunction$dates (smalldatetime)
AS RANGE LEFT FOR VALUES ('20020101','20030101');
                --set based on recent version of
                --AdventureWorks2008.Sales.SalesOrderHeader table to show
                --partition utilization
```

Specifying the function as RANGE LEFT says that the values in the comma-delimited list should be considered the boundary on the side listed. So in this case, the ranges would be as follows:

- value <= '20020101'
- value > '20020101' and value <= '20060101'
- value > '20060101'

Specifying the function as RANGE RIGHT would have meant that the values lie to the right of the values listed, in the case of our ranges, for example:

- value < '20020101'
- value >= '20020101' and value < '20060101'
- value >= '20060101'

Next, use that partition function to create a partitioning scheme:

```
CREATE PARTITION SCHEME PartitonScheme$dates
                AS PARTITION PartitionFunction$dates ALL to ( [PRIMARY] )
```

With the CREATE PARTITION SCHEME command, you can place each of the partitions you previously defined on a specific filegroup. I placed them all on the same filegroup for clarity and ease (and laziness so I could create this example in tempdb), but in practice, you usually want them on different filegroups, depending on the purpose of the partitioning. For example, if you were partitioning just to keep the often-active data in a smaller structure, placing all partitions on the same filegroup might be fine. But if you want to improve parallelism or be able to just back up one partition with a filegroup backup, you would want to place your partitions on different filegroups.

Next, you can apply the partitioning to a new table. You'll need a clustered index involving the partition key. You apply the partitioning to that index. Following is the statement to create the partitioned table:

```
CREATE TABLE salesOrder
(
    salesOrderId    int,
    customerId      int,
    orderAmount     decimal(10,2),
    orderDate       smalldatetime,
    constraint PKsalesOrder primary key nonclustered (salesOrderId)
                                                ON [Primary],
    constraint AKsalesOrder unique clustered (salesOrderId, orderDate)
) on PartitonScheme$dates (orderDate)
```

Next, load some data from the AdventureWorks2008.Sales.SalesOrderHeader table to make looking at the metadata more interesting. You can do that using an INSERT statement such as the following:

```
INSERT INTO salesOrder
SELECT SalesOrderId, CustomerId, TotalDue, OrderDate
FROM   AdventureWorks2008.Sales.SalesOrderHeader
```

You can see what partition each row falls in using the $partition function. You suffix the $partition function with the partition function name and the name of the partition key (or a partition value) to see what partition a row's values are in, for example:

```
SELECT *, $partition.PartitionFunction$dates(orderDate) as partiton
FROM   salesOrder
```

You can also view the partitions that are set up through the sys.partitions catalog view. The following query displays the partitions for our newly created table:

```
SELECT  partitions.partition_number, partitions.index_id,
        partitions.rows, indexes.name, indexes.type_desc
FROM    sys.partitions as partitions
            JOIN sys.indexes as indexes
                on indexes.object_id = partitions.object_id
                    and indexes.index_id = partitions.index_id
WHERE   partitions.object_id = object_id('salesOrder')
```

This will return the following:

| partition_number | index_id | rows | name | type_desc |
|---|---|---|---|---|
| 1 | 1 | 1424 | AKsalesOrder | CLUSTERED |
| 2 | 1 | 3720 | AKsalesOrder | CLUSTERED |
| 3 | 1 | 26321 | AKsalesOrder | CLUSTERED |
| 1 | 2 | 31465 | PKsalesOrder | NONCLUSTERED |

Partitioning is not a general purpose tool that should be used on every table, which is one of the reasons why it is only included in Enterprise Edition (not to mention that Microsoft can charge you more for it—I'm just saying).

# Indexes Overview

Indexes allow the SQL Server engine to perform fast, targeted data retrieval rather than simply scanning though the entire table. A well-placed index can speed up data retrieval by orders of magnitude (and a haphazard approach to indexing can actually have the opposite effect when creating, updating, or deleting data).

Indexing your data effectively requires a sound knowledge of how that data will change over time, the sort of questions that will be asked of it, and the volume of data that you expect to be dealing with. Unfortunately, this is what makes any topic about physical tuning so challenging. To index effectively, you need knowledge of your hardware and your exact data usage patterns. Nothing in life is free, and the creation and maintenance of indexes can be costly. When deciding to (or not to) use an index to improve the performance of one query, you have to consider the effect on the overall performance of the system.

In the upcoming sections, I'll do the following:

- Introduce the basic structure of an index.

- Discuss the two fundamental types of indexes and how their structure heavily affects the structure of the table.

- Demonstrate basic index usage, introducing you to the basic syntax and usage of indexes.

- Show you how to determine whether SQL Server is likely to use your index and how to see if SQL Server has used your index.

# Basic Index Structure

An index is an object that SQL Server can maintain to optimize access to the physical data in a table. You can build an index on one or more columns of a table. In essence, an index in SQL Server works on the same principle as the index of a book. It organizes the data from the column (or columns) of data in a manner that's conducive to fast, efficient searching, so you can find a row or set of rows without looking at the entire table. It provides a means to jump quickly to a specific piece of data, rather than just starting on page one each time you search the table and scanning through until you find what you're looking for. Even worse, unless SQL Server knows *exactly* how many rows it is looking for, it has no way to know if it can stop scanning data when one row had been found. Also, like the index of a book, an index is a separate entity from the actual table (or chapters) being indexed.

As an example, consider that you have a completely unordered list of employees and their details. If you had to search this list for persons named Davidson, you would have to look at every single name on every single page. Soon after doing this, I don't know, *once*, you would immediately start trying to devise some better manner of searching. On first pass, you would probably sort the list alphabetically. But what happens if you needed to search for an employee by an employee identification number? Well, you would spend a bunch of time searching through the list sorted by last name for the employee number. Eventually, you could create a list of last names and the pages you could find them on, and another list with the employee numbers and their pages. Following this pattern, you would build indexes for any other type of search you'd regularly perform on the list. (Of course, I am assuming that you don't get paid by the hour to search this list. I have seen people do less intelligent things!)

Now, consider this in terms of a table like an `Employee` table. You might execute a query such as the following:

```
SELECT LastName, <EmployeeDetails>
FROM Employee
WHERE LastName = 'Davidson'
```

In the absence of an index to rapidly search, SQL Server will perform a scan of the data in the entire table (referred to as a full table scan) on the `Employee` table, looking for rows that satisfy the query predicate. A full table scan generally won't cause you too many problems with small tables, but it can cause poor performance for large tables with many pages of data, much like it would if you had to manually look through 20 values versus 2,000.

Now, creating an index on the `LastName` column, the index sorts the `LastName` rows in some logical fashion (probably in ascending alphabetical order) so that the database engine can move directly to rows where the last name is Davidson and retrieve the required data quickly and efficiently. And even if there are 10 people with the last name of Davidson, SQL Server knows to stop when it hits `'Davidton'`.

Of course, as you might imagine, the engineer types who invented the concept of indexing and searching data structures don't simply make lists to search through. Instead, indexes are implemented using what is known as a *balanced tree* (B-tree) structure. The index is made up of index pages structured, again, much like an index of a book or a phone book. Each index page contains the first value in a range and a pointer to the next lower page in the index. The last level in the index is referred to as the *leaf page*, which contains the actual data values that are being indexed, plus either the data for the row or pointers to the data.

---

■**Note**  I'll discuss the leaf pages in later sections on clustered and nonclustered indexes.

---

Figure 9-8 shows an example of the type of B-tree that SQL Server uses for indexes. Each of the outer rectangles is an 8K index page, just as we discussed earlier. The three values—A, J, and P— are the *index keys* in this top-level page of the index. The index page has as many index keys as is possible. To decide which path to follow to reach the lower level of the index, we have to decide if the value requested is between two of the keys: A to I, J to P, or greater than P. For example, say the value we want to find in the index happens to be I. We go to the first page in the index. The database determines that I doesn't come after J, so it follows the A pointer to the next index page. Here, it determines that I comes after C, so it follows the G pointer to the leaf page

Each of these pages is 8K in size. Depending on the size of the key (determined by summing the data lengths of the columns in the key, up to a maximum of 900 bytes), it's possible to have anywhere from 8 entries to over 1,000 on a single page. The more keys you can fit on a page, the greater the number of pages you can have on each level of the index. The more pages are linked from each level to the next, the fewer numbers of steps from the top page of the index to reach the leaf.

B-tree indexes are extremely efficient, because for an index that stores only 500 different values on a page—a reasonable number for a typical index of an integer—it has 500 pointers on the next level in the index, and the second level has 500 pages with 500 values each. That makes 250,000 different pointers on that level, and the next level has up to 250,000 × 500 pointers. That's 125,000,000 different values in just a three-level index! Obviously, there's overhead to each index key, and this is just a rough estimation of the number of levels in the index.

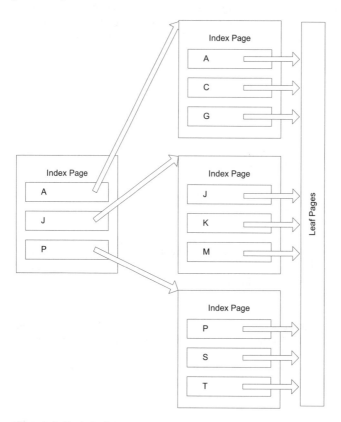

**Figure 9-8.** *Basic index structure*

Another term that's mentioned occasionally is how *balanced* the tree is. If the tree is perfectly balanced, every index page would have exactly the same number of keys on it. Once the index has lots of data on one end, or data gets moved around on it for insertions or deletions, the tree becomes *ragged*, with one end having one level, and another many levels. This is why you have to do some basic maintenance on the indexes, something I have mentioned already.

# Index Types

How indexes are structured internally is based on the existence (or nonexistence) of a clustered index. For the nonleaf pages of an index, everything is the same for all indexes. However, at the leaf node, the indexes get quite different—and the type of index used plays a large part in how the data in a table is physically organized.

There are two different types of indexes:

- *Clustered*: This type orders the physical table in the order of the index.

- *Nonclustered*: These are completely separate structures that simply speed access.

In the upcoming sections, I'll discuss how the different types of indexes affect the table structure and which is best in which situation.

# Clustered Indexes

A clustered index physically orders the pages of the data table. The leaf pages of the clustered indexes are the data pages of the table. Each of the data pages is then linked to the next page in a doubly linked list. The leaf pages of the clustered index are the actual data pages. In other words, the data rows in the table are sorted according to the columns used in the index. Tables with clustered indexes are referred to as *clustered tables*.

The key of a clustered index is referred to as the *clustering key*, and this key will have additional uses that will be mentioned later in this chapter. For clustered indexes that aren't defined as unique, each record has a 4-byte value (commonly known as a *uniquifier*) added to each value in the index where duplicate values exist. For example, if the values were A, B, C, you would be fine. But, if you added another value B, the values internally would be A, B + 4ByteValue, B + Different4ByteValue, and C. Clearly, it is not optimal to get stuck with 4 bytes on top of the other value you are dealing with in every level of the index, so in general, you should try to use the clustered index on a set of columns where the values are unique.

Figure 9-9 shows, at a high level, what a clustered index might look like.

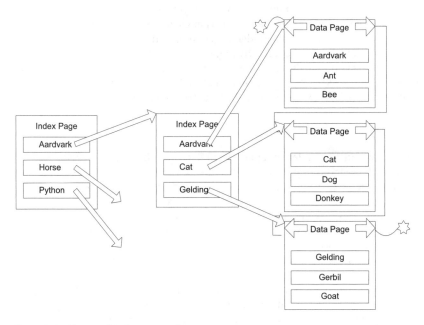

**Figure 9-9.** *Clustered index example*

You can have only a single clustered index on a table, because the table cannot be ordered in more than one direction. (Remember this; it is one of the most fun interview questions. Answering anything other than "one clustered index per table" leads to a fun line of questioning.) This organization saves having to go from the index structure to the data pages for queries, making the clustered index one of the most important performance choices you can make for your data access plan.

A good real-world example of a clustered index would be a set of old-fashioned encyclopedias. Each book is a level of the index, and on each page, there is another level that denotes the things you can find on each page (e.g., "Office–Officer.") Then each topic is the leaf level of the index. These books are "clustered" on the topics in the encyclopedia, just as the example was clustered on the name of the animal. In essence, the entire set of books was a table of information in clustered ordered. (Yes, they are also partitioned to enhance parallel use. And, Junior, if the word *encyclopedia* is unknown to you, whip open your favorite web browser, and look it up on Wikipedia.)

Now, consider a dictionary. Why are the words sorted, rather than just having a separate index with the words not in order? I presume that at least part of the reason is to let the readers scan through words they don't know exactly how to spell, checking the definition to see if the word matches what they expect. SQL Server does something like this when you do a search. For example, back in Figure 9-9, if you were looking for a cat named George, you could use the clustered index to find rows where animal = 'Cat', then scan the data pages for the matching pages for any rows where name = 'George'.

I must caution you that although it's true, physically speaking, that tables have order, logically speaking, tables must be thought of as having no order (I know I promised to not mention this again, but it really is an important thing to remember). This lack of order is a fundamental truth of relational programming: *you aren't required to get back data in the same order when you run the same query twice.* The ordering of the physical data can be used by the query processor to enhance your performance, but during intermediate processing, the data can be moved around in any manner that results in faster processing the answer to your query. It's true that you do almost always get the same rows back in the same order, mostly because the optimizer is almost always going to put together the same plan every time the same query is executed under the same conditions. However, load the server up with many requests, and the order of the data might change so SQL Server can best use its resources, regardless of the data's order in the structures. SQL Server can choose to return data to us in any order that's fastest for it. If disk drives are busy in part of a table and it can fetch a different part, it will. If order matters, use ORDER BY clauses to make sure that data is returned as you want.

## Nonclustered Indexes

Nonclustered index structures are fully independent of the underlying table. Where a clustered index is like a dictionary with the index physically linked to the table (since the leaf pages of the index are a part of the table), nonclustered indexes are more like indexes in a textbook. A nonclustered index is completely separate from the data, and on the leaf page, there are pointers to go to the data pages much like the index of a book contains page numbers.

Each leaf page in a nonclustered index contains some form of pointer to the rows on the data page. The pointer from the index to a data row is known as a *row locator*. Exactly how the row locator of a nonclustered indexes is structured is based on whether or not the underlying table has a clustered index.

In this section, I will first show an abstract representation of the nonclustered index and then show the differences between the implementation of a nonclustered index when you do and do not also have a clustered index. At an abstract level, all nonclustered indexes follow the form shown in Figure 9-10.

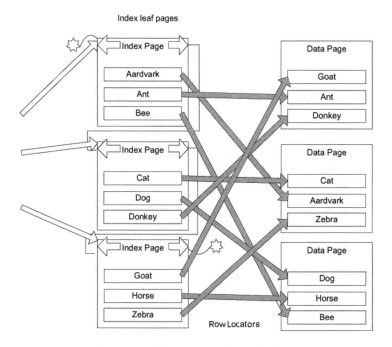

**Figure 9-10.** *Sample nonclustered index*

The major difference between the two possibilities comes down to the row locator being different based on whether the underlying table has a clustered index. There are two different types of pointer that will be used:

- *Tables with a clustered index*: Clustering key
- *Tables without a clustered index*: Pointer to physical location of the data

In the next two sections, I'll explain these in more detail.

---

**Tip**  You can place nonclustered indexes on a different filegroup than the data pages to maximize the use of your disk subsystem in parallel. Note that the filegroup you place the indexes on likely ought to be on a different controller channel than the table; otherwise, there will likely be minimal or no gain.

---

## Nonclustered Indexes on Clustered Tables

When a clustered index exists on the table, the row locator for the leaf node of any nonclustered index is the clustering key from the clustered index. In Figure 9-10, the structure on the right side is the clustered index, and on the left is the nonclustered index. To find a value, you start at the leaf node of the index and traverse the leaf pages. This time, you get the clustering key, rather than a pointer. You then use the clustering key to traverse the clustered index to reach the data, as shown in Figure 9-11.

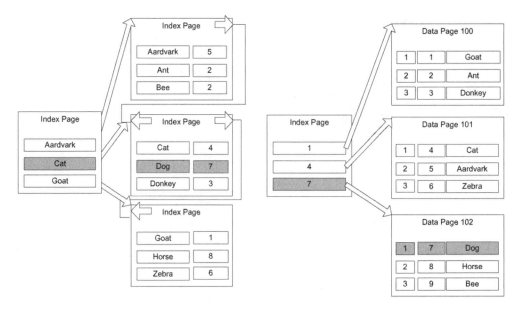

**Figure 9-11.** *Nonclustered index on a clustered table*

The overhead of the operation I've just described is minimal as long as you keep your clustering key optimal. While having to scan two indexes probably seems like more work; overall, it's usually better than having direct pointers to the table because only minimal reorganization is required for any modification of the values in the table. Also, very little hardware-based information lingers in the structure of the index (which caused all manners of corruption in our indexes in early versions, before the big physical changes implemented in version 7.0 allowed us to start using this clustering key strategy for nonclustered indexes). And let's face it, the people with better understanding of such things also tell us that when the size of the clustering key is adequately small, this method is faster overall than having pointers directly to the table.

The benefit of the key structure is certainly true when we talk about modification operations. Because the clustering key is the same regardless of physical location, only the lowest level of the clustered index need know where the physical data is. Add to this that the data is organized sequentially, and the overhead of modifying indexes is significantly lowered. Of course, this benefit is only true if the clustering key rarely, or never, changes. Therefore, the general suggestion is to make the clustering key a small nonchanging value, such as an identity column (but the advice section is still a few pages away).

## Nonclustered Indexes on a Heap

If a table does not have a clustered index, the table is physically referred to as a *heap*. One definition of a heap is, "a group of things placed or thrown one on top of the other" (yes, your first car was probably a heap, but that was a totally different meaning of the word). This is a great way to explain what happens in a table when you have no clustered index: SQL Server simply puts every new row on the end of the last page for the table. Once that page is filled up, it puts a data on the next page or a new page as needed.

When building a nonclustered index on a heap, the row locator is a pointer to the physical page and row that contains the row. As an example, take the example structure from the previous section with a nonclustered index on the name column of an animal table, represented in Figure 9-12.

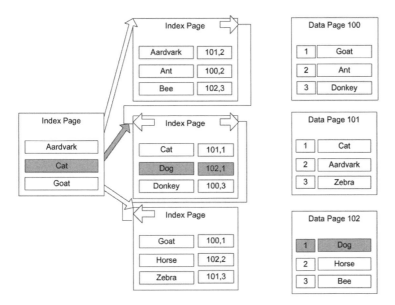

**Figure 9-12.** *Nonclustered index on a heap*

If you want to find the row where name ='Dog', you first find the path through the index from the top-level page to the leaf page. Once you get to the leaf page, you get a pointer to the page that has a row with the value, in this case Page 102, Row 1. This pointer consists of the page location and the record number on the page to find the row values (the pages are numbered from 0, and the offset is numbered from 1). The most important fact about this pointer is that it points directly to the row on the page that has the values you're looking for. The pointer for a table with a clustered index (a clustered table) is different, and this distinction is important to understand because it affects how well the different types of indexes perform.

One of the worst aspects of the heap structure is that when a row must be moved to a different physical location, the pointers in the index aren't changed. Instead, the data is moved to a different page, and on the original location of the data, a *forwarding pointer* is left to point to the new page where the data is now. So if the row where name ='Dog' had moved (for example, due to a large varchar(3000) column being updated), you might end up with following situation to extend the number of steps required to pick up the data. In Figure 9-13, this type of forwarding pointer is illustrated.

All existing indexes that have the old pointer simply go to the old page and follow the new pointer on that page to the new location of the data. If you are careful with your structures, data should rarely be moved around within a heap, but you have to be careful if you're often updating data to a larger value in a variable length column that's used as an index key, it's possible that a row may be moved to a different page. This adds another step to finding the data, and if the data is moved to a page on a different extent, another read to the database. This forwarding pointer is immediately followed when scanning the table, causing possible horrible performance over time if it's not managed.

Space is not reused in the heap without rebuilding the table (by selecting into another table, adding a clustered index temporarily, or in 2008, using the ALTER TABLE command with the REBUILD option).

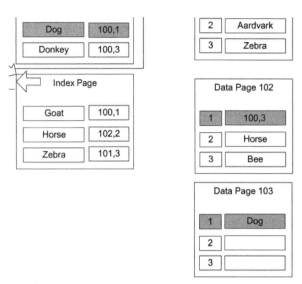

**Figure 9-13.** *Fowarding pointer*

# Basics of Index Creation

The basic syntax for creating an index is as follows:

```
CREATE [UNIQUE] INDEX [CLUSTERED | NONCLUSTERED] <indexName>
  ON <tableName> (<columnList>)
```

As you can see, you can specify either a clustered or nonclustered index, with nonclustered being the default type. Each type of index can be unique or nonunique. If you specify that your index must be unique, then every row in the indexed column must have a different value—no duplicate entries are accepted.

The `<columnList>` is a comma-delimited list of columns in the table. Each column can be specified either in ascending (ASC) or descending (DESC) order for each column, with ascending being the default. SQL Server can traverse the index in either direction for searches, so the direction is generally only important when you have multiple columns in the index (more on that later).

For example, the following statement creates an index called `XtableA_column1AndColumn2` on `column1` and `column2` of `tableA`, with ascending order for `column1` and descending order for `column2`:

```
CREATE INDEX XtableA_column1AndColumn2 ON tableA (column1, column2 DESC)
```

Let's take a look at a more full example. First, we need to create a base table. Use whatever database you desire. I used `tempdb` on my test machine and included the `USE` statement in the code download.

```
CREATE SCHEMA produce
go
CREATE TABLE produce.vegetable
(
    --PK constraint defaults to clustered
    vegetableId int CONSTRAINT PKproduce_vegetable PRIMARY KEY,
    name varchar(15)
                CONSTRAINT AKproduce_vegetable_name UNIQUE,
```

```
    color varchar(10),
    consistency varchar(10),
    filler char(4000) default (replicate('a', 4000))
)
```

---

■**Note** I included a huge column in the produce table to exacerbate the issues with indexing the table in lieu of having tons of rows to work with. This causes the data to be spread among several data pages, and as such, forces some queries to perform more like a table with a lot more data. I will not return this filler column or acknowledge it much in the chapter, but this is its purpose. Obviously, creating a filler column is not a performance tuning best practice, but it is a common trick to force a table's data pages to take up more space in a demonstration.

---

Now, we create two single-column nonclustered indexes on the color and consistency columns, respectively:

```
CREATE INDEX Xproduce_vegetable_color ON produce.vegetable(color)
CREATE INDEX Xproduce_vegetable_consistency ON produce.vegetable(consistency)
```

Then, we create a unique composite index on the vegetableID and color columns. We make this index unique, not to guarantee uniqueness of the values in the columns but because the values in vegetableId must be unique because it's part of the PRIMARY KEY constraint. Making this unique signals to the optimizer that the values in the index are unique (note that this index is probably not very useful but is created to demonstrate a unique index that isn't a constraint).

```
CREATE UNIQUE INDEX Xproduce_vegetable_vegetableId_color
      ON produce.vegetable(vegetableId, color)
```

Finally, we add some test data:

```
INSERT INTO produce.vegetable(vegetableId, name, color, consistency)
VALUES (1,'carrot','orange','crunchy'), (2,'broccoli','green','leafy'),
       (3,'mushroom','brown','squishy'), (4,'pea','green','squishy'),
       (5,'asparagus','green','crunchy'), (6,'sprouts','green','leafy'),
       (7,'lettuce','green','leafy'),( 8,'brussels sprout','green','leafy'),
       (9,'spinach','green','leafy'), (10,'pumpkin','orange','solid'),
       (11,'cucumber','green','solid'), (12,'bell pepper','green','solid'),
       (13,'squash','yellow','squishy'), (14,'canteloupe','orange','squishy'),
        (15,'onion','white','solid'), (16,'garlic','white','solid')
```

To see the indexes on the table, we check the following query:

```
SELECT  name, type_desc, is_unique
FROM    sys.indexes
WHERE   object_id('produce.vegetable') = object_id
```

This returns the following results:

---

| name | type_desc | is_unique |
| --- | --- | --- |
| PKproduce_vegetable | CLUSTERED | 1 |
| AKproduce_vegetable_name | NONCLUSTERED | 1 |
| Xproduce_vegetable_color | NONCLUSTERED | 0 |
| Xproduce_vegetable_consistency | NONCLUSTERED | 0 |
| Xproduce_vegetable_vegetableId_color | NONCLUSTERED | 1 |

---

One thing to note here is that PRIMARY KEY and UNIQUE constraints were implemented behind the scenes using indexes. The PK constraint is, by default, implemented using a clustered index and the UNIQUE constraint via a nonclustered index. As the primary key is generally chosen to be an optimally small value, it tends to make a nice clustering key.

---

■**Note** Foreign key constraints aren't automatically implemented using an index, though indexes on migrated foreign key columns are often useful for performance reasons. I'll return to this topic later when I discuss the relationship between foreign keys and indexes.

---

The remaining entries in the output show the three nonclustered indexes that we explicitly created and that the last index was implemented as unique since it included the unique key values as one of the columns. Before moving on, briefly note that to drop an index, use the DROP INDEX statement, like this one to drop the Xproduce_vegetable_consistency index we just created:

```
DROP INDEX Xproduce_vegetable_consistency ON produce.vegetable
```

One last thing I want to mention on the basic index creation is a new feature to 2008. That new feature is the ability to create *filtered indexes*. By including a WHERE clause in the CREATE INDEX statement, you can restrict the index such that the only values that will be included in the leaf nodes of the index are from rows that meet the where clause. We built a filtered index back in Chapter 5 when I introduced selective uniqueness, and I will mention them again in this chapter to show how to optimize for certain WHERE clauses.

The options I have shown so far are clearly not all of the options for indexes in SQL Server, nor are these the only types of indexes available. For example, there are options to place indexes on different filegroups from tables. Also at your disposal are filestream data (mentioned in Chapter 7), data compression, the maximum degree of parallelism to use with an index, locking (page or row locks), rebuilding, and several other features. There are also XML and spatial index types. This book focuses specifically on relational databases, so relational indexes are really all that I am covering in any depth.

# Basic Index Usage Patterns

In this section, I'll look at some of the basic usage patterns of the different index types, as well as how to see the use of the index within a query plan:

- *Clustered indexes*: I'll discuss the choices you need to make when choosing which columns in which to put the clustered index.

- *Nonclustered indexes*: After the clustered index is applied, you need to decide where to apply nonclustered indexes.

- *Unique indexes*: I'll look at why it's important to use unique indexes as frequently as possible.

All plans that I present were obtained using the SET SHOWPLAN_TEXT ON statement. When you're doing this locally, it can be easier to use the graphical showplan from Management Studio. However, when you need to post the plan or include it in a document, use one of the SET SHOWPLAN_TEXT commands. You can read about this more in SQL Server Books Online. Note that using SET SHOWPLAN_TEXT (or the other versions of SET SHOWPLAN that are available, such as SET SHOWPLAN_XML), do not actually execute the statement/batch; rather, they show the estimated plan. If you need to execute the statement (like to get some dynamic SQL statements to execute to see the plan), you can use SET STATISTICS PROFILE ON to get the plan and some other pertinent information about what has been executed. Each of these session settings will need to be turned OFF explicitly once you have finished, or they will continue executing giving you plans.

For example, say you execute the following query:

```
SET SHOWPLAN_TEXT ON
GO
SELECT *
FROM    produce.vegetable
GO
SET SHOWPLAN_TEXT OFF
GO
```

Running these statements echoes the query as a single column result set of StmtText and then returns another with the same column name that displays the plan:

```
|--Clustered Index Scan
            (OBJECT:([tempdb].[produce].[vegetable].[PKproduce_vegetable]))
```

Although this is the best way to communicate the plan in text (for example, to post to the MSDN/ Technet (or any other) forums to get help on why your query is so slow), it is not the richest experience or the easiest. In SSMS, clicking the Query menu and choosing Display Estimated Execution Plan (Ctrl+L), you'll see the plan in a more interesting way, as shown in Figure 9-14, or by choosing Include Actual Execution Plan, you can see exactly what SQL Server did (which is analogous to SET STATISTICS PROFILE ON).

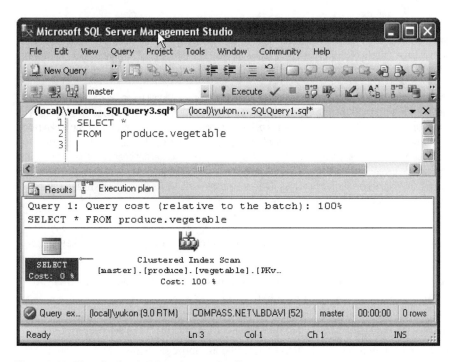

**Figure 9-14.** *Plan display in Management Studio*

Before digging into indexes, a few terms need to be introduced:

- *Scan*: This refers to an unordered search, where SQL Server scans the leaf pages of the index looking for a value. Generally speaking, all leaf pages would be considered in the process.

- *Seek*: This refers to an ordered search, in that the index pages are used to go to a certain point in the index and then a scan is done on a range of values. For a unique index, this would always return a single value.

- *Lookup*: The clustered index is used to look up a value for the nonclustered index.

## Using Clustered Indexes

The column you use for the clustered index will (because the key is used as the row locator), become a part of every index for your table, so it has heavy implications for all indexes. Because of this, for a typical OLTP system, a very common practice is to choose a surrogate key value, often the primary key of the table, since the surrogate can be kept very small.

Using the surrogate key as the clustering key is great, not only because is it a small key (most often the datatype is an integer that requires only 4 bytes or possibly less using compression) but because it's always a unique value. As mentioned earlier, a nonunique clustering key has a 4-byte uniquifier tacked onto its value when keys are not unique. It also helps the optimizer that an index has only unique values, because it knows immediately that for an equality operator, either 1 or 0 values will match. Because the surrogate key is often used in joins, it's helpful to have smaller keys for the primary key.

---

■**Caution**  Using a GUID for a surrogate key is becoming the vogue these days, but be careful. GUIDs are 16 bytes wide, which is a fairly large amount of space, but that is really the least of the problem. They are random values, in that they generally aren't monotonically increasing, and a new GUID could sort anywhere in a list of other GUIDs.

Clustering on a random value is generally horrible for inserts, because if you don't leave spaces on each page for new rows, you are likely to have page splitting. If you have a very active system, the constant page splitting can destroy your system, and the opposite effect, to leave lots of empty space, can be just as painful, as you make reads far less effective. The only way to make GUIDs a reasonably acceptable type is to use the NEWSEQUENTIALID() function (or one of your own) to build sequential GUIDS, but it only works with uniqueidentifier columns in a default constraint. Seldom will the person architecting a solution that is based on GUID surrogates want to be tied down to using a default constraint to generate surrogate values. The ability to generate GUIDs from anywhere and ensure their uniqueness is part of the lure of the siren call of the 16-byte value.

---

The clustered index won't always be used for the surrogate key or even the primary key. Other possible uses can fall under the following types:

- *Range queries*: Having all the data in order usually makes sense when there's data that you often need to get a range, such as from A to F.

- *Data that's always accessed sequentially*: Obviously, if the data needs to be accessed in a given order, having the data already sorted in that order will significantly improve performance.

- *Queries that return large result sets*: This point will make more sense once I cover nonclustered indexes, but for now, note that having the data on the leaf index page saves overhead.

The choice of how to pick the clustered index depends on a couple factors, such as how many other indexes will be derived from this index, how big the key for the index will be, and how often the value will change. When a clustered index value changes, every index on the table must also be touched and changed, and if the value can grow larger, well, then we might be talking page splits. This goes back to understanding the users of your data and testing the heck out of the system to verify that your index choices don't hurt overall performance more than they help. Speeding up one query by using one clustering key could hurt all queries that use the nonclustered indexes, especially if you chose a large key for the clustered index.

Frankly, in an OLTP setting, in all but the most unusual cases I stick with a surrogate key, usually one of the integer types or sometimes even the uniqueidentifier (GUID) type. I use the surrogate key because so many of the queries you do for modification (the general goal of the OLTP system) will access the data via the primary key. You then just have to optimize retrievals, which should also be of generally small numbers of rows, and doing so is usually pretty easy.

Another thing that is good about using the clustered index on a monotonously increasing value is that page splits over the entire index are greatly decreased. The table grows only on one end of the index, and while it does need to be rebuilt occasionally using ALTER INDEX REORGANIZE or ALTER INDEX REBUILD, you don't end up with page splits all over the table. You can decide which to do by using the criteria stated by SQL Server Books Online. By looking in the dynamic management view sys.dm_db_index_physical_stats, you can use REBUILD on indexes with greater than 30 percent fragmentation and use REORGANIZE otherwise. Now, let's look at an example of a clustered index in use. If you have a clustered index on a table, instead of Table Scan, you'll see a Clustered Index Scan in the plan:

```
SELECT *
FROM    produce.vegetable
```

The plan for this query is as follows:

```
|--Clustered Index Scan
            (OBJECT:([tempdb].[produce].[vegetable].[PKproduce_vegetable]))
```

If you query on a value of the clustered index key, the scan will likely change to a seek. Although a scan touches all the data pages, a clustered index seek uses the index structure to find a starting place for the scan and knows just how far to scan. For a unique index with an equality operator, a seek would be used to touch one page in each level of the index to find (or not find) a single value on a single data page, for example:

```
SELECT *
FROM    produce.vegetable
WHERE   vegetableId = 4
```

The plan for this query now does a seek:

```
|--Clustered Index Seek
        (OBJECT:([tempdb].[produce].[vegetable].[PKproduce_vegetable]),
            SEEK:([tempdb].[produce].[vegetable].[vegetableId]=
            CONVERT_IMPLICIT(int,[@1],0)) ORDERED FORWARD)
```

In this case, you're seeking in the clustered index based on the SEEK predicate of vegetableId = 1. Search for two rows:

```
SELECT *
FROM    produce.vegetable
WHERE   vegetableId in (1,4)
```

And in this case, pretty much the same plan is used, except the seek criteria now has an OR in it:

```
|--Clustered Index Seek
      (OBJECT:([tempdb].[produce].[vegetable].[PKproduce_vegetable]),
       SEEK:([tempdb].[produce].[vegetable].[vegetableId]=(1) OR
       [tempdb].[produce].[vegetable].[vegetableId]=(4)) ORDERED FORWARD)
```

But whether any given query uses a seek or a scan, or even two seeks, can be a pretty complex question. Why it is so complex will become clearer over the rest of the chapter, and it will become instantly clearer how useful a clustered index seek is in the next section, "Using Nonclustered Indexes."

**Tip** You might have noticed the differences between this plan:

```
CONVERT_IMPLICIT(int,[@1],0)) ORDERED FORWARD)
```

and this one:

```
([tempdb].[produce].[vegetable].[vegetableId]=(1) OR
[tempdb].[produce].[vegetable].[vegetableId]=(4)
```

This is part of the parameterization feature of SQL Server. The first query was parameterized by the query optimizer such that other queries can use the same plan. The second one wasn't, because the WHERE clause was more complex. Parameterization of ad hoc SQL is a great feature that I'll cover in Chapter 11.

# Using Nonclustered Indexes

After you have made the ever important choice of what to use for the clustered index, all other indexes will be nonclustered. In this section, I will cover nonclustered indexes in the following areas:

- General considerations
- Composite index considerations
- Nonclustered indexes with clustered tables
- Nonclustered indexes on heaps

## General Considerations

We generally know that indexes are needed because queries are slow. Lack of indexes is clearly not the only reason that queries are slow. Here are some of the obvious reasons for slow queries:

- Extra heavy user load
- Hardware load
- Network load

After looking for the existence of the preceding reasons, we can pull out Management Studio and start to look at the plans of the slow queries. Most often, slow queries are apparent because either |--Clustered Index Scan or |--Table Scan shows up in the query plan, and those operations take a large percentage of time to execute. Simple, right? Essentially, it is a true enough statement that index and table scans are time consuming, but unfortunately, that really doesn't give a full picture of the process. It's hard to make specific indexing changes before knowing about usage, because the usage pattern will greatly affect these decisions, for example:

- Is a query executed once a day, once an hour, or once a minute?

- Is a background process inserting into a table rapidly? Or perhaps inserts are taking place during off hours?

Using Profiler and the Dynamic Management Views, you can watch the usage patterns of the queries that access your database, looking for slowly executing queries, poor plans, and so on. After you do this and you start to understand the usage patterns for your database, you now need to use that information to consider where to apply indexes—the final goal being that you use the information you can gather about usage and tailor an index plan to solve the overall picture.

You can't just throw indexes around to fix individual queries. Nothing comes without a price, and indexes definitely have a cost. You need to consider how indexes help and hurt the different types of operations in different ways:

- SELECT: Indexes can only have a beneficial effect on SELECT queries.

- INSERT: An index can only hurt the process of inserting new data into the table. As data is created in the table, there's a chance that the index will have to be modified and reorganized to accommodate the new values.

- UPDATE: An update requires two or three steps: find the row(s) and change the row(s), or find the row(s), delete them, and reinsert them. During the phase of finding the row, the index is beneficial, such as for a SELECT. Whether or not it hurts during the second phase depends on several factors; for example:

  - Did the index key value change such that it needs to be moved around to different leaf nodes?

  - Will the new value fit on an existing page, or will it require a page split? (More on that later in this section.)

- DELETE: The delete requires two steps: to find the row and to remove it. Indexes are beneficial to find the row, but on deletion, you might have to do some reshuffling to accommodate the deleted values from the indexes.

You should also realize that for INSERT, UPDATE, or DELETE operations, if triggers on the table exist (or constraints exist that execute functions that reference tables), indexes will affect those operations in the same ways as in the list. For this reason, I'm going to shy away from any generic advice about what types of columns to index. In practice, there are just too many variables to consider.

---

**Tip** Too many people index without considering the costs. Just be wary that every index you add has to be maintained. Sometimes, a query taking 1 second to execute is OK when getting it down to .1 seconds might slow down other operations. The real question lies in how often each operation occurs and how much cost you are willing to suffer. The hardest part is keeping your tuning hat off until you can really get a decent profile of what operations are taking place.

---

For a good idea of how your current indexes and/or tables are currently being used, you can query the dynamic management view sys.dm_db_index_usage_stats:

```
SELECT object_name(i.object_id) as object_name
     , case when i.is_unique = 1 then 'UNIQUE ' else '' end +
           i.type_desc as index_type
     , i.name as index_name
     , user_seeks, user_scans, user_lookups,user_updates
```

```
FROM  sys.indexes i
        left outer join sys.dm_db_index_usage_stats s
            on i.object_id = s.object_id
              and i.index_id = s.index_id
              and database_id = db_id()
WHERE  objectproperty(i.object_id , 'IsUserTable') = 1
ORDER  BY 1,3
```

This query will return the name of each object, an index type, an index name, plus the number of

- *User seeks*: The number of times the index was used in a seek operation
- *User scans*: The number of times the index was scanned in answering a query
- *User lookups*: For clustered indexes, the number of times the index was used to resolve the row locator of a nonclustered index search
- *User updates*: The number of times the index was changed by a user query

This information is very important when trying to get a feel for which indexes might need to be tuned and especially which ones are not doing their jobs because they are mostly getting updated. You could probably boil performance tuning to a math equation if you had an advanced degree in math and a lot of time, but truthfully it would take longer than just testing in most cases (especially if you have a good performance-testing plan for your system). Even once you know the customer's answer to these questions, you should test your database code on your performance-testing platform. Performance testing is a tricky art, but it doesn't usually take tremendous amounts of time to identify your hot spots and optimize them, and to do the inevitable tuning of queries in production.

## Determining Index Usefulness

It might seem at this point that all you need to do is look at the plans of queries, look for the search arguments, put an index on the columns, and things will improve. There's a bit of truth to this, but indexes have to be useful to be used by a query. What if the index of this book had two entries:

General Topics Page 1

Determining Index Usefulness Page 417

This means that one page was classified such that the topic started on this page, and all other pages covered general topics. This would be useless to you, unless you needed to know about indexes. One thing is for sure: you could determine that the index was useless pretty quickly. Another thing we all do with the index of a book to see if it's useful is to take a value and look it up in the index. If what you're looking for is in there (or something close), you go to the page and check it out.

SQL Server determines whether or not to use your index in much the same way. It has two specific measurements that it uses to decide if an index is useful: the *density* of values (sometimes known as the *selectivity*), and a histogram of a sample of values in the table to check against.

You can see these in detail for indexes by using DBCC SHOW_STATISTICS. Our table is very small, so it doesn't need stats to decide which to use. Instead, we'll look at an index in the AdventureWorks2008 database:

```
DBCC SHOW_STATISTICS('AdventureWorks2008.Production.WorkOrder',
                     'IX_WorkOrder_ProductID') WITH DENSITY_VECTOR
DBCC SHOW_STATISTICS('AdventureWorks2008.Production.WorkOrder',
                     'IX_WorkOrder_ProductID') WITH HISTOGRAM
```

This returns the following sets (truncated for space), the first of which tells us the size and density of the keys. The second shows the histogram of where the table was sampled to find representative values:

| All density | Average Length | Columns |
| --- | --- | --- |
| 0.004201681 | 4 | ProductID |
| 1.377581E-05 | 8 | ProductID, WorkOrderID |

| RANGE_HI_KEY | RANGE_ROWS | EQ_ROWS | DISTINCT_RANGE_ROWS | AVG_RANGE_ROWS |
| --- | --- | --- | --- | --- |
| 3 | 0 | 1093 | 0 | 1 |
| 316 | 0 | 1093 | 0 | 1 |
| 324 | 0 | 1093 | 0 | 1 |
| ... | | | | |
| 730 | 0 | 127 | 0 | 1 |
| 731 | 0 | 12 | 0 | 1 |
| 733 | 21 | 21 | 1 | 21 |
| 736 | 24 | 340 | 2 | 12 |
| 737 | 0 | 311 | 0 | 1 |
| 738 | 0 | 374 | 0 | 1 |
| 739 | 0 | 458 | 0 | 1 |
| 742 | 111 | 412 | 2 | 55.5 |
| 743 | 0 | 485 | 0 | 1 |
| 744 | 0 | 69 | 0 | 1 |
| ... | | | | |
| 996 | 0 | 1084 | 0 | 1 |
| 997 | 0 | 236 | 0 | 1 |
| 998 | 0 | 236 | 0 | 1 |
| 999 | 0 | 233 | 0 | 1 |

I won't cover the DBCC SHOW_STATISTICS command in great detail, but there are a couple important things to understand. First, consider the density of each column set. The ProductId column is the only column that is actually declared in the index, but note that it includes the density of the index column and the clustered index key as well (it's known as the *clustering key*, which I'll cover more later in this chapter).

All the density is calculated approximately by 1/ number of distinct rows, as shown here for the same columns as I just checked the density on:

```
--Used isnull as it is easier if the column can be null
--value you translate to should be impossible for the column
--ProductId is an identity with seed of 1 and increment of 1
--so this should be safe (unless a dba does something weird)
SELECT 1.0/ count(distinct isnull(ProductId,-1)) as density,
          count(distinct isnull(ProductId,-1)) as distinctRowCount,

       1.0/ count(*) as uniqueDensity,
          count(*) as allRowCount
FROM   AdventureWorks2008.Production.WorkOrder
```

This returns the following:

| density | distinctRowCount | uniqueDensity | allRowCount |
| --- | --- | --- | --- |
| 0.004201680672 | 238 | 0.000013775812 | 72591 |

You can see that the densities match (the queries density is in a numeric type, while the DBCC is using a float, which is why they are formatted differently, but they are the same value!). The smaller the number, the better the index, and the more likely it will be easily chosen for use. There's no magic number, per se, but this value fits into the calculations of which way is best to execute the query. (The actual numbers returned from this query might vary slightly from the DBCC value, as a sampled number might be used for the distinct count.)

The second thing to understand in the DBCC SHOW_STATISTICS output is the histogram. Even if the density of the index isn't low, SQL Server can check a given value (or set of values) in the histogram to see how many rows will likely be returned. SQL Server keeps statistics about columns in a table as well as in indexes, so it can make informed decisions as to how to employ indexes or table columns. For example, consider the following rows from the histogram (I have faked some of these results for demonstration purposes):

| RANGE_HI_KEY | RANGE_ROWS | EQ_ROWS | DISTINCT_RANGE_ROWS | AVG_RANGE_ROWS |
|---|---|---|---|---|
| ... | | | | |
| 989 | 111 | 58 | 2 | 55.5 |
| 992 | 117 | 67 | 2 | 58.5 |

In the second row, the row values tell us the following:

- RANGE_HI_KEY: The sampled ProductId values were 989 and 992.

- RANGE_ROWS: There are 117 rows where the value was between 989 and 992 (noninclusive of the endpoints). These values would not be known. However, if a user used 990 as a search argument, the optimizer can now know that a maximum of 117 rows would be returned. This is one of the ways that the query plan gets the estimated number of rows for each step in a query and is one of the ways to determine if an index will be useful for an individual query.

- EQ_ROWS: There were exactly 67 rows where ProductId = 992.

- DISTINCT_RANGE_ROWS: For the row with 989, it is estimated that there are two distinct values between 989 and 992.

- AVG_RANGE_ROWS: This is the average number of duplicate values in the range, excluding the upper and lower bounds. This value is what the optimizer can expect to be the average number of rows. Note that this is calculated by RANGE_ROWS / DISTINCT_RANGE_ROWS.

One thing that having this histogram can do is allow a seemingly useless index to become valuable in some cases. For example, say you want to index a column with only two values. If the values are evenly distributed, the index would be useless. However, if there are only a few of a certain value, it could be useful (going back to the tempdb):

```
CREATE TABLE testIndex
(
    testIndex int identity(1,1) constraint PKtestIndex primary key,
    bitValue bit,
    filler char(2000) not null default (replicate('A',2000))
)
CREATE INDEX XtestIndex_bitValue on testIndex(bitValue)
go
SET NOCOUNT ON
INSERT INTO testIndex(bitValue)
VALUES (0)
GO 50000 --runs current batch 20000 times in Management Studio.
INSERT INTO testIndex(bitValue)
VALUES (1)
GO 100 --puts 100 rows into table with value 1
```

You can guess that few rows will be returned if the only value desired is 1. Check the plan for bitValue = 0:

```
SELECT *
FROM    testIndex
WHERE   bitValue = 0
```

This shows a clustered index scan:

```
|--Clustered Index Scan(OBJECT:([tempdb].[dbo].[testIndex].[PKtestIndex]),
                        WHERE:([tempdb].[dbo].[testIndex].[bitValue]=(0)))
```

However, change the 0 to a 1 and the optimizer chooses an index seek. This means that it performed a seek into the index to the first row that had a 1 as a value and worked its way through the values:

```
|--Nested Loops(Inner Join,
        OUTER REFERENCES:([tempdb].[dbo].[testIndex].[testIndex]) OPTIMIZED)
    |--Index Seek(OBJECT:([tempdb].[dbo].[testIndex].[XtestIndex_bitValue]),
            SEEK:([tempdb].[dbo].[testIndex].[bitValue]=(1)) ORDERED FORWARD)
    |--Clustered Index
        Seek(OBJECT:([tempdb].[dbo].[testIndex].[PKtestIndex]),
                SEEK:([tempdb].[dbo].[testIndex].[testIndex]=
                    [tempdb].[dbo].[testIndex].[testIndex])
                    LOOKUP ORDERED FORWARD)
```

Note that this may look a bit odd, but this plan shows that the query processor will do the index seek to find the rows that match and then a nested loop join to the clustered index to get the rest of the data for the row (because we chose to do SELECT *), getting the entire data row (more on how to avoid the clustered seek in the next section).

You can see why in the histogram:

```
UPDATE STATISTICS dbo.testIndex
DBCC SHOW_STATISTICS('dbo.testIndex', 'XtestIndex_bitValue')
                                    WITH HISTOGRAM
```

This returns the following results (your actual values will likely vary, and in fact, in some tests, only the 0 rows showed up in the output):

| RANGE_HI_KEY | RANGE_ROWS | EQ_ROWS | DISTINCT_RANGE_ROWS | AVG_RANGE_ROWS |
| --- | --- | --- | --- | --- |
| 0 | 0 | 50020.19 | 0 | 1 |
| 1 | 0 | 79.80884 | 0 | 1 |

The statistics gathered estimated that about 80 rows match for bitValue = 1. That's because statistics gathering isn't an exact science—it uses a sampling mechanism rather than checking every value (your values might vary as well). Check out the TABLESAMPLE clause, and you can use the same mechanisms to gather random samples of your data.

The optimizer knew that it would be advantageous to use the index when looking for bitValue = 1, because approximately 80 rows are returned when the index key with a value of 1 is desired, but 50020 are returned for 0.

This demonstration of the histogram is good, but in practice in SQL Server 2008, actually building a filtered index to optimize this query may be a better practice (I introduced filtered indexes back in Chapter 5 to implement selective uniqueness). You might build an index such as this:

```
CREATE INDEX XtestIndex_bitValueOneOnly
    ON testIndex(bitValue) WHERE bitValue = 1
```

The histogram for this index is definitely by far a clearer good match:

| RANGE_HI_KEY | RANGE_ROWS | EQ_ROWS | DISTINCT_RANGE_ROWS | AVG_RANGE_ROWS |
|---|---|---|---|---|
| 1 | 0 | 81 | 0 | 1 |

Whether or not the query actually uses this index will likely depend on how badly the other index would perform, which can also be dependent on hardware conditions. A histogram is, however, another tool that you can use when optimizing your SQL to see what the optimizer is using to make its choices.

---

■**Tip** Whether or not the histogram includes any data where the bitValue = 1 is largely a matter of chance. I have done this example several times, and one time no rows were shown unless I used the FULLSCAN option on the UPDATE STATISTICS command (which isn't feasible on very large tables unless you have quite a bit of time).

---

## Indexing and Multiple Columns

So far, the indexes I've talked about were mostly on single columns, but it isn't all that often that you only need performance enhancing indexes on single columns. When multiple columns are included in the WHERE clause of a query on the same table, there are several possible ways you can enhance your queries:

- Having one composite index on all columns
- Creating *covering indexes* by including all columns that a query touches
- Having multiple indexes on separate columns
- Adjusting key sort order to optimize sort operations

### Composite Indexes

When you include more than one column in an index, it's referred to as a *composite index*. As the number of columns grows, or the number of bytes in the key grows, the effectiveness of the index is reduced. The problem is that the index is sorted by the first column values. So the second column in the index is more or less only useful if you need the first column as well. Even so, a composite index is often good to have when users are querying with predicates on all of the columns involved.

The order of the columns in a query is important with respect to whether a composite can and will be used. There are a couple important considerations:

- *Which column is most selective?* If one column includes unique or mostly unique values, this is possibly a good candidate for the first column. The key is that the first column is the one by which the index is sorted. Searching on the second column only is less valuable (though queries using only the second column can scan the index leaf pages for values).

- *Which column is used most often without the other columns?* One composite index can be useful to several different queries, even if only the first column of the index is all that is being used in those queries.

For example, consider this query:

```
SELECT vegetableId, name, color, consistency
FROM produce.vegetable
WHERE color = 'green'
  and consistency = 'crunchy'
```

---

■**Note** I included all columns in the results for demonstration purposes. In some cases demonstrating the different uses of indexes will require me to force the use of a particular index or to use some odd query pattern to get
the kind of results desired.

---

An index on color or consistency alone might not do the job well enough (of course, it will
in this case, as vegetable is a very small table). If the plan that is being produced by the optimizer
is to do a table scan, you might consider adding a composite index on color and consistency. This
isn't a bad idea to consider, and composite indexes are great tools, but just how useful such an
index will be is completely dependent on how many rows will be returned by color = 'green' and
consistency = 'crunchy'.

The preceding query with existing indexes (clustered primary key on produceId, alternate key
on Name, indexes on color and consistency, plus a composite index on vegetable and color_) is
optimized with the following plan:

---

```
|--Clustered Index
    Scan(OBJECT:([tempdb].[produce].[vegetable].[PKproduct_vegetable]),
        WHERE:([tempdb].[produce].[vegetable].[color]='green' AND
            [tempdb].[produce].[vegetable].[consistency]='crunchy'))
```

---

Adding an index on color and consistency might seem like a good way to further optimize the
query, but first, you should look at the data for these columns (consider future usage of the index
too, but existing data is a good place to start):

---

| color | consistency |
| --------- | ----------- |
| orange | crunchy |
| green | leafy |
| brown | squishy |
| green | squishy |
| green | crunchy |
| green | leafy |
| green | leafy |
| green | leafy |
| green | leafy |
| orange | solid |
| green | solid |
| green | solid |
| yellow | squishy |
| orange | squishy |
| white | solid |
| white | solid |

---

A good idea is to see which of the columns has more distinct values:

```
SELECT COUNT(Distinct color) as color,
       COUNT(Distinct consistency) as consistency
FROM   produce.vegetable
```

This query returns the following:

| color | consistency |
| ----------- | ----------- |
| 5 | 4 |

The column consistency has the most unique values (though not tremendously, in real practice, the difference in the number of values will often be much greater). So we add the following index:

```
CREATE INDEX Xproduce_vegetable_consistencyAndColor
       ON produce.vegetable(consistency, color)
```

The plan changes to the following (well, it would if there were lots more data in the table, so I have forced the plan to generate this particular example; otherwise, because there is such a small amount of data, the clustered index would always be used for all queries):

```
|--Nested Loops(Inner Join, OUTER REFERENCES:
                      ([tempdb].[produce].[vegetable].[vegetableId]))
   |--Index Seek(OBJECT:
          ([tempdb].[produce].[vegetable].[Xvegetable_consistencyAndColor]),
          SEEK:([tempdb].[produce].[vegetable].[consistency]='crunchy'
              AND [tempdb].[produce].[vegetable].[color]='orange')
                      ORDERED FORWARD)
   |--Clustered Index Seek(OBJECT:
          ([tempdb].[produce].[vegetable].[PKproduce_vegetable]),
          SEEK:([tempdb].[produce].[vegetable].[vegetableId]=
                      [tempdb].[produce].[vegetable].[vegetableId])
                      LOOKUP ORDERED FORWARD)
```

The execution plan does an index seek on the Xvegetable_consistencyAndColor index, and it uses the clustered index named PKproduce_vegetable to fetch the other parts of the row that were not included in the Xvegetable_consistencyAndColor index (which is why the clustered index seek is noted as **LOOKUP** ORDERED FORWARD).

In the next section, I will show how you can eliminate the clustered index scan, but in general, having the scan isn't the worst thing in the world unless you are matching lots of rows. In this case, for example, the two single-row seeks would result in better performance than a full scan through the table. When the number of rows found using the nonclustered index grows large, however, a plan such as the preceding one can become very costly.

### Covering Indexes

When only retrieving data from a table, if an index exists that has all the data values that are needed for a query, the base table needn't be touched. Back in Figure 9-10, there was a nonclustered index on the type of animal. If the name of the animal was the only data the query needed to touch, the data pages of the table wouldn't need to be accessed directly. The index *covers* all the data needed for the query and is commonly referred to as a *covering index*. The ability to create covering indexes is a nice feature, and the approach even works with clustered indexes (though with clustered indexes, SQL Server scans the lowest index structure page, because scanning the leaf nodes of the clustered index is the same as a table scan).

As a baseline to the example, let's run the following query:

```
select name, color
from produce.vegetable
where color = 'green'
```

The resulting plan is a simple clustered index scan:

```
|--Clustered Index Scan
        (OBJECT:([tempdb].[produce].[vegetable].[PKproduce_vegetable]),
        WHERE:([tempdb].[produce].[vegetable].[color]='green'))
```

We could do a couple of things to improve the performance of the query. First, we could create a composite index on the color and name columns. If you will be filtering on the name column in some cases, that would be the best thing to do.

However, in SQL Server 2005, a new feature was added to the index-creation syntax to improve the ability to implement covering indexes—the INCLUDE (<columns>) clause of the CREATE INDEX statement. The included columns can be almost any datatype, even (max)-type columns. In fact, the only types that aren't allowed are text, ntext, and image datatypes, but you shouldn't use these types anyhow, as they're in the process of being deprecated (you should expect them to be completely removed from the product in the version after 2008).

Using the INCLUDE keyword gives you the ability to add columns to cover a query without including those columns in the index pages, and thus without causing overhead in the use of the index. Instead, the data in the INCLUDE columns is added only to the leaf pages of the index. The INCLUDE columns won't help in index seeking, but they do eliminate the need to go to the data pages to get the data being sought.

To demonstrate, let's modify the index on vegetable color and include the name column:

```
DROP INDEX Xproduce_vegetable_color ON produce.vegetable
CREATE INDEX Xproduce_vegetable_color ON produce.vegetable(color) INCLUDE (name)
```

Now the query goes back to scanning the index, because it has all the data in the index, and this time it doesn't even need to go to the clustered index to pick up the name column.

```
|--Index Seek(OBJECT:([tempdb].[produce].[vegetable].[Xvegetable_color]),
SEEK:([tempdb].[produce].[vegetable].[color]=[@1]) ORDERED FORWARD)
```

This ability to include columns only in the leaf pages of covering indexes is incredibly useful in a lot of situations. Too many indexes with overly large keys were created to cover a query to avoid accessing the base table and were generally only good for one situation, wasting valuable resources. Now, using INCLUDE, you get the benefits of a covering index without the overhead of bloating the nonleaf pages of the index with values that are useless from a row-accessing standpoint.

Be careful not to use covering indexes unless you can see a large benefit from them. The INCLUDE feature costs less to maintain than including the values in the index structure, but it doesn't make the index structure free to maintain.

---

**Caution** I must include a caution about overusing covering indexes, because their use does incur a fairly heavy cost. Be careful to test that the additional overhead of duplicating data in indexes doesn't harm performance more than it helps it.

---

## Multiple Indexes

Sometimes, we might not have a single index on a table that meets the given situation for the query optimizer to do an optimum job. In this case, SQL Server can sometimes use two or more indexes to meet the need. When processing a query with multiple indexes, SQL Server uses the indexes as if they were tables, joins them together, and returns a set of rows. The more indexes used, the larger the cost, but using multiple indexes can be dramatically faster in some cases.

Multiple indexes aren't usually something to rely on to optimize known queries. It's almost always better to support a known query with a single index. However, if you need to support *ad hoc* queries that cannot be foretold as a system designer, having several indexes including multiple situations might be the best idea. If you're building a read-only table, a decent starting strategy might be to index every column that might be used as a filter for a query.

My focus throughout this book has been on OLTP databases, and for that type of database, it isn't usual to use multiple indexes in a single query. However, it's possible that the need for using multiple indexes will arise if you have a table with several columns that you'll allow users to query against in any combination.

For example, consider that you want data from four columns in a table that contains telephone listings. You might create a table for holding phone numbers called phoneListing, with these columns: phoneListingId, firstName, lastName, zipCode, areaCode, exchange, and number (assuming US-style phone numbers).

You have a clustered primary key index on phoneListingId, nonclustered composite indexes on lastName and firstName, one on areaCode and exchange, and another on the zipCode. From these indexes, you can effectively perform a large variety of searches, though generally speaking none of these will be perfect standing alone.

For less typical names (such as Joe Shlabotnik, for example), a person can find this name without knowing the location. For other names, there are hundreds and thousands of other people with the same first and last name. I always thought I was the only schmuck with the name Louis Davidson, but it turns out that there are others!

We could build a variety of indexes on these columns, such that SQL Server would only need a single index. However, not only would these indexes have a lot of columns in them but you'd need several indexes. A composite index can be useful for searches on the second and third columns, but if the first column is not included in the filtering criteria, it will require a scan of the index, rather than a seek. Instead, for large sets, SQL Server can find the set of data that meets one index's criteria and then join it to the set of rows that matches the other index's criteria.

This technique can be useful when dealing with large sets of data, especially when users are doing *ad hoc* querying, and you cannot anticipate what columns they'll need until runtime. Users have to realize that they need to specify as few columns as possible, because if the multiple indexes can cover a query such as the one in the last section, the indexes will be far more likely to be used.

As an example, we'll use the data already created, and add an index on the consistency column:

```
CREATE INDEX Xproduce_vegetable_consistency ON produce.vegetable(consistency)
--existing index repeated as a reminder
--CREATE INDEX Xproduce_vegetable_color ON produce.vegetable(color) INCLUDE (name)
```

We'll force the optimizer to use multiple indexes (because the sample table is far too small to require multiple indexes):

```
SELECT consistency, color
FROM   produce.vegetable with (index=Xproduce_vegetable_color,
                               index=Xproduce_vegetable_consistency)
WHERE  color = 'green'
 and   consistency = 'leafy'
```

This produces the following plan (I've only included the portion of the plan pertaining to the indexes):

```
|--Merge Join(Inner Join, MERGE:([tempdb].[produce].[vegetable].[vegetableId])
            =([tempdb].[produce].[vegetable].[vegetableId]),
            RESIDUAL:([tempdb].[produce].[vegetable].[vegetableId] =
            [tempdb].[produce].[vegetable].[vegetableId]))
     |--Index Seek(OBJECT:
        ([tempdb].[produce].[vegetable].[Xproduce_vegetable_color]),
        SEEK:([tempdb].[produce].[vegetable].[color]='green') ORDERED FORWARD)
     |--Index Seek(OBJECT:
          ([tempdb].[produce].[vegetable].[Xproduce_vegetable_consistency]),
          SEEK:([tempdb].[produce].[vegetable].[consistency]='leafy')
          ORDERED FORWARD)
```

Looking at a snippet of the plan for this query, you can see that there are two index seeks to find rows where color = 'green' and consistency = 'leafy'. These seeks would be fast on even a very large set, as long as the index was reasonably selective. Then a join is done between the sets using a merge join, because the sets can be ordered by the clustered index (there's a clustered index on the table, so the clustering key is included in the index keys).

### Sort Order of Index Keys

While SQL Server can traverse an index in either direction (since it is a doubly linked list), sometimes sorting the keys of an index to match the sort order of some desired output can be valuable. For example, consider the case where you want to look at the hire dates of your employees, in descending order by hire date. To do that, execute the following query (in the AdventureWorks2008 database):

```
SELECT maritalStatus, hiredate
FROM   Adventureworks2008.HumanResources.Employee
ORDER BY maritalStatus ASC, hireDate DESC
```

The plan for this query follows:

```
|--Sort(ORDER BY:(
        [AdventureWorks2008].[HumanResources].[Employee].[MaritalStatus] ASC,
        [AdventureWorks2008].[HumanResources].[Employee].[HireDate] DESC))
     |--Clustered Index
          Scan(OBJECT:([AdventureWorks2008].[HumanResources].[Employee].
             [PK_Employee_EmployeeID]))
```

Next, create a typical index with the default (ascending) sort order:

```
CREATE INDEX Xemployee_maritalStatus_hireDate ON
     Adventureworks2008.HumanResources.Employee (maritalStatus,hiredate)
```

Rechecking the plan, you will see that the plan changes to an index scan (since it can use the index to cover the query), but it still requires a sort operation.

```
|--Sort(ORDER BY:(
        [AdventureWorks2008].[HumanResources].[Employee].[MaritalStatus] ASC,
        [AdventureWorks2008].[HumanResources].[Employee].[HireDate] DESC))
     |--Index Scan(OBJECT:([AdventureWorks2008].[HumanResources].[Employee].
             [Xemployee_maritalStatus_hireDate]))
```

Better, but still not quite what we want. Change the index we just added to be sorted in the direction that the output is desired in:

```
DROP INDEX Xemployee_maritalStatus_hireDate ON
        Adventureworks2008.HumanResources.Employee
GO
CREATE INDEX Xemployee_maritalStatus_hireDate ON
    AdventureWorks2008.HumanResources.Employee(maritalStatus ASC,hiredate DESC)
```

Now, reexecute the query, and the sort is gone:

```
|--Index Scan(OBJECT:([AdventureWorks2008].[HumanResources].[Employee].
                [Xemployee_maritalStatus_hireDate]), ORDERED FORWARD)
```

Tweaking index sorting is not necessarily the best thing to do just to tune a single query. Doing so creates an index that will need to be maintained, and in the end, it may end costing more than just paying the cost of the clustered index scan. Creating an index in a sort order to match a query's ORDER BY clause is, however, another tool in the belt to enhance query performance. Consider it when an ORDER BY operation is done frequently enough and at a cost that is otherwise too much to bear.

## Nonclustered Indexes on a Heap

Although there are rarely compelling use cases for leaving a table as a heap structure in a production OLTP database, I do want at least to show you how this works. As an example of using a nonclustered index with a heap, we'll drop the primary key on our table and replace it with a nonclustered version of the PRIMARY KEY constraint:

```
ALTER TABLE produce.vegetable
    DROP CONSTRAINT PKproduce_vegetable

ALTER TABLE produce.vegetable
    ADD CONSTRAINT PKproduce_vegetable PRIMARY KEY NONCLUSTERED (vegetableID)
```

Now we look for a single value in the table:

```
SELECT *
FROM    produce.vegetable
WHERE   vegetableId = 4
```

We optimize this query with the following plan:

```
|--Nested Loops(Inner Join, OUTER REFERENCES:([Bmk1000]))
    |--Index Seek(
            OBJECT:([tempdb].[produce].[vegetable].[PKproduce_vegetable]),
        SEEK:([tempdb].[produce].[vegetable].[vegetableId]=
        CONVERT_IMPLICIT(int,[@1],0)) ORDERED FORWARD)
    |--RID Lookup(OBJECT:([tempdb].[produce].[vegetable]),
        SEEK:([Bmk1000]=[Bmk1000]) LOOKUP ORDERED FORWARD)
```

First we probe the index for the value; then we have to look up the row from the row ID (RID) in the index (the RID lookup operator.) The most important thing I wanted to show in this section was the RID lookup operator, so you can identify this on a plan and understand what is going on.

## Using Unique Indexes

An important index setting is `UNIQUE`. In the design of the tables, `UNIQUE` and `PRIMARY KEY` constraints were created to enforce keys. Behind the scenes, SQL Server employs unique indexes to enforce uniqueness over a column or group of columns. The reason that SQL Server uses them for this purpose is because, to determine if a value is unique, you have to look it up in the table. Because SQL Server uses indexes to speed access to the data, you have the perfect match.

Enforcing uniqueness is a business rule, and as I covered in Chapter 6, the rule of thumb is to use `UNIQUE` or `PRIMARY` constraints to enforce uniqueness on a set of columns. Now, as you're improving performance, use unique indexes when the data you're indexing allows it.

For example, say you're building an index that happens to include a column (or columns) that is already a part of another unique index. Another possibility might be if you're indexing a column that's naturally unique, such as a GUID. It's up to the designer to decide if this GUID is a key or not, and that depends completely on what it's used for. Using unique indexes lets the optimizer determine more easily the number of rows it has to deal with in an equality operation.

Also note that it's important for the performance of your systems that you use unique indexes whenever possible, as they enhance the SQL Server optimizer's chances of predicting how many rows will be returned from a query that uses the index. If the index is unique, the maximum number of rows that can be returned from a query that requires equality is one. This is common when working with joins.

# Advanced Index Usage Scenarios

So far we've dealt with the mechanics of indexes, and basic situations where they're useful. Now we need to talk about a few special uses of indexes that deserve some preplanning or understanding to use.

I'll discuss the following topics:

- Indexing foreign keys
- Indexing views to optimize denormalization

## Foreign Key Indexes

Foreign key columns are a special case where often we need an index of some sort. This is because we build foreign keys so we can match up rows in one table to rows in another. For this, we have to take a value in one table and match it to another.

In an OLTP database that has proper constraints on alternate keys, it's often the case that we won't need to index foreign keys beyond what we're given with the unique indexes that are built as part of the structure of the database. This is probably why SQL Server 2005 doesn't implement unique indexes for us when creating a foreign key constraint.

However, it's important to make sure that any time you have a foreign key constraint declared, there's the potential for need of an index whenever you have a parent table and you want to see the children of the row. A special and important case where this type of access is essential is when you have to delete the parent row in any relationship, even one of a domain type. I know other architects who apply an index to all foreign keys as a default, only removing the index if it is obvious that it is not helping performance. However, I generally use a more pragmatic approach based on the type of relationship and usage.

For example, say you have five values in the parent table and five million in the child. For example, consider the case of a click log for a sales database, a snippet of which is shown in Figure 9-15.

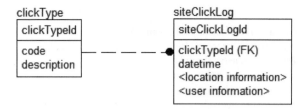

**Figure 9-15.** *Sample foreign key relationship*

Consider that you want to delete a `clickType` that someone added inadvertently. Creating the row took several milliseconds. Deleting it shouldn't take long at all, right? Well, even if there isn't a single value in the table, if you don't have an index on the foreign key in the `siteClickLog` table, it will take just over 10 seconds longer than eternity will take (or just 5 seconds longer than the line to ride Space Mountain at Disney World on a hot summer's day!). Even though the value doesn't exist in the table, the query processor would need to touch and check the entire five million rows for the value. However, if you have an index, deleting the row (or knowing that you can't delete it) will take a very short period of time, because in the upper pages of the index, you'll have all the unique values in the index, in this case five values. There will be a fairly substantial set of leaf pages for the index, because each row needs to be pointed to, but if there are only a few `clickType` rows, the top page of the index tree will have all of the distinct values found in the `clickType` table. Hence, deciding if the row can be deleted takes no time at all. And if you have cascading operations enabled for the relationship, having an index can be even more compelling. The cascading options will need the index to find the rows to cascade to. When `NO ACTION` is specified for the relationship, if just one row is found, the operation could be stopped.

This adds more decisions when building indexes. Is the cost of building and maintaining the index during creation of `siteClickLog` rows justified, or do you just bite the bullet and do deletes during off hours? Add a trigger such as the following (ignoring error handling in this example for brevity):

```
CREATE TRIGGER clickType$insteadOfDelete
ON clickType
INSTEAD OF DELETE
AS
    INSERT INTO clickType_deleteQueue (clickTypeId)
    SELECT clickTypeId
    FROM   inserted
```

Then you let your queries that return lists of `clickType` rows check this table when presenting rows to the users:

```
SELECT code, description, clickTypeId
FROM    clickType
WHERE   not exists (SELECT *
                    FROM    clickType_deleteQueue
                    WHERE   clickType.clickTypeId =
                                clickType_deleteQueue.clickTypeId)
```

Now (assuming all code follows this pattern), the users will never see the value, so it won't be an issue, and you can delete the row during the wee hours of the night without building the index.

Whether or not an index proves useful depends on the purpose of the foreign key. I'll mention specific types of foreign keys individually, each with their own signature usage:

- *Domain tables*: Used to implement a defined set of values and their descriptions

- *Ownership*: Used to implement a multivalued attribute of the parent

- *Many-to-many resolution*: Used to implement a many-to-many relationship physically
- *One-to-one relationships*: Cases where a parent may have only a single value in the related table

We'll look at examples of these types and discuss when it's appropriate to index them before the typical trial-and-error performance tuning, where the rule of thumb is to add indexes to make queries faster, while not slowing down other operations that create data.

In all cases, deleting the parent row requires a table scan of the child if there's no index on the child row. This is an important consideration if there are deletes.

## Domain Tables

You use a domain table to enforce a domain using a table, rather than using a scalar value with a constraint. This is often done to enable a greater level of data about the domain value, such as a descriptive value. For example, consider the tables in Figure 9-16.

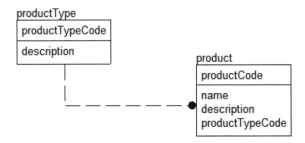

**Figure 9-16.** *Sample domain table relationship*

In this case, there are a small number of rows in the `productType` table. It's unlikely that an index on the `product.productTypeCode` column would be of any value in a join. That's because you'll generally be getting a `productType` row for every row you fetch from the `product` table.

What about the other direction, when you want to find all products of a single type? This can be useful if there aren't many products, but in general, with domain tables there aren't enough unique values to merit an index. The general advice is that tables of this sort don't need an index on the foreign key values, by default. Of course, deleting `productType` rows would need to scan the entire `productType`.

On the other hand, as discussed, sometimes an index can be useful when there are limited numbers of some value. For example, consider a `user` to `userStatus` relationship illustrated in Figure 9-17.

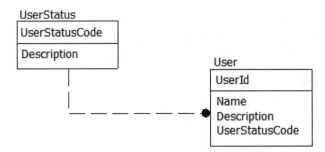

**Figure 9-17.** *Sample domain table relationship with low cardinality*

In this case, most users would be in the database with an active status. However, when a user was deactivated, you might need to do some action for that user. Since the number of inactive users would be far fewer than active users, it might be useful to have an index on the `userStatusCode` column for that purpose.

## Ownership Relationships

You use an ownership relationship to implement multivalued attributes of an object. The main performance characteristic of this situation is that most of the time when the parent row is retrieved, the child rows are retrieved as well. It's less likely that you'll need to retrieve a child row and then look for the parent row.

For example, take the case of an invoice and its line items in Figure 9-18.

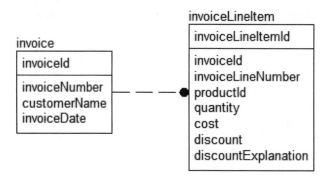

**Figure 9-18.** *Sample ownership relationship*

In this case, it's essential to have an index on the `invoiceLineItem.invoiceId` column. Most access to the `invoiceLineItem` table results from a user's need to get an invoice first. What also makes this an ideal situation for an index is that, generally speaking, this is a very selective index (unless you have large numbers of items and few sales).

Note that you should already have a `UNIQUE` constraint (and a unique index as a consequence of this) on the alternate key for the table, in this case `invoiceId` and `invoiceLineNumber`. As such, you probably wouldn't need to have an index on just `invoiceId`. This is largely based on the size of your key values, and the usage of the data, of course, but generally speaking if you had the AK composite index, that would probably suffice. Of course, if the other columns in the constraint index are large and the foreign key is small, adding an index on just the foreign key column might be valuable. Your mileage will vary, but in general, I stick with the `UNIQUE` constraint unless it turns out that it isn't useful for common queries.

## Many-to-Many Resolution Table Relationships

When we have a many-to-many relationship, there certainly needs to be an index on the two migrated keys from the two parent tables. Think back to our previous examples of games owned on a given platform (diagram repeated in Figure 9-19).

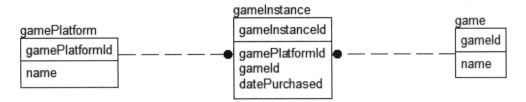

**Figure 9-19.** *Sample many-to-many relationship*

There's certainly a need for a composite UNIQUE constraint (and accompanying index) on the gamePlatformId and gameId columns, as well as the primary key on gameInstanceId. In some cases, you might want to add an index to individual columns if neither direction is dominant and you have a lot of data. Just as in all cases, testing is the key when adding most performance-based indexes.

Again, in this case, you would already have a unique index on gamePlatformId and gameId, and one of the two will be necessary to be first in the composite index. If you need to search for both keys independently of one another, you may want to create an index on each column individually.

Take this example. If we usually look up a game by name (which would be alternate key indexed) and then get the platforms for this game, an index only on gameInstance.gameId would be much more useful and two-thirds the size of the alternate key index (assuming a clustering key of gameInstanceId).

## One-to-One Relationships

One-to-one relationships generally require some form of unique index on the key in the parent table as well as on the migrated key in the child table. For example, consider the subclass example of a bankAccount, shown in Figure 9-20.

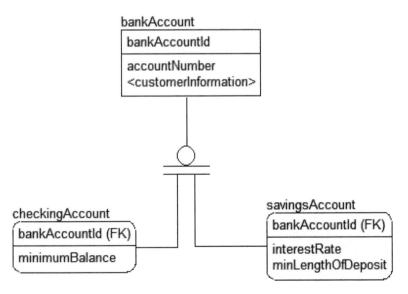

**Figure 9-20.** *Sample one-to-one relationship*

In this case, because these are one-to-one relationships, and there are already indexes on the primary key of each table, no other indexes would need to be added for the relationship.

## Indexed Views

I mentioned the use of persisted calculated columns in Chapter 5 for optimizing denormalizations for a single row, but sometimes, your denormalizations need to span multiple rows and include things like summarizations. In this section, I will introduce a way to take denormalization to the next level, using *indexed views*.

Indexing a view basically takes the virtual structure of the view and makes it a physical entity. The data to resolve queries with the view is generated as data is modified in the table, so access to the results from the view is just as fast as if it were an actual table. Indexed views give you the ability to build summary tables without any kind of manual operation or trigger; SQL Server automatically maintains the summary data for you. Creating indexed views is as easy as writing a query.

The benefits are twofold when using indexed views. In the Enterprise Edition, SQL Server automatically considers the use of an indexed view whenever you execute any query, even if you haven't specified a particular view to use, and even if the query doesn't reference the view! SQL Server accomplishes this index view assumption by matching the executed query to each indexed view to see whether that view already has the answer to something you are asking for. In other editions, you have to specify a table hint (NOEXPAND) when using an indexed view in queries to have the optimizer use the view's index rather than expanding the view text as part of the query (the normal behavior for using views in queries).

For example, going back to our item and sales tables from earlier in the chapter, we could create the following view. Note that only schema-bound views can be indexed (a more full list of requirements is presented after the example). This makes certain that the tables and structures that the index is created upon won't change underneath the view. Consider the following example on the AdventureWorks2008 database (note, you actually have to be in the AdventureWorks2008 database, unlike other examples where I have addressed items to the database):

```
CREATE VIEW Production.ProductAverageSales
WITH SCHEMABINDING
AS
SELECT  Product.productNumber,
        SUM(SalesOrderDetail.lineTotal) as totalSales,
        COUNT_BIG(*) as countSales
FROM    Production.Product as Product
            JOIN Sales.SalesOrderDetail as SalesOrderDetail
                ON product.ProductID=SalesOrderDetail.ProductID
GROUP   BY Product.productNumber
```

This would do the calculations at execution time. We run the following query:

```
SELECT productNumber, totalSales, countSales
FROM    Production.ProductAverageSales
```

The plan looks like this:

```
----------------------------------------------------------------------------
|--Hash Match(Inner Join, HASH:([SalesOrderDetail].[ProductID])=
                                    ([Product].[ProductID]))
     |--Hash Match(Aggregate, HASH:([SalesOrderDetail].[ProductID])
                    DEFINE:([Expr1004]=SUM([AdventureWorks2008].[Sales].
                    [SalesOrderDetail].[LineTotal] as
                    [SalesOrderDetail].[LineTotal]), [Expr1005]=COUNT(*)))
```

```
| |--Compute Scalar(DEFINE:([SalesOrderDetail].[LineTotal]=
        [AdventureWorks2008].[Sales].[SalesOrderDetail].[LineTotal] as
                                [SalesOrderDetail].[LineTotal]))
|          |--Compute Scalar(DEFINE:([SalesOrderDetail].[LineTotal]=
              isnull((CONVERT_IMPLICIT(numeric(19,4),
        [AdventureWorks2008].[Sales].[SalesOrderDetail].[UnitPrice] as
              [SalesOrderDetail].[UnitPrice],0)*
              ((1.0)-CONVERT_IMPLICIT(numeric(19,4),
              [AdventureWorks2008].[Sales].[SalesOrderDetail].
              [UnitPriceDiscount] as [SalesOrderDetail].
              [UnitPriceDiscount],0)))* CONVERT_IMPLICIT(numeric(5,0),
              [AdventureWorks2008].[Sales].[SalesOrderDetail].[OrderQty]
                   as  [SalesOrderDetail].[OrderQty],0),(0.000000))))
|              |--Clustered Index
                  Scan(OBJECT:(
                  [AdventureWorks2008].[Sales].[SalesOrderDetail].
                  [PK_SalesOrderDetail_SalesOrderID_SalesOrderDetailID]
                  AS [SalesOrderDetail]))
|--Index Scan(OBJECT:([AdventureWorks2008].[Production].[Product].
                  [AK_Product_ProductNumber] AS [Product]))
```

This is a big plan for such a small query, for sure, and hard to follow, but it scans the SalesOrderDetail table, computes our scalar values, then does a hash match aggregate and a hash match join to join the two sets together. For further reading on the join types, consider the book *Inside SQL Server 2005 Query Processing and Optimization* by Kalen Delaney (Microsoft Press) and her forthcoming *SQL Server 2008 Internals*.

This query executes pretty fast on my 1.8 GHz 2GB laptop, but there's a noticeable delay. Say this query wasn't fast enough, or it used too many resources to execute, or it was used extremely often. In this case, we might add an index on the view. Note that it is a clustered index, as the data pages will be ordered based on the key we chose. Consider your structure of the index just like you would on a physical table.

```
CREATE UNIQUE CLUSTERED INDEX XPKProductAverageSales on
                    Production.ProductAverageSales(productNumber)
```

SQL Server would then materialize the view and store it. Now our queries to the view will be *very* fast. However, although we've avoided all the coding issues involved with storing summary data, we have to keep our data up to date. Every time data changes in the underlying tables, the index on the view changes its data, so there's a performance hit due to maintaining the index for the view. Hence, indexing views means that performance is great for reading, but not necessarily for updating.

Now, run the query again:

```
SELECT productNumber, totalSales, countSales
FROM   Production.ProductAverageSales
```

The plan looks like the following:

```
---------------------------------------------------------------------
|--Clustered Index
        Scan(OBJECT:([AdventureWorks2008].[Production].
        [ProductAverageSales].[XPKProductAverageSales]))
```

Big deal, right? We expected this result because we directly queried the view. On my test system, running the Developer Edition (which is functionally comparable to the Enterprise Edition), you get a great insight into how cool this feature is in the following query for getting the average sales per product:

```
SELECT Product.productNumber, sum(SalesOrderDetail.lineTotal) / COUNT(*)
FROM   Production.Product as Product
          JOIN Sales.SalesOrderDetail as SalesOrderDetail
                ON product.ProductID=SalesOrderDetail.ProductID
GROUP  BY Product.productNumber
```

We'd expect the plan for this query to be the same as the first query of the view was, because we haven't referenced anything other than the base tables, right? I already told you the answer, so here's the plan:

```
|--Compute
   Scalar(DEFINE:(
       [Expr1006]=[AdventureWorks2008].[Production].ProductAverageSales].
       [totalSales]/CONVERT_IMPLICIT(numeric(10,0),[Expr1005],0)))
    |--Compute Scalar(DEFINE:([Expr1005]=
           CONVERT_IMPLICIT(int,[AdventureWorks2008].[Production].
           [ProductAverageSales].[averageTotal],0)))
       |--Clustered Index
             Scan(OBJECT:([AdventureWorks2008].[Production].
             [ProductAverageSales].[XPKProductAverageSales]))
```

There are two scalar computes—one for the division, one to convert the bigint from the COUNT_BIG(*) to an integer—and the other to scan through the indexed view's clustered index. The ability to use the optimizations from an indexed view indirectly is a neat feature that allows you to build in some guesses as to what *ad hoc* users will be doing with the data, and giving them performance they didn't even ask for.

---

■ **Tip** The indexed view feature in the Enterprise Edition can also come in handy for tuning third-party systems that work on an API that is not tuneable in a direct manner (that is, to change the text of a query to make it more efficient).

---

There are some pretty heavy caveats, though. The restrictions on what can be used in a view, prior to it being indexed, are fairly tight. The most important things that cannot be done are as follows:

- Use the SELECT * syntax—columns must be explicitly named.
- Use a CLR user defined aggregate.
- Use UNION, EXCEPT, or INTERSECT in the view.
- Use any subqueries.
- Use any outer joins or recursively join back to the same table.
- Specify TOP in the SELECT clause.
- Use DISTINCT.
- Include a SUM() function if it references more than one column.
- Use COUNT(*), though COUNT_BIG(*) is allowed.
- Use almost any aggregate function against a nullable expression.
- Reference any other views, or use CTEs or derived table.

- Reference any nondeterministic functions.

- Reference data outside the database.

- Reference tables owned by a different owner.

And this isn't all. You must meet several pages of requirements, documented in SQL Server Books Online in the section "Creating Indexed Views," but these are the most significant ones that you need to consider before using indexed views.

Although this might all seem pretty restrictive, there are good reasons for all these rules. Maintaining the indexed view is analogous to writing our own denormalized data maintenance functions. Simply put, the more complex the query to build the denormalized data, the greater the complexity in maintaining it. Adding one row to the base table might cause the view to need to recalculate, touching thousands of rows.

Indexed views are particularly useful when you have a view that's costly to run, but the data on which it's based doesn't change a tremendous amount. As an example, consider a decision-support system where you load data once a day. There's overhead either maintaining the index, or possibly just rebuilding it, but if you can build the index during off hours, you can omit the cost of redoing joins and calculations for every view usage.

---

**Tip** With all the caveats, indexed views can prove useless for some circumstances. An alternative method is to materialize the results of the data by inserting the data into a permanent table. For example, for our sample query we'd create a table with three columns (productNumber, totalSales, and countSales), then we'd do an INSERT INTO ProductAverageSales SELECT . . . We'd put the results of the query in this table. Any query works here, not just one that meets the strict guidelines. It doesn't help out *ad hoc* users who don't directly query the data in the table, but it certainly improves performance of queries that directly access the data, particularly if perfect results are not needed, since data will usually be a little bit old due to the time required to refresh the data.

---

# Best Practices

Indexing is a complex subject, and even though this is not a small chapter, we've only scratched the surface. The following best practices are what I use as a rule of thumb when creating a new database solution. Note that I assume that you've applied UNIQUE constraints in all places where they make logical sense. These constraints most likely should be there, even if they slow down your application (there are exceptions, but if a set of values needs to be unique, it needs to be unique). From there, it's all a big tradeoff. The first rule is the most important.

- *There are few reasons to add indexes to tables without testing*: Add nonconstraint indexes to your tables only as needed to enhance performance. In many cases it will turn out that no index is needed to achieve decent performance. A caveat can be foreign key indexes.

- *Choose clustered index keys wisely*: All nonclustered indexes will use the clustering key as their row locator, so the performance of the clustered index will affect all other index utilization. If the clustered index is not extremely useful, it can affect the other indexes as well.

- *Keep indexes as thin as possible*: Only index the columns that are selective enough in the main part of the index. Use the INCLUDE clause on the CREATE INDEX statement if you want to include columns only to cover the data used by a query.

- *Consider several thin indexes rather than one monolithic index*: SQL Server can use multiple indexes in a query efficiently. This can be a good tool to support *ad hoc* access where the users can choose between multiple situations.

- *Be careful of the cost of adding an index*: When you insert, update, or delete rows from a table with an index, there's a definite cost to maintaining the index. New data added might require page splits, and inserts, updates, and deletes can cause a reshuffling of the index pages.

- *Carefully consider foreign key indexes*: If child rows are selected because of a parent row (including on a foreign key checking for children on a delete operation), then an index on the columns in a foreign key is generally a good idea.

- UNIQUE *constraints are used to enforce uniqueness, not unique indexes*: Unique indexes are used to enhance performance by telling the optimizer that an index will only return one row in equality comparisons. Users shouldn't get error messages from a unique *index* violation.

# Summary

Indexing, like the entire gamut of performance-tuning topics, is hard to cover with any specificity on a written page. I've given you some information about the mechanics of tables and indexes, and a few best practices, but to be realistic, it's never going to be enough without you working with a realistic, active working test system.

Tuning with indexes requires a lot of basic knowledge applied on a large scale. Joins decide whether or not to use an index based on many factors, and the indexes available to a query affect the join operators chosen. The best teacher for this is the school of "having to wait for a five-hour query to process." Most people, when starting out, start on small systems and code any way they want, slap indexes on everything, and it works great. SQL Server has a very advanced optimizer that covers a multitude of such sins, particularly on a low-concurrency, low-usage system. As your system grows and requires more and more resources, it becomes more and more difficult to do performance tuning haphazardly.

The steps I generally suggest for indexing are straightforward:

- Apply all the UNIQUE constraints that can need to be added without annoying the users by enforcing uniqueness that they don't care about.

- Minimally, index all foreign key constraints where the parent table is likely to be the driving force behind fetching rows in the child (such as invoice ➤ line item).

- Start performance testing, running load tests to see how things perform.

- Identify queries that are slow, and consider the following:

    - Adding indexes.

    - Eliminating clustered index row lookups by covering queries, possibly using the new INCLUDE keyword on indexes.

    - Materializing query results, either by indexed view or by putting results into permanent tables.

    - Working on data location strategies with filegroups.

Do this last step over and over, adding indexes and removing indexes, moving data around to different disk channels, and so on until you arrive at the happy medium. Every added index is more overhead, but it can greatly improve performance of reads. Only you can decide if your system does more reads or writes, and even more important, which delay bothers you most. If queries take 10 seconds, but users only need results within 20, who cares? But if a query takes 500 milliseconds, and you have a machine that you feel could be working at 100 milliseconds per operation, then you might be tempted to optimize for that performance at all costs. Once you optimize this query, ten others might be affected negatively.

Be very aware that performance tuning is a balancing act, and most every performance gain is also going to hurt some other performance. Luckily it is not a one-to-one match, performance gain to loss. An optimization that saves you 1,000 ms per query may cost you 10 ms in another. Of course, don't forget frequency. Saving 30 minutes of nightly processing probably isn't worth making your online queries run one second longer each—not if these queries are run 10,000 times a day. (That's 2.7 hours of lost work a day!).

Indexes are an important step to building high-performance systems, and highly concurrent ones with many users executing simultaneously. In the next chapter, I'll look at some of the other concerns for concurrency. Having moderate- to high-level server-class hardware with fast RAID arrays and multiple channels to the disk storage, you can spread the data out over multiple file-groups, as I discussed in the basic table structure section earlier. However, if you only have one hard disk on your server, or a single array of disks, you won't get much, if any, benefit out of moving your data around on the disk.

# CHAPTER 10

■ ■ ■

# Coding for Concurrency

*"Time is the scarcest resource, and unless it is managed, nothing else can be managed."*

—Peter F. Drucker

**C**oncurrency is all about having the computer utilize all of its resources simultaneously, or basically having more than one thing done at the same time when serving multiple users (technically, in SQL Server, you open multiple requests, on one or more connections). Even if you haven't done much with multiple users, if you know anything about computing you probably are familiar with the term *multitasking*. The key here is that when multiple processes or users are accessing the same resources, each user expects to see a consistent view of the data and certainly expects that other users will not be stomping on his or her results.

The topics of this chapter will center on understanding why and how you should write your database code or design your objects to make them accessible concurrently by as many users as you have in your system. In this chapter, I'll discuss the following:

- *Query optimization basics*: The basics of how queries get optimized and then executed by the query engine.

- *OS and hardware issues*: I'll briefly discuss various issues that are out of the control of SQL code.

- *Transactions*: I'll give an overview of how transactions work and how to code them in T-SQL code.

- *SQL Server concurrency controls*: In this section, I'll explain locks and isolation levels.

- *Coding for concurrency*: I'll discuss methods of coding data access to protect from users simultaneously making changes to data and placing data into less-than-adequate situations. You'll also learn how to deal with users stepping on one another, and how to maximize concurrency.

The key goal of this chapter is to acquaint you with many of the kinds of things SQL Server does to make it fast and safe to have multiple users doing the same sorts of tasks with the same resources and how you can optimize your code to make it easier for this to happen.

---

**RESOURCE GOVERNOR**

SQL Server 2008 has a new feature that is concurrency related (especially as it relates to performance tuning), though it is more of a management tool than it is a design concern. The feature is called Resource Governor, and it allows you to partition the workload of the entire server by specifying maximum and minimum resource allocations (memory, CPU, concurrent requests, etc.) to users or groups of users. You can classify users into groups using a simple user-defined function that, in turn, takes advantage of the basic server-level functions you have for identifying users and applications (IS_SRVROLEMEMBER, APP_NAME, SYSTEM_USER, etc.). Like many of the high-end features of SQL Server 2008, Resource Governor is only available with the Enterprise Edition.

Using Resource Governor, you can group together and limit the users of a reporting application, of Management Studio, or of any other application to a specific percentage of the CPU, a certain percentage and number of processors, and limited requests at one time.

One nice thing about Resource Governor is that some settings only apply when the server is under a load. So if the reporting user is the only active process, that user might get the entire server's power. But if the server is being heavily used, users would be limited to the configured amounts. I won't talk about Resource Governor anymore in this chapter, but it is definitely a feature that you might want to consider if you are dealing with different types of users in your applications.

---

# What Is Concurrency?

The concept of concurrency can be boiled down to the following statement:

*Maximize the amount of work that can be done by all users at the same time, and most importantly, make all users feel like they're important.*

Because of the need to balance the amount of work with the user's perception of the amount of work being done, there are going to be the following tradeoffs:

- *Number of concurrent users:* How many users can (or need to) be served at the same time
- *Overhead*: How complex the algorithms are to maintain concurrency
- *Accuracy*: How correct results must be
- *Performance*: How fast each process finishes
- *Cost*: How much you're willing to spend on hardware and programming time

As you can probably guess, if all the users of a database system never needed to run queries at the same time, life in database-system–design land would be far simpler. You would have no need to be concerned with what other users might want to do. The only real performance goal would be to run one process really fast and move to the next process. However, in building database solutions, there's always more to it. If no one ever shared resources, multitasking servers would be unnecessary. All files could be places on a user's local computer, and that would be enough. And single-threading activities could result in more work being done by the computer, but just like the old days, people would sit around waiting for their turns (yes, with mainframes, people actually did that sort of thing). Internally, the situation is still technically the same in a way, as a computer cannot process more individual instructions than it has cores in its CPUs, but it can run and swap around fast enough to make hundreds or thousands of people feel like they are the only users. This is especially true if your system engineer builds computers that are good as SQL Server machines (and not just file servers) and the architects/programmers build systems that meet the requirements for a relational database (and not just what seems expedient at the time).

A common scenario for a multiuser database involves a sales and shipping application. You might have 50 salespeople in a call center trying to sell the last 25 closeout items that are in stock. It isn't desirable to promise the last physical item accidentally to multiple customers, since two users might happen to read that it was available at the same time, and then are both allowed to place an order for it. In this case, stopping the first order wouldn't be necessary, but you would want to disallow or otherwise prevent the second (or subsequent) orders from being placed, since they cannot be fulfilled immediately.

Most programmers instinctively write code to check for this condition and to try to make sure that this sort of thing doesn't happen. Code is generally written that does something along these lines:

- Check to make sure that there's adequate stock.

- Create a shipping row.

Simple enough, but what if one person checks to see if the product is available at the same time as another, and more orders are placed than you have adequate stock for? This is a far more common possibility than you might imagine. Is this acceptable? If you've ever ordered a product that you were promised in two days, and then you found out your items are on backorder for a month, you know the answer to this question, "No! It is very unacceptable." When this happens, you try another retailer next time, right?

I should also note that the problems presented by concurrency aren't quite the same as those for *parallelism*, which is having one task split up and done by multiple resources at the same time. Parallelism involves a whole different set of problems and luckily is more or less not your problem. In writing SQL Server code, parallelism is done automatically, as tasks can be split among resources (sometimes you will need to adjust just how many parallel operations can take place, but in practice, SQL Server does *most* of that work for you). When I refer to concurrency, I generally mean having multiple *different* operations happening at the same time by different connections to SQL Server.

---

**Tip** In SQL Server 2005, a new way to execute multiple batches of SQL code from the same connection simultaneously was added, known as Multiple Active Result Sets (MARS). It allows interleaved execution of several statements, such as SELECT, FETCH, RECEIVE READTEXT, or BULK INSERT. As the product continues to mature, you will start to see the term *request* being used in the place where we commonly thought of *connection* in SQL Server 2000 and earlier. Admittedly, this is going to be a hard change that will take several versions to become embedded in people's thought processes, but in some places (like in the Dynamic Management Views), you need to understand the difference.

MARS is principally a client technology and must be enabled by a connection, but it can change some of the ways that SQL Server handles concurrency. I'll note the places where MARS affects the fundamentals of concurrency.

---

# Query Optimization Basics

SQL Server is a batch-oriented system. A batch of commands is sent to the server, then the client waits for messages and tabular data sets to be returned. Nothing should be done in an interactive manner at all. Each batch executes sequentially, one statement at a time (even in MARS, each batch is sequentially executed, though you can execute multiple batches from the same connection). SQL Server can spawn multiple threads to perform a single operation, but each operation gets executed one at a time.

To optimize the query, SQL Server takes the text of the query and parses it. The query is then compiled down to a series of *operators*. Operators are essentially black-box modules that have inputs (usually one or two) and a single output. For every query, many operators are used to handle I/O, messaging, and algorithms. We, as database programmers, generally deal with the algorithm type of operator most of all, as I/O and messaging are pretty much internal.

To understand this, it's best to look at the execution plan of a query. It isn't the first time we've done this, as we looked at many plans to show index usage in Chapter 9. Take the following query in the AdventureWorks2008 database:

```
SELECT  productModel.name as productModel,
        product.name as productName
FROM    AdventureWorks2008.production.product as product
          join AdventureWorks2008.production.productModel as productModel
            on productModel.productModelId = product.productModelId
WHERE   product.name like '%glove%'
```

SQL Server's optimizer breaks this down into several operations. You can see a graphical representation of this by selecting the Query ➤ Display Estimated Execution Plan menu item in SQL Server Management Studio, with this code in the edit window. The graphic in Figure 10-1 is displayed (or something close, as optimization can be more than just the query and database objects, depending on hardware).

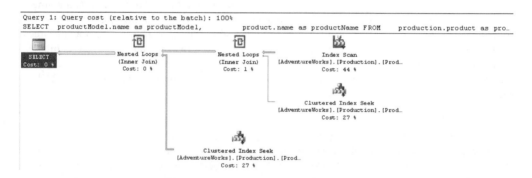

**Figure 10-1.** *Sample graphical query plan*

Each of the items in Figure 10-1 is a query operator. Hovering over any of the operators brings up a dialog like the one in Figure 10-2.

The numbers represent costs and size and are generally good for comparisons to the other values for nodes. (Look up SHOWPLAN—and _ALL, _TEXT, and _XML derivatives—in SQL Server Books Online for alternative ways to view the plan and for more detailed explanations of each of these values.) In general, the goal is to reduce all these values as much as possible and to end up with a smooth plan. Often in a plan, something will jump out at you as the major issue in the query. In this plan, we had one operator at 39 percent and two others at 29 percent. If this query executed in a reasonable time, I would be inclined to expect that it was more or less optimal, or at least good enough.

Plans are executed right to left, and there's always a single operator on the left that's the final output or result. SQL Server can take any of these operations and spread them across multiple processors, but you have little control over this happening (other than limiting the maximum degree of parallelism).

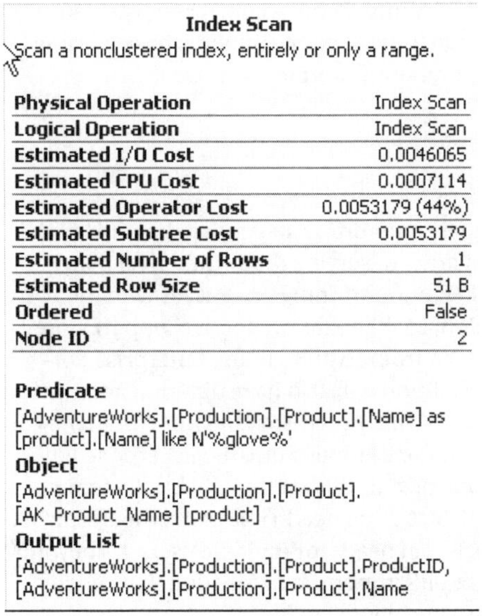

**Index Scan**
Scan a nonclustered index, entirely or only a range.

| | |
|---|---|
| **Physical Operation** | Index Scan |
| **Logical Operation** | Index Scan |
| **Estimated I/O Cost** | 0.0046065 |
| **Estimated CPU Cost** | 0.0007114 |
| **Estimated Operator Cost** | 0.0053179 (44%) |
| **Estimated Subtree Cost** | 0.0053179 |
| **Estimated Number of Rows** | 1 |
| **Estimated Row Size** | 51 B |
| **Ordered** | False |
| **Node ID** | 2 |

**Predicate**
[AdventureWorks].[Production].[Product].[Name] as
[product].[Name] like N'%glove%'
**Object**
[AdventureWorks].[Production].[Product].
[AK_Product_Name] [product]
**Output List**
[AdventureWorks].[Production].[Product].ProductID,
[AdventureWorks].[Production].[Product].Name

**Figure 10-2.** *Sample query plan operator detail*

There are operators for all sorts of things; for example:

- *Scans*: Scanning a data set, such as index leaf nodes or tables.

- *Seeks*: Seeking into an index structure using the B-tree structures to find items.

- *Joins*: Taking two sets of data and forming one set, based on connecting rows one to the other on some criteria.

- *Computing values*: Evaluating functions or expressions to return a scalar value for a column.

- *Output*: Sending tabular data sets to the client, or DML operations such as INSERT, UPDATE, and DELETE. There's always one output from each query.

Each of these types of operators can have many different types of actions. You can see from the preceding plan that data of some form flows from one operator to the next, leading to the final output. Hovering over the lines in the plan will tell you the number of rows expected (or the number of actual rows, depending on whether or not you are looking at the estimated plan), the size per row, and the expected total amount of data sent between operators.

What all this means is that each of these operators must be executed in some order, because (using the logical ordering imposed by the graphical plan) every single operator on the right side needs be executed before the one directly on its left. Because code isn't executed while time stands still, this brings up questions that I'll try to answer in the rest of this chapter, such as the following (considering our small query plan):

- What effect will there be if a query modifies rows that have already been used by a query in a different batch?

- What if the other query creates new rows that would have been important to the other batch's query? What if the other query deletes others?

- Most importantly, can one query corrupt another's results?

You must consider a few more questions as well. Just how important is concurrency to you, and how much are you willing to pay in performance? The whole topic of concurrency is basically a set of tradeoffs between performance, consistency, and the number of simultaneous users.

# OS and Hardware Issues

SQL Server is designed to run on a variety of hardware types that's pretty staggering. Essentially the same basic code runs on a low-end PC and on a clustered array of servers that would rival many supercomputers. There's even the SQL Server 2008 Mobile Edition running on devices with the Windows Mobile OS and the Tablet PC OS (in its current version, Mobile Edition doesn't support stored procedures). Every machine running a version of SQL Server, from Express to the Enterprise Edition, can have a vastly different concurrency profile. Each edition will also have different amounts of hardware it can support: Express supports 1GB of RAM and one processor (still more than our first SQL Server that had 16MB of RAM), and at the other end of the spectrum, the Enterprise Edition can handle as much hardware as you can stuff into one box. In this section, I'll briefly touch upon some of the issues governing concurrency that our T-SQL code needn't be concerned with.

SQL Server and the OS balance all the different requests and needs for multiple users. It's beyond the scope of this book to delve too deeply into the details, but it's important to mention that concurrency is heavily tied to hardware architecture. For example, consider the following subsystems:

- *Processor*: The heart of the system is the CPU. It controls the other subsystems, as well as doing any calculations needed. If you have too few processors, excessive time can be wasted switching between requests.

- *Disk subsystem*: This is usually the biggest I/O issue to be dealt with. A slow disk subsystem is the downfall of many systems, particularly because doing it right can be quite expensive. Each drive can only read one sector at a time, so to do concurrent disk access, it's necessary to have multiple disk drives, and even multiple controllers or channels to disk drive arrays. Especially important is the choice between RAID systems, which take multiple disks and configure them for performance and redundancy:

  - *0*: Striping across all disks with no redundancy, performance only.

  - *1*: Mirroring between two disks, redundancy only.

  - *5*: Striping with distributed parity; excellent for reading, but can be slow for writing. Not typically suggested for most SQL Server OLTP usage, though it isn't horrible for lighter loads.

  - *0+1*: Mirrored stripes. Two RAID 1 arrays, mirrored. Great for performance, but not tremendously redundant.

  - *1+0 (also known as 10)*: Striped mirrors. Some number of RAID 0 mirrored arrays, then striped across the mirrors. Usually the best mix of performance and redundancy for an OLTP SQL Server installation.

- *Network interface*: Bandwidth to the users is critical, but is usually less of a problem than disk access. However, it's important to attempt to limit the number of round trips between the server and the client. This is highly dependent on whether the client is connecting over a dialup connection or a gigabit Ethernet (or even multiple network interface cards). Turning on SET NOCOUNT in all stored procedures and triggers is a good first step, because otherwise a message is sent to the client for each query executed, requiring bandwidth (and processing) to deal with them.

- *Memory*: One of the cheapest commodities is memory. SQL Server 2008 can use a tremendous amount of memory (whatever your hardware can support for the Standard and Enterprise Editions).

Each of these subsystems needs to be in balance to work properly. You could theoretically have 100 CPUs and 128GB of RAM and your system could still be slow. In this case, ending up with a slow disk subsystem and could mean ending up with a slow system too (and *slow* is possibly the most relative term of them all, since it is largely based on what your server is used for). The goal is to maximize utilization of all these subsystems—the faster the better—but it's useless to have super-fast CPUs with a super-slow disk subsystem. Ideally, as your load increases, disk, CPU, and memory usage would increase proportionally, though this is a heck of a hard thing to do. The bottom line is that the number of CPUs, disk channels and disk drives, network cards, and the amount of RAM you have all affect concurrency.

Monitoring hardware and OS performance issues is a job primarily for `perfmon` and/or the Data Collector. Watching counters for CPU, memory, SQL Server, and so on lets you see the balance between all the different subsystems. In the end, poor hardware configuration can kill you just as quickly as can poor SQL Server implementation.

For the rest of this chapter, I'm going to ignore these types of issues, and leave them to others with a deeper hardware focus, such as the MSDN website (`http://msdn.microsoft.com`) or `http://www.sql-server-performance.com`. I'll be focusing on software-coding–related issues pertaining to how to code better SQL to manage concurrency between SQL Server processes.

# Transactions

No discussion of concurrency can really have much meaning without an understanding of the transaction. Transactions are a mechanism that allows one or more statements to be guaranteed either to be fully completed or to fail totally. It is an internal SQL Server mechanism that is used to keep the data that's written to and read from tables consistent throughout a batch, as required by the user.

Whenever data is modified in the database, the changes are not only written to the physical tables, but a log of every change is written to the transaction log. You have to be cognizant that every modification operation is logged when considering how large to make your transaction log. The log also needs to be on a very fast disk-drive subsystem because it will be written every time you write to your database.

The purpose of transactions is to provide a mechanism to allow multiple processes access to the same data simultaneously, while ensuring that logical operations are either carried out entirely or not at all. To explain the purpose of transactions, there's a common acronym: ACID. It stands for the following:

- *Atomicity*: Every operation within a transaction is treated as a singular operation; either all its data modifications are performed, or none of them is performed.

- *Consistency*: Once the transaction is completed, the system must be left in a consistent state. This means that all the constraints on the data that are part of the RDBMS definition must be honored.

- *Isolation*: This means that the operations within a transaction must be suitably isolated from other transactions. In other words, no other transactions should see data in the intermediate state, within the transaction, until it's finalized. This is done by using locks (for details on locks, refer to the section "SQL Server Concurrency Controls," later in this chapter).

- *Durability*: Once a transaction is completed, all changes must be persisted as requested. The modifications should persist even in the event of a system failure.

Transactions are used in two different ways. First, every statement that's executed in SQL Server is run within the control of a transaction. This includes INSERT, UPDATE, DELETE, and even SELECT statements to provide for isolation between processes. For modification statements such as

INSERT, UPDATE, and DELETE, locks are placed and all system changes are recorded in the transaction log. If any operation fails, or if the user asks for an operation to be undone, SQL Server uses the transaction log to undo the operations already performed.

Second, the programmer can use transaction commands to batch together multiple commands into one logical unit of work. This section is specifically about defining and demonstrating this syntax.

The key for using transactions is that when writing statements to modify data using one or more SQL statements, you need to make use of transactions to ensure that data is written safely and securely. A typical problem with procedures and operations in T-SQL code is to underuse transactions, so that when unexpected errors (such as security problems, constraint failures, hardware glitches, and so on) occur, orphaned or inconsistent data is the result. And when a few weeks later users are complaining about inconsistent results, you have to track down the issues; you lose some sleep; and your client loses confidence in the system you have created and even in you.

How long the log is stored is based on the recovery model under which your database is operating. There are three models:

- *Simple*: The log is maintained only until the operation is executed and a checkpoint is executed (done by SQL Server automatically or manually).

- *Full*: The log is maintained until you explicitly clear it out.

- *Bulk logged*: This keeps a log much like the full recovery model but doesn't log some operations, such as SELECT INTO, bulk loads, index creations, or text operations.

Even in the simple model, you must be careful about log space, because if large numbers of changes are made in a single transaction, the log rows must be stored at least until all transactions are committed and a checkpoint takes place. This is clearly just a taste of transaction log management; for a more complete explanation, please see SQL Server 2008 Books Online.

# Transaction Syntax

The syntax to start and stop transactions is pretty simple. I'll cover four variants of the transaction syntax in this section:

- *Basic transactions*: The syntax of how to start and complete a transaction

- *Nested transactions*: How transactions are affected when one is started when another is already executing

- *Savepoints*: Used to selectively cancel part of a transaction

- *Distributed transactions*: Using transactions to control saving data on multiple SQL Servers

These sections will give you the foundation needed to move ahead and start building proper code, ensuring that each modification is done properly, even when multiple SQL statements are necessary to form a single-user operation.

## Basic Transactions

In their basic form, three commands are required: BEGIN TRANSACTION (to start the transaction), COMMIT TRANSACTION (to save the data), and ROLLBACK TRANSACTION (to undo the changes that were made). It's as simple as that.

For example, consider the case of building a stored procedure to modify two tables. Call these tables table1 and table2. You'll modify table1, check the error status, and then modify table2 (these aren't real tables, just examples):

```
BEGIN TRY
    BEGIN TRANSACTION
        UPDATE table1
        SET    value = 'value'

        UPDATE table2
        SET value = 'value'
        COMMIT TRANSACTION
END TRY
BEGIN CATCH
    ROLLBACK TRANSACTION
    RAISERROR ('An error occurred',16,1)
END CATCH
```

Now, in case some unforeseen error occurs while updating either table1 or table2, you won't get into the case where the update of table1 happens and not the update of table2. It's also imperative not to forget to close the transaction (either save the changes with COMMIT TRANSACTION, or undo the changes with ROLLBACK TRANSACTION), because the open transaction that contains your work is in a state of limbo and if you don't either complete it or roll it back, it can cause a lot of issues. For example, if the transaction stays open and other operations get executed within that transaction, you might end up losing all work done on that connection. You may also cause other connections to not get their work done, because each connection is isolated from one another messing up or looking at their unfinished work. Another user who needed the affected rows in table1 or table2 would have to wait (more on why this is throughout the chapter).

There's an additional setting for simple transactions known as *named transactions*, which I'll introduce for completeness, (ironically, this explanation will take more ink than introducing the more useful transaction syntax, but it is something good to know!). You can extend the functionality of transactions by adding a transaction name, as shown:

```
BEGIN TRANSACTION <tranName> or <@tranvariable>
```

This can be a confusing extension to the BEGIN TRANSACTION statement. It names the transaction to make sure you roll back to it, for example:

```
BEGIN TRANSACTION one
ROLLBACK TRANSACTION one
```

Only the first transaction mark is registered in the log, so the following code returns an error:

```
BEGIN TRANSACTION one
BEGIN TRANSACTION two
ROLLBACK TRANSACTION two
```

The error message is as follows:

```
Server: Msg 6401, Level 16, State 1, Line 3
Cannot roll back two. No transaction or savepoint of that name was found.
```

**■Note** In the downloads I have included a ROLLBACK TRANSACTION statement as the previous code sample would leave open a transaction. A very good practice in testing your code that deals with transactions is to make sure that there are no transactions by executing ROLLBACK TRANSACTION until you see the message: "The ROLLBACK TRANSACTION request has no corresponding BEGIN TRANSACTION" returned. At that point, you can feel safe that you are outside a transaction. In code you should use @@trancount to check, which I will demonstrate later in this chapter.

Unfortunately, after this error has occurred, the transaction is still left open. For this reason, it's seldom a good practice to use named transactions in your code unless you have a very specific purpose. The specific use that makes named transactions interesting is when named transactions use the WITH MARK setting. This allows marking the transaction log, which can be used when restoring a transaction log instead of a date and time. A common use of the marked transaction is to restore several databases back to the same condition and then restore all of the databases to a common mark.

The mark is only registered if data is modified within the transaction. A good example of its use might be to build a process that marks the transaction log every day before some daily batch process, especially one where the database is in single-user mode. The log is marked, then you run the process, and if there are any troubles, the database log can be restored to just before the mark in the log, no matter when the process was executed. Using the AdventureWorks2008 database, I'll demonstrate this capability. You can do the same, but be careful to do this somewhere where you know you have a proper backup (just in case something goes wrong).

We first set up the scenario by putting the AdventureWorks2008 database in Full recovery model.

---

■**Tip** You can see the current setting using the following code:

```
SELECT   recovery_model_desc
FROM     sys.databases
WHERE    name = 'AdventureWorks2008'
```

---

```
USE Master
GO

ALTER DATABASE AdventureWorks2008
     SET RECOVERY FULL
```

Next, we create a couple of backup devices to hold the backups we're going to do:

```
EXEC sp_addumpdevice 'disk', 'TestAdventureWorks2008',
                           'C:\Temp\AdventureWorks2008.bak'
EXEC sp_addumpdevice 'disk', 'TestAdventureWorks2008Log',
                           'C:\Temp\AdventureWorks2008Log.bak'
```

Next, we back up the database to the dump device we created:

```
BACKUP DATABASE AdventureWorks2008 TO TestAdventureWorks2008
```

Now, we change to the AdventureWorks2008 database and delete some data from a table:

```
USE AdventureWorks2008
GO
SELECT count(*)
FROM   Sales.SalesTaxRate

BEGIN TRANSACTION Test WITH MARK 'Test'
DELETE Sales.SalesTaxRate
COMMIT TRANSACTION
```

This returns 29. Run SELECT again, and it will return 0. Next back up the transaction log to the other backup device:

```
BACKUP LOG AdventureWorks2008 to TestAdventureWorks2008Log
```

Now we can restore the database using the RESTORE DATABASE command (the NORECOVERY setting keeps the database in a state ready to add transaction logs). We apply the log with RESTORE LOG. For the example, we'll only restore up to before the mark that was placed, not the entire log:

```
USE Master
GO
RESTORE DATABASE AdventureWorks2008 FROM TestAdventureWorks2008
                                          WITH REPLACE, NORECOVERY

RESTORE LOG AdventureWorks2008 FROM TestAdventureWorks2008Log
                                          WITH STOPBEFOREMARK = 'Test'
```

Now execute the counting query again and you can see that the 29 rows are in there.

```
USE AdventureWorks2008
GO
SELECT count(*)
FROM   Sales.SalesTaxRate
```

If you wanted to include the actions within the mark, you could use STOPATMARK instead of STOPBEFOREMARK. You can find the log marks that have been made in the MSDB database in the logmarkhistory table.

## Nesting Transactions

Yes, I am aware that the title of this section probably sounds a bit like Marlin Perkins is going to take over and start telling of the mating habits of transactions, but I am referring to the fact that you can nest the starting of transactions like this:

```
BEGIN TRANSACTION
    BEGIN TRANSACTION
        BEGIN TRANSACTION
```

Technically speaking, there is really only one transaction being started, but an internal counter is keeping up with how many logical transactions have been started. To commit the transactions, you have to execute the same number of COMMIT TRANSACTION commands as the number of BEGIN TRANSACTION commands that have been executed. To tell how many BEGIN TRANSACTION commands have been executed, without being committed, you can use the @@TRANCOUNT global variable. When it's equal to one, then one BEGIN TRANSACTION has been executed, if it's equal to two then two, and so on. When @@TRANCOUNT equals zero, you are no longer within a transaction context.

The limit to the number of transactions that can be nested is extremely large (the limit is 2,147,483,647, which took about 1.75 hours to reach in a tight loop on my 2.27-GHz laptop with 2GB of RAM—clearly way, way more than *any* process should ever need).

As an example, execute the following:

```
SELECT @@TRANCOUNT AS zeroDeep
BEGIN TRANSACTION
SELECT @@TRANCOUNT AS oneDeep
```

It returns the following results:

```
zeroDeep
-----------
0

oneDeep
-----------
1
```

Then, nest another transaction, and check @@TRANCOUNT to see whether it has incremented. Afterward, commit that transaction and check @@TRANCOUNT again:

```
BEGIN TRANSACTION
SELECT @@TRANCOUNT AS twoDeep
COMMIT TRANSACTION --commits very last transaction started with BEGIN TRANSACTION
SELECT @@TRANCOUNT AS oneDeep
```

This returns the following results:

```
twoDeep
-----------
2

oneDeep
-----------
1
```

Finally, close the final transaction:

```
COMMIT TRANSACTION
SELECT @@TRANCOUNT AS zeroDeep
```

It returns the following result:

```
zeroDeep
-----------
0
```

As I mentioned earlier in this section, technically only one transaction is being started. Hence, it only takes one ROLLBACK TRANSACTION command to roll back as many transactions as you have nested. So, if you've coded up a set of statements that end up nesting 100 transactions (man, that would be fun code to debug, eh?), and you issue one rollback transaction, all transactions are rolled back, for example:

```
BEGIN TRANSACTION
BEGIN TRANSACTION
BEGIN TRANSACTION
BEGIN TRANSACTION
BEGIN TRANSACTION
BEGIN TRANSACTION
BEGIN TRANSACTION
SELECT @@trancount as InTran
ROLLBACK TRANSACTION
SELECT @@trancount as OutTran
```

This returns the following results:

```
InTran
-----------
7

OutTran
-----------
0
```

This is by far the trickiest part of using transactions in your code leading to some messy error handling. It's a bad idea to just issue a ROLLBACK TRANSACTION command without being cognizant of what will occur once you do—especially the command's influence on the following code. If code is written expecting it to be within a transaction and it isn't, your data can get corrupted.

In the preceding example, if an UPDATE statement had been executed immediately after the ROLLBACK command, it wouldn't be executed within an explicit transaction. Also, if a COMMIT TRANSACTION is executed immediately after the ROLLBACK command, the following error will occur:

```
Server: Msg 3902, Level 16, State 1, Line 12
The COMMIT TRANSACTION request has no corresponding BEGIN TRANSACTION.
```

## Savepoints

In the last section, I explained that all open transactions are rolled back using a ROLLBACK TRANSACTION call. This isn't always desirable, so a tool is available to roll back only certain parts of a transaction. Unfortunately, it requires forethought and a special syntax. *Savepoints* are used to provide "selective" rollback.

For this, from within a transaction, issue the following statement:

```
SAVE TRANSACTION <savePointName> --savepoint names must follow the same rules for
                                 --identifiers as other objects
```

For example, use the following code in whatever database you desire. In the source code, I'll continue to place it in the tempdb since the examples are pretty self contained.

```
CREATE SCHEMA arts
CREATE TABLE arts.performer
(
    performerId int identity,
    name varchar(100)
)
GO
BEGIN TRANSACTION
INSERT INTO arts.performer(name) VALUES ('Elvis Costello')

SAVE TRANSACTION savePoint

INSERT INTO arts.performer(name) VALUES ('Air Supply')

--don't insert Air Supply, yuck! ...
ROLLBACK TRANSACTION savePoint

COMMIT TRANSACTION

SELECT *
FROM arts.performer
```

The output of this listing is as follows:

```
performerId   name
-----------   ---------------
1             Elvis Costello
```

In the code, there were two INSERT statements within our transaction, but in the output there's only one row. Obviously, the row that was rolled back to the savepoint wasn't persisted.

Note that you don't commit a savepoint; SQL Server simply places a mark in the transaction log to tell itself where to roll back to if the user asks for a rollback to the savepoint. The rest of the operations in the overall transaction aren't affected. Savepoints don't affect the value of @@trancount, nor do they release any locks that might have been held by the operations that are rolled back, until all nested transactions have been committed or rolled back.

Savepoints give the power to effect changes on only part of the operations transaction, giving you more control over what to do if you're deep in a large number of operations.

I'll mention savepoints later in this chapter when writing stored procedures, as they allow the rolling back of all the actions of a single stored procedure without affecting the transaction state of the stored procedure caller, though in most cases, it is usually just easier to roll back the entire transaction. Savepoints do, however, allow you to perform some operation, check to see if it is to your liking, and if it's not, roll it back.

You can't use savepoints in a couple situations:

- When using MARS and you're executing more than one batch at a time

- When the transaction is enlisted into a distributed transaction (the next section discusses this)

---

### HOW MARS AFFECTS TRANSACTIONS

There's a slight wrinkle in how multiple statements can behave when using OLE DB or ODBC native client drivers to retrieve rows in SQL Server 2005 or later. When executing batches under MARS, there can be a couple scenarios:

- *Connections set to automatically commit*: Each executed batch is within its own transaction, so there are multiple transaction contexts on a single connection.

- *Connections set to be manually committed*: All executed batches are part of one transaction.

When MARS is enabled for a connection, any batch or stored procedure that starts a transaction (either implicitly in any statement or by executing BEGIN TRANSACTION) must commit the transaction; if not, the transaction will be rolled back. These transactions were new to SQL Server 2005 and are referred to as *batch-scoped transactions*.

---

## Distributed Transactions

It would be wrong not to at least bring up the subject of distributed transactions. Occasionally, you might need to update data on a different server, from the one on which your code resides. The Microsoft Distributed Transaction Coordinator service (MS DTC) gives us this ability.

If your servers are running the MS DTC service, you can use the BEGIN DISTRIBUTED TRANSACTION command to start a transaction that covers the data residing on your server, as well as the remote server. If the server configuration 'remote proc trans' is set to 1, then any transaction that touches a linked server will start a distributed transaction without actually calling the BEGIN DISTRIBUTED TRANSACTION command. However, I would strongly suggest you know if you will be using another server in a transaction (check sys.configurations or sp_configure for the current setting, and set the value using sp_configure). Note also that savepoints aren't supported for distributed transactions.

The following code is just pseudocode and won't run as is, but this is representative of the code needed to do a distributed transaction:

```
BEGIN TRY
    BEGIN DISTRIBUTED TRANSACTION

    --remote server is a server set up as a linked server

    UPDATE remoteServer.dbName.schemaName.tableName
    SET value = 'new value'
    WHERE keyColumn = 'value'

    --local server
    UPDATE dbName.schemaName.tableName
    SET value = 'new value'
    WHERE keyColumn = 'value'

    COMMIT TRANSACTION
END TRY
BEGIN CATCH
    ROLLBACK TRANSACTION
    DECLARE @ERRORMessage varchar(2000)
    SET @ERRORMessage = ERROR_MESSAGE()
    RAISERROR (@ERRORMessage,16,1)
END CATCH
```

The distributed transaction syntax also covers the local transaction. As mentioned, setting the configuration option 'remote proc trans' automatically upgrades a BEGIN TRANSACTION command to a BEGIN DISTRIBUTED TRANSACTION command. This is useful if you frequently use distributed transactions. Without this setting, the remote command is executed, but it won't be a part of the current transaction.

## Explicit vs. Implicit Transactions

Before finishing the discussion of transactions, there's one last thing that needs to be covered for the sake of completeness. I've alluded to the fact that every statement is executed in a transaction (again, this includes even SELECT statements). This is an important point that must be understood when writing code. Internally, SQL Server starts a transaction every time a SQL statement is started. Even if a transaction isn't started explicitly with a COMMIT TRANSACTION statement, SQL Server automatically starts a new transaction whenever a statement starts, and commits or rolls it back depending on whether or not any errors occur. This is known as an *autocommit* transaction, when the SQL Server engine commits the transaction it starts for each statement-level transaction.

SQL Server gives us a setting to change this behavior of automatically committing the transaction: SET IMPLICIT_TRANSACTIONS. When this setting is turned on and the execution context isn't already within an explicitly declared transaction using BEGIN TRANSACTION, a BEGIN TRANSACTION is automatically (logically) executed when any of the following commands are executed: INSERT, UPDATE, DELETE, SELECT, TRUNCATE TABLE, DROP, ALTER TABLE, REVOKE, CREATE, GRANT, FETCH, or OPEN. This will mean that a COMMIT TRANSACTION or ROLLBACK TRANSACTION command has to be executed to end the transaction. Otherwise, once the connection terminates, all data is lost (and until the transaction terminates, locks that have been accumulated are held, other users are blocked, and pandemonium might occur).

SET IMPLICIT_TRANSACTIONS isn't a typical setting used by SQL Server administrators, but is worth mentioning, because if you change the setting of ANSI_DEFAULTS to ON, IMPLICIT_TRANSACTIONS will be enabled.

I've mentioned that every SELECT statement is executed within a transaction, but this deserves a bit more explanation. The entire process of rows being considered for output, then transporting them from the server to the client—all this is inside a transaction. The SELECT statement isn't finished until the entire result set is exhausted (or the client cancels the fetching of rows), so the transaction doesn't end either. This is an important point that will come back up in the "Isolation Levels" section, as I discuss how this transaction can seriously affect concurrency based on how isolated you need your queries to be.

# Compiled SQL Server Code

Now that I've discussed the basics of transactions, it's important to understand some of the slight differences involved in using them within compiled code. It's almost the same, but there are some subtle differences. You can't use transactions in user-defined functions (you can't change system state in a function, so they aren't necessary anyhow), but it is important to understand the caveats when you use them in

- Stored procedures
- Triggers

## Stored Procedures

Stored procedures, simply being compiled batches of code, use transactions as previously discussed, with one caveat. The transaction nesting level cannot be affected during the execution of a procedure. In other words, you must commit as many transactions as you begin in a stored procedure.

Although you can roll back any transaction, you shouldn't roll it back unless the @@TRANCOUNT was zero when the procedure started. However, it's better not to execute a ROLLBACK TRANSACTION command at all in a stored procedure, so there's no chance of rolling back to a transaction count that's different from when the procedure started. This protects you from the situation where the procedure is executed in another transaction. Rather, it's generally best to start a transaction, then follow it by a savepoint. Later, if the changes made in the procedure need to be backed out, simply roll back to the savepoint, and commit the transaction. It's then up to the stored procedure to signal to any caller that it has failed, and to do whatever it wants with the transaction.

As an example, let's build the following simple procedure that does nothing but execute a BEGIN TRANSACTION and a ROLLBACK TRANSACTION:

```
CREATE PROCEDURE tranTest
AS
BEGIN
  SELECT @@TRANCOUNT AS trancount

  BEGIN TRANSACTION
  ROLLBACK TRANSACTION
END
```

Executing this procedure outside a transaction is fine and returns a single row with a 0 value. However, say you execute it as follows:

```
BEGIN TRANSACTION
EXECUTE tranTest
COMMIT TRANSACTION
```

The procedure returns the following results:

```
Server: Msg 266, Level 16, State 2, Procedure tranTest, Line 5
Transaction count after EXECUTE indicates that a COMMIT or ROLLBACK TRANSACTION
statement is missing. Previous count = 1, current count = 0.

Server: Msg 3902, Level 16, State 1, Line 3
The COMMIT TRANSACTION request has no corresponding BEGIN TRANSACTION.
```

The errors occur because the transaction depth has changed, while rolling back the transaction inside the procedure.

Finally, say you recode the procedure as follows:

```
ALTER PROCEDURE tranTest
AS
BEGIN
   --gives us a unique savepoint name, trim it to 125 characters if the
   --user named the procedure really really large, to allow for nestlevel
   DECLARE @savepoint nvarchar(128) =
      cast(object_name(@@procid) AS nvarchar(125)) +
                        cast(@@nestlevel AS nvarchar(3))

   BEGIN TRANSACTION
   SAVE TRANSACTION @savepoint
     --do something here
   ROLLBACK TRANSACTION @savepoint
   COMMIT TRANSACTION
END
```

Now, you can execute it from within any number of transactions, and it will never fail, and it will never actually do anything either. You can call procedures from other procedures (even recursively from the same procedure) or external programs. It's important to take these precautions to make sure that the code is safe under any calling circumstances.

---

■**Caution** As mentioned in the "Savepoints" section, you can't use savepoints with distributed transactions or when sending multiple batches over a MARS-enabled connection. To make the most out of MARS, you might not be able to use this strategy. Frankly speaking, it might simply be prudent to execute modification procedures one at a time, anyhow.

---

Naming savepoints is important. As savepoints aren't scoped to a procedure, you must ensure that they're always unique. I tend to use the procedure name (retrieved here by using the object_name function called for the @@procId, but you could just enter it textually) and the current transaction nesting level. This guarantees that I can never have the same savepoint active, even if calling the same procedure recursively. It would be also possible to use @@nestLevel, as it would always be unique in the calling chain for a given connection.

Let's look briefly at how to code this into procedures using proper error handling:

```
ALTER PROCEDURE tranTest
AS
BEGIN
   --gives us a unique savepoint name, trim it to 125
   --characters if the user named it really large
   DECLARE @savepoint nvarchar(128) =
            cast(object_name(@@procid) AS nvarchar(125)) +
                              cast(@@nestlevel AS nvarchar(3))
   --get initial entry level, so we can do a rollback on a doomed transaction
   DECLARE @entryTrancount int = @@trancount

   BEGIN TRY
     BEGIN TRANSACTION
     SAVE TRANSACTION @savepoint

     --do something here
     RAISERROR ('Invalid Operation',16,1)
```

```
      COMMIT TRANSACTION
   END TRY
   BEGIN CATCH

     --if the tran is doomed, and the entryTrancount was 0,
     --we have to roll back
     IF xact_state()= -1 and @entryTrancount = 0
          roll back transaction
     --otherwise, we can still save the other activities in the
     --transaction.
     ELSE IF xact_state() = 1 --transaction not doomed, but open
        BEGIN
           ROLLBACK TRANSACTION @savepoint
           COMMIT TRANSACTION
        END

     DECLARE @ERRORmessage nvarchar(4000)
     SET @ERRORmessage = 'Error occurred in procedure ''' + object_name(@@procid)
                        + ''', Original Message: ''' + ERROR_MESSAGE() + ''''
     RAISERROR (@ERRORmessage,16,1)
     RETURN -100
   END CATCH
END
```

In the CATCH block, instead of rolling back the transaction, I checked for a doomed transaction, and if we were not in a transaction at the start of the procedure, I rolled back. A *doomed transaction* is a transaction where some operation has made it impossible to do anything other than roll back the transaction. A common cause is a trigger-based error message. It is still technically an active transaction, giving you the chance to roll it back and not have operations occur outside of the expected transaction space.

If the transaction was not doomed, I simply rolled back the savepoint. An error is returned for the caller to deal with. You could also eliminate the RAISERROR altogether if the error wasn't critical and the caller needn't ever know of the rollback. You can place any form of error handling in the CATCH block, and as long as you don't roll back the entire transaction and the transaction does not become doomed, you can keep going and later commit the transaction.

If this procedure called another procedure that used the same error handling, it would roll back its part of the transaction. It would then raise an error, which in turn would cause the CATCH block to be called, and roll back the savepoint and commit the transaction (which at that point wouldn't contain any changes at all). If the transaction was doomed, when you get to the top level, it is rolled back. You might ask, why go through this exercise if you're just going to roll back the transaction anyhow? The key is that each level of the calling structure can decide what to do with its part of the transaction. Plus, in the error handler we have created, we get the basic call stack for debugging purposes.

As an example of how this works, consider the following schema and table (create it in any database you desire, likely tempdb, as this sample is isolated to this section):

```
CREATE SCHEMA menu
CREATE TABLE menu.foodItem
(
    foodItemId int not null IDENTITY(1,1)
        CONSTRAINT PKmenu_foodItem PRIMARY KEY,
    name varchar(30) not null
        CONSTRAINT AKmenu_foodItem_name UNIQUE,
    description varchar(60) not null,
        CONSTRAINT CHKmenu_foodItem_name CHECK (name <> ''),
        CONSTRAINT CHKmenu_foodItem_description CHECK (description <> '')
)
```

Now create a procedure to do the insert:

```
CREATE PROCEDURE menu.foodItem$insert
(
    @name       varchar(30),
    @description varchar(60),
    @newFoodItemId int = null output --we will send back the new id here
)
AS
BEGIN
  SET NOCOUNT ON

  --gives us a unique savepoint name, trim it to 125
  --characters if the user named it really large
  DECLARE @savepoint nvarchar(128) =
              cast(object_name(@@procid) AS nvarchar(125)) +
                              cast(@@nestlevel AS nvarchar(3))
  --get initial entry level, so we can do a rollback on a doomed transaction
  DECLARE @entryTrancount int = @@trancount

  BEGIN TRY
    BEGIN TRANSACTION
    SAVE TRANSACTION @savepoint

    INSERT INTO menu.foodItem(name, description)
    VALUES (@name, @description)

    SET @newFoodItemId = scope_identity() --if you use an instead of trigger,
                                --you will have to use name as a key
                                --to do the identity "grab" in a SELECT
                                --query
    COMMIT TRANSACTION
  END TRY
  BEGIN CATCH

    --if the tran is doomed, and the entryTrancount was 0,
    --we have to roll back
    IF xact_state()= -1 and @entryTrancount = 0
        roll back transaction
    --otherwise, we can still save the other activities in the
    --transaction.
    ELSE IF xact_state() = 1 --transaction not doomed, but open
        BEGIN
          ROLLBACK TRANSACTION @savepoint
          COMMIT TRANSACTION
        END

    DECLARE @ERRORmessage nvarchar(4000)
    SET @ERRORmessage = 'Error Occurred in procedure ''' + object_name(@@procid)
                    + ''', Original Message: ''' + ERROR_MESSAGE() + ''''
    RAISERROR (@ERRORmessage,16,1)
    RETURN -100
  END CATCH
END
```

Now try out the code:

```
DECLARE @foodItemId int, @retval int
EXECUTE @retval = menu.foodItem$insert  @name ='Burger',
                                        @description = 'Mmmm Burger',
                                        @newFoodItemId = @foodItemId output
SELECT  @retval as returnValue
IF @retval >= 0
    SELECT  foodItemId, name, description
    FROM    menu.foodItem
    where   foodItemId = @foodItemId
```

There's no error, so the row we created is returned:

| foodItemId | name   | description |
| ---------- | ------ | ----------- |
| 1          | Burger | Mmmm Burger |

Now try out the code with an error:

```
DECLARE @foodItemId int, @retval int
EXECUTE @retval = menu.foodItem$insert  @name ='Big Burger',
                                        @description = '',
                                        @newFoodItemId = @foodItemId output
SELECT  @retval as returnValue
IF @retval >= 0
    SELECT  foodItemId, name, description
    FROM    menu.foodItem
    where   foodItemId = @foodItemId
```

Because the description is blank, an error is returned:

```
Msg 50000, Level 16, State 1, Procedure foodItem$insert, Line 47
Error Occurred in procedure 'foodItem$insert', Original Message: 'The INSERT
statement conflicted with the CHECK constraint "CHKmenu_foodItem_description".
The conflict occurred in database "tempdb", table "menu.foodItem",
column 'description'.'

returnValue
-----------
-100
```

## Triggers

Just as in stored procedures, you can start transactions, set savepoints, and roll back to a savepoint. However, if you execute a ROLLBACK TRANSACTION statement in a trigger, two things can occur:

- Outside a TRY-CATCH block, the entire batch of SQL statements is canceled.
- Inside a TRY-CATCH block, the batch isn't canceled, but the transaction count is back to zero.

Back in Chapter 6, we discussed and implemented triggers that consistently used rollbacks when any error occurred. If not using TRY-CATCH blocks, this approach is generally exactly what's desired, but when using TRY-CATCH blocks, it can make things more tricky. To handle this, in the CATCH block of stored procedures I've included this code:

```
--if the tran is doomed, and the entryTrancount was 0,
--we have to roll back
 IF xact_state()= -1 and @entryTrancount = 0
     roll back transaction
--otherwise, we can still save the other activities in the
--transaction.
 ELSE IF xact_state() = 1 --transaction not doomed, but open
     BEGIN
       ROLLBACK TRANSACTION @savepoint
       COMMIT TRANSACTION
     END
```

This is an effective, if perhaps limited method of working with errors from triggers that works in most any situation. Removing all ROLLBACK TRANSACTION commands but just raising an error from a trigger dooms the transaction, which is just as much trouble as the rollback. The key is to understand how this might affect the code that you're working with, and to make sure that errors are handled in an understandable way. More than anything, test all types of errors in your system (trigger, constraint, and so on).

---

■**Caution** If a trigger causes a rollback to occur, there's a chance that you might receive a 266 error message—"Transaction count after EXECUTE indicates that a COMMIT or ROLLBACK"—if you execute this code within a transaction and outside a TRY-CATCH block. This won't be the first error message, and isn't harmful, but processing will continue, so you need to understand this situation.

---

For an example, I will create a trigger based on the framework we set up back in Chapter 6. Instead of any validations, I will just immediately cause an error: RAISERROR ('FoodItem''s cannot be done that way',16,1). Note that my trigger template does do a rollback in the trigger, assuming that users of these triggers follow the error handing set up here, rather than just dooming the transaction. Dooming the transaction could be a safer way to go if you do not have full control over error handling.

```
CREATE TRIGGER menu.foodItem$InsertTrigger
ON menu.foodItem
AFTER INSERT
AS
BEGIN
    DECLARE @rowsAffected int,    --stores the number of rows affected
            @msg varchar(2000)    --used to hold the error message

    SET @rowsAffected = @@rowcount

    --no need to continue on if no rows affected
    IF @rowsAffected = 0 return

    SET NOCOUNT ON --to avoid the rowcount messages
    SET ROWCOUNT 0 --in case the client has modified the rowcount

    BEGIN TRY
        --[validation blocks][validation section]
        RAISERROR ('FoodItem''s cannot be done that way',16,1)
        --[modification blocks][modification section]
    END TRY
```

```
BEGIN CATCH
        IF @@trancount > 0
            ROLLBACK TRANSACTION

        DECLARE @ERROR_MESSAGE nvarchar(4000)
        SET @ERROR_MESSAGE = ERROR_MESSAGE()
        RAISERROR (@ERROR_MESSAGE,16,1)

    END CATCH
END
```

In the downloadable code, I have modified the error handling in the stored procedure to put out markers, so you can see what branch of the code is being executed:

```
SELECT 'In error handler'

--if the tran is doomed, and the entryTrancount was 0,
--we have to roll back
 IF xact_state()= -1 and @entryTrancount = 0
  begin
     SELECT 'Transaction Doomed'
     ROLLBACK TRANSACTION
  end
--otherwise, we can still save the other activities in the
--transaction.
 ELSE IF xact_state() = 1 --transaction not doomed, but open
    BEGIN
        SELECT 'Savepoint Rollback'
        ROLLBACK TRANSACTION @savepoint
        COMMIT TRANSACTION
    END
```

So, executing the code that contains an error that the constraints catch:

```
DECLARE @foodItemId int, @retval int
EXECUTE @retval = menu.foodItem$insert  @name ='Big Burger',
                                        @description = '',
                                        @newFoodItemId = @foodItemId output
SELECT @retval
```

This is the output:

```
----------------
In error handler
------------------
Savepoint Rollback

Msg 50000, Level 16, State 1, Procedure foodItem$insert, Line 51
Error Occurred in procedure 'foodItem$insert', Original Message: 'The INSERT
statement conflicted with the CHECK constraint "CHKmenu_foodItem_description".
The conflict occurred in database "tempdb", table "menu.foodItem", column
'description'.'

returnValue
-----------
-100
```

You can see the constraint message, after the template error. Now, try to enter some data that is technically correct, but is blocked by the trigger with the ROLLBACK:

```
DECLARE @foodItemId int, @retval int
EXECUTE @retval = menu.foodItem$insert  @name ='Big Burger',
                                        @description = 'Yummy Big Burger',
                                        @newFoodItemId = @foodItemId output
SELECT @retval
```

These results are a bit more mysterious, though the transaction is clearly in an error state. Since the rollback operation occurs in the trigger, once we reach the error handler, there is no need to do any savepoint or rollback, so it just finishes:

```
----------------
In error handler

Msg 50000, Level 16, State 1, Procedure foodItem$insert, Line 51
Error Occurred in procedure 'foodItem$insert', Original Message: 'FoodItem's
cannot be done that way'

returnValue
-----------
-100
```

For the final demonstration, I will change the trigger to just do a RAISERROR, with no other error handling:

```
ALTER TRIGGER menu.foodItem$InsertTrigger
ON menu.foodItem
AFTER INSERT
AS
BEGIN
    DECLARE @rowsAffected int,      --stores the number of rows affected
            @msg varchar(2000)      --used to hold the error message

    SET @rowsAffected = @@rowcount

    --no need to continue on if no rows affected
    IF @rowsAffected = 0 return

    SET NOCOUNT ON --to avoid the rowcount messages
    SET ROWCOUNT 0 --in case the client has modified the rowcount

    RAISERROR ('FoodItem''s cannot be done that way',16,1)

END
```

Then, reexecute the previous statement that caused the trigger error:

```
----------------
In error handler

------------------
Transaction Doomed

Msg 50000, Level 16, State 1, Procedure foodItem$insert, Line 51
Error occurred in procedure 'foodItem$insert', Original Message: 'FoodItem's
cannot be done that way'

returnValue
-----------
-100
```

Hence, our error handler covered all of the different bases of what can occur for errors. In each case, we got an error message that would let us know where an error was occurring and that it was an error. The main thing I wanted to show in this section is that triggers, while useful, do complicate the error handling process, so I would certainly use constraints as much as possible (emphasizing the same thing I said in Chapter 6.)

# SQL Server Concurrency Controls

In the previous section, I introduced transactions, but the real goal of this chapter is to demonstrate how multiple users can be manipulating and modifying the exact same data, making sure that all users get consistent usage of the data.

To understand the basics of the Isolation part of the ACID properties discussed earlier, this section will introduce a couple important concepts that are essential to building concurrent applications:

- *Locks*: These are "holds" put by SQL Server on objects that are being used by users.

- *Isolation levels*: These are settings used to control the length of time for which SQL Server holds onto the locks.

These two important things work together to allow you to control and optimize a server's concurrency, allowing users to work at the same time, on the same resources, while still maintaining consistency. However, just how consistent your data remains is the important thing, and that is what you will see in the "Isolation Levels" section.

## Locks

Locks are tokens laid down by the SQL Server processes to "stake their claim" to the different resources available, so as to prevent one process from stomping on another and causing inconsistencies. They are a lot like the "Diver Down" markers that deep sea divers place on top of the water when working below the water. They do this to alert other divers, pleasure boaters, fishermen, and so on, that they're below. Every SQL Server process applies a lock to almost anything it does, to try to make sure that other user processes know what they *are* doing as well as what they are *planning* to do.

The most common illustration of why locks are needed is called the *lost update*; see Figure 10-3.

```
BEGIN TRANSACTION

SELECT balance
FROM    table
where acct = '1111'
(balance = 500)
                                        BEGIN TRANSACTION
--Perform operations to determine
--how much to increase (500)           SELECT balance
                                        FROM    table
                                        WHERE   acct = '1111'
                                        (balance = 500)
Update table                           --Perform calculations to determine
set balance = 500 (old value)          --how much to decrease (30)
            +500 (calculate value)
where acct = '1111'                    Update table
                                        set balance = 500 (old value)
COMMIT TRANSACTION                                  - 30 (calculate value)
                                        from table
                                        where acct = '1111'

                                        COMMIT TRANSACTION
```

*Figure 10-3. A lost update illustration (probably one of the major inspirations for the other definition of multitasking: "screwing everything up simultaneously")*

In the scenario in Figure 10-3, you have two concurrent users. Each of these executes some SQL statements, but in the end, the final value is going to be the wrong value, and 500 will be lost. Why? Because each user fetched a reality from the database that was correct at the time, and then acted on it as if it would always be true. Locks act as a message to other processes that a resource is being used, or at least probably being used. Think of a railroad-crossing sign. When the bar crosses the road, it acts as a lock to tell you not to drive across the tracks because the train is going to use the resource. Even if the train stops and never reaches the road, the bar comes down, and the lights flash like it is Christmas at Disney World. This lock *can* be ignored (as can SQL Server locks), but it's generally not advisable to do so, since if the train does come you may not have the ability to go back to Disney World, except perhaps to the Haunted Mansion. (Ignoring locks isn't usually as messy as ignoring a train-crossing signal, but you could be creating the system that controls that warning signal. Ignore locks—ouch.)

Locks are made up of two things: the type of lock and the mode of the lock. These elements include what's being locked, and just how locked it is, respectively. If you've been around for a few versions of SQL Server, you probably know that since SQL Server 7.0, SQL Server primarily uses row-level locks. That is, a user locking some resource in SQL Server does it on individual rows of data, rather than on pages of data, or even on complete tables.

However, thinking that SQL Server only locks at the row level is misleading, as SQL Server can use six different types of locks to lock varying portions of the database, with the row being the finest type of lock, all the way up to a full database lock. And each of them will be used quite often. The types of locks in Table 10-1 are supported.

**Table 10-1.** *Lock Types*

| Type of Lock | Granularity |
|---|---|
| Row or row identifier (RID) | A single row in a table |
| Key or key range | A single value or range of values (for example, to lock rows with values from A–M, even if no rows currently exist) |
| Page | An 8K index or data page |
| Extent | A group of eight 8K pages (64K), generally only used when allocating new space to the database |
| Table | An entire table, including all rows and indexes |
| Database | The entire database |

■**Tip** In terms of locks, database object locks are all you have much knowledge of or control over in SQL Server, so this is all I'll cover. However, you should be aware that many more locks are in play, as SQL Server manages its hardware and internal needs as you execute queries. Hardware locks are referred to as *latches*, and you'll occasionally see them referenced in SQL Server Books Online, though little is explained about them. You have little control over them, because they control physical resources, like the lock on the lavatory door in an airplane. Like the lavatory, though, you generally only want one user accessing a physical resource at a time.

At the point of request, SQL Server determines approximately how many of the database resources (a table, a row, a key, a key range, and so on) are needed to satisfy the request. This is calculated on the basis of several factors, the specifics of which are unpublished. Some of these factors include the cost of acquiring the lock, the amount of resources needed, and how long the locks will be held (the next major section, "Isolation Levels," will discuss the factors surrounding the question "how long?"). It's also possible for the query processor to upgrade the lock from a more granular lock to a less specific type if the query is unexpectedly taking up large quantities of resources.

For example, if a large percentage of the rows in a table are locked with row locks, the query processor might switch to a table lock to finish out the process. Or, if you're adding large numbers of rows into a clustered table in sequential order, you might use a page lock on the new pages that are being added. Although the type of lock defines the amount of the database to lock, the second part of the lock is the mode. It refers to how strict the lock is when dealing with other locks. Table 10-2 lists these available modes.

**Table 10-2.** *Lock Modes*

| Mode | Description |
|---|---|
| Shared | Generally used when users are looking at the data but not editing. It's called *shared* because multiple processes can have a shared lock on the same resource, allowing read-only access to the resource. However, sharing resources prevents other processes from modifying the resource. |
| Exclusive | As the name implies, this gives exclusive access to a resource. Only one process may have an active exclusive lock on a resource. |
| Update | Used to inform other processes that you're planning to modify the data, but aren't quite ready to do so. Other connections may also issue shared locks while still preparing to do the modification, but not update or exclusive. Update locks are used to prevent deadlocks (I'll cover them later in this section) by marking rows that a statement will possibly update, rather than upgrading from shared directly to an exclusive lock. |

| Mode | Description |
|------|-------------|
| Intent | Communicates to other objects that it might be necessary to take one of the previously listed modes. You might see these as intent shared, intent exclusive, or shared with intent exclusive. |
| Schema | Used to lock the structure of an object when it's in use. That's so you cannot alter a table when a user is reading data from it. |

Each of these modes, coupled with the granularity, describes a locking situation. For example, an exclusive table lock would mean that no other user can access any data in the table. An update table lock would say that other users could look at the data in the table, but any statement that might modify data in the table would have to wait until after this process has been completed.

The next concept to discuss is lock compatibility. Each lock mode may be compatible or not with the other lock mode on the same resource. If the types are compatible, then two or more users may lock the same resource. Incompatible lock types would require the second user(s) simply to wait until the incompatible lock(s) has been released.

Table 10-3 shows which types are compatible with which others.

**Table 10-3.** *Lock Compatibility Modes*

| Mode | IS | S | U | IX | SIX | X |
|------|----|----|----|----|-----|----|
| Intent shared (IS) | • | • | • | • | • | |
| Shared (S) | • | • | • | | | |
| Update (U) | • | • | | | | |
| Intent exclusive (IX) | • | | | • | | |
| Shared with intent exclusive (SIX) | • | | | | | |
| Exclusive (X) | | | | | | |

Although locks are great for data consistency, as far as concurrency is considered, locked resources stink. Whenever a resource is locked with an incompatible lock type and another process cannot use it to complete its processing, concurrency is lowered, as the process must wait for the other to complete before it can continue. This is generally referred to as *blocking*: one process is blocking another from doing something, so the blocked process must wait its turn, no matter how long it takes.

Simply put, locks allow consistent views of the data by only letting a single process modify a single resource at a time, while allowing multiple viewers. Locks are a necessary part of SQL Server architecture, as is blocking to honor those locks when needed, to make sure one user doesn't trample on the other's data, ending up with invalid data in some cases.

In the next section, I'll discuss isolation levels, which determine how long locks are held. Executing SELECT * FROM sys.dm_os_waiting_tasks gives you a list of all processes that tells you if any users are blocking, and which user is doing the blocking. Executing SELECT * FROM sys.dm_tran_locks lets you see locks that are being held. SQL Server Management Studio has a decent Activity Monitor, accessible via the Object Explorer in the Management folder.

It's possible to force SQL Server to use a different type of lock than it might ordinarily choose, by using *table hints* on your queries. For individual tables in a FROM clause, you can set the type of lock to be used for the single query like so:

```
FROM    table1 [WITH] (<tableHintList>)
            join table2 [WITH] (<tableHintList>)
```

Note that these hints work on all query types. In the case of locking, you can use quite a few. A partial list of the more common hints follows:

- PageLock: Forces the optimizer to choose page locks for the given table.
- NoLock: Leaves no locks, and honors no locks for the given table.
- RowLock: Forces row-level locks to be used for the table.
- Tablock: Goes directly to table locks, rather than row or even page locks. This can speed some operations, but seriously lowers write concurrency.
- TablockX: Same as Tablock, but it always uses exclusive locks (whether it would have normally done so or not).
- XLock: Uses exclusive locks.
- UpdLock: Uses update locks.

Note that SQL Server can override your hints if necessary. For example, take the case where a query sets the table hint of NoLock, but then rows are modified in the table in the execution of the query. No shared locks are taken or honored, but exclusive locks are taken and held on the table for the rows that are modified, though not on rows that are only read (this is true even for resources that are read as part of a trigger).

One term that's often bandied about is *deadlocks*. A deadlock is a circumstance where two processes are trying to use the same objects, but neither will ever be able to complete because it's blocked by the other connection. For example, consider two processes (Processes 1 and 2), and two resources (Resources A and B). The following steps lead to a deadlock:

- Process 1 takes a lock on Resource A, and at the same time Process 2 takes a lock on Resource B.
- Process 1 tries to get access to Resource B. As it's locked by Process 2, Process 1 goes into a wait state.
- Process 2 tries to get access to Resource A. Because it's locked by Process 1, Process 2 goes into a wait state.

At this point, there's no way to resolve this issue without ending one of the processes. SQL Server arbitrarily kills one of the processes (unless one of the processes has voluntarily raised the likelihood of being the killed process by setting DEADLOCK_PRIORITY to a lower value than the other. Values can be between integers –10 and 10, or LOW (equal to –5), NORMAL (0), or HIGH (5). SQL Server raises error 1205 to the client to tell the client that the process was stopped:

```
Server: Msg 1205, Level 13, State 1, Line 4
Transaction (Process ID 55) was deadlocked on lock resources with another process
 and has been chosen as the deadlock victim. Rerun the transaction.
```

At this point, you could resubmit the request, as long as the call was coded such that any data access was treated as an atomic operation. This all assumes that a transaction was used for multiple data modifications, and the program can tell what was rolled back.

■**Tip** Proper deadlock handling requires that you build your applications in such a way that you can easily tell how much of an operation succeeded or failed. This is done by proper use of transactions. A good practice is to send one transaction per batch from a client application. Keep in mind the engine views nested transactions as one transaction, so what I mean here is to start and complete a high-level transaction per batch.

Deadlocks can be hard to diagnose, as you can deadlock on many things, even hardware access. A common trick to try to alleviate frequent deadlocks between pieces of code is to order object access in the same order, if possible. This makes it more likely that locks taken are taken in the same order. Note that I said "alleviate *frequent* deadlocks." Most often, if you are running a very busy server, the best thing to do is handle deadlocks by resubmitting the last transaction executed (too many applications just raise the deadlock as an error that users don't understand).

Using SQL Server Profiler, you can add the DeadLock Graph event class to see deadlock events, which helps diagnose them. For more information about Profiler, check SQL Server Books Online.

---

■**Note**  There's also a Bulk Update mode that I didn't mention, which you use to lock the table when inserting data in bulk into the table and applying the TABLOCK hint. It's analogous to an exclusive table lock for concurrency issues.

---

## Isolation Levels

In the previous section on locks, I made this statement: "Every SQL Server process applies a lock to almost anything it does, to try to make sure that no other users can affect the operation that SQL Server is doing." Why did I say "try to make sure"? Locks are placed to make sure that while SQL Server is using the resource, the resource is protected. The *isolation level* is the setting that tells SQL Server how long to hold these locks, or even whether or not to take them.

The safest method to provide consistency in operations would be to take an exclusive lock on the entire database, do your operations, and then release the lock. Then the next user does the same thing. Although this was relatively common in early file-based systems, it isn't a reasonable alternative when you need to support 20,000 concurrent users (or even just a few automated users who do thousands of operations per second), no matter how beefy your hardware platform may be.

To improve concurrency, locks are held for the minimum time necessary to provide a reasonable amount of data consistency. (If the word "reasonable" concerns you, read on, because SQL Server defaults don't provide perfect coverage.) Isolation levels control how long locks are held, and there are five distinct levels. From inside a transaction, locks can be held for a variable amount of time to protect the data that's being worked with. For example, consider the following hypothetical code snippet that illustrates an extremely typical mistake made by people just getting started (note that code like this in version 2008 or later should be migrated to use the new MERGE syntax, but this is going to remain a very common coding problem for years to come, I will imagine):

```
BEGIN TRANSACTION
SAVE TRANSACTION savePoint

IF EXISTS ( SELECT * FROM tableA WHERE tableAId = 'value' )
BEGIN
  UPDATE tableB
  SET status = 'UPDATED'
  WHERE tableAId = 'value'

  IF @@error <> 0
  BEGIN
    RAISERROR ('Error updating tableB',16,1)
    ROLLBACK TRANSACTION savePoint
  END
END
--usually followed by an insert
COMMIT TRANSACTION
```

First, check to see if a value exists in tableA, then if it does, update a value in tableB. On first glance, this seems safe—if a record exists when checked for in tableA, it will exist once the execution gets to the tableB update. However, how well this works is based solely on how long the locks are held on the SELECT from tableA, coupled with how long it takes to get to the UPDATE statement. Although the row might exist when the IF EXISTS block executed, what if a table lock exists on tableB when you try to execute the update of tableB, and the process gets blocked waiting for the lock to be cleared? During this period of time waiting for the table lock on tableB to be cleared, the key row that previously existed could have been deleted from tableA, if the lock isn't maintained on the row in tableA until the transaction is completed.

Here's what the major problem is and why this is usually a major problem: under the default isolation level in which SQL Server connections operate, no lock would have been kept on tableA, leaving a potential hole in your data integrity if another user makes a change to the table before your transaction is complete. Usually however, if you have checks on tableA that validate the effects on tableB's integrity, the locks from the modification operations will protect you from integrity issues.

Deeply ingrained in the concepts of isolation levels are the concepts of *repeatable reads* and *phantom rows*. Consider that you execute a statement such as the following:

```
SELECT * FROM table
```

The following rows are returned:

```
ColumnName
----------
row1
row2
```

For this SELECT statement to claim to support repeatable reads within a transaction, you must be able to execute it multiple times and get back *at least the same results*. This means that no other user could change the data that had been retrieved in the operation. Other users are allowed to create new rows, so you might get back the following results:

```
ColumnName
----------
row1
row2
row3
```

Note that the term "repeatable read" can seem confusing, because the exact results of the read weren't repeatable, but that's how it's defined. The value row3 is a phantom row.

The following bulleted list contains the isolation levels to adjust how long locks are held to prevent phantom rows and nonrepeatable reads:

- READ UNCOMMITTED: Doesn't honor or take locks, unless data is modified.

- READ COMMITTED: Takes and honors locks, but releases read locks after data is retrieved. Allows phantom rows and nonrepeatable reads.

- REPEATABLE READ: Holds locks for the duration of the transaction to prevent users from changing data. Disallows nonrepeatable reads but allows phantom rows.

- SERIALIZABLE: Like REPEATABLE READ, but adds locks on ranges of data to make sure no new data is added. Holds these locks until the transaction is completed. Disallows phantom rows and nonrepeatable reads.

- SNAPSHOT: Allows the user to look at data as it was when the transaction started (existed as of SQL Server 2005).

The syntax for setting the isolation level is as follows:

```
SET TRANSACTION ISOLATION LEVEL <level>
```

`<level>` is any of the five preceding settings. The default isolation level is READ COMMITTED, and is a good balance between concurrency and integrity. It does bear mentioning that READ COMMITTED isn't always the proper setting. Quite often when only reading data, the SNAPSHOT isolation level gives the best results, though not setting your servers up properly can have some serious performance implications (more on the reasons for that in the section dedicated to SNAPSHOT).

Referring to the previous example code block—checking that a value exists in one table, then modifying another—keep in mind that the types of tables that tableA and tableB represent will greatly affect the isolation level. In that case, using REPEATABLE READ isolation level would suffice, because you are looking for the case where the row existed. REPEATABLE READ will allow phantoms, but if one row exists and you add another, existence is still guaranteed if another row is created.

Keep in mind that locks aren't just held for operations that you directly execute. They can be held for any constraints that fire to check existence in other tables, and any code executed in trigger code. The isolation level in effect also controls how long these locks are held. Understanding that fact alone will make you a much better performance tuner, because you won't just look on the surface but will know to dig deep into the code to figure out what is going on.

When considering solutions, you must keep in mind locking and isolation levels. As more and more critical solutions are being built upon SQL Server, it's imperative to make absolutely sure to protect data at a level that's commensurate with the value of the data. If you are building procedures to support a system on a space shuttle or a life support system, this becomes more important than it would be in the case of a sales system, or even a pediatrician's schedule. In the next major section, "Coding for Integrity and Concurrency," I'll look at coding schemes aimed at improving the concurrency of your stored procedure programs.

---

**■Tip** The IF EXISTS() THEN . . . ELSE . . . scenario mentioned earlier cannot be managed simply with isolation levels. In the next section, when I discuss pessimistic locking, I will present a solution using application locks that can be fitted to perform the "perfect" single threading solution.

---

In the next subsections, I'll briefly discuss the different isolation levels and demonstrate how they work using the following table. (Again, build these in any database of your choice. I'll create them in tempdb.)

```
CREATE TABLE dbo.testIsolationLevel
(
    testIsolationLevelId int identity(1,1)
                CONSTRAINT PKtestIsolationLevel PRIMARY KEY,
    value varchar(10)
)

INSERT dbo.testIsolationLevel(value)
VALUES ('Value1'),
       ('Value2')
```

---

**■Tip** Just as for locking modes, there are table query hints to apply an isolation level only to a given table in a query, rather than an entire query. These hints are READUNCOMMITTED, READCOMMITTED, REPEATABLEREAD, SNAPSHOT, and SERIALIZABLE, and they behave as their corresponding isolation levels do, only with respect to a single table in a query.

---

When you are coding or testing, checking to see what isolation level you are currently executing under can be useful. To do this, you can look at the results from sys.dm_exec_sessions:

```
SELECT  case transaction_isolation_level
            when 1 then 'Read Uncomitted'      when 2 then 'Read Committed'
            when 3 then 'Repeatable Read'      when 4 then 'Serializable'
            when 5 then 'Snapshot'             else 'Unspecified'
        end
FROM    sys.dm_exec_sessions
WHERE   session_id = @@spid
```

Unless you have already changed it, the default (and what you should get from executing this query in your connection) is Read Committed. Change the isolation level to serializable like so:

```
SET TRANSACTION ISOLATION LEVEL SERIALIZABLE
```

Then reexecute the query, and the results will now show that the isolation level is currently serializable. In the following sections, I will show you why you would want to change the isolation level at all.

---

■**Tip** I have included all of the code for these chapters in a single file, but you will want to start your own connections for CONNECTION A and CONNECTION B. All of the example code requires multiple connections to execute, in order to allow for concurrency.

---

## READ UNCOMMITTED

Ignore all locks, and don't issue locks. Queries can see any data that has been saved to the table, regardless of whether or not it's part of a transaction that hasn't been committed (hence the name). However, READ UNCOMMITTED still leaves exclusive locks if you do modify data, to keep other users from changing data that you haven't committed.

For the most part, READ UNCOMMITTED is a good tool for developers to use to check the progress of operations, and to look at production systems when SNAPSHOT isn't available. For example, say you execute the following code on one connection:

```
--CONNECTION A
SET TRANSACTION ISOLATION LEVEL READ COMMITTED --this is the default, just
                                               --setting for emphasis
BEGIN TRANSACTION
INSERT INTO dbo.testIsolationLevel(value)
VALUES('Value3')
```

Then execute on a second connection:

```
--CONNECTION B
SET TRANSACTION ISOLATION LEVEL READ UNCOMMITTED
SELECT *
FROM dbo.testIsolationLevel
```

This returns the following results:

```
testIsolationLevelId value
-------------------- ----------
1                    Value1
2                    Value2
3                    Value3
```

Being able to see locked data is quite valuable, especially when you're in the middle of a long-running process. That's because you won't block the process that's running, but you can see the data being modified. There is no guarantee that the data you see will be correct (it might fail checks and be rolled back), but for looking around and some reporting needs, this data might be good enough.

Finally, commit the transaction you started earlier:

```
--CONNECTION A

COMMIT TRANSACTION
```

---

CAUTION  Ignoring locks using READ UNCOMMITTED is almost never a *good* way to build highly concurrent database systems! Yes, it is possible to make your applications screamingly fast, because they never have to wait for other processes. There is a reason for this waiting. Consistency of the data you read is highly important and should not be taken lightly. Using SNAPSHOT or READ COMMITTED SNAPSHOT, which I will cover later in the chapter, will give you sort of the same concurrency without reading dirty data.

---

## READ COMMITTED

READ COMMITTED improves on READ UNCOMMITTED in that it doesn't allow you to see uncommitted data. It is the default isolation level as far as SQL Server is concerned. Be careful that your toolset may or may not use it as its default (some toolsets use SERIALIZABLE as the default, which, as you will see is pretty tight and is not great for concurrency). All shared and update locks are released as soon as the process is finished using the resource. Exclusive locks are held until the end of the transaction. Data modifications are usually executed under this isolation level. However, understand that this isolation level isn't perfect, as there isn't protection for repeatable reads or phantom rows. This means that as the length of the transaction increases, there's a growing possibility that some data that was read during the first operations within a transaction might have been changed or deleted by the end of the transaction. It happens extremely rarely when transactions are kept short, so it's generally considered an acceptable risk.

For example:

```
--CONNECTION A

SET TRANSACTION ISOLATION LEVEL READ COMMITTED

BEGIN TRANSACTION
SELECT * FROM dbo.testIsolationLevel
```

You see all the rows in the table from the previous section (though the testIsolationLevelId might be different if you had errors when you built your code). Then on the second connection, delete a row:

```
--CONNECTION B

DELETE FROM dbo.testIsolationLevel
WHERE testIsolationLevelId = 1
```

Finally, go back to the other connection and execute, still within the transaction:

```
--CONNECTION A
SELECT *
FROM dbo.testIsolationLevel
COMMIT TRANSACTION
```

This returns the following results:

```
testIsolationLevelId value
-------------------- ----------
2                    Value2
3                    Value3
```

Since most referential integrity checks are done based on the existence of some data, the impact of READ COMMITTED is lessened by the fact that most operations in an OLTP database system are inserts and updates. The impact is further lessened because relationships are pretty well guarded by the fact that deleting the parent or child row in a relationship requires a lock on the other row(s). So if someone tries to modify the parent and someone else tries to modify the child, one process will be locked by the other.

However, the key to the success of using READ COMMITTED isolation is simple probability. The chances of two users stepping on each other's processes within milliseconds is pretty unlikely, even less likely is the scenario that one user will do the exact thing that would cause inconsistency. However, the longer your transactions and the higher the concurrent number of users on the system, the more likely that READ COMMITTED will produce anomalies.

In my 15 years of using SQL Server, the primary issues I have found with READ COMMITTED have centered exclusively on checking/retrieving a value, then going back later and using that value. If you do much of that, and it is important that the situation remain the same until you use the value, consider implementing your code using a higher level of isolation.

For example, consider the issues involved in implementing a system to track drugs given to a patient in a hospital. For a system such as this, you'd never want to give a user too much medicine accidentally, because when you started a process to set up a schedule via a batch system, a nurse was administering the dosage off schedule. Although this situation is unlikely, as you will see in the next few sections, an adjustment in isolation level would prevent it from occurring at all.

## REPEATABLE READ

The REPEATABLE READ isolation level includes protection from data being deleted from under your operation. Shared locks are now held during the entire transaction, to prevent other users from modifying the data that has been read. You would be most likely to use this isolation level if your concern is the absolute guarantee of existence of some data when you finish your operation.

As an example on one connection, execute the following statement:

```
--CONNECTION A

SET TRANSACTION ISOLATION LEVEL REPEATABLE READ

BEGIN TRANSACTION
SELECT * FROM dbo.testIsolationLevel
```

This returns the following:

```
testIsolationLevelId value
-------------------- ----------
2                    Value2
3                    Value3
```

Then, on a different connection, run the following:

```
--CONNECTION B

INSERT INTO dbo.testIsolationLevel(value)
VALUES ('Value4')
```

This executes, but try executing the following code:

```
--CONNECTION B
DELETE FROM dbo.testIsolationLevel
WHERE value = 'Value3'
```

You go into a blocked state, because CONNECTION B will need an exclusive lock on that particular value, because deleting that value would cause the results from CONNECTION A to return fewer rows. Back on the other connection, run the following code:

```
--CONNECTION A

SELECT * FROM dbo.testIsolationLevel
COMMIT TRANSACTION
```

This will return the following:

```
testIsolationLevelId value
-------------------- ----------
2                    Value2
3                    Value3
4                    Value4
```

And immediately, the batch on the other connection will complete. Now viewing the data (from either connection) returns this:

```
testIsolationLevelId value
-------------------- ----------
2                    Value2
4                    Value4
```

The fact that other users may be changing the data you have locked can be a very serious concern for the perceived integrity of the data. If the user on connection A goes right back and the row is deleted, they will be confused. Of course, there is really nothing that can be done to solve this problem, as it is just a fact of life. In the section on "Optimistic Locking," I will present a method of making sure that one user doesn't crush the changes of another user, and it could be extended to viewed data, but generally this is not the case for performance reasons. In the end, you can implement most any scheme to protect the data, but all you are doing is widening the window of time where users are protected. No matter what, once the user relinquishes transactional control on a row, it will be fair game to other users without some form of workflow system in place (a topic that is well beyond the scope of my book, though once you are finished reading my book, you could design and create one!)

## SERIALIZABLE

SERIALIZABLE takes everything from REPEATABLE READ, and adds in phantom-row protection. SQL Server does this by not only taking locks on existing data that it has read, but now taking key locks on any ranges of data that *could possibly* match any SQL statement executed. This is the most restrictive isolation level, and is the best in any case where data integrity is absolutely necessary. It can cause lots of blocking; for example, consider what would happen if you executed the following query under the SERIALIZABLE isolation level:

```
SELECT *
FROM dbo.testIsolationLevel
```

No other user will be able to modify the table until all rows have been returned and the transaction it was executing within (implicit or explicit) is completed.

---

■**Note** Be careful. I said, "No other user will be able to *modify* the table;" I didn't say "read." Readers leave shared locks, not exclusive ones. This caveat is something that can be confusing at times when we are trying to write safe but concurrent SQL code.

---

If lots of users are viewing data in the table under any of the previously mentioned isolation levels, it can be difficult to get any modifications done. If you're going to use SERIALIZABLE, you need to be careful with your code that it only uses the minimum number of rows needed (especially if you are not using SNAPSHOT isolation level for read processes, as covered in the next section).

Now, execute this statement on a connection to simulate a user with a table locked:

```
--CONNECTION A

SET TRANSACTION ISOLATION LEVEL SERIALIZABLE

BEGIN TRANSACTION
SELECT * FROM dbo.testIsolationLevel
```

Then try to add a new row to the table:

```
--CONNECTION B

INSERT INTO dbo.testIsolationLevel(value)
VALUES ('Value5')
```

Your insert is blocked. Commit the transaction on the A connection:

```
--CONNECTION A

SELECT * FROM dbo.testIsolationLevel
COMMIT TRANSACTION
```

This returns the following:

```
testIsolationLevelId value
-------------------- ----------
2                    Value2
4                    Value4
```

The results are the same. However, this unblocks the CONNECTION B work, and by running the SELECT again, you will see that the contents of the table are now the following:

```
testIsolationLevelId value
-------------------- ----------
2                    Value2
4                    Value4
5                    Value5
```

It is important to be careful with the SERIALIZABLE isolation level. I can't stress enough that multiple readers can read the same data, but no one can update it while others are reading. Too often, people take this to mean that they can read some data and be guaranteed that no other user might have read it also, leading to the occasional inconsistent results and more frequent deadlocking issues.

## SNAPSHOT

SNAPSHOT isolation was one of the major cool new features in SQL Server 2005, and it continues to be one of my favorites (especially the READ COMMITTED SNAPSHOT variant that is mentioned later in this section). It lets you read the data as it was when the transaction started, regardless of any changes. It's a special case, because although it doesn't allow for phantom rows, nonrepeatable reads, or dirty reads from any queries within the transaction, it doesn't represent the current state of the data. You might check a value in a table at the beginning of the transaction and it's in the physical table, but later you requery the table. As long as you are inside the same transaction, even though the value exists in your virtual table, it needn't exist in the physical table any longer (in fact, the physical table needn't exist either!). This provides that the results of your query will reflect a consistent state of the database at some time, which is generally very desirable.

What makes SNAPSHOT particularly useful is that it doesn't use locks in the normal way, as it looks at the data as it was at the start of the transaction. Modifying data under this isolation level has its share of problems, which I'll demonstrate later in this section. However, I don't want to scare you off, as this isolation level can become a major part of a highly concurrent design strategy (particularly useful for reads in an optimistic locking strategy, which the last sections of this chapter cover).

The largest downside is performance. This history data is written not only to the log, but the data that will be used to support other users that are in a SNAPSHOT isolation level transaction is written to the tempdb. Hence, if this is going to be a very active server, you have to make sure that your tempdb is up to the challenge, especially if you're supporting large numbers of concurrent users. The good news is that if set up correctly, data readers will no longer block data writers, and they will always get a transactionally consistent view of the data. So when the vice president of the company decides to write a 20-table join query in the middle of the busiest part of the day, all other users won't get stuck behind him with data locks. The better news is that he won't see the mistaken ten-million-dollar entry that one of the data-entry clerks added to the data that the check constraint hasn't had time to deny yet (the vice president would have seen the error if using the READ UNCOMMITTED solution). The bad news is that eventually his query might take up all the resources and cause a major system slowdown that way. (Hey, if it was too easy, companies wouldn't need DBAs. And I, for one, wouldn't survive in a nontechnical field.)

To use (and demonstrate) SNAPSHOT isolation level, you have to alter the database you're working with (you can even do this to tempdb):

```
ALTER DATABASE tempDb
SET ALLOW_SNAPSHOT_ISOLATION ON
```

Now the SNAPSHOT isolation level is available for queries.

---

■**Caution** SNAPSHOT isolation level uses copies of changed data placed into the tempdb. Because of this, you should make sure that your tempdb is set up optimally. For more on setting up hardware, consider checking out the website http://www.sql-server-performance.com.

---

Let's look at an example. On the first connection, start a transaction and select from the testIsolationLevel table:

```
--CONNECTION A

SET TRANSACTION ISOLATION LEVEL SNAPSHOT
BEGIN TRANSACTION
SELECT * from dbo.testIsolationLevel
```

This returns the following results:

```
testIsolationLevelId value
-------------------- ----------
2                    Value2
4                    Value4
5                    Value5
```

On a second connection, run the following:

```
--CONNECTION B

SET TRANSACTION ISOLATION LEVEL READ COMMITTED
INSERT INTO dbo.testIsolationLevel(value)
VALUES ('Value6')
```

This executes with no waiting. Going back to the other connection, reexecuting the SELECT returns the same set as before. Now, still on the second connection, run the following code:

```
--CONNECTION B

DELETE FROM dbo.testIsolationLevel
WHERE  value = 'Value4'
```

This doesn't have to wait either. Going back to the other connection again, nothing has changed. So what about modifying data in SNAPSHOT isolation level? If no one else has modified the row, you can make any change:

```
--CONNECTION A

UPDATE  dbo.testIsolationLevel
SET     value = 'Value2-mod'
WHERE   testIsolationLevelId = 2
```

This runs, but going back to the B connection, if you try to select this row, it will be blocked, and the connection is forced to wait, because this row is new and has an exclusive lock on it, and B is not in SNAPSHOT ISOLATION level.

Commit the transaction in CONNECTION A and you'll see rows such as these:

```
--CONNECTION A

COMMIT TRANSACTION
SELECT * from dbo.testIsolationLevel
```

This returns the current contents of the table:

```
testIsolationLevelId value
-------------------- ----------
2                    Value2-mod
5                    Value5
6                    Value6
```

The messy/troubling bit with modifying data under the SNAPSHOT isolation level is what happens when one user modifies a row that another user has also modified, and committed the transaction for it. To see this, in CONNECTION A run the following, simulating a user fetching some data into the cache:

```
--CONNECTION A
SET TRANSACTION ISOLATION LEVEL SNAPSHOT
BEGIN TRANSACTION

--touch the data
SELECT * FROM dbo.testIsolationLevel
```

This returns the same results as just shown. Then a second user changes the value:

```
--CONNECTION B
SET TRANSACTION ISOLATION LEVEL READ COMMITTED --any will do

UPDATE dbo.testIsolationLevel
SET    value = 'Value5-mod'
WHERE  testIsolationLevelId = 5 --might be different in yours
```

Then the user on CONNECTION A tries to update the row also:

```
--CONNECTION A
UPDATE dbo.testIsolationLevel
SET    value = 'Value5-mod'
WHERE testIsolationLevelId = 5 --might be different in yours
```

As this row has been deleted by a different connection, the following error message rears its ugly head:

```
Msg 3960, Level 16, State 2, Line 1
Snapshot isolation transaction aborted due to update conflict. You cannot use
snapshot isolation to access table 'dbo.testIsolationLevel' directly or
indirectly in database 'tempdb' to update, delete, or insert the row
that has been modified or deleted by another transaction. Retry the transaction
or change the isolation level for the update/delete statement.
```

As such, strictly for simplicity's sake, it's my recommendation that almost all retrieval-only operations can execute under the SNAPSHOT isolation level, and the procedures that do data modifications execute under the READ COMMITTED isolation level. As long as data is only read, the connection will see the state of the database as it was when the data was first read.

A strong word of caution—if you do data validations under SNAPSHOT isolation level and you do data-checking logic such as in a trigger or procedure, the data might already be invalid in the live database, especially if the transaction runs long. This invalid data is far worse than REPEATABLE READ, where the data is always valid when the check is done but might be changed after the violation. However, you should note that FOREIGN KEY constraints, when doing a modification, are smart enough to use the same sorts of locks as READ COMMITTED would to protect against this sort of issue. My suggestion (if you ignore the suggestion not to do writes under SNAPSHOT) would be to manually code SET TRANSACTION ISOLATION LEVEL READ COMMITTED or REPEATABLE READ or SERIALIZABLE where necessary in your modification procedures or triggers to avoid this sort of issue.

## Read Committed Snapshot

The database setting READ_COMMITTED_SNAPSHOT changes the isolation level of READ COMMITTED to behave very much like SNAPSHOT isolation level on a statement level.

Note that I said "statement" and not "transaction." In SNAPSHOT isolation level, once you start a transaction, you get a consistent view of the database *as it was* when the transaction started until you close it. READ_COMMITTED_SNAPSHOT gives you a consistent view of the database for a single statement. Set the database into this mode as follows:

```
--must be no active connections other than the connection executing
--this ALTER command
ALTER DATABASE <databasename>
    SET READ_COMMITTED_SNAPSHOT ON
```

By doing this, every *statement* is now in SNAPSHOT isolation level by default. For example, imagine you're at the midpoint of the following pseudo-batch:

```
BEGIN TRANSACTION
SELECT column FROM table1
--midpoint
SELECT column FROM table1
COMMIT TRANSACTION
```

If you're in SNAPSHOT isolation level, table1 could change completely—even get dropped—and you wouldn't be able to tell when you execute the second SELECT statement. You're given a consistent view of the database for reading. With the READ_COMMITTED_SNAPSHOT database setting turned on, and in a READ COMMITTED transaction, your view of table1 would be consistent with how it looked when you started reading, but when you started the second pass through the table, it might not match the data the first time you read through. This behavior is similar to plain READ COMMITTED, except that you don't see any new phantoms or nonrepeatable reads while retrieving rows produced during the individual statement (other users can delete and add rows while you scan through the table, but you won't be affected by the changes), and SQL Server doesn't need to take locks or block other users.

This can actually be tremendously better than just using READ COMMITTED, though it does suffer from the same issues with data consistency as did plain READ COMMITTED, and maybe just a bit worse. You should remember that in the previous section on READ COMMITTED, I noted that because SQL Server releases locks immediately after reading the data, another user could come behind you and change data that you just finished using to do some validation. This same thing is true for READ_COMMITTED_SNAPSHOT, but the window of time can be slightly longer because it reads only history as it passes through different tables. This amount of time is generally insignificant and usually isn't anything to worry about, but it *can* be important based on the type of system you're creating. For places where you might need more safety, consider using the higher isolation levels, such as REPEATABLE READ or SERIALIZABLE. I would certainly suggest that, in the triggers and modification procedures that you build using this isolation level, you consider the upgraded isolation level. The best part is that basic readers who just want to see data for a query or report will not be affected. Later in the chapter when I present the mechanism for optimistic locking, you will see that whether or not a reading user gets an old version doesn't really matter. Users will never be allowed to modify anything but the row that looks exactly like the one that they fetched.

SNAPSHOT isolation level and the READ_COMMITTED_SNAPSHOT settings are very important aspects of SQL Server's concurrency feature set. They cut down on blocking and the need to use the dirty reads to look at active OLTP data for small reports and for read-only queries to cache data for user-interface processes.

---

■**Note** READ COMMITTED SNAPSHOT is the feature that saved one of the major projects I worked on after version 2005 was released. We tried and tried to optimize the system under basic READ COMMITTED, but it was not possible, mostly due to the fact that we had no control over the API building the queries that were used to access the database.

---

# Coding for Integrity and Concurrency

When building database systems, you must consider that multiple users will be attempting to modify your data, at the same time. So far in this chapter, I've talked at length about the different mechanisms, such as transactions, isolation levels, and so on, for protecting your data. Now I'll present some of the different coding mechanisms to keep your users from stepping on one another.

The general progression of events for most applications is the same: fetch some data for a user or a process to look at, operate on this data, make changes to the data, or make some decision based on the retrieved values. Once the users have performed their operations, they'll either commit their changes to the database, or possibly save data to a different table based on their decision.

Our coding decisions generally surround how to deal with the lag time while the users have the data cached on their client. For example, what happens if a different user wants the data, and wants to make a change to the same data?

For this situation, you can use a couple common schemes while coding your database application:

- *Pessimistic locking*: Assume it's likely that users will try to modify the same data, so single-thread access to important resources.

- *Optimistic locking*: Assume it's unlikely that users will try to modify the exact same row at the same time another user wants to. Only verify that the cached data is valid when the user wants to change the data.

Using one or parts of both these schemes, it's usually possible to protect data in a multiuser system at an acceptable level of integrity and concurrency.

## Pessimistic Locking

A pessimistic locking scheme is restrictive. Generally, the idea is straightforward: begin a transaction, most likely a serializable one; fetch the data; manipulate the data; modify the data; and finally commit the transaction. The goal is to serialize or single-thread all access to the resource in which the process is interested, making sure that no other user can modify or even view the data being worked on.

The main concern is blocking all access to given resources. This sounds easy and reasonable, but the main issue is that any query to a locked resource has to wait for the user to complete access. Even if the parts of the resource won't be involved in the answer to a query, if a locked resource *might* be involved, there's a possibility that unnecessary blocking will occur.

For example, say one user has a single row locked in a table. The next user executes a different query that requires a table scan on the same table. Even if the results of this query needn't use the locked row, the second user will be blocked until the other connection has completed, as SQL Server won't know if the next user needs the row until it's unlocked.

---

■**Note**  You might be thinking that SQL Server could simply check to see if the locked resource would be needed. However, this cannot be known, because once a row is locked with a noncompatible lock, all other users must assume that the values might change. Hence, you're forced to wait until the lock is dropped.

---

Any users who need data that this next user has locked also have to wait, and soon a chain of users is waiting on one particular user.

Except for one thing—time—all this might even be reasonable. If the lock only lasted milliseconds (or possibly seconds), this would be fine. Small applications based on file managers have implemented concurrency this way for years. However, what if the user decides to take a break? (This can be a common issue with smaller systems.) All other users have to wait until this user finishes his or her access to the data, and if this user has modified one piece of data (possibly with complex triggers), and still has more to go, access might be blocked to most of the system data because a user was forgetful and didn't press the Save button.

It's possible to relieve some of the long-term stress on the system by reducing the time locks can be held for, such as setting time limits on how long the user can keep the data before rolling back the transaction. However, either way, it's necessary to block access to large quantities of data for a more-than-reasonable period of time. That's because you'd need to lock any domain tables that the users will rely on to choose values for their table, so that users change no related table values or any related data that other users might need.

Implementing pessimistic locks isn't all that easy, as you have to go out of your way to force locks on data that keep other users from even viewing the data. One method is to lock data using exclusive lock hints, coupled with the SERIALIZABLE isolation level, when you fetch data and maintain the connection to the server as you modify the data. This is messy, and will likely cause lots of undesired locks if you aren't extremely careful how you write queries to minimize locking.

---

■**Caution** If the page has not been dirtied, even if an exclusive lock exists on the row/page, another reader can get access to the row for viewing. You need to actually modify the row to dirty the page if you want to hold the lock, or use a PAGELOCK and XLOCK hint (Microsoft KB Article 324417), though this will lock the entire page.

---

SQL Server does have a built-in method you can use to implement a form of pessimistic locking: SQL Server *application locks*. These locks, just like other locks, must be taken inside a transaction (executing the procedures without a transaction will get you a nasty error message). The real downside is that enforcement and compliance are completely optional. If you write code that doesn't follow the rules and use the proper application lock, you will get no error letting you know. The commands that you have to work with application locks are as follows:

- sp_getAppLock: Places a lock on an application resource. The programmer names application resources, and they can be named with any string value. In the string, you could name single values, or even a range

- sp_releaseAppLock: Releases locks taken inside a transaction.

- APPLOCK_MODE: Used to check the mode of the application lock.

- APPLOCK_TEST: Used to see if you could take an application lock before starting the lock and getting blocked.

As an example, we'll run the following code. We'll implement this on a resource named 'invoiceId=1', which represents an invoice that we'll lock. We'll set it as an exclusive lock so no other user can touch it. In one connection, we run the following code:

```
--CONNECTION A

BEGIN TRANSACTION
    DECLARE @result int
    EXEC @result = sp_getapplock @Resource = 'invoiceId=1', @LockMode = 'Exclusive'
    SELECT @result
```

This returns 0, stating that the lock was taken successfully. Now, if another user tries to execute the same code to take the same lock, their process has to wait until the user has finished with the resource 'invoiceId=1':

```
--CONNECTION B
BEGIN TRANSACTION
    DECLARE @result int
    EXEC @result = sp_getapplock @Resource = 'invoiceId=1', @LockMode = 'Exclusive'
    PRINT @result
```

This transaction has to wait. Let's cancel the execution, and then execute the following code using the APPLOCK_TEST function to see if we can take the lock (allowing the application to check before taking the lock):

```
--CONNECTION B

BEGIN TRANSACTION
SELECT APPLOCK_TEST('public','invoiceId=1','Exclusive','Transaction')
                                                    as CanTakeLock

ROLLBACK TRANSACTION
```

This returns 0, meaning we cannot take this lock currently. APPLOCKs can be a great resource for building locks that don't fit into the mold of SQL Server locks, and could be used by a user interface to lock access to a given screen in an application. The key is that every application must implement the locking mechanism, and every application must honor the locks taken. In the next section, I will show you how to use a pessimistic lock based on the application lock to single thread access to a given block of code.

---

■**Tip** You can use application locks to implement more than just pessimistic locks using different lock modes other than exclusive, but exclusive is what you'd use to implement a pessimistic locking mechanism. For more information about application locks, SQL Server Books Online gives some good examples and a full reference to using application locks.

---

# Implementing a Single Threaded Code Block

The problem of the critical section is a very common problem. Very often, it is troublesome for more than one connection to have access to a given section of code. For example, you might need to fetch a value, increment it, and keep the result unique among other callers that could be calling simultaneously.

The general solution to the single threading problem is to exclusively lock the resources that you need to be able to work with, forcing all other users to wait even for reading. In some cases, this technique will work great, but it can be troublesome in cases like the following:

- The code is part of a larger set of code that may have other code locked in a transaction, blocking users' access to more than you expect

- Only one minor section of code needs to be single threaded, and you can allow simultaneous access otherwise.

- The speed in which the data is accessed is so fast that two processes are likely to fetch the same data within microseconds of each other

- When the single threading is not for table access. For example, you may want to write to a file of some sort or use some other resource that is not table based.

The following technique will leave the tables unlocked while single threading access to a code block (in this case, getting and setting a value) manually, using an application lock to lock a section of code.

---

■**Note** An application lock must be used and honored manually in every piece of code where the need to lock the data matters, so there is a loss of safety associated with using application locks rather than data-oriented locks. If there is any concern with what other processes might do, be sure to still assign proper concurrency and locking hints to that code also.

---

To demonstrate a very common problem of building a unique value without using identities (for example, if you have to create an account number with special formatting/processing), I have created the following table:

```
CREATE TABLE applock
(
    applockId int primary key,   --the value that we will be generating
                                 --with the procedure
    connectionId int,            --holds the spid of the connection so you can
                                 --who creates the row
    insertTime datetime default (getdate()) --the time the row was created, so
                                            --you can see the progression
)
```

Next, a procedure that starts an application lock fetches some data from the table, increments the value, and stores it in a variable. I added a delay parameter, so you can tune up the problems by making the delay between increment and insert more pronounced. There is also a parameter to turn the application lock (noted as @useApplockFlag in the parameters) on and off, as that parameter will help you test to see how it behaves with and without the application lock.

```
CREATE PROCEDURE applock$test
(
    @connectionId int,
    @useApplockFlag bit = 1,
    @stepDelay varchar(10) = '00:00:00'
) as
SET NOCOUNT ON
BEGIN TRY
    BEGIN TRANSACTION
        declare @retval int = 1
        if @useApplockFlag = 1 --turns on and off the applock for testing
            begin
                exec @retval = sp_getapplock @Resource = 'applock$test',
                                             @LockMode = 'exclusive';
                if @retval < 0
                    begin
                        declare @errorMessage nvarchar(200)
                        set @errorMessage = case @retval
                                when -1 then 'Applock request timed out.'
                                when -2 then 'Applock request canceled.'
                                when -3 then 'Applock involved in deadlock'
                            else 'Parameter validation or other call error.'
                                end
                        raiserror (@errorMessage,16,1)
                    end
            end
```

```
    --get the next primary key value
    declare @applockId int
    set @applockId = coalesce((select max(applockId) from applock),0) + 1

    --delay for parameterized amount of time to slow down operations
    --and guarantee concurrency problems
    waitfor delay @stepDelay

    --insert the next value
    insert into applock(applockId, connectionId)
    values (@applockId, @connectionId)

    --won't have much effect on this code, since the row will now be
    --exclusively locked, and the max will need to see the new row to
    --be of any effect.
    exec @retval = sp_releaseapplock @Resource = 'applock$test'

    --this releases the applock too
    commit transaction
END TRY
BEGIN CATCH
    --if there is an error, roll back and display it.
    if @@trancount > 0
        rollback transaction
        select cast(error_number() as varchar(10)) + ':' + error_message()
END CATCH
```

Now, you can set up a few connections using this stored procedure, varying the parameters to get more or less clashing of values. Since we're running the procedure in such a tight loop, it is not surprising that two connections will often get the same value and try to insert new rows using that value:

```
WAITFOR TIME '23:46' --set for a time to run so multiple batches
                          --can simultaneously execute
go
EXEC applock$test @@spid, 1 -- <1=use applock, 0 = don't use applock>,
            ,'00:00:00.001'--'delay in hours:minutes:seconds.parts of seconds'
GO 10000 --runs the batch 10000 times in SSMS
```

You will probably be amazed at how many clashes you get when you have application locks turned off. Doing 10,000 iterations of this procedure on three connections on a Pentium 4, 2.1 GHz-laptop, I got over 1,000 clashes pretty much constantly. With application locks turned on, all rows were inserted in very close to the same amount of time.

To solidify the point that every connection has to follow the rules, turn off application locks on a connection or two and see the havoc that will result. The critical section will now no longer be honored, and you will get tons of clashes quickly, especially if you use any delay.

This is not the only method of implementing the solution to the incrementing values problem. The more common method is to change the code where you get the maximum value to increment and apply locking hints:

```
SET @applockId =
        coalesce((select max(applockId)
                    from applock with (UPDLOCK,PAGLOCK)),0) + 1
```

Changing the code to do this will cause update locks to be held because of the UPDLOCK hint, and the PAGLOCK hint causes page locks to be held (SQL Server can ignore locks when a row is locked and it has not been modified, even if it were to be exclusively locked).

The solution I presented is a very generic solution for single threading a code segment in T-SQL code, allowing that the one procedure is the only one single threading. It does not take any locks that will block others until it needs to update the data (if there is no changing of data, it won't block any other users, *ever*). This works great for a hotspot where you can clearly cordon off the things being utilized at a given level, like in this example, where all users of this procedure are getting the maximum of the same rows.

On the other hand, in Appendix C, when I implement this kind of solution for the `hierarchyId` examples, I will use the `UPDLOCK`, because the same procedure will be used to lock values all over the table, which may not be such a reading hot spot. Hence, if ten people wanted to insert a new row into the hierarchy, they may not block one another, whereas in the code in this section, all users of this procedure need one particular value. These two techniques together allow you to decide how to implement a safe, single-threaded operation based on how each will perform under a given load.

## Optimistic Locking

The opposite of pessimistic locking is optimistic locking (I make this statement merely to win the obvious statement of the year award). Here, the premise is simply to assume that the likelihood of users stepping on one another is limited. Instead of locking resources, locks are only taken during actual data-modification activities, because most of the time users just look around, and even if the data they're looking at is slightly out of date, it won't hurt anything (this is where the `SNAPSHOT` isolation level is perfect). Plus, the likelihood of two users editing the same data (in most systems) is reasonably low. If this is not the case, then pessimistic locking might be a better choice.

This is true of almost all applications, especially OLTP-style applications. It is very unlikely that the same person is calling into your sales call center on two lines talking to two different users. Even scenarios like giving a customer an inventory amount is a place where a sort of optimistic lock is acceptable. If you tell a customer that you have 1,000 of some item on hand and Joey Bigbucks walks up and buys all 1,000 of them, your first customer will be left out in the cold. Use a pessimistic lock (like the application lock example) when you need to implement that critical section of the code in which inventory is being decremented (or even selectively implement a pessimistic lock when your inventory levels are getting so you can tell the other customer that you *might* have inventory).

The idea behind optimistic locking is that, in all cases, only lock the data at the point where the user modifies the data. Data is protected in the server using constraints, triggers, and so on. Choose the best isolation level depending upon how important perfection is. That's because, as noted in the section "Isolation Levels," the default of READ UNCOMMITTED is flawed, because for some amount of time (hopefully milliseconds), it leaves open the possibility that one user can change data on which your transaction is dependent. For the most part, it's considered appropriate to use the default, as it greatly enhances concurrency, and the probability of someone modifying data that your transaction is reliant on is close to the chances of being hit by lightning on ten sunny days in a row. It could happen, but it's a slim chance.

Thinking back to the normal progression of events when a user works in an application, the user fetches data, modifies data, and finally commits data to the database. There can easily be a long interval between fetching the data and committing the changes to the database. In fact, it's also possible that other users could have also fetched and modified the data during the same period of time. Because of this, you need to implement some method to make sure that the data that the client originally fetched matches the data that's stored in the database. Otherwise, the new changes could trample important changes made by another user.

So, instead of locking the data by using SQL Server locks, simply employ one of the following schemes to leave data unlocked after it has been fetched to the client. Later, after the user makes desired changes and goes back to update the data, one of the following schemes is employed:

- *Unchecked*: Just let it happen. If two users modify the same row in the database, then the last user wins. It's not the best idea, as the first user might have had something important to say, and this method rejects the first user's changes. I won't cover this any further because it's straightforward. Note that many systems use no locking mechanism at all and just let clashes happen, and their users are as happy as they can be. Such an approach is never what I suggest for controlling your important data resources, but so far, I have not been elected data emperor, just data architect.

- *Row-based*: Protect your data at the row level, by checking to see if the rows being modified are the same as in the table. If not, refresh the data from the table, showing the user what was changed. When optimistic locking is implemented, this is by far the most common method used.

- *Logical unit of work*: A logical unit of work is used to group a parent record with all its child data to allow a single optimistic lock to cover multiple tables. For example, you'd group an invoice and the line items for that invoice. Treat modifications to the line items the same way as a modification to the invoice, for locking purposes.

Although it isn't typically a good idea to ignore the problem of users overwriting one another altogether, this is a commonly *decided* upon method for some companies. On the other hand, the best plan is optimally a mixture of the row-based solution for most tables, and a logical unit of work for major groups of tables that make up some common object. If you remember back to Chapter 6, the reasons for using a logical-unit-of-work solution mirror the reasons to use cascading operations between two tables. If multiple tables compose a larger entity, such as an invoice and line items, then it might make sense to implement this method. However, any situation that can use a row-based solution is fine. It's completely based upon what you desire, as the architect.

Before discussing the details of how to modify our data, let's briefly discuss details of the isolation level for retrieving and modifying data. I mentioned earlier that using the SNAPSHOT isolation level gives us "lock-free" operations that won't block other users. This makes it perfect for optimistic locking situations, because we expect that no two users will want to modify the same rows, but they often might want to look at the same rows. For this reason, I suggest using the following:

- SNAPSHOT *isolation level*: Use for all retrieval operations where no data is going to be modified; for example, when you want to fetch a row or set of rows to possibly modify. This includes reporting, editors (especially when you're going to use ADO disconnected recordsets), and so on.

- READ COMMITTED *isolation level*: Use for update operations, as it's the best balance of safe operations and performance.

- *Higher isolation levels*: Use as needed when the situation merits.

An important point about optimistic locking is that it isn't enforced by the database, and must be coded into every query that's executed against the tables. If the user has a row with an older optimistic lock value, SQL Server won't deny access to the data. It's all up to the programmers to follow the rules that the database architect lays down.

In the following sections, I'll cover row-based locking and the logical unit of work. The unchecked method ignores the concern that two people might modify the same row twice, so there's no coding (or thinking!) required.

# Row-Based Locking

You must implement a row-based scheme to check on a row-by-row basis whether or not the data that the user has retrieved is still the same as the one that's in the database. The order of events now is fetch data, modify data, check to see that the row (or rows) of data are still the same as they were, and then commit the changes.

There are three common methods to implement row-based optimistic locking:

- *Check all columns in the table*: If you cannot modify the table structure, which the next two methods require, you can check to make sure that all the data you had fetched is still the same, and then modify the data. This method is the most difficult, because any procedure you write must contain parameters for the previous values of the data, which isn't a good idea. Checking all columns is useful when building bound data-grid types of applications, where there are direct updates to tables, especially if not all tables can follow the rather strict rules of the next two methods.

- *Add a date and time column to the table*: Set the datetime value when the table is inserted and subsequently updated. Every procedure for modifying or deleting data from the table needs a column for the previous value of the timestamp. Every update to the table is required to modify the value in the table to set the updateDatetime column. Generally, it's best to use a trigger for keeping the datetime column up to date, and often it's nice to include a column to tell which user last modified the data (you need someone to blame!). Later in this section, I'll demonstrate a simple INSTEAD OF trigger to support this approach.

- *Use a* rowversion *column*: In the previous method, you used a manually controlled value to manage the optimistic lock value. This method uses column with a rowversion datatype. The rowversion datatype automatically gets a new value for every command used to modify a given row in a table.

The next two sections cover adding the optimistic lock columns to your tables, and then using them in your code.

## Adding Optimistic Lock Columns

In this section, we'll add an optimistic lock column to a table to support either adding the datetime column or the rowversion column. The first method mentioned, checking all columns, needs no table modifications.

As an example, let's create a new simple table, in this case hr.person (again, use any database you like; the sample again uses tempdb). Here's the structure:

```
CREATE SCHEMA hr
CREATE TABLE hr.person
(
    personId int IDENTITY(1,1) CONSTRAINT PKperson primary key,
    firstName varchar(60) NOT NULL,
    middleName varchar(60) NOT NULL,
    lastName varchar(60) NOT NULL,

    dateOfBirth date NOT NULL,
    rowLastModifyTime datetime NOT NULL
        CONSTRAINT DFLTperson_rowLastModifyTime default getdate(),
    rowModifiedByUserIdentifier nvarchar(128) NOT NULL
        CONSTRAINT DFLTperson_rowModifiedByUserIdentifier default suser_sname()

)
```

Note the two columns for our optimistic lock, named rowLastModifyTime and rowModifiedByUserIdentifier. I'll use these to hold the last date and time of modification, and the SQL Server's login name of the principal that changed the row. There are a couple ways to implement this:

- *Let the manipulation layer manage the value like any other column*: This is often what client programmers like to do, and it's acceptable, as long as you're using trusted computers to manage the timestamps. I feel it's inadvisable to allow workstations to set such values, as it can cause confusing results. For example, say your application displays a message stating that another user has made changes, and the time the changes were made is in the future, based on the client's computer. Then the user checks out his or her PC clock, and it's set perfectly.

- *Using SQL Server code*: For the most part, triggers are implemented to fire on any modification to data.

As an example of using SQL Server code (my general method of doing this), I'll implement an INSTEAD OF trigger on the update of the hr.person table (note that the errorLog$insert procedure was created back in Chapter 6, and has been commented out for this demonstration in case you don't have it available):

```
CREATE TRIGGER hr.person$InsteadOfUpdate
ON hr.person
INSTEAD OF UPDATE AS
BEGIN

    --stores the number of rows affected
    DECLARE @rowsAffected int = @@rowcount,
            @msg varchar(2000) = ''    --used to hold the error message

    --no need to continue on if no rows affected
    IF @rowsAffected = 0 return

    SET NOCOUNT ON --to avoid the rowcount messages
    SET ROWCOUNT 0 --in case the client has modified the rowcount

    BEGIN TRY
            --[validation blocks]
            --[modification blocks]
            --remember to update ALL columns when building instead of triggers
            UPDATE hr.person
            SET    firstName = inserted.firstName,
                   middleName = inserted.middleName,
                   lastName = inserted.lastName,
                   dateOfBirth = inserted.dateOfBirth,
                   rowLastModifyTime = default, -- set the value to the default
                   rowModifiedByUserIdentifier = default
            FROM   hr.person
                      JOIN inserted
                          on hr.person.personId = inserted.personId
    END TRY
    BEGIN CATCH
            IF @@trancount > 0
               ROLLBACK TRANSACTION

            --EXECUTE dbo.errorLog$insert
```

```
          DECLARE @ERROR_MESSAGE varchar(8000)
          SET @ERROR_MESSAGE = ERROR_MESSAGE()
          RAISERROR (@ERROR_MESSAGE,16,1)

      END CATCH
END
```

Then insert a row into the table:

```
INSERT INTO hr.person (firstName, middleName, lastName, dateOfBirth)
VALUES ('Paige','O','Anxtent','19391212')

SELECT *
FROM   hr.person
```

Now you can see that the data has been created:

| personId | firstName | middleName | lastName | dateOfBirth |
|----------|-----------|------------|----------|-------------|
| 1 | Paige | O | Anxtent | 1939-**12**-12 |

| rowLastModifyTime | rowModifiedByUserIdentifier |
|-------------------|------------------------------|
| 2008-**07**-30 01:**26**:10.780 | **<username>** |

Now update the row:

```
UPDATE hr.person
SET    middleName = 'Ona'
WHERE  personId = 1

SELECT rowLastModifyTime
FROM   hr.person
```

You should see that the update date has changed (in my case, it was pretty doggone late at night, but such is the life):

```
rowLastModifyTime
-----------------------
2008-07-30 01:28:28.397
```

If you want to set the value on insert, or implement rowCreatedByDate or userIdentifier columns, the code would be similar. Because this has been implemented in an INSTEAD OF trigger, the user or even the programmer cannot overwrite the values, even if they include it in the column list of an INSERT.

As previously mentioned, the other method that requires table modification is to use a rowversion column. In my opinion, this is the best way to go, and I almost always use a rowversion. I usually have the row modification columns on there as well, for the user's benefit. I find that the modification columns take on other uses and have a tendency to migrate to the control of the application developer, and rowversion columns never do. Plus, even if the triggers don't make it on the table for one reason or another, the rowversion column continues to work. Sometimes you may be prohibited from using INSTEAD OF insert triggers for some reason (recently I couldn't use them in a project I worked on because they invalidate the identity functions).

Let's add a `rowversion` column to our table to demonstrate using it as an optimistic lock:

```
ALTER TABLE hr.person
  ADD rowversion rowversion
GO
SELECT personId, rowversion
FROM   hr.person
```

You can see now that the `rowversion` has been added and magically updated:

```
personId    rowversion
----------- ------------------
1           0x00000000000007D1
```

Now, when the row gets updated, the `rowversion` is modified:

```
UPDATE  hr.person
SET     firstName = 'Paige' --no actual change occurs
WHERE   personId = 1
```

Then, looking at the output, you can see that the value of the `rowversion` has changed:

```
SELECT personId, rowversion
FROM   hr.person
```

This returns the following result:

```
personId    rowversion
----------- ------------------
1           0x00000000000007D2
```

## Coding for Row-Level Optimistic Locking

Next, include the checking code in your stored procedure. Using the `hr.person` table previously created, the following code snippets will demonstrate each of the methods (note that I'll only use the optimistic locking columns germane to each example, and not include the others).

Check all the cached values for the columns:

```
UPDATE  hr.person
SET     firstName = 'Headley'
WHERE   personId = 1  --include the key
  and   firstName = 'Paige'
```

```
and    middleName = 'ona'
and    lastName = 'Anxtent'
and    dateOfBirth = '19391212'
```

Note that it's a good practice to check your rowcount after an update with an optimistic lock to see how many rows have changed. If it is 0, you could check to see if the row exists with that primary key:

```
IF EXISTS ( SELECT *
            FROM   hr.person
            WHERE  personId = 1) --check for existence of the primary key
  --raise an error stating that the row no longer exists
ELSE
  --raise an error stating that another user has changed the row
```

Use a date column:

```
UPDATE  hr.person
SET     firstName = 'Fred'
WHERE   personId = 1  --include the key
  and   rowLastModifyTime = '2005-07-30 00:28:28.397'
```

Use a rowversion column:

```
UPDATE  hr.person
SET     firstName = 'Fred'
WHERE   personId = 1
  and   rowversion = 0x00000000000007D3
```

Which is better performance-wise? Either of these generally performs just as well as the other, because in all cases you're going to be using the primary key to do the bulk of the work fetching the row and then your update. There's a bit less overhead with the last two columns because you don't have to pass as much data into the statement, but that difference is negligible.

Deletions use the same WHERE clause, because if another user has modified the row, it's probably a good idea to see if that user's changes make the row still valuable.

If you want to delete the row, you'd use the same WHERE clause:

```
DELETE FROM hr.person
WHERE   personId = 1
  And   rowversion = 0x00000000000007D3
```

I typically prefer using a rowversion column because it requires the least amount of work to always work perfectly. On the other hand, many client programmers prefer to have the manipulation layer of the application set a datetime value, largely because the datetime value has meaning to them to let them see when the row was last updated. Truthfully, I too like keeping these automatically modifying values in the table for diagnostic purposes. However, I prefer to rely on the rowversion column for locking because it is far simpler and safer and cannot be overridden by any code, no matter how you implement the other columns.

## Logical Unit of Work

Although row-based optimistic locks are helpful, they do have a slight downfall. In many cases, several tables together make one "object." A good example is an invoice and line items. The idea behind a logical unit of work is that instead of having a row-based lock on the invoice and all the line items, you might only implement one on the invoice, and use the same value for the line items. This does require that the user always fetch not only the invoice line items, but at least the invoice's timestamp into the client's cache when dealing with the invoice line items. Assuming you're using a rowversion column, I'd just use the same kind of logic as previously used on the hr.person table. In this example, we'll build the procedure to do the modifications.

When the user wants to insert, update, or delete line items for the invoice, the procedure requires the @objectVersion parameter, and checks the value against the invoice, prior to update. Consider that there are two tables, minimally defined as follows:

```
CREATE SCHEMA invoicing
go
--leaving off who invoice is for
CREATE TABLE invoicing.invoice
(
    invoiceId int IDENTITY(1,1),
    number varchar(20) NOT NULL,
    objectVersion rowversion not null,
    constraint PKinvoicing_invoice primary key (invoiceId)
)
--also forgetting what product that the line item is for
CREATE TABLE invoicing.invoiceLineItem

(
    invoiceLineItemId int NOT NULL,
    invoiceId int NULL,
    itemCount int NOT NULL,
    cost int NOT NULL,
     constraint PKinvoicing_invoiceLineItem primary key (invoiceLineItemId),
     constraint FKinvoicing_invoiceLineItem$references$invoicing_invoice
          foreign key (invoiceId) references invoicing.invoice(invoiceId)
)
```

For our delete procedure for the invoice line item, the parameters would have the key of the invoice and the line item, plus the rowversion value:

```
CREATE PROCEDURE invoiceLineItem$del
(
    @invoiceId int, --we pass this because the client should have it
                    --with the invoiceLineItem row
    @invoiceLineItemId int,
    @objectVersion rowversion
) as
  BEGIN
    --gives us a unique savepoint name, trim it to 125
    --characters if the user named it really large
    DECLARE @savepoint nvarchar(128) =
                        cast(object_name(@@procid) AS nvarchar(125)) +
                                    cast(@@nestlevel AS nvarchar(3))
    --get initial entry level, so we can do a rollback on a doomed transaction
    DECLARE @entryTrancount int = @@trancount

    BEGIN TRY
        BEGIN TRANSACTION
        SAVE TRANSACTION @savepoint

        UPDATE  invoice
        SET     number = number
        WHERE   invoiceId = @invoiceId
          And   objectVersion = @objectVersion
```

```
        DELETE  invoiceLineItem
        FROM    invoiceLineItem
        WHERE   invoiceLineItemId = @invoiceLineItemId

        COMMIT TRANSACTION

    END TRY
    BEGIN CATCH

        --if the tran is doomed, and the entryTrancount was 0,
        --we have to roll back
        IF xact_state()= -1 and @entryTrancount = 0
            roll back transaction
        --otherwise, we can still save the other activities in the
        --transaction.
        ELSE IF xact_state() = 1 --transaction not doomed, but open
          BEGIN
                ROLLBACK TRANSACTION @savepoint
                COMMIT TRANSACTION
          END

    DECLARE @ERRORmessage nvarchar(4000)
    SET @ERRORmessage = 'Error occurred in procedure ''' +
            object_name(@@procid) + ''', Original Message: '''
            + ERROR_MESSAGE() + ''''
    RAISERROR (@ERRORmessage,16,1)
    RETURN -100

    END CATCH
END
```

Instead of checking the rowversion on an invoiceLineItem row, we check the rowversion (in the objectVersion column) on the invoice table. Additionally, we must update the rowversion value on the invoice table when we make our change, so we update the invoice row, simply setting a single column to the same value. There's a bit more overhead when working this way, but it's normal to update multiple rows at a time from the client. You'd probably want to architect your solution with multiple procedures, one to update and check the optimistic lock, and then others to do the insert, update, and delete operations.

---

■**Tip** Using Table Parameters, you could build a single procedure that accepted a list of id values as parameters that included rowversion values quite easily. This would be yet another way to implement proper optimistic locking on a group of rows.

---

# Best Practices

The number-one issue when it comes to concurrency is data quality. Maintaining consistent data is why you go through the work of building a database in the first place. Generally speaking, if the only way to get consistent results was to have every call single threaded, it would be worth it. Of course, we don't have to do that except in rare situations, and SQL Server gives us tools to make it happen with the isolation levels. Use them as needed. It's the data that matters:

- *Use transactions as liberally as needed*: It's important to protect your data, 100 percent of the time. Each time data is modified, it isn't a bad practice to enclose the operation in a transaction. This gives you a chance to check status, number of rows modified, and so on, and if necessary, roll back the modification.

- *Keep transactions as short as possible*: The smaller the transaction, the less chance there is of it holding locks. Try not to declare variables, create temporary tables, and so on inside a transaction unless it's necessary. Make sure that all table access within transactions is required to be executed as an atomic operation.

- *Recognize the difference between hardware limitations and SQL Server concurrency issues*: If the hardware is maxed out (excessive disk queuing, 90-percent–plus CPU usage, and so on), consider adding more hardware. However, if you're single-threading calls through your database due to locking issues, you could add 20 processors and a terabyte of RAM and still see little improvement.

- *Fetch all rows from a query as fast as possible*: Depending on the isolation level and editability of the rows being returned, locks held can interfere with other users' ability to modify or even read rows.

- *Make sure that all queries use reasonable execution plans*: The better all queries execute, the faster the queries will execute, and it follows that more code can be executed.

- *Use some form of optimistic locking mechanism*: Do optimistic locking, preferably using a rowversion column, as it requires the smallest amount of coding, and is managed entirely by SQL Server. The only code that's required when programming is to validate the value in the rowversion column.

- *Consider using some form of the* SNAPSHOT *isolation level:* Either code all your optimistic-locked retrieval operations with SET SNAPSHOT ISOLATION LEVEL, or change the database setting for READ_COMMITTED_SNAPSHOT to ON. This alters how the READ COMMITTED isolation level reads snapshot information at the statement level. Be careful to test existing applications if you're going to make this change, because these settings do alter how SQL Server works, and might negatively alter how your programs work. I suggest using full SNAPSHOT isolation level for read-only operations anyhow, if it's reasonable for you to do so.

# Summary

Concurrency is an important topic, and also a difficult one. It seems easy enough: keep the amount of time a user needs to be in the database to a minimum; have adequate resources on your machine.

The fact is, concurrency is a juggling act for SQL Server, Windows, the disk system, the CPUs, and so on. If you have reasonable hardware for your situation, use the SNAPSHOT isolation level for retrieval and READ COMMITTED for other calls, and you should have no trouble with large-scale blocking on your server. This sounds perfect, but the greater the number of users, the more difficult a time you'll have making things perform the way you want. Concurrency is one of the fun jobs for a DBA, because it's truly a science that has a good deal of artsy qualities. You can predict only so much about how your user will use the system, and then experience comes in to tune queries, tune hardware, and tweak settings until you have it right.

I discussed some of the basics of how SQL Server implements controls to support concurrent programming, such that many users can be supported using the same data with locks and transactions. Then I covered isolation levels, which allow you to tweak the kinds of locks taken and how long they're held on a resource. The most important part of the chapter was the part on optimistic locking. As the trend for implementing systems is to use cached data sets, modify that set, and then flush it back, you must make sure that other users haven't made changes to the data while it's cached.

■■■

# Considering Data Access Strategies

*Arguments are to be avoided; they are always vulgar and often convincing.*

—Oscar Wilde

**A**t this point in the process of covering the topic of database design, we have designed and implemented the database, devised effective security and indexing strategies, and taken care of all of the other bits and pieces that go along with these tasks. The next logical step is to decide on the data-access strategy and how best to implement and distribute data-centric business logic (of course, in reality, design is not really a linear process, as performance tuning and indexing require a test plan, and this usually requires that some form of UI has been created to get an idea of how the data is going to be accessed).

Regardless of whether your application is a traditional client-server application or a multitier web application, data must be stored in and retrieved from tables. Therefore, most of the advice presented in this chapter will be relevant regardless of the type of application you're building. One way or another, you are going to have to build some interface between the data and the applications that use them.

The really good arguments tend to get started about the topics in this chapter. Take every squabble to decide whether or not to use surrogate keys as primary keys, add to it all of the discussions about whether or not to use triggers in the application, and then multiply that by the number of managers it takes to screw in a light bulb, which I calculate as about 3.5. That is about how many times I have argued with a system implementer to decide whether stored procedures were a good idea.

---

■**Note** The number of managers required to screw in a light bulb, depending on the size of the organization, would generally be a minimum of three or four: one manager to manage the person who notices the burnt out bulb, the manager of building services, and the shift manager of the person who actually changes light bulbs. Sometimes, the manager of the two managers might have to get involved to actually make things happen, so figure about three and a half.

---

I will present my opinions on how to use stored procedures, *ad hoc* SQL, and the CLR. Each of these opinions is based on 15 years of experience working with SQL Server technologies, but I am not so set in my ways that I cannot see the point of the people on the other side of any fence—anyone whose mind cannot be changed is no longer learning. I made up my mind at a young age that I would keep my mind open, even when it comes to firmly held religious beliefs. If your beliefs cannot come under scrutiny, you believe in something that is dangerous. So if you disagree with this chapter, flame away; you won't hurt my feelings.

In this chapter, I'll tackle the question of how to code the data-access part of the system. I am going to discuss the following topics:

- *Using ad hoc SQL*: Formulating queries in the application's presentation and manipulation layer (typically functional code stored in objects, such as .NET or Java, and run on a server or a client machine).

- *Using stored procedures*: Creating an interface between the presentation/manipulation layer and the data layer of the application. Note that views and functions, as well as procedures, also form part of this data-access interface. You can use all three of these object types.

- *Using CLR in T-SQL:* In this section, I will present some basic opinions on the usage of the CLR within the realm of T-SQL.

Each section will analyze some of the pros and cons of each approach, in terms of flexibility, security, performance, and so on. Along the way, I'll offer some personal opinions on optimal architecture and give advice on how best to implement both types of access. Bear in mind that a lot of this is just my personal opinion.

I should note that the first two of these, *ad hoc* SQL and stored procedures, have been locked in mortal combat for years to determine which is the best. Clearly, that topic is a polarizing one, and discussing it has been the cause of many a programmer-versus-DBA 15-round cage match, where neither side comes out a winner. Toss in some CLR contentions into the mix, and it's likely that some of you will disagree with my advice, which is totally expected; we can't all be right.

---

■**Note** You may also be thinking that another thing I might discuss is object-relational mapping tools, like Hibernate, Spring, or even the ADO.NET Entity Framework. In the end, however, these tools are really using *ad hoc* access, in that they are generating SQL on the fly. For the sake of this book, they should be lumped into the *ad hoc* group, unless they are used with stored procedures (which is pretty rare).

---

My personal feeling is that the real arguments are not so much about right and wrong, but rather it turns into a question of which method is easier to program and maintain. SQL Server and Visual Studio .NET give you lots of handy dandy tools to build your applications, mapping objects to data, and with 2008, this becomes even truer with the ADO.NET Entity Framework and with new techniques like LINQ sounding more and more exciting.

The problem is that these tools don't always take enough advantage of SQL Server's best practices to build applications. Doing things in a best practice manner would mean doing a lot of coding manually, without the ease of tools to help you. Some organizations do this manual work with great results, but such work is rarely going to be popular with developers who have never hit the wall of having to support an application that is extremely hard to optimize once the system is in production.

A point that I really should make clear is that I feel that the choice of data-access strategy shouldn't really be linked to the methods used for data validation, nor should it be linked to whether you use (or how much you use) check constraints, triggers, and suchlike. I feel that you should do every possible data validation on the SQL Server data that can be done without making a maintenance nightmare. As mentioned throughout the book, fundamental data rules that are cast in stone should be done on the database server in constraints and triggers at all times, so that these rules can be trusted by the user (for example, an ETL process). On the other hand, procedures or client code may be used to enforce mutable business rules to some level, but in either situation, the rule can be circumvented by using a different access path.

My experience is different from yours, and often it's different from that of other people whose opinions I look to for advice about architecture. I wish there were an easy, straightforward answer for all situations, but it's impossible to be that rigid, even when working for a small company where you're the only architect. Everyone who has any experience building data-oriented systems will likely have some strong opinions on what's right, but as a consultant, I always have to be flexible and ready to work with anything, even situations that I might find abhorrent.

# Ad Hoc SQL

*Ad hoc* SQL is sometimes referred to as "straight SQL" and generally refers to the formulation of SELECT, INSERT, UPDATE, and DELETE statements (as well as any others) in the client. These statements are then sent to SQL Server either individually or in batches of multiple statements to be syntax checked, compiled, optimized (producing a plan), and executed.

SQL Server may use a cached plan from a previous execution, but it will have to match the text of one call to another to do so.

I will make no distinction between *ad hoc* calls that are generated manually and those that use a middleware setup like LINQ: from SQL Server's standpoint, a string of characters is sent to the server and interpreted at runtime. So whether your method of generating these statements is good or poor is of no concern to me in *this* discussion, as long as the SQL generated is well formed and protected from users' malicious actions (for example, injection attacks are generally the biggest offender). The reason I don't care where the *ad hoc* statements come from is that the advantages and disadvantages for the database support professionals are pretty much the same, and in fact, statements generated from a middleware tool can be worse, because you may not be able to change the format or makeup of the statements, leaving you with no easy way to tune statements, even if you can modify the source code.

Sending queries as strings of text is the way that most tools tend to converse with SQL Server, and is, for example, how SQL Server Management Studio does all of its interaction with the server metadata. (If you have never used Profiler to watch the SQL that Management Studio uses, you should; just don't use it as your guide for building your OLTP system. It is, however, a good way to learn where some bits of metadata that you can't figure out come from.) There's no question that users will perform some *ad hoc* queries against your system, especially when you simply want to write a query and execute it just once. However, the more pertinent question is: should you be using *ad hoc* SQL when building the permanent interface to an OLTP system's data?

---

■**Note** This topic doesn't include *ad hoc* SQL statements executed from stored procedures (commonly called dynamic SQL), which I'll discuss in the section "Stored Procedures."

---

## Advantages

Using uncompiled *ad hoc* SQL has some advantages over building compiled stored procedures:

- *Runtime control over queries*: Queries are built at runtime, without having to know every possible query that might be executed. This can lead to better performance as queries can be formed at runtime; you can retrieve only necessary data for SELECT queries or modify data that's changed for UPDATE operations.

- *Flexibility over Shared Plans and Parameterization*: Because you have control over the queries, you can more easily build queries at runtime that use the same plans, and even can be parameterized as desired, based on the situation. versions of SQL Server before 7.0, shared plans and parameterization would have been major downfalls of *ad hoc* SQL.

### Runtime Control Over Queries

Unlike stored procedures, which are prebuilt and stored in the SQL Server system tables, *ad hoc* SQL is formed at the time it's needed: at runtime. Hence, it doesn't suffer from some of the inflexible requirements of stored procedures. For example, say you want to build a user interface to a list of customers. You can add several columns to the SELECT clause, based on the tables listed in the FROM clause. It's simple to build a list of columns into the user interface that the user can use to customize his or her own list. Then the program can issue the list request with only the columns in the SELECT list that are requested by the user. Because some columns might be large and contain quite a bit of data, it's better to send back only the columns that the user really desires instead of a bunch of columns the user doesn't care about.

For instance, consider that you have the following table to document contacts to prospective customers (it's barebones for this example). In each query, you might return the primary key but show or not show it to the user based on whether the primary key is implemented as a surrogate or natural key (it isn't important to our example either way). You can create this table in any database you like. (In the sample code, I've created a database named architectureChapter):

```
CREATE SCHEMA sales
GO
CREATE TABLE sales.contact
(
    contactId   int CONSTRAINT PKsales_contact PRIMARY KEY,
    firstName   varchar(30),
    lastName    varchar(30),
    companyName varchar(100),
    salesLevelId  int, --real table would implement as a foreign key
    contactNotes  varchar(max),
    personalNotes varchar(max),
    CONSTRAINT AKsales_contact UNIQUE (firstName, lastName, companyName)
)
```

One user might want to see the person's name and the company, plus the end of the contact-Notes, in his or her view of the data:

```
SELECT  contactId, firstName, lastName, companyName, salesLevelId,
            right(contactNotes,500) as notesEnd
FROM    sales.contact
```

Another user might want (or need) to see less:

```
SELECT contactId, firstName, lastName, companyName
FROM sales.contact
```

Allowing the user to choose the columns for output can be useful. Consider how the file-listing dialog works in Windows, as shown in Figure 11-1.

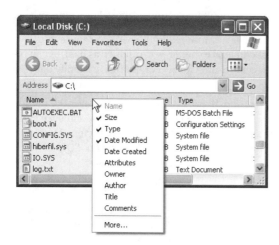

**Figure 11-1.** *The Windows file-listing dialog*

You can see as many or as few of the attributes of a file in the list as you like, based on some metadata you set on the directory. This is a useful method of letting the users choose what they want to see. Let's take this one step further. Consider that the contact table is then related to a table that tells us if a contact has purchased something:

```
CREATE TABLE sales.purchase
(
    purchaseId int CONSTRAINT PKsales_purchase PRIMARY KEY,
    amount        numeric(10,2),
    purchaseDate datetime,
    contactId    int
        CONSTRAINT FKsales_contact$hasPurchasesIn$sales_purchase
            REFERENCES sales.contact(contactId)
)
```

Now consider that you want to calculate the sales totals and dates for the contact and add these columns to the allowed pool of choices. By tailoring the output when transmitting the results of the query back to the user, you can save bandwidth, CPU, and disk I/O. As I've stressed, values such as this should usually be calculated rather than stored, especially when working on an OLTP system.

In this case, consider the following two possibilities. If the user asks for a sales summary column, then the client will send the whole query:

```
SELECT  contact.contactId, contact.firstName, contact.lastName,
                sales.yearToDateSales, sales.lastSaleDate
FROM    sales.contact as contact
            LEFT OUTER JOIN
                (SELECT contactId,
                        SUM(amount) AS yearToDateSales,
                        MAX(purchaseDate) AS lastSaleDate
                FROM    sales.purchase
                WHERE   purchaseDate >= --the first day of the current year
                            cast(datepart(year,getdate()) as char(4)) + '0101'
                GROUP  by contactId) AS sales
                ON contact.contactId = sales.contactId
WHERE    contact.lastName like 'Johns%'
```

If the user doesn't ask for a sales summary column, the client will send only the bolded query:

```
SELECT  contact.contactId, contact.firstName, contact.lastName
                --,sales.yearToDateSales, sales.lastSaleDate
FROM    sales.contact as contact
--            LEFT OUTER JOIN
--                (SELECT contactId,
--                        SUM(amount) AS yearToDateSales,
--                        MAX(purchaseDate) AS lastSaleDate
--                FROM    sales.purchase
--                WHERE   purchaseDate >= --the first day of the current year
--                            cast(datepart(year,getdate()) as char(4)) + '0101'
--                GROUP  by contactId) AS sales
--                ON contact.contactId = sales.contactId
WHERE    contact.lastName like 'Johns%'
```

In this way, you have the flexibility to execute only the code that's needed.

■**Note**  Conversely, you will find it hard to vary the columns, especially the INSERT and UPDATE lists, in your stored procedure code without resorting to implementing *ad hoc* calls in your procedures, which has its own set of issues, particularly doing this kind of selective join criteria based on user input.

In the same vein, when using *ad hoc* calls, it's trivial (from a SQL standpoint) to build UPDATE statements that include only the columns that have *changed* in the set lists, rather than updating all columns, as can be necessary for a stored procedure. For example, take the customer columns from earlier: customerId, name, and number. You could just update all columns:

```
UPDATE sales.contact
SET    firstName = 'First Name',
       lastName = 'Last Name',
       salesLevelId = 1,
       companyName = 'Company Name',
       contactNotes = 'Notes about the contact',
       personalNotes = 'Notes about the person'
WHERE contactId = 1
```

But what if only the firstName column changed? What if the company column is part of an index, and it has data validations that take three seconds to execute? How do you deal with varchar(max) columns (or other long types)? The notes columns could contain 3MB each. Execution could take far more time than is desirable if the application passes the entire value back and forth each time. Using straight SQL, to update the firstName column only, you can simply execute the following code:

```
UPDATE sales.contact
SET    firstName = 'First Name'
WHERE  contactId = 1
```

Some of this can be done with dynamic SQL calls built into the stored procedure, but it's far easier to know if data changed right at the source where the data is being edited, rather than having to check the data beforehand. For example, you could have every data-bound control implement a "data changed" property, and perform a column update only when the original value doesn't match the value currently displayed. In a stored-procedure-only architecture, having multiple update procedures is not necessarily out of the question, particularly when it is very costly to modify a given column.

One place where using *ad hoc* SQL can produce more reasonable code is in the area of optional parameters. Say that, in your query to the sales.contact table, your UI allowed you to filter on either firstName, lastName, or both. For example, take the following code to filter on both firstName and lastName:

```
SELECT firstName, lastName, companyName
FROM    sales.contact
WHERE   firstName like 'firstNameValue%'
  AND   lastName like 'lastNamevalue%'
```

What if the user only needed to filter by last name? Sending the '%' wildcard for firstName can cause code to perform less than adequately, especially when the query is parameterized. (I'll cover query parameterization in the next section, "Performance.")

```
SELECT firstName, lastName, companyName
FROM    sales.contact
WHERE   firstName like '%'
  AND   lastName like 'lastNamevalue%'
```

This query would be fine if an index was on lastName, firstName, but if it was firstName, lastName, the index would be more or less useless for the query. You could have two indexes, but what happens when this is reality and there are 10–20 different criteria that the client "needs" to filter by? Using *ad hoc* SQL, you can simply change the code to the following:

```
SELECT firstName, lastName, companyName
FROM   sales.contact
WHERE  lastName like 'lastNamevalue%'
```

This doesn't require any difficult coding. Just remove one of the criteria from the WHERE clause, and the optimizer needn't consider the other. Now it can choose what index to use. What if you want to OR the criteria instead? Simply build the query with OR instead of AND. This kind of flexibility is one of the biggest positives to using *ad hoc* SQL calls.

---

■**Note** The ability to change the statement programmatically does sort of play to the downside of any dynamically built statement, as now, with just two parameters, we have three possible variants of the statement to be used, so we have to consider performance for all three when we are building our test cases.

---

For a stored procedure, you might need to write code such as the following:

```
IF @firstNameValue <> '%'
        SELECT firstName, lastName, companyName
        FROM   sales.contact
        WHERE  firstName like @firstNameValue
          AND  lastName like @lastNameValue
ELSE
        SELECT firstName, lastName, companyName
        FROM   sales.contact
        WHERE  lastName like @lastNameValue
```

Or you can do something along these lines in your WHERE clause:

```
WHERE  Firstname like isnull(nullif(ltrim(@FirstNamevalue) +'%','%'),Firstname)
  and  Lastname like isnull(nullif(ltrim(@LastNamevalue) +'%','%'),Lastname)
```

Unfortunately though, this often does not optimize very well—leading to the need for the branching solution mentioned previously. A better way to do this with stored procedures might be to create two stored procedures—one with the first query and another with the second query—especially if you are needing extremely high performance access to the data. You'd change this to the following code:

```
IF @firstNameValue <> '%'
        EXECUTE sales.contact$get @firstNameValue, @lastNameValue
ELSE
        EXECUTE sales.contact$getLastOnly @lastNameValue
```

You can do some of this kind of *ad hoc* SQL writing using dynamic SQL in stored procedures. However, you might have to do a good bit of these sorts of IF blocks to arrive at which parameters aren't applicable in various datatypes. Because you know which parameters are applicable, due to knowing what the user filled in, it can be far easier to handle this situation using *ad hoc* SQL. Getting this kind of flexibility is the main reason that I use an *ad hoc* SQL call in an application (usually embedded in a stored procedure): you can omit parts of queries that don't make sense in some cases, and it's easier to avoid executing unnecessary code.

## Flexibility over Shared Plans and Parameterization

Queries formed at runtime, using proper techniques, can actually be better for performance in many ways than using stored procedures. Because you have control over the queries, you can more easily build queries at runtime that use the same plans, and even can be parameterized as desired, based on the situation. In earlier versions of SQL Server, shared plans and parameterization would have been major downfalls of *ad hoc* SQL.

This is not to say that it is the most favorable way of implementing (if you want to know the whole picture you have to read the whole section on *ad hoc* and stored procedures). However, the fact is that *ad hoc* access tends to get a bad reputation as being bad for something that Microsoft fixed several versions back. In the following sections:

- Shared Execution Plans
- Parameterization

I will take a look at the good points and the caveats you will deal with when building *ad hoc* queries and executing them on the server.

### Shared Execution Plans

The age-old reason that people used stored procedures was that the query processor cached their plans. Every time you executed a procedure, you didn't have to decide the best way to execute the query. As of SQL Server 7.0, cached plans were extended to include *ad hoc* SQL. However, the standard for what can be cached is pretty strict. For two calls to the server to use the same plan, the statements that are sent must be identical, except possibly for the scalar values in search arguments. Identical means identical; add a comment, change the case, or even add a space character, and the plan is blown. SQL Server can build query plans that have parameters, which allow plan reuse by subsequent calls. However, overall, stored procedures are better when it comes to using cached plans for performance, primarily because the matching and parameterization are easier for the optimizer to do, since it can be done by object_id, rather than having to match larger blobs of text.

A fairly major caveat is that for *ad hoc* queries to use the same plan, they must be exactly the same, other than any values that can be parameterized (which I will demonstrate in the next section). For example, consider the following two queries (using AdventureWorks2008 tables for this example, as that database has a nice amount of data to work with):

```
SELECT  address.AddressLine1, address.AddressLine2,
        address.City, state.StateProvinceCode, address.PostalCode
FROM    Person.Address as address
          join Person.StateProvince as state
                on address.stateProvinceId = state.stateProvinceId
WHERE   address.AddressLine1 = '1, rue Pierre-Demoulin'
```

Next, run the following query. See whether you can spot the difference between the two queries.

```
SELECT  address.AddressLine1, address.AddressLine2,
        address.City, state.StateProvinceCode, address.PostalCode
FROM    Person.Address AS address
          join Person.StateProvince AS state
                on address.stateProvinceId = state.stateProvinceId
WHERE   address.AddressLine1 = '1, rue Pierre-Demoulin'
```

These queries can't share plans because the AS in the first query is lowercase, but in the second, it's uppercase. Using the sys.dm_exec_query_stats dynamic management view, you can see that the case difference does cause two plans by running:

```
SELECT *
FROM   (SELECT execution_count,
            SUBSTRING(st.text, (qs.statement_start_offset/2)+1,
                ((CASE qs.statement_end_offset
                  WHEN -1 THEN DATALENGTH(st.text)
                  ELSE qs.statement_end_offset
                  END - qs.statement_start_offset)/2) + 1) AS statement_text
        FROM sys.dm_exec_query_stats AS qs
                CROSS APPLY sys.dm_exec_sql_text(qs.sql_handle) AS st
       ) as queryStats
WHERE queryStats.statement_text like 'SELECT address.AddressLine1%'
```

This SELECT statement will return two rows (or more, you might have to adjust the WHERE clause, depending on what other queries you might have executed), one for each query you have just executed. Hence, trying to use some method to make sure that every query sent that is essentially the same query is formatted the same is important: queries must use the same format, capitalization, and so forth.

### Parameterization

The next performance topic to discuss is *parameterization*. When a query is parameterized, only one version of the plan is needed to service many queriers. Stored procedures are parameterized in all cases, but SQL Server does parameterize *ad hoc* SQL statements too. By default, the optimizer doesn't parameterize most queries, and caches most plans as straight text, unless the query is simple. For example, it can only reference a single table (check for "Forced Parameterization" in Books Online for the complete details). When the query meets the strict requirements, it changes each literal it finds in the query string into a parameter. The next time the query is executed with different literal values, the same plan can be used. For example, take this simpler form of the previous query:

```
SELECT address.AddressLine1, address.AddressLine2
FROM   Person.Address AS address
WHERE  address.AddressLine1 = '1, rue Pierre-Demoulin'
```

The plan (from using showplan_text on) is as follows:

```
|--Index Seek(OBJECT:([AdventureWorks2008].[Person].[Address].
   [IX_Address_AddressLine1_AddressLine2_City_StateProvinceID_PostalCode]
                                                    AS [address]),
       SEEK:([address].[AddressLine1]=CONVERT_IMPLICIT(nvarchar(4000),[@1],0))
                                                    ORDERED FORWARD)
```

The value of N'1, rue Pierre-Demoulin' has been changed to @1 (which is in bold in the plan), and the value is filled in from the literal at execute time. However, try executing this query:

```
SELECT address.AddressLine1, address.AddressLine2,
       address.City, state.StateProvinceCode, address.PostalCode
FROM   Person.Address AS address
        join Person.StateProvince AS state
            on address.stateProvinceId = state.stateProvinceId
WHERE  address.AddressLine1 ='1, rue Pierre-Demoulin'
```

The plan won't recognize the literal and parameterize it:

```
|--Nested Loops(Inner Join, OUTER REFERENCES:([address].[StateProvinceID]))
    |--Index Seek(OBJECT:([AdventureWorks].[Person].[Address].
       [IX_Address_AddressLine1_AddressLine2_City_StateProvinceID_PostalCode]
                                                         AS [address]),
          SEEK:([address].[AddressLine1]=N'1, rue Pierre-Demoulin')
                                                ORDERED FORWARD)
    |--Clustered Index
          Seek(OBJECT:([AdventureWorks2008].[Person].[StateProvince].
                       [PK_StateProvince_StateProvinceID] AS [state]),
                SEEK:([state].[StateProvinceID]=
                   [AdventureWorks].[Person].[Address].[StateProvinceID]
                        as [address].[StateProvinceID]) ORDERED FORWARD)
```

Note that the literal (which is bolded in this plan) from the query is still in the plan, rather than a parameter. Both plans are cached, but the first one can be used regardless of the literal value included in the WHERE clause. In the second, the plan won't be reused unless the precise literal value of N'1, rue Pierre-Demoulin' is passed in.

If you want the optimizer to be more liberal in parameterizing queries, you can use the ALTER DATABASE command to force the optimizer to parameterize:

```
ALTER DATABASE AdventureWorks
    SET PARAMETERIZATION FORCED
```

Try the plan of the query with the join. It now has replaced the N'1, rue Pierre-Demoulin' with CONVERT_IMPLICIT(nvarchar(4000),[@0],0). Now the query processor can reuse this plan no matter what the value for the literal is. This *can* be a costly operation in comparison to normal, text-only plans, so not every system should use this setting. However, if your system is running the same, reasonably complex-looking queries over and over, this can be a wonderful setting to avoid the need to pay for the query optimization.

Not every query will be parameterized when forced parameterization is enabled. For example, change the equality to a LIKE condition:

```
SELECT address.AddressLine1, address.AddressLine2,
       address.City, state.StateProvinceCode, address.PostalCode
FROM   Person.Address AS address
         JOIN Person.StateProvince as state
             ON address.stateProvinceId = state.stateProvinceId
WHERE  address.AddressLine1 like '1, rue Pierre-Demoulin'
```

The plan will contains the literal, rather than the parameter, because it cannot parameterize the second and third arguments of the LIKE operator (the arguments are arg1 LIKE arg2 [ESCAPE arg3]). If you change the query to end with WHERE '1, rue Pierre-Demoulin' like address.AddressLine1, it would be parameterized, but that construct is rarely what is desired.

For your applications, another method is to use parameterized calls from the data access layer. Basically using ADO.NET, this would entail using T-SQL variables in your query strings, and then using a SqlCommand object and its Parameters collection. The plan that will be created from SQL parameterized on the client will in turn be parameterized in the plan that is saved.

The myth that performance is definitely worse with *ad hoc* calls is just not quite true (certainly after 7.0). Performance can certainly be less of a worry than you might have been led to believe when using *ad hoc* calls to the SQL Server in your applications. However, don't stop reading here. While performance may not suffer tremendously, performance tuning is one of the pitfalls, since once you have compiled that query into your application, changing the query is never as easy as it might seem during the development cycle.

■**Tip** The better solution for parameterizing complex statements is a stored procedure. Generally, the only way this makes sense as a best practice is when you cannot use procedures, perhaps because of your tool choice or using a third-party application.

# Pitfalls

I'm glad you didn't stop reading at the end of the previous section, because although I have covered the good points of using *ad hoc* SQL, there are significant pitfalls as well:

- Low cohesion, high coupling
- Batches of statements
- Security issues
- SQL injection
- Performance tuning difficulties

I'll discuss each of these in the following sections.

## Low Cohesion, High Coupling

The number-one pitfall of using *ad hoc* SQL as your interface relates to what you learned back in Programming 101: strive for high cohesion, low coupling. *Cohesion* means that the different parts of the system work together to form a meaningful unit. This is a good thing, as you don't want to include lots of irrelevant code in the system, or be all over the place. On the other hand, *coupling* refers to how connected the different parts of a system are to one another. It's considered bad when a change in one part of a system breaks other parts of a system. (If you aren't too familiar with these terms, I suggest you go to http://www.wikipedia.org and search for these terms. You should build all the code you create with these concepts in mind.)

When issuing T-SQL statements directly from the application, the structures in the database are tied directly to the client interface. This sounds perfectly normal and acceptable at the beginning of a project, but it means that any change in database structure might require a change in the user interface. This makes making small changes to the system just as costly as large ones, because a full testing cycle is required.

■**Note** When I started this section, I told you that I wouldn't make any distinction between toolsets used. This is still true. Whether you use a horribly manually coded system or the best object-relational mapping system, that the tier knows the structure of the database is just as inflexible in the way that matters here. Though stored procedures are similarly inflexible, they are stored with the data, allowing the disparate systems to be decoupled: the code on the database tier can be structurally dependent on the objects in the same tier without completely sacrificing your loose coupling.

For example, consider that you've created an employee table, and you're storing the employee's spouse's name, as shown in Figure 11-2.

**Figure 11-2.** *An employee table*

Now some new regulation appears that you have to include the ability to have more than one spouse, which requires a new table, as shown in Figure 11-3.

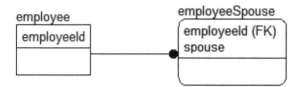

**Figure 11-3.** *Adding the ability to have more than one spouse*

The user interface must immediately be morphed to deal with this case, or at the least, you need to add some code to abstract this new way of storing data. In a scenario such as this, where the condition is quite rare (certainly most everyone will have zero or one spouse), a likely solution would be simply to encapsulate the one spouse into the `employee` table via a view and support some sort of `otherSpouse` functionality that would be used if the employee had more than one spouse. Then the original UI would continue to work, but a new form would be built for the case where `count(spouse) > 1`.

## Batches of More Than One Statement

A major problem with *ad hoc* SQL access is that when you need to do multiple commands and treat them as a single operation, it becomes increasingly more difficult to build the mechanisms in the application code to execute multiple statements as a batch, particularly when you need to group statements together in a transaction. When you have only individual statements, it's easy to manage *ad hoc* SQL for the most part. Some queries can get mighty complicated and difficult, but generally speaking, things pretty much work great when you have single statements. However, as complexity rises in the things you need to accomplish in a transaction, things get tougher. What about the case where you have 20 rows to insert, update, and/or delete at one time and all in one transaction?

Two different things usually occur in this case. The first way to deal with this situation is to start a transaction using functional code. For the most part, as discussed in Chapter 10, the best practice was stated as never to let transactions span batches, and you should minimize starting transactions using an ADO.NET object (or something like it). This isn't a hard and fast rule, as it's usually fine to do this with a middle-tier object that requires no user interaction. However, if something occurs during the execution of the object, you can still leave open connections to the server.

The second way to deal with this is to build a batching mechanism for batching SQL calls. Implementing the first method is self explanatory, but the second is to build a code-wrapping mechanism, such as the following:

```
BEGIN TRY
BEGIN TRANSACTION
```

```
      <-- statements go here

COMMIT TRANSACTION
END TRY
BEGIN CATCH
    ROLLBACK TRANSACTION
    RAISERROR ('<describe what happened>',16,1)
END CATCH
```

For example, if you wanted to send a new invoice and line items, use the following code:

```
BEGIN TRY
BEGIN TRANSACTION

        INSERT invoice (columns) values (values)

        INSERT invoiceLineItem (columns) values (values)
        INSERT invoiceLineItem (columns) values (values)
        INSERT invoiceLineItem (columns) values (values)

COMMIT TRANSACTION
END TRY
BEGIN CATCH
    ROLLBACK TRANSACTION
    EXECUTE dbo.errorLog$insert --from back in chapter 6
    RAISERROR ('Invoice creation did not succeed',16,1)
END CATCH
```

Now, executing multiple statements in a transaction is done solely on the server, and no matter what the client does, the transaction either completes or not. There's no chance that you'll end up with a transaction swinging in the wind, ready to block the next user who needs to access the locked row (even in a table scan for unrelated items!). A downside is that it does stop you from using any interim values from your statements, but starting transactions outside of the batch you commit them is asking for blocking and locking due to longer batch times. And certainly you'll find transactions blocked if the application code fails in the process of dealing with interim values.

Starting the transaction outside of the server is likely easier, but building this sort of batching interface is always the preferred way to go. First, it's better for concurrency, because only one batch needs to be executed instead of many little ones. Second, the execution of this batch won't have to wait on communications back and forth from the server before sending the next command. It's all there and happens in the single batch of statements.

---

■**Note**  The problem I have run into in almost all cases was that building a batch of multiple SQL statements is a very unnatural thing for the object oriented code to do. The way the code is generally set up is more one table to one object , where the `invoice` and `invoiceLineItem` objects have the responsibility of saving themselves.

---

## Security Issues

Security is one of the biggest downsides to using *ad hoc* access. For a user to use his or her own Windows login to access the server, you have to grant too many rights to the system, whereas with stored procedures, you can simply give access to the stored procedures. Using *ad hoc* T-SQL, you have to go with one of three possible security patterns, each with their own downsides:

- *Use one login for the application:* This, of course, means that you have to code your own security system rather than using what SQL Server gives you. This even includes some form of login and password for application access, as well as individual object access.

- *Use application roles:* This is slightly better: while you have to implement security in your code since all application users will have the same database security, at the very least, you can let SQL server handle the data access via normal logins and passwords (probably using Windows authentication). Using application roles can be better as having only the one password for users to log in with usually avoids the mass of sticky notes embossed in bold letters all around the office: **payroll system ID: fred, password: fredswifesname**.

- *Give the user direct access to the tables, or possibly views:* This unfortunately opens up your tables to users who discover the magical world of Management Studio, where they can open a table and immediately start editing it without any of those pesky UI data checks or business rules that only exist in your data access layer.

Usually, almost all applications follow the first of the three methods. Building your own security mechanisms is just considered a part of the process, and just about as often, it is considered part of the user interface's responsibilities. At the very least, by not giving *all* users direct access to the tables, the likelihood of them mucking around in the tables editing data all willy nilly is greatly minimized. With procedures, you can give the users access to stored procedures, which are not natural for them to use and certainly would not allow them to accidentally delete data from a table.

The other issues security-wise are basically performance related. SQL Server must evaluate security for every object as it's used, rather than once at the object level for stored procedures (if the owner of the procedure owns all objects, that is). This isn't generally a big issue, but as your need for greater concurrency increases, everything becomes an issue!

---

**■Caution** If you use the single-application login method, make sure not to use an account with system administration or database owner privileges. Doing so opens up your application to programmers making mistakes, and if you miss something that allows SQL injection attacks, which I describe in the next section, you could be in a world of hurt.

---

## SQL Injection

Another issue is your query being hacked by a SQL injection attack. Unless you (and/or your toolset) program your *ad hoc* SQL intelligently, a user can inject something such as the following:

```
' + char(13) + char(10) + ';SHUTDOWN WITH NOWAIT;' + '--'
```

In this case, the command might just shut down the server if the user has rights, but clearly, you can see far greater attack possibilities. Preventing this kind of attack is a user interface issue, but there are methods of preventing this sort of problem out there. I'll discuss more about injection attacks and how to avoid them in the "Stored Procedures" section. When using *ad hoc* SQL, you must be careful to avoid these types of issues for *every* call.

A SQL injection attack is not terribly hard to beat, if you are very careful in every statement you create to escape any single quote characters that a user passes in. For general text entry, like a name, commonly if the user passes in a string like "O'Malley", you know to change this to `'O''Malley'`. However, what isn't quite so obvious is that you have to do this for *every single string*, even if the string value could never legally have a single quote in it. If you don't double up on the quotes, the person could put in a single quote and then a string of SQL commands—this is where you get hit by the injection attack.

If you employ *ad hoc* SQL in your applications, I strongly suggest you do some more reading on the subject of SQL injection, and then go in and look at the places where SQL commands can be sent to the server to make sure you are covered. SQL injection is especially dangerous if the accounts being used by your application have too much power, because you didn't set up particularly granular security.

### Difficulty Tuning for Performance

Performance tuning is far more difficult when having to deal with *ad hoc* requests, for a few reasons:

- *Unknown queries*: The application can be programmed to send any query it wants, in any way. Unless very extensive testing is done, slow or dangerous scenarios can slip through. With procedures, you have a tidy catalog of possible queries that might be executed. Of course, this concern can be mitigated by having a single module where SQL code can be created and a method to list all possible queries that the application layer can execute.

- *Tuning often requires people from multiple teams*: It may seem silly, but when something is running slower, it is always SQL Server's fault. With *ad hoc* calls, the best thing that the database administrator can do is use a profiler to capture the query that is executed, see if an index could help, and call for a programmer, leading to the issue in the next bullet.

- *You cannot change queries without a recompile*: Hence, if you want to add a tip to a query to use an index, a rebuild and a redeploy are required. For stored procedures, you'd simply modify the query without the client knowing.

These reasons seem small during the development phase, but often they're the real killers for tuning, especially when you get a third-party application and its developers have implemented a dumb query that you could easily change, but doing so isn't possible (not that this regularly happens; no, not at all).

SQL Server 2005 gave us plan guides (and there are some improvements in their usability in 2008) that can be used to force a plan for queries, *ad hoc* calls, and procedures when you have troublesome queries that don't optimize naturally, but the fact is, going in and editing a query to tune is far easier than using these objects.

# Stored Procedures

Stored procedures are compiled batches of SQL code that can be parameterized to allow for easy reuse. The basic structure of stored procedures follows (check SQL Server Books Online for a complete reference):

```
CREATE PROCEDURE <procedureName>
[(
        @parameter1  <datatype> [ = <defaultvalue> [OUTPUT]]
        @parameter2  <datatype> [ = <defaultvalue> [OUTPUT]]
        ...
        @parameterN  <datatype> [ = <defaultvalue> [OUTPUT]]
)]
AS
<T-SQL statements> | <CLR Assembly reference>
```

There isn't much more to it. You can put any statements that could have been sent as *ad hoc* calls to the server into a stored procedure and call them as a reusable unit. You can return an integer value from the procedure by using the RETURN statement, or return any datatype by declaring the parameter as an output parameter (other than text or image, though you should be using (max) datatypes instead as they will not likely even exist in the version after 2008). After the AS, you can execute any T-SQL commands you need to, using the parameters like variables. (You can also declare an object that's part of a CLR assembly, which I'll mention again in the last major section of the chapter.)

Here's an example of a basic procedure to retrieve rows from a table (continuing to use the AdventureWorks2008 tables for these examples):

```
CREATE PROCEDURE person.address$select
(
    @addressLine1 nvarchar(120) = '%',
    @city         nvarchar(60) = '%',
    @state        nchar(3) = '___', --special because it is a char column
    @postalCode   nvarchar(8) = '%'
) AS
--simple procedure to execute a single query
SELECT address.AddressLine1, address.AddressLine2,
       address.City, state.StateProvinceCode, address.PostalCode
FROM   Person.Address as address
         join Person.StateProvince as state
            on address.stateProvinceId = state.stateProvinceId
WHERE  address.AddressLine1 like @addressLine1
  AND  address.City like @city
  AND  state.StateProvinceCode like @state
  AND  address.PostalCode like @postalCode
```

Now instead of having the client programs formulate a query by knowing the table structures, the client can simply issue a command, knowing a procedure name and the parameters. Clients can choose from four possible criteria to select the addresses they want. For example, they'd use this if they want to find people in London:

```
person.address$select @city = 'London'
```

Or they could use the other parameters:

```
person.address$select @postalCode = '98%', @addressLine1 = '%Hilltop%'
```

The client doesn't know whether the database or the code is well built or even if it's horribly designed. Originally our state value might have been a part of the address table but changed to its own table when we realized that it was necessary to store more information about a state than a simple code. The same might be true for the city, the postalCode, and so on. Often, the tasks the client needs to do won't change based on the database structures, so why should the client need to know the database structures?

For much greater detail about how to write stored procedures and good T-SQL, consider the books *Pro T-SQL 2008 Programmer's Guide* by Michael Coles (Apress 2008), *Inside Microsoft SQL Server 2005: T-SQL Programming* by Itzik Ben-Gan et al. (Microsoft Press, 2006), or search for "stored procedures" in Books Online. In this section, I'll look at some of the characteristics of using stored procedures as our *only* interface between client and data. I'll discuss the following topics:

- *Encapsulation*: Limits client knowledge of the database structure by providing a simple interface for known operations

- *Dynamic procedures*: Gives the best of both worlds, allowing for *ad hoc*–style code without giving *ad hoc* access to the database

- *Security*: Provides a well-formed interface for known operations that allows you to apply security only to this interface and disallow other access to the database

- *Performance*: Allows for efficient parameterization of any query, as well as tweaks to the performance of any query, without changes to the client interface

- *Pitfalls*: Drawbacks associated with the stored-procedure–access architecture

# Encapsulation

To me, encapsulation is the primary reason for using stored procedures, and it's the leading reason behind all the other topics that I'll discuss. When talking about encapsulation, the idea is to hide the working details from processes that have no need to know about the details. Encapsulation is a large part of the desired "low coupling" of our code that I discussed in the pitfalls of *ad hoc* access. Some software is going to have to be coupled to the data structures, of course, but locating that code with the structures makes it easier to manage. Plus, the people who generally manage the SQL Server code on the server are not the same people who manage the compiled code.

For example, when we coded the `person.address$select` procedure, it's unimportant to the client how the procedure was coded. We could have built it based on a view and selected from it, or the procedure could call 16 different stored procedures to improve performance for different parameter combinations. We could even have used the dreaded cursor version that you find in some production systems:

```
--pseudocode:
CREATE PROCEDURE person.address$select
...
Create temp table
Declare cursor for (select all rows from the address table)
Fetch first row
While not end of cursor (@@fetch_status)
 Begin
        Check columns for a match to parameters
        If match, put into temp table
        Fetch next row
 End
SELECT * from temp table
```

This would be horrible, horrible code to be sure. I didn't give real code so it wouldn't be confused for a positive example and imitated (and somebody would end up blaming me, though definitely not you!). However, it certainly could be built to return correct data and possibly could even be fast enough for smaller data sets. Even better, when the client executes the following code, they get the *same* result, regardless of the internal code:

```
person.address$select @city = 'london'
```

What makes this great is that you can rewrite the guts of the procedure without any concern for breaking any client code. This means that anything can change, including table structures, column names, and coding method (cursor, join, and so on), and no client code need change. You'll see this even more clearly in the next section, "Dynamic SQL," as I'll re-create this procedure in a different way.

This concept of having easy access to the code may seem like an insignificant consideration, especially if you generally only work with limited sized sets of data. The problem is, as data set sizes fluctuate, the types of queries that will work often vary greatly. When you start dealing with increasing orders of magnitude in the number of rows in your tables, queries that seemed just fine somewhere at ten thousand rows start to fail to produce the kinds of performance that you need, so you have to tweak the queries to get results in an amount of time that users won't complain to your boss about. I will cover more about performance tuning in a later section.

---

■**Note** Some of the benefits of building your objects in the way that I describe can also be achieved by building a solid middle-tier architecture with a data layer that is flexible enough to deal with change. However, I will always submit to you that it is easier to build your data access layer in the T-SQL code that is built specifically for data access. Unfortunately, it doesn't solve the code ownership issues (functional versus relational programmers,) nor does it solve the issue with performance tuning the code.

---

## Dynamic Procedures

You can dynamically create and execute code in a stored procedure, just like you can from the front end. Often, this is necessary when it's just too hard to get a good answer using the rigid requirements of precompiled stored procedures. For example, say you need a procedure that needs a lot of optional parameters. It can be easier to only include parameters where the user passes in a value and let the compilation be done at execution time, especially if the procedure isn't used all that often. The same parameter sets will get their own plan saved in the plan cache anyhow, just like for typical *ad hoc* SQL.

Clearly, some of the problems of straight *ad hoc* SQL pertain here as well, most notably SQL injection. You must always make sure that no input users can enter can allow them to return their own results, allowing them to poke around your system without anyone knowing. As mentioned before, a common way to avoid this sort of thing is always to check the parameter values and immediately double up the single quotes so that the caller can't inject the old `' + ;SHUTDOWN WITH NOWAIT; + '`, or any other far more malicious code.

Make sure that any parameters that don't need quotes (such as numbers) are placed into the correct datatype. If you use a string value for a number, you can insert things such as `'novalue'` and check for it in your code, but another user could put in the injection attack value and be in like Flynn. For example, take the sample procedure from earlier, and turn it into a dynamic SQL statement in a stored procedure:

```
ALTER PROCEDURE person.address$select
(
    @addressLine1 nvarchar(120) = '%',
    @city         nvarchar(60) = '%',
    @state        nchar(3) = '___',
    @postalCode   nvarchar(50) = '%'
) AS
BEGIN
    DECLARE @query varchar(max)
    SET @query =
            'SELECT address.AddressLine1, address.AddressLine2,
                    address.City, state.StateProvinceCode, address.PostalCode
            FROM    Person.Address as address
                    join Person.StateProvince as state
                        on address.stateProvinceId = state.stateProvinceId
            WHERE   address.City like ''' + @city + '''
                AND state.StateProvinceCode like ''' + @state + '''
                AND address.PostalCode like ''' + @postalCode + '''
                --this param is last because it is largest
                --to make the example
                --easier as this column is very large
                AND address.AddressLine1 like ''' + @addressLine1 + ''''
```

```
    SELECT @query --just for testing purposes
    EXECUTE (@query)
END
```

There are two problems with this procedure. The first is that you don't get the full benefit, because in the final query you can end up with useless parameters used as search arguments that make using indexes more difficult (this is one of the main reasons I use dynamic procedures). I'll fix that in the next version of the procedure, but the most important problem is the injection attack. For example, let's assume that the user who's running the application has dbo powers or rights to sysusers. The user executes the following statement:

```
EXECUTE person.address$select
                        @addressLine1 = '~''select name from sysusers--'
```

This returns three result sets: the two (including the test SELECT) from before plus a list of all of the users in the AdventureWorks2008 database. No rows will be returned to the proper result sets, because no address lines happen to be equal to '~', but the list of users is not a good thing (with some work, a decent hacker could probably figure out how to use a UNION and get back the users as part of the normal result set).

The easy way to correct this is to use the quotename() function to make sure that all values that need to be surrounded by single quotes are formatted in such a way that no matter what a user sends to the parameter, it cannot cause a problem.

In the next code block, I will change the procedure to safely deal with invalid quote characters, plus instead of just blindly using the parameters, if the parameter value is the same as the default, I will leave off the values from the WHERE clause.

```
ALTER PROCEDURE person.address$select
(
    @addressLine1   nvarchar(120) = '%',
    @city           nvarchar(60) = '%',
    @state          nchar(3) = '___',
    @postalCode     nvarchar(50) = '%'
) AS
BEGIN
    DECLARE @query varchar(max)
    SET @query =
                'SELECT address.AddressLine1, address.AddressLine2,
                        address.City, state.StateProvinceCode, address.PostalCode
                FROM    Person.Address as address
                        join Person.StateProvince as state
                            on address.stateProvinceId = state.stateProvinceId
                WHERE   1=1'
    IF @city <> '%'
        SET @query = @query + ' AND address.City like ' + quotename(@city,'''')
    IF @state <> '___'
        SET @query = @query + ' AND state.StateProvinceCode like ' +
                                                quotename(@state,'''')
    IF @postalCode <> '%'
        SET @query = @query + ' AND address.City like ' + quotename(@city,'''')
    IF @addressLine1 <> '%'
        SET @query = @query + ' AND address.addressLine1 like ' +
                                        quotename(@addressLine1;'''')
    SELECT  @query
    EXECUTE (@query)
END
```

Now you might get a much better plan, especially if there are several useful indexes on the table. That's because SQL Server can make the determination of what indexes to use at runtime, rather than using a stored plan. You also don't have to worry about injection attacks, because it's impossible to put something into any parameter that will be anything other than a search argument, and that will execute any code other than what you expect. Basically this version of a stored procedure is the answer to the flexibility of using ad hoc SQL, though it is a bit more messy to write. However, it is located right on the server where it can be tweaked as necessary.

Try executing the evil version of the query, and look at the WHERE clause it fashions:

```
WHERE    1=1
         AND address.addressLine1 like '~''select name from sysusers--'
```

The query that is formed, when executed will now just return two result sets (one for the query and one for the results), and no rows for the executed query. This is because you are looking for rows where address.addressLine1 is like ~'select name from sysusers--. While not being exactly *impossible*, this is certainly very, very unlikely.

I should also note that in previous versions of SQL Server, using dynamic SQL procedures would break the security chain, and you'd have to grant a lot of extra rights to objects just used in a stored procedure. This little fact was enough to make using dynamic SQL not a best practice for SQL Server 2000 and earlier versions. However, in SQL Server 2005 you no longer had to grant these extra rights, as I'll explain in the next section (hint: you can EXECUTE AS someone else).

# Security

The second most important reason for using stored-procedure access is security (as previously discussed in Chapter 8). You can grant access to just the stored procedure, instead of giving users the rights to all the different resources used by the stored procedure. Granting users rights to all the objects in the database gives them the ability to open Management Studio and do the same things (and more) that the application allows them to do. This is rarely the desired effect, as an untrained user let loose on base tables can wreak havoc on the data. ("Oooh, I should change that. Oooh, I should delete that row. Hey, weren't there more rows in this table before?") I should note that if the database is properly designed, users can't violate core structural business rules, but they can circumvent business rules in the middle tier and can execute poorly formed queries that chew up important resources.

---

■**Note** In general, it is best to keep your users away from the power tools like Management Studio and keep them in a sandbox where even if they have advanced powers (like because they are CEO) they cannot accidentally delete a lot of data. Provide tools that hold user's hands and keep them from shooting off their big toe.

---

Now, you have a far clearer surface area on which to manage security, rather than tables, columns, groups of rows (row-level security), and actions (SELECT, UPDATE, INSERT, DELETE), so you can give rights to just a single operation, in a single way. For example, the question of whether users should be able to delete a contact is wide open, but should they be able to delete their own contacts? Sure, so give them rights to execute deletePersonalContact (meaning a contact that the user owned). Making this choice easy would be based on how well you name your procedures. I use a naming convention of <tablename | subject area>$<action>. For example, to delete a contact, the procedure might be contact$delete, if users were allowed to delete any contact. How you name objects is completely a personal choice, as long as you follow a standard that is meaningful to you and others.

As discussed back in the *ad hoc* section, a lot of architects simply avoid this issue altogether by letting objects connect to the database as a single user (or being forced into this by political pressure, either way), and let the application handle security. That is fine, and the security implications of this are the same for stored procedures or *ad hoc* usage. Using stored procedures still clarifies what you can or cannot apply security to.

In SQL Server 2005, the EXECUTE AS clause was added on the procedure declaration. In versions before SQL Server 2005, if a different user owned any object in the procedure (or function, view, or trigger), the caller of the procedure had to have explicit rights to the resource. This was particularly annoying when having to do some small dynamic SQL operation in a procedure, as discussed in the previous section.

The EXECUTE AS clause gives the programmer of the procedure the ability to build procedures where the procedure caller has the same rights in the procedure code as the owner of the procedure—or if permissions have been granted, the same rights as any user or login in the system.

For example, consider that you need to do a dynamic SQL call to a table (in reality it ought to be more complex, like needing to use a sensitive resource). First, create a test user:

```
CREATE USER  fred WITHOUT LOGIN
```

Next, create a simple stored procedure:

```
CREATE PROCEDURE testChaining
AS
EXECUTE ('SELECT CustomerId, StoreId, AccountNumber
        FROM    Sales.Customer')
GO
GRANT EXECUTE ON testChaining TO fred
```

Now execute the procedure (changing your security context to be this user):

```
EXECUTE AS user = 'fred'
EXECUTE testChaining
REVERT
```

You're greeted with the following error:

---

```
Msg 229, Level 14, State 5, Line 1
SELECT permission denied on object 'Customer',
database 'AdventureWorks', schema 'Sales'.
```

---

You could grant rights to the user directly to the object, but this gives users more usage than just from this procedure, which is probably not desirable. Now change the procedure to EXECUTE AS SELF:

```
ALTER PROCEDURE testChaining
WITH EXECUTE AS SELF
AS
EXECUTE ('SELECT CustomerId, StoreId, AccountNumber
                  FROM Sales.Customer')
```

Now, go back to the context of user Fred and try again. Just like when Fred had access directly, you get back data. You use SELF to set the context the same as the principal creating the procedure. OWNER is usually the same as SELF, and you can only specify a single user in the database (it can't be a group).

---

■**Tip** The value of SUSER_SNAME(), which is typically used for logging user actions, won't be usable if you use WITH EXECUTE AS in procedures. That's because after the EXECUTE AS, this function returns the login of the user that you've changed security context to. Use ORIGINAL_LOGIN() instead.

---

Warning: the EXECUTE AS clause can easily be abused. Consider the following query, which is obviously a gross exaggeration of what you might hope to see but not beyond possibility:

```
CREATE PROCEDURE dbo.doAnything
(
    @query nvarchar(4000)
)
WITH EXECUTE AS SELF
AS
EXECUTE (@query)
```

This procedure gives the person that has access to execute it full access to the database. Bear in mind that *any* query can be executed (DROP TABLE? Sure, why not?), easily allowing improper code to be executed on the database. Now, consider a little math problem; add together the following items:

- EXECUTE AS SELF
- Client executing code as the database owner (a very typical bad practice).
- The code for dbo.doAnything
- An injection-susceptible procedure, with a parameter that can hold approximately 120 characters (the length of the dbo.doAnything procedure plus punctuation to create it)

What do you get? If you guessed no danger at all, please e-mail me your social security number, address, and a major credit card number. If you realize that the only one that you really have control over is the fourth one and that hackers, once the dbo.doAnything procedure was created, could execute any code they wanted as the owner of the database, you get the gold star. So be careful to block code open to injection.

---

**■Tip** I am not suggesting that you should avoid the EXECUTE AS setting completely, just that its use must be scrutinized a bit more than the average stored procedure along the lines of when a #temp table is used. Why was EXECUTE AS used? Is the use proper? You must be careful to understand that in the wrong hands this command can be harmful to security.

---

# Performance

There are a couple reasons why stored procedures are great for performance:

- Parameterization of complex plans is controlled by you at design time rather than controlled by the optimizer at compile time.
- You can performance-tune your queries without making invasive program changes.

## Parameterization of Complex Plans

Stored procedures, unlike *ad hoc* SQL, always have parameterized plans for maximum reuse of the plans. This lets you avoid the cost of recompilation, as well as the advanced costs of looking for parameters in the code. Any literals are always literal, and any variable is always a parameter. This can lead to some performance issues as well, as occasionally the plan for a stored procedure that gets picked by the optimizer might not be as good of a plan as might be picked for an *ad hoc* procedure.

The interesting thing here is that, although you can save the plan of a single query with *ad hoc* calls, with procedures you can save the plan for a large number of statements. With all the join types, possible tables, indexes, view text expansions, and so on, optimizing a query is a nontrivial task that might take quite a few milliseconds. Now, admittedly, when building a single-user application, you might say, "Who cares?" However, as user counts go up, the amount of time begins to add up. With stored procedures, this only has to be done once. (Or perhaps a bit more frequently. SQL Server can create multiple copies of the plan if the procedure is heavily used.)

Of course, stored procedure parameterization isn't always a perfect thing. When you pass values to your stored procedure, SQL Server uses *parameter sniffing* to take the set of parameters and plug them into the queries being used to build the plan. This is fine and dandy, except when you have a situation where you have some values that will work nicely for a query but others that work pitifully. Much like I talked about in Chapter 9 on indexing, two different values that are being searched for can end up creating two different plans. Often, this is where you might pass in a value that tells the query that there are no values, and SQL Server uses that value to build the plan. When you pass in a real value, it takes far too long to execute. Using `WITH RECOMPILE` at the object level or the `RECOMPILE` statement-level hint can avoid the problems of parameter sniffing, but then you have to wait for the plan to be created for each execute, which can be costly. It's possible to branch the code out to allow for both cases, but this can get costly if you have a couple of different scenarios to deal with.

---

■**Note** This section, after I reread it several times, seems to suggest parameterization is negative. The fact is, while there are a few caveats, they are very few and far between. And lucky for the person that has to deal with this, our next topic is about tuning procedures without changing the procedure's public interface. You can use the tricks mentioned to fix the performance issue without the client's knowledge.

---

## Fine-Tuning Without Program Changes

Even if you didn't have the performance capabilities of parameterization for stored procedures (say every query in your procedure was forced to do dynamic SQL), the ability to fine-tune the queries in the stored procedure without making *any* changes to the client code is of incredible value. Of course, this is the value of encapsulation, but again, fine-tuning is such an important thing.

Often, a third-party system is purchased that doesn't use stored procedures. If you're a support person for this type of application, you know that there's little you can do other than to add an index here and there.

"But," you're probably thinking, "shouldn't the third party have planned for all possible cases?" Sure they should, because the performance characteristics of a system with 10 rows are identical to one with 100,000. And then there is the outlier, like the organization that pumped 10 million new rows per hour into that system that was only expected to do 100,000 per day. The fact is, SQL Server is built to operate on a large variety of hardware. A system running on a one-processor laptop with its slow disk subsystem behaves exactly like a RAID 10 system with 20 high-speed 32-GB drives, right? (Another gold star if you just said something witty about how dumb that sounded.)

The answer is no. In general, the performance characteristics of database systems vary wildly based on usage characteristics, hardware, and data sizing issues. By using stored procedures, it's possible to tweak how queries are written, as the needs change from small dataset to massive dataset. For example, I've seen many queries that ran great with 10,000 rows, but when the needs grew to millions of rows, the queries ran for hours. Rewriting the queries using proper query techniques, or sometimes using temporary tables gave performance that was several orders of magnitude better. And I have had the converse be true, where I have removed temporary tables and consolidated queries into a single statement to get better performance. The user of the procedures did not even know.

This ability to fine-tune without program changes is such an important thing. Particularly as a corporate developer, when the system is running slow and you identify the query or procedure causing the issue, fixing it can either be a one-hour task or a one-week task. If the problem is a procedure, you can modify, test, and distribute the one piece of code. Even following all of the rules of proper code management, your modify/test/distribute cycle can be a very fast operation. However, if application code has to be modified, you have to coordinate multiple groups (DBAs and programmers, at least) and discuss the problem and the code has to be rewritten and tested (for many more permutations of parameters and settings than for the one procedure).

For smaller organizations, it can be overly expensive to get a really good test area, so if the code doesn't work quite right in production, you can tune it easily then. Tuning a procedure is easy, even modification procedures, you can just execute the code in a transaction and roll it back. Keep changing the code until satisfied, compile the code in the production database, and move on to the next problem (note that this is not best practice, but it is something I have to do from time to time).

# Pitfalls

So far, everything has been all sunshine and lollipops for using stored procedures, but this isn't always true. There are several pitfalls I will discuss:

- The high initial effort to create procedures can be prohibitive.
- It isn't always easy to implement optional parameters in searches in an optimum manner.
- It's more difficult to affect only certain columns in an operation.

One pitfall that I won't cover too much in this chapter is cross-platform coding. If you're going to build a data layer that needs to be portable to different platforms such as Oracle or MySQL, this need for cross-platform coding can complicate your effort (though it can still be worthwhile in some cases). Chapter 12 covers the differences and similarities between the SQL dialects and the procedure methodologies of each different platform. (Chapter 12 is a bonus downloadable chapter available on the Apress website.)

## High Initial Effort

Of all the pros and cons, initial effort is most often the straw that breaks the camel's proverbial back in the argument for or against stored procedures. For every time I've failed to get stored procedure access established as the method of access, this is the reason given. There are lots of tools out there that can map a database to objects or screens to reduce development time. The problem is that they suffer from some or all of the issues discussed in the *ad hoc* SQL pitfalls.

It's an indefensible stance that writing lots of stored procedures takes less time up front—quite often, it takes quite a bit more time for initial development. Writing stored procedures is definitely an extra step in the process of getting an application up and running.

An extra step takes extra time, and extra time means extra money. You see where this is going, because people like activities where they see results, not infrastructure. When a charismatic programmer comes in and promises results, it can be hard to back up claims that stored procedures are certainly the best way to go. The best defenses are knowing the pros and cons and especially understanding the application development infrastructure you'll be dealing with.

## Difficulty Supporting Optional Parameters in Searches

I already mentioned something similar to optional parameters earlier when talking about dynamic SQL. In those examples, all of the parameters used simple LIKE parameters with character strings. But what about integer values? Or numeric ones? As mentioned earlier in the *ad hoc* sections, a possible solution is to pass NULL into the variable values by doing something along the lines of the following code:

```
WHERE  (integerColumn = @integerColumn or @integerColumn is null)
  AND  (numericColumn = @numericColumn or @numericColumn is null)
  AND  (characterColumn like @characterColumn)
```

Generally speaking, it's possible to come up with some scheme along these lines to implement optional parameters alongside the rigid needs of procedures in stored procedures. Note too that using NULL as your get everything parameter value means it is then hard to get only NULL values. For character strings you can use LIKE '%'. You can even use additional parameters to state: @returnAll-TypeFlag to return all rows of a certain type.

It isn't possible to come up with a scheme (especially a scheme that can be optimized). However, you can always fall back on using dynamic SQL for these types of queries using optional parameters, just like I did in the *ad hoc* section. One thing that can help this process is to add the WITH RECOMPILE clause to the stored-procedure declaration. This tells the procedure to create a new plan for every execution of the procedure.

Although I try to avoid dynamic SQL because of the coding complexity and maintenance difficulties, if the set of columns you need to deal with is large, dynamic SQL can be the best way to deal with the situation. Using dynamically built stored procedures is generally the same speed as using *ad hoc* access from the client, so the benefits from encapsulation still exist.

## Difficulty Affecting Only Certain Columns in an Operation

When you're coding stored procedures without dynamic SQL, the code you'll write is going to be pretty rigid. If you want to write a stored procedure to modify a row in the table created earlier in the chapter—sales.contact—you'd write something along the lines of this skeleton procedure (back in the architectureChapter database):

```
CREATE PROCEDURE sales.contact$update
(
    @contactId    int,
    @firstName    varchar(30),
    @lastName     varchar(30),
    @companyName  varchar(100),
    @salesLevelId int,
    @personalNotes varchar(max),
    @contactNotes  varchar(max)
)
AS
    DECLARE @entryTrancount int = @@trancount

    BEGIN TRY
        UPDATE sales.contact
        SET          firstName = @firstName,
                     lastName = @lastName,
                     companyName = @companyName,
                     salesLevelId = @salesLevelId,
                     personalNotes = @personalNotes,
                     contactNotes = @contactNotes
        WHERE   contactId = @contactId
    END TRY
    BEGIN CATCH

        --if the tran is doomed, and the entryTrancount was 0
        --we have to rollback
        IF xact_state()= -1 and @entryTrancount = 0
            rollback transaction
```

```
    DECLARE @ERRORmessage nvarchar(4000)
    SET @ERRORmessage = 'Error occurred in procedure ''' +
                object_name(@@procid) + ''', Original Message: '''
                + ERROR_MESSAGE() + ''''
    RAISERROR (@ERRORmessage,16,1)
    RETURN -100

END CATCH
```

A procedure such as this is fine *most* of the time, because it usually isn't a big performance concern just to pass all values and modify those values, even setting them to the same value and revalidating. However, in some cases, validating every column can be a performance issue because not every validation is the same as the next.

For example, say that the salesLevelId column was a very important column for the corporate sales process. And it needed to validate in the sales data if the customer could, in fact, actually be that level. A trigger might be created to do that validation, and it could take a relatively large amount of time. (Note that when the average operation takes 1 millisecond, 100 milliseconds can actually be "a long time." It is all relative to what else is taking place and how many times a minute things are occurring.) You could easily turn this into a dynamic SQL procedure, though since you don't know if the value of salesLevel has changed, you will have to check that first:

```
ALTER PROCEDURE sales.contact$update
(
    @contactId    int,
    @firstName    varchar(30),
    @lastName     varchar(30),
    @companyName varchar(100),
    @salesLevelId int,
    @personalNotes varchar(max),
    @contactNotes  varchar(max)
)
WITH EXECUTE AS SELF
AS
    DECLARE @entryTrancount int = @@trancount

    BEGIN TRY
        --declare variable to use to tell whether to include the
        DECLARE @salesOrderIdChangedFlag bit =
                    case when (select salesLevelId
                                    from    sales.contact
                                    where   contactId = @contactId) =
                                                        @salesLevelId
                            then 0 else 1 end

        DECLARE @query nvarchar(max)
        SET @query = '
        UPDATE sales.contact
        SET         firstName = ' + quoteName(@firstName,'''') + ',
                    lastName = ' + quoteName(@lastName,'''') + ',
                    companyName = ' + quoteName(@companyName, '''') + ',
                    '+ case when @salesOrderIdChangedFlag = 1 then
                    'salesLevelId = ' + quoteName(@salesLevelId, '''') + ',
                    ' else '' end +  'personalNotes = ' + quoteName(@personalNotes,
                                                                    '''') + ',
                    contactNotes = ' + quoteName(@contactNotes,'''') + '
```

```
            WHERE  contactId = ' + cast(@contactId as varchar(10))
            EXECUTE (@query)
        END TRY
        BEGIN CATCH

            --if the tran is doomed, and the entryTrancount was 0
            --we have to rollback
            IF xact_state()= -1 and @entryTrancount = 0
                rollback transaction

          DECLARE @ERRORmessage nvarchar(4000)
          SET @ERRORmessage = 'Error occurred in procedure ''' +
                    object_name(@@procid) + ''', Original Message: '''
                    + ERROR_MESSAGE() + ''''
          RAISERROR (@ERRORmessage,16,1)
          RETURN -100

        END CATCH
GO
```

This is a pretty simple example, and as you can see the code is getting pretty darn ugly. Of course, the advantage of encapsulation is still intact, since the user will be able to do exactly the same operation as before with no change to the public interface, but the code is immediately less manageable at the module level.

An alternative you might consider would be an INSTEAD OF trigger to conditionally do the update on the column in question if the inserted and deleted columns don't match:

```
CREATE TRIGGER sales.contact$insteadOfUpdate
ON sales.contact
INSTEAD OF UPDATE
AS
BEGIN
    DECLARE @rowsAffected int,    --stores the number of rows affected
            @msg varchar(2000)    --used to hold the error message
    SET @rowsAffected = @@rowcount
    --no need to continue on if no rows affected
    IF @rowsAffected = 0 return
    SET NOCOUNT ON --to avoid the rowcount messages
    SET ROWCOUNT 0 --in case the client has modified the rowcount
    BEGIN TRY
            --[validation blocks]
            --[modification blocks]
            --<perform action>

        UPDATE contact
        SET    firstName = inserted.firstName,
                lastName = inserted.lastName,
                companyName = inserted.companyName,
                personalNotes = inserted.personalNotes,
                contactNotes = inserted.contactNotes
        FROM   sales.contact as contact
                JOIN inserted
                    on inserted.contactId = contact.contactId
```

```
            IF UPDATE(salesLevelId) --this column requires heavy validation
                                    --only want to update if necessary
                UPDATE contact
                SET    salesLevelId = inserted.salesLevelId
                FROM   sales.contact as contact
                            JOIN inserted
                                ON inserted.contactId = contact.contactId

            --this correlated subquery checks for rows that have changed
            WHERE  EXISTS (SELECT *
                                    FROM   deleted
                                    WHERE  deleted.contactId =
                                            inserted.contactId
                                        AND   deleted. salesLevelId <>
                                            inserted. salesLevelId)
    END TRY
    BEGIN CATCH
            IF @@trancount > 0
                ROLLBACK TRANSACTION

            --optional
            --EXECUTE utility.ErrorLog$insert

            DECLARE @ERROR_MESSAGE nvarchar(4000)
            SET @ERROR_MESSAGE = ERROR_MESSAGE()
            RAISERROR (@ERROR_MESSAGE,16,1)
    END CATCH
END
```

This is a lot of code, but it's simple. This is one of the rare uses of INSTEAD OF triggers, but it's pretty simple to follow. Just update the simple columns and not the "high cost" columns, unless it has changed.

## Opinions

If the opinions in the previous two sections were not enough (and they weren't), this section lays out my opinions on what is good and bad about using *ad hoc* SQL and stored procedures. As Oscar Wilde was quoted as saying, "It is only about things that do not interest one that one can give a really unbiased opinion, which is no doubt the reason why an unbiased opinion is always absolutely valueless." This is a topic that I care about, and I have firm feelings about what is right and wrong. Of course, it is also true that many viable, profitable, and stable systems don't follow any of these opinions. That said, let's recap the pros and cons I have given for the different approaches. The pros of using *ad hoc* SQL are as follows:

- It gives a great deal of flexibility over the code, as the code can be generated right at runtime, based on metadata, or even the user's desires. The modification statement can only update column values that have changed.

- It can give adequate or even improved performance by only caching and parameterizing obviously matching queries. It also can be much easier to tailor queries in which you have wildly varying parameter and join needs.

- The other major benefit is that it's just fast to do. If the programmer can write a SQL statement or use an API that does, there's less overhead learning about how to write stored procedures.

The cons are as follows:

- Your client code and database structures are tightly coupled, and when any little thing changes (column name for example) in the database, it's often required to make a change to the client code, requiring greater costs in deploying changes.

- Tying multiple statements together can be cumbersome, especially when transactions are required.

- API-generated queries often are not optimal, causing performance and especially maintenance issues when the database administrator has to optimize queries that cannot be modified.

- Performance-tuning database calls can be much harder to do, because modifying a statement, even to add a query hint, requires a recompile.

For stored procedure access, the pros are as follows:

- The encapsulation of database code reduces what the user interface needs to know about the implemented database structures. If they need to change, often you can change the structures and tweak a procedure, and the client needn't know.

- You can easily manage security at the procedure level, with no need whatsoever to grant rights to base tables. This way, users don't have to have rights to modify any physical tables.

- You have the ability to do dynamic SQL in your procedures. In SQL Server 2005 and later, you can do this without the need to grant rights to objects using `EXECUTE AS`.

- Performance is improved, due to the parameterizing of all plans (unless otherwise specified).

- Performance tuning is made far simpler, due to the ability to tune a procedure without the client knowing the difference.

The cons for stored-procedure access are as follows:

- The rigid code of precompiled stored procedures can make coding them difficult (though you can use dynamic SQL to optimize certain parts of the code as needed).

- You can't effectively vary the columns affected by any T-SQL statement.

- There's a larger initial effort required to create the procedures.

With no outside influence other than this list of pros and cons and experience, I can state without hesitation that stored procedures are the way to go, if for no other reason other than the encapsulation angle. By separating the database code from the client code, you get an effective separation of data-access code from application code.

Keep in mind that I'm not suggesting that *all* code that works with data should be in stored procedures. Too often when stored procedures are used as the complete data interface, the people doing the programming have a tendency to start putting all sorts of procedural code in the procedures, making them hard to write and hard to maintain. The next step is moaning that procedures are terrible, slow, and inflexible. This is often one of the sticking points between the two different opinions on how to do things. More or less, what's called for when building a user interface is to build stored procedures that replace T-SQL statements that you would have built in an *ad hoc* manner, using T-SQL control of flow language at a minimum. Several types of code act on data that shouldn't be in stored procedures or T-SQL:

- *Mutable business logic and rules*: T-SQL is a rigid language that can be difficult to work with. Even writing CLR SQL Server objects (covered in the next major section of this chapter) is unwieldy in comparison to building an adequate business layer in your application.

- *Formatting data*: When you want to present a value in some format, it's best to leave this to the presentation layer or user interface of the application. You should use SQL Server primarily to do set-based operations using basic DML, and have as little of the T-SQL control of flow language as possible.

In my opinion (again, this is my book, and we are getting near the end, so if you made it this far, I probably am not going to alienate you now!) probably the biggest drawback to using procedures in earlier versions of SQL Server was eliminated in 2005 in the EXECUTE AS clause on the procedure creation. By carefully using the EXECUTE AS clause, you can change the security context of the executor of a procedure when the ownership chain is broken. So, in any places where a dynamic call is needed, you can make a dynamic call, and it will look to the user exactly as a normal precompiled stored procedure would (again, making sure to avoid the very dangerous SQL Injection errors that are far too common).

I don't want to sound as if any system largely based on *ad hoc* SQL is permanently flawed and just a festering pile of the smelly bits of an orangutan. Many systems have been built on letting the application handle all the code, especially when tools are built that need to run on multiple platforms. (Chapter 12 covers multiplatform considerations.) This kind of access is exactly what SQL-based servers were originally designed for, so it isn't going to hurt anything. At worst, you're simply not using one of the advanced features that SQL Server gives you in stored procedures.

The one thing that often tips the scales to using *ad hoc* access is time. The initial effort required to build stored procedures is going to be increased over just using *ad hoc* SQL. In fact, for every system I've been involved with where our access plan was to use *ad hoc* SQL, the primary factor was time: "It takes too long to build the procedures," or "it takes too long to develop code to access the stored procedures." Or even, "The tool we are using doesn't support stored procedures." All this inevitably swings to the statement that "the DBA is being too rigid. Why do we want to . . ."

These responses are a large part of why this section of the chapter needed to be written. It's never good to state that the *ad hoc* SQL is just plain wrong, because that's clearly not true. The issue is which is better, and stored procedures greatly tip the scale, at least until outside forces and developer talents are brought in.

# T-SQL and the CLR

Many world-class and mission-critical corporate applications have been created using T-SQL and SQL Server, so why integrate SQL Server with the CLR? The fact is, integrating the CLR provides a host of benefits to developers and DBAs that wasn't possible or wasn't easy with SQL Server 2000 and earlier. It also opens up a plethora of questions about the applicability of this reasonably new technology.

In the last two sections, I approached the topic of stored procedures and *ad hoc* access to data, but as of SQL Server 2005, there's another interesting architectural option to consider. Beyond using T-SQL to code objects, you can use a .NET language to write your objects to run not in interpreted manner that T-SQL objects do but rather in what is known as the SQLCLR, which is a SQL version of the CLR that is used as the platform for the .NET languages to build objects that can be leveraged by SQL Server just like T-SQL objects.

Using the SQLCLR, Microsoft provides a choice in how to program objects by using the enhanced programming architecture of the CLR for SQL Server objects. By hosting the CLR inside SQL Server, developers and DBAs can develop SQL Server objects using any .NET-compatible language, such as C# or Visual Basic. This opens up an entire new world of possibilities for programming SQL Server objects and makes the integration of the CLR one of the most powerful new development features of SQL Server.

Back when the CLR was introduced to us database types, it was probably the most feared new feature of SQL Server. As adoption of SQL Server 2005 increases, and SQL Server 2008 finds its way into more and more developers' hands, use of the CLR still may be the problem we suspected. One reason is that it's a new thing that isn't fully understood, but it's also feared because the programmers who use the CLR languages aren't generally accustomed to writing set-based code. Properly built objects written in the CLR need to follow many of the same principals as T-SQL.

Microsoft chose to host the CLR inside SQL Server for many reasons; some of the most important motivations follow:

- *Rich language support*: .NET integration allows developers and DBAs to use any .NET-compatible language for coding SQL Server objects. This includes such popular languages as C# and VB.NET.

- *Complex procedural logic and computations*: T-SQL is great at set-based logic, but .NET languages are superior for procedural/functional code. .NET languages have enhanced looping constructs that are more flexible and perform far better than T-SQL. You can more easily factor .NET code into functions, and it has much better error handling than T-SQL. T-SQL has some computational commands, but .NET has a much larger selection of computational commands. Most important for complex code, .NET ultimately compiles into native code while T-SQL is an interpreted language. This can result in huge performance wins for .NET code.

- *String manipulation, complex statistical calculations, custom encryption, and so on*: As discussed earlier, heavy computational requirements such as string manipulation, complex statistical calculations, and custom encryption algorithms that don't use the native SQL Server 2005 encryption fare better with .NET than with T-SQL in terms of both performance and flexibility.

- *.NET Framework classes*: The .NET Framework provides a wealth of functionality within its many classes, including classes for data access, file access, registry access, network functions, XML, string manipulation, diagnostics, regular expressions, arrays, and encryption.

- *Leveraging existing skills*: Developers familiar with .NET can be productive immediately in coding SQL Server objects. Familiarity with languages such as C# and VB.NET, as well as being familiar with the .NET Framework is of great value. Microsoft has made the server-side data-access model in ADO.NET similar to the client-side model, using many of the same classes to ease the transition. This is a double-edged sword, as it's necessary to determine where using .NET inside SQL Server provides an advantage over using T-SQL. I'll consider this topic further throughout this section.

- *Easier and safer substitute for extended stored procedures*: You can write extended stored procedures in C++ to provide additional functionality to SQL Server. This ability necessitates an experienced developer fluent in C++ and able to handle the risk of writing code that can crash the SQL Server engine. Stored procedures written in .NET that extend SQL Server's functionality can operate in a managed environment, which eliminates the risk of code crashing SQL Server and allows developers to pick the .NET language with which they're most comfortable.

- *New SQL Server objects and functionality*: If you want to create user-defined aggregates or user-defined types (UDTs) that extend the SQL Server type system, .NET is your only choice. You can't create these objects with T-SQL. There's also some new functionality only available to .NET code that allows for streaming table-valued functions. I'll cover streaming table-valued functions later in this chapter in the "User-Defined Functions" section.

- *Integration with Visual Studio*: Visual Studio is the premier development environment from Microsoft for developing .NET code. This environment has many productivity enhancements for developers. The Professional and higher versions also include a new SQL Server project, with code templates for developing SQL Server objects with .NET. These templates significantly ease the development of .NET SQL Server objects. Visual Studio .NET also makes it easier to debug and deploy .NET SQL Server objects.

---

■**Note** In 2008, some improvements have been made to the SQL CLR implementation, but the largest one is that the amount of data that can be serialized has increased from 8000 bytes to a full 2GB. This comes into play if you want to build a larger user-defined type and often when building user-defined aggregates.

---

However, while these are all good reasons for the *concept* of mixing of the two platforms, it isn't as if the CLR objects and T-SQL objects are equivalent. As such, it is important to consider the reasons that you might choose the CLR over T-SQL, and vice versa, when building objects. The inclusion of the CLR inside SQL Server offers an excellent enabling technology that brings with it power, flexibility, and design choices. And of course, as we DBA types are cautious people, there's a concern that the CLR is unnecessary and will be misused by developers. Although any technology has the possibility of misuse, you shouldn't dismiss the SQLCLR without consideration as to where it can be leveraged as an effective tool to improve your database designs.

What really makes using the CLR for T-SQL objects is that in some cases, T-SQL just does not provide native access to the type of coding you need without looping and doing all sorts of machinations. In T-SQL it is the SQL queries and smooth handling of data that make it a wonderful language to work with. In almost every case, if you can fashion a SQL query to do the work you need, T-SQL will be your best bet. However, once you have to start using cursors and/or T-SQL control of flow language (for example, looping through the characters of a string or through rows in a table,) performance will suffer mightily. This is because T-SQL is an interpreted language. In a well-thought-out T-SQL object, you may have a few non-SQL statements, variable declarations, and so on. Your statements will not execute as fast as they could in a CLR object, but the difference will often just be milliseconds if not microseconds.

The real difference comes if you start to perform looping operations, as the numbers of operations grow fast and really start to cost. In the CLR, the code is compiled and runs very fast. For example, I needed to get the maximum time that a row had been modified from a join of multiple tables. There were three ways to get that information. The first method is to issue a correlated subquery in the SELECT clause:

```
SELECT a.<columns>, b.<columns>,..., n.<columns>,
                (SELECT MAX(lastUpdateTime)
                 FROM   (SELECT a.lastUpdateTime
                         UNION ALL
                         SELECT b.lastUpdateTime
                         UNION ALL
                         ...
                         UNION ALL
                         SELECT n.lastUpdateTime) as dates) as lastUpdateTime
FROM    a
        JOIN b
            ON a.akey = b.akey
        ...
        JOIN n
            ON a.akey = n.akey
```

Yes, Oracle users will probably note that this subquery performs the task that their GREATEST function will (or so I have been told many times). The approach in this query is a very good approach, and works adequately for most cases, but it is not necessarily the fastest way to answer the question that I've posed. A second, and a far more natural, approach for most programmers is to build a T-SQL scalar user-defined function:

```
CREATE FUNCTION date$getGreatest
(
    @date1    datetime,
    @date2    datetime,
    @date3    datetime = NULL,
    @date4    datetime = NULL
)
RETURNS datetime
AS
  BEGIN
    RETURN (SELECT MAX(dateValue)
            FROM  ( SELECT @date1 as dateValue
                          UNION ALL
                          SELECT @date2
                          UNION ALL
                          SELECT @date3
                          UNION ALL
                          SELECT @date4 ) as dates)

END
```

This is a pretty decent approach, though it is actually slower to execute than the native T-SQL approach in the tests I have run, as there is some overhead in using user-defined functions, and since the algorithm is the same, you are merely costing yourself. The third method is to employ a CLR user-defined function. The function I will create is pretty basic and uses what is really a brute force algorithm:

```
<SqlFunction(IsDeterministic:=True, DataAccess:=DataAccessKind.None, _
                              Name:="date$getMax_CLR", _
                              IsPrecise:=True)> _
Public Shared Function MaxDate(ByVal inputDate1 As SqlDateTime, _
                            ByVal inputDate2 As SqlDateTime, _
                            ByVal inputDate3 As SqlDateTime, _
                          ByVal inputDate4 As SqlDateTime _
                              ) As SqlDateTime

    Dim outputDate As SqlDateTime

    If inputDate2 > inputDate1 Then outputDate = inputDate2
                              Else outputDate = inputDate1
    If inputDate3 > outputDate Then outputDate = inputDate3
    If inputDate4 > outputDate Then outputDate = inputDate4

    Return New SqlDateTime(outputDate.Value)

End Function
```

Generally, I just let VS .NET build and deploy the object into tempdb for me and script it out to distribute to other databases (I have included the script in the downloads, as well as the project in VS .NET). For cases where the number of data parameters is great (ten or so in my testing on moderate, enterprise-level hardware), the CLR version will execute several times faster than either of the other versions. This is very true in most cases where you have to do some very functional-like logic, rather than using set-based logic. In the date example, I force a set-based solution to make T-SQL better, but in the end, the CLR solution operates faster because doing individual comparison operations will be faster in the compiled language.

Ignoring for a moment the performance factors, some problems are just easier to solve using the CLR, and the solution is just as good, if not better than using T-SQL. For example, to get a value from a comma-delimited list in T-SQL requires either a looping operation or the use of techniques requiring a sequence table (as introduced in Chapter 7). This technique is slightly difficult to follow and is too large to reproduce here as an illustration.

However, in .NET, getting a comma-delimited value from a list is a built-in operation:

```
Dim tokens() As String = Strings.Split(s.ToString(), delimiter.ToString(), _
                                         -1, CompareMethod.Text)

    ' return string at array position specified by parameter
    If tokenNumber > 0 AndAlso tokens.Length >= tokenNumber.Value Then
    Return tokens(tokenNumber.Value - 1).Trim()
```

In this section, I have made the CLR implementation sound like sunshine and puppy dogs. Well, sometimes, the sun gives you cancer, and puppy dogs bite and mess up carpets. I did this to impress upon you that the CLR is *not bad* in and of itself. It is, however, not a replacement for T-SQL. It is a complementary technology that can be used to help programmers do some of the things that T-SQL does not necessarily do well.

The basic thing to remember is that while the CLR offers some great value, T-SQL is the language on which most all of your objects should be based. A good practice is to continue writing your routines using T-SQL until you find that it is just too difficult or slow to get done using T-SQL; then try the CLR.

In the next two sections, I will cover the guidelines for choosing either T-SQL or the CLR.

# Guidelines for Choosing T-SQL

Let's get one thing straight: T-SQL isn't going away anytime soon. On the contrary, it's being enhanced, along with the addition of the CLR. Much of the same code that you write today with T-SQL in SQL Server 7 or 2000 is still best done the same way with SQL Server 2005. If your routines primarily access data, I would first consider using T-SQL. The CLR is a complementary technology that will allow you to optimize some situations that could not be optimized well enough using T-SQL.

The exception to this guideline of using T-SQL for SQL Server routines that access data is if the routine contains a significant amount of conditional logic, looping constructs, and/or complex procedural code that isn't suited to set-based programming. What's a significant amount? You must review that on a case-by-case basis. It is also important to ask yourself, "Is this task even something that should be done in the data layer, or is the design perhaps suboptimal and a different application layer should be doing the work?

If there are performance gains or the routine is much easier to code and maintain when using .NET, it's worth considering a .NET approach instead of T-SQL. T-SQL is the best tool for set-based logic and should be your first consideration if your routine calls for set-based functionality. I suggest avoiding rewriting your T-SQL routines in .NET unless there's a definite benefit. If you are rewriting routines, do so only after trying a T-SQL option and asking in the newsgroups and forums if there is a better way to do it. T-SQL is a very powerful language that can do amazing things if you understand it. But if you have loops or algorithms that can't be done easily, the CLR is there to get you compiled and ready to go.

Keep in mind that T-SQL is constantly being enhanced with such features as MERGE, table parameters, row constructors in 2008, and in 2005, we got CTEs (which gave us recursive queries), the ability to PIVOT data, new TRY-CATCH syntax for improved error handling, and other various features we can now take advantage of. If there are new T-SQL features you can use to make code faster, easier to write, and/or easier to maintain, you should consider this approach before trying to write the equivalent functionality in .NET.

---

■**Note**  Truthfully, if T-SQL is used correctly with a well designed database, almost all of your code will fit nicely into T-SQL code with only a function or two possibly needing to be created using the CLR.

---

## Guidelines for Choosing .NET

The integration of .NET is an enabling technology. It's not best suited for all occasions, but it has some advantages over T-SQL that merit consideration. As we've discussed, .NET compiles to native code, and is better suited to complex logic and CPU-intensive code than T-SQL. One of the best scenarios for the CLR approach to code is writing scalar functions that don't need to access data. Typically, these will perform an order (or orders) of magnitude faster than their T-SQL counterparts. .NET user-defined functions can take advantage of the rich support of the .NET Framework, which includes optimized classes for functions such as string manipulation, regular expressions, and math functions. In addition to .NET scalar functions, streaming table-valued functions is another great use of .NET. This allows you to expose arbitrary data structures—such as the file system or registry—as rowsets, and allows the query processor to understand the data.

Another excellent use for .NET is as a safe and relatively easy alternative to coding extended stored procedures. .NET provides access to a host of classes in the .NET Framework, and is a much safer environment than using C++, as I discussed earlier in this chapter. "Regular" stored procedures that access data are most often written with T-SQL. The exception discussed in the preceding section is when the stored procedure contains a lot of procedural code and moves a lot of data around close to the server.

The next two scenarios where .NET can be useful are user-defined aggregates and .NET-based UDTs. You can only write user-defined aggregates with .NET. They allow a developer to perform any aggregate such as SUM or COUNT that SQL Server doesn't already do. Complex statistical aggregations would be a good example. I've already discussed .NET UDTs. These have a definite benefit when used to extend the type system with additional primitives such as point, SSN, and date (without time) types. As I discussed in Chapter 5, you shouldn't use .NET UDTs to define business objects in the database.

## CLR Object Types

This section provides a brief discussion of each of the different types of objects you can create with the CLR. You'll also find additional discussion about the merits (or disadvantages) of using the CLR for each type.

You can build any of the following types of objects using the CLR, including:

- User-defined functions
- Stored procedures
- Triggers
- User-defined aggregates
- User-defined types

---

■**Note** If you owned the previous version of this book, you may remember that I gave full examples of each type of object. They were new in 2005, and I felt including those examples was a good idea. In this edition, I give only prescriptive advice for each type, though I will still provide the example code for each type of object in a download on the Apress website for you to try out.

---

## User-Defined Functions

When the CLR was added to SQL Server, using it would have been worth the effort had it allowed you only to implement user-defined functions. Scalar user-defined functions that are highly computational are the sweet spot of coding SQL Server objects with .NET, particularly when you have more than a statement or two executing such functions. In fact, functions are the only type of objects that I have personally created using the CLR. Those functions have been a tremendous tool for improving performance of several key portions of the systems I have worked with.

You can make both table value and scalar functions, and they will often be many times faster than corresponding T-SQL objects when there is no need for data other than what you pass in via parameters. CLR functions that have to query data via SQL become cumbersome to program, and usually coding them in T-SQL will simply be easier. Examples of functions that I have built using the CLR include:

- *Date functions*: Especially those for getting time zone information
- *Comparison functions*: For comparing several values to one another, like the date$getMax function shown earlier, though with more like 30 parameters instead of 4.
- *Calculation functions*: Performing math functions or building a custom soundex-style function for comparing strings, and so forth

Of all of the CLR object types, the user-defined functions are definitely the ones that you should consider using to replace your T-SQL objects, particularly when you are not interacting with data in SQL.

## Stored Procedures

As a replacement for extended stored procedures, .NET stored procedures provide a safe and relatively easy means to extend the functionality of SQL Server. Examples of extended stored procedures include xp_sendmail, xp_cmdshell, and xp_regread. Traditionally, extended stored procedures required writing code in a language such as C++ and ran in-process with the sqlservr.exe process. .NET stored procedures have the same capabilities as traditional, extended stored procedures, but they're easier to code and run in the safer environment of managed code. Of course, the more external resources that you access, the less safe your CLR object will be. The fact is that extended stored procedures were very often a dangerous choice, no matter how many resources you used outside of SQL server.

Another means of extending SQL Server was using the extended stored procedures beginning with sp_OA%. These used OLE automation to allow you to access COM objects that could be used to do things that T-SQL was unable to accomplish on its own. These objects were always slow and often unreliable. .NET is an admirable replacement for the sp_OA% procedures and COM objects, as you can now use the .NET Framework classes to perform the same functionality as COM objects can.

If you are iterating through a set (perhaps using a cursor) performing some row-wise logic, you might try using .NET and the SqlDataReader class as it can be faster than using cursors. That said, it's best to start with T-SQL for your stored procedures that access SQL Server data, since there is very little that you cannot do using setwise manipulations, especially using ROW_NUMBER and the other ranking functions.

If performance of the stored procedure becomes a factor and there's lots of *necessary* procedural and computational logic within the stored procedure, experimenting with rewriting the stored procedure using .NET might be worthwhile

Quite often, if you find yourself doing too much in T-SQL code, you might be doing too much in the data layer, and perhaps you should move the procedural and computational logic away from the database to the middle tier and use the T-SQL stored procedure(s) primarily for data-access routines.

## Triggers

If you choose to use triggers in your database architecture, they're almost the exclusive domain of T-SQL. I felt this when I first heard of CLR triggers, and I feel this now. There is really not a good mainstream scenario where .NET triggers are going to be better than a well written T-SQL trigger. For any complex validation that might be done in a trigger, a better option is probably to use a .NET scalar function and call it from within a T-SQL trigger. Perhaps if there's significant procedural logic in a trigger, .NET would be a better choice than T-SQL.

However, be careful when using complex triggers. Almost any complex activity in a trigger is probably a cause for moving to use some form of queue where the trigger pushes rows off to some layer that operates asynchronously from the current transaction.

---

■**Note** Refer to Chapter 6 for more information about triggers in general.

---

## User-Defined Aggregates

User-defined aggregates are a feature that have been desired for many years, and in 2005, with the introduction of the CLR, we were finally able to create our own aggregate functions. SQL Server already includes the most commonly used aggregate functions such as SUM, COUNT, and AVG. There might be a time when your particular business needs a special type of aggregate, or you need a complex statistical aggregate not supplied out of the box by SQL Server. Aggregates you create are not limited to numeric values either. An aggregate that I've always wanted is one similar to Sybase's List() aggregate that concatenates a list of strings in a column, separating them by commas.

In the download for this book, you will find the code for the following aggregate function, called string$list (I also include the assembly in the T-SQL code for those of you who are purists who think VB and C# are for others). Once the function's code is compiled and loaded into SQL server, you can do something like this:

```
SELECT  dbo.string$list(name) as names
FROM    (VALUES('Name'),('Name2'),('Name3')) as Names (name)
```

This will return:

---
-------------------------------------------------------------------------

Name, Name2, Name3

---

In informal testing, running code like this using a custom aggregate can give an order of magnitude performance improvement over the T-SQL alternatives of using XML or over any trick you can do with variables and concatenation. A good part of the reason that the CLR version runs faster is that the T-SQL version is going to run a query for each group of values desired, while the CLR version is simply aggregating the products returned from the single query, using techniques that are natural to the SQL engine.

Versions of Visual Studio 2005 or 2008 Professional and higher provide a SQL Server project and template that includes the stub for the functions that must be included as part of the contract for coding a .NET user-defined aggregate. For each aggregate, you must implement the `Init`, `Accumulate`, `Merge`, and `Terminate` functions. Besides the obvious performance benefit, there's also the flexibility benefit of being able to use such an aggregate with any column of any table. That is definitely unlike the T-SQL options where you need to hard-code which column and table are being aggregated.

---

■**Note** In SQL Server 2008, you can now pass more than one parameter to your aggregate function, allowing you to perform far more interesting aggregations involving multiple values from each individual row returned by a query.

---

## User-Defined Types

The case for user-defined types was made back in Chapter 5, and I included a sample for them that implemented a United States social security number. Microsoft has also built several types into SQL Server 2008 using the CLR. These are the `hierarchyId` and the spatial types. The fact is, though, that you should hesitate to base all of your datatypes on CLR types. The intrinsic, built-in datatypes will suffice for nearly every situation you will find, but if you have a need for a richer type with some complex handling, they are definitely available.

One thing that makes me feel better about using the CLR for types in 2008 versus 2005 is the types that Microsoft has built using them. In 2005, Microsoft tried to include a few datatypes in the product that were based on the CLR (`date` and `time` types), and those datatypes did not make it into the final product. No matter the actual reasons for them not making it into the product, it did not make it seem overly safe to make large use of these types in our systems. The more that Microsoft uses a feature, the better it gets tested and used by the general public, and the more bulletproof it becomes.

Finally, one thing to remember about using CLR user-defined types. In order to get the full experience using the types, you will need to have the client set up to use them. To access the properties and methods of a UDT on the client and take full advantage of the new datatype, each client must have a copy of the UDT available in an assembly accessible by the client. If the .NET code for a UDT is updated on SQL Server, the UDT class that's registered on each client that makes use of the UDT should be kept in sync with the server version to avoid any data problems. If the client does not have the UDT class available (like when you return the value of a column based on a UDT in Management Studio), the value will be returned as a hexadecimal value, unless you use the `.ToString` method on the type (which is a requirement for building a type that I demonstrated in Chapter 5 when I built the SSN type).

# Best Practices

The first half of the chapter discussed the two primary methods of architecting a SQL Server application, either by using stored procedures as the primary interface, or by using *ad hoc* calls built outside the server. Either is acceptable, but in my opinion the best way to go is to use stored procedures as much as possible. There are a few reasons:

- As precompiled batches of SQL statements that are known at design and implementation time, you get a great interface to the database that encapsulates the details of the database from the caller.

- They can be a performance boost, primarily because tuning is on a known set of queries, and not just on any query that the programmer might have written that slips by untested (not even maliciously; it could just be a bit of functionality that only gets used "occasionally").

- They allow you to define a consistent interface for security that lets you give users access to a table in one situation but not in another. Plus, if procedures are consistently named, giving access to database resources is far easier.

However, not every system is written using stored procedures. *Ad hoc* access can serve to build a fine system as well. You certainly can build a flexible architecture, but it can also lead to hard-to-maintain code that ends up with the client tools being tightly coupled with the database structures. At the very least, if you balk at the use of procedures, make sure to architect in a manner that makes tuning your queries reasonable without full regression testing of the application.

I wish I could give you definitive best practices, but there are so many possibilities, and either method has pros and cons (plus, there would be a mob with torches and pitchforks at my door, no matter how I said things must be done). This topic will continue to be hotly contested, and rightly so. In the last few releases of SQL Server, Microsoft continues to improve the use of *ad hoc* SQL, but it's still considered a best practice to use stored procedures if you can. I realize that in a large percentage of systems that are created, stored procedures are only used when there's a compelling reason to do so.

Whether or not you decide to use stored-procedure access or use *ad hoc* calls instead, you'll probably want to code some objects for use in the database. New to SQL Server 2005, there's another interesting decision to make regarding what language and technology to use when building several of these database objects. The best practices for the CLR usage are a bit more clear cut:

- *User-defined functions*: When there's no data access, the CLR is almost always a better way to build user-defined functions. When data access is required, it will be dependent on the types of operations being done in the function, but most data access functions would be best at least done initially in T-SQL.

- *Stored procedures*: For typical data-oriented stored procedures, T-SQL is usually the best course of action. On the other hand, when using the CLR, it's far easier and much safer to create replacements for extended stored procedures (procedures typically named xp_) that do more than simply touch data.

- *User-defined types*: For the most part, the advice here is to avoid them, unless you have a compelling reason to use them. For example, you might need complex datatypes that have operations defined between them (such as calculating the distance between two points) that can be encapsulated into the type. The client needs the datatype installed to get a natural interface; otherwise the clunky .NET-like methods need to be used (they aren't SQL-like).

- *User-defined aggregates*: You can only create these types of objects using .NET. User-defined aggregates allow for some interesting capabilities for operating on groups of data, like the example of a string aggregation.

- *Triggers*: There seems to be little reason to use triggers built into a CLR language. Triggers are about data manipulation. Even with DDL triggers, the primary goal is usually to insert data into a table to make note of a situation.

# Summary

In this chapter full of opinions, what's clear is that SQL Server 2005 and 2008 have continued to increase the number of options for writing code that accesses data. I've covered two topics that you need to consider when architecting your relational database applications using SQL Server. Designing the structure of the database is (reasonably) easy enough. Follow the principles set out by normalization to ensure that you have limited, if any, redundancy of data and limited anomalies when you modify or create data. On the other hand, once you have the database architected from an internal standpoint, you have to write code to access this data, and this is where you have a couple of seemingly difficult choices.

The case for using stored procedures is compelling (at least to many SQL architects), but it isn't a definite. Many programmers use *ad hoc* T-SQL calls to access SQL Server (including those made from middleware tools), and this isn't ever likely to change completely. This topic is frequently debated in blogs, forums, newsgroups, and church picnics with little budge from either side. I strongly suggest stored procedures for the reasons laid out in this chapter, but I do concede that it isn't the only way.

I then introduced the new CLR features, and presented examples and opinions about how and when to use them. I dare say that some of the opinions concerning the CLR in this chapter might shift a little over time (especially as service packs begin to arrive), but for the most part, the CLR is going to be most valuable as a tool to supercharge parts of queries, especially in places where T-SQL was poor because it was interpreted at runtime, rather than compiled. Usually this isn't a problem, because decent T-SQL usually has few functional statements, and all the real work is done in set-based SQL statements.

However, at times, in T-SQL you'd need to loop through a set, iterate over the characters in a string, or something along these lines, where it would seemingly take forever to do a single operation. Add onto this putting a function that did some heavy computing into a SELECT or WHERE clause, and life got worse. Proper application of a CLR user-defined function speeds up many slow-running queries where the user-defined functions based on T-SQL were ill-advised at best. The CLR can add performance benefits and additional functionality to your database solutions when used with care.

The primary thing to take from this chapter is that lots of tools are provided to access the data in your databases. Use them wisely, and your results will be excellent. Use them poorly, and your results will be poor. Hopefully this advice will be of value to you, but as you were warned at the start of the chapter, a good amount of this chapter was opinion.

Last, the decision about the data-access method (i.e., *ad hoc* SQL code versus stored procedures and how much to use the CLR) should be chosen for a given project up front, when considering high-level design. For the sake of consistency, I would hope that the decision would be enforced across all components of the application(s). Nothing is worse than having to figure out the application as you dig into it.

---

■**Note** A resource that I want to point out for further reading after this chapter is from Erland Sommarskog. His website (http://www.sommarskog.se/) contains a plethora of information regarding many of the topics I have covered in this chapter and in far deeper detail. I would consider most of what I have said the introductory-level course, while his papers are nearly graduate-level courses in the topics he covers.

---

# APPENDIX A

■■■

# Codd's 12 Rules for an RDBMS

**A**lthough most of us think that any database that supports SQL is automatically considered a relational database, this isn't always the case—at least not completely. In Chapter 1, I discussed the basics and foundations of relational theory, but no discussion on this subject would be complete without looking at the rules that were formulated in 1985 in a two-part article published by *Computerworld* magazine ("Is Your DBMS Really Relational?" and "Does Your DBMS Run By the Rules?" by E. F. Codd, *Computerworld*, October 14 and October 21, 1985). Many websites also outline these rules. These rules go beyond relational theory and defines more specific criteria that need to be met in an RDBMS, if it's to be truly relational.

It might seem like old news, but the same criteria can still be used today to measure how relational a database is. These rules are frequently brought up in conversations when discussing how well a particular database server is implemented. I present the rules in this appendix, along with brief comments as to whether SQL Server 2008 meets each of them, or otherwise. Relational theory has come a long way since these rules were first published, and "serious" theorists have enhanced and refined relational theory tremendously since then, as you'd expect. A good place for more serious learning is the website http://www.dbdebunk.com, run by C. J. Date and Fabian Pascal, or any of their books. If you want to see the debates on theory, the newsgroup comp.databases.theory is a truly interesting place. Of course, as the cover of this book states, my goal is practicality, with a foundation on theory, so I won't delve too deeply into theory here at all. I present these 12 rules simply to set a basis for what a relational database started out to be and largely what it is and what it should be even today.

All these rules are based upon what's sometimes referred to as the *foundation principle*, which states that for any system to be called a relational database management system, the relational capabilities must be able to manage it completely.

For the rest of this appendix, I'll treat SQL Server 2008 specifically as a relational database engine, not in any of the other configurations in which it might be used, such as a plain data store, a document storage device, or whatever other way you might use SQL Server as a storage engine.

## Rule 1: The Information Rule

*All information in the relational database is represented in exactly one and only one way—by values in tables.*

This rule is an informal definition of a relational database and indicates that every piece of data that we permanently store in a database is located in a table.

In general, SQL Server fulfills this rule, because we cannot store any information in anything other than a table. We can't use the variables in this code to persist any data, and therefore they're scoped to a single batch.

# Rule 2: Guaranteed Access Rule

*Each and every datum (atomic value) is guaranteed to be logically accessible by resorting to a combination of table name, primary key value, and column name.*

This rule stresses the importance of primary keys for locating data in the database. The table name locates the correct table, the column name finds the correct column, and the primary key value finds the row containing an individual data item of interest. In other words, each (atomic) piece of data is accessible by the combination of table name, primary key value, and column name. This rule exactly specifies how we access data using an access language such as Transact-SQL (T-SQL) in SQL Server.

Using SQL, we can search for the primary key value (which is guaranteed to be unique, based on relational theory, as long as it has been defined), and once we have the row, the data is accessed via the column name. We can also access data by any of the columns in the table, though we aren't always guaranteed to receive a single row back.

# Rule 3: Systematic Treatment of NULL Values

NULL *values (distinct from empty character string or a string of blank characters and distinct from zero or any other number) are supported in the fully relational RDBMS for representing missing information in a systematic way, independent of data type.*

This rule requires that the RDBMS support a distinct NULL placeholder, regardless of datatype. NULLs are distinct from an empty character string or any other number, and they are always to be considered as unknown values.

NULLs must propagate through mathematic operations as well as string operations. NULL + <anything> = NULL, the logic being that NULL means "unknown." If you add something known to something unknown, you still don't know what you have, so it's still unknown.

There are a few settings in SQL Server that can customize how NULLs are treated. Most of these settings exist because of some poor practices that were allowed in early versions of SQL Server:

- ANSI_NULLS: Determines how NULL comparisons are handled. When OFF, then NULL = NULL is True for the comparison, and when ON (the default), NULL = NULL returns UNKNOWN.

- CONCAT_NULL_YIELDS_NULL: When the CONCAT_NULL_YIELDS_NULL setting is set ON, NULLs are treated properly, such that NULL + 'String Value' = NULL. If the CONCAT_NULL_YIELDS_NULL setting is OFF, which is allowed for backward compatibility with SQL Server, NULLs are treated in a nonstandard way such that NULL + 'String Value' = 'String Value'.

# Rule 4: Dynamic Online Catalog Based on the Relational Model

*The database description is represented at the logical level in the same way as ordinary data, so authorized users can apply the same relational language to its interrogation as they apply to regular data.*

This rule requires that a relational database be self-describing. In other words, the database must contain certain system tables whose columns describe the structure of the database itself, or alternatively, the database description is contained in user-accessible tables.

This rule is becoming more of a reality in each new version of SQL Server, as with the implementation of the INFORMATION_SCHEMA system views. The INFORMATION_SCHEMA is a schema that has a set of views to look at much of the metadata for the tables, the relationships, the constraints, and even the code in the database.

Anything else you need to know can most likely be viewed in the system views (in the SYS schema). They're the system views that replaced the system tables in 2005 that we had used since the beginning of SQL Server time. These views are far easier to read and use, and most all the data is self-explanatory, rather than requiring bitwise operations on some columns to find the value.

# Rule 5: Comprehensive Data Sublanguage Rule

*A relational system may support several languages and various modes of terminal use. However, there must be at least one language whose statements are expressible, per some well-defined syntax, as character strings and whose ability to support all of the following is comprehensible: a. data definition b. view definition c. data manipulation (interactive and by program) d. integrity constraints e. authorization f. transaction boundaries (begin, commit, and rollback).*

This rule mandates the existence of a relational database language, such as SQL, to manipulate data. SQL as such isn't specifically required. The language must be able to support all the central functions of a DBMS: creating a database, retrieving and entering data, implementing database security, and so on. T-SQL fulfils this function for SQL Server and carries out all the data definition and manipulation tasks required to access data.

SQL is a nonprocedural language, in that you don't specify "how" things happen, or even where. You simply ask a question of the relational server, and it does the work.

# Rule 6: View Updating Rule

*All views that are theoretically updateable are also updateable by the system.*

This rule deals with views, which are virtual tables used to give various users of a database different views of its structure. It's one of the most challenging rules to implement in practice, and no commercial product fully satisfies it today.

A view is theoretically updateable as long as it's made up of columns that directly correspond to real table columns. In SQL Server, views are updateable as long as you don't update more than a single table in the statement; neither can you update a derived or constant field. SQL Server 2000 also implemented INSTEAD OF triggers that you can apply to a view (see Chapter 6). Hence, this rule can be technically fulfilled using INSTEAD OF triggers, but in what can be a less-than-straightforward manner. You need to take care when considering how to apply updates, especially if the view contains a GROUP BY clause and possibly aggregates.

# Rule 7: High-Level Insert, Update, and Delete

*The capability of handling a base relation or a derived relation as a single operand applies not only to the retrieval of data but also to the insertion, update, and deletion of data.*

This rule stresses the set-oriented nature of a relational database. It requires that rows be treated as sets in insert, delete, and update operations. The rule is designed to prohibit implementations that support only row-at-a-time, navigational modification of the database. The SQL language covers this via the INSERT, UPDATE, and DELETE statements.

Even the CLR doesn't allow you to access the physical files where the data is stored, but BCP does kind of go around this. As always, you have to be extra careful when you use the low-level tools that can modify the data without going through the typical SQL syntax, because it can ignore the rules you have set up, introducing inconsistencies into your data.

# Rule 8: Physical Data Independence

*Application programs and terminal activities remain logically unimpaired whenever any changes are made in either storage representation or access methods.*

Applications must still work using the same syntax, even when changes are made to the way in which the database internally implements data storage and access methods. This rule implies that the way the data is stored physically must be independent of the logical manner in which it's accessed. This is saying that users shouldn't be concerned about how the data is stored or how it's accessed. In fact, users of the data need only be able to get the basic definition of the data they need.

Other things that shouldn't affect the user's view of the data are as follows:

- *Adding indexes*: Indexes determine how the data is stored, yet the user, through SQL, will never know that indexes are being used.

- *Changing the filegroup of an object*: Just moving a table to a new filegroup will not affect the application. You access the data in the same way no matter where it is physically located.

- *Using partitioning*: Beyond moving entire tables around to different filegroups, you can move parts of a table around by using partitioning technologies to spread access around to different independent subsystems to enhance performance.

- *Modifying the storage engine*: From time to time, Microsoft has to modify how SQL Server operates (especially in major version upgrades). However, SQL statements must appear to access the data in the same manner as they did in any previous version, only (we hope) faster.

Microsoft has put a lot of work into this area, because SQL Server has a separate relational engine and storage engine, and OLE DB is used to pass data between the two. Further reading on this topic is available in SQL Server 2008 Books Online in the "Database Engine Components" topic or in *Inside Microsoft SQL Server 2005: The Storage Engine* by Kalen Delaney (Microsoft Press, 2006).

# Rule 9: Logical Data Independence

*Application programs and terminal activities remain logically unimpaired when informa-tion preserving changes of any kind that theoretically permit unimpairment are made to the base tables.*

Along with rule 8, this rule insulates the user or application program from the low-level implemen-tation of the database. Together, they specify that specific access or storage techniques used by the RDBMS—and even changes to the structure of the tables in the database—shouldn't affect the user's ability to work with the data.

In this way, if you add a column to a table and if tables are split in a manner that doesn't add or subtract columns, then the application programs that call the database should be unimpaired.

For example, say you have the table in Figure A-1.

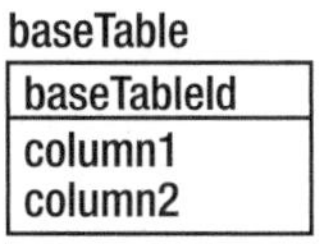

baseTable

| baseTableId |
| --- |
| column1 |
| column2 |

**Figure A-1.** *Small sample table*

Then, say you vertically break it up into two tables (see Figure A-2).

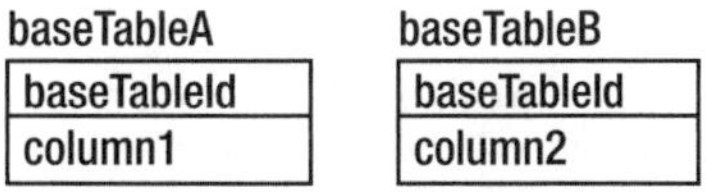

baseTableA          baseTableB

| baseTableId |
| --- |
| column1 |

| baseTableId |
| --- |
| column2 |

**Figure A-2.** *Small sample table split into two tables*

You then could create this view:

```
CREATE VIEW baseTable
AS
SELECT baseTableId, column1, column2
FROM   baseTableA
         JOIN baseTableB
             ON baseTableA.baseTableId = baseTableB.baseTableId
```

The user should be unaffected. If you were to implement `INSTEAD OF` triggers on the view that had the same number of columns with the same names, you could seamlessly meet the need to manage the view in the exact manner the table was managed. Note that the handling of identity columns can be tricky in views, because they require data to be entered, even when the data won't be used. See Chapter 6 for more details on creating `INSTEAD OF` triggers.

Of course, you cannot always make this rule work if columns or tables are removed from the system, but you can make the rule work if columns and data are simply added.

---

■**Tip** Always access data from the RDBMS by name, and not by position or by using the `SELECT *` wildcard. The order of columns shouldn't make a difference to the application.

---

# Rule 10: Integrity Independence

*Integrity constraints specific to a particular relational database must be definable in the relational data sublanguage and storable in the catalog, not in the application programs.*

The database must support a minimum of the following two integrity constraints:

- *Entity integrity*: No component of a primary key is allowed to have a NULL value.
- *Referential integrity*: For each distinct non-NULL foreign key value in a relational database, there must exist a matching primary key value from the same domain.

This rule says that the database language should support integrity constraints that restrict the data that can be entered into the database and the database modifications that can be made. In other words, the RDBMS must internally support the definition and enforcement of entity integrity (primary keys) and referential integrity (foreign keys).

It requires that the database be able to implement constraints to protect the data from invalid values and that careful database design is needed to ensure that referential integrity is achieved. SQL Server 2008 does a great job of providing the tools to make this rule a reality. We can protect our data from invalid values for most any possible case using constraints and triggers. Most of Chapter 6 was spent covering the methods that we can use in SQL Server to implement integrity independence.

# Rule 11: Distribution Independence

*The data manipulation sublanguage of a relational DBMS must enable application programs and terminal activities to remain logically unimpaired whether and whenever data are physically centralized or distributed.*

This rule says that the database language must be able to manipulate data located on other computer systems. In essence, we should be able to split the data on the RDBMS out onto multiple physical systems without the user realizing it. SQL Server 2008 supports distributed transactions among SQL Server sources, as well as other types of sources using the Microsoft Distributed Transaction Coordinator service.

Another distribution-independence possibility is a group of database servers working together more or less as one. Database servers working together like this are considered to be *federated*. With every new SQL Server version, the notion of federated database servers seamlessly sharing the load is becoming a definite reality. More reading on this subject can be found in the SQL Server 2008 Books Online in the "Federated Database Servers" topic.

# Rule 12: Non-Subversion Rule

*If a relational system has or supports a low-level (single-record-at-a-time) language, that low-level language cannot be used to subvert or bypass the integrity rules or constraints expressed in the higher-level (multiple-records-at-a-time) relational language.*

This rule requires that alternate methods of accessing the data are not able to bypass integrity constraints, which means that users can't violate the rules of the database in any way. For most SQL

Server 2008 applications, this rule is followed, because there are no methods of getting to the raw data and changing values other than by the methods prescribed by the database. However, SQL Server 2008 violates this rule in two places:

- *Bulk copy*: By default, you can use the bulk copy routines to insert data into the table directly and around the database server validations.

- *Disabling constraints and triggers*: There's syntax to disable constraints and triggers, thereby subverting this rule.

It's always good practice to make sure you use these two features carefully. They leave gaping holes in the integrity of your data, because they allow any values to be inserted in any column. Because you're expecting the data to be protected by the constraint you've applied, data value errors might occur in the programs that use the data, without revalidating it first.

# Summary

Codd's 12 rules for relational databases can be used to explain much about how SQL Server operates today. These rules were a major step forward in determining whether a database vendor could call his system "relational" and presented stiff implementation challenges for database developers. Fifteen years on, even the implementation of the most complex of these rules is becoming achievable, though SQL Server (and other RDBMSs) still fall short of achieving all their objectives.

# APPENDIX B

■■■

# Scalar Datatype Reference

**C**hoosing proper datatypes to match the domain to satisfy logical modeling is an important task. One datatype might be more efficient than another of a similar type. For example, you can store integer data in an integer datatype, a numeric datatype, a floating point datatype, a character type, or even a binary column, but these datatypes certainly aren't alike in implementation or performance.

In this appendix, I'll introduce you to all the intrinsic datatypes that Microsoft provides and discuss the situations where they're best used. The following is a list of the datatypes I'll cover. I'll discuss when to use them and in some cases why not to use them.

- *Precise numeric data*: Stores data with no loss of precision due to storage.
    - bit: Stores either 1, 0, or NULL. Used for Boolean-type columns.
    - tinyint: Non-negative values between 0 and 255.
    - smallint: Integers between -32,768 and 32,767.
    - int: Integers between 2,147,483,648 and 2,147,483,647 ($-2^{31}$ to $2^{31} - 1$).
    - bigint: Integers between 9,223,372,036,854,775,808 and 9,223,372,036,854,775,807 (that is, $-2^{63}$ to $2^{63} - 1$).
    - decimal: Values between $-10^{38} + 1$ through $10^{38} - 1$.
    - money: Values from -922,337,203,685,477.5808 through 922,337,203,685,477.5807.
    - smallmoney: Values from -214,748.3648 through +214,748.3647.
- *Approximate numeric data*: Stores approximations of numbers. Provides for a large range of values.
    - float (N): Values in the range from -1.79E + 308 through 1.79E + 308.
    - real: Values in the range from -3.40E + 38 through 3.40E + 38. real is a synonym for a float(24) datatype.
- *Date and time*: Stores date values, including time of day.
    - date: Date-only values from January 1, 0001, to December 31, 9999 (3 bytes).
    - time: Time of day–only values to 100 nanoseconds (3–5 bytes). Note that the range of this type is from 0:00 to 23:59:59 and some fraction of a second based on the precision you select.
    - smalldatetime: Dates from January 1, 1900, through June 6, 2079, with accuracy to 1 minute (4 bytes).
    - datetime: Dates from January 1, 1753, to December 31, 9999, with accuracy to ~3 milliseconds (stored in increments of .000, .003, or .007 seconds) (8 bytes).

- `datetime2`: Despite the hideous name, this type will store dates from January 1, 0001, to December 31, 9999, to 100-nanosecond accuracy (6–8 bytes). The accuracy is based on the precision you select.

- `datetimeoffset`: Same as `datetime2` but includes an offset from UTC time (8–10 bytes).

- *Character (or string) data*: Used to store textual data, such as names, descriptions, notes, and so on.

  - `char`: Fixed-length character data up to 8,000 characters long.

  - `varchar`: Variable-length character data up to 8,000 characters long.

  - `varchar(max)`: Large variable-length character data; maximum length of $2^{31} - 1$ (2,147,483,647) bytes, or 2GB.

  - `text`: Large text values; maximum length of $2^{31} - 1$ (2,147,483,647) bytes, or 2GB. (Note that this datatype is outdated and should be phased out in favor of the `varchar(max)` datatype.)

  - `nchar`, `nvarchar`, `ntext`: Unicode equivalents of `char`, `varchar`, and `text` (with the same deprecation warning for `ntext` as for `text`).

- *Binary data*: Data stored in bytes, rather than as human-readable values, for example, files or images.

  - `binary`: Fixed-length binary data up to 8,000 bytes long.

  - `varbinary`: Variable-length binary data up to 8,000 bytes long.

  - `varbinary(max)`: Large binary data; maximum length of $2^{31} - 1$ (2,147,483,647) bytes, or 2GB.

  - `image`: Large binary data; maximum length of $2^{31} - 1$ (2,147,483,647) bytes, or 2GB. (Note that this datatype is outdated and should be phased out for the `varbinary(max)` datatype.)

- *Other scalar datatypes*: Datatypes that don't fit into any other groups nicely but are still interesting.

  - `timestamp` (or `rowversion`): Used for optimistic locking.

  - `uniqueidentifier`: Stores a globally unique identifier (GUID) value.

  - `cursor`: Datatype used to store a cursor reference in a variable. Cannot be used as a column in a table.

  - `table`: Used to hold a reference to a local temporary table. Cannot be used as a column in a table.

  - `sql_variant`: Stores data of most any datatype.

- *Not simply scalar*: For completeness, I will mention these types, but they will be covered on their own in Appendix C (which will be available as bonus downloadable content). These types are `XML`, `hierarchyId`, and the spatial types (`geometry` and `geography`).

Although you'll look at all these datatypes, this doesn't mean you'll have a need for all of them. Choosing a datatype needs to be a specific task to meet the needs of the client with the proper datatype. You could just store everything in unlimited-length character strings (this was how some systems worked in the old days), but this is clearly not optimal. From the list, you'll choose the best datatype, and if you cannot find one good enough, you can use the CLR and implement your own (I cover this in Chapter 5). The proper datatype choice is the first step in making sure the proper data is stored for a column.

---

■**Note**  I include information in each section about how the types are affected by using compression. This information refers to row-level compression only. For page-level compression information, see Chapter 9. Also note that compression is available only in the Enterprise Edition of SQL Server 2008.

---

# Precise Numeric Data

You can store numerical data in many base datatypes. There are two different types of numeric data: precise and approximate. The differences are important and must be well understood by any architect who's building a system that stores readings, measurements, or other numeric data.

Precise values have no error in the way they're stored, from integer to floating point values, because they have a fixed number of digits before and after the decimal point (or *radix*). It might seem odd to need to say that, but as I'll discuss in the next major section, some datatypes are considered approximate in that they don't always store exactly what you expect them to store. However, they aren't as bad as they sound and are useful for scientific and other applications where the range of values varies greatly.

The precise numeric values include the bit, int, bigint, smallint, tinyint, decimal, and money datatypes (money and smallmoney). I'll break these down again into two additional subsections: whole numbers and fractional numbers. This is done so we can isolate some of the discussion down to the values that allow fractional parts to be stored, because quite a few mathematical "quirks" need to be understood surrounding using those datatypes. I'll mention a few of these quirks, most importantly with the money datatypes. However, when you do any math with computers, you must be careful how rounding is achieved and how this affects your results.

## Integer Values

Whole numbers are, for the most part, integers stored using base-2 values. You can do bitwise operations on them, though generally it's frowned upon in SQL (think back to Chapter 4 in the First Normal Form sections, if you don't remember why). Math performed with integers is generally fast because the CPU can perform it directly using registers. I'll cover five integer sizes: bit, tinyint, smallint, int, and bigint.

### bit

*Domain*: 0, 1, or NULL.

*Storage*: A bit column requires 1 byte of storage per eight instances in a table. Hence, having eight bit columns will cause your table to be no larger than if your table had only a single bit column.

*Discussion*:

You use bit values as a kind of imitation Boolean value. A bit isn't a Boolean value, in that it has values 0 and 1, not True and False. This is a minor distinction but one that needs to be made. You cannot execute code such as this:

```
IF (bitValue) DO SOMETHING
```

A better term than a Boolean is a *flag*. A value of 1 means the flag has been set (such as a value that tells us that a customer does want e-mail promotions). Many programmers like to use character values 'yes' or 'no' for this, because this can be easier for viewing, but it can be harder to program with using built-in programming methods. In fact, the use of the bit datatype as a Boolean value has occurred primarily because many programming languages usually use 0 for False and nonzero for True (some use 1 or –1 explicitly).

You can index a bit column, but usually it isn't of any value only to index it. Having only two distinct values in an index (technically three with NULL) makes for a poor index. (See Chapter 9 for more information about indexes. You may be able to use a filtered index to make some indexes on bit columns useful.) Clearly, a bit value most often should be indexed in conjunction with other columns.

*Row Compression Effect:*

This will require 4 bits because of the metadata overhead of compression.

---

■**Tip** There's always a ton of discussion on the newsgroups about using the bit datatype. It isn't a standard datatype, but in my opinion it's no different in usage than an integer that has been constrained to the values 0, 1, or NULL.

It's often asked why we don't have a Boolean datatype. This is largely because of the idea that datatypes need to support NULL in RDBMSs, and a Boolean datatype would have to support UNKNOWN and NULL, resulting in four valued logic tables that are difficult to contemplate (without taking a long nap) and hard to deal with. So, we have what we have, and it works well enough.

---

## tinyint

*Domain*: Non-negative whole numbers from 0 through 255.

*Storage*: 1 byte.

*Discussion*:

tinyints are used to store small non-negative integer values. When using a single byte for storage, if the values you'll be dealing with are guaranteed always to be in this range, a tinyint is perfect. A great use for this is for the primary key of a domain table that can be guaranteed to have only a couple values. The tinyint datatype is especially useful in a data warehouse to keep the surrogate keys small. However, you have to make sure that there will never be more than 256 values, so unless the need for performance is incredibly great (such as if the key will migrate to tables with billions and billions of rows), it's best to use a larger datatype.

*Row Compression Effect:*

No effect, because 1 byte is the minimum for the integer types other than bit.

## smallint

*Domain*: Whole numbers from -32,768 through 32,767 (or $-2^{15}$ through $2^{15} - 1$).

*Storage*: 2 bytes.

*Discussion*:

If you can be guaranteed to need values only in this range, the smallint can be a useful type. It requires 2 bytes of storage.

Just as before with tinyint, it's often a bad idea to use a smallint for a primary key. Uniformity (just using int) makes your database code more consistent. This might seem like a small point, but in most average systems it's much easier to code when you automatically know what the datatype is.

One use of a smallint that crops up from time to time is as a Boolean. This is because, in earlier versions of Visual Basic, 0 equals False and -1 equals True (technically, VB would treat any nonzero value as True, but it used -1 as a False). Storing data in this manner is not only a tremendous waste of space—2 bytes versus potentially 1/8th of a byte for a bit, or even a single byte for a char(1)—'Y' or 'N'. It's also confusing to all the other SQL Server programmers. ODBC and OLE DB drivers do this translation for you, but even if they didn't, it's worth the time to write a method or a function in VB to translate True to a value of 1.

*Row Compression Effect:*

The value will be stored in the smallest number of bytes required to represent the value. For example, if the value is 10, it would fit in a single byte; then it would use 1 byte, and so forth, up to 2 bytes.

## int

*Domain*: Whole numbers from -2,147,483,648 to 2,147,483,647 (that is, $-2^{31}$ to $2^{31} - 1$).

*Storage*: 4 bytes.

*Discussion*:

The integer datatype is frequently employed as a primary key for tables, because it's small (it requires 4 bytes of storage) and efficient to store and retrieve.

One downfall of the int datatype is that it doesn't include an unsigned version, which for a 32-bit version could store non-negative values from 0 to 4,294,967,296 ($2^{32}$). Because most primary key values start out at 1, this would give you more than 2 billion extra values for a primary key value without having to involve negative numbers that can be confusing to the user. This might seem unnecessary, but systems that have billions of rows are becoming more and more common.

An application where the storage of the int column plays an important part is the storage of IP addresses as integers. An IP address is simply a 32-bit integer broken down into four octets. For example, if you had an IP address of 234.23.45.123, you would take $(234 * 2^3) + (23 * 2^2) + (45 * 2^1) + (123 * 2^0)$. This value fits nicely into an unsigned 32-bit integer, but not into a signed one. However, the 64-bit integer (bigint, which is covered next) in SQL Server covers the current IP address standard nicely but requires twice as much storage. Of course, bigint will fall down in the same manner when we get to IPv6 (the forthcoming Internet addressing protocol), because it uses a full 64-bit unsigned integer.

*Row Compression Effect:*

The value will be stored in the smallest number of bytes required to represent the value. For example, if the value is 10, it would fit in a single byte; then it would use 1 byte, and so forth, up to 4 bytes.

## bigint

*Domain*: Whole numbers from -9,223,372,036,854,775,808 to 9,223,372,036,854,775,807 (that is, $-2^{63}$ to $2^{63} - 1$).

*Storage*: 8 bytes.

*Discussion*:

One of the common reasons to use the 64-bit datatype is as a primary key for tables where you'll have more than 2 billion rows, or if the situation directly dictates it, such as the IP address situation I previously discussed. Of course, there are some companies where a billion isn't really a very large number of things to store or count, so using a `bigint` will be commonplace to them. As usual, the important thing is to size your utilization of any type to the situation, not using too small or even too large of a type than is necessary.

*Row Compression Effect:*

The value will be stored in the smallest number of bytes required to represent the value. For example, if the value is 10, it would fit in a single byte; then it would use 1 byte, and so forth, up to 4 bytes.

# Decimal Values

The `decimal` datatype is precise, in that whatever value you store, you can always retrieve it from the table. However, when you must store fractional values in precise datatypes, you pay a performance and storage cost in the way they're stored and dealt with. The reason for this is that you have to perform math with the precise decimal values using SQL Server engine code. On the other hand, math with IEEE floating point values (the `float` and `real` datatypes) can use the floating point unit (FPU), which is part of the core processor in all modern computers. This isn't to say that the `decimal` type is slow, *per se*, but if you're dealing with data that doesn't require the perfect precision of the `decimal` type, use the `float` datatype. I'll discuss the `float` and `real` datatypes more in the "Approximate Numeric Data" section.

## decimal (or Numeric)

*Domain*: All numeric data (including fractional parts) between $-10^{38} + 1$ through $10^{38} - 1$.

*Storage*: Based on precision (the number of significant digits): 1–9 digits, 5 bytes; 10–19 digits, 9 bytes; 20–28 digits, 13 bytes; and 29–38 digits, 17 bytes.

*Discussion*:

The `decimal` datatype is a precise datatype because it's stored in a manner that's like character data (as if the data had only 12 characters, 0 to 9 and the minus and decimal point symbols). The way it's stored prevents the kind of imprecision you'll see with the `float` and `real` datatypes a bit later. However, `decimal` does incur an additional cost in getting and doing math on the values, because there's no hardware to do the mathematics.

To specify a decimal number, you need to define the precision and the scale:

- *Precision* is the total number of significant digits in the number. For example, 10 would need a precision of 2, and 43.00000004 would need a precision of 10. The precision may be as small as 1 or as large as 38.
- *Scale* is the possible number of significant digits to the right of the decimal point. Reusing the previous example, 10 would have a scale of 0, and 43.00000004 would need 8.

Numeric datatypes are bound by this precision and scale to define how large the data is. For example, take the following declaration of a numeric variable:

```
DECLARE @testvar decimal(3,1)
```

This allows you to enter any numeric values greater than -99.94 and less than 99.94. Entering 99.949999 works, but entering 99.95 doesn't, because it's rounded up to 100.0, which can't be displayed by decimal(3,1). Take the following, for example:

```
SELECT @testvar = -10.155555555
SELECT @testvar
```

This returns the following result:

```
------------
-10.2
```

This rounding behavior is both a blessing and a curse. You must be careful when butting up to the edge of the datatype's allowable values. Note that a setting—SET NUMERIC_ROUNDABORT ON—causes an error to be generated when a loss of precision would occur from an implicit data conversion. That's kind of like what happens when you try to put too many characters into a character value.

Take the following code:

```
SET NUMERIC_ROUNDABORT ON
DECLARE @testvar decimal(3,1)
SELECT @testvar = -10.155555555
```

This causes the following error:

```
Msg 8115, Level 16, State 7, Line 5
Arithmetic overflow error converting numeric to data type numeric.
```

SET NUMERIC_ROUNDABORT can be quite dangerous to use and might throw off applications using SQL Server if set to ON. However, if you need to prevent implicit round-off due to system constraints, it's there.

As far as usage is concerned, you should generally use the decimal datatype as sparingly as possible, and I don't mean this negatively. There's nothing wrong with the type at all, but it does take that little bit more processing than integers or real data, and hence there's a performance hit. You should use it when you have specific values that you want to store where you can't accept any loss of precision. Again, I'll deal with the topic of loss of precision in more detail in the section "Approximate Numeric Data." The decimal type is commonly used as a replacement for the money type, because it has certain round-off issues that decimal does not.

*Row Compression Effect:*

The value will be stored in the smallest number of bytes that are necessary to provide the precision necessary, plus 2 bytes overhead per row. For example, if you are storing the value of 2 in a numeric(28,2) column, it needn't use all the possible space; it can use the space of a numeric(3,2), plus the 2 bytes overhead.

## Money Types

There are two intrinsic datatypes that are for storing monetary values. Both are based on integer types, with a fixed four decimal places. These types are as follows:

- money
    - *Domain*: -922,337,203,685,477.5808 to 922,337,203,685,477.5807
    - *Storage*: 8 bytes
- smallmoney
    - *Domain*: -214,748.3648 to 214,748.3647
    - *Storage*: 4 bytes

The money datatypes are generally considered a poor choice of datatype, even for storing monetary values, because they have a few inconsistencies that can cause a good deal of confusion. First, you can specify units, such as $ or £, but the units are of no real value. For example:

```
CREATE TABLE dbo.testMoney
(
    moneyValue money
)
go

INSERT INTO dbo.testMoney
VALUES ($100)
INSERT INTO dbo.testMoney
VALUES (100)
INSERT INTO dbo.testMoney
VALUES (£100)
GO
SELECT * FROM dbo.testMoney
```

The query at the end of this code example returns the following results:

```
moneyValue
---------------------
100.00
100.00
100.00
```

The second problem is that the money datatypes have well-known rounding issues with math. I mentioned that these types are based on integers (the range for smallmoney is -214,748.3648 to 214,748.3647, and the range for an integer is 2,147,483,648 to 2,147,483,647). Unfortunately, as I will demonstrate, intermediate results are stored in the same types, causing unexpected rounding errors. For example:

```
DECLARE @money1 money, @money2 money

SET     @money1 = 1.00
SET     @money2 = 800.00
SELECT cast(@money1/@money2 as money)
```

This returns the following result:

```
---------------------
0.0012
```

However, try the following code:

```
DECLARE @decimal1 decimal(19,4), @decimal2 decimal(19,4)
SET     @decimal1 = 1.00
SET     @decimal2 = 800.00
SELECT  cast(@decimal1/@decimal2 as decimal(19,4))
```

It returns the following result:

```
---------------------------------------
0.0013
```

Why? Because money uses only four decimal places for intermediate results, where decimal uses a much larger precision:

```
SELECT  @money1/@money2
SELECT  @decimal1/@decimal2
```

This code returns the following results:

```
---------------------
0.0012
```

```
---------------------------------------
0.0012500000000000000
```

That's why there are round-off issues. The common consensus among database architects is to avoid the money datatype and use a numeric type instead, because of the following reasons:

- It gives the answers to math problems in the natural manner that's expected.

- It has no built-in units to confuse matters.

Even in the previous version of SQL Server, the following statement was included in the monetary data section: "If a greater number of decimal places are required, use the decimal datatype instead." Using a decimal type instead gives you the precision needed. To replicate the range for money, use DECIMAL(19,4), or for smallmoney, use DECIMAL (10,4). However, you needn't use such large values if you don't need them. Otherwise, if you happen to be calculating the national debt or my yearly gadget allowance, you might need to use a larger value.

*Row Compression Effect:*

The money types are simply integer types with their decimal places shifted. As such, they are compressed in the same manner that integer types would be. However, since the values would be larger than they appear (because of the value 10 being stored as 10.000, or 10000 in the physical storage), the compression would be less than for an integer of the same magnitude.

# Approximate Numeric Data

Approximate numeric values contain a decimal point and are stored in a format that's fast to manipulate. They are called *floating point* because they have a fixed number of significant digits, but the placement of the decimal point "floats," allowing for really small numbers or really large numbers. Approximate numeric values have some important advantages, as you'll see later in this appendix.

*Approximate* is such a negative term, but it's technically the proper term. It refers to the real and float datatypes, which are IEEE 75454 standard single- and double-precision floating point values. The number is stored as a 32-bit or 64-bit value, with four parts:

- *Sign*: Determines whether this is a positive or negative value.

- *Exponent*: The exponent in base-2 of the mantissa.

- *Mantissa*: Stores the actual number that's multiplied by the exponent (also known as the *coefficient* or *significand*).

- *Bias*: Determines whether the exponent is positive or negative.

A complete description of how these datatypes are formed is beyond the scope of this book but may be obtained from the IEEE body at http://www.ieee.org.

- float [ (N) ]

  - *Domain*: $-1.79E + 308$ through $1.79E + 308$. The float datatype allows you to specify a certain number of bits to use in the mantissa, from 1 to 53. You specify this number of bits with the value in N. The default is 53.

  - *Storage*: See Table B-1.

- real

  - real is a synonym for float(24).

**Table B-1.** *Floating Point Precision and Storage Requirements*

| N (Number of Mantissa Bits for Float) | | Precision | Storage Size |
|---|---|---|---|
| 1–24 | 7 | 4 bytes | |
| 25–53 | 15 | 8 bytes | |

At this point, SQL Server rounds all values of N up to either 24 or 53. This is the reason that the storage and precision are the same for each of the values.

---

■**Note** There's another approximate datatype named real. It's a synonym for a float(24) datatype. It can store values in the range from $-3.40E + 38$ through $3.40E + 38$.

---

*Discussion:*

Using these datatypes, you can represent most values from $-1.79E + 308$ to $1.79E + 308$ with a maximum of 15 significant digits. This isn't as many significant digits as the numeric datatypes can deal with, but the range is enormous and is plenty for almost any scientific application. These datatypes have a *much* larger range of values than any other datatype. This is because the decimal point isn't fixed in the representation. In numeric types, you always have a pattern such as NNNNNNN.DDDD for numbers. You can't store more digits than this to the left or right of the decimal point. However, with float values, you can have values that fit the following patterns (and much larger):

- 0.DDDDDDDDDDDDDDD

- NNNNN.DDDDDDDDD

- 0.00000000000000000000000000000DDDDDDDDDDDDDDD

- NNNNNNNNNNNNNNNN000000000000000000

So, you have the ability to store tiny numbers, or large ones. This is important for scientific applications where you need to store and do math on an extreme range of values. The float datatypes are well suited for this usage.

*Row Compression Effect:*

The least significant bytes with all zeros are not stored. This is applicable mostly to non-fractional values in the mantissa.

# Date and Time Data

There are two datatypes for working with date and time values: datetime and smalldatetime. Both have a time element and a date element, and you cannot separate them. Not having a simple date or time datatype can be a real bother at times, because often we want to store just the time of an event, or just the date of the event. For date-only values, it's simple: we just ignore the time by making sure that the time value is exactly midnight, and it works OK. Time values can be more of an issue. Although we can set the date to some arbitrary date and just use the time value, the date value then looks funny when viewed without formatting. We often build our own datatype for these values. I'll discuss this in this section as well.

## date

*Domain*: Date-only values from January 1, 0001, to December 31, 9999.

*Storage*: 3-byte integer, storing the offset from January 1, 0001.

*Accuracy*: One day.

*Discussion*:

Of all the features added to SQL Server in 2008, this one datatype is worth the price of the upgrade (especially since I don't have to whip out my wallet and pay for it). The problem of how to store date values without time has plagued T-SQL programmers since the beginning of time (a.k.a. version 1.0).

With this type, you will be able to avoid the goofy tricks you have needed to go through to ensure that date types had no time in order to store just a date value. In the past versions of the book, I have even advocated the creation of your own pseudodate values stored in an integer value. That worked, but you could not use the built-in date functions without doing some "tricks."

*Row Compression Effect:*

Technically you get the same compression as for any integer value, but dates in the "normal" range of dates require 3 bytes, meaning no compression is realized.

## time [(precision)]

*Domain*: Time of day only (note this is not a quantity of time, but a point in time on the clock).

*Storage*: 3–5 bytes, depending on precision.

*Accuracy*: To 100 nanoseconds, depending on how it is declared. `time(0)` is accurate to 1 second, `time(1)` to .1 seconds, up to `time(7)` as .0000001. The default is 100-nanosecond accuracy.

*Discussion*:

Where the `date` type was earth-shattering, the `time` type is handy to have but generally less useful. It will seem like a good idea to store a point in time, but in that case you will have to make sure that both times are for the same day. Rather, for the most part when you want to store a time value, it is a point in time, and you need one of the date + time types.

The time value can be useful for storing a time for a recurring activity, for example, where the time is for multiple days rather than a single point in time.

*Row Compression Effect:*

Technically you get the same compression as for any integer value, but time values generally use most of the bytes of the integer storage, so very little compression should be expected for time values.

# smalldatetime

*Domain*: Date and time data values between January 1, 1900, and June 6, 2079.

*Storage*: 4 bytes (two 2-byte integers: one for the day offset from January 1, 1900, the other for the number of minutes past midnight).

*Accuracy*: One minute.

*Discussion*:

The `smalldatetime` datatype is accurate to 1 minute. It requires 4 bytes of storage. `smalldatetime` values are the best choice when you need to store just the date, and possibly the time, of some event where accuracy of a minute isn't a problem.

*Row Compression Effect:*

When there is no time stored, 2 bytes can be saved, and times less than 4 a.m. can save 1 byte.

# datetime

*Domain*: Date and time data values between January 1, 1753, and December 31, 9999.

*Storage*: 8 bytes (two 4-byte integers: one for the day offset from January 1, 1753, and the other for the number of 3.33-millisecond periods past midnight).

*Accuracy*: 3.33 milliseconds.

*Discussion*:

Using 8 bytes, `datetime` does require a sizable chunk of memory. There are few cases where you need this kind of precision. A primary example of where you do need this kind of precision is a timestamp column (not to be confused with the `timestamp` datatype, which I'll discuss in a later section), used to denote exactly when an operation takes place. This isn't uncommon if you need to get timing information, such as the time taken between two activities in seconds, or if you want to use the `datetime` value in a concurrency control mechanism.

*Row Compression Effect:*

For the date part of the type, dates before 2079 can save 1 byte. For the time part, 4 bytes are saved when there is no time saved, and it uses the first 2 bytes after the first 2 minutes and reaches the fourth byte after 4 a.m. After 4 a.m., compression can generally save 1 byte.

# datetime2 [(precision)]

*Domain:* Dates from January 1, 0001, to December 31, 9999, with a time component.

*Storage:* Between 6 and 8 bytes. The first 4 bytes are used to store the date, and the others an offset from midnight, depending on the accuracy.

*Accuracy:* To 100 nanoseconds, depending on how it is declared. `datetime(0)` is accurate to 1 second, `datetime(1)` to .1 seconds, up to `datetime(7)` as .0000001. The default is 100-nanosecond accuracy.

*Discussion:*

`datetime2`: Despite the hideous Oracle-looking name, this is a much better datatype than `datetime`. Technically you get far better time support without being limited by the .003 accuracy issues that datetime is. The only downside I currently see is support for the type in your API.

What I see as the immediate benefit of this type is to fix the amount of accuracy that your users actually desire. Most of the time a user doesn't desire fractional seconds, unless the purpose of the type is something scientific or technical. With `datetime2`, you can choose 1-second accuracy. Also, you can store .999 seconds, unlike datetime, which would round .999 up to 1, whereas .998 would round down to .997.

*Row Compression Effect:*

For the date part of the type, dates before 2079 can save 1 byte of the 4 bytes for the date. Little compression should be expected for the time portion.

# datetimeoffset [(precision)]

The `datetimeoffset` is the same as `datetime2`, but it includes an offset from UTC time (8–10 bytes).

*Domain:* Dates from January 1, 0001, to December 31, 9999, with a time component. Includes the offset from the UTC time, in a format of [+|-] hh:mm. (Note that this is not time zone/daylight saving time aware. It simply stores the offset at the time of storage.)

*Storage:* Between 8 and 10 bytes. The first 4 bytes are used to store the date, and just like `datetime2`, 2–4 will be used for the time, depending on the accuracy. The UTC offset is stored in the additional 2 bytes.

*Accuracy:* To 100 nanoseconds, depending on how it is declared. `datetimeoffset(0)` is accurate to 1 second, `datetimeoffset (1)` to .1 seconds, up to `datetimeoffset (7)` as .0000001. The default is 100-nanosecond accuracy.

*Discussion:*

The offset seems quite useful but in many ways is more cumbersome than using two date columns, one for UTC and one for local (though this will save a bit of space). Its true value is that it defines an exact point in time better than the regular `datetime` type, since there is no ambiguity as to where the time was stored.

A useful operation is to translate the date from its local offset to UTC, like this:

```
DECLARE @LocalTime DateTimeOffset
SET @LocalTime = SYSDATETIMEOFFSET()
SELECT @LocalTime
SELECT SWITCHOFFSET(@LocalTime, '+00:00') As UTCTime
```

The true downside is that it stores an offset, not the time zone, so daylight saving time will still need to be handled manually.

*Row Compression Effect:*

For the date part of the type, dates before 2079 can save 1 byte of the 4 bytes for the date. Little compression should be expected for the time portion.

# Discussion on All Date Types

Date types are often some of the most troublesome types for people to deal with. In this section, I'll lightly address the following problem areas:

- Date functions
- Date ranges
- Representing dates in text formats

## Date Functions

With the creation of new date and time (and datetime) types in SQL Server 2008, there needed to be more functions to work with. Microsoft has added functions that return and modify dates and time with more precision than GETDATE or GETUTCDATE:

- SYSDATETIME: Returns system time to the nearest fraction of a second, with seven places of scale in the return value
- SYSDATETIMEOFFSET: Same as SYSDATETIME but returns the offset of the server in the return value
- SYSUTCDATETIME: Same as SYSDATETIME but returns the UTC date time rather than local time
- SWITCHOFFSET: Changes the offset for a datetimeoffset value
- TODATETIMEOFFSET: Converts a local date and time value to a given time zone

There have been a few changes to the basic date functions as well:

- DATENAME: Includes values for microsecond, nanosecond, and TZoffset. These will work differently for the different types. For example, TZoffset will work with datetime2 and datetimeoffset, but not the other types.
- DATEPART: Includes microsecond, nanosecond, TZoffset, and ISO_WEEK. ISO_WEEK is a feature that has been long desired by programmers who need to know the week of the year, rather than the nonstandard week value that SQL Server has previously provided.
- DATEADD: Supports micro and nanoseconds.

With all the date functions, you really have to be careful that you are cognizant of what you are requesting. For an example, how old is this person? Say you know that a person was born on December 31, 2008, and on January 3, 2009, you want to know their age (yes, this seems like a very easy question, but the answer is kind of interesting). Common sense says to look for a function to take the difference between two dates. You are in luck—there is a DATEDIFF function. Executing the following:

```
DECLARE @time1 date = '20081231',
        @time2 date = '20090102'
SELECT DATEDIFF(yy,@time1,@time2)
```

You see that the person is 0 years old right? Wrong! It returns 1. Well, maybe. But if that is true, then the following should probably return 2, right?

```
DECLARE @time1 date = '20080101',
        @time2 date = '20091231'
SELECT DATEDIFF(yy,@time1,@time2)
```

No, shucks, that also returns 1. So, no matter whether the date values are 1 day apart or 730, you get the same result? Yes, because the DATEDIFF function is fairly dumb in that it is taking the difference of the year value, not the difference in years. Then, to find out the age, you will need to use several functions.

So, what is the answer? We could do something more fancy, likely by coming up with an algorithm based on the number of days, or months, or shifting dates to some common value, but that is way more like work than the really straightforward answer. Build a table of dates, commonly called a *calendar* (a calendar table is introduced in Chapter 7).

## Date Ranges

This topic will probably seem really elementary, but the fact is that one of the largest blunders in the database implementation world is working with ranges of dates. The problem is that when you want to do inclusive ranges, you have always needed to consider the time in the equation. For example, the following criteria:

```
WHERE pointInTimeValue between '2008-01-01' and '2008-12-31'
```

means something different based on whether the values stored in dateValue have, or do not have, a time part stored. With the introduction of the date type, the need to worry about this issue of date ranges will probably become a thing of the past, but it is still an issue that you'll need to worry about in the near-term at least.

Thinking back to the example WHERE clause, the problem is that any value with the same date as the end value plus a time (such as '2008-12-31 12:00:00') does not fit within the preceding selecting criteria. So, this value will be left out of the results. Of course, the next criteria to try would logically be the following:

```
WHERE pointInTimeValue between '2009-01-01' and '2009-12-31'
```

But now you have actually missed all the activity that occurred on December 31 that wasn't at midnight. And of course, this problem gets worse when you move toward smaller ranges of time.

There are two ways to deal with this. Either code your WHERE clause like this:

```
WHERE pointInTimeValue >= '2009-01-01' and pointInTimeValue < '2010-01-01'
```

or use a calculated column to translate point-in-time values in your tables to date-only values (like dateValue as cast(pointInTimeValue as date)). Having done that, a value such as '2008-12-31 12:00:00' will be truncated to '2008-12-31 00:00:00', and a row containing that value will be picked up by selection criteria such as this:

```
WHERE pointInTimeValue between '2008-01-01' and '2008-12-31'
```

A common solution that I don't generally suggest is to use a between range like this:

```
WHERE pointInTimeValue between '2009-01-01' and '2009-12-31 23:59:59.9999999'
```

The idea is that if the second value is less than the next day, then values for the next day won't be returned. The major problem with this solution has to do with the conversion of 23:59:59.9999999 to some date datatype. For example, if `pointInTimeValue` were a `Datetime`, it would be rounded up to the next day because the maximum time for a datetime is 23:59:59.997. For the range to work with a datetime, you would use this:

```
WHERE pointInTimeValue between '2009-01-01' and '2009-12-31 23:59:59.997'
```

However, for a `smalldatetime` value, it would need to be this:

```
WHERE pointInTimeValue between '2009-01-01' and '2009-12-31 23:59'
```

and so on, for all of the different date types, which gets complicated by the new types where you can specify precision. We strongly suggest you avoid trying to use a maximum date value like this unless you are tremendously careful with the types of data and how their values round off.

For more information about how date and time data work with one another and converting from one type to another, read the topic "Using Date and Time Data" in Books Online.

## Representing Dates in Text Formats

When working with date values in text, using a standard format is always best. There are many different formats used around the world for dates, most confusingly MMDDYYYY and DDMMYYYY (is 01022004 or 02012004 the same day, or a different day?). Although SQL Server uses the locale information on your server to decide how to interpret your date input, using one of the following formats ensures that SQL Server doesn't mistake the input regardless of where the value is entered.

Generally speaking, it is best to stick with one of the standard date formats that are recognized regardless of where the user is. This prevents any issues when sharing data with international clients, or even with sharing it with others on the Web when looking for help.

There are several standards formats that will work:

- ANSI SQL Standard
    - *No time zone offset*: 'YYYY-MM-DD HH:MM:SS'
    - *With time zone*: 'YYYY-MM-DD HH:MM:SS -OH:OM' (Z can be used to indicate the time zone is 00:00)
- ISO 8601
    - *Unseparated*: 'YYYYMMDD'
    - *Numeric*: 'YYYY-MM-DD'
    - *Time*: 'HH:MM:SS.sssssss' (SS and .sssssss are optional)
    - *Date and time*: 'YYYY-MM-DDTHH:MM:SS.sssssss'
    - *Date and time with offset*: 'YYYY-MM-DDTHH:MM:SS.sssssss -OH:OM'
- ODBC
    - *Date*: {d 'YYYY-MM-DD'}
    - *Time*: {t 'HH:MM:SS'}
    - *Date and time*: {ts 'YYYY-MM-DD HH:MM:SS'}

Using the ANSI SQL Standard or the ISO 8601 formats is generally considered the best practice for specifying date values. It will definitely feel odd when you first begin typing '2008-08-09' for a date value, but once you get used to it, it will feel natural.

The following are some examples using the ANSI and ISO formats:

```
select cast ('2009-01-01' as smalldatetime) as dateOnly
select cast('2009-01-01 14:23:00.003' as datetime) as withTime
```

You might also see values that are close to this format, such as the following:

```
select cast ('20090101' as smalldatetime) as dateOnly
select cast('2009-01-01T14:23:00.120' as datetime) as withTime
```

These are acceptable variations. For more information, check SQL Server 2008 Books Online under "Using Date and Time Data."

# Character Strings

Most data that's stored in SQL Server uses character datatypes. In fact, usually far too much data is stored in character datatypes. Frequently, character columns are used to hold noncharacter data, such as numbers and dates. Although this might not be technically wrong, it isn't ideal. For starters, storing a number with eight digits in a character string requires at least 8 bytes, but as an integer it requires 4 bytes. Searching on integers is far easier because 1 always precedes 2, whereas 11 comes before 2 in character strings. Additionally, integers are stored in a format that can be manipulated using intrinsic processor functions, as opposed to having SQL Server–specific functions deal with the data.

## char[(length)]

*Domain*: ASCII characters, up to 8,000 characters long.

*Storage*: 1 byte * length.

*Discussion*:

The char datatype is used for fixed-length character data. Every value will be stored with the same number of characters, up to a maximum of 8,000 bytes. Storage is exactly the number of bytes as per the column definition, regardless of actual data stored; any remaining space to the right of the last character of the data is padded with spaces. The default size if not specified is 1 (it is best practice to include the size).

You can see the possible characters by executing the following query:

```
SELECT number, CHAR(number)
FROM   utility.sequence
WHERE  number >=0 and number <= 255
```

---

■**Tip** The sequence table is a common table that every database should have. It's a table of integers that can be used for many utility purposes. In Chapter 7, I present a sequence table that you can use for this query.

---

The maximum limit for a char is 8,000 bytes, but if you ever get within a mile of this limit for a fixed-width character value, you're likely making a big design mistake because it's very rare to have massive character strings of exactly the same length. You should employ the char datatype only in cases where you're guaranteed to have exactly the same number of characters in every row.

The char datatype is most often used for codes and identifiers, such as customer numbers or invoice numbers where the number includes alpha characters as well as integer data. An example is a vehicle identification number (VIN), which is stamped on most every vehicle produced around the world. Note that this is a composite attribute, because you can determine many things about the automobile from its VIN.

Another example where a char column is usually found is in Social Security numbers (SSNs), which always have nine characters and two dashes embedded.

*Row Compression Effect:*

Instead of storing the padding characters, it removes them for storage and adds them back whenever the data is actually used.

---

**■Note** The setting ANSI_PADDING determines exactly how padding is handled. If this setting is ON, the table is as I've described; if not, data will be stored as I'll discuss in the "varchar[](length)" section that follows. It's best practice to leave this ANSI setting ON.

---

# varchar[(length)]

*Domain*: ASCII characters, up to 8,000 characters long.

*Storage*: 1 byte * length + 2 bytes (for overhead).

*Discussion*:

For the varchar datatype, you choose the maximum length of the data you want to store, up to 8,000 bytes. The varchar datatype is far more useful than char, because the data doesn't have to be of the same length and SQL Server doesn't pad out excess memory with spaces. There's some reasonably minor overhead in storing variable-length data. First, it costs an additional 2 bytes per column. Second, it's a bit more difficult to get to the data, because it isn't always in the same location of the physical record. The default size if not specified is 1 (it is best practice to include the size).

Use the varchar datatype when your character data varies in length. The good thing about varchar columns is that, no matter how long you make the maximum, the space used by the column is based on the actual size of the characters being stored plus the few extra bytes that specify how long the data is.

You'll generally want to choose a maximum limit for your datatype that's a reasonable value, large enough to handle most situations, but not too large as to be impractical to deal with in your applications and reports. For example, take people's first names. These obviously require the varchar type, but how long should you allow the data to be? First names tend to be a maximum of 15 characters long, though you might want to specify 20 or 30 characters for the unlikely exception.

The most prevalent storage type for non-key values that you'll use is varchar data, because, generally speaking, the size of the data is one of the most important factors in performance tuning. The smaller the amount of data, the less has to be read and written. This means less disk access, which is one of the two most important bottlenecks we have to deal with (networking speed is the other).

*Row Compression Effect:*

No effect.

# varchar(max)

*Domain*: ASCII characters, up to $2^{31} - 1$ characters (that is a maximum of 2GB worth of text!).

*Storage*: There are a couple possibilities for storage based on the setting of the table option 'large value types out of row', which is set with the sp_tableoption system stored procedure:

- OFF or 0 =: The data for all the columns fits in a single row, and the data is stored in the row with the same storage costs for non-max varchar values. Once the data is too big to fit in a single row, data can be placed on more than one row. This is the default setting.
- ON or 1 =: You store varchar(max) values using 16-byte pointers to separate pages outside the table. Use this setting if the varchar(max) data will only seldom be used in queries.

*Discussion*:

The varchar(max) datatype is possibly the greatest thing since someone said, "Meat and fire—I wonder if they might go together?" Too long we struggled with the painful text datatype and all its quirks. You can deal with varchar(max) values using mostly the same functions and methods that you use with normal varchar values. There's a minor difference, though. As the size of your varchar(max) column grows toward the upper boundary, it's likely true that you aren't going to want to be sending the entire value back and forth over the network most of the time. I know that even on my 100MB LAN, sending 2GB is no instantaneous operation, for sure.

There are a couple things to look at, which I'll just touch on here:

- The UPDATE statement has a .WRITE() clause to write chunks of data to the (max) datatypes. This is also true of varbinary(max).
- Unlike text and image values, (max) datatypes are accessible in AFTER triggers.

One word of warning for when your code mixes normal varchar and varchar(max) values in the same statement: normal varchar values do not automatically change datatype to a (max) type when the data being manipulated grows beyond 8,000 characters. For example, write a statement such as the following:

```
DECLARE @value varchar(max)
SET @value = replicate('X',8000) + replicate('X',8000)
SELECT len(@value)
```

This returns the following result, which you would expect to be 16000, since you have two 8,000-character strings:

```
--------------------
8000
```

The reason is that the type of the REPLICATE function is varchar, when replicating normal char values. Adding two varchar values together doesn't result in a varchar(max) value. However, most of the functions return varchar(max) values when working with varchar(max) values. For example:

```
DECLARE @value varchar(max)
SET @value = replicate(cast('X' as varchar(max)),16000)
SELECT len(@value)
```

This returns the following result:

```
--------------------
16000
```

*Row Compression Effect:*

No effect.

## text

Don't use the text datatype for any reason in new designs. It might not exist in the next version of SQL Server. Replace with varchar(max) whenever you possibly can. See SQL Server Books Online for more information.

# Unicode Character Strings: nchar, nvarchar, nvarchar(max), ntext

*Domain*: ASCII characters, up to $2^{15} - 1$ characters (2GB of storage).

*Storage*: Same as other character datatypes, though every character takes 2 bytes rather than 1. (Note there is no support for any of the variable-length Unicode storage.)

*Discussion*:

So far, the character datatypes we've been discussing have been for storing typical ASCII data. In SQL Server 7.0 (and NT 4.0), Microsoft implemented a new standard character format called Unicode. This specifies a 16-bit character format that can store characters beyond just the Latin character set. In ASCII—a 7-bit character system (with the 8 bits for Latin extensions)—you were limited to 256 distinct characters. This was fine for most English-speaking people but was insufficient for other languages. Asian languages have a character for each different syllable and are nonalphabetic; Middle Eastern languages use several different symbols for the same letter according to its position in the word. Unicode expanded the amount of characters and eliminated the need for code pages to allow for a vastly expanded character set (which allowed you to have multiple character sets in an 8-character encoding set in ASCII). SQL Server supports the Unicode Standard, version 3.2.

For these datatypes, you have the nchar, nvarchar, nvarchar(max), and ntext datatypes. They are the same as the similarly named types (without the n) that we've already described, except for one thing: Unicode uses double the number of bytes to store the information, so it takes twice the space, thus cutting by half the number of characters that can be stored.

One quick tip: if you want to specify a Unicode value in a string, you append an N to the front of the string, like so:

```
SELECT N'Unicode Value'
```

---

■**Tip** You should migrate away from ntext as a datatype just as you should for the text datatype.

---

*Row Compression Effect:*

Same as their ASCII counterparts. This has no effect on the variable types and doesn't store trailing blanks for the fixed-length types.

# Binary Data

Binary data allows you to store a string of bytes. It's useful for storing just about anything, especially data from a client that might or might not fit into a character or numeric datatype. In SQL Server 2005, binary columns have become even more useful, because you can use them when storing encrypted data. In Chapter 7, you'll learn about the encryption capabilities of SQL Server 2005.

One of the restrictions of binary datatypes is that they don't support bitwise operators, which would allow you to do some powerful bitmask storage by being able to compare two binary columns to see not only whether they differ, but how they differ. The whole idea of the binary datatypes is that they store strings of bits. The bitwise operators can operate on integers, which are physically stored as bits. The reason for this inconsistency is fairly clear from the point of view of the internal query processor. The bitwise operations are operations that are handled in the processor, whereas the binary datatypes are SQL Server specific.

Binary literal values are specified as 0xB1B2B3 . . . BN. 0x tells you that it's a hexadecimal value. B1 specifies the first single byte in hexadecimal.

## binary[(length)]

*Domain*: Fixed-length binary data with a maximum length of 8,000 bytes.

*Storage*: Number of bytes the value is defined for. The default length is 1, if not specified (it is best practice to include a size).

*Discussion*:

The use of binary columns is fairly limited. You can use them to store any binary values that aren't dealt with by SQL Server. Data stored in binary is simply a string of bytes:

```
declare @value binary(10)
set @value = cast('helloworld' as binary(10))
select @value
```

This returns the following result:

```
----------------------
0x68656C6C6F776F726C64
```

Now you can reverse the process:

```
select cast(0x68656C6C6F776F726C64 as varchar(10))
```

This returns the following result:

```
----------
helloworld
```

Note that casting the value HELLOWORLD gives you a different value:

```
----------------------
0x48454C4C4F574F524C44
```

This fact that these two binary values are different, even for textual data that would be considered equivalent on a case-insensitive collation, has been one use for the binary datatype: case-sensitive searches. It's far more efficient to use the COLLATE keyword and use a different collation if you want to do a case-insensitive comparison on text data.

*Row Compression Effect:*

Trailing zeros are not stored but are returned when the values are used.

# varbinary[(length)]

*Domain*: Variable-length binary data with a maximum length of 8,000 bytes.

*Storage*: Number of bytes the value is defined for, plus 2 bytes for variable-length overhead. The default length is 1, if not specified (it is a best practice to include a size).

*Discussion*:

The usage is the same as binary, except the number of bytes is variable.

*Row Compression Effect:*

No effect.

# varbinary(max)

*Domain*: Binary data, up to $2^{31} - 1$ bytes (up to 2GB for storage) when data is stored in SQL Server files, up to the max of the storage for data stored in the filestream. For more information and examples about the filestream, check Chapter 7.

*Storage*: There are a couple possibilities for storage based on whether the data is stored using the filestream setting, as well as the setting of the table option 'large value types out of row':

- OFF =: If the data for all the columns fits in a single row, the data is stored in the row with the same storage costs for non-max varchar values. Once the data is too big to fit in a single row, data can be placed on greater than one row.

- ON =: You store varbinary(max) values using 16-byte pointers to separate pages outside the table. Use this setting if the varchar(max) data will only seldom be used in queries.

*Discussion*:

The varbinary(max) datatype provides the same kinds of benefits for large binary values as the varchar(max) does for text. Pretty much you can deal with varbinary(max) values using the same functions and the same methods as you do with the normal varbinary values.

What's cool is that you can store text, JPEG and GIF images, and even Word documents and Excel spreadsheet data using the varbinary(max) type. On the other hand, it can be much slower and more programming work to use SQL Server as a storage mechanism for files, mostly because it's slow to retrieve really large values from the database as compared to from the file system. You can, however, use a filestream access to get the best of both possible worlds by using Win32 access to a file in a directory within the context of a transaction. This approach is described in greater detail in Chapter 7.

*Row Compression Effect:*

No effect.

## image

Just like the text datatype, the image datatype has always been a real bother and is being deprecated in this version of SQL Server. Don't use the image datatype in new designs if at all possible. It very well may not exist in the next version of SQL Server. Replace with varbinary(max) in any location you can. See SQL Server Books Online for more information or if you have existing image column data that you need to manipulate.

# Other Datatypes

The following datatypes are somewhat less easy to categorize but are still commonly employed in OLTP systems:

- rowversion (timestamp)
- uniqueidentifier
- cursor
- table
- sql_variant

## rowversion (a.k.a. timestamp)

The rowversion datatype is a database-wide unique number. When you have a rowversion column in a table, the value of the rowversion column changes for each modification to each row. The value in the rowversion column is guaranteed to be unique across all tables in the datatype. It's also known as a timestamp value, but it doesn't have any time implications—it's merely a unique value to tell you that your row has changed.

---

■**Tip** In the SQL standards, a timestamp datatype is equivalent to what you know as a datetime datatype. To avoid confusion, Microsoft now recommends that you specify rowversion rather than timestamp.

---

The rowversion column of a table (you may have only one) is usually used as the data for an optimistic locking mechanism. The rowversion datatype is a mixed blessing. It's stored as an 8-byte varbinary value. Binary values aren't always easy to deal with, and their use depends on which mechanism you're using to access your data.

As an example of how the rowversion datatype works, consider the following batch:

```
SET nocount on
CREATE TABLE testRowversion
(
   value    varchar(20) NOT NULL,
   auto_rv   rowversion NOT NULL
)

INSERT INTO testRowversion (value) values ('Insert')

SELECT value, auto_rv FROM testRowversion
UPDATE testRowversion
SET value = 'First Update'
```

```
SELECT value, auto_rv from testRowversion
UPDATE testRowversion
SET value = 'Last Update'

SELECT value, auto_rv FROM testRowversion
```

This batch returns the following results:

| value | auto_rv |
| --- | --- |
| Insert | 0x00000000000007D1 |

| value | auto_rv |
| --- | --- |
| First Update | 0x00000000000007D2 |

| value | auto_rv |
| --- | --- |
| Last Update | 0x00000000000007D3 |

You didn't touch the auto_rv column, and yet it incremented itself twice. However, you can't bank on the order of the rowversion values being sequential, because updates of other tables will change the value as well. All rowversion values in a database draw from the same pool of values. It's also in your best interest not to assume in your code that a rowversion number is an incrementing value. How rowversions are implemented is a detail that will likely change in the future. If a better method of building database-wide unique values comes along that's even a hair faster, Microsoft will likely use it.

You can create variables of the rowversion type for holding rowversion values, and you can retrieve the last-used rowversion via the @@dbts configuration function. Rowversion columns are used in Chapter 9, when I demonstrate optimistic locking.

*Row Compression Effect:*

Uses an integer representation of the value, using 8 bytes. Then it can be compressed just like the bigint type.

# uniqueidentifier

Globally unique identifiers are fast becoming a mainstay of Microsoft computing. The name says it all—these identifiers are globally unique. According to the way that GUIDs are formed, there's a tremendously remote chance that there will ever be any duplication in their values. They're generated by a formula that includes the current date and time, a unique number from the CPU clock, and some other "magic numbers."

In your databases, these GUID values are stored in the uniqueidentifier type. An interesting use is to have a key value that's guaranteed to be unique across databases and servers. You can generate a GUID value in T-SQL using the newid function.

```
DECLARE @guidVar uniqueidentifier
SET @guidVar = newid()

SELECT @guidVar as guidVar
```

```
returns

guidVar
------------------------------------------------------------
6C7119D5-D48F-475C-8B60-50D0C41B6EBF
```

GUIDs are stored as 16-byte binary values. Note that a GUID isn't exactly a straight 16-byte binary value. You cannot put just any binary value into a uniqueidentifier column, because the value must meet the criteria for the generation of a GUID, which aren't well documented, for obvious reasons. (For more information, a good resource is http://en.wikipedia.org/wiki/guid.)

If you need to create a uniqueidentifier column that's autogenerating, you can set a property in the CREATE TABLE statement (or ALTER TABLE, for that matter). It's the rowguidcol property, and it's used like so:

```
CREATE TABLE guidPrimaryKey
(
    guidPrimaryKeyId uniqueidentifier NOT NULL rowguidcol DEFAULT newId(),
    value varchar(10)
)
```

I've introduced a couple new things here: rowguidcol and default values. Suffice it to say that if you don't provide a value for a column in an insert operation, the default operation will provide it. In this case, you use the newId() function to get a new uniqueidentifier. Execute the following INSERT statement:

```
INSERT INTO guidPrimaryKey(value)
VALUES ('Test')
```

Then run the following command to view the data entered:

```
SELECT *
FROM guidPrimaryKey
```

This returns the following result (though of course your key value will be different):

| guidPrimaryKeyId | value |
| --- | --- |
| 8A57C8CD-7407-47C5-AC2F-E6A884C7B646 | Test |

The rowguidcol property of a column built with the uniqueidentifier notifies the system that this is just like an identity column value for the table—a unique pointer to a row in a table. Note that neither the identity nor the rowguidcol properties guarantee uniqueness. To provide such a guarantee, you have to implement your tables using UNIQUE constraints.

It would seem that the uniqueidentifier would be a better way of implementing primary keys, because when they're created, they're unique across all databases, servers, and platforms. However, there are two main reasons why you won't use uniqueidentifier columns to implement all your primary keys:

- *Storage requirements*: Because they're 16 bytes in size, they're considerably more bloated than a typical integer column.

- *Typeability*: Because there are 36 characters in the textual version of the GUID, it's hard to type the value of the GUID into a query, and it isn't easy to enter.

If you're using the GUID values for the primary key of a table and you're clustering on this value, you can use another function to generate the values: newSequentialId(). You can use this function only in a default constraint. It's used to guarantee that the next GUID chosen will be greater than the previous value:

```
DROP TABLE guidPrimaryKey
go
CREATE TABLE guidPrimaryKey
(
    guidPrimaryKeyId uniqueidentifier NOT NULL
                     rowguidcol DEFAULT newSequentialId(),
    value varchar(10)
)
GO
INSERT INTO guidPrimaryKey(value)
SELECT 'Test'
UNION ALL
SELECT 'Test1'
UNION ALL
SELECT 'Test2'
GO

SELECT *
FROM guidPrimaryKey
```

This returns something like the following:

```
guidPrimaryKeyId                      value
------------------------------------- ----------
AA52457C-339B-DA11-9A3C-001422E6CCC3  Test
AB52457C-339B-DA11-9A3C-001422E6CCC3  Test1
AC52457C-339B-DA11-9A3C-001422E6CCC3  Test2
```

■**Note** You may notice that the increasing value appears to be in the letters to the far left. To the naked eye, it would appear that we could be pretty close to running out of values, since the progression of AA, AB, AC would run out pretty quickly. The fact is, the values are not being sorted on the text representation of the GUID, but on the internal binary value. If you are interested in learning more about the internals of GUIDS, check http://en.wikipedia.org/wiki/guid.

Now, using a GUID for a primary key is just about as good as using an identity column for building a surrogate key, particularly one with a clustered index (they are still rather large at 16 bytes versus 4 for an integer, or even 8 for a bigint). That's because all new values will be added to the end of the index rather than randomly throughout the index. (Chapter 8 covers indexes, but be cognizant that a random value distributed throughout your rows can cause fragmentation unless you provide a fill factor that allows for adding rows to pages.) Values in the uniqueidentifier type will still be four times as large as an integer column, hence requiring four times the storage space. This makes using a uniqueidentifier a less than favorable index candidate from the database storage layer's perspective. However, the fact that it can be generated by any client and be guaranteed unique is a major plus, rather than requiring you to generate them in a single threaded manner to ensure uniqueness.

*Row Compression Effect:*

No effect.

# cursor

A cursor is a mechanism that allows row-wise operations instead of using the normal set-wise way. You use the cursor datatype to hold a reference to a SQL Server T-SQL cursor. You may not use a cursor datatype as a column in a table. Its only use is in T-SQL code to hold a reference to a cursor, which can be passed as a parameter to a stored procedure.

*Row Compression Effect:*

No effect.

# table

The table type is kind of two different things now in 2008. First you have the table type that is essentially a temporary table that you can declare like a variable at runtime, and you can define its characteristics. Second (and new to 2008), you have table types that are defined and stored for later use, for example, as table-valued parameters. I have broken these two different types of uses down into two sections. Neither usage is affected by row compression.

## Table Variables

The table variable has a few things in common with the cursor datatype, but instead of a cursor, it holds a reference to a result set. The name of the datatype is a pretty bad choice, because it will make functional programmers think that they can store a pointer to a table. It's actually used to store a result set as a temporary table. In fact, the table is exactly like a temporary table in implementation. However, you don't get any kind of statistics on the table, nor are you able to index the table datatype, other than to apply PRIMARY KEY and UNIQUE constraints in the table declaration. You can also have CHECK and DEFAULT constraints.

Unlike local temporary tables (those declared with # preceding the name), table datatype variables won't cause recompiles in stored procedures that use them, because they don't have any statistics to change the plan anyway. Use them only for modestly small sets of data (hundreds of rows, not thousands, generally), such as when all the data in the table can fit on a single data page.

The following is an example of the syntax needed to employ the table variable type:

```
DECLARE @tableVar TABLE
(
    id int IDENTITY PRIMARY KEY,
    value varchar(100)
)
INSERT INTO @tableVar (value)
VALUES ('This is a cool test')

SELECT id, value
FROM @tableVar
```

This returns the following result:

```
id          value
---- --------------------------------------
1           This is a cool test
```

As with the cursor datatype, you may not use the table datatype as a column in a table, and it can be used only in T-SQL code to hold a set of data. One of the primary purposes for the table datatype is for returning a table from a user-defined function, as in the following example:

```
CREATE FUNCTION table$testFunction
(
    @returnValue varchar(100)

)
RETURNS @tableVar table
(
    value varchar(100)
)
AS
BEGIN
    INSERT INTO @tableVar (value)
    VALUES (@returnValue)

    RETURN
END
```

Once created, you can use the table datatype returned by the function using typical SELECT syntax:

```
SELECT *
FROM dbo.table$testFunction('testValue')
```

This returns the following result:

```
value
-------------
testValue
```

One interesting thing about the table datatype is that it isn't subject to transactions. For example:

```
DECLARE @tableVar TABLE
(
    id int IDENTITY,
    value varchar(100)
)
BEGIN TRANSACTION
    INSERT INTO @tableVar (value)
    VALUES ('This will still be there')
ROLLBACK TRANSACTION

SELECT id, value
FROM @tableVar
```

This returns the following result:

```
id          value
----------- ---------------------------------------
1           This will still be there
```

For this reason, these tables are useful for logging errors, because the data is still available after the ROLLBACK TRANSACTION.

## Table Valued Parameters

One of the oft-requested features for SQL Server was the ability to pass in a table of values to a stored procedure. Using the table type, you can now do this, but not in as free a manner as you probably would have initially hoped. Instead of being able to define your table on the fly, you are required to use a type that you predefine.

The table type you will define is the same as the datatype alias we discussed in Chapter 5, except you specify an entire table, with all of the same things that a table variable can have, including PRIMARY KEY, UNIQUE, CHECK, and DEFAULT constraints.

An example that I imagine will be very commonly imitated is the generic table type with a list of integer values to pass as a parameter or to use in a query instead of an IN clause:

```
CREATE TYPE GenericIdList AS TABLE
(
    Id Int Primary Key
)
```

You declare the table variable just like any other and then load and use the variable with data just like any other local variable table:

```
DECLARE @ProductIdList GenericIdList

INSERT INTO @productIDList
VALUES (1),(2),(3),(4)

SELECT ProductID, Name, ProductNumber
FROM   AdventureWorks2008.Production.product
        JOIN @productIDList as list
            on Product.ProductID = List.Id
```

This returns the following:

| ProductID | Name | ProductNumber |
| --- | --- | --- |
| 1 | Adjustable Race | AR-5381 |
| 2 | Bearing Ball | BA-8327 |
| 3 | BB Ball Bearing | BE-2349 |
| 4 | Headset Ball Bearings | BE-2908 |

Of course, you can then use the type in your stored procedure creation statements as well:

```
CREATE PROCEDURE product$list
(
    @productIdList GenericIdList READONLY
)
AS
SELECT ProductID, Name, ProductNumber
FROM   AdventureWorks2008.Production.product
        JOIN @productIDList as list
            on Product.ProductID = List.Id
```

Unfortunately, you cannot pass a set of row constructors to the stored procedure; instead, you will need to declare and load a table variable to use this construct from T-SQL.

```
DECLARE @ProductIdList GenericIdList

INSERT INTO @productIDList
VALUES (1),(2),(3),(4)

EXEC product$list @ProductIdList
```

What makes this really nice is that in ADO.NET, you can declare a DataTable object and pass it to the procedure as a parameter, just like any other value now. This will make the ability to insert multiple items at a time or SELECT multiple rows far easier than ever before. In the past, we used a kludgy comma-delimited list or XML to do this, and it worked, but not in a natural manner we are accustomed to, and it was generally slow. This method will now work in a natural manner, allowing us to finally support multiple operations in a single transaction from an easy-to-build ADO.NET construct.

## sql_variant

The catchall datatype, the sql_variant type, allows you to store a value of almost any datatype that I've discussed. This ability allows you to create a column or variable where you don't know ahead of time exactly what kind of data will be stored. The sql_variant datatype allows you to store values of various SQL Server–supported datatypes, except for varchar(max), varbinary(max), xml, text, ntext, rowversion/timestamp, and sql_variant.

---

**■Note** Although the rowversion datatype cannot be stored directly in a sql_variant, a rowversion value can be stored in a binary(8) variable, which can in turn be stored in a sql_variant variable. Also, it might seem strange that you can't store a variant in a variant, but this is just saying that the sql_variant datatype doesn't exist as such—SQL Server chooses the best type of storage in which to store the value you give to it.

---

Generally, sql_variant is a datatype to steer clear of unless you really cannot know the datatype of a given value until the user enters the value. I used the sql_variant in Chapter 7 when I implemented the user-specified data storage using the entity-attribute-value solution. This allowed the user to enter any type of data and then have the system store the data in the most appropriate method.

The sql_variant type has some obvious value, and I used it earlier in Chapter 7 when building an entity-attribute-value solution for an open schema solution. By not needing to know the type at design time, you can allow the user to insert any type of data that they might want.

However, the positives lead directly to the negatives to the sql_variant type. Although simple storage and viewing of the data isn't too hard, it isn't easy to manipulate data once it has been stored in a sql_variant column. I'll leave it to you to read the information fully in the parts of SQL Server Books Online that deal with variant data, but some issues to consider are as follows:

- *Difficulties assigning data from a sql_variant column to a stronger typed datatype*: You have to be careful, because the rules for casting a variable from one datatype to another are difficult and might cause errors if the data can't be cast. For example, you can't cast the varchar(10) value 'Not a Date' to a datetime datatype. Such problems become an issue when you start to retrieve the variant data out of the sql_variant datatype and try to manipulate it.

- *NULL sql_variant values are considered to have no datatype*: Hence, you'll have to deal with sql_variant NULLs differently from nulls in other datatypes.

- *Comparisons of variants to other datatypes could cause difficult-to-catch programmatic errors, because of the sql_variant value instance's datatype*: Usually, the compiler will know whether you try to run a statement that compares two incompatible datatypes, such as @intVar = @varcharVar. However, if the two variables in question were defined as sql_variants and the datatypes don't match, then the values won't match because of the datatype incompatibilities.

When working with `sql_variant` variables or columns, you can use the `SQL_VARIANT_PROPERTY` function to discover the datatype of a given `sql_variant` value. For example:

```
DECLARE @varcharVariant sql_variant
SET @varcharVariant = '1234567890'
SELECT @varcharVariant AS varcharVariant,
   SQL_VARIANT_PROPERTY(@varcharVariant,'BaseType') as baseType,
   SQL_VARIANT_PROPERTY(@varcharVariant,'MaxLength') as maxLength,
   SQL_VARIANT_PROPERTY(@varcharVariant,'Collation') as collation
```

The preceding statement returns the following result:

| VarcharVariant | baseType | maxLength | collation |
| --- | --- | --- | --- |
| 1234567890 | varchar | 10 | SQL_Latin1_General_CP1_CI_AS |

For numeric data, you can also find the precision and scale:

```
DECLARE @numericVariant sql_variant
SET @numericVariant = 123456.789
SELECT @numericVariant AS numericVariant,
   SQL_VARIANT_PROPERTY(@numericVariant,'BaseType') as baseType,
   SQL_VARIANT_PROPERTY(@numericVariant,'Precision') as precision,
   SQL_VARIANT_PROPERTY(@numericVariant,'Scale') as scale
```

This returns the following result:

| numericVariant | baseType | precision | scale |
| --- | --- | --- | --- |
| 123456.789 | numeric | 9 | 3 |

# Not Simply Scalar Datatypes

This section will deal with the class of datatypes that have been implemented by Microsoft that aren't really scalar values. Another common term for these datatypes that have cropped up around the Internet is *beyond relational*, but to many people this is a confusing term. In one way of thinking, these are perfectly scalar types, but in yet another they really aren't.

The non-scalar types include the following:

- `hierarchyId`: Used to help build and manage a tree structure. It is very close to being a scalar type with several methods that can be applied to traverse and work with a hierarchy.

- Spatial types: `geometry` for dealing with planar/Euclidean (flat-Earth) data; `geography` for ellipsoidal (round-Earth) data, such as GPS longitude and latitude data. The spatial types technically hold arrays of values that represent sets on their own (and as you will see, you can join two shapes to see whether they overlap).

- `XML`: Used to store and manipulate XML values. A single XML column can more or less implement a database almost on its own.

One thing cannot be argued. Each of these types has some value to someone and fills a void that cannot be straightforwardly represented with the relational model, at least not as easily. I am a prude in many ways when it comes to normalization, but not every situation calls for strict adherence to the first normal form. What is, however, important is to know what you are doing and how you are violating the normal forms when you do and when it is appropriate.

So, are these bad things? My feeling on the matter is that it really depends upon usage. Since these types each have a lot more about them than simply what they can store, I have chosen to split them out into their own appendix. These types are mentioned here for completeness but will be covered in Appendix C (which will be available as a bonus download.)

# Index

# You Need the Companion eBook

**Your purchase of this book entitles you to buy the companion PDF-version eBook for only $10. Take the weightless companion with you anywhere.**

We believe this Apress title will prove so indispensable that you'll want to carry it with you everywhere, which is why we are offering the companion eBook (in PDF format) for $10 to customers who purchase this book now. Convenient and fully searchable, the PDF version of any content-rich, page-heavy Apress book makes a valuable addition to your programming library. You can easily find and copy code—or perform examples by quickly toggling between instructions and the application. Even simultaneously tackling a donut, diet soda, and complex code becomes simplified with hands-free eBooks!

Once you purchase your book, getting the $10 companion eBook is simple:

❶ Visit **www.apress.com/promo/tendollars/**.

❷ Complete a basic registration form to receive a randomly generated question about this title.

❸ Answer the question correctly in 60 seconds, and you will receive a promotional code to redeem for the $10.00 eBook.

THE EXPERT'S VOICE™

2855 TELEGRAPH AVENUE | SUITE 600 | BERKELEY, CA 94705

**Offer valid through 2/25/09.**